Societies and Cultures
IN WORLD HISTORY

Societies and Cultures
IN WORLD HISTORY
VOLUME I   TO 1715

MARK KISHLANSKY
Harvard University

PATRICK GEARY
University of California, Los Angeles

PATRICIA O'BRIEN
University of California, Irvine

R. BIN WONG
University of California, Irvine

With

ROY MOTTAHEDEH
Harvard University

LEROY VAIL
Harvard University

ANN WALTNER
University of Minnesota

MARK WASSERMAN
Rutgers University

JAMES GELVIN
Massachusetts Institute
of Technology

HarperCollinsCollegePublishers

Executive Editor: Bruce Borland
Development Editor: Barbara Muller
Project Coordination: Ruttle, Shaw & Wetherill, Inc.
Cover Design: Mary McDonnell
Text Design: Anne O'Donnell
Photo Research: Sandy Schneider
Cartographer: Maps produced by Mapping Specialists, Inc.
Manufacturing Manager: Willie Lane
Compositor: Publication Services, Inc.
Printer and Binder: R.R. Donnelley & Sons Company
Cover Printer: The Lehigh Press, Inc.

For permission to use copyrighted material, grateful acknowledgment is made to the copyright holders on pp. C-1–C-10, which are hereby made part of this copyright page.

Cover and Frontispiece: Immortals in the Mountain Palace, ca. 1100 C.E. Chinese silk painting. Scala/Art Resource, NY.

Library of Congress Cataloging-in-Publication Data
  Societies and cultures in world history / Mark Kishlansky ... [et al.] ;
      p.   cm.
  Includes indexes.
  Contents: v. 1. To 1715 — v. 2. 1500 to the present.
  ISBN 0-06-500351-9 (v. 1).—ISBN 0-06-500352-7 (v. 2)
    1. Civilization—History. I. Kishlansky, Mark A.
  CB69.S632   1995
  909—dc20   93-49368
                                                            CIP

94 95 96 97 9 8 7 6 5 4 3 2 1

CONTENTS

DOCUMENTS

MAPS

CHARTS, TABLES, AND FIGURES

COLOR ESSAYS

PREFACE

There is no more difficult subject for an introductory textbook than world history. While textbook writers are always faced with the dilemma of what to include and what to leave out, for the authors of a world history text this choice usually involves entire civilizations across centuries. And now more than ever—with the explosion in scholarship on world societies over the past decade—there are no easy answers. Decisions once made on the basis of too little knowledge to reconstruct a story must now be made on other grounds. It is an extraordinarily daunting task.

In writing *Societies and Cultures in World History*, we first considered how the book would be used among the variety of courses currently taught under the title World Civilizations. We designed the book for courses that combine the teaching of Western and world civilizations. It devotes more space to the history of the West, broadly construed, than to that of any other civilization. This design will give students a base of knowledge from which to compare and contrast the experiences of other civilizations as well as to help them understand the impact (for good or ill) that the West has had on the rest of the world. In coverage of world civilizations, we have allocated most space to Asian civilizations and have attempted to treat equally Africa, the Middle East, and Latin America. Although this presentation conforms to the broad outlines of most world civilization courses, we recognize there are nearly as many configurations of the course as there are places where it is taught. We hope the strengths of our presentation will outweigh its shortcomings.

We believe our book offers two outstanding distinctions: an intellectual respect for the integrity of all civilizations and a concern for the demands placed on student users. In planning our world civilization text, we decided not to follow the well-beaten path of adding one or two specialists to the author team and requiring them to write about civilizations (or epochs) in which they had neither scholarly training nor teaching experience. Instead we have contributions from a diverse team of experts—specialists in African, Latin American, and Middle Eastern history, as well as in early and modern Asia. This means that *Societies and Cultures in World History* has the benefit of the most up-to-date knowledge of world societies presented by experts on those societies.

Ann Waltner of the University of Minnesota has written on early Asia for part or all of Chapters 1, 4, 8, and 11. Leroy Vail of Harvard University has written on Africa for part or all of Chapters 1, 7, 14, 18, 19, 27, and 33. Mark Wasserman of Rutgers University has written on Latin America for part or all of Chapters 1, 14, 28, and 33. Roy Mottahedeh of Harvard University has written on early Islamic civilization for part or all of Chapters 15, 19, and 33; and James Gelvin of the Massachusetts Institute of Technology has written on modern Islamic civilization for part or all of Chapters 19 and 33.

Secondly, we are acutely aware that studying world history can be as daunting as reconstructing it, and throughout the process we have been concerned that the book meet the diverse needs and abilities of the students who will study it. We have tried to write a book that students will want to read. A number of decisions contributed to our goal. First, we would not write an encyclopedia of world civilization. Information would never be included in a chapter unless it fit within the themes of that chapter. There would be no information for information's sake and we would need to defend the inclusion of names, dates, and events whenever we met to critique our chapters. To our surprise, we found that by adhering to the principle that information appear only to illustrate a particular point or a dominating theme, we included as much, if not more, than books that habitually listed names, places, and dates with no other context. In addition, we were committed to integrating the history of women and of ordinary people into the narrative. In this endeavor, we had the assistance of two reviewers who were assigned no other responsibilities than to evaluate our chapters for the inclusion and integration of these materials within our chapters.

To construct a book that students would want to read, we needed to develop fresh ideas about how to involve the readers with the material, how to transform them from passive recipients to active participants. From computer science we borrowed the concept of "user friendly." Seeking ways to stimulate the imagination of the student, we realized the most dynamic way to do this was visually. Thus we initiated the technique of the pictorial chapter opener. At the beginning of each chapter, we explore a picture, guiding students across a canvas or an artifact or a photograph, helping them see things that are not immediately apparent, unfolding both an image and a theme. In some chapters we highlight details in the manner of an art history course, pulling out a section of the original picture to take a closer look. In others we attempt to shock readers into recognition of horror or beauty. Some openers are designed to make students ask, "What was it like to be there?" All are chosen to illustrate a dominant theme within the chapter, and the lingering impression they make helps reinforce that theme. We believe the combination of words and images will actively involve our readers—grabbing their attention and drawing them into the narrative.

To reinforce our emphasis on involving readers through visual learning, we included eight color inserts, built around the single theme, "Gender and Culture." The images and essays were prepared by Debra Mancoff, Professor and Chair of the Art History Department at Beloit College. Professor Mancoff has contributed her scholarly expertise in writing and teaching about representations of women to a compelling set of images that students will be able to compare and contrast over time and across cultures. These pictorial essays are substantive—not merely decorative—text, and we hope instructors will build on students' experience in reading the chapter pictorial features to analyze these photographs.

Similarly, we have taken an image-based approach to our presentation of geography. When teachers of world civilization courses are surveyed, no single area of need is highlighted more often than geography. Students simply have no mental image of the world beyond its shape, no familiarity with the geophysical features that are a fundamental part of the realities of world history. No world civilization textbook is without maps and ancillary map programs, yet no survey of teachers shows satisfaction with the effectiveness of these presentations. In *Societies and Cultures in World History*, we have tried to ensure that each place identified in the text is also identified in a map located within the chapter. The second device we developed to engage students with historical subjects is the in-depth chapter feature. These two-page, illustrated essays focus on a single event or personality chosen to demonstrate or enhance the students' sense that history is as real and exciting as life itself. They are written with more drama or sympathy or wonder than would be appropriate in the body of the text, and we believe they will captivate the imagination of their readers.

Finally, so that students can grasp the past first-hand, we have provided a wide variety of excerpts from primary source documents. Two criteria guided the selection of these excerpts: accessibility and immediacy. We believe students will be able to engage with these primary sources with no further introduction than that provided by the contextual headnotes that introduce each selection. In choosing these excerpts, we

have tapped the widest variety of genres—literature, popular culture, philosophy, religion, and all manner of political accounts. For those instructors who wish to make primary materials more central to their course, *Societies and Cultures in World History* also comes with a two-volume supplementary source book, *Sources of World History*.

Although our text includes much that is new and out of the ordinary, we do not mean to suggest that we have attempted to appeal to students only by adding "whistles and bells." *Societies and Cultures in World History* is a mainstream text in which most of the authors' energies have been placed in developing a solid, readable narrative of world civilizations that integrates women and the masses into the traditional sequence of periods and major events. We have highlighted personalities while identifying trends. We have spotlighted social history while maintaining a firm grip on political developments. We hope there are many qualities in this book that every teacher of world civilization will find valuable. But we also hope that there are things here you will disagree with, themes you can develop better, arguments and ideas that will provoke you. A textbook is only one part of a course, and it is always less important than a teacher. We have attempted to produce a book that your students will read so that you will not need to read it to them. We hope that by doing our job successfully we have made your job easier and your students' job more enjoyable.

Mark Kishlansky
Patrick Geary
Patricia O'Brien
R. Bin Wong

ACKNOWLEDGMENTS

We wish to thank the many conscientious historians who reviewed our manuscript and gave generously of their time and knowledge. Their valuable critiques and suggestions have contributed greatly to the final product. We are grateful to the following:

Mark Bartusis
Northern State University

Doris L. Bergen
University of Vermont

Martin Berger
Youngstown State University

Timothy Brook
University of Toronto

Charles J. Bussey
Western Kentucky University

Lee Cassanelli
University of Pennsylvania

Weston F. Cook, Jr.
Kutztown University

Todd A. Diacon
University of Tennessee at Knoxville

Ross E. Dunn
San Diego State University

Ainslie T. Embree
Columbia University

Charles T. Evans
Northern Virginia Community College-Loudoun

William Edward Ezzell
DeKalb College-Central Campus

Jonathan Goldstein
West Georgia College

Joseph Gowaskie
Rider College

John Mason Hart
University of Houston

Kandice Hauf
Babson College

Gerald Herman
Northeastern University

Mark C. Herman
Edison Community College

Ira M. Lapidus
University of California, Berkeley

Alan LeBaron
Kennesaw State College

Geri H. Malandra
University of Minnesota

Jon E. Mandaville
Portland State University

Patrick Manning
Northeastern University

Thomas Metcalf
University of California, Berkeley

James A. Miller
Clemson University

Joseph C. Miller
University of Virginia

Barbara A. Moss
University of Georgia

On-cho Ng
Penn State University

Donathon C. Olliff
Auburn University

James B. Palais
Jackson School of International Studies at the University of Washington

Peter C. Perdue
Massachusetts Institute of Technology

Paul J. Smith
Haverford College

Alexander Sydorenko
Arkansas State University

Steven C. Topik
University of California, Irvine

Karen Turner
College of the Holy Cross

Anne Walthall
University of California, Irvine

Eric L. Wake
Cumberland College

Allen Wells
Bowdoin College

David L. White
Appalachian State University

Alexander Woodside
University of British Columbia

Madeline C. Zilfi
University of Maryland

SUPPLEMENTS

The following supplements are available for use in conjunction with this book:

For the Instructor

Instructor's Resource Guide, by George F. Jewsbury, Oklahoma State University. This unique Instructor's Resource Guide provides new materials not found in the text through the use of lecture modules, lecture launchers, critical thinking exercises relating to the text's primary documents, detailed chapter summaries, test questions, and listings of additional resources for videos and films. As a **special feature**, there are six essays by Dr. Robert Edgar, Professor of African History at Howard University which incorporate the African history portions of the text into the lectures and discuss many of the most important and controversial issues in the teaching of world history.

Discovering World History Through Maps and Views, by Gerald Danzer of the University of Illinois at Chicago, winner of the AHA's 1990 James Harvey Robinson Prize for his work in the development of map transparencies. This set of 100 four-color transparencies from selected sources is bound in a three-ring binder and available free to adopters. It also contains an introduction on teaching history with maps and detailed commentary on each transparency. The collection includes cartographic and pictorial maps, views and photos, urban plans, building diagrams, classic maps, and works of art.

Test Bank, by John Paul Bischoff, Oklahoma State University. A total of 2000 questions, including 50 multiple-choice questions and five essay questions per text chapter. Each test item is referenced by topic, type, and text page number. Available in print and computerized format.

TestMaster Computerized Testing System. This flexible, easy-to-master computer test bank includes all the test items in the printed test bank. The TestMaster software allows you to edit existing questions and add your own items. Available for IBM and Macintosh computers.

QuizMaster. The new program enables you to design TestMaster generated tests that your students can take on a computer rather than in printed form. QuizMaster is available separate from TestMaster and can be obtained free through your sales representative. *Grades*. A grade-keeping and classroom management software program that maintains data for up to 200 students.

Map Transparencies. A set of 40 transparencies of maps taken from the text.

The HarperCollins World Civilization Media Program. A wide variety of media enhancements for use in teaching world civilization courses. Offered to qualified adopters of HarperCollins world history texts.

For the Student

Study Guide, in two volumes. Volume I (Chapters 1 through 16) and Volume II (Chapters 14 through 35), prepared by John Paul Bischoff, Oklahoma State University. Includes chapter outlines; timeline; map exercises; lists of important terms, people and events; and sections on "Making Connections" and "Putting Larger Concepts Together."

World History Map Workbook: Geographic and Critical Thinking Exercises, in two volumes. Prepared by Glee Wilson of Kent State University, each volume of this workbook contains 40 maps accompanied by over 120 pages of exercises. Each of the two volumes is designed to teach the students the location of various countries and their relationship to one another and events. Also included are numerous exercises aimed at enhancing students' critical thinking abilities.

Sources of World History, by Mark Kishlansky, a collection of primary source documents available in two volumes. These volumes provide a balance among constitutional documents, political theory, philosophy, imaginative literature, and social description. Represented are examples of the works of each of the major civilization complexes, Asia, Africa, Latin America, and the Islamic world as well as the central works of Western Civilization. Each volume includes the introductory essay, "How to Read a Document," which leads students step by step through the experience of using historical documents. *Super-Shell II Computerized Tutorial*, prepared by John Paul Bischoff,

Oklahoma State University. This interactive program for IBM computers helps students learn the major facts and concepts through drill and practice exercises and diagnostic feedback. SuperShell II provides immediate correct answers; the text page number on which the material is discussed, and a running score of the student's performance is maintained on the screen throughout the session. This free supplement is available to instructors through their sales representative. *TimeLink Computer Atlas of World History*, by William Hamblin, Brigham Young University. This HyperCard Macintosh program presents three views of the world—Europe/Africa, Asia, and the Americas—on a simulated globe. Students can spin the globe, select a time period, and see a map of the world at that time, including the names of major political units. Special topics such as the conquests of Alexander the Great are shown through animated sequences that depict the dynamic changes in geopolitical history. A comprehensive index and quizzes are also included.

Mapping World History: Student Activities, a free student map workbook by Gerald Danzer of the University of Illinois at Chicago. It features numerous map skill exercises written to enhance students' basic geographical literacy. The exercises provide ample opportunities for interpreting maps and analyzing cartographic materials as historical documents. The instructor is entitled to one free copy of *Mapping World History* for each copy of the text purchased from HarperCollins.

ABOUT THE AUTHORS

MARK KISHLANSKY

Recently appointed Professor of History at Harvard University, Mark Kishlansky is among today's leading young scholars. Professor Kishlansky received his Ph.D. from Brown University and is a member of the Harvard University faculty. A Fellow of the Royal Historical Society, his primary area of expertise is seventeenth-century English political history. Among his main publications are *Parliamentary Selection: Social and Political Choice in Early Modern England* and *The Rise of the New Model Army*. He is the editor of the *Journal of British Studies* and the recipient of the 1989 Most Distinguished Alumnus Award from SUNY Stony Brook.

PATRICK GEARY

Holding a Ph.D. in Medieval Studies from Yale University, Patrick Geary is both a noted scholar and teacher. Professor Geary was named outstanding undergraduate history teacher for the 1986–87 year at the University of Florida. He currently teaches at the University of California, Los Angeles, where he is Director for the Center for Medieval and Renaissance Studies. He has also held academic positions at the École des Hautes Études en Sciences Sociales, Paris; the Universitat Wien; and Princeton University. His many publications include *Readings in Medieval History; Before France and Germany: The Creation and Transformation of the Merovingian World; Aristocracy in Provence: the Rhone Basin at the Dawn of the Carolingian Age;* and *Furta Sacra: Thefts of Relics in the Central Middle Ages.*

PATRICIA O'BRIEN

Professor O'Brien teaches at the University of California, Irvine, and is Associate Vice Chancellor in the Office of Research and Graduate Studies. Professor O'Brien holds a Ph.D. from Columbia University in modern European history. Among her many publications are *The Promise of Punishment: Prisons in 19th Century France; "l'Embastillement de Paris: The Fortification of Paris During the July Monarchy";* and *"Crime and Punishment as Historical Problems."*

R. BIN WONG

R. Bin Wong holds a Ph.D. from Harvard University where he studied both Chinese and European history. In addition to research publications in the United States, which include *Nourish the People: The State Civilian Granary System in China, 1650–1850* (with Pierre-Etienne Will), he has published articles in mainland China, Taiwan, Japan, France, and Holland. He has held a number of research and teaching positions, including ones in the Society of Fellows, the University of Michigan; the Institute of Economics, Chinese Academy of Social Sciences; Institute of Oriental Culture, University of Tokyo; and the École des Hautes Études en Sciences Sociales in Paris. Currently, Professor Wong teaches history and directs a research program in Asian Studies at the University of California, Irvine.

JAMES L. GELVIN

Holding a Ph.D. in History and Middle Eastern Studies from Harvard University, James L. Gelvin's particular field of interest is Syrian history during the late nineteenth and twentieth centuries. An award-winning teacher, Professor Gelvin has taught history and politics at Harvard University, Boston College, and Massachusetts Institute of Technology.

ROY P. MOTTAHEDEH

Professor of History at Harvard University, Roy Mottahedeh has served as Director of the Center for Middle Eastern Studies and is currently Chair of the Committee on Islamic Studies at that University. He received his B.A. and Ph.D. at Harvard University and taught for many years at Princeton University. His publications include *Loyalty and Leadership in an Early Islamic Society* and *The Mantle of the Prophet: Religion and Politics in Iran.*

LEROY VAIL

Professor of African History at Harvard University, Leroy Vail is a leading scholar of Africa. Having received his Ph.D. from the University of Wisconsin (Madison), he spent a dozen years in Africa, teaching at the Universities of Malawi and Zambia and carrying out research on the languages and history of southeast Africa. He is the author of numerous articles on the region's history and linguistics. In collaboration with Landeg White, he has written *Capitalism and Colonialism in Mozambique* and *Power and the Praise Poem: Southern African Voices in History*. He has also edited the important *The Creation of Tribalism in Southern Africa* and is currently editing a dictionary of Lakeside Tonga, a language of Malawi.

ANN WALTNER

An Associate Professor of History at the University of Minnesota and Director of Graduate Studies there, Professor Waltner holds a Ph.D. in Chinese history from the University of California at Berkeley. Her research interests center on the social and intellectual history of China in the sixteenth and seventeenth century, and include topics such as gender, kinship, and religion. She is presently completing a book on Tanyangzi, a young woman mystic who lived in south China in the sixteenth century. Her publications include numerous articles, as well as *Getting an Heir: Adoption and the Construction of Kinship in Late Imperial China*.

MARK WASSERMAN

With his Ph.D. from the University of Chicago, Mark Wasserman is professor of history at Rutgers, The State University of New Jersey. He has won prestigious post-doctoral fellowships from the Social Science Research Council, the Tinker Foundation, the American Philosophical Society, and the U.S. Department of Education. Among his main publications are *Capitalists, Caciques and Revolution: The Native Elite and Foreign Enterprise in Chihuahua, Mexico, 1854–1911, Persistent Oligarchs: Elites and Politics in Chihuahua, Mexico, 1910–1940, A History of Latin America*, and *Provinces of the Revolution: Essays on Regional Mexican History, 1910–1929*. He won the Arthur P. Whitaker Prize in 1984 from the Middle Atlantic Council of Latin American Studies for *Capitalists, Caciques, and Revolution*.

CHAPTER 1

The First Civilizations

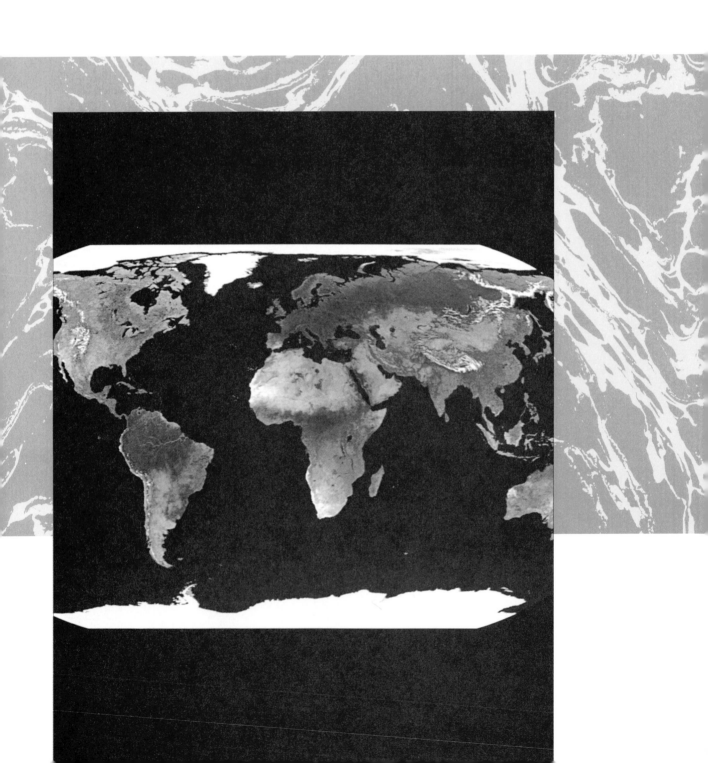

THE IDEA OF CIVILIZATION

An astronaut viewing the terrestrial sphere can make out the forms of Africa, bounded by the Atlantic, the Indian Ocean, the Red Sea, and the Mediterranean. Australia, the Americas, and even Antarctica are distinct patches in the darker waters that surround them. But while the physical contours of the world are visible from space, the richness and complexity of its civilizations are not. Civilization, unlike continents, rivers, and mountain ranges, belongs more to the mental than the physical world, even though men and women have slowly altered the physical environment in accord with their cultural values, their quest for power, their restlessness, their dreams. Still the meaning of civilization is as elusive when we look for it in history as when we search for it in space.

The word *civilization* itself does not have a long history, although it is ultimately derived from the ancient Greek term for those who reside in a particular place, its citizens. When *civilization* first entered the English language in the late eighteenth century, it was used to contrast the society and culture of Europe with what the British saw as the chaotic barbarity of much of the world. In the past two centuries, such a narrow and judgmental view of the world and the nature of human society has given way to broader understandings of civilization. Generally, it refers to those forms of complex social and cultural development characterized by innovative agricultural technology, demographic density, settled patterns of habitation in towns or cities, complex commercial networks, hierarchically organized political and social systems, and, often, the development of a literate culture wherever these characteristics have appeared. The history of civilization has been understood as the spread of these forms of culture (primarily from North Africa, western Asia, Europe, India, Mesoamerica, and China) to the rest of the world. But even this description is too restrictive. People in many parts of the world developed successful strategies to deal with the challenges of their geographical, climatological, and social circumstances without recourse to these characteristics of "civilization." In sub-Saharan Africa, for example, agricultural techniques remained basic because simple tools such as hoes were better suited to soil conditions than more "advanced" plows. People developed extensive commercial and communication networks without political centralization. In southern Africa, towns boasting elaborate stone buildings were constructed without recourse to either external models or literate traditions. Such alternatives to the European or Chinese model remind us of the variety of human experience and the wide spectrum of options by which people have faced the challenges of their existence. A history of civilization that omitted such alternative ways of constructing human culture would not only ignore an important part of the human experience but, in so doing, fail to put the uniqueness of traditional "civilizations" in their proper perspective.

Traditional civilizations appeared around the world at roughly the same time, ca. 3500 B.C.E. (before the common era, which begins with the traditional but erroneous date of the birth of Jesus), but under different circumstances and in forms so varied that scholars attempting to apply models of civilization based on European experience have been hard-pressed to recognize some of these early civilizations for what they were. For thousands of years they developed in relative isolation, only occasionally cross-fertilized by trade and sporadic travelers. Military conquerors such as Alexander the Great (336–323 B.C.E.) and Genghis Khan (ca. 1162–1227) temporarily united portions of these civilizations into short-lived empires. Religion provided a more lasting cultural bond, particularly Islam which, beginning in the seventh century of the common era, spread from Arabia to southern Europe and India, sub-Saharan Africa, and eventually China. Then, in the fifteenth century, European merchants, missionaries, and adventurers established enduring contact with the civilizations of Africa, Asia, and the Americas. These initial contacts, often brutal and destructive, began a process of mutual transformation that profoundly changed all human civilizations and affected the lives of everyone in the world.

At the end of the twentieth century, we all live in a world culture in which the legacies of ancient civilizations, for good and for evil, are an integral part. Much of the world is fed by crops first cultivated by the first civilizations of Africa, Asia, and the Americas; Asian social and cultural values have transformed international industry and trade and art; European science and technology have made it possible to lengthen life expectancy, harness the forces of nature, and conquer disease.

Many of today's most pressing problems are also part of the legacy of civilization. The remnants of European and Asian colonialism have left deep hostilities around the globe. The integration of developing nations into the world economy keeps much of humanity in a seemingly hopeless cycle of poverty. The technological advances of civilization endanger our very existence, polluting the world's air, water, and soil. And yet it is this same technology that allows us to view our world from outer space.

How did we get here? In this book we attempt to answer this question. This history of civilization is not simply the triumphal story of progress, the creation of a better world. Even in areas in which we can see development—such as agriculture, technology, communications, and social complexity—change is not always for the better. However, it would be equally inaccurate to view civilization as a progressive decline from a mythical golden age of the human race. The roughly three hundred generations since the origins of civilization have bequeathed a rich and contradictory heritage to the present. Inherited political and social institutions, cultural forms, and religious and philosophical traditions form the framework within which the future must be created. The past does not determine the future, but it is the raw material from which the future will be made. To use this legacy properly, we must first understand it, not because the past is the key to the future, but because understanding yesterday frees us to create tomorrow.

Before Civilization

The human race was already ancient by the time civilization first appeared. The first humanlike creatures whose remains have been discovered date from as long as five million years ago. One of the best-known finds, nicknamed "Lucy" by the scientist who discovered her skeleton in 1974, stood only about four feet tall and lived on the edge of a lake in what is now Ethiopia. Lucy and her band did not have brains that were as well developed as those of modern humans. They did, however, use simple tools such as sticks, bone clubs, and perhaps chipped rocks. Although small and relatively weak compared with other animals, Lucy's species of creatures—neither fully apes nor human—survived for over four million years.

Varieties of the modern species of humans, *Homo sapiens* (thinking human), appeared well over one hundred thousand years ago and spread across the Eurasian landmass and Africa. The earliest *Homo sapiens* in Europe, the *Neanderthal*, differed little from us today.

Although the term *Neanderthal* has gained a negative image in the popular imagination, these early humans were roughly the same size and had the same cranial capacity as we. They spread throughout much of Africa, Europe, and Asia during the last great ice age. To survive in the harsh tundra landscape, they developed a cultural system that enabled them to modify their environment. Customs such as the burial of their dead with food offerings indicate that Neanderthals may have developed a belief in an afterlife. Thus they apparently had the capacity for carrying on intellectual activities such as abstract and symbolic thought.

No one knows why or how the Neanderthals were replaced by our subspecies, *Homo sapiens sapiens* (thinking thinking human), around forty thousand years ago. Whatever the reason and whatever the process—extinction, evolution, interbreeding, or extermination—this last arrival on the human scene was universally successful. All humans today, whether Scandinavians, Australian aborigines, Africans, Japanese, or Native Americans, belong to this same subspecies. Differences in skin color, type of hair, or build are minor variations on the same theme. The identification of races, while selectively based on some of these physical variations, is, like civilization itself, a fact not of biology but of culture.

Early *Homo sapiens sapiens* lived in small kin groups of twenty or thirty, following game and seeking shelter in tents, lean-tos, and caves. People of the Paleolithic era, or Old Stone Age (ca. 600,000–10,000 B.C.E.), worked together for hunting and defense and apparently formed emotional bonds based on more than sex or economic necessity. During the upper or late Paleolithic era (ca. 35,000–10,000 B.C.E.), culture, meaning everything about humans not inherited biologically, was increasingly determinant in human life. Paleolithic people were not on an endless and all-consuming quest to provide for the necessities of life. They spent less time on such things than we do today. Thus they found time to develop speech, religion, and artistic expression. Wall paintings, small clay and stone figurines of female figures (which may reflect concerns about fertility), and finely decorated stone and bone tools indicate not just artistic ability but also abstract and symbolic thought.

Sometime after 10,000 B.C.E., hunter-gatherers living in what is now the Zhejiang province of China, in the plain of the Indus River in modern Pakistan, in sub-Saharan Africa, along the coastal plains of what is today Syria and Israel, and in the valleys and the hill country near the Zagros Mountains between modern Iran and

Before Civilization	
ca. 100,000 B.C.E.	*Homo sapiens*
ca. 40,000 B.C.E.	*Homo sapiens sapiens*
ca. 35,000–10,000 B.C.E.	Late Paleolithic era (Old Stone Age)
ca. 8000–6500 B.C.E.	Neolithic era (New Stone Age)
ca. 3500 B.C.E.	Civilization begins

Iraq began to develop specialized strategies that led, by accident, to a transformation in human culture. Rather than constantly traveling in search of food, people began to stay put and exploited the various seasonal sources of food, fish, wild grains, fruits, and game.

No one really knows why settlement led to agriculture, which is, after all, a riskier venture than hunting and gathering. Specialization in only a few species of plants or animals could spell starvation if severe weather

Sculptured skulls found at Jericho date from between 7000 and 6000 B.C.E. They are actual human skulls whose faces have been reconstituted with molded and tinted plaster. Pieces of seashells represented the eyes.

caused that crop to fail or if disease destroyed herds. Some scholars speculate that the push to take nature in hand came from population growth and the development of a political hierarchy that reduced the natural breaking away of groups when clans or tribes became too large for the natural resources of an area to support. In settled communities, infant mortality decreased and life expectancy rose. In part, these changes occurred because life in a fixed location was less exhausting than constant wandering for the very young and the very old.

The ability to domesticate goats, sheep, pigs, and cattle and to cultivate barley, wheat, and vegetables changed human communities from passive harvesters of nature to active partners with it. These peoples of the Neolithic era, or New Stone Age, approximately 8000–6500 B.C.E., organized sizable villages. Jericho, which had been settled before the agricultural revolution, grew into a fortified town complete with ditch, stone walls, and towers and sheltered perhaps two thousand inhabitants. Catal Hüyük in southern Turkey may have been even larger.

The really revolutionary aspect of agriculture was not simply that it ensured settled communities a food supply. The true innovation was that agriculture was portable. For the first time, rather than looking for a place that provided them with the necessities of life, humans could carry with them what they needed to make a site inhabitable. This portability also meant the rapid spread of agriculture throughout the region.

Agricultural societies brought changes in the form and organization of formal religious cults. In these larger communities the bonds of kinship that had united small hunter-gatherer bands were being supplemented by religious organization, which helped control and regulate social behavior. The nature of this religion is a matter of speculation. Images of a female deity found in some early sites and interpreted as a guardian of animals, suggest the religious importance of fertility and women's role in it.

Sub-Saharan Africa to 700 C.E.

In sub-Saharan Africa people shifted gradually from their earlier hunting and gathering existence to systematic stock breeding, fishing, and farming. This more settled life stood at the core of the Neolithic food-producing revolution that occurred in the Sahara/Sudanic zones. Once such changes had taken place

there, Neolithic people moved into other parts of the continent, displacing or absorbing the hunters and gatherers they encountered and creating more-complex political institutions. Yet in the new process of state building one can discern patterns of a uniquely African style of history, with Africa's physical environment demanding the durability of the village and the town and ensuring the transitory nature of ruling dynasties and empires.

The Diffusion of an African Food-Producing Revolution

A change in climate some 10,000 years ago in the eastern and central parts of the Sahara/Sudanic region resulted in a sharp increase in rain. The eastern and central Sahara became a fertile grassland full of wild animals while, to the south, the Sudanic region's rivers and lakes grew ever larger. In the Sudanic zone some hunting and gathering peoples added aquatic creatures such as fish, otters, and hippopotamuses to their diet. They developed boats and rafts, harpoons and nets, bone hooks and fishing lines, and, to cook and store their food, they made pottery. Because of the richness of the environment, populations increased, with people settling down in

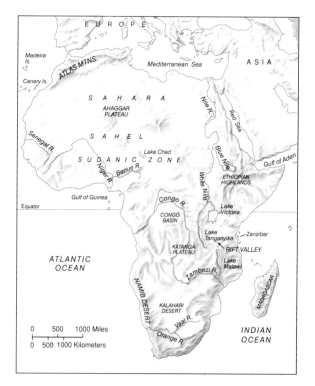

Africa

In this cave painting at Tassili in northern Africa, animal magic evokes help from the spirit world in ensuring the prosperity of the cattle herd. A similar ceremony is still performed by members of the Fulani tribes in the Sahel, on the southern fringe of the Sahara.

communities of up to one hundred or so and experimenting with improved gathering of wild grains such as millet, sorghum, and rice.

With its hospitable climate, the central and eastern Sahara/Sudanic zone was also an ideal area for the spread of innovations in food production that had already occurred in southwest Asia. Except in Egypt and North Africa, Africans could not grow Asian wheat and barley because they were unsuitable for tropical conditions, but they did adopt the domesticated goats, sheep, and cattle that had been developed in Asia. By about 5000 B.C.E. these animals had spread into the eastern Saharan grasslands, and between 4000 B.C.E. and 2500 B.C.E. they provided the basis of a new pastoral way of life based on herding. In subsequent centuries, pastoralists spread southward, particularly in eastern Africa, into highland areas of Ethiopia and northern Kenya.

After about 3500 B.C.E., the climate of the Sahara/ Sudanic zone began to revert to its earlier dryness, becoming progressively less hospitable. The Sudanic belt's rivers and lakes also began to shrink. As a consequence, people began to move southward in search of better living conditions in less dry climates. In the process, carriers of the new food-producing techniques expanded into areas up to then inhabited only by hunters and gatherers. In East Africa, for example, pastoralists

moved southward along the interior highlands into central and southern Kenya and Tanzania. From the central Sudanic region pastoralists also moved into the environs of Lake Chad and, apparently for the first time, into the western Sudanic regions as well. While pastoralists migrated in southerly and westerly directions, people versed in the fishing technologies originally pioneered on Sudanic rivers and lakes penetrated the West African forests to take advantage of the opportunities offered by their many rivers. Sometime during this process of movement into the forests—and certainly by 2000 B.C.E.—actual agricultural production based on yams and other root crops was established as a supplement to fishing in the forest zones. In the drier areas of the savanna, people had also begun to cultivate millet, sorghum, and rice.

In effect, the wet phase that occurred in the central and eastern Sahara/Sudanic zone between about 8000 B.C.E. and around 3500 B.C.E. fostered important innovations in food production, ranging from domestication of animals to fishing and experimental agriculture, all supplemented by some continued hunting and gathering. The growing dryness of the period after 3500 B.C.E. pushed the new ways of life southward into areas of Africa still only sparsely occupied by hunters and gatherers. Virtually everywhere such movement occurred, earlier occupants were either absorbed into the new

The Nok culture flourished along the Niger River from 500 B.C.E. until about 200 C.E. Nok artists produced fine terra-cotta sculptures of human and animal figures. This example is hollow, with perforations for the eyes, nostrils, and mouth.

population or displaced to marginal areas, as they were too weak to mount effective resistance.

As part of this broad southerly expansion, one of the most important population movements in all human history occurred. This was the migration of speakers of a Niger-Congo language known as proto-Bantu, the ancestor of the hundreds of languages in the Bantu linguistic family that are spoken today. They moved from the forest area along the Nigeria/Cameroon border and gradually spread into almost all of Africa south of the equator. This process resulted in a gigantic area of Africa being occupied by speakers of highly similar languages.

The Bantu migrations took a long time to complete and involved great complexity. They appear to have begun in the second millennium B.C.E., with people spreading in two main directions from the forested areas of the Nigeria/Cameroon borderlands. Some moved south and east, along the many rivers that crossed the Congo basin's rain forests, ultimately reaching the grass-

land regions of Zaire, Angola, and Zambia south of the forest. These migrants brought with them pottery and basketry, bows and arrows, domesticated goats and chickens, techniques of boating and fishing, and an agriculture based on root crops such as yams.

Others spread eastward along the northernmost fringes of the Congo forest into East Africa. As they did so, they acquired from Central Sudanic peoples whom they encountered techniques of raising sheep and cattle, information about growing grains, and, of immense importance, the knowledge of how to work iron and other metals, a discovery that rapidly spread back to West Africa. Once the Bantu speakers had reached East Africa, further migrations took place southward along two secondary routes throughout the first millennium B.C.E. One went near the coast, through Kenya, Tanzania, Mozambique, and Malawi, and it seems that migrants reached South Africa's Transvaal area by the fourth century C.E. The second was situated farther to the west, along the eastern upland fringes of the Congo basin and then into central and eastern Zambia and Zimbabwe.

Yet even after these initial migrations were completed by around 900 C.E., there were immense areas of Africa south of the equator still occupied by hunters and gatherers. Only with the passage of centuries did groups of Bantu-speaking agriculturalists grow in size, divide, and expand their internal frontiers to occupy new areas. In areas that the Bantu speakers considered undesirable, however, hunters and gatherers persisted, living on down to the present as such groups as the Mbuti people of the deep Congo rain forest and the Khoisan peoples of the southwest corner of Africa and the Kalahari Desert. By 1500 C.E. Bantu speakers occupied fully ninety per cent of the habitable land area south of the equator, having brought to it the complex material culture that had developed initially in the eastern and central Saharan/Sudanic areas, that had been enriched by the knowledge of metalworking, and that they elaborated into a myriad of new forms as they adapted to their varied new environments.

Ecology, Labor Power, and the Politics of Kinship

It is clearly impossible to make valid generalizations that apply to every part of a continent as large and diverse as Africa. Yet, while the continent had clearly been hospitable to earlier hunters and gatherers, it is fair to say that the history of Africa's agricultural and pastoral peoples has been significantly more difficult, shaped by their having to come to terms with an environment that, taken as a whole, must be considered one of the world's most difficult. This is especially true for agriculturalists, as they have had great problems in maintaining the soil's fertility.

Except for the North African coast and the area around the Cape of Good Hope, which have a temperate Mediterranean climate, all of Africa is tropical. In the tropics rains generally fall daily during four or five months of the year. This period is followed by a long dry season of up to seven or eight months. If the rains are too light or too heavy, crop yields suffer, and in a typical decade hunger is a problem in at least three years. When rains fail for two or three years in succession, famine results and people starve to death. Because African agriculture is dependent on fickle rainfall, it has always been a risky endeavor except in equatorial zones, where rains are more reliable and in certain West African river valleys, where water is perennially available.

Most of the soils of the African continent are inhospitable to agriculture. In the tropical rain forests of the Congo basin, the soil is thin and poor, with most of the nutrients locked up in living plants and animals. In cleared areas, soil nutrients are soon leached away by the heavy rains. The vast areas of grassland and savanna to the north, south, and west of the rain forests are low in fertility and have long dry seasons. Africans have managed these problems by using a system of shifting cultivation. A piece of land is cleared, used for three to five years, and then abandoned to lie fallow to recover its fertility, and a new piece of land is cleared for cultivation. This process continues with other pieces of land, until, after perhaps as long as twenty-five or thirty years, the fertility of the soil is restored to a point at which it may be used to grow crops once again for another brief period. Because most land in Africa, except for some West African areas and rare places where good volcanic soils exist such as Uganda, was used in this fashion, the carrying capacity of the soil—the number of people who could live on a unit of land—has been historically quite small. In rain forest areas, where the soils are exceptionally poor, it has been extremely low.

Finally, diseases such as endemic malaria, bilharzia, parasitical worms, and smallpox restricted productivity. Perhaps the most important disease, however, has been carried by the tsetse fly. When a tsetse bites a domesticated animal, it delivers a parasite called a trypanosome, which gradually destroys the animal's nervous system. The animal dies from sleeping sickness, or trypanosomiasis, in a matter of months. As a result, in areas where the tsetse exists it has been impossible to use draft animals for agriculture, and all agricultural work has had to be carried out by hand using only simple tools. This situation has sharply limited productivity. Ironically, the areas where tsetse flies are not found, such as in the Sudanic zone, are often those with such uncertain rainfall that pastoralism, not agriculture, is the more reliable way to survive.

With climate and problems of soil management and disease limiting the carrying capacity of its land, until the twentieth century Africa was characterized by an abundance of land and a relative shortage of labor to work it. Success in dealing with the difficult environment required effective use of available labor, especially in areas where draft animals could not be used. This fact has had a crucial impact upon the nature of politics throughout sub-Saharan Africa.

Because of Africa's relatively sparse population, and because of difficulties of transport and communication, labor mobilization for agricultural work has historically best been done on a relatively small scale, not through the intervention of large-scale state structures. If one is to understand Africa's past, then one must break away from the assumption that the state is a necessity and imagine a situation in which there is actually little need for it for day-to-day survival. When the influence of state

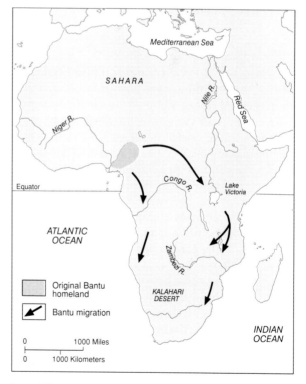

Bantu Migrations

structures was minimal or wholly absent, relations within families served to organize virtually all African societies. They defined the roles of people and placed them in situations in which they could be mobilized as workers to ensure that the family household unit, the extended family, and, ultimately, society as a whole survived in difficult ecological conditions. The emphasis on the family was also important for a second, closely related, reason. In a situation of chronic labor shortage, family members worked without pay.

Central to this system were women. In most African societies women performed a large part of the agricultural work. The more women in a lineage, the more productive it was. Moreover, women bore the children who were crucial for the lineage's survival. When female children reached maturity, they were exchanged in marriage with other lineages. Male children remained within the lineage and attracted wives, thereby strengthening it and making it more likely to prosper and grow. In sum, then, family membership did not merely encompass existing biological relationships, but it also served as a way of ensuring that work was done at little cost. Greatest local power lay with the family head, usually a senior member, for he both shaped his family into an efficient productive unit by directing its day-to-day work and arranged marriages with other families to ensure its continuity.

"Big Men" and Political Change

Not all families were equal, however. To the extent that wealth existed in Africa, it was not usually equated with the possession of material goods. Basic wealth lay in control over people. A poor man had a wife and a child or two and, if cattle existed in the area, a cow or two. A wealthy man was one who had accumulated power over many people and, if possible, many cattle. It was to augment one's power over people—not to satisfy sexual passion—that polygyny was important in Africa. It not only ensured many children to a man, but it was also a way for him to build important alliances with other families by contracting marriages for himself and his children.

Yet while it is accurate to see economic and political power as having existed primarily at the local level and as having resided with family heads, much of the history of Africa nonetheless has been the history of the growth of states, their dynasties, and the wars they have sponsored. This has been so largely because, even at the local level, there were always people who were known—as they are still today—as "big men" (in Swahili, for example, such a person was called a *bwana mkubwa*). Although women occasionally became powerful, when they did so they were usually considered socially as "men" and are hence considered as part of the overall category of "big men."

Their control over people through their families made such persons wealthy and powerful. Because of their power, poor people, weak people, or immigrants to the area also turned to them as patrons for protection and for access to food or land. In this way, even at the local level, some family heads were able to extend their powers beyond their own family's members and territory, often expressing their expanded powers in the terminology of family relationships. This situation resulted in the existence of thousands of highly localized microstates throughout Africa.

A second step toward the transformation of an embryonic microstate to a mature larger one occurred when circumstances changed in such a way that new opportunities for amassing additional power appeared. When this happened, the big men who were already powerful could take advantage of the new opportunities. When the opportunities were great enough, they could use their new power to dominate other, weaker families by force if necessary, making their states influential in regional politics.

Surveying Africa's history, one is struck by the frequency with which the catalyst for such rapid political change has been the growth of trade with outside peoples. Time and again, the creation of a market for a particular item to which local society has access—such as gold in Ghana and Zimbabwe, salt in Mali, slaves in West Africa, iron in Tanzania, or copper in Angola and Zaire—provided the opportunity for an enlargement of

Sub-Saharan Africa to 700 C.E.	
8000–2000 B.C.E.	Wet phase in central and eastern Sahara/Sudanic zone
2000 B.C.E.	Beginning of drying phase in central and eastern Sahara/Sudanic zone
2000–1000 B.C.E.	Beginning of Bantu migrations

economic scale. The new economic activity naturally fell into the hands of those in the society with the greatest access to labor power, the big men, and the way was opened for state building. Given the opportunity and the appropriate catalyst, African societies showed a remarkable ability to change quickly, with the big men becoming chiefs, kings, and even emperors, able to pass on their power and authority to successors. Single individuals or aristocracies used their advantaged economic position to reinforce and expand their political power. Ties of kinship or clientage were reinforced by religious sanctions or coercion and, in the process, a state, dominated by a king or council of important people, emerged. Although standing armies were rare, the new state often developed military capabilities as well.

When such an increase in scale occurred, the state's demands challenged family relationships. Equally clearly, however, at the local level families remained the basic unit for mobilizing labor needed for daily survival. As a consequence, situations frequently arose in which the apparatus of the large state hovered over the villages or, in West Africa, the towns it encompassed, tapping into them from time to time for tribute or taxes, or to levy labor power, but remaining generally distant from them. Because of the persistent vitality of the villages and towns, and because their interests were often different from those of the larger state, tensions were built into the relationship between the two. These tensions often led to resistance, rebellion, or local secession when the coercive power of the distant state weakened. Moreover, because states usually relied upon access to markets beyond their borders to obtain their wealth and because they often lacked adequate transport and communications and an institutionalized bureaucracy, they tended to be at the mercy of forces beyond their rulers' immediate control. The true history of Africa, it might be argued, lies in the life of the enduring local villages and towns rather than in the often glittering achievements of states and empires ruled by successful big men who had become chiefs, kings, or emperors.

Mesopotamia: The Land Between the Two Rivers

As in Africa, geography and climate helped determine the forms of social organization in western Asia. However, in this region, which today comprises Iran and Iraq, need drove the inhabitants of Mesopotamia to create a civilization. The name *Mesopotamia* means "between the rivers," and was used for that featureless plain stretching to the marshes near the mouths of the Tigris and Euphrates rivers. Nature itself offered little for human comfort or prosperity in this harsh environment. The upland regions of the north receive most of the rainfall, but the soil is thin and poor. In the south, the soil is fertile but rainfall is almost nonexistent. There the twin rivers provide life-giving water, but also bring destructive floods that normally arrive at harvest time. Thus agriculture is impossible without irrigation. But irrigation systems, if not properly maintained, deposit harsh alkaline chemicals on the soil, gradually reducing its fertility. In addition, Mesopotamia's only natural resource is clay. It has no metals, no workable stone, no valuable minerals of use to ancient people. These very obstacles pressed the people to cooperative, innovative, and organized measures for survival. Survival in the region required planning and the mobilization of human resources possible only through centralization.

Until around 3500 B.C.E., the inhabitants of the lower Tigris and Euphrates lived in scattered villages and small towns. Then the population of the region, known as Sumer, began to increase rapidly. Small settlements became increasingly common, then towns such as Eridu and Uruk (in modern Iraq) began to grow rapidly. These towns developed in part because of the need to concentrate and organize population in order to carry on the extensive irrigation systems necessary to support Mesopotamian agriculture. In most cases, the earlier role of particular villages as important religious centers favored their growth into towns. These towns soon spread their control out to the surrounding cultivated areas, incorporating the small towns and villages of the region. They also fortified themselves against the hostile intentions of their neighbors.

Nomadic peoples inhabited the arid steppes of Mesopotamia, constantly trading with and occasionally threatening settled villages and towns. But nomads were a minor threat compared with the dangers posed by raids from settled neighbors. Victims sought protection within the ramparts of the settlements that had grown up around religious centers. As a result, the population of the towns rose along with their towering temples, largely at the expense of the countryside. Between ca. 3500 and 3000 B.C.E., the population of Uruk quadrupled, from ten to forty thousand. Other Mesopotamian cities developed along the same general lines as they concentrated water supplies within their districts with artificial canals and dikes. At the same time, the number of smaller towns and villages in the vicinity decreased

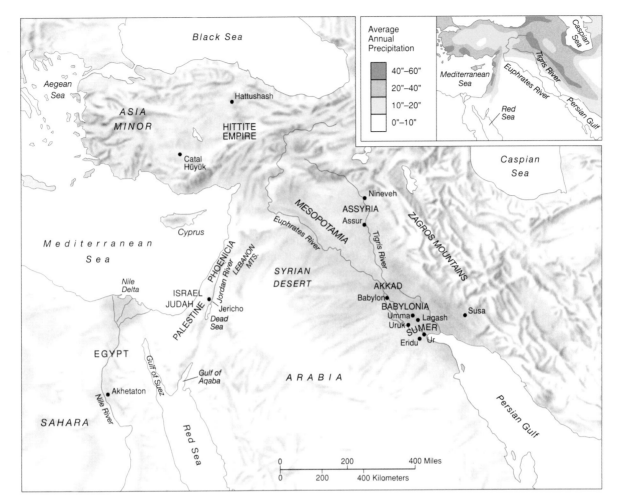

The Ancient Near East

rapidly. The city had become the dominant force in the organization of economy and society, and the growth of the Sumerian cities established a precedent that would continue throughout history.

The Ramparts of Uruk

Cities did more than simply concentrate population. Within the walls of the city, men and women developed new technologies and new social and political structures. They created cultural traditions such as writing and literature. The pride of the first city dwellers is captured in a passage from the *Epic of Gilgamesh*, the first great heroic poem, which was composed sometime before 2000 B.C.E. In the poem, the hero Gilgamesh boasts of the mighty walls he had built to encircle his city, Uruk:

Go up and walk on the ramparts of Uruk
Inspect the base terrace, examine the brickwork:
Is not its brickwork of burnt brick?
Did not the Seven Sages lay its foundations?

Gilgamesh was justly proud of his city. In his day (ca. 2700 B.C.E.) these walls were marvels of military engineering and even now their ruins remain a tribute to the age. Archaeologists have uncovered the remains of the ramparts of Uruk, which stretched over five miles and were protected by some nine hundred semicircular towers. These protective walls enclosed about two square miles of houses, palaces, workshops, and temples. For the first time, a true urban environment had appeared in western Eurasia, and Uruk was its first city. Within Uruk's walls, the peculiar circumstances of urban life changed the traditional social structure of Mesopotamia. In Neolithic times, social and

THE CODE OF HAMMURABI

■ *The society revealed in the Code of Hammurabi was a complex world of landed aristocrats, merchants, and simple workers and shopkeepers. Its economy functioned on a complex system of credit relationships binding the various members of the society together, as seen in the following selections.*

If a merchant lent grain at interest, he shall receive sixty *qu* of grain per *jur* as interest (= 20% rate of interest.) If he lent money at interest, he shall receive one-sixth shekel six *se* (i.e., one-fifth shekel) per shekel of silver as interest.

If a seignior, who incurred a debt, does not have the money to pay it back, but has the grain, the merchant shall take grain for his money with its interest in accordance with the ratio fixed by the king.

If a seignior gave money to another seignior for a partnership, they shall divide equally in the presence of god the profit or loss which was incurred.

If a woman wine seller, instead of receiving grain for the price of a drink has received money by the large weight and so has made the value of the drink less than the value of the grain, they shall prove it against that wine seller and throw her into the water.

If an obligation came due against a seignior and he sold the services of his wife, his son, or his daughter, or he has been bound over to service, they shall work in the house of their purchaser or obligee for three years, with their freedom reestablished in the fourth year.

If an obligation came due against a seignior and he has accordingly sold the services of his female slave who bore him children, the owner of the female slave may repay the money which the merchant paid out and thus redeem his female slave.

economic differences within society had been minimal. Urban immigration increased the power, wealth, and status of two groups, the religious authorities responsible for the temples and the emerging military and administrative elites.

Whether they lived inside the city or on the farmland it controlled, Mesopotamians formed a highly stratified society that shared unequally in the benefits of civilization. Slaves, who did most of the unskilled labor within the city, were the primary victims of civilization. Most were prisoners of war, but some were people forced by debt to sell themselves or their children. Most of the remaining rural people were peasants who were little better than slaves. Better off were soldiers, merchants, and workers and artisans who served the temple or palace. At the next level were landowning free persons. Above all of these were the priests responsible for temple services and the rulers. Rulers included the *ensi*, or city ruler, and the *lugal*, or king, the earthly representative of the gods. Kings were powerful and feared.

Urban life also redefined the role and status of women, who in the Neolithic period had enjoyed roughly the same roles and status as men. In cities, women tended to exercise private authority over children and servants within the household, while men controlled the household and dealt in the wider world. This change in roles resulted in part from the economic basis of the first civilization. Southern Mesopotamia has no sources of metal or stone. To acquire these precious commodities, trade networks were extended into Syria, the Arabian Peninsula, and even India. The primary commodities that Mesopotamians produced for trade were textiles, and these were largely produced by women captured in wars with neighboring city-states. Some historians suggest that the disproportionate numbers of low-status women in Mesopotamian cities affected the status of women in general. Although women could own property and even appear as heads of households, by roughly 1500 B.C.E. the pattern of patriarchal households predominated. Throughout western Eurasian history, while individual women might at times exercise great power, they did so largely in the private sphere.

Changes in society brought changes in technology. The need to feed, clothe, protect, and govern growing urban populations led to major technological and conceptual discoveries. Canals and systems of dikes partially harnessed water supplies. Farmers began to work their fields with improved plows and to haul their produce to town, first on sleds and ultimately on carts. These land-transport devices, along with sailing ships, made it possible for farmers not only to produce greater agricultural surplus but also to move this surplus to distant markets. Craft workers used a refined potter's wheel to produce ceramic vessels of great beauty. Government officials and private individuals began to use cylinder seals, small stone cylinders engraved with a pattern, to mark ownership. Metalworkers fashioned gold and silver into valuable items of adornment and prestige. They also began to cast bronze, an alloy of copper and tin, which came into use for tools and weapons about 3000 B.C.E.

Perhaps the greatest invention of early cities was writing. As early as 7000 B.C.E., small clay or stone tokens with distinctive shapes or markings were being used to keep track of animals, goods, and fruits in inventories and bartering. By 3500 B.C.E., government and temple administrators were using simplified drawings, today termed *pictograms*, which were derived from these tokens, to assist them in keeping records of their transactions. Scribes used sharp reeds to impress the pictograms on clay tablets. Thousands of these tablets have survived in the ruins of Mesopotamian cities.

The first tablets were written in Sumerian, a language related to no other known tongue. Each pictogram represented a single sound, which corresponded to a single object or idea. In time, these pictograms developed into a true system of writing, called cuneiform (from the Latin *cuneus*, "wedge") after the wedge shape of the characters. Finally, scribes took a radical step. Rather than simply using pictograms to indicate single objects, they began to use cuneiform characters to represent concepts. For example, the pictogram for "foot" could also mean "to stand." Ultimately, pictograms came to represent sounds divorced from any particular meaning.

The implications of the development of cuneiform writing were revolutionary. Since symbols were liberated from meaning, they could be used to record any language. Over the next thousand years, scribes used these same symbols to write not only in Sumerian but also in the other languages of Mesopotamia, such as Akkadian, Babylonian, and Persian. Writing soon allowed those who had mastered it to achieve greater centralization and control of government, to communicate over enormous distances, to preserve and transmit information, and to express religious and cultural beliefs. Writing reinforced memory, consolidating and expanding the achievements of the first civilization and transmitting them to the future. Writing was power, and for much of subsequent history a small minority of merchants and elites and the scribes in their employ wielded this power. In Mesopotamia, this power served to increase the strength of the king, the servant of the gods.

Gods and Mortals in Mesopotamia

Uruk had begun as a village like any other. Its rise to importance resulted from its significance as a religious site. A world of many cities, Mesopotamia was also a world of many gods, and Mesopotamian cities bore the imprint of the cult of their gods.

The gods were like the people who worshiped them. They lived in a replica of human society, and each god had a particular responsibility. Every object and element from the sky to the brick or the plow had its own active god. The gods had the physical appearance and personalities of humans as well as human virtues and vices. Greater gods like Nanna and Ufu were the protectors of Ur and Sippar. Others, such as Inanna, or Ishtar, the goddess of love, fertility, and wars, and her husband Dumuzi, were worshiped throughout Mesopotamia. Finally, at the top of the pantheon were the gods of the sky, the air, and the rivers.

Mesopotamians believed that the role of mortals was to serve the gods and to feed them through sacrifice. Towns had first developed around the gods' temples for this purpose. By around 2500 B.C.E., although military lords and kings had gained political power at the expense of the temple priests, the temples still controlled a major portion of economic resources. They owned vast estates where peasants cultivated wheat and barley as well as vegetable gardens, vineyards, flocks of sheep, and herds of cattle and pigs. The produce from temple lands and flocks supported the priests, scribes, craft workers, laborers, farmers, teamsters, smiths, and weavers who operated these complex religious centers. At Lagash, for example, the temple of the goddess Bau owned over eleven thousand acres of land. The king held a quarter of this land for his own use. The priests divided the remainder into individual plots of about thirty-five acres, each to be cultivated for the support of the temple workers or rented out to free peasants. At a time when the total population was approximately forty thousand, the temple employed more than twelve hundred workers of various sorts, supervised by an administrator and an inspector appointed by the priests. The temple of Bau was only one of twenty temples in Lagash—and not the largest or most wealthy among them.

By around 2000 B.C.E., a ziggurat, or tiered tower, dedicated to the god stood near many temples. The great Ziggurat of Ur, for example, measured nearly two thousand square feet at its base and originally stood more than 120 feet high. It is easy to see why people of a later age thought that the people who had built the ziggurats wanted a tower that would reach to heaven—the origin of the biblical story of the Tower of Babel.

Although Mesopotamians looked to hundreds of personal divinities for assistance, they did not attempt to establish personal relationships with their great gods. However, since they assumed that the gods lived in a structured world that operated rationally, they believed that mortals could deal with them and enlist their aid by following the right rituals. Rites centered on the worship of idols. The most important care was feeding. At the temple of Uruk, the idols of the gods were offered two meals a day, each consisting of two courses served in regal quantity and style.

Through the proper rituals, a person could buy the god's protection and favor. Still, mortal life was harsh and the gods offered little solace to the great issues of human existence. This attitude is powerfully presented in the *Epic of Gilgamesh* which, while not an accurate picture of Mesopotamian religion, still conveys much of the values of this civilization. In this popular legend Gilgamesh, king of Uruk, civilizes the wild man Enkidu, who had been sent by the gods to temper the king's harshness. Gilgamesh and Enkidu become friends and undertake a series of adventures. However, even their great feats cannot overcome death. Enkidu displeases the gods and dies. Gilgamesh then sets out to find the magic plant of eternal life with which to return his friend from the somber underworld. On his journey he meets Ut-napishtim, the Mesopotamian Noah, who recounts the story of the Great Flood and tells him where to find the plant. Gilgamesh follows Ut-napishtim's advice and is successful but loses the plant on his journey home. The message is that only the gods are immortal, and the human afterlife is at best a shadowy and mournful existence.

Sargon and Mesopotamian Expansion

The temple was one center of the city; the palace was the other. As representative of the city's god, the king was the ruler and highest judge. He was responsible for the construction and maintenance of religious buildings and the complex system of canals that maintained the

The southwestern side of the ruins of the Ziggurat of Ur. On top of a main platform fifty feet high, two successively smaller stages were built. The top stage was a temple containing a religious shrine. Ramplike stairways led up to the shrine from the ground.

precarious balance between swamp and arid steppe. Finally, he commanded the army, defending his community against its neighbors and leading his forces against rival cities.

The cultural and economic developments of early Mesopotamia occurred within the context of almost constant warfare. From around 3000 B.C.E. until 2300 B.C.E., the rulers of Ur, Lagash, Uruk, and Umma fought among themselves for control of Sumer, their name for the southern region of Mesopotamia. The population was a mixture of Sumerians and Semites—peoples speaking Semitic languages related to modern Arabic or Hebrew—all jealously protective of their cities and gods and eager to extend their domination over their weaker neighbors.

The extraordinary developments in this small corner of the Middle East might have remained isolated phenomena were it not for Sargon (ca. 2334–2279 B.C.E.), king of Akkad and the most important figure in Mesopotamian history. During his long reign of fifty-five years, Sargon built on the conquests and confederacies of the past to unite, transform, and expand Mesopotamian civilization. Born in obscurity, after his death he was worshiped as a god. Sargon was the son of a priestess and an unknown father. In his youth he was the cupbearer to the king of Kish. Later, he overthrew his master and conquered Uruk, Ur, Lagash, and Umma. This made him lord of Sumer. Such glory had satisfied his predecessors, but not Sargon. Instead he extended his military operations east across the Tigris, west along the Euphrates, and north into modern Syria, thus creating the Akkadian state—the first great multiethnic empire state—so named by contemporary historians for Sargon's capital at Akkad.

Sargon attempted to rule a vast and heterogeneous collection of city-states and territories by transforming the traditions of royal government. Rather than eradicating the traditions of conquered cities, he allowed them to maintain their own institutions, but replaced many of their autonomous ruling aristocracies with his own functionaries. He also reduced the economic power of local temples in favor of his supporters. At the same time, however, he tried to win the loyalty of the ancient cities of Sumer by naming his daughter high priestess of the moon god Nanna at Ur. He was thus the first in a long tradition of western Asian rulers who sought to unite his disparate conquests into a true state.

Sargon did more than just conquer cities. Although a Semite, he spread the achievements of Sumerian civilization throughout his vast state. Akkadian scribes used cuneiform to write the Semitic Akkadian language. So important did Sargon's successors deem his accomplishments that they ordered him worshiped as a god.

The Akkadian nation-state proved as ephemeral as Sargon's accomplishments were lasting. All Mesopotamian states tended to undergo a cycle of rising rapidly under a gifted military commander and then beginning to crumble under the internal stresses of dynastic disputes and regional assertions of autonomy. Thus weakened, they could then be conquered by other expanding states. First Ur, under its Sumerian king and first law-codifier, Shulgi (2094–2047 B.C.E.), and then Amoritic Babylonia, under its great ruler, Hammurabi (1792–1750 B.C.E.), assumed dominance in the land between the rivers. From about 2000 B.C.E. on, the political and economic centers of Mesopotamia were in Babylonia and in Assyria, the region to the north at the foot of the Zagros Mountains.

Hammurabi and the Old Babylonian Empire

In the tradition of Sargon, Hammurabi expanded his state through arms and diplomacy. He expanded his power south as far as Uruk and north to Assyria. In the tradition of Shulgi, he promulgated an important body of law, known as the Code of Hammurabi. In the words of its prologue, this code sought:

> To cause justice to prevail in the country
> To destroy the wicked and the evil,
> That the strong may not oppress the weak.

As the favored agent of the gods, the king held responsibility for regulating all aspects of Babylonian life, including dowries and contracts, agricultural prices and wages, commerce and money lending, and even professional standards for physicians, veterinarians, and architects. Hammurabi's code thus offers a view of many aspects of Babylonian life, although always from the perspective of the royal law. This law lists offenses and prescribes penalties, which vary according to the social status of the victim and the perpetrator. The code creates a picture of a prosperous society composed of three legally defined social strata: a well-to-do elite, the mass of the population, and slaves. Each group had its own rights and obligations in proportion to its status. Even slaves enjoyed some legal rights and protection, could marry free persons, and might eventually obtain freedom.

Much of the code sought to protect women and children from arbitrary and unfair treatment. Husbands ruled their households, but they did not have unlimited authority over their wives. Women could initiate their

A seven-foot-high diorite stele, dating from about 1750 B.C.E., is inscribed with the law code of Hammurabi. The relief at the top shows Hammurabi standing at left in the presence of the sun-god, perhaps explaining his code of laws.

own court cases, practice various trades, and even hold public positions. Upon marriage, husbands gave their fathers-in-law a payment in silver or in furnishings. The father of the wife gave her a dowry over which she had full control. Some elite women personally controlled great wealth.

The Code of Hammurabi was less a royal attempt to restructure Babylonian society than an effort to reorga-nize, consolidate, and preserve previous laws in order to maintain the established social and economic order. What innovation it did show was in the extent of such punitive measures as death or mutilation. Penalties in earlier codes had been primarily compensation in silver or valuables.

Law was not the only area in which the Old Babylonian kingdom began an important tradition. In order to handle the economics of business and government administration, Babylonians developed the most sophisticated mathematical system known prior to the fifteenth century C.E. Babylonian mathematics was based on the number sixty (we still divide hours and minutes into sixty units today). Babylonian mathematicians devised multiplication tables and tables of reciprocals. They also devised tables of squares and square roots, cubes and cube roots, and other calculations needed for computing such important figures as compound interest. Although Babylonian mathematicians were not primarily interested in theoretical problems and were seldom given to abstraction, their technical proficiency indicates the complex level of sophistication with which Hammurabi's contemporaries could tackle the problems of living in a complex society.

For all its successes, Hammurabi's state was no more successful than those of his predecessors at defending itself against internal conflicts or external enemies. Despite his efforts, the traditional organization inherited from his Sumerian and Akkadian predecessors could not ensure orderly administration of a far-flung collection of cities. Hammurabi's son lost over half of his father's kingdom to internal revolts. Weakened by internal dissension, the kingdom fell to a new and potent force—the Hittites.

From their capital of Hattushash (modern Bogazköy in Turkey), the Hittites established a centralized state based on agriculture and trade in the metals mined from the ore-rich mountains of Anatolia and exported to Mesopotamia. Perfecting the light, horse-drawn war chariot, the Hittites expanded into northern Mesopotamia and along the Syrian coast. They were able to destroy the Babylonian state around 1600 B.C.E. Unlike the Sumerians, the Semitic nomads, the Akkadians, and the Babylonians, the Hittites were an Indo-European people, speaking a language that was part of a linguistic family that includes most modern European languages as well as Persian, Greek, Latin, and Sanskrit. The Hittites' gradual expansion south along the coast was checked at the battle of Kadesh around 1300 B.C.E., when they encountered the army of an even greater and more ancient power—the Egypt of Ramses II.

Mesopotamia: Between the Two Rivers

ca. 3500 B.C.E.	Pictograms appear
ca. 3000–2316 B.C.E.	War for control of Sumer
ca. 2334–2279 B.C.E.	Sargon
ca. 2700 B.C.E.	Gilgamesh
1792–1750 B.C.E.	Hammurabi
ca. 1600 B.C.E.	Hittites destroy Old Babylonian state
ca. 1286 B.C.E.	Battle of Kadesh

Egypt: The Gift of the Nile

Like that of the Tigris and Euphrates valleys, the rich soil of the Nile Valley can support a dense population. There, however, the similarities end. Unlike the Mesopotamian, the Nile floodplain required little effort to make the land productive. Each year the river flooded at exactly the right moment to irrigate crops and to deposit a layer of rich, fertile silt. South of the last cataracts, the fertile region called Upper Egypt is about eight miles wide and is flanked by high desert plateaus. Near the Mediterranean in Lower Egypt, the Nile spreads across a lush, marshy delta more than a hundred miles wide. Egypt knew only two environments, the fertile Nile Valley and the vast wastes of the Sahara surrounding it. This inhospitable and largely uninhabitable region limited Egypt's contact with outside influences. Thus while trade, communication, and violent conquest characterized Mesopotamian civilization, Egypt knew self-sufficiency, an inward focus in culture and society, and stability. In its art, political structure, society, and religion, the Egyptian universe was static. Nothing was ever to change.

The earliest sedentary communities in the Nile Valley appeared on the western margin of the Delta around 4000 B.C.E. In villages, some of which had populations of around ten thousand, huts constructed of poles and adobe bricks huddled together near *wadis*, fertile riverbeds that were dry except during the rainy season. Farther south, in Upper Egypt, similar communities developed somewhat later but achieved an earlier political

unity and a higher level of culture. By around 3200 B.C.E., Upper Egypt was in contact with Mesopotamia and had apparently borrowed something of that region's artistic and architectural traditions. During the same period, Upper Egypt developed a pictographic script.

These cultural achievements coincided with the political centralization of Upper Egypt under a series of kings. Probably around 3150 B.C.E., King Narmer or one of his predecessors in Upper Egypt expanded control over the fragmented south, uniting Upper and Lower Egypt and establishing a capital at Memphis on the border between these two regions. For over twenty-five hundred years this lush corner of Africa—the Nile Valley, from the first cataract to the Mediterranean—enjoyed the most stable civilization the Western world has ever known.

Tending the Cattle of God

Historians divide the vast sweep of Egyptian history into thirty-one dynasties, regrouped in turn into four periods of political centralization: pre- and early dynastic Egypt (ca. 3150–2770 B.C.E.), the Old Kingdom (ca. 2770–2200 B.C.E.), the Middle Kingdom (ca. 2050–1786 B.C.E.), and the New Kingdom (ca. 1560–1087 B.C.E.). The time gaps between kingdoms were periods of disruption and political confusion termed intermediate periods. While minor changes in social, political, and cultural life certainly occurred during these centuries, the changes were less significant than the astonishing stability and continuity of the civilization that developed along the banks of the Nile.

Divine kingship was the cornerstone of Egyptian life. The king lived in the royal city of Memphis in the splendor of a *Per-ao* or "great house," from which comes the word *pharaoh*, the Hebrew term for the Egyptian king. Initially, the king was regarded as the incarnation of Horus, a sky and falcon god. Later, the king was identified with the sun god Ra (subsequently known as Amen-Re, the great god), as well as with Osiris, the god of the dead. As divine incarnation, the king was obliged above all to care for his people. It was he who assured the annual flooding of the Nile, which brought water to the parched land. His commands preserved *maat*, the ideal state of the universe and society, a condition of harmony and justice. In the poetry of the Old Kingdom, the king was the divine herdsman, while the people were the cattle of god:

> Well tended are men, the cattle of god.
> He made heaven and earth according to their desire

and repelled the demon of the waters . . .
He made for them rulers (even) in the egg,
a supporter to support the back of the disabled.

Unlike the rulers in Mesopotamia, the kings of the Old Kingdom were not warriors but divine administrators. Protected by the Sahara, Egypt had few external enemies and no standing army. A vast bureaucracy of literate court officials and provincial administrators assisted the god-king. They wielded wide authority as religious leaders, judicial officers, and, when necessary, military leaders. A host of subordinate overseers, scribes, metalworkers, stonemasons, artisans, and tax collectors rounded out the royal administration. At the local level, governors administered provinces called *nomes*, the basic units of Egyptian local government.

Women of ancient Egypt were more independent and involved in public life than were those of Mesopotamia. Egyptian women owned property, conducted their own business, entered legal contracts, and brought lawsuits. They shared in the economic and professional life of the country at every level except one. Women were apparently excluded from formal education. The professional bureaucracy was open only to those who could read and write. As a result, the primary route to public power was closed to women, and the bureaucratic machinery remained firmly in the hands of men. The role of this bureaucracy was to administer estates, collect taxes, and channel revenues and labor toward vast public works projects. These construction projects focused on the king.

During the Old and Middle kingdoms, great pyramid temple-tomb complexes were built for the kings. Within the temples priests and servants performed rituals to serve the dead kings just as they had served the kings when they were alive. Even death did not disrupt the continuity so vital to Egyptian civilization. The cults of dead kings reinforced the monarchy, since veneration of past rulers meant veneration of the kings' ancestors. The founder of the Old Kingdom, King Zoser, who was an approximate contemporary of Gilgamesh, built the first pyramid-temple, the Step Pyramid at Sakkara.

Building and equipping the pyramids focused and transformed Egypt's material and human resources. Artists and craft workers had to be trained, engineering and transportation problems solved, quarrying and stoneworking techniques perfected, and laborers recruited. In the Old Kingdom, whose population has been estimated at perhaps 1.5 million, more than seventy thousand workers at a time were employed in building these

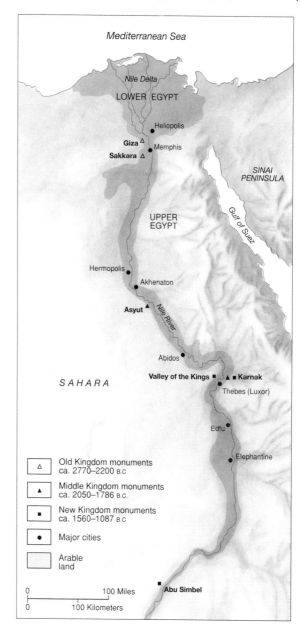

Ancient Egypt

great temple-tombs. The largest, the Great Pyramid of Khufu (ca. 2000 B.C.E.), stood 481 feet high and contained almost 6 million tons of stone. In comparison, the great Ziggurat of Ur rose only some 120 feet above the Mesopotamian plain.

Feeding the masses of laborers absorbed most of the country's agricultural surplus. Equipping the temples and pyramids provided a constant demand for the highest-quality luxury goods, since royal tombs and

The pyramids at Giza, near modern Cairo. The three largest pyramids, which were built around 2600–2500 B.C.E., are the tombs of the pharaohs Khufu, Khafre, and Menkure.

temples were furnished as luxuriously as palaces. Thus the construction and maintenance of these vast complexes focused the organization and production of Egypt's economy and government.

Democratization of the Afterlife

In the Old Kingdom, future life was available only to the king or through the king. The graves of thousands of his attendants and servants surrounded his temple. All the wealth, labor, and expertise of the kingdom thus flowed into these temples, reinforcing the position of the king. Like the tip of a pyramid, the king was the summit, supported by all of society.

Gradually, however, the absolute power of the king declined. The increasing demands for consumption by the court and the cults forced agricultural expansion into areas where returns were poor, thus decreasing the flow of wealth. As bureaucrats increased their efforts to supply the voracious needs of living and dead kings and their attendants, they neglected the maintenance of the economic system that supplied these needs. The royal government was not protecting society, the "cattle of god" were not being well tended. Finally, tax-exempt religious foundations, established to ensure the perpetual cult of the dead, received donations of vast amounts of property and came to rival the power of the king. This removed an ever greater amount of the

country's wealth from the control of the king and his agents. Thus the wealth and power of the kings declined at roughly the time that Sargon was expanding his Akkadian state in Mesopotamia. By around 2200 B.C.E., Egyptian royal authority collapsed entirely, leaving political and religious power in the hands of provincial governors.

After almost two hundred years of fragmentation, the governors of Thebes in Upper Egypt reestablished centralized royal traditions, but with a difference. Kings continued to build vast temples, but they did not resume the tremendous investments in pyramid complexes on the scale of the Old Kingdom. The bureaucracy was opened to all men, even sons of peasants, who could master the complex pictographic writing. Private temple-tombs proliferated and with them new pious foundations. These promised eternal care by which anyone with sufficient wealth could enjoy a comfortable afterlife.

The memory of the shortcomings of the Old Kingdom introduced a new ethical perspective expressed in the literature written by the elite. For the first time, the elite voiced the concern that justice might not always be served and that the innocent might suffer at the hands of royal agents. In the story of Sinuhe, a popular tale from around 1900 B.C.E., an official of Amenemhet I (d. 1962 B.C.E.) flees Egypt after the death of his king. He fears that through false reports of his actions he will incur the wrath of Amenemhet's son, Senusert I. Only in his old age, after years in Syria and Palestine, does Sinuhe dare to return to his beloved Egypt. There, through the intercession of the royal children, Senusert receives him honorably and grants him the ultimate favor, his own pyramid-tomb. The moral is clear: The state system at times failed in its responsibility to safeguard *maat*.

The greater access to power and privilege in the Middle Kingdom benefited foreigners as well as Egyptians. Assimilated Semites from Palestine rose to important administrative positions. By around 1600 B.C.E., when the Hittite armies were destroying the state of Hammurabi's successors, large bands of Palestinians had settled in the eastern Delta, setting the stage for the first foreign conquest of Egypt. A series of kings referred to by Egyptian sources as "rulers of foreign lands," or *Hyksos*, overran the country and ruled the Nile Valley as far south as Memphis. These foreigners adopted the traditions of Egyptian kingship and continued the tradition of divine rule.

The Hyksos kings introduced their military technology and organization into Egypt. In particular, they brought with them the light, horse-drawn war chariot. This mobile fighting platform, manned by warriors armed with bows, bronze swords of a type previously unknown in Egypt, and lances, transformed Egyptian military tactics. These innovations remained even after the Hyksos were expelled by Ahmose I (1552–1527 B.C.E.), the Theban founder of the Eighteenth Dynasty, with whose reign the New Kingdom began.

This painted limestone head of Hatshepsut was originally from a statue. She is shown wearing the crown of Egypt and the stylized "beard" that symbolized royalty and was often seen on the statues and death masks of pharaohs.

The Egyptian Empire

Ahmose did not stop with the liberation of Egypt. He forged an empire. He and his successors used their new-found military might to extend the frontiers of Egypt south up the Nile beyond the fourth cataract and well into Nubia, solidifying Egypt's contacts with other regions of Africa. To the east they absorbed the caravan routes to the Red Sea, from which they were able to send ships to Punt (probably modern Somalia), the source of the myrrh and frankincense needed for funeral and religious rituals. Most important was the Egyptian expansion into Canaanite Palestine and Syria. Here Egyptian chariots crushed their foes as kings pressed on as far as the Euphrates. Thutmose I (1506–1494 B.C.E.) proclaimed, "I have made the boundaries of Egypt as far as that which the sun encircles."

Thutmose's immediate successors were his children, Thutmose II (1494–1490 B.C.E.) and Hatshepsut (1490–1468 B.C.E.), who married her brother. Such brother-sister marriages, although not unknown in polygamous Egyptian society, were rare. After the death of Thutmose II, Hatshepsut ruled both as regent for her stepson Thutmose III (1490–1468 B.C.E.) and as co-ruler. She was by all accounts a capable ruler, preserving stability and even personally leading the army on several occasions to protect the empire.

In spite of the efforts of Hatshepsut and her successors, the Egyptian empire was never as grand as its kings proclaimed. Many of the northern expeditions were raids rather than conquests. Still, the expanded political frontiers meant increased trade and unprecedented interaction with the rest of the ancient world. The cargo excavated from the wreck of a ship that sank off the coast of modern Turkey around 1350 B.C.E. vividly portrays the breadth of international exchange in the New Kingdom. The nationality of the ship, its origins, and its destination are unknown, but it carried a cargo of priceless and exotic merchandise from around the Mediterranean world. The lost ship was probably not a merchant vessel in the modern sense; private merchants were virtually unknown in the Egyptian empire. Instead, most precious commodities circulated through royal ventures or as gifts and tribute.

Religion was both the heart of royal power and its only limiting force. Though the king was the embodiment of the religious tradition, he was also bound by that tradition, as it was interpreted by an ancient and powerful system of priesthoods, pious foundations, and cults. The intimate relationship between royal absolutism and religious cult culminated in the reign of Amenhotep IV (1364–1347 B.C.E.), the most controversial and enigmatic ruler of the New Kingdom, who challenged the very basis of royal religious control. In a calculated break with over a thousand years of Egyptian religious custom, Amenhotep attempted to abolish the cult of Amen-Re along with all of the other traditional gods, their priesthoods, and their festivals. In their place he promoted a new divinity, the sun-disk god Aten. Amenhotep moved his capital from Thebes to a new temple city, modern Tell al-'Amarna, and changed his own name to Akhenaten ("It pleases Aten").

Akhenaten has been called the first monotheist, a reformer who sought to revitalize a religion that had decayed into superstition and magic. Yet his monotheism was not complete. The god Aten shared divine status with Akhenaten himself. Akhenaten attacked other cults, especially that of Amen-Re, to consolidate royal power and to replace the old priesthoods with his own family members and supporters.

In attempting to reestablish royal divinity, Akhenaten temporarily transformed the aesthetics of Egyptian court life. Traditional archaic language gave way to the everyday speech of the fourteenth century B.C.E. Wall paintings and statues showed people in the clothing that they actually wore rather than in stylized parade dress. This new naturalism rendered the king at once more human and more divine. It differentiated him from the long line of preceding kings, emphasizing his uniqueness and his royal power.

The strength of royal power was so great that during his reign Akhenaten could command acceptance of his radical break with Egyptian stability. However, his ambitious plan did not long survive his death. His innovations annoyed the Egyptian elite, while his abolition of traditional festivals alienated the masses. His son-in-law, Tutankhamen (1347–1337 B.C.E.), the son of Akhenaten's predecessor, was a child when he became king upon Akhenaten's death. Under the influence of his court advisors, probably inherited from his father's reign, he restored the ancient religious traditions and

abandoned the new capital of Amarna for his father's palace at Thebes.

Return to the old ways meant return to the old problems. Powerful pious foundations controlled fully ten percent of the population. Dynastic continuity ended after Tutankhamen and a new military dynasty seized the throne. These internal problems provided an opportunity for the Hittite state in Asia Minor to expand south at the expense of Egypt. Ramses II (1289–1224 B.C.E.) checked the Hittite expansion at the battle of Kadesh, but the battle was actually a draw. Eventually, Ramses and the Hittite king Hattusilis III signed a peace treaty whose terms included nonaggression and mutual defense. The agreement marked the failure of both states to unify the Fertile Crescent, the region stretching from the Persian Gulf northwest through Mesopotamia and down the Mediterranean coast to Egypt.

The mutual standoff at Kadesh did not long precede the disintegration of both Egypt and the Hittite state. Within a century, states large and small along the Mediterranean coast from Anatolia to the Delta and from the Aegean Sea in the west to the Zagros Mountains in the east collapsed or were destroyed in what seems to have been a general crisis of the civilized world. The various raiders, sometimes erroneously called the "Sea Peoples," who struck Egypt, Syria, the Hittite state, and elsewhere were not the primary cause of the crisis. It

Egypt: The Gift of the Nile

ca. 3150–2770 B.C.E.	Predynastic and early dynastic Egypt
ca. 2770–2200 B.C.E.	Old Kingdom
ca. 2600 B.C.E.	Pyramid of Khufu
ca. 2050–1786 B.C.E.	Middle Kingdom
ca. 1560–1087 B.C.E.	New Kingdom
1552–1527 B.C.E.	Ahmose I
1506–1494 B.C.E.	Thutmose I
1494–1490 B.C.E.	Thutmose II
1490–1468 B.C.E.	Hatshepsut
1364–1347 B.C.E.	Amenhotep IV (Akhenaten)
1347–1337 B.C.E.	Tutankhamen
1289–1224 B.C.E.	Ramses II

was rather internal political, economic, and social strains within both of these great states that provided the opportunity for various groups—including Anatolians, Greeks, Israelites, and others—to raid the ancient centers of civilization. In the ensuing confusion, the small Semitic kingdoms of Syria and Palestine developed a precarious independence in the shadow of the great powers.

Israel: Between Two Worlds

Urban forms of civilization were an endangered species throughout antiquity. Just beyond the well-tilled fields of Mesopotamia and the fertile delta of the Nile lay the world of anticivilization—that of the Semitic tribes of seminomadic shepherds and traders. Of course, not all Semites were nonurban. Many had formed part of the heterogeneous population of the Sumerian world. Sargon's Semitic Akkadians and Hammurabi's Amorites created great Mesopotamian nation-states, adopting the ancient Sumerian cultural traditions. Along the coast of Palestine, other Semitic groups established towns modeled on those of Mesopotamia, which were involved in the trade between Egypt and the north. But the majority of Semitic peoples continued to live a life radically different from that of the floodplain civilizations. From these, one small group, the Hebrews, emerged to establish a religious and cultural tradition unique in antiquity.

A Wandering Aramaean Was My Father

Sometime after 2000 B.C.E., small Semitic bands under the leadership of patriarchal chieftains spread into what is today Syria and Palestine. These bands crisscrossed the Fertile Crescent, searching for pasture for their flocks. Occasionally they participated in the trade uniting Mesopotamia and the towns of the Mediterranean coast. For the most part, however, they pitched their tents on the outskirts of towns only briefly, moving on when their sheep and goats had exhausted the supply of pasturage. Semitic Aramaeans and Chaldeans brought with them not only their flocks and families, but Mesopotamian culture as well. Hebrew history records such Mesopotamian traditions as the story of the flood (Genesis, chapters 6–10), legal traditions strongly reminis-

cent of those of Hammurabi, and the worship of the gods on high places. Stories such as that of the Tower of Babel (Genesis, chapter 11) and the garden of Eden (Genesis, chapters 2–4) likewise have a Mesopotamian flavor, but with a difference. For these wandering shepherds, civilization was a curse. In the Hebrew Bible (the Christian Old Testament), the first city was built by Cain, the first murderer. The Tower of Babel, probably a ziggurat, was a symbol not of human achievement but of human pride.

At least some of these wandering Aramaeans, among them the biblical patriarch Abraham, rejected the gods of Mesopotamia. Religion among these nomadic groups focused on the specific divinity of the clan. In the case of Abraham, this was the god El. Abraham and his successors were not monotheists. They did not deny the existence of other gods. They simply believed that they had a personal pact with their own god.

In its social organization and cultural traditions, Abraham's clan was no different from its neighbors. These independent clans were ruled by a senior male (hence the Greek term *patriarch*—rule by the father). Women, whether wives, concubines, or slaves, were treated as distinctly inferior, virtually as property.

Some of Abraham's descendants must have joined the steady migration from Palestine into Egypt that took place during the Middle Kingdom and the Hyksos period. Although initially well treated, after the expulsion of the Hyksos in the sixteenth century B.C.E., many of the Semitic settlers in Egypt were reduced to slavery. Around the thirteenth century B.C.E., a small band of Semitic slaves numbering perhaps less than one thousand left Egypt for Sinai and Palestine under the leadership of Moses. The memory of this departure, known as the Exodus, became the formative experience of the descendants of those who had taken part and those who later joined them. Moses, a Semite who carried an Egyptian name and who, according to tradition, had been raised in the royal court, was the founder of the Israelite people.

During the years that they spent wandering in the desert and then slowly conquering Palestine, the Israelites forged a new identity and a new faith. From the Midianites of the Sinai Peninsula, they adopted the god Yahweh as their own. Although composed of various Semitic and even Egyptian groups, the Israelites adopted the oral traditions of the clan of Abraham as their common ancestor and identified his god, El, with Yahweh. They interpreted their extraordinary escape from Egypt as evidence of a covenant with this god, a treaty similar to those concluded between the

THE KINGDOM OF ISRAEL

Hebrew scriptures preserve two accounts of the establishment of the monarchy and the selection of Saul by Samuel as the first king (ca. 1020 B.C.E.). The first, from 1 Samuel 9, is favorable to the monarchy, describing how Saul was privately anointed by Samuel. The second, from 1 Samuel 8, is hostile to the monarchy, suggesting that by desiring a king the people of Israel were rejecting the traditional leadership of God alone.

1 Samuel 9-10. The Lord revealed to Samuel: "Tomorrow about this time I will send to you a man from the land of Benjamin, and you shall anoint him to be prince over my people Israel. He shall save my people from the hand of the Philistines; for I have seen the affliction of my people because their cry has come to me" . . . Then Samuel took a vial of oil and poured it on his head and kissed him and said, "Has not the Lord anointed you to be prince over his people Israel? And you shall reign over the people of the Lord and you will save them from the hand of their enemies round about."

1 Samuel 8. All the elders of Israel gathered together and came to Samuel at Ramah, and said to him . . . "Appoint for us a king to govern us like all the nations" . . . And Samuel prayed to the Lord. And the Lord said to Samuel, "Hearken to the voice of the people in all that they say to you; for they have not rejected you, but they have rejected me from being king over them." . . . So Samuel told all the words of the Lord to the people who were asking for a king from him. He said, "These will be the ways of the king who will reign over you: He will take your sons and appoint them to his chariots and to be his horsemen, and to run before his chariots; and he will appoint for himself commanders of thousands and commanders of fifties, and some to plow his ground and to reap his harvest, and to make his implements of war and the equipment of his chariots. He will take your daughters to be perfumers and cooks and bakers. He will take the best of your fields and vineyards and olive orchards and give them to his servants. He will take the tenth of your grain and of your vineyards and give it to his officers and to his servants . . . And in that day you will cry out because of your king, whom you have chosen for yourselves; but the Lord will not answer you in that day."

But the people refused to listen to the voice of Samuel; and they said, "No! but we will have a king over us, that we also may be like all the nations, and that our king may govern us and go out before us and fight our battles."

From The Holy Bible, Revised Standard

Hittite kings and their dependents. Yahweh was to be the Israelites' exclusive god; they were to make no alliances with any others. They were to preserve peace among themselves, and they were obligated to serve Yahweh with arms. This covenant was embodied in the law of Moses, a series of terse, absolute commands ("Thou shall not . . .") quite unlike the conditional laws of Hammurabi. Inspired by their new identity and their new religion, the Israelites swept into Palestine. Taking advantage of the vacuum of power left by the Hittite-Egyptian standoff following the battle of Kadesh, they destroyed or captured the cities of the region.

A King Like All the Nations

During its first centuries, Israel was a loosely organized confederation of tribes whose only focal point was the religious shrine at Shiloh. This shrine, in contrast with the temples of other ancient peoples, housed no idols, but only a chest, known as the Ark of the Covenant, which contained the law of Moses and mementos of the Exodus. At times of danger temporary leaders would lead united tribal armies. The power of these leaders, called judges in the Hebrew Bible, rested solely on their personal leadership qualities.

This "charisma" indicated that the spirit of Yahweh was with the leader. Yahweh alone was the ruler of the people.

By the eleventh century B.C.E., this disorganized political tradition placed the Israelites at a disadvantage in fighting their neighbors. The Philistines, who dominated the Palestinian seacoast and had expanded inland, posed the greatest threat. By 1050 B.C.E., the Philistines had defeated the Israelites, captured the Ark of the Covenant, and occupied most of their territory. Many Israelites clamored for "a king like all the nations" to lead them to victory. To consolidate their forces, the Israelite religious leaders reluctantly established a kingdom. Its first king was Saul and its second was David.

David (ca. 1000–962 B.C.E.) and his son and successor, Solomon (ca. 961–922 B.C.E.), brought the kingdom of Israel to its peak of power, prestige, and territorial expansion. David defeated and expelled the Philistines, subdued Israel's other enemies, and created a united state that included all of Palestine from the desert to the sea. He established Jerusalem as the political and religious capital. Solomon went still further, building a magnificent temple complex to house the Ark of the Covenant and to serve as Israel's national shrine. David and Solomon restructured Israel from a tribal to a monarchical society. The old tribal structure remained only as a religious tradition. Solomon centralized land divisions, raised taxes, and increased military service in order to strengthen the monarchy.

The cost of this transformation was high. The kingdom under David and especially under Solomon grew more tyrannical as it grew more powerful. Solomon behaved like any other king of his time. He contracted marriage alliances with neighboring princes and allowed his wives to practice their own cults. He demanded extraordinary taxes and services from his people to pay for his lavish building projects. When he was unable to pay his Phoenician creditors for supplies and craft workers, he deported Israelites to work as slaves in Phoenician mines. Not surprisingly, the united kingdom did not survive Solomon's death. The northern region broke off to become the Kingdom of Israel with its capital in Shechem. The south, the Kingdom of Judah, continued the tradition of David from his capital of Jerusalem.

Beginning in the ninth century B.C.E., a new Mesopotamian power, the Assyrians, began a campaign of conquest and unprecedented brutality throughout western Asia. The Hebrew kingdoms were among their many victims. In 722 B.C.E., the Assyrians destroyed the Kingdom of Israel and deported thousands of its people to upper Mesopotamia. In 586 B.C.E., the Kingdom of Ju-

Kingdoms of Israel and Judah

dah was conquered by Assyria's destroyers, the New Babylonian Empire under King Nebuchadnezzar II (604–562 B.C.E.). The temple of Solomon was destroyed, Jerusalem was burned, and Judah's elite were deported to Babylon. This Babylonian captivity ended some fifty years later when the Persians, who had conquered Babylonia, allowed the people of Judah to return to their homeland.

The Law and the Prophets

The religious significance of the people of Israel is as great as their political significance is small. The faith of the Israelites is the direct source of the three great Western religions: Judaism, Christianity, and Islam. Gradually, the relationship between Yahweh and the

In this gypsum bas-relief panel, Israelite refugees are seen sadly departing their home city of Lachish after its subjugation by the Assyrians in 701 B.C.E. The sculpture was commissioned by the tyrant Sennacherib to commemorate his victory.

people of Israel was transformed from one of simple exclusivity to monotheism. Particularly after the Babylonian captivity, Yahweh was not simply one god among many but rather the one universal god, creator and ruler of the universe. Yahweh was so beyond human understanding that he could not be depicted in any image.

Although beyond all earthly powers, Yahweh intervened in human history to accomplish his goals. He formed a covenant with Abraham and renewed it with Moses. The covenant promised that Israel would be Yahweh's special people, but in return for this favor he demanded not simply sacrifices but righteousness. Thus ethics was a central aspect of Israel's religion.

Religious leaders, termed *prophets*, constantly explained historical events in terms of the faithfulness of the Israelite or, later, Jewish people (the term *Jew* means a descendant of those who occupied the Kingdom of Judah) to their covenant with Yahweh. The prophets were independent of royal control and spoke out constantly against any ruler whose immorality compromised the terms of the covenant. They called upon rulers and people to reform their lives and to return to Yahweh. The prophet Jeremiah (ca. 650–570 B.C.E.) boldly accused King Jehoiakim (ca. 609–598 B.C.E.) of Judah of reviving the cult of Ishtar and practicing child sacrifice and warned that Yahweh would send Babylon to destroy him. In Egypt or Mesopotamia, such dissenters would have been liquidated. Even in Israel and Judah, prophets often met with persecution. Some prophets were killed. Still they persisted, establishing a tradition of religious opposition to royal absolutism, a tradition that, like monotheism itself, is an enduring legacy.

Nineveh and Babylon

The Assyrian state that destroyed Israel accomplished what no other power had ever achieved. It tied together the floodplain civilizations of Mesopotamia and Egypt. But the Assyrian state was not just larger than the nation-states that had preceded it; it differed in nature as well as in size. The nation-states of Akkadia, Babylonia, the Hittites, and even the Egyptian empire were essentially diverse collections of city-states. Each preserved its own institutions and cultural traditions while diverting its economic resources to the capital. The Assyrian Empire was an integrated state in which conquered regions were reorganized and remade along the model of the central government. By the middle of the seventh century B.C.E., the Assyrian Empire stretched from the headwaters of the Tigris and Euphrates rivers to the Persian Gulf, along the coast from Syria to beyond the Delta, and up the Nile to Thebes.

The Assyrian plain north of Babylonia had long been a small Mesopotamian state threatened by seminomads and great powers such as the Babylonians and later the Hittites. When King Assur-dan II mounted the throne in 934 B.C.E., his country was, as he himself later said, exhausted. Gradually he and his successors began to strengthen the state against its enemies and to allow its population to rebuild its agricultural and commercial base. The Assyrian army, forged by constant warfare into a formidable military machine, began to extend the frontiers of the kingdom both toward the Mediterranean and down the twin rivers toward the Persian Gulf. However, like its predecessors, within a century this empire seemed destined for collapse.

Rapid growth and unprecedented wealth had created a new class of noble warriors, who were resented and mistrusted by the petty nobility of the old heartland of the Assyrian kingdom. The old nobility demanded a greater share in the imperial wealth and a more direct role in the administration of the empire. When the emperors ignored their demands, they began a long and bitter revolt that lasted from 827 B.C.E. until 750 B.C.E. This internal crisis put Assyria at the mercy of its external enemies, who seemed on the verge of destroying the Assyrian state. Instead, the revolt paved the way for the ascension of Tiglath-pileser III (746–727 B.C.E.), the greatest empire builder of Mesopotamia since Sargon. Tiglath-pileser and his successors transformed the structure of the Assyrian state and expanded its empire. They created a model for empire that would later be copied by Persia, Macedonia, and Rome. In the sense that the Assyrians not only conquered but created an administrative system by which to rule, theirs was the first true empire.

From his capital at Nineveh, Tiglath-pileser combined all of the traditional elements of Mesopotamian statecraft with a new religious ideology and social system to create the framework for a lasting, multiethnic imperial system. This system rested on five bases: a transformed army, a new religious military ideology, a novel administrative system, a social policy involving large-scale population movements, and the calculated use of massive terror.

The heart of Tiglath-pileser's program was the most modern army the world had ever seen. In place of traditional armies of peasants and slaves supplied by great aristocrats, he raised professional armies from the conquered lands of the empire, commanded by Assyrian generals. The Assyrian army was also the first to use iron weapons on a massive scale. Assyrian armies were also well balanced, including not only infantry, cavalry, and chariots, but also engineering units for constructing the siege equipment needed to capture towns. Warfare had become a science.

In addition to the professional army, Tiglath-pileser created the most developed military-religious ideology of any ancient people. Kings had long been agents of the gods, but Ashur, the god of the Assyrians, had but one command: enlarge the empire! Thus warfare was the mission and duty of all, a sacred command paralleled through the centuries in the cries of "God wills it" of the Christian crusaders and the "God is great" of Muslims.

Tiglath-pileser restructured his empire, both at home in Assyria and abroad, so that revolts of the sort that had nearly destroyed it would be less possible. Within Assyria, he increased the number of administrative districts, thus decreasing the strength of each. This reduced the likelihood of successful rebellions launched by dissatisfied governors. Outside Assyria proper, whenever possible the king executed traditional leaders and appointed Assyrian governors, or at least assigned loyal overseers to protect his interests. Even then he did not allow governors and overseers unlimited authority or discretion; instead, he kept close contact with local administrators through a system of royal messengers.

In order to shatter regional identities, which could lead to separatist movements, Tiglath-pileser deported and resettled conquered peoples on a massive scale. He transported the Hebrews to Babylon, sent thirty thousand Syrians to the Zagros Mountains, and moved eighteen thousand Aramaeans from the Tigris to Syria. The resettled peoples, cut off from their homelands by hundreds of miles and surrounded by people speaking different languages and practicing different religions, posed no threat to the stability of the empire.

Finally, in the tradition of his Assyrian predecessors, Tiglath-pileser and his successors maintained control of conquered peoples through a policy of unprecedented cruelty and brutality. One, for example, boasted of once having flayed an enemy's chiefs and using their skins to cover a great pillar he erected at their city gate and on which he impaled his victims.

Ironically, while the imperial military and administrative system created by the Assyrians became in time the blueprint for future empires, its very ferocity led to its downfall. The hatred inspired by such brutality led to the destruction of the Assyrian Empire at the hands of a coalition of its subjects. In what is today Iran, Indo-European tribes coalesced around the Median dynasty. Egypt shook off its Assyrian lords under the leadership

of the pharaoh Psamtik I (664–610 B.C.E.). In Babylon, which had always proven difficult for the Assyrians to control, a new Aramaean dynasty began to oppose Assyrian rule. In 612 B.C.E., the Medes and Babylonians joined forces to attack and destroy Nineveh. Once more, the pattern begun by Sargon, of imperial expansion, consolidation, decay, and destruction, was repeated.

However, the lessons that the Assyrians taught the world were not forgotten by the Babylonians, who modeled their imperial system on that of their predecessors. Administration of the New Babylonian Empire, which extended roughly over the length of the Tigris and extended west into Syria and Palestine, owed much to Assyrian tradition. The Code of Hammurabi once more formed the fundamental basis for justice. Babylonian kings restored and enriched temples to the Babylonian gods, and temple lands, administered by priests appointed by the king, played an important role in Babylonian economy and culture. Babylonian priests, using the mathematical methods developed during the Old Kingdom, made important advances in mathematical astronomy.

Under King Nebuchadnezzar II, the city of Babylon reached its zenith, covering some five hundred acres and containing a population of over one hundred thousand, over twice the population of Uruk at its height.

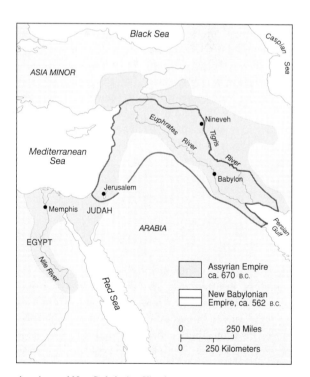

Assyrian and New Babylonian Kingdoms

Israel: Between Two Worlds

ca. 1050 B.C.E.	Philistines defeat the Israelites
ca. 1000–961 B.C.E.	David, king of Israel
ca. 961–922 B.C.E.	Solomon, king of Israel
827–750 B.C.E.	Revolt of Assyrian petty nobility
746–727 B.C.E.	Tiglath-pileser III
722 B.C.E.	Assyrians destroy Kingdom of Israel
612 B.C.E.	Medes and Babylonians take Nineveh
604–562 B.C.E.	Nebuchadnezzar II
586 B.C.E.	Nebuchadnezzar II conquers Kingdom of Judah
539 B.C.E.	Cyrus II of Persia takes the city of Babylon

The city walls, counted among the seven wonders of the world by the later Greeks, were so wide that two chariots could ride abreast on them. And yet this magnificent fortification was never tested. In 539 B.C.E., a Persian army under King Cyrus II (ca. 585–ca. 529 B.C.E.), who had ousted the Median dynasty in 550 B.C.E., slipped into the city through the Euphrates riverbed at low water and took the city by surprise.

The Foundations of Indian Culture, 3000–1000 B.C.E.

The civilizations of ancient India are in some ways very similar and in other ways very different from those of ancient western Asia. As in both Africa and western Asia, geography was an important determinant of ancient Indian civilization. India can be divided into two large geographical regions: the broad plains of the Indus and Ganges rivers in the north, and the peninsular south, which is subdivided into many smaller regions by moun-

tains, plateaus and river valleys. The agricultural season is governed by the monsoon, seasonal rains that fall from June to October. These geographical and climatic factors have important implications for agriculture, and are important in providing a backdrop for India's regional diversity.

The earliest civilizations in ancient India arose in the Indus River valley, in what is today Pakistan. The first of these was the Harappan civilization, named after Harappa, one of the most important ancient cities. The civilization comprised an area of half a million square miles, and encompassed many local cultures that maintained a degree of regional difference yet shared common features. In about 1500 B.C.E., a group of seminomadic people calling themselves Aryans invaded the Indian subcontinent from the north.

Harappa was a lost city, and its achievements and those of the civilization that bears its name were unknown to later generations of Indians. Not until archaeologists uncovered its ruins in the early twentieth century did the magnitude of the earliest civilizations in India become clear. But the culture established by the Aryans, the second civilization of ancient India, preserved in texts called Vedas, or "Books of Knowledge," has had a profound influence on subsequent Indian memory and imagination.

The Lost Civilizations of Harappa and Mohenjo-Daro

Most of our knowledge of Harappan civilization comes from archaeological excavations that began in the early 1900s and continue to the present day. Our conclusions change frequently as new finds are made, interpreted, and reinterpreted. To reconstruct the life of a people through their burial practices, their ruined cities, and fragments of their pottery or metal objects is not a precise science and lively controversy abounds. One of the liveliest controversies surrounds the deciphering of the Harappan writing system.

Sometime in the early third millennium B.C.E., Neolithic settlers from the hills of Baluchistan began to spread to the valley of the Indus River, a valley rich with silt. Farmers planted some crops, like wheat and barley, at the end of the monsoon. Those fields required neither plowing nor fertilizing, nor did the crops require additional water. Farmers planted other crops, such as cotton and sesame, at the beginning of the monsoon and harvested them at its end. To regulate the amount of

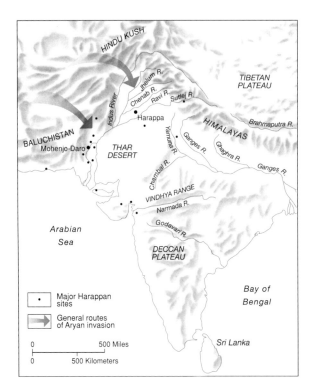

India 3000–1000 B.C.E.

water that reached these crops, farmers built embankments around fields. Thus these earliest settlers manipulated their environment to obtain a living from the soil. Although the land was fertile and the rains regular, Harappan life cannot have been easy. Analysis of human skeletons found at Harappan sites shows that the average age at death was about thirty.

The city of Harappa had a population of from thirty-five thousand to forty thousand people. A second city, Mohenjo-Daro, was somewhat smaller. In addition to several other large cities, archaeologists have found a thousand small sites. Thus, although there was an important urban component to Harappan civilization, the geographical range and the dispersal of the Harappan culture mark it as different from the city-states of western Asia.

In spite of the differences among the sites, an identifiable Harappan culture style had become dominant by the late third millennium B.C.E. The Harappan cultural style is marked by several features, including town planning, a uniform system of weights and measures, and writing. The streets of both Harappa and Mohenjo-Daro were laid out in a gridlike fashion, and the bricks used in construction are of standardized sizes. Large-scale public works, such as granaries, drainage ditches

(some covered with brick slabs) and sewage facilities, also indicate a degree of centralized power and central planning. In the strata (or layers) excavated at Mohenjo-Daro, the layout of the streets is remarkably consistent from one layer to another, indicating considerable continuity. In addition, ceramics produced at various Harappan sites share common stylistic features. One of the most widespread of Harappan ceramics is small carts modelled in clay, possibly toys for the children of ancient India.

The Harappan writing system remains a tantalizing puzzle. The script bears no relationship to any surviving writing system, and has not yet been clearly deciphered. Samples of Harappan writing are preserved on small stone and clay seals, probably used in trading. The inscriptions are short, the longest being twenty-one characters long. About four hundred symbols have been identified to date. The writing system is what linguists refer to as logo-syllabic, which means that some symbols refer to whole words and others to sounds. (Both Egyptian hieroglyphics and modern Japanese characters are also logo-syllabic writing systems.) The stone and clay seals may have identified goods, and the texts on them the occupation, social status, geographical location, and given name or lineage of the owner of the seal. Although much about the language remains uncertain,

Seals from Mohenjo-Daro often featured mythical beasts. The writing may have identified the owner. Such seals have been found as far afield as Mesopotamia.

it appears to be related to a south Indian language family called Dravidian.

The most important economic activities concerned food production. Wheat was the most important grain, but Harappan farmers also cultivated rice. More important to the Harappan economy than agriculture was cattle breeding. Skeletal remains indicate extensive animal domestication. Indeed, these Indians were the first to domesticate the chicken, and most of today's breeds are descendants of birds first domesticated in India long ago. Exotic birds were among the products exported to Sumer.

Handicrafts were also important to the Harappan economy. Samples of dyed cloth have been found at Mohenjo-Daro. Harappans began spinning and weaving cotton about 2000 B.C.E. At Mohenjo-Daro the craftsmen's quarters seem to have been spread throughout the city, whereas at Chanhu-Daro, a much smaller city, they were clustered in the center of the city. This clustered settlement pattern may imply a system of social stratification, in which some residents had more power and prestige than others.

A careful reading of the physical remains can lead us to a variety of conclusions about the religious life of the Harappan people. A large brick tank at Mohenjo-Daro may be a pool that was used for ritualized bathing. Ritual bathing has been an important part of subsequent Indian religious practice. Hundreds of images of women with prominent breasts and hips have been discovered, suggesting that Harappans may have worshiped a mother goddess. Phallic images indicate that fertility, both of the land and of its inhabitants, was important to these early inhabitants of India.

Harappan civilization was a literate, sedentary, sophisticated culture, spread out over much of the Indus valley. About 1750 B.C.E., the civilization seems to have begun to decline, although the reasons for the decline are unclear. Thirty or so skeletons found at Mohenjo-Daro were not buried but were trapped, perhaps fleeing some catastrophe. Perhaps they were fleeing the flooding Indus River, perhaps an earthquake. Whatever the cause of the crisis, the delicate balance upon which Harappan civilization rested crumbled, and the civilization began its decline.

The Aryan Invasion and the Roots of Vedic Culture

Shortly after Harappan civilization fell into decline, the Aryans entered the Indian subcontinent from the northwest. The language they brought with them, an ante-

cedent of Sanskrit, is one of the family of Indo-European languages. (One can see the relationship between the Sanskrit and Latin words for king, for example: the former is *raja*, the latter is *rex*.) They were seminomadic and illiterate. But they had superior military technology: the horse and chariot. The Aryans are but the first in a long line of examples of horse-riding invaders who conquered and transformed sedentary cultures.

The main source for the history of this period is the four collections of "Books of Knowledge," or Vedas, that were collected and preserved by priestly lineages. The oldest of these, the *Rig Veda*, consists of 1,017 Sanskrit

This bronze figure from Mohenjo-Daro is called the Dancing Girl.

poems and is the oldest surviving piece of Indo-European literature. According to tradition it was composed around 1500 B.C.E., though it was not written down until much later. Each priestly lineage would memorize the Vedas and pass them on orally to the next generation. Because the texts were sacred, great importance was attached to transmitting them unchanged from generation to generation.

The Vedas reveal a complex religious system and a rich pantheon of gods. Vedic religion had an important influence on later Hinduism, but it is distinct from it. Vedic religion emphasized the afterlife. The House of Clay, presided over by Varuna, the king of universal order, was the Vedic place of eternal punishment. The House of the Fathers was a place of eternal reward. The Vedas provide a rich pantheon of deities. In addition to Varuna, Aryans worshiped Indra, the thunderbolt-wielding young god of war; Rudra, the storm god; Agni, the fire god; and Ushas, the goddess of dawn.

The Vedic deities are not infallible. They are subject to emotion and error. The deities and the members of the human race each have their own specific duties. As long as god and mortal each perform these allotted duties, the cosmos is in balance. But gods and mortals are not the only inhabitants of the cosmos: there are also demons. And demons are constantly battling the gods, trying to upset the cosmic order. One of the chief ritual acts human priests perform in the Vedas is sacrifice to the gods, to obtain their favor and to restore the cosmic balance. The sacrifice was often of an animal. Central to the ritual was the consuming of soma, an intoxicating drink. The mythological origins of kingship are linked to this cosmic struggle between gods and demons. One such myth relates that during the course of a protracted battle between gods and demons, the gods selected a king to lead them in battle. Thus religion is deeply implicated in the political order.

Although the Vedas are primarily religious texts, we can derive some information on social life from them. Aryan society was firmly patrilineal and patriarchal. Fathers governed their families, and kin groups claiming descent from a common male ancestor comprised the fundamental unit of society. Earlier Vedic societies (late

THE CREATION OF THE UNIVERSE IN THE *RIG VEDA*

■ *This short hymn is a meditation on the mystery of the creation of the universe. It poses questions rather than providing answers. It suggests that the gods cannot be responsible for the creation of the universe, because creation preceded them. A creative force, referred to as "that one," is posited in this hymn.*

In this text, desire is seen as fundamental to cosmic generation. Male seed-givers and female powers are contrasted: the process of cosmic creation is analogized to human reproduction. As the end of the verse makes clear, the cosmic creative force, the one who looked down upon it, is not necessarily omniscient: he may hold the secrets of creation, or then again, he may not.

There was neither nonexistence nor existence then; there was neither the realm of space nor the sky which is beyond. What stirred? Where? In whose protection? Was there water, bottomlessly deep?

There was neither death nor immortality then. There was no distinguishing sign of night or day. That one breathed, windless, by its own impulse. Other than that there was nothing beyond.

Darkness was hidden by darkness in the beginning; with no distinguishing sign, all this was water. The life force that was covered by emptiness, that one arose through the power of heat.

Desire came upon that one in the beginning; that was the first seed of the mind. Poets seeking in their heart with wisdom found the bond of existence in nonexistence.

The cord was extended across. Was there below? Was there above? There were seed-placers; there were powers. There was impulse beneath; there was giving-forth above.

Who really knows? Who will here proclaim it? Whence was it produced? Whence is this creation? The gods came afterwards, with the creation of this universe. Who then knows whence it has arisen?

Whence this creation has arisen—perhaps it formed itself, or perhaps it did not—the one who looked down on it, in the highest heaven—only he knows—and perhaps he does not know.

second to early first millennium B.C.E.) were tribal or lineage-based. The economy was largely pastoral. But by the late Vedic period (800–600 B.C.E.), the tribes and lineages had coalesced into kingdoms, typically ruled by a warrior-king. There were no regularized legal institutions: custom served as law, and its arbiters were the king and his priests.

When the Aryans arrived in India, they divided their society into three groups: the ruling warriors known as Kshatriyas; the priests, or Brahmans; and the cultivators. The non-Aryan inhabitants of India formed a fourth group. The first three groups were known as the twice-born, because males in the group underwent an initiation to adulthood. Only members of these highest three groups—both male and female—could perform Vedic sacrifices. This hierarchical way of organizing society and social interactions was the beginning of the caste system, which would be elaborated and made much more rigid in later Indian history.

In this early period, some key aspects of Indian culture were established. The Vedas would remain crucial religious texts in later eras. The language of the Vedas, Sanskrit, was to function as the classical language of later India. And the caste system was to be one of the determining aspects of Indian civilization. Regional variation is another theme we will see again in the history of the Indian subcontinent. The cultures of the Indian subcontinent are marked by a complex mixture of elements the Aryans brought with them and elements from the time before the conquest.

The Foundations of Indian Culture

3000–1500 B.C.E.	Indus Valley civilizations of Harappa and Mohenjo-Daro
1750 B.C.E.	Beginning of Aryan invasions
1500–500 B.C.E.	Vedic societies

Cradles of Chinese Civilization, 5000–1000 B.C.E.

If Indian civilization is marked by the sharp discontinuity of the Aryan invasions and by great regional diversity, Chinese civilization reveals a remarkable level of continuity and cultural uniformity. We can see elements of this even in the earliest periods. The writing system devised during the Shang dynasty four thousand years ago is clearly related to modern Chinese writing. And writing is not the only aspect of identifiably "Chinese" culture to be established in those early days. Chinese culture is not unchanging, but there is a durability to Chinese cultural forms that we rarely see elsewhere in the world.

Neolithic Villages

Chinese civilization has several cradles. Around 5000 B.C.E., when the Yangshao culture was emerging in the north, villagers farther south in Homudu (in present-day Zhejiang province) began to cultivate rice and construct complex wooden houses. In what is now Vietnam, coastal peoples developed their own distinctive agricultural and craft traditions.

The Neolithic Yangshao culture centered on small villages, frequently built on hills to avoid floods. The villagers built their houses of tamped earth with thatched roofs. They practiced slash-and-burn agriculture, a form of cultivation in which land is cleared (the growth is slashed and burned), and then cultivated. After a few years, the land is abandoned, and new land is brought into cultivation. As long as land is plentiful, this method of cultivation is reasonably productive, but it ceases to be efficient after the population reaches a certain level.

Yangshao farmers domesticated dogs and pigs. Cut silkworm cocoons found at Yangshao sites indicate that sericulture (the cultivation of silk) is as old in China as sedentary agriculture itself. Yangshao people used tools made of polished and chipped stone. Their kilns were capable of temperatures of between 1000 and 1500 degrees Fahrenheit. Yangshao painted pottery, decorated with designs of fish and birds, was elaborate and beautiful, but there is no evidence that it was cast on a potter's wheel.

The Yangshao people had elaborate burial practices that give evidence that their society was stratified. They buried the dead in special burial grounds and buried

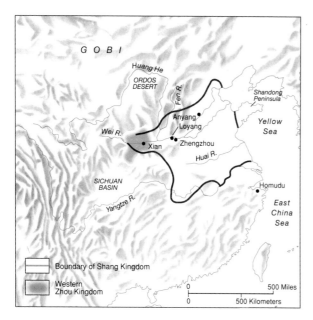

Cradles of Chinese Civilization

women and men separately. In some sites a high percentage of women's graves are richly endowed with grave goods, sometimes more elaborate than those of their male counterparts, raising the possibility that China in antiquity may have been a matriarchal society. In a matriarchal society, the family is the crucial social unit, and the most powerful person in the family is the mother. Later Chinese societies were strongly patriarchal.

Another north Chinese Neolithic culture, called the Longshan, followed the Yangshao. Longshan villages, also built on hills, were typically fortified with tamped-earth ramparts and surrounded by moatlike ditches. The Longshan people produced distinctive black pottery, using a potter's wheel. Potter's marks on many Longshan pots may be prototypes of numbers. Some pots bear phallic symbols and were probably objects of fertility cults. Longshan farmers domesticated the sheep and the ox, as well as the dog and the pig. Despite the importance of agriculture, hunting and fishing remained important to the economy of Longshan villages.

In addition to the northern Chinese Neolithic sites of Yangshao and Longshan, there were also important southern sites. For example, a Neolithic site at Homudu, which can be dated to about 5000 B.C.E., features rice, hand-made pottery, and distinctive wooden mortise-and-tenon architecture. Sites on the southeast coast include Bo-nam and Con Moong, in what is now Vietnam. The southeast coastal sites had a common culture, using similar pottery and stone tools. They also

shared a common diet of taro, yams, and other roots. We know less about the southern Neolithic cultures because the region's high humidity destroys artifacts and the archaeological record is meager. Nonetheless the southern cultures significantly influenced the formation of what would become Chinese civilization.

Certain aspects of the Chinese Neolithic were common to Neolithic villages worldwide: villagers practiced sedentary agriculture and produced rudimentary tools and pottery. But other artifacts from Chinese villages reveal that distinctive Chinese practices were beginning to emerge: the cultivation of rice and silk, for example.

The Shang Dynasty

With the Shang dynasty, more elements of a distinctively Chinese culture emerged. The writing system, ancestor worship, and a political system characterized by both king and bureaucracy are three of the most important of these cultural traits.

The traditional Chinese written record extends about twenty-five hundred years into the past. The earliest texts describe events that happened thousands of years before their compilation. Until recently, scholars considered the first two dynasties in the written record, the Xia (2005–1784 B.C.E.) and the Shang (1784–1050 B.C.E.) to be legendary. But archaeology has radically transformed our view of China's antiquity, firmly establishing the historical existence of the Shang and suggesting that of the Xia. Ongoing archaeological research in the People's Republic of China will continue to illuminate and amplify our views of the past.

In the early twentieth century, scholars discovered Shang "texts" that are contemporary to the events they describe. These texts are called oracle bones, and are among the most remarkable aspects of Shang culture. They are the product of Shang dynasty divination practices, in which a priest inscribed a question on a turtle shell or sheep's shoulder bone (or scapula, hence the term for this kind of divination, scapulimancy). The diviner then placed the shell or bone into a fire, and interpreted the resulting cracks as the gods' or ancestors' answer to the question. A pit containing 107,000 of these bones was found at Anyang, and smaller finds have been made elsewhere. The oracle bones are an extremely important source for Shang history. They are particularly rich in information about the ruling house, about warfare, and about religion.

Inscribed bronze vessels, dating from about 2000 B.C.E., are another important source for Shang history.

EARLY CHINESE ORACLE BONE

■ The text of the oracle bone reproduced below can be divided into four parts: a preface, a charge, a prognostication, and a verification. The text begins by giving the date according to a traditional system of reckoning. The diviner gives his name. The charge, which is here not in the form of a question, follows. It is the king who reads the cracks in the bones and interprets them. His interpretation is inscribed on the bone. Later, a verification that the king's gloom was justified was inscribed on the bone. Relations with border peoples were a constant source of anxiety for the Shang. The Tufang, who are the subject of the alarming news in this inscription, are a persistent problem.

Preface: Crack-making on guisi day (day 30), Chue divined:

Charge: "In the (next) ten days there will be no disaster."

Prognostication: The king, reading the cracks, said: "There will be harm; there will perhaps be the coming of alarming news."

Verification: When it came to the fifth day, dingyou, there really was the coming of alarming news from the west. Zhi Guo, reporting, said, "The Tufang are besieging in our eastern borders and have harmed two settlements. The Gongfang also raided the fields of our western borders."

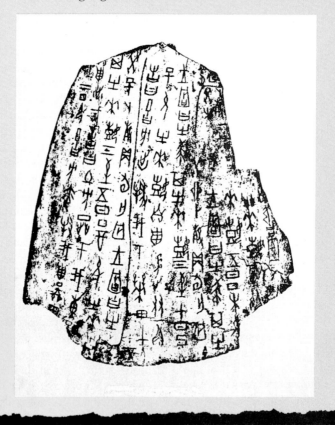

The vessels celebrated ceremonial occasions—succession to the throne, military victory, and so on. The inscriptions describe military exploits and political alliances.

The language inscribed on the bones and bronzes is quite different from modern Chinese, but it is clearly recognizable as Chinese. The Chinese language is written with characters, rather than with an alphabet. Each character represents a word. Many, though not all, of the characters are pictographic. The forms of the characters have been modified somewhat, as have some of the fine points of grammar. But the language written by Shang diviners thousands of years ago can be deciphered by speakers of modern Chinese with a minimum of specialized training, much as native speakers of English need some training to read the Old English of *Beowulf*.

Shang civilization was urban. Excavations beginning in 1928 at Anyang revealed a walled city, since identified as the last Shang capital. And an earlier capital, one at Zhengzhou, was excavated during the 1950s. (The site of the first capital has not yet been located, though a joint Chinese-American team is currently searching for it.) The walls at Zhengzhou, built with tamped-earth construction, are massive. Archaeologists estimate that it took 13 million workdays to construct them, suggesting a political power with a formidable capacity to marshal resources.

The people who built such large-scale fortifications also built elaborate royal tombs. The most spectacular of these was found in 1976 at Anyang. The grave goods were of a richness never before imagined for the Shang—two hundred bronze vessels were found in the burial chamber itself. The tomb belongs to Fu Hao, a consort of the Shang king Wu Ding. The *Book of Odes*, a text compiled between the ninth and the sixth centuries B.C.E., describes the splendor of the Shang under Wu Ding:

> Even his inner domains measured a thousand leagues,
> In him the people found sure support.
> They opened up new lands as far as the four seas,
> Men from the four seas came in homage.

It is not surprising that his consort had a splendid burial.

It is not only from Fu Hao's tomb that we know about this extraordinary woman. Her momentous achievements (she gave birth to several children and she led armies in battle) and her trivial afflictions (she was prone to toothaches) are described in oracle bones.

The data from bones, bronzes, and later textual accounts paint an interesting picture of Shang society. The presence of walled cities, massive bronzes, and chariots implies the existence of an aristocratic class defined by its participation in sacrifices and war. Bronze metallurgy implies a stratified society not only because the technology of casting is so complex, but because of the requirements of mining. Different kinds of burial also imply a degree of social stratification, as do more puzzling finds, like caches of agricultural tools. A cache of 444 stone sickles unearthed at Anyang indi-

cates that there might have been some centralized control of agriculture.

At the pinnacle of Shang society was a king, who had unified religious and secular duties. Under the king was a group of officials who performed specialized functions, but we have no idea how they were selected, paid, or trained. The importance of the minister, a trusted advisor to the king, perhaps one of the defining characteristics of traditional Chinese political culture, can be discerned as early as the Shang. Among the most important of the officials was a priestly class, the diviners. One hundred and twenty of these diviners have left their names on the oracle bones.

The Shang polity in no way resembled a modern state. It was more like a network of linked towns, perhaps a thousand of them. Indeed, the polity was probably defined by the personal power of the king and his officials and their kinship association rather than in terms of control of territory. Outside the core area, the Shang divided their world into friendly and nonfriendly powers. At least one hundred areas sent tribute goods to the Shang king, and these friendly areas were regarded by the king as Shang. The king did not control their territory, but allegiance was signified by the payment of tribute. But all neighbors were not friendly, and the Shang frequently engaged in warfare with peoples on their borders. We can conclude from the accounts of warfare on oracle bones and on bronzes that the king had extensive military power.

The oracle bones reveal a complicated Shang religion. The premise behind the divination practices is that the dead ancestors of the king retain an interest in as well as a power over the world of the living, who can

Cradles of Chinese Civilization

5000 B.C.E.	Beginnings of Yangshao and Longshan civilizations in north China
5000 B.C.E.	Beginnings of Homudu civilization in south China
2005 B.C.E.–1784 B.C.E.	Xia dynasty
1784 B.C.E.–1050 B.C.E.	Shang dynasty

This exquisite jade bird was found in the Shang dynasty tomb of the lady-commander Fu Hao.

communicate with them by divination and placate them by sacrifice. The chief Shang deity is called Di or Shang-di (the word *Shang* is written with a different Chinese character than is the word for Shang dynasty), and he is the ancestor of the ruling house. Throughout Chinese history we will see a lively interaction between the world of spirits and the human world.

By the fall of the Shang dynasty in about 1000 B.C.E., many of the characteristics we have come to think of as Chinese were established. The writing system, the importance of ancestors, and belief in a spirit world that interacts with the world of humans were all established.

Middle and South America to 700 C.E.

The first humans came to the New World over a land bridge between Siberia and Alaska in a series of migra-tions that probably began 40,000 years ago and ended in approximately 10,000 B.C.E., when the end of the Ice Age raised the sea level. Within a thousand years these nomads had reached southernmost South America. Although the first of these people likely originated mostly in northern China, they consisted of a mixture of Mongoloid, Caucasian, and Negroid types from all over Asia. The gradual transformation from hunting and gathering to sedentary agriculture began at roughly the same time as elsewhere in the world, between 9000 and 7000 B.C.E., when drastic alterations in climate caused large game animals to disappear, making it necessary for humans to find other sources of food.

The first civilizations arose in two areas—Mesoamerica, the region comprised of modern-day central and southern Mexico, Guatemala, Honduras, and Belize; and the central Andes, comprised of modern Peru, Bolivia, and Ecuador. (See Special Feature, "The Origins of America's First Civilizations," pp. 36–37.) These civilizations grew in two types of geographic and climatic areas: the coastal lowlands and the highland plateaus. The exchange of technology, art, and commodities between them was a crucial part of the development of their respective societies.

The principal factor in the creation of human civilization in the New World, as in the Old, was the transformation from nomadic hunting and gathering to sedentary agriculture. Sometime between 9000 and 5000 B.C.E. humans began to cultivate the avocado pear, chili pepper, amaranth (a grain), and squash. Between 3500 B.C.E. and 2500 B.C.E. they domesticated beans and maize, settled in villages, and started to make pottery and weave cotton in complex designs.

Because the earliest peoples left no written record and archaeological discoveries reveal only small segments of the past, there are many more unanswered than answered questions about the first civilizations of the New World. Great gaps exist in our knowledge about the rise and fall of empires, as well as everyday life and custom. Archaeologists only recently have come to understand much of the record that exists and historians must constantly revise their interpretations.

For the most part, great advancements took place later in the New World than in the Old and they evolved more gradually. The most notable lag was in the technologies of transport and agriculture, for pre-Columbian civilizations lacked the wheel and the plow. We know that Mesoamerican peoples mastered the technology of the wheel, for archaeologists have unearthed toylike artifacts with wheels, but since there were no large mammals to pull wheeled vehicles and the terrain was often too difficult for them, there was no need to adapt this technology. Relatively primitive metallurgy and the lack of large mammals to pull it also stymied the development of the plow. Moreover, the plow was not usable on terraces and *chinampas* (floating gardens), the most productive methods of agriculture. Nonetheless, the accomplishments of the great preclassic and classic civilizations of Mesoamerica and Peru in art, architecture, mathematics, astronomy, and hydraulic engineering were remarkable and in many ways surpassed those of contemporary civilizations in Europe and Asia.

Society in Mesoamerica and the central Andes evolved increasingly complex social hierarchies and states, which rose in response to the need for intense agriculture. Civilization resulted from success in producing food surpluses. Work, custom, and religion revolved around agriculture and its cycles.

The Olmecs and Teotihuacanos of Mesoamerica

Mesoamerica includes widely diverse climatic, topographic, and ecological regions. The two principal areas in which civilization arose were the central highlands and the southern lowlands. The highlands consisted of mountains, fertile valleys, and plains. The Valley of Mexico, with its network of lakes, was particularly fertile and was strategically located to dominate the area. Other important plateaus were the Oaxaca Valley and the plain of Guatemala. The lowlands, located along the Caribbean and Pacific coasts, were tropical jungle, for the most part disagreeable for human habitation, with the exception of the dry areas of the Yucatán Peninsula.

Nothing in the historical record proves any theory other than that the Americas gave birth to their own remarkable civilizations independent from the Old World. However, given what we do not yet know, and given the recent, radical changes in interpretation of the nature of these earliest peoples, the possibility of exchanges, perhaps extensive, between them is certainly not out of the question.

Archaeologists divide pre-Columbian Mesoamerican civilizations into three historical periods: the pre-Classic, or Formative (2000 B.C.E.–1 B.C.E.), the Classic (250–900 C.E.), and the post-Classic (900–1519 C.E.). In the Formative era villages became larger and residents built the first temple mounds and ceremonial centers, painted their first hieroglyphics, invented a special religious calendar, played a ritual ball game, and practiced human sacrifice.

The so-called "mother" civilization of Mesoamerica, the Olmec (1200 B.C.E.–200 C.E.), arose along the Caribbean in the lowlands of southern Veracruz and Tabasco, a most unlikely region, where the hot, humid climate is unsuitable for human habitation. They constructed three major centers, San Lorenzo, La Venta, and Tres Zapotes. La Venta was situated on an island in the middle of marshland. Tropical soils, cultivated by slash-and-burn agriculture of the sort practiced in much of sub-Saharan Africa and in early Asia, produced food surpluses but did not support a dense population. A total of approximately 350,000 people lived in the Olmec region.

We know little of the Olmecs' origins or rise. We do know that their society spawned a stratified social structure in which kings and, perhaps, warriors ruled where there had been clans and villages, a transformation similar to that in Mesopotamia. This centralized social and political system allowed the Olmecs to organize labor and technology to construct the earliest Mesoamerican ceremonial centers, pyramids, and palaces. San Lorenzo had an elaborate water drainage system, the first form of water control known in the New World.

Their most astounding artistic accomplishments were giant heads, sculpted from stone, weighing many tons. These enormous sculptures represent not only colossal artistic achievements but notable engineering feats as well, for the Olmecs hauled the massive stones a considerable distance to their sites. The Olmecs are also well-known for "were-jaguars," part human and part jaguar figures. These objects, made from jade in varying sizes, represent humans with flat noses, snarling mouths, and jaguar fangs. The Olmecs invented the art of writing and recording calendar dates on stone, bar and dot dates, and glyphic writing.

They initiated the crucial interchange of commodities, crafts, customs, and ideas between highland and lowland peoples. The lowlands provided the highlands with luxury and religious goods, such as precious jewels, bird feathers, jaguar skins, and cacao. The highlands sent corn and other staples.

The Olmecs also provided the first cultural unity to Mesoamerica, introducing many of the gods, myths, and rituals later found among their successors, just as the Sumerians did for subsequent civilizations in western Asia. This spread of Olmec culture is evident, but not the mechanisms by which it took place. However, since it is unlikely that the Olmec region's relatively small population could have sustained conquests of large scope, and archaeological evidence suggests that Olmecs did not live outside their central region in any

Close-fitting headgear and flattened facial features are characteristic of Olmec stone heads. Four of these colossal basalt sculptures were found at La Venta in 1940.

The Origins of America's First Civilizations

What were the origins of the great civilizations of Latin America? Did they arise independently or did they derive from contact with the Old World? One theory suggests that Egyptians migrated to the Americas and founded civilizations. Another posits that the people of the Americas were descendants of the inhabitants of the lost conti-nent of Atlantis, which is supposed to have once existed in the Atlan-tic Ocean. Yet a third theory maintains that Native Americans were the offspring of the ten lost tribes of Israel. While none of these ideas has much validity in light of modern research, there is ample, though by no means con-clusive, evidence that there was contact between Asia and the early American civilizations. The exist-ence, timing, and extent of such contacts is an unending source of debate.

At the heart of the controversy about contacts between the Old and New worlds before 1492 are two contradictory views of the origins of civilization. One main-tains that all human innovations were made only once and then "diffused" through the rest of the world. The other claims that such discoveries have been made in different places independently. Currently, there is considerable agreement that some form of contact took place between Old and New worlds before Colum-bus's voyages, but little evidence supports the idea that external visitors gave birth to American civilizations.

The notion that there were prehistoric relations between Old and New worlds before 1492 (other than the migrations across the Bering Strait land bridge that ended around 10,000 B.C.E.) relies primarily on a number of technical and stylistic similarities between cultures, including architectural structures, artwork (especially pottery), language, and religion, and biological links in the form of cultivated plants, such as sweet potatoes, maize (corn), and cotton.

Various theories abound about transoceanic voyages. One claims that a succession of migrants from Japan, south China, Indochina, and Indonesia continued through 1200 C.E. But no record exists of such voyages on either side of the ocean. The Chinese chroniclers, so pro-lific and painstaking in their record keeping, make no mention whatso-ever. Moreover, no artifact of Asian origin has been found in the

Americas nor any American artifact in Asia. Another question arises as to whether or not the level of sailing expertise was sufficient for such arduous trips. The best case is made for exchanges between the Pacific Ocean islands and the west coast of South America. Thor Heyerdahl, the well-known adventurer, proved that travel across the Pacific from Peru to Polynesia was possible with pre-Columbian technology when he sailed such a route in the raft Kon-Tiki in the late 1940s. Innumerable customs and utensils with similar traits were prevalent in both regions, such as wooden pillows and blowguns. The most convincing proof of interrelation was the presence of the sweet potato in Polynesia before 1492. This plant unquestionably originated in America and very probably was brought to the Pacific islands by humans.

Other controversies surround maize and cotton. Current research indicates that maize was first raised in Mexico around 3500 B.C.E. and then brought to Peru about a thousand years later. Some suggest it spread from China. Two factors argue against this latter theory. Corn was not found among the remains of early agriculturalists in China. Moreover, the speed by which China adopted corn once it was introduced indicates that an earlier arrival would have been sufficiently dramatic to earn recognition in the historical record, which it did not. Cotton was cultivated first in Peru (around 3000 B.C.E.) and four hundred years later in Mexico. Asian strains of the plant abound. But cotton, unlike corn, can be carried by birds. Humans were not necessary to transport its seeds.

During the 1950s, archaeologists at a site in Valdivia, Ecuador, discovered pottery that dated to approximately 3000 B.C.E. They observed that it bore a striking resemblance to pottery of a similar time in Japan and concluded that Japanese fishermen, taken by serendipitous winds across the Pacific, had reached Ecuador and introduced pottery. On closer scrutiny, however, their theory falls apart. There may be closer resemblance to other American artifacts than to the Japanese. More recent discoveries indicate that pottery was present before the Valdivia find and, therefore, the technology was not brought in from abroad. Finally, it is unlikely that a small boatload of fishermen could have begun a technological change of this magnitude.

A lively debate arose over the origins of the Olmecs of Mesomerica. The facial traits characteristic of their sculpture—full lips and broad, flat noses—have led to speculation that there was a migration of Phoenicians or Africans. Although there is some question as to whether one can describe the features as negroid, more importantly, the physical traits exhibited were not necssarily African. Similar heads are found in Southeast Asia. Most likely, the people who crossed over the Bering Strait land bridge originated in these areas of Asia. Archaeologists, noting that Chavín's artwork felines parallel Chinese artifacts, have posited the origins of the Chavín culture of Peru somewhere in Asia. But recent carbon dating indicates that Chavín predated the Chinese discoveries.

Nothing in the historical record proves any theory other than that the Americas gave birth to their own remarkable civilizations independent from the Old World. However, given what we do not yet know, and given the recent, radical changes in interpretation of the nature of these earliest peoples, the possibility of exchanges, perhaps extensive, between them is certainly not out of the question.

significant numbers, this spread probably resulted from trade rather than conquest.

We know as little about the decline of the Olmecs as about their origins. Around 950 B.C.E. the monuments at San Lorenzo suffered mutilation and burial according to deliberate plan. Olmec influence seems to have waned thereafter, though La Venta lasted to 600 B.C.E.

The Olmec heritage of deities, large temples, rituals, glyphs, and widespread commerce was received and raised to its greatest heights in Teotihuacán (200–700 C.E.). A city with remarkable art and architecture, Teotihuacán dominated the central plateau of Mexico, reaching a size larger in area than Rome, its contemporary, and housing perhaps 200,000 inhabitants. Its spectacular architecture included two gigantic constructions, the Pyramid of the Sun and the Pyramid of the Moon along the Street of the Dead, 600 other pyramids, the temple of Quetzalcoatl, two thousand apartment compounds, and five hundred workshops. Its obsidian crafts and "thin orange" pottery (made from fine, polished orange clay) were unsurpassed. Because its excavation has been more thorough than that of any other site in Mesoamerica, our knowledge of the city is extensive. Its exquisite wall paintings reveal a city that was "austere . . . gay and graceful, and intensely religious." Teotihuacán was also an enormous economic power, which like the Olmec, seems to have spread its influence through trade, not warfare. The city's large-scale construction points to a sophisticated state apparatus and hierarchial social structure.

We do not know why Teotihuacán declined. Between 650 and 750 C.E., the main buildings were burned and wrecked and the population scattered. Possibly a combination of ecological and agricultural deterioration, such as deforestation and soil erosion, caused its downfall. Or perhaps Teotihuacán was conquered. In either case, its collapse, like the fall of other great states, "left in its wake a disordered world, whose surviving cities were like planets in orbit around an extinct sun."

The Rise and Fall of the Maya, 300 B.C.E.–900 C.E.

More than in the case of any other early American civilization, our knowledge of the Maya has altered radically in light of recent excavations and discoveries. Whereas once we thought that their enormous achievements in mathematics, astronomy, art, and architecture were based on a sparse population and precarious agricultural base, we have learned that by means of a complicated system of canals, reservoirs, and raised fields, the Maya supported a far larger number of people than previously thought possible. We also once believed that the Maya were peaceful. Now we know from the recent translation of their hieroglyphics that scores of independent city-states, like those of Mesopotamia, lived in constant warfare. Archaeological evidence has changed the view that the Maya resided in villages and that the large, excavated sites were only ceremonial centers; new discoveries indicate that the ceremonial centers had densely populated suburbs.

Central to the reinterpretation of Maya civilization are recent archaeological excavations and the deciphering of the hieroglyphics painted on stone pillars, fig-bark paper, and ceramic vessels. Cracking the Maya code (which had no key to its code, as did the the Egyptian Rosetta Stone, to interpret it) involved three new approaches: recognition that the glyphs were phonetically based, that they are related to present-day Maya language, and that they relate not myths but actual history.

Terrain and climate—swampland and tropical rains—created the conditions for much of the Maya innovations. They had to learn to manage the great quantities of water and to use the swampland for farming. Overcoming these obstacles demanded a stratified society, occupational specialization, and a ruling elite.

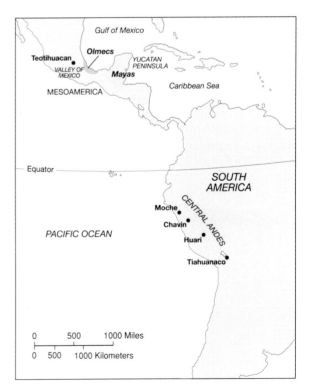

Middle and South America

The Maya solved these problems through enormous, complex systems of reservoirs and canals. Maya agriculture included a system of raised fields and canals constructed by excavating the swamps and piling the muck. The canals held water and fish, whose excretions provided fertilizer for the fields. The complex system was difficult to build and maintain, but produced two or three crops a year.

Maya architecture, literature, measurement of time, and mathematics were as impressive as Maya agriculture. In this, the early Maya were heavily influenced by the Olmecs and later by Teotihuacán. The first great Maya pyramids rose at Tikal and El Mirador sometime after 250 B.C.E. These pyramids were notable for their false arches, carved stone facades, ornamental roofs, and frescoes. Maya hieroglyphics are the only surviving written literature from a pre-Columbian civilization. Much of it consisted of sacred books written on bark paper, only three of which survived the conquest. In the words of one scholar, "writing was a sacred proposition that had the capacity to capture the order of the cosmos, to inform history, to give form to ritual, and to transform the profane material of everyday life into the supernatural."

The Maya calendar was more accurate than the European. There were two cycles of days. The first was ceremonial. It contained 260 days and consisted of 20 months of 13 days each. Another cycle had 365 days divided into 18 months of 20 days, with an extra 5-day month. Completion of the two cycles coincided every 52 years. The Maya also compiled an era-based calendar of 360 days known as the Long Count. They used a bar-dot system for indicating the number of years since the base date. Maya mathematics consisted of units of 1, 5, 20, the dot indicating 1, a bar 5, and positions 20. They also invented the zero.

To the Maya the world consisted of three overlapping domains, heaven, a middle world of humans and earth, and a dark underworld, all of which were interrelated. The world of earth was connected to the underworld through the king.

The lowland kingdoms of the Maya collapsed in the ninth century C.E.. We have only a few clues to explain why this occurred. In some cases the written record actually ends in mid-sentence, suggesting sudden disruptions. The root cause may have been that at some point the population grew to an extent that it overwhelmed the capacity to feed it. Because of social strife or increased warfare, the raised-field agricultural system was neglected and fell into decay. Simultaneously, the Maya evidently lost faith in their kings, whose legitimacy depended on their ability to communicate with the gods. Warfare among the kingdoms grew more intense, a result, perhaps, of pressure from a growing nobility to further its privileges. In the end the Maya gradually stopped building, ceased maintaining their agriculture, scattered into the countryside, and even abandoned literacy.

Although the civilization of the southern lowlands collapsed, this did not end Maya civilization. The kingdoms of the lowlands of the northern Yucatán Peninsula, the greatest of which was Chitzén Itzá, depended not on raised-field agriculture but on rainfall and were thus able to flourish in the ninth, tenth, and eleventh centuries. There was a final resurgence of Maya culture after 1200, lasting until 1441 under the auspices of the state of Mayapán.

The Civilizations of the Andes

Though the area is divided into highlands and lowlands, Andean geography and ecology differ substantially from those of Mesoamerica. The transformation from hunting and gathering to sedentary agriculture took place in the central Andean coastal region between 2500 and 1800 B.C.E. In the Peruvian coastal lowlands rivers traversed deserts, making irrigation necessary for agriculture. Civilizations arose first in the valleys of the north coast which were larger than those in the south. Irrigation required an organized central authority, which gave rise to state bureaucracies and stratified social structures. In the Andes, the altitude and harshly cold climate precluded the cultivation of maize, the staple crop of Mesoamerica. Potatoes were suitable for the environment and became the staple of the Andean highlands, which also supported large mammals—the llama and alpaca—which provided both meat and transportation.

In the Andes no one region dominated in the way that the Valley of Mexico dominated Mesoamerica. Thus a vast increase in food production increased population and gave rise to classic civilization and great achievements, but people lived for the most part in dispersed settlements with ceremonial centers, not in cities as in Mesoamerica. Valleys united as units to maintain their irrigation agriculture. Such dispersed communities housed large populations but did not encroach on farmland.

One of the most important features of Andean life was the colonization by one group, such as a state, community, or even family, of a number of different ecological zones. Highlanders, for example, might establish a

POPOL VUH: THE SACRED BOOK OF THE ANCIENT QUICHE MAYA

■ *The* Popol Vuh *is the Maya equivalent of the Christian and Hebrew bibles. A Spanish priest found the surviving version in the seventeenth century. It features the great hero twins of Maya myth, Hunahpu and Xbalanque. The* Popol Vuh *is, perhaps, the greatest example of Native American literature. The excerpt relates the decision to create humans.*

And the creation of all the four-footed animals and the birds being finished, they were told by the Creator and the Maker and the Forefathers: "Speak, cry, warble, call, speak each according to your variety, each according to your kind." So it was said to the deer, the birds, pumas, jaguars, and serpents.

"Speak, then, our names, praise us, your mother, your father. Invoke then . . . the Creator, the Maker, the Forefathers; speak, invoke us, adore us," they were told.

But they could not make them speak like men; they only hissed and screamed and cackled; they were unable to make words, and each screamed in a different way.

When the Creator and the Maker saw that it was impossible for them to talk to each other, they said: "It is impossible for them to say our names, the names of us, their Creators and Makers." "This is not well," said the Forefathers to each other.

Then they said to them: "Because it is not possible for you to talk you shall be changed. We have changed our minds: Your food, your pasture, your homes, and your nests you shall have; they shall be the ravines and the woods, because it has not been possible for you to adore us or invoke us. There shall be those who adore us, we shall make other [beings] who shall be obedient."

They wished to give them another trial . . .
But they could not understand each other's speech . . .
For this reason another attempt had to be made to create
and make men by the Creator, the Maker, and the Forefathers.

From the translation of Adrian Recinos, in the English version by Delia Goetz and Sylvanus G. Morley.

colony on the coast to assure supplies of fish or elsewhere in the lowlands to acquire coca or other tropical plants. The basic exchange, however, was lowland maize and cotton for highland potatoes and wool. Colonization sometimes allowed states to extend political control over large territories.

The first civilization in the Andes was the Chavín, a religious cult that probably spread through conversion rather than warfare. Around 900 B.C.E., Chavín art and architecture began to spread throughout northern Peru. Typically, these included stone carvings with mouths, eyes, and snakes intermingled, and stylized human, animal or deity figures in geometric forms. The animals were often ferocious jaguars or hawks, giving rise to theories of Olmec influence. The Chavín peoples erected pyramids which, though not as large as those in Mesoamerica, were constructed with rooms and passages. Around 300 B.C.E., the Chavín culture abruptly disappeared.

The Moche (or Mochica) culture, which peaked around 300 C.E., exemplified the great achievements of Peruvian civilization and marked the acme of Peruvian population density, art, and technology. The Mochicas are noted for exquisite art work: magnificent pottery, especially stirrup spout bottles, figure painting, and sculpture. Mochica pottery reveals a realistic view of life at the time and provides more information about its culture than exists for any other society of the region. The paintings on the pottery, often very erotic, portray scenes of everyday life, including hunting, fishing, farming, and warfare, as well as images of gods and scenes from myths. They illustrate social classes through differences in dress. The Mochicas were also highly accomplished at weaving and their metallurgy was more advanced than elsewhere in the region.

In addition to their great artistic achievements, the Mochicas were accomplished engineers. Theirs was the only great pre-Columbian state structure in the Americas that developed solely dependent on artificial irrigation. The construction and maintenance of these large irrigation systems spawned a powerful state bureaucracy, since the state owned the land and controlled the water. Irrigation thus intensified and fixed the differences between rulers and ruled. Violence accompanied this social stratification, and the era of the Mochicas also marked a time when warfare emerged as an important part of Andean life, and Mochica cities were protected with stone walls.

Of the cities built in the era before the Inca in the fourteenth century C.E., the best known is Tiahuanaco, on the southern shores of Lake Titicaca in present-day Bolivia. This ceremonial center of perhaps 10,000 inhabitants is noted for its stone statues and stelae. Tiahuanaco, along with Huari, was one of the two empires that arose around 600 C.E. and brought the first unity to Peru, a unity that lasted two centuries. We know nothing of the reasons for their decline, but by 800 C.E. there were no more cities in southern Peru and there would be none for nearly 700 years. Instead, the entire population lived in villages and small towns.

Regional Fragmentation and War

The end of the classic cultures in both Mesoamerica and the Andes brought a long interlude of fragmentation until the rise of the great empires of the Incas in Peru and the Aztecs in the Valley of Mexico some 600 years later. In Mesoamerica, the collapse of Teotihuacán and the decline of the Maya meant the end of significant high culture. Between 950 and 1150 the Toltecs, a grim, warlike people, dominated central Mexico from their capital of Tula northwest of present-day Mexico City. They were the predecessors of the Aztecs, the greatest warrior state of Mesoamerica. The end of classic culture in the Andes was not as catastrophic as in Mesoamerica for several reasons. First, it was not accompanied by fatal crises in food production or ecology as in the case of the Maya. Second, the Andean ruling classes were evidently not as vulnerable as their Mesoamerican contemporaries, perhaps because their position was founded not on serving as intermediaries between the gods and their people but rather on their control of vital irrigation.

The first civilizations of the Americas ultimately rose and fell on the strength of their ability to produce agricultural surpluses. Despite their sometimes precarious ecological bases, they succeeded to a remarkable extent. A complex of social classes and governmental systems developed around agriculture. Priests contended with deities, bureaucrats organized labor to build and

Mayan Temple I at Tikal. The huge temple-pyramids at the Tikal ceremonial center were built in the eighth century C.E.

operate irrigation works, and craft workers provided goods for trade. In Mesoamerica the environment was evidently unable to sustain great states and their achievements without cyclical catastrophes. In the Andes, geography dictated a dispersed population that for millennia precluded powerful, centralized states.

The legacy of the first three thousand years of civilization is more than a tradition of imperial conquest, exploitation, and cruelty. It goes beyond a mere catalog of discoveries, inventions, and achievements, impressive as they are. The legacy includes the basic structure of modern civilization. The floodplain civilizations and their neighbors provided the first solutions to problems of social and political organization and complex government. Pastoralists and agriculturalists in Asia, Africa, and the Americas found ways to support complex societies in spite of climatic and geographical limitations. These societies built what we now recognize to have been the first cities, city-states, nation-states, and finally, multinational empires. They attacked the problems of uneven distribution of natural resources through irrigation, long-distance trade, and communication.

Middle and South America

40,000 B.C.E.–10,000 B.C.E.	Migration across the Bering Sea
5000 B.C.E.	First agriculture in Mesoamerica
4000 B.C.E.	First agriculture in Andes
1200–200 B.C.E.	Olmec civilization in Mexico
900–300 B.C.E.	Chavín civilization in Andes
200–700 C.E.	Height of Teoti-huacán civilization
300 C.E.	Height of Mochica civilization in Andes
600–800 C.E.	Tiahuanaco civiliza-tion in Andes
300–900 C.E.	Maya civilization in Yucatán
950–1150 C.E.	Toltec civilization in central Mexico

Mochica stirrup-spout portrait vessel. Such vessels have been found in graves and were probably designed as burial goods.

Their religious traditions, from polytheism to monotheism, provided patterns for subsequent world religious traditions. Mesopotamian astronomy and mathematics and Egyptian engineering and building were fundamental for future civilizations.

SUGGESTIONS FOR FURTHER READING

GENERAL READING

Cambridge Ancient History, Vol. 1, Part 1 (Cambridge: Cambridge University Press, 1970). Contains essays on every aspect of ancient civilizations.

* A. Bernard Knapp, *The History and Culture of Ancient Western Asia and Egypt* (Chicago: Dorsey Press, 1987). A good general survey of the entire period.

* Gerda Lerner, *The Creation of Patriarchy* (New York: Oxford University Press, 1986). A study of gender and politics in antiquity by a leading feminist historian.

* Barbara Lesko, "Women of Egypt and the Ancient Near East," in Renate Bridenthal, Claudia Koonz, and Susan Stuart, eds., *Becoming Visible*, 2d ed. (Boston: Houghton Mifflin, 1987). A general survey of women in ancient civilizations.

BEFORE CIVILIZATION

* Lewis R. Binford, *In Pursuit of the Past* (New York: Thames & Hudson, 1988). A general introduction to prehistoric archaeology, intended for a general audience by an expert.

Peter Ucko and G. W. Dimbleby, *The Domestication and Exploitation of Plants and Animals* (Chicago: Aldine, 1969). Technical essays on the origins of domestication.

SUB-SAHARAN AFRICA TO 700 C.E.

* Philip Curtin, Steven Feierman, Leonard Thompson, and Jan Vansina, *African History* (London: Longman, 1978). A standard text of African history that, though somewhat dated, is still useful.

* Jan Vansina, *Paths in the Rainforests* (Madison, WI: University of Wisconsin Press, 1990). A difficult but important discussion of Bantu migrations into the Congo basin.

Roland Oliver, *the African Experience* (New York: HarperCollins, 1991). A highly stimulating overview of the main themes in all African history.

MESOPOTAMIA: THE LAND BETWEEN THE TWO RIVERS

Hans J. Nissen, *The Early History of the Ancient Near East 9000-2000 B.C.* (Chicago: University of Chicago Press, 1988). An up-to-date survey of early Mesopotamia.

* A. L. Oppenheim, *Ancient Mesopotamia*, 2d ed. (Chicago: University of Chicago Press, 1977). Another general introduction by an expert.

* Georges Roux, *Ancient Iraq* (New York: Penguin Books, 1980). A very readable general introduction intended for a broad audience.

Morris Silver, *Economic Structures of the Ancient Near East* (New York: B&N Imports, 1985). A controversial analysis of ancient Near Eastern economy.

* O. Neugebauer, *The Exact Sciences in Antiquity* (New York: Dover, 1970). A series of technical essays on ancient mathematics and astronomy.

EGYPT: THE GIFT OF THE NILE

H. Frankfort, *Ancient Egyptian Religion* (New York: Harper & Row, 1961). A classic study of Egyptian religion.

* B. B. G. Trigger et al., *Ancient Egypt: A Social History* (Cambridge: Cambridge University Press, 1983). A current survey of ancient Egyptian social history by a group of experts.

ISRAEL: BETWEEN TWO WORLDS

John Bright, *A History of Israel*, 3d ed. (Louisville, KY: Westminster John Knox Press, 1981). A standard history of the Israelites until the middle of the second century B.C.E.

A. T. Olmstead, *History of Assyria* (Chicago: University of Chicago Press, 1975). The fundamental survey of the Assyrian Empire.

H. W. F. Saggs, *Everyday Life in Babylonia and Assyria* (New York: Putnam, 1965). A readable account of Babylonian and Assyrian society.

THE FOUNDATIONS OF INDIAN CULTURE, 3000-1000 B.C.E.

Gregory L. Possehl, "Revolution in the Urban Revolution: The Emergence of Indus Urbanization," *Annual Reviews of Anthropology 19* (1990), pp. 261-82. A summary of recent scholarship and controversies.

Bridget and Raymond Allchin, *The Rise of Civilization in India and Pakistan* (New York: Cambridge University Press, 1982). A standard work.

Walter Fairservis, *The Harappan Civilization and Its Writing: A Model for the Decipherment of the Indus State* (Leiden: E.J. Brill, 1992). A detailed account of one approach to the deciphering of the Harappa script.

Romila Thapar, *From Lineage to State: Social Formation in the First Millennium B.C. in the Ganga Valley* (Bombay: Oxford University Press, 1984). A lucid account of state formation in early India.

Wendy Doniger O'Flaherty, *The Rig Veda* (New York: Penguin, 1982) An annotated translation of the classic text.

CRADLES OF CHINESE CIVILIZATION, 5000-1000 B.C.E.

Chang Kwang-chih, *The Archaeology of Ancient China*, 4th ed. (New Haven, CT: Yale University Press, 1986). The single most authoritative source on Chinese archaeology.

David N. Keightley, "Early Civilization in China: Reflections on How It Became Chinese," in Paul Ropp, ed., *Heritage of China: Contemporary Perspectives on Chinese Civilization* (Berkeley and Los Angeles: University of California Press, 1990), pp. 15-54. A stimulating article that explicitly contrasts ancient Chinese and Greek civilizations, and examines what is distinctive about each.

Chang Kwang-chih, *Shang Civilization* (New Haven: Yale University Press, 1980). A synthetic interpretation of what was known about the Shang as of 1980.

David N. Keightley, *Sources of Shang History: The Oracle Bone Inscriptions of Bronze Age China* (Berkeley and Los Angeles: University of California Press, 1978). A survey and explanation of the oracle bone documentation.

Chang Kwang-chih, *Art, Myth and Ritual: The Path to Political Authority in Ancient China* (Cambridge: Harvard University Press, 1983). A highly readable interpretation of early Chinese art and politics.

MIDDLE AND SOUTH AMERICA TO 700 C.E.

Richard E. W. Adams, *Prehistoric Mesoamerica. Rev. ed.* (Norman, OK: University of Oklahoma Press, 1991). Thorough overview for those interested in archaeology.

* Shirley Gorenstein, Richard G. Forbis, Paul Tolstoy, and Edward P. Lanning, *Prehispanic America* (New York: St. Martin's Press, 1974). Contains excellent essays on preconquest peoples of the Americas.

* Nigel Davies, *The Ancient Kingdoms of Mexico* (New York: Penguin Books, 1992). Lively survey of the civilizations of the Mesoamerican highlands.

* Linda Schele and David Freidel, *A Forest of Kings: the Untold Story of the Ancient Maya* (New York: William Morrow, 1990). Magnificent drawings and illustrations of architecture, sculpture, and stelae. The most up-to-date information on the radically new interpretation of Mayan history.

Friedrich Katz, *The Ancient American Civilizations* (New York: Praeger Publishers, 1972). Though the archaeological information is dated, it still provides an excellent framework for comparing Mesoamerican and Andean pre-Columbian civilizations.

Edward P. Lanning, *Peru Before the Incas* (Englewood Cliffs, NJ: Prentice-Hall, 1967). The best survey of pre-Inca civilizations.

---

* Indicates paperback edition available.

CHAPTER 2

Early Greece, 2500–500 B.C.E.

HECUBA AND ACHILLES

The wrath of the warrior Achilles is the subject of the *Iliad*, the great epic poem written at the close of the Dark Ages, shortly after 750 B.C.E., but recalling events that occurred during the semimythical Trojan War, which took place ca. 1220 B.C.E. during the last century of Mycenaean civilization. Episodes from the *Iliad* appear frequently in Greek literature and art, as for example on this magnificent sixth-century B.C.E. *hydria*, or water pitcher.

Angered by a perceived slight to his honor, Achilles sulks in his tent while the other Achaeans, or Greeks, fight a desperate and losing battle against the Trojans. Only after his friend Patroclus is slain by the Trojan prince Hector does Achilles return to the battle to propel the Achaeans to victory. Near the end of the epic, after he has slain Hector in hand-to-hand combat, Achilles ties his foe's body to the back of his chariot and drags it around Patroclus' tomb to appease his friend's spirit. The gods are horrified at this demeaning treatment of the body. Zeus, the chief god, sends his messenger Iris to Hector's mourning parents, his father, Priam, king of Troy, and his mother, Hecuba. Iris urges them to ransom their son's body from Achilles. Moved by the message, Priam goes to Achilles' tent to plead for Hector's body. Achilles, moved by pity and grief for his own father and for Patroclus, grants the old king his request.

The first portions of this episode are brilliantly rendered on this clay pitcher. At the center, Achilles leaps into his chariot. The naked body of Hector stretches below him and the chariot rushes around the burial mound of Achilles' friend, represented by the white hill to the right. Above it, the small winged spirit of Patroclus watches. In death he is a pale reflection, a shade, of his former self, still attired in the clothing and arms of a warrior. But even as Achilles carries out his deed of vengeance, Iris, the winged messenger of Zeus, rushes to Hector's parents, who are shown under a columned portico, which represents Troy. Typically, the artist has taken some liberty with the story. It is not the grieving father the artist has chosen to feature but rather Hecuba, Hector's disconsolate mother. In a vivid manner, totally alien to previous artistic traditions, the Greek artist, like the Greek poet, has captured the essentials of human tragedy.

The epic, traditionally ascribed to Homer, summarizes the essential values of Archaic Greek civilization. First, for all its violent action, the *Iliad* is concerned less with what people do than with how they face the great moments of their life, their time of suffering, their time of death. Second, while the gods are ever present in the *Iliad*, men and women must work out their own lives, struggling against fate rather than acquiescing to it. Third, the essential sphere of human action is the city, the *polis*, the fundamental unit of government and culture. Finally, the variations in the poetic and artistic representations of the scene show at once the importance of the Homeric myths in unifying the Greek world and the fierce independence that artists and others displayed in expressing that unity. Such sentiments, expressed by the poet and restated by the anonymous painter, became an enduring legacy of Greek civilization to its successors. In the small, fragile, and violent communities of Greek speakers spread across the Mediterranean, citizen-soldiers first struggled with these fundamental issues that continue to confront humankind today.

Marble statue of a seated harp player from the Cyclades Islands, dating from the third millennium B.C.E. The statue is executed in great detail despite the primitive tools at the sculptor's disposal.

Greece in the Bronze Age to 700 B.C.E.

Early in the *Iliad* Homer pauses to list the captains and ships of the besieging forces. The roll call of heroes and their homelands is more than a literary device. It is the distant echo of a vanished world, the world of "the goodly citadel of Athens, wealthy Corinth, Knossos and Gortys of the great walls, and the established fortress of Mycenae." The poet lived in an age of illiterate warrior herdsmen, of impoverished, scattered, and sparsely populated villages. Still, in the depths of this "Dark Age," roughly from 1200 to 700 B.C.E., the distant memory of a time of rich palaces, teeming cities, and powerful kings lived on. Homer and his contemporaries could not know that these confused memories were of the last great Bronze Age (ca. 3500–1200 B.C.E.) civilization of the Mediterranean. During this long period, distinctive political and cultural traditions developed both on the

mainland and on the islands of the Aegean Sea. Still less could they have imagined that they were preparing the foundations of a far greater and lasting civilization, that of classical Greece.

Unlike the rich floodplains of Mesopotamia and Egypt, Greece is a stark world of mountains and sea. The rugged terrain of Greece, only ten percent of which is flat, and the scores of islands that dot the Aegean and Ionian seas favor the development of small, self-contained agricultural societies. The Greek climate is uncertain, constantly threatening Greek farmers with failure. Rainfall varies enormously from year to year, and arid summers alternate with cool, wet winters. Greek farmers struggled to produce the Mediterranean triad of grains, olives, and wine, which first began to dominate agriculture around 3000 B.C.E. Wheat, barley, and beans were the staples of Greek life. Constant fluctuations in climate and weather from region to region helped break down the geographical isolation by forcing isolated communities to build contacts with a wider world in order to survive and to establish colonies and communities across the Mediterranean from what is now France to modern Turkey. Throughout its history, Greece was less a geographical than a cultural designation.

Cycladic and Minoan Society: Islands of Peace

To Homer, the Greeks were all Achaeans no matter whether they came from the Greek mainland, the islands in the Aegean Sea, or the coast of Asia Minor. Since the late nineteenth century, archaeologists have discerned three fairly distinct late Bronze Age cultures—the Cycladic, the Minoan, and the Mycenaean—that flourished in the Mediterranean prior to the end of the twelfth century B.C.E.

The first culture appeared on the Cyclades, the rugged islands strewn across the bottom of the Aegean from the Greek mainland to the coast of Asia Minor. As early as 2500 B.C.E., craft workers in small settlements on the islands of Naxos and Melos developed a high level of metallurgical and artistic skill.

Cycladic society was not concentrated into towns, nor apparently was it particularly warlike. Many of the largest Cycladic settlements were unfortified. Cycladic religion, to judge from fragments of large clay statues of female figures found in a temple, focused on female deities, perhaps fertility goddesses.

This early Bronze Age society faded slowly and imperceptibly, but not before influencing its neighbors, especially Crete, the large Mediterranean island to the

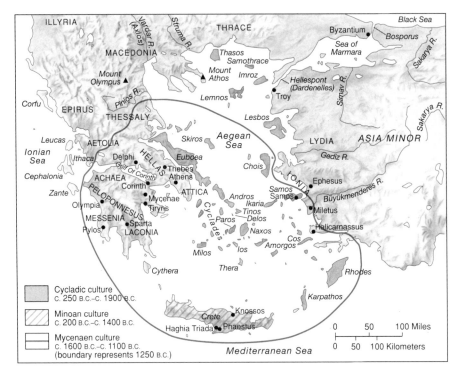

ILLYRIA
THRACE
Black Sea
MACEDONIA
Byzantium
Bosporus
Thasos
Sea of
Marmara
Samothrace
Mount
Imroz
Olympus ▲
Mount
Athos
Hellespont
(Dardenelles)
Troy
Corfu
Lemnos
EPIRUS
Pinios R.
THESSALY
Lesbos
LYDIA
ASIA MINOR
Leucas
Skiros
Aegean
Sea
Ionian
AETOLIA
Sea
HELLAS
Euboea
Chois
Gediz R.
Ithaca
Delphi
Cephalonia
Thebes
IONIA
Ephesus
ACHAEA
Athens
Samos
Büyükmenderes R.
Corinth
ATTICA
Samos
Zante
Andros
Miletus
Olympia
Mycenae
Ikaria
PELOPONNESUS
Tiryns
Cyclades
Tinos
Halicarnassus
MESSENIA
Sparta
Paros
Delos
Cos
Pylos
LACONIA
Naxos
Amorgos
Milos
Ios
Cythera
Thera
Rhodes
Karpathos

Early Greece

Cycladic culture
c. 250 B.C.–c. 1900 B.C.

Minoan culture
c. 200 B.C.–c. 1400 B.C.

Mycenaen culture
c. 1600 B.C.–c. 1100 B.C.
(boundary represents 1250 B.C.)

Crete
Knossos
Haghia Triada
Phaestus

0   50   100 Miles
0   50   100 Kilometers

Mediterranean Sea

south. There, beginning around 2500 B.C.E., developed a remarkably sophisticated centralized civilization termed Minoan after the legendary King Minos of Crete.

Knowledge of Minoan civilization burst upon the modern world suddenly in 1899. In that year the English archaeologist Sir Arthur Evans made the first of a series of extraordinary archaeological discoveries at Knossos, the legendary palace of Minos. Crete's location between the civilizations of the Fertile Crescent and the less urbanized worlds of the north and west made the island a natural point of exchange and amalgamation of cultures. Still, during the golden age of Crete, roughly between 2000 and 1550 B.C.E., the island developed its unique traditions of monumental architecture, social stratification, peace, and the participation of women in public life.

Great palace complexes were constructed at Knossos, Phaistos, Hagia Triada, and elsewhere on the island. They appear as a maze of storerooms, workrooms, and living quarters clustered around a central square. Larger public rooms may have existed at an upper level, but all traces of them have disappeared. Palace bureaucrats, using a unique form of syllabic writing known as Linear A, controlled agricultural production and distribution as well as the work of skilled artisans in their surrounding

areas. Towns with well-organized street plans, drainage systems, and clear hierarchies of elite and lesser homes dotted the landscape.

Like other ancient civilizations, Minoan Crete was a strongly stratified system in which the vast peasantry paid a heavy tribute in olive oil and other produce. Tribute or taxes flowed to local and regional palaces and ultimately to Knossos, which stood at the pinnacle of a four-tier network uniting the island. To some extent, the palace elites redistributed this wealth back down the system through their patterns of consumption.

Though the system may have been exploitative, it was not militaristic. None of the palaces or towns of Crete was fortified. Nor was the cult of the ruler particularly emphasized. Monumental architecture and sculpture designed to exalt the ruler and to overwhelm the commoner is entirely absent from Crete. A key to this unique social tone may be Cretan religion and, with it, the unusually high status of women. Although male gods received veneration, Cretans particularly worshiped female deities. Bulls and bull horns as well as the double-headed ax, or *labris*, played an important if today mysterious role in the worship of the gods. Chief among the female deities was the mother goddess, who was the source of good and evil. However, one must be careful not to paint too idyllic an image of Cretan religion.

Children's bones found in excavations of the palace of Knossos show traces of butchering and the removal of slices of flesh.

Although evidence such as the frequent appearance of women participating in or watching public ceremonies and the widespread worship of female deities cannot lead to the conclusion that Minoan society was a form of matriarchy, it does suggest that Minoan civilization differed considerably from the floodplain civilizations of the Near East and the societies developing on the mainland. At least until the fourteenth century B.C.E., Cretan society was truly unique. Both men and women seem to have shared important roles in religious and public life and together built a structured society without the need for vast armies or warrior kings.

Around 1450 B.C.E., a wave of destruction engulfed all of the Cretan cities except Knossos, which finally met destruction around 1375 B.C.E. The causes of this catastrophe continue to inspire historical debate. Some argue that a natural disaster such as an earthquake or the eruption of a powerful volcano on Thera was responsible for the destruction. More likely, given the martial traditions of the continent and their total absence on Crete, the destruction was the work of mainland Greeks taking control of Knossos and other Minoan centers. An Egyptian tomb painting from the fifteenth century B.C.E. graphically illustrates the transition. An ambassador in Cretan dress was overpainted by one wearing a kilt characteristic of that worn by mainland Greeks. Around this same time, true warrior graves equipped with weapons and armor begin to appear on Crete and at Knossos for the first time. Following this violent conquest, only Knossos and Phaistos were rebuilt, presumably by Greek lords who had eliminated the other political centers on the island. A final destruction hit Knossos around 1200 B.C.E.

Mycenaean Civilization: Mainland of War

Around 1600 B.C.E., a new and powerful warrior civilization arose on the Peloponnesus at Mycenae. The only remains of the first phase of this civilization are thirty graves found at the bottom of deep shafts arranged in two circles. The swords, axes, and armor that fill the graves emphasize the warrior lives of their occupants. By 1500 B.C.E., mainland Greeks were using huge beehive-shaped tombs for royal burials. These structures were magnificent achievements of architecture and masonry, far beyond anything seen previously in Europe. Over fifty such tombs have been found on the Greek mainland, as have the remains of over five hundred villages and great palaces at Mycenae, Tiryns, Athens, Thebes, and Pylos. This entire civilization, which encompassed not only the mainland but also parts of the coast of Asia Minor, is called Mycenaean, although there is no evidence that the city of Mycenae actually ruled all of Greece.

The Mycenaeans quickly adopted artisanal and architectural techniques from neighboring cultures, especially from the Hittites and from Crete. However, the Mycenaeans incorporated these techniques into a distinctive tradition of their own. Unlike the open Cretan palaces and towns, Mycenaean palaces were strongly walled fortresses. From these palaces Mycenaean kings, aided by a small military elite, organized and controlled the collection of taxes and tribute from subordinate towns and rural districts. Their palace administrators adopted the Linear A script of Crete, transforming it to write their own language, a Greek dialect, in

Faience statuette of a priestess, or perhaps a deity, from the Palace of Minos, holding two squirming snakes. The stiff, flounced skirt and bare breasts are typical of female figures found in Cretan frescoes and on gold signet rings.

a writing known as Linear B, which appears to have been used almost exclusively for record-keeping in palaces.

Mycenaean domination did not last for long. Around 1200 B.C.E., many of the mainland and island fortresses and cities were sacked and totally destroyed. In some areas, such as Pylos, the population fell to roughly ten percent of what it had been previously. Centralized government, literacy, urban life, civilization itself disappeared from Greece for over four hundred years. Why and how this happened is one of the great mysteries of world history.

In later centuries the Greeks believed that following the Trojan War, new peoples, especially the Dorians, had migrated into Greece, destroying Mycenae and most of the other Achaean cities. More recently, some historians have argued that catastrophic climatic changes, volcanic eruptions, or some other natural disaster wrecked the cities and brought famine and tremendous social unrest in its wake. Neither theory is accurate. Mycenaean Greece was destroyed neither by barbarian invaders nor by natural disasters. It self-destructed. Its disintegration was part of the widespread crisis affecting the eastern Mediterranean in the twelfth century B.C.E. (see chapter 1, p. 44). The pyramid of Mycenaean lordship, built by small military elites commanding maritime commercial networks, was always threatened with collapse. Overpopulation, the fragility of the agrarian base, the risks of overspecialization in cash crops such as grain in Messenia and in sheep raising in Crete, and rivalry among states—all made Mycenaean culture vulnerable. The disintegration of the Hittite empire and the near-collapse of the Egyptian disrupted Mediterranean commerce, exacerbating hostilities among Greek states. As internal warfare raged, the delicate structures of elite lordship disappeared in the mutual sackings and destructions of the palace fortresses. The Dark Age poet Hesiod (ca. 800 B.C.E.), although writing about his own time, probably got it about right:

> Father will have no common bond with son
> Neither will guest with host, nor friend with friend
> The brother-love of past days will be gone . . .
> Men will destroy the towns of other men.

The Dark Age: 1200–700 B.C.E.

With the collapse of the administrative and political system on which Mycenaean civilization was built, the tiny elite that had ruled it vanished as well. Some of these rulers probably migrated to the islands, especially Cyprus, and the eastern Mediterranean. Others took to piracy. What later Greeks remembered as the Trojan War may have been a cloudy recollection of the last raids of freebooters along the edge of the collapsing Hittite empire. From roughly 1200 until 700 B.C.E., the Aegean world entered what is generally termed the Dark Age, a confused and little-known period during which Greece returned to a more primitive level of culture and society.

In the wake of the Mycenaean collapse, bands of northerners moved slowly into the Peloponnesus, while other Greeks migrated out from the mainland to the islands and the coast of Asia Minor. As these tribal groups merged with the indigenous populations, they gave certain regions distinctive dialectic and cultural characteristics. Thus the Dorians settled in much of the Peloponnesus, Crete, and southwest Asia Minor. Ionians made Attica, Euboea, and the Aegean islands their home, while a mixed group called Aeolians began to migrate to central and northwest Asia Minor. As a result, from the eleventh century B.C.E., both shores of the Aegean became part of a Greek-speaking world. Still later, Greeks established colonies in what is today southern Russia, Italy, North Africa, Spain, and France.

Everywhere in this world, between roughly 1100 and 1000 B.C.E., architecture, urban traditions, even writing disappeared along with the elites whose exclusive benefit these achievements had served. The Greece of this Dark Age was much poorer, more rural, and more simply organized. It was also a society of ironworkers. Iron began to replace bronze as the most common metal for ornaments, tools, and weapons. At first this was a simple necessity. The collapse of long-distance trade deprived Greeks of access to tin and copper, the essential ingredients of bronze. Gradually, however, the quality of iron tools and weapons began to improve as smiths learned to work hot iron into a primitive steel.

What little is known of this period must be gleaned from archaeology and from two great epic poems written down around 750 B.C.E., near the end of the Dark Age. The archaeological record is bleak. Pictorial representation of humans and animals almost disappears. Luxury goods and most imports are gone from tombs. Pottery made at the beginning of the Dark Age shows little innovation, crudely imitating forms of Mycenaean production.

Gradually, beginning in the eleventh century B.C.E., things began to change a bit. New geometric forms of decoration begin to appear on pottery. New types of iron pins, weapons, and decorations appeared, which owe little or nothing to the Mycenaean tradition. Cultural changes accompanied these material changes. Around the middle of the eleventh century B.C.E., Greeks in some locations stopped burying their dead and began to practice cremation. Whatever the meaning of these changes, they signaled something new on the shores of the Aegean.

The two epic poems, the *Iliad* and the *Odyssey*, hint at this something new. The *Iliad* is the older poem, dating probably to the second half of the eighth century B.C.E. The *Odyssey* dates from perhaps fifty years later. Traditionally ascribed to Homer, these epics were actually the work of oral bards, or performers who composed as they chanted. The world in which the action of the Homeric epics takes place was already passing away when the poems were composed, but the world described is not really that of the late Bronze Age. Although the poems explicitly harken back to the Mycenaean age, much of the description of life, society, and culture actually reflects Dark Age conditions.

Homer's heroes were petty kings, chieftains, and nobles, whose position rested on their wealth, measured in land and flocks, on personal prowess, on networks of kin and allies, and on military followings. The Homeric hero Odysseus is typical of these Dark Age chieftains. In the *Iliad* and the *Odyssey* he is king of Ithaca, a small island on the west coast of Greece. To the Homeric poets he was "goodly Odysseus" as well as "the man of wiles" and "the waster of cities." He retained command of his men only as long as he could lead them to victory in the raids against their neighbors, which formed the most honorable source of wealth. Odysseus describes with pride his departure for home after the fall of Troy:

"The wind that bore me from Ilios brought me . . . to Ismarus, whereupon I sacked their city and slew the people. And from the city we took their wives and much goods, and divided them among us, that none through me might go lacking his proper share."

Present, the king was judge, gift giver, lawgiver, and commander. Absent, no legal or governmental institutions preserved his authority. Instead the nobility, lesser warriors who were constantly at odds with the king, sought to take his place. In the *Odyssey* only their mutual rivalry saves Odysseus' wife, Penelope, from being forced to marry one of these haughty aristocrats eager to replace the king.

These nobles, warriors wealthy enough to possess horses and weapons, lived to prove their strength and honor in combat against their equals, the one true test of social value. The existence of chieftains such as Odysseus was a threat to their honor, and by the eighth century B.C.E., the aristocracy had eliminated kings in most places. Ranking beneath these proud warriors was the populace. Some of this group were slaves, but most were shepherds or farmers too mired down in the laborious work of subsistence agriculture to participate in the heroic lifestyle of their social betters. Still, even the populace were not entirely excluded from public life. Odysseus' son Telemachus summoned the assembly of the people, the *demos*, to listen to his complaints against the noble suitors of his mother. This does not mean that the assembly was particularly effective. They listened to both sides and did nothing. Still, a time was coming

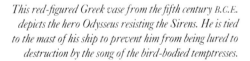

This red-figured Greek vase from the fifth century B.C.E. depicts the hero Odysseus resisting the Sirens. He is tied to the mast of his ship to prevent him from being lured to destruction by the song of the bird-bodied temptresses.

HECTOR AND ANDROMACHE

■ *The Trojan hero Hector is almost as central to the* Iliad *of Homer as is Achilles. Unlike the latter, Hector is a dutiful, reliable support to his city and to Andromache, who is not only his wife but his closest and dearest companion. The description of their last meeting is one of the great expressions of the heroic ethos and of the bonds of man and woman in that culture.*

At last his own generous wife came running to meet him, Andromache, the daughter of high-hearted Eëation, . . . She came to him there, and beside her went an attendant carrying the boy in the fold of her bosom, a little child, only a baby, Hector's son, the admired, beautiful as a star shining. . . . Andromache, stood close beside him, letting her tears fall, and clung to his hand and called him by name and spoke to him: "Dearest, your own great strength will be your death, and you have no pity on your little son, nor on me, ill-starred, who soon must be your widow" . . .

Then tall Hector of the shining helm answered her: "All these things are in my mind also, lady; yet I would feel deep shame before the Trojans, and the Trojan women with trailing garments, if like a coward I were to shrink aside from fighting . . . But it is not so much the pain to come of the Trojans that troubles me, . . . as the thought of you, when some bronze-armored Achaian leads you off, taking away your day of liberty in tears; and in Argos you must work at the loom of another" . . . Then taking up his dear son he tossed him about in his arms and kissed him, and lifted his voice in prayer to Zeus and the other immortals: "Zeus, and you other immortals, grant that this boy, who is my son, may be as I am, pre-eminent among the Trojans,

great in strength, as I am, and rule strongly over Ilion;
And some day let them say of him: "He is better by far than his father,"
as he comes from the fighting; and let him kill his enemy
and bring home the blooded spoils, and delight the heart of his mother."

From *The Iliad of Homer*, Book VI.

when changes in society would give a new and hitherto unimagined power to the silent farmers and herdsmen of the Dark Age.

From the Bronze Age civilizations, Greek speakers had inherited distant memories of an original, highly organized urban civilization grafted onto the rural, aristocratic warrior society of the Dark Age. Most importantly, this common, dimly recollected past gave all Greek-speaking inhabitants of the Mediterranean world common myths, values, and identity.

Archaic Greece, 700–500 B.C.E.

Between roughly 700 and 500 B.C.E., extraordinary changes took place in the Greek world. The descendants of the farmers and herdsmen of Homer's Dark Age brought about a revolution in political organization, artistic traditions, intellectual values, and social structures. In a burst of creativity forged in conflict and competition, Greeks of the Archaic Age (ca. 700–500 B.C.E.) laid the foundations for the Western notions of politics, abstract thought, and the individual.

The first sign of radical change in Greece was a major increase in population in the eighth century B.C.E. In Attica, for example, between 780 and 720 B.C.E., the population increased perhaps sevenfold. The reasons for this extraordinary increase are obscure, but it may have resulted from a shift from herding to agriculture. In any case the consequences were enormous. First, population increase meant more villages and towns, greater communication among them, and thus the more rapid circulation of ideas and skills. Second, the rising population placed impossible demands on the agricultural system of much of Greece. Third, it led to greater division of labor and, with an increasingly diverse population, to fundamental changes in political systems. The

Greece in the Bronze Age

ca. 2500 B.C.E.	Beginning of Minoan civilization in Crete
ca. 2000–1500 B.C.E.	Golden Age of Crete
ca. 1600 B.C.E.	Beginning of Mycenaean civilization in Greece
ca. 1450 B.C.E.	Cretan cities, except Knossos, destroyed
ca. 1375 B.C.E.	Knossos destroyed
ca. 1200–700 B.C.E.	Greek Dark Age
ca. 1200 B.C.E.	Mycenaean sites in Greece destroyed; Knossos destroyed again
ca. 1100–1000 B.C.E.	Writing disappears from Greece

old structure of loosely organized tribes and chieftains became inadequate to deal with the more complex nature of the new society.

The multiplicity of political and social forms developing in the Archaic Age set the framework in which developed the first flowering of Greek culture. Economic and political transformations laid the basis for intellectual advance by creating a broad class with the prosperity to enjoy sufficient leisure for thought and creative activity. Finally, maritime relations brought people and ideas from around the Greek world together, cross-fertilizing artists and intellectuals in a way never before seen in Western Eurasia.

Ethnos and Polis

In general, two forms of political organization developed in response to the population explosion of the eighth century B.C.E. On the mainland and in much of the western Peloponnesus, people continued to live in large territorial units called *ethne* (sing. *ethnos*). In each ethnos people lived in villages and small towns scattered across a wide region. Common customs and a common religion focusing on a central religious sanctuary united them. The ethnos was governed by an elite, or *oligarchy*, meaning "rule by the few," made up of major landowners who

met from time to time in one or another town within the region. This form of government, which had its roots in the Dark Age, continued to exist throughout the classical period.

A much more innovative form of political organization, which developed on the shores of the Aegean and on the islands, was the *polis* (pl. *poleis*), or city-state. Initially, *polis* meant simply "citadel." Villages clustered around these fortifications, which were both protective structures and cult centers for specific deities. These high, fortified sites—*acropolis* means "high citadel"—were sacred to specific gods: in Athens and Sparta, to Athena; in Argos and Samos, to Hera; at Corinth and Thermon, to Apollo. In addition to protection, the polis offered a marketplace, or *agora*, where farmers and artisans could trade and conduct business. The rapid population growth of the eighth century B.C.E. led to the fusion of these villages and the formation of real towns. Each town was independent, each was ruled by a monarch or an oligarchy, and each controlled the surrounding region, the inhabitants of which were on an equal footing with the townspeople. At times of political or military crisis, the rulers might summon an assembly of the free males of the community to the agora to participate in or to witness the decision-making process. In

A Greek hoplite. With shield, lance, and bronze armor, these foot soldiers were expected to "stand near and take the enemy."

the following centuries, these city-states became the center for that most dramatic Greek experiment in government—democracy.

The general model of the polis may have been borrowed from the eastern Mediterranean Phoenicians, the merchant society responsible for much of the contact Greeks of the eighth century B.C.E. had with the surrounding world. The Phoenicians were certainly the source of an equally important innovation that appeared in Greece at the same time: the reintroduction of writing. The Linear B script had entirely disappeared, along with the complex palace systems that it had served. Sometime in the eighth century B.C.E., Greeks adopted the Phoenician writing system. But this time the purpose was not primarily central administrative record keeping. From the start this writing system was intended for private, personal use and was available to virtually anyone. The Greeks radically transformed the Phoenician system, making its Semitic characters stand for arbitrary sounds and adding vowel notation in order to record poetry. Soon this writing system was being used to indicate ownership of objects, to record religious and secular vows, and even to entertain.

Within the polis, political power was not the monopoly of the aristocracy. The gradual expansion of the politically active population resulted largely from the demands of warfare. In the Dark Age, warfare had been dominated by heavily armed, mounted aristocrats who engaged their equals in single combat. In the Archaic Age, such individual combat between aristocratic warriors gave way to battles decided by the use of well-disciplined ranks of infantrymen called *phalange* (sing. *phalanx*). While few Greeks could afford costly weapons, armor, and horses, between 25 and 40 percent of the landowners could provide the shields, lances, and bronze armor needed by the infantryman, or *hoplites*.

The democratization of war led gradually to the democratization of political life. Those who brought victory in the phalanx were unwilling to accept total domination by the aristocracy in the agora. The rapid growth of the urban population, the increasing impoverishment of the rural peasantry, and the rise of a new class of wealthy merchant commoners were all challenges that traditional forms of government failed to meet. Everywhere traditional aristocratic rule was being undermined, and cities searched for ways to resolve this social conflict. No one solution emerged, and one of the outstanding achievements of Archaic Greece was the almost limitless variety of political forms elaborated in its city-states.

Colonists and Tyrants

Colonization and tyranny were two intertwined results of the political and social turmoil of the seventh century B.C.E. Population growth, changes in economy, and opposition to aristocratic power led Greeks to seek change externally through emigration and internally through political restructuring.

Late in the eleventh century B.C.E., Greeks began to migrate to new homes on the islands and along the coast of Asia Minor, in search of commercial advantages or a better life. By the eighth century B.C.E., Greeks had pushed east as far as Al Mina in northern Syria and Tarsus in eastern Asia Minor.

Beginning around 750 B.C.E., a new form of colonization began in the western Mediterranean. The impetus for this expansion was not primarily trade, but rather the need to reduce population pressure at home. The first noteworthy colony, Cumae near Naples, was founded by emigrants from Euboea. Soon other cities sent colonists to southern Italy and Sicily. Around 700 B.C.E., similar colonies appeared in the northeast in Thrace, on the shores of the Black Sea, and as far as the mouth of the Don River.

Colonists were not always volunteers. At Thera, for example, young men were chosen by lot to colonize Cyrene. The penalty for refusing to participate was death and confiscation of property. Usually colonists included only single males, the most volatile portion of the community. Colonies were thus a safety valve to release the pressures of population growth and political friction. Although colonies remained attached culturally to their mother cities, they were politically independent. The men who settled them were warriors as well as farmers or traders and carved out their new cities at the expense of the local population.

Colonization relieved some of the population pressure on Greek communities, but it did not solve the problem of political conflict. As opposition to entrenched aristocracies grew, first in Argos, then at Corinth, Sicyon, Elis, Mytilene, and elsewhere, individuals supported by those opposed to aristocratic rule seized power. These rulers were known as *tyrants*, a term that originally meant the same as *king*. In the course of the later sixth century B.C.E., *tyrant* came to designate those who had achieved supreme power without benefit of official position. Often, this rise to power came through popularity with hoplite armies. However, the term *tyrant* did not carry the negative connotation associated with it today. Early tyrants were generally welcomed by their fellow citizens and played a crucial role

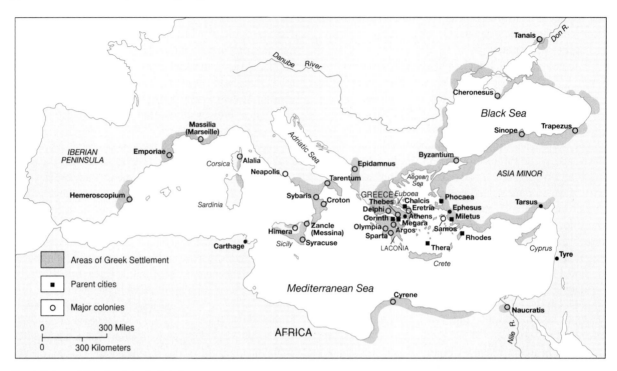

Greek Cities and Colonies of the Archaic Age

Greek commerce expanded along with the colonies. In the painting on the interior of the Arkesilas Cup, dating from around 560 B.C.E., the king of Cyrene, a Greek colony in North Africa, is shown supervising the preparation of hemp or flax for export.

in the destruction of aristocratic government and the creation of civic traditions.

Generally, tyrants were motivated not so much by great civic spirit as they were by the desire to win and maintain power. Still, to this end they weakened the power of entrenched aristocratic groups, promoted the prosperity of their supporters by protecting farmers and encouraging trade, undertook public works projects, founded colonies, and entered marriage alliances with rulers of other cities, which provided some external peace. Although they stood outside the traditional organs of government, tyrants were frequently content to govern through them, leaving magistracies and offices intact but ensuring that through elections these offices were filled with the tyrant's supporters. Thus at Corinth, Mytilene, Athens, and elsewhere, tyrants preserved and even strengthened constitutional structures as a hedge against the return to power of aristocratic factions.

The great weakness of tyrannies was that they depended for their success on the individual qualities of the ruler. Tyrants tended to pass their powers on to their sons and, as tyrannies became hereditary, cities came to resent incompetent or excessively harsh heirs' arbitrary control of government. As popular tyranny gave way to harsh and arbitrary rule, opposition brought on civil war and the deposition or abdication of the tyrant. Gradually tyranny acquired the meaning it bears today, and new forms of government emerged. Still, in spite of the bitter memory Greek tyranny left in people's minds, in many cities tyrants had for a time solved the crisis of political order and had cleared the way for broader participation in public life than had ever before been known.

Gender and Power

Military, political, and cultural life in the city-states became more democratic, but this democratization did not extend to women. Greek attitudes toward gender roles and sexuality were rigid. Except in a few cities, and in certain religious cults, women played no public role in the life of the community. They remained firmly under male control throughout their lives, passing from the authority of their fathers to that of their husbands. For the most part friendship existed only between members of the same sex, and these friendships were often intensely sexual. Thus bisexuality was the norm in Greek society, although neither Greek homosexuality nor heterosexuality were the same as they are in modern society. Rather, both coexisted within a sexuality of domination by those considered superior in age, rank, or sex over others. Mature men took young boys as their lovers, helped educate them, and inspired them by word and deed to grow into ideal warriors and citizens. We know less about such practices among women, but teachers such as Sappho of Lesbos (ca. 610–ca. 580 B.C.E.) formed similar bonds with their pupils, even while preparing them for marriage.

Those women who were in public life were mostly slaves, frequently prostitutes. These ranged from impoverished streetwalkers to educated, sophisticated courtesans who entertained men at *symposia* (sing. *symposion*), or male banquets, which were the centers of cultural and social life. Greek society did not condemn or even question infanticide, prostitution, and sexual exploitation of women and slave boys. These practices formed part of the complex and varied social systems of the developing city-states.

Gods and Mortals

Greeks and their gods enjoyed an ambivalent, peculiar, almost irreverent relationship. On the one hand, Greeks made regular offerings to the gods, pleaded with them for help, and gave them thanks for assistance. On the

other, the gods were thoroughly human, sharing in an exaggerated manner not only human strengths and virtues but also weaknesses and vices.

Greeks offered sacrifices to the gods on altars, which were raised everywhere—in homes, in fields, in sacred groves. No group had the sort of monopoly on the cult of the gods enjoyed by Mesopotamian and Egyptian priests. Unlike the temples of other societies, Greek temples were houses of the gods, especially the gods seen to have a particular relationship with individual cities, not centers of ritual. The so-called Doric temple, which housed a statue of the god, consisted of an oblong or rectangular room covered by a pitched roof and circled by columns. These temples reflected the wealth and patriotism of the city. They stood as monuments to the human community rather than to the divine.

Vase painting showing the Pythia, the priestess of Delphi, seated on her tripod. She holds a branch of the laurel plant, which is sacred to her patron, the god Apollo. The petitioner standing at right will most likely receive an enigmatic reply to his question.

This detail of a sixth-century B.C.E. relief sculpture shows Greek youths wrestling.

The Agony of Athletics

The Greeks did not play sports. Our word *play* is related to the Greek word *pais* (child), and there was nothing childish about Greek athletics. The Greek word was *agonia*, and our modern derivation, *agony*, hits closer to the mark. From Homeric times, sports were a deadly serious affair. Poets, philosophers, and statesmen placed athletic victories above all other human achievements. "There is no greater glory for a man, no matter how long his life," proclaimed Homer, "than what he achieves with his hands and feet."

Athletic contests took place within a religious context, honoring the gods but glorifying the human victors. By 500 B.C.E., there were fifty sets of games across the Greek world held at regular intervals. Among the most prestigious contests were the so-called Crown Games at Delphis, Corinth, and Nemea; the most important were those held every four years as part of the cult of Zeus at Olympia. The most important event of the Olympic Games was the 192-meter race, or *stade*, from which comes the word *stadium*. So important was victory in this event that the name of the victor provided the basic system of Greek dating. Years were reckoned from the last Olympiad and were recorded as "three years after Epitelidas of Sparta won the stade" (577 B.C.E.), or "the year in which Phanias of Pellene won the stade" (512 B.C.E.). In time, other events were added to the Olympics—other footraces (including one in which the contestants wore armor), throwing of the discus and javelin, the long jump, horse races, and chariot races. The *pankration* combined wrestling and boxing in a no-holds-barred contest. The pentathlon included five events: discus, jumping, javelin, running, and wrestling.

The serious nature of sport was equaled by its danger. One inscription from a statue erected at Olympia reads simply, "Here he died, boxing in the stadium, having prayed to Zeus for either the crown or death." The most celebrated pankration hero was Arrichion, who won but died in victory. Although his opponent was slowly strangling him, Arrichion managed to kick his adversary in such a way as to force the ball of his ankle free from its socket. The excruciating pain caused the opponent to signal defeat just as Arrichion died, victorious.

The ultimate disgrace was not injury or even death, but defeat. As one contemporary author put it, "In the Olympic Games you cannot just be beaten and then depart, but first of all, you will be disgraced not only before the people of Athens or Sparta or Nicopolis but before the whole world." Greeks did not honor good losers, only winners. As Pindar, the great lyric poet who celebrated victorious athletes, wrote, "As they [the losers] returned to their mothers no laughter sweet brought them pleasure, but they crept along the backroads, avoiding their enemies, bitten by misfortune."

If failure was bitter, victory was sweet indeed. Victors received enduring fame and enormous fortune. Poets composed odes in their honor, crowds hurried to meet them on their return home. Most games carried considerable cash prizes. At the four big games, winners received only crowns of olive or laurel leaves, but their home cities gave them more substantial gifts. Athens, for example, paid Olympic victors the equivalent of five hundred bushels of grain. This fabulous sum put the winner—for one year at least—in the ranks of the wealthiest Athenians. Most cities granted winners public honors and allowed them to eat at public expense for the rest of their lives. Thus the best athletes were essentially professionals, traveling from game to game. The Thasian boxer and pankratiast Theogenes claimed to have won over thirteen hundred victories during a professional career that spanned more than two decades. After his death he received the ultimate accolade: he was worshiped in Thasos as a god.

Competition among cities to field winning athletes was as sharp as the competition among the athletes themselves. Cities hired coaches, often themselves former Olympic champions, and actively recruited athletes from rival neighboring cities. The colony of Croton in Italy, for example, won the stade 44 percent of the time between 588 B.C.E. and 484 B.C.E. Then Croton's leading sprinter, Astylos, was lured to Syracuse and won three races, including the stade, for that city. Croton never again achieved an Olympia victory. Presumably its best athletes had been bought off.

In keeping with the rest of male-dominated Greece, only men were allowed to participate in or attend the Olympic games. Separate games dedicated to Zeus' wife, Hera, were held for unmarried women at Olympia. Women competed only in footraces over a shortened track. While men competed naked, their bodies rubbed down with olive oil, in the Heraia women wore a short tunic. Victors in the Heraia did not receive the same honors as their male counterparts, but at least one woman found an indirect way to win a victory at the male Olympics. Cynisca, the daughter of a Spartan king, entered a team of horses in the race, encouraged, the story goes, by her brother, who wanted to show that victory in these events "required no excellence but was a victory of money and expense." Whatever her motivation, Cynisca was certainly proud of her achievement. Following the victory won for her by her male driver, she erected a statue of herself at Olympia.

The Greeks' passion for games is unique in antiquity, and the progressive interest of Romans and "barbarians" in athletics was a sure sign of their absorption of Greek culture. Perhaps the best explanation of the place of athletics in the Greek world was that the single athlete, standing along and naked and striving with all his being for excellence, was the purest expression of the individualism that animated Hellenic society.

On special occasions, festivals celebrated at sanctuaries honored the gods of the city with processions, athletic contests, and feasts. Some of these celebrations drew participants from all of the Greek world. The two greatest pan-Hellenic (meaning "all Greek," from *Hellas*, the Greek word for Greece) sanctuaries were Olympia and Delphi. Because both were remote from centers of political power, they were insulated from interstate rivalry and provided neutral ground on which hostile neighbors could meet in peace.

Beginning in 776 B.C.E., every four years, wars and conflicts were temporarily suspended while athletes from the whole Greek world met at Olympia to participate in contests in honor of Zeus. (See Special Feature, "The Agony of Athletics," pp. 56-57.) The religious nature of the contests lowered neither their heated interstate rivalry nor the violence with which they were pursued. Wrestling in particular could be deadly, since matches continued until one participant signaled that he had had enough. Many wrestlers chose death rather than defeat. Victors were seen as ideal humans, the perfect triumph of body and soul, and Olympic victors were treated as national heroes. Delphi, the site of the shrine of Apollo, god of music, archery, medicine, and prophecy, was the second pan-Hellenic cult center. Like Olympia, Delphi drew athletes from the whole Greek world to its athletic contests. However, Delphi's real fame lay in its oracle, or spokeswoman for the god Apollo. From the eighth century B.C.E., before undertaking any important decision such as establishing a colony, beginning a war, or even contracting a marriage, individuals and representatives of distant cities traveled to Delphi to ask Apollo's advice or to seek purification from the guilt attached to shedding others' blood and reconciliation with their fellow citizens. For a stiff fee, visitors were allowed to address questions to the god through a female medium. She entered a trance state and uttered a reply, which lay priests at the shrine then put into verse form and transmitted to the petitioner. The ambiguity of the Delphic replies was legendary.

Though gods were petitioned, placated, and pampered, they were not privileged or protected. Unlike the awe-inspiring gods of the Mesopotamians and Egyptians, the traditional Greek gods, inherited from the Dark Age, were represented in ways that showed them as all too human, vicious, and frequently ridiculous. Zeus was infamous for his frequent rapes of boys and girls. His lust was matched only by the fury of his jealous wife, Hera. The Greek gods were immortal, superhuman in strength, and able to interfere in human affairs. But in all things, they reflected the values and weaknesses of the Greek mortals, who could bargain with them, placate them, and even trick them.

Religious cults were not under the exclusive control of any priesthood or political group. Thus, there were no official versions of stories of gods and goddesses. This is evident both from Greek poetry, which often presents contradictory stories of the gods, and from pottery, which bears pictorial versions of myths that differ greatly from written ones. No one group or sacred site enjoyed a monopoly on access to the gods. Like literacy and government, the gods belonged to all.

Myth and Reason

The glue holding together the individual and frequently hostile Greek poleis and ethne scattered throughout the Mediterranean was their common stock of myths and a common fascination with the Homeric legends. Stories of gods and heroes, told and retold, were fashioned into *mythoi* (myths, literally, "formulated speech"), which explained and described the world both as it was and as it should be. Myths were told about every city, shrine, river, mountain, and island. Myths explained the origins of cities, festivals, the world itself. What is the place of humans in the cosmos? They stand between beasts and gods because Prometheus tricked Zeus and gave men fire with which they cook their food and offer the bones and fat of sacrificial animals to the gods. Why is there evil and misfortune? Because, Greek men explained, in revenge for Prometheus' trickery, Zeus offered man Pandora (the name means "all gifts"), the first woman, whose beauty hid her evil nature. By accepting this gift, humans brought evil and misfortune on themselves. Such stories were more than simply fanciful explanations of how things came to be. Myths sanctioned and supported the authority of social, political, and religious traditions. They presented how things had come to be in a manner that prescribed how they were to remain. In the process of revising and retelling, myths became a powerful and dynamic tool for reasoning about the world.

Archaic Greeks showed a similar combination of veneration and liberty in dealing with the Homeric legends. Thoughtful Greeks approached the heroic ideals of these epics with a sense of detachment and criticism. Some mothers might tell their sons as they marched off to war, "Return with your shield or on it," that is, victorious or dead. But Archilochus, a seventh-century B.C.E. lyric poet, could take a very different view of shields and honor:

The François Vase is a large krater, a vessel for mixing wine. It comes from the Greek colonies of Sicily and dates from around 570 B.C.E. The krater is decorated with bands on which are depicted martial and mythological scenes.

> A perfect shield bedecks some Thracian now;
> I had no choice, I left it in a wood.
> Ah, well, I saved my skin, so let it go!
> A new one's just as good.

The new, open examination of traditional values extended into all areas of investigation. By the sixth century B.C.E., a number of Ionian Greeks began to investigate the origins and nature of the universe, not in terms of myth or religion, but by observation and rational thought. Living on the coast of Asia Minor, these Ionians were in contact with the ancient civilizations of Mesopotamia and learned much from the Babylonian traditions of astronomy, mathematics, and science. However, their primary interest went beyond observing and recording to speculating. They were the first philosophers, intellectuals who sought natural explanations for the world around them.

Thales of Miletus (ca. 625–ca. 547 B.C.E.) regarded water as the fundamental substance of the universe. For Anaximander (610–ca. 527 B.C.E.) the primary substance

was matter—eternal and indestructible. It was Anaximenes of Miletus (fl. ca. 545 B.C.E.) who regarded air as the primary substance of the universe. Heraclitus of Ephesus (ca. 540–ca. 480 B.C.E.) saw the universe not as one unchanging substance but rather as change itself. For him, the universe is constantly in flux, changing like a flickering fire. Thus all is constantly in a state of becoming, not in a static state of being. And yet this constant change is not random. The cosmic tension between stability and flux is regulated by laws that human reason can determine. The universe is rational.

The significance of such speculative thought was not in the conclusions reached, but rather in the method employed. The Ionian philosophers no longer spoke in myth but rather in plain language. They reached their conclusions through observation and rational thought in which religion and the gods played no direct role. As significant as their original speculations was the manner in which these philosophers were received. Although as late as the fourth century B.C.E., intellectuals still occasionally fell prey to persecution, by the sixth century B.C.E., much of Greek society was ready to tolerate such nonreligious, rational teaching, which in other times and places would have been thought scandalous or atheistic.

Art and the Individual

Archaic Greeks borrowed from everywhere and transformed all that they borrowed. Just as they adopted and adapted the Phoenician alphabet and Mesopotamian science, they took Near Eastern and Egyptian painting and sculpture and made them their own. During the Dark Age, the Mycenaean traditions of art had entirely disappeared. Pottery showed only geometric decorations; sculpture was unknown. Gradually, from the ninth century B.C.E., stylized human and animal figures, lions, griffins, and other strange beasts began to appear within the tightly composed geometric patterns. But by the eighth century B.C.E., such exotic subjects had given way to the Greek passion for human images taken from their own myths and legends. The preferred technique was the so-called black figure style developed first at Corinth. Subjects were painted in black silhouette on red clay and then details were cut with a sharp point so that the background could show through. As the popularity of these mythic and heroic scenes increased, so too did the artists' technical competence. Greek artists competed with one another to overcome technical problems of perspective and foreshortening. From the sixth century B.C.E., many of the finest examples were signed.

ALL THINGS CHANGE

■ *The thought of Heraclitus of Ephesus is preserved entirely in fragmentary, oracular-like aphorisms. These brief statements nevertheless convey a sense of his reflections on the nature of the universe.*

1. It is wise to hearken, not to me, but to my Word, and to confess that all things are one.

2. Though this Word is true evermore, yet men are as unable to understand it when they hear it for the first time as before they have heard it at all. For, though all things come to pass in accordance with this Word, men seem as if they had no experience of them, when they make trial of words and deeds such as I set forth, dividing each thing according to its kind and showing how it truly is. But other men know not what they are doing when awake, even as they forget what they do in sleep.

39. Cold things become warm, and what is warm cools, what is wet dries, and the parched is moistened.

41. You cannot step twice into the same rivers; for fresh waters are ever flowing in upon you.

43. Homer was wrong in saying: "Would that strife might perish from among gods and men!" He did not see that he was praying for the destruction of the universe; for if his prayer were heard, all things would pass away.

Such masterpieces celebrated not only the heroes of the past but also the artist as individual and as the interpreter of culture no less original than the poet.

Greek sculpture underwent a similar dramatic development. The earliest and most common subject of archaic sculpture was the standing male nude, or *kouros* (pl. *kouroi*) figure, which was in wide demand as grave monument, dedication to a god, or even cult statue of male deity. In Egypt, seventh-century B.C.E. Greeks had seen colossal statues and had learned to work stone. They brought these techniques home, improved on them by using iron tools (the Egyptians knew only bronze ones), and began to create their own human images. The rigidly formulaic position of the kouros—standing, arms by the sides, looking straight ahead, left foot extended—followed Egyptian tradition and left little room for originality. Thus sculptors sought to give their statues originality and individuality, not as representations of individuals, but as the creations of the individual sculptor. To this end, they experimented with increasingly natural molding of limbs and body and began signing their works. Thus, as in vase painting, Greek sculpture reflected the importance of the individual, not in its subject matter, but in its creator. The female counterparts of the kouros figures, called *korai*, followed similarly rigid traditions to which sculptors added female attributes.

The real challenges in sculpture came in the portrayal of narrative in decorations on monuments, primarily temples. Unlike kouroi, which were usually private commissions intended to adorn the tombs of aristocrats, these public buildings were constructed as expressions of civic pride and were accessible to everyone. Here the creativity and dynamism of Greek cities could be paralleled in stone. Figures such as the Calf-Bearer (ca. 590 B.C.E.) from the Athenian acropolis are daring in the complexity of composition and the delicacy of execution. These are statues that tell stories. In the Calf-Bearer, a master farmer carries a calf to be sacrificed to Athena. The two gentle heads, the cross formed by the farmer's hands and the calf's legs are individual traits without precedent in ancient art. Although formally intended for religious purposes, these figures serve not only the gods and the aristocratic elite, but the whole community.

A Tale of Three Cities

The political, social, and cultural transformations that occurred in the Archaic Age took different forms across the Greek world. No community or city-state was typical of Greece. The best way to understand the diversity of Archaic Greece is to examine three very different cities that, by the end of the sixth century B.C.E., had become leading centers of Greek civilization. Corinth, Sparta, and Athens present something of the spectrum of political, cultural, and social models of the Hellenic world. Corinth, like many cities, developed into a commercial center in which the assembly of citizens was dominated by an oligarchy. Sparta developed into a state in which citizenship was radically egalitarian but restricted to a small military elite. In Athens, the Archaic Age saw the foundations of an equally radical democracy.

Archaic Greece

ca. 780–720 B.C.E.	Population increase in Greece
776 B.C.E.	First Olympic Games held
ca. 750–700 B.C.E.	Greeks develop writing system based on Phoenician model; Greeks begin colonizing western Mediterranean
ca. 700–500 B.C.E.	Archaic Age of Greece
ca. 700 B.C.E.	First stone temples appear in Greece
ca. 650 B.C.E.	Cypselus breaks rule of Bacchiads in Corinth; rules city as tyrant
594 B.C.E.	Solon elected chief archon of Athens; institutes social and political reforms
586 B.C.E.	Death of Periander ends tyrants' rule in Corinth
499 B.C.E.	Ionian cities revolt

Kouros figure from the Greek Archaic period, seventh century B.C.E. Egyptian influence can be seen in the stiff, formal pose, the broad, square shoulders, and the rigid symmetry of the design.

Wealthy Corinth

Corinth owed its prosperity to its privileged site, dominating both a rich coastal plain and the narrow isthmus connecting the Peloponnesus to the mainland. In the eighth century B.C.E., as Greeks turned their attention to the west, Corinthians led the way. Corinthian pottery appeared throughout western Greece and southern Italy. Corinthian trade led to colonization, and settlers from Corinth founded Syracuse and other cities in Sicily and Italy, which served as markets for Corinthian products. Even more important to Corinthian prosperity was its role in the transport of other cities' products from east to west. By carrying goods across the isthmus and loading them onto other ships, merchants could avoid the long and dangerous passage around the Peloponnesus.

The precise details of early Corinthian government are uncertain. Still, it appears that in Corinth as in many other cities, a tyranny replaced a ruling clan and in time this tyranny ended with an oligarchic government. Until the middle of the seventh century B.C.E., Corinth and its wealth were ruled in typical Dark Age fashion by an aristocratic clan known as the Bacchiads. Corinth began

The Calf-Bearer was commissioned for the temple of Athena, which was destroyed by the Persians in 480 B.C.E, when they captured Athens and burned the Acropolis.

its rise under this aristocratic rule, and individual Bacchiads led colonizing expeditions to Italy and Sicily. However, the increasing pressures of population growth, rapidly expanding wealth, and dramatic changes in the economy produced social tensions that the traditional aristocratic rulers were unable to handle. As in cities throughout the Greek world, these tensions led to the creation of a new order.

The early history of Corinth is obscure, but apparently around 650 B.C.E. a revolution, led by a dissident Bacchiad named Cypselus (ca. 657–627 B.C.E.) and supported by non-Bacchiad aristocrats and other Corinthians, broke the Bacchiads' grip on the city. The revolution led to the establishment of Cypselus as tyrant. Cypselus and his son Periander (ca. 627–

586 B.C.E.) seem to have been generally popular with most Corinthians.

In Corinth, as in many other cities, the tyrants restructured taxes, relying primarily on customs duties, which were less of a burden on the peasantry. Around 600 B.C.E., Periander began construction of a causeway across the isthmus on which ships could be hauled from the Aegean to the western Mediterranean. This causeway eventually became a major source of Corinth's wealth. Periander attacked conspicuous consumption on the part of the aristocracy. He introduced laws against idleness and put thousands of Corinthians to work in extensive building programs. He erected temples and sent colonists to Italy. Under his leadership the Corinthian fleet developed into the most powerful naval force in the Adriatic and Aegean seas. Under its tyrants, Corinth led the Greek world in the production of black figure pottery, which spread throughout the Mediterranean.

The tyrants also laid the foundation for broader political participation. Cypselus divided the population into eight tribes, based not on traditional ethnic divisions, but on arbitrary groupings by region. All of Corinth was divided into three large regions. The population of each region was distributed among each of the eight tribes. This assignment prevented the emergence of political factions based on regional disputes. Ten representatives from each tribe formed a council of eighty men. Under the tyrants, this council was largely advisory and provided a connection between the autocratic rulers and the citizens.

In Corinth as elsewhere, the strength or weakness of tyranny rested on the abilities and personality of individual tyrants. Cypselus had been a beloved liberator. His son Periander, in spite of his accomplishments, was remembered for his cruelty and violence. Shortly after Periander's death in 586 B.C.E., a revolt killed his successor and tyranny in Corinth ended.

The new government continued the tribal and council system established by Cypselus. From the sixth century B.C.E. until its conquest by Macedonia in 338 B.C.E., Corinth was ruled by an oligarchy. Although an assembly of the *demos*, or adult males, met occasionally, actual government was in the hands of eight deliberators and nine other men from each tribe, who together formed the council of eighty. The oligarchs who made up the council avoided the kind of exclusive and arbitrary tendencies that had destroyed both the Bacchiads and the tyrants. They were remarkably successful in maintaining popular support among the citizens and provided a reliable and effective government.

Bronze statue of a Greek warrior from the sixth century B.C.E. The figure is slightly less than six inches high and stands on a base of red marble. The warrior is draped in a cloak and wears a helmet of the Corinthian type, covering the head and face.

Thus Corinth flourished, a city more open to commerce and wealth than most, moderate in its political institutions and eager for stability. As one fourth-century B.C.E. poet wrote:

> (There) lawfulness dwells, and her sister,
> Safe foundation of cities,
> Justice, and Peace, who was bred with her;
> They dispense wealth to men.

Martial Sparta

At the beginning of the eighth century B.C.E., the Peloponnesus around Sparta and Laconia faced circumstances similar to those of Corinth and other Greek communities. Population growth, increasing disparity between rich and poor, and an expanding economy created powerful tensions. However, while Corinthian society developed into a complex mix of aristocrats, merchants, artisans, and peasants, ruled by an oligarchy, the Spartan solution presented a rigid, two-tiered social structure. By the end of the Archaic Age, a small, homogeneous class of warriors called equals ruled a vast population of state serfs, or *helots*. The two classes lived in mutual fear and mistrust. Spartans controlled the helots through terror and ritual murder. The helots in turn were "an enemy constantly waiting for the disasters of the Spartans." And yet, throughout antiquity the Spartans were the Greeks most praised for their courage, simplicity of life, and service to the state.

War was the center of Spartan life, and war lay at the origin of the Spartans' extraordinary social and political organization. In the eighth century B.C.E., the Spartans conquered the fertile region of Messenia and compelled the vanquished Messenians to turn over one-half of their harvests. The spoils were not divided equally, but went to increase the wealth of the aristocracy, thus creating resentment among the less privileged. Early in the seventh century B.C.E., the Spartans attempted a similar campaign to take the plain of Thyreatis from the city of Argos. This time they were defeated, and resentment of the ordinary warriors toward their aristocratic leaders flared into open conflict. The Messenians seized this opportunity to revolt, and for a time Sparta was forced to fight for its very existence at home and abroad. In many cities, such crises gave rise to tyrants. In Sparta, the crisis led to radical political and social reforms that transformed the polis into a unique military system.

The Spartans attributed these reforms to the legendary lawgiver Lycurgus (seventh century B.C.E.). Whether or not Lycurgus ever existed and was responsible for all of the reforms, they saved the city. But in the process Sparta abandoned the mainstream of Greek development. Traditionally, Greeks had placed personal honor above communal concerns. During the crisis of the second Messenian war, Spartans of all social ranks were urged to look not to individual interest but to good order and obedience to the laws, which alone could unite Spartans and bring victory.

United, the Spartans crushed the Messenians. In return for obedience, poor citizens received equality before the law and benefited from a land distribution that relieved their poverty. Conquered land, especially that in Messenia, was divided and distributed to Spartan warriors. However, the Spartan warriors were not expected to work the land themselves. Instead, the state reduced the defeated Messenians to the status of helots and assigned them to individual Spartans. While this system did not erase all economic inequalities among the Spartans (aristocrats continued to hold more land than others), it did decrease some of the disparity. It also provided a minimum source of wealth for all Spartan citizens and allowed them to devote themselves to full-time military service.

This land reform was coupled with a political reform that incorporated elements of monarchy, oligarchy, and democracy. The state was governed by two hereditary kings and a council of elders, the *gerousia*. In peacetime, the authority of the two royal families was limited to familial and religious affairs. In war, they commanded the army and held the power of life and death.

In theory at least, the central institution of Spartan government was the gerousia, which was composed of thirty men at least sixty years of age and included the two kings. The gerousia directed all political activity, especially foreign affairs, and served as high court. Members were elected for life by the assembly, which was composed of all equals over the age of thirty and which approved decisions of the gerousia. However, this approval, made by acclamation, could easily be manipulated, as could the course of debate within the gerousia itself. Wealth, cunning, and patronage were more important in the direction of the Spartan state than were its formal structures.

Actual administration was in the hands of five magistrates termed *ephors*. Their powers were extremely broad. They presided over joint sessions of the gerousia and assembly. They held supreme authority over the kings during wartime and acted as judges for noncitizens. Finally, the ephors controlled the *krypteia*, or secret police, a band of youths who practiced state terrorism as part of their rite of passage to the status of equal. On the orders of the ephors, the krypteia assassinated, intrigued, arrested powerful people, and terrorized helots. Service in this corps was considered a necessary part of a youth's education.

The key to the success of Sparta's political reform was an even more radical social reform that placed everyone under the direct supervision and service of the state from birth until death. Although admiring aristocratic visitors often exaggerated their accounts of Spartan life, the main outlines are clear enough. Good order and obedience to the laws was the sole guiding principle, and service to the state came before family, social class, and every other duty or occupation.

Spartan equals were made, not born. True, only a man born of free Spartan parents could hope to become an equal, but birth alone was no guarantee of admission to this select body, or even of the right to live. Public officials examined infants and decided whether they were sufficiently strong to be allowed to live or should be exposed on a hillside to die. From birth until age seven, a boy lived with his mother, but then he entered the state education system, living in barracks with his

contemporaries and enduring thirteen years of rigorous military training.

At age twelve, training with swords and spears became more intense, as did the rigors of the lifestyle. Boys were given only a single cloak to wear and slept on thin rush mats. They were encouraged to supplement their meager diet by stealing food, although if caught they were severely whipped, not for the theft but for the failure. All of this they were expected to endure in silence.

Much of the actual education of the youths was entrusted to older accomplished warriors who selected boys as their homosexual lovers. Not only did the lover serve as tutor and role model, but in time the two became a fighting team, each inspiring the other to show the utmost valor. At age twenty, Spartan youths were enrolled in the krypteia. Each was sent out into the countryside with nothing but a cloak and a knife and forbidden to return until he had killed a helot.

If a youth survived the rigors of his training until age thirty, he could at last be incorporated into the rank of equals, provided he could pass the last obstacle. He had to be able to furnish a sufficient amount of food from his own lands for the communal dining group to which he would be assigned. This food might come from inherited property or, if he had proved himself an outstanding warrior, from the state. Those who passed this final qualification became full members of the assembly, but they continued to live with the other warriors. Men could marry at age twenty, but family life in the usual sense was nonexistent. A man could not live with his wife until age thirty because he was bound to the barracks.

Although their training was not as rigorous as that of males, Spartan women were given an education and allowed a sphere of activity unknown elsewhere in Greece. Girls, like boys, were trained in athletic competition and, again like them, competed naked in wrestling, footraces, and spear throwing. This training was based not on a belief in the equality of the sexes but simply on the desire to improve the physical stamina and child-bearing abilities of Spartan women. Women were able to own land and to participate widely in business and agricultural affairs, the reason being that since men were entirely involved in military pursuits, women were expected to look after economic and household affairs.

Few inhabitants of Sparta ever became equals. In addition to the great numbers of helots, there were many inhabitants of the region who were free citizens of their local communities but were not allowed into the state educational system. Others were washed out, unable to endure the harsh life, and still others lacked the property qualifications to supply their share of the communal meals. Thus for all the trappings of egalitarianism, equality in Sparta was the privilege of a tiny minority.

The total dedication to military life was reinforced by a deliberate rejection of other activities. From the time of the second Messenian war, Sparta withdrew from the mainstream of Greek civilization. Equals could not engage in crafts, trade, or any other forms of eco-nomic activity. Because Sparta banned silver and gold coinage, it could not participate in the growing commercial network of the Greek world. Although a group of free citizens of subject towns could engage in such activities, the role of Sparta in the economic, architectural, and cultural life of Greece was negligible after the seventh century B.C.E. Militarily, Sparta cast a long shadow across the Peloponnesus and beyond, but the

TWO FACES OF TYRANNY

■ *The spectrum of tyrannies in Archaic Greece is shown in the lives of Periander of Corinth and Peisistratus of Athens. The description of Periander is that of Herodotus; the description of Peisistratus comes from the* Athenian Constitution, *one of over a hundred constitutions compiled by Aristotle and his students between 328 and 325 B.C.E. as part of the research for his* Politics.

Now Periander at the first was of milder mood than his father; but after he had held converse by messengers with Thrasybulus the despot of Miletus, he became much more blood-thirsty than Cypselus. For he sent a herald to Thrasybulus and enquired how he should most safely so order all matters as best to govern his city. Thrasybulus led the man who had come from Periander outside the town, and entered into a sown field; where, while he walked through the corn and plied the herald with still-repeated questions anent his coming from Corinth, he would ever cut off the tallest that he saw of the stalks, and cast away what he cut off, till by so doing he had destroyed the best and richest of the crop; then, having passed through the place and spoken no word of counsel, he sent the herald away . . . But Periander understood what had been done, and perceived that Thrasybulus had counseled him to slay those of his townsmen who stood highest' and with that he began to deal very evilly with his citizens. For whatever act of slaughter or banishment Cypselus had left undone, that did Periander bring to accomplishment.

From Herodotus, Book V, ch. 92.

The factions were three: one was the part of the Men of the Coast . . . and they were thought chiefly to aim at the middle form of constitution; another was the party of the Men of the Plain, who desired the oligarchy . . . third was the party of the Hillmen, which had appointed Peisistratus over it, as he was thought to be an extreme advocate of the people. And on the side of this party were also arrayed, from the motive of poverty, those who had been deprived of the debts due to them, and, from the motive of fear, those who were not of pure descent . . . Peisistratus inflicted a wound on himself with his own hand and then gave out that it had been done by the members of the opposite factions, and so persuaded the people to give him a bodyguard . . . He was given the retainers called Club-Bearers, and with their aid he rose against the people and seized the Acropolis . . .

Peisistratus' administration of the state was . . . moderate, and more constitutional than tyrannic; he was kindly and mild in everything, and in particular he was merciful to offenders, and moreover he advanced loans of money to the poor for their industries, so that they might support themselves by farming. In doing this he had two objects, to prevent their stopping in the city and make them stay scattered about the country and to cause them to have a moderate competence and be engaged in their private affairs, so as not to desire nor to have time to attend to public business.

From Aristotle, *Athenian Constitution.*

number of equals was always too small to allow Sparta both to create a vast empire and to maintain control over the helots at home. Instead, Sparta created a network of alliances and nonaggression pacts with oligarchic neighbors. In time this network came to be known as the Peloponnesian League.

Democratic Athens

Athens did not enjoy the advantages of a strategic site such as that of Corinth, nor was it surrounded by rich plains like Sparta. However, the "goodly citadel of Athens" was one of the few Mycenaean cities to have escaped destruction at the start of the Dark Age. Gradually Athens united the whole surrounding region of Attica into a single polis, by far the largest in the Greek world. Well into the seventh century B.C.E., Athens followed the general pattern of the polis seen in Corinth and Sparta. Like other Dark Age communities, Athens was ruled by aristocratic clans, particularly the Alcmaeonids. Only the members of these clans could participate in the *areopagus*, or council, which they entered after serving a year as one of the nine *archons*, or magistrates, elected yearly. Until the seventh century B.C.E., Athens escaped the social pressures brought on by population growth and economic prosperity that led to civil strife, colonialism, and tyranny elsewhere. This was due largely to its relative abundance of arable land and its commercial prosperity based on the export of grain.

By the late seventh century B.C.E., however, Athens began to suffer from the same class conflict that had shaken other cities. Sometime around 630 B.C.E., an aristocrat named Cylon attempted to seize power as tyrant. His attempt failed, but when he was murdered by one of the Alcmaeonids, popular revulsion drove the Alcmaeonids from the city. A decade of strife ensued as aristocratic clans, wealthy merchants, and farmers fought for control of the city. Violence between groups and families threatened to tear the community apart. In 621 B.C.E., the Athenians granted a judge, Draco, extraordinary powers to revise and systematize traditional laws concerning vengeance and homicide. His restructuring of procedures for limiting vengeance and preventing bloodshed were harsh enough to add the term *Draconian* to Western legal vocabulary. When asked why death was the most common penalty he imposed, Draco explained that minor offenses merited death and he knew of no more severe penalty for major ones. Still, these measures did nothing to solve the central problems of political control. Finally in 594 B.C.E., Solon (ca. 630–ca. 560 B.C.E.), an aristocratic merchant, was

elected chief archon and charged with restructuring the city's government. Solon based his reform on the ideal of eunomia, as had the Spartans, but he followed a very different path to secure good order.

In Sparta, Lycurgus had begun with a radical redistribution of land. In Athens, Solon began with the less extreme measure of eliminating debt bondage. Athenians who had been forced into slavery or into sharecropping because of their debts were restored to freedom. A law forbade mortgaging free men and women as security for debts. Athenians might be poor, but they would be free. This free peasantry formed the basis of Athenian society throughout its history.

Solon also reorganized the rest of the social hierarchy and broke the aristocracy's exclusive control of the areopagus by dividing the society into four classes based on wealth rather than birth and opening the archonship to the top two classes. He further weakened the areopagus by establishing a council of four hundred members drawn from all four classes, to which citizens could appeal decisions of the magistrates.

Although Solon's reforms established the framework for a resolution of Athens' social tensions, they did not entirely succeed. Solon himself did not consider his new constitution perfect, only practical. Resistance from the still-powerful aristocracy prompted some Athenians to urge Solon to assume the powers of a tyrant in order to force through his reforms. He refused, but after his death, Peisistratus (d. 527 B.C.E.), an aristocrat strongly supported by the peasants against his own class, hired a mercenary force to seize control of the city. After two abortive attempts, Peisistratus ruled as tyrant from 545 B.C.E. until his death.

Peisistratus might have governed the city, for a while at least, as an absolute tyrant. Instead, he and later his son Hippias (d. 490 B.C.E.), who succeeded him until 510 B.C.E., continued to rule through Solon's constitution

Athenian silver coin called a tetradrachm, dating from the fifth century B.C.E. The owl is the symbol of the goddess Athena.

but simply ensured that the archons elected each year were their agents.

Peisistratus and Hippias drew their support from the demos, or people at large, rather than from an aristocratic faction. They claimed divine justification for their rule and made a great show of devotion to the Athenian gods. Peisistratus promoted annual festivals, and in so doing began the great tradition of Athenian literature. At the festival of Athena, professional reciters of epic poetry recited large portions of the *Iliad* and the *Odyssey*. During a festival in honor of the god Dionysus, actors performed the first tragedies and comedies. The tyrants also directed a series of popular, nationalistic public works programs that beautified the city, increased national pride, and provided work for the poor. They rebuilt the temple of Athena on the acropolis, for which the statue of the Calf-Bearer was commissioned. These internal measures were accompanied by support for commerce and export, particularly of grain. Soon, Athens was challenging Corinth as the leading commercial power and trading in grain as far away as the Black Sea.

Peisistratus was firm. His son Hippias was harsh. Still, even Hippias enjoyed the support of the majority of the citizens of both popular and aristocratic factions. Only after the assassination of his younger brother did Hippias become sufficiently oppressive to drive his opponents into exile. Some of these exiles obtained the assistance of Sparta and returned to overthrow Hippias in 510 B.C.E. Hippias' defeat ended the tyrants' rule in Athens and won for Sparta an undeserved reputation as the opponent of all tyranny.

Following the expulsion of Hippias, some aristocrats attempted to return to the "good old days" of aristocratic rule. However, for more than eighty years, Athenians had been accustomed to Solon's constitution and were unwilling to give it up. Moreover, the tyrants had created a fierce sense of nationalistic pride among all ranks of Athenians, and few were willing to turn over government to the hands of only a few. Thus, when the aristocrats made their bid to recover power, their primary opponent, Cleisthenes (ca. 570–ca. 507 B.C.E.), "made the demos his faction" and pushed through a final constitutional reform that became the basis for Athenian democracy.

The essence of Cleisthenes' reform lay in his reorganization of the major political units by which members of the council were selected. Previously, each citizen had belonged to one of four tribes, further broken down into twelve brotherhoods, which were administrative and religious units. In a manner similar to that of Cypselus in Corinth, Cleisthenes reshuffled these brotherhoods into thirty territorial units comprising urban, inland, or coastal regions. These thirty units in turn were grouped into ten tribes, each consisting of one unit from each of the urban, inland, and coastal regions. The tribes elected the members of the council, military commanders, jurors, and magistrates. As in Corinth, this reorganization destroyed the traditional kin-based social and political pattern and integrated people of differing social, economic, and regional backgrounds. Aristocrats, merchants, and poor farmers had to work together to find common ground for political action, both regionally and nationally. With this new, integrated democracy and its strong sense of nationalism, Athens emerged from the Archaic Age as the leading city of the Hellenic world.

Neither Corinth, Sparta, nor Athens was a typical archaic Greek city—there was no such thing. However each faced similar problems: deep conflict between old aristocratic families and wider society, growing population pressure, and threats from within and from without. Their solutions, a period of tyranny in Corinth and Athens followed by oligarchy in the former and radical democracy in the latter or, in the case of Sparta, the creation of a small but egalitarian military elite, suggest the spectrum of alternatives from which cities across the Greek world sought to meet these challenges.

The Coming of Persia and the End of the Archaic Age

By the end of the sixth century B.C.E., the products of Greek experimentation were evident throughout the Mediterranean. Greek city-states had resolved the crises of class conflict. Greek merchants and artisans had found ways to flourish despite poor soil and uncertain climate. Greek philosophers, poets, and artists had begun to celebrate the human form and the human spirit. Still, these achievements were the product of small, independent, and relatively weak communities on the fringe of the civilized world.

In the second half of the sixth century B.C.E., this changed. The Persian Empire, under its dynamic king Cyrus II, began a process of conquest and expansion west into Asia Minor. The Persian Empire, which eventually reached from what is today western Turkey to India, was an extraordinary amalgam of ancient imperial traditions of Mesopotamia, the dynamic Zoroastrian religion of the supreme deity Ahura Mazda, and an eagerness to tolerate wide varieties of religious and cultural

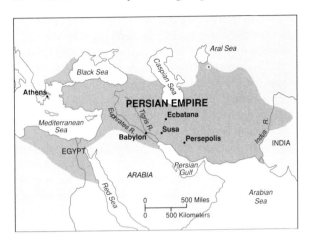

The Persian Empire, 500 B.C.E.

traditions. Cyrus granted the provinces of his empire great autonomy and preserved local forms of government wherever possible, being careful only to impose governors, or satraps, loyal to him and his Achaemenid dynasty. In keeping with this tradition, when he absorbed the kingdom of Lydia and Ionia on the coast of Asia Minor, he put tyrants loyal to Cyrus to rule over these Greek communities. For a few decades these centers of Greek culture and thought accepted foreign control, but in 499 B.C.E., the passion for democracy, which had swept much of mainland Greece, reached Ionia. Cities such as Miletus, Ephesus, Chios, and Samos revolted, expelled their Persian-appointed tyrants, established democracies, and sent ambassadors to the mainland to seek assistance. Eretria and Athens, two mainland cities with Ionian roots, responded, sending ships and men to aid the Ionian rebels. Athenian interests were more than simple solidarity with their Ionian cousins. Athens depended on grain from the Black Sea region and felt its direct interests to lie with the area. The success of the revolt was short-lived. The puny Greek cities were dealing with the largest empire the West had yet known. By 500 B.C.E., the Persian Empire included Asia Minor, Mesopotamia, Palestine, and Egypt, uniting all the peoples from the Caucasus to the Sudan.

The giant Persian Empire responded slowly, but with force, to the Greek revolt. King Darius I (522–486 B.C.E.) gathered a vast, international force from throughout his empire and set about to recapture the rebellious cities. The war lasted five years and ended in a Persian victory. By 494 B.C.E., the Persians had retaken the cities of the coast and nearby islands. In the cities deemed most responsible for the revolt, the population was

herded together, the boys were castrated and made into royal eunuchs, the girls sent to Darius' court, the remainder of the population sold into slavery, and the towns burnt to the ground. Once the rebels had been disposed of, Darius set out to punish their supporters on the mainland, Eretria and Athens. With the same meticulous planning and deliberate pace, the Persian king turned his vast armies toward the Greek mainland.

Civilization developed much later in the Mediterranean world than it had in the floodplains of the Near East. The earliest Bronze Age societies of Greece and the neighboring islands, while influenced by contact with the great civilizations of Mesopotamia and Egypt, developed distinctive societies and cultures tied closely to the sea around them. Still, they too were caught up in the general cataclysm of the twelfth century B.C.E. Out of the ruins emerged a society much less centralized, wealthy, or powerful, but possessing an extraordinary dynamism.

The Archaic Age was an age of experimentation. Greeks, propelled by demographic and political pressures and inspired by the legends of vanished heroes, began in the eighth century B.C.E. to recast traditions and techniques acquired from their ancient neighbors into new forms. The multiplicity of independent communities, their relative isolation, and their differing traditions created a wide spectrum of political forms, social structures, and cultural values. And yet from Sicily to Asia Minor, Greeks felt themselves united by a common language, a common cultural heritage, and a common commitment to individual freedom within the community, whether that freedom was protected within a monarchy, a tyranny, an oligarchy, or a democracy. That commitment to freedom, fostered in the hoplite ranks, protected in the assembly, and increasingly expressed in poetry and sculpture, hung in the balance as Darius and the Persians marched west.

SUGGESTIONS FOR FURTHER READING

GENERAL READING

John Boardman, Jasper Griffin, and Oswyn Murray, *Greece and the Hellenistic World* (Oxford: Oxford University Press, 1988). An excellent collection of essays on Greek civilization by British scholars.

Cambridge Ancient History, Vol. 4. Contains more detailed essays on all aspects of early Greek history.

GREECE IN THE BRONZE AGE TO 700 B.C.E.

* M. I. Finley, *Early Greece: The Bronze and Archaic Ages*, 2d ed. (New York: W.W. Norton, 1982). A very readable overview by a leading Greek historian.

* N. K. Sandars, *The Sea Peoples* (New York: Thames & Hudson, 1985). A recent survey of the controversy over the crisis of the twelfth century B.C.E.

* Emily Vermeule, *Greece in the Bronze Age* (Chicago: University of Chicago Press, 1964). A standard though somewhat dated study, particularly for the early material.

O. Krzyszkowska and L. Nixon, eds., *Minoan Society* (Bristol: Bristol Classical Press, 1983). Excellent collection of essays on early Crete.

J. T. Hooker, *Mycenaean Greece* (New York: Routledge, Chapman & Hall, 1976). The best introduction to Mycenaean history.

* M. I. Finley, *The World of Odysseus*, 2d. rev. ed. (New York: Penguin Books, 1979). A brilliant analysis of the Dark Age through the Homeric epics.

ARCHAIC GREECE, 700–500 B.C.E.

Anthony Snodgrass, *Archaic Greece: The Age of Experiment* (Totowa, NJ: Biblio Distribution Center, 1980). Excellent survey of the creative achievements of the Archaic period.

* John Boardman, *The Greeks Overseas* (New York: Thames & Hudson, 1982). Description of varieties of Greek involvement abroad and their effects on Greece by a distinguished archaeologist.

* A. J. Graham, *Colony and Mother City in Ancient Greece* (Chicago: Ares, 1983). A synthetic look at Greek colonies.

G. E. R. Lloyd, *Magic, Reason and Experience* (New York: Cambridge University Press, 1979). Enlightening analysis of early Greek thought and culture.

E. Hussey, *The Presocratics* (New York: Scribners, 1972). Standard study of early Greek philosophers.

* Walter Burkert, *Structure and History in Greek Mythology and Ritual* (Berkeley: University of California Press, 1980). Relates myth and religion to society and history.

W. G. Forrest, *The Emergence of Greek Democracy* (New York: McGraw-Hill, 1966). Covers the politics of the Archaic period.

A. Andrewes, *The Greek Tyrants* (Atlantic Highlands, NJ: Humanities Press International, 1956). Standard survey of Greek tyranny.

Eva. C. Keuls, *The Reign of the Phallus: Sexual Politics in Ancient Athens* (New York: Harper & Row, 1985). Controversial study of sexual politics.

* S. B. Pomeroy, *Goddesses, Whores, Wives, and Slaves: Women in Classical Antiquity* (New York: Schocken Books, 1975). Pioneering study of gender in antiquity.

T. B. L. Webster, *Everyday Life in Classical Athens* (New York: Putnam, 1969). A general look at ordinary life but concentrating on the classic period.

W. B. Dinsmoor, *The Architecture of Ancient Greece* (New York: W. W. Norton, 1952). An old but still valuable survey.

* J. Boardman, *Preclassical Style and Civilization* (Harmondsworth: Penguin Books, 1967). A study of early Greek art by a leading archaeologist.

J. Boardman, *Greek Sculpture: Archaic Period* (New York: Thames & Hudson, 1985). A well-illustrated survey of early Greek sculpture.

R. M. Cook, *Greek Painted Pottery*, 2d ed. (Routledge, Chapman & Hall, 1972). The basic handbook of Greek vase painting.

A TALE OF THREE CITIES

David Whitehead, *The Demes of Attica (ca. 508-250 B.C.)* (Princeton, NJ: Princeton University Press, 1986). An excellent, recent study of Athenian politics and society.

Paul Cartledge, *Sparta and Lakonia: A Regional History 1300-362 B.C.* (New York: Routledge, Chapman & Hall, 1978). The best survey of Spartan history.

J. R. Salmon, *Wealthy Corinth: A History of the City to 338 B.C.* (New York: Oxford University Press, 1984). A comprehensive history of early Corinth.

THE COMING OF PERSIA AND THE END OF THE ARCHAIC AGE

A. R. Burn, *Persia and the Greeks: The Defense of the West c. 546-478 B.C.* (Stanford, CA: Stanford University Press, 1984). A standard account of the conflict but largely from the Greek perspective.

* Indicates paperback edition available.

CHAPTER 3

Classical and Hellenistic Greece, 500–100 B.C.E.

ALEXANDER AT ISSUS

War with Persia opened and closed the centuries of Greek glory. In 490 B.C.E. the invasion of the Greek mainland by Darius I pitted the greatest empire the West had ever known against a few small, mutually suspicious states. The victory of the Greeks convinced them of the superiority of their world over the barbarian and of free men over Eastern despots. One hundred fifty-seven years later, Darius III (336–330 B.C.E.) suffered a far more devastating defeat than his ancestor at the hands of Alexander the Great (336–323 B.C.E.) and a combined Greek army. Darius I had lost his pride. Darius III lost his empire and, shortly afterward, his life.

Alexander had announced his expedition as a campaign to punish the Persians for their invasion of Greece a century and a half earlier. Greeks rightly viewed Alexander's victory at Issus in 333 B.C.E. as the beginning of the end for the Persians, and it was long celebrated by Greek poets and artists. The most famous of these was Philoxenus of Eretria, whose paintings marked the high point of Greek pictorial art. His masterpiece, like all other Greek paintings executed on wood, is long vanished. However sometime in the first century B.C.E., a wealthy Roman commissioned a mosaic copy of the painting for his villa at Pompeii in southern Italy. The mosaic, measuring some sixteen feet by eight feet and containing a million and a half stones, each the size of a grain of rice, is itself a masterpiece. It is also a faithful copy of Philoxenus' painting, which a Roman critic had characterized as "surpassed by none."

Alexander, with reckless disregard for his own safety, had led his right wing across a small stream at a gallop and routed the Persians' left flank. At the same time the Persian center, which consisted of Greek mercenaries, managed to push Alexander's center back into the stream. Finally, Alexander and his right wing swung left, cutting Darius' Greeks to pieces, scattering his Persian guard, and forcing Darius to flee for his life.

In muted tones of red, brown, black, and yellow, Philoxenus brings all the skills developed through two centuries of Greek art to capture this most dramatic moment of the battle. The action takes place on a dusty and barren plain. The only landscape features are a lone dead tree and a forest of spears. Bold foreshortening, first used in the previous century, renders the rear of the horse in the center almost three-dimensional as it runs in blind fury toward Darius' chariot. Although the entire scene is wildly chaotic, each man and each mount is portrayed as an individual, with his own expression of emotion and his own part to play in the violent action.

The young Alexander, his hair blowing free and his eye fixed not on Darius but on his greater destiny, exudes the reckless courage and violence for which he was so famous. And yet he is not the center of the composition. That place of honor goes to Darius, whose kindly, tortured face looks back as his horses pull his chariot to safety. His hand stretches out in helpless sympathy toward the young Persian who has thrown himself between his king and Alexander, taking through his chest the spear that the Greek king had intended for the Persian ruler.

The effect of the painting is at once heroic and disconcerting. Who is the hero of the battle? Is it the wild-eyed Alexander in his moment of victory, or is it the aged Persian monarch, whose infinite sadness at his moment of defeat is not for himself but for his young aide, who has given his life so that Darius might live? The picture here is no simple juxtaposition of civilization against barbarity. Greeks fought on both sides at Issus, just as they had in the Persian wars of the fifth century B.C.E. Nor did Alexander's warriors despise their Persian enemies. Alexander told Darius' mother, captured after the battle, that he felt no personal bitterness toward her son. By the fourth century B.C.E., Greeks had learned that right and wrong, good and evil, civilized and barbarian were not simple issues. In the past century and a half, they had seen many wars, many leaders, and many defeats. Greek intellectuals had explored the complexity of human existence, agreeing with the philosopher Socrates that the unexplored life was not worth living. Greek dramatists had taught that suffering brought

wisdom. Philoxenus' depictions of Darius and Alexander reflect the same complexity. Who is the hero here? Who is the man of wisdom?

Learning to ask these questions was a painful education for Greeks of the fifth and fourth centuries. The victories over the Persian forces of Darius and his successors brought an unprecedented period of political and cultural freedom and creativity, but also deadly rivalry between Athens and Sparta, the leaders of the victorious Greeks. Democratic Athens transformed its wartime alliance into an empire, and only a generation after Athenian and Spartan troops had faced the Persians, they fought each other in a long and futile war, which left the Greek world exhausted and easy prey for the ambitious Macedonian dynasty.

War and Politics in the Fifth Century

The vast Persian army, moving west in 490 B.C.E., threatened the fruits of three centuries of Greek political, social, and cultural experimentation. The shared ideal of freedom within community and the common bond of language and culture seemed no basis on which to build an effective resistance to the great Persian Empire. Moreover, Darius I was not marching against the Greeks as such but against the allies of the rebellious Ionian cities. Few Greek states other than Athens had supported the Ionians against their Persian conquerors. Many Greeks saw the Persians as potential allies or even rulers preferable to their more powerful Greek neighbors and rivals within their own states. Separated by political traditions, intercity rivalries, and cultural differences, the Greeks felt no sense of national or ethnic unity. Particular interest, rather than patriotism or love of freedom, determined which cities opposed the Persian march. In the end, only Eretria, a badly divided Athens, and the small town of Plataea were prepared to

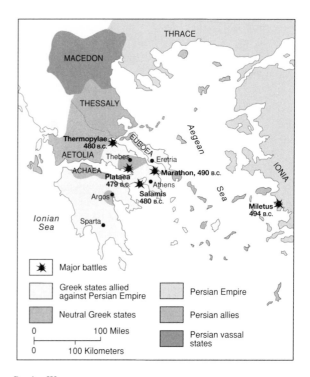

Persian Wars

refuse the Persian king's demand for gifts of earth and water, the traditional symbols of submission.

The Persian Wars

Initially, the Persian campaign followed the pattern established in Ionia. In the autumn of 490 B.C.E., Darius quickly destroyed the city of Eretria and carried off its population in captivity. The victorious Persian forces, numbering perhaps twenty thousand infantrymen and mounted archers, then landed at the Bay of Marathon. The total Athenian and Plataean force was no more than half that of its enemies, but the Greeks were better armed and commanded the hills facing the Marathon plain on which the Persian troops had massed. The Athenians also benefited from the leadership of Miltiades (ca. 544–489 B.C.E.), an experienced soldier who had served Darius and who knew the Persian's strengths and weaknesses. For over a week the two armies faced each other in a battle of nerves. Growing dissension in the Athenian ranks finally led the Greek generals to make a desperate and unexpected move. Abandoning the high ground, the Athenian hoplites rushed in disciplined phalanxes over almost a mile of open fields and then attacked the amazed Persian forces at a run. Although the Persians broke through the center of the Greek lines, the Athenians routed the Persian flanks and then turned in, enveloping the invaders in a deadly trap. In a few hours it was all over. Six thousand Persians lay dead, while fewer than two hundred Athenians were buried in the heroes' grave that still marks the Marathon plain. The Persians retreated to their ships and sailed for the Bay of Phalerum near Athens, hoping to attack the city itself before its victorious troops could return. However, the Athenians, though exhausted from the battle, rushed the twenty-three miles home in under eight hours, beating the Persian fleet. When the Persians learned that they had lost the race, they turned their ships for Asia.

The almost miraculous victory at Marathon had three enormous consequences for Athens and for Greece in general. First, it established the superiority of the hoplite phalanx as the finest infantry formation in the Mediterranean world. Second, Greeks expanded this belief in military superiority to a faith in the general superiority of Greeks over the "barbarians" (those who spoke other languages). Finally, by proving the value of the citizen army, the victory of the Athenians solidified and enhanced the democratic reforms of Cleisthenes.

Common citizens were determined that the victory won by the hoplite phalanx at Marathon should not be

This ostrakon was found in the Athenian agora. It was used to cast a vote to choose a person who would be ostracized—banished—from Athens for a period of ten years. The name on the first line is Themistocles.

lost to an aristocratic faction at home. To guard against this danger, the Athenian assembly began to practice *ostracism*, ten-year exile without loss of property, imposed on those who threatened to undermine the constitution of Cleisthenes. Each year every Athenian citizen had the opportunity to write on a potsherd (in Greek, *ostrakon*) the name of the man he most wished to leave Attica. If at least six thousand citizens voted, the state sent the individual receiving the most votes into temporary exile. No charges or accusations had to be made, much less proven. Anyone who had offended the Athenians or who, by his prominence, seemed a threat to democracy, could be ostracized. At the same time, Athenians also began to select their chief officers not simply by direct election but by lot. This practice prevented any individual from rising to power by creating a powerful faction.

For six years Persia was occupied by problems elsewhere in their vast empire and paid little attention to Greece. After the unexpected death of Darius I in 486 B.C.E., his son Xerxes (486–465 B.C.E.) began to amass foodstuffs, weapons, and armies for a land assault on his Greek enemies. In response to these preparations, Greek cities attempted to close ranks against the invaders. However, many Greek communities still saw their neighbors as greater threats than the Persians. Some states, including Thebes, Argos, and Thessaly, more or less willingly allied with the Persians against Athens or Sparta. North of the Peloponnesus only Athens, Plataea, and a few other small states were willing to fight the Persians. Sparta was prepared to defend itself and its league, but was not interested in campaigns far from home. Finally, in 481 B.C.E., when the Persian invasion was imminent, representatives of what a contemporary called "the Greeks who had the best thoughts for Greece" met in Sparta to plan resistance. The allies agreed that the Spartans would take command of the combined land and sea forces, which totaled roughly 35,000 helots, 5,000 hoplites, and 378 ships.

Although larger than those mustered by Athens against Darius, the Greek forces were puny compared with Xerxes' estimated two hundred thousand infantry and one thousand light and highly maneuverable Ionian and Phoenician ships. The Spartan commanders sought a strategic point at which the numerical superiority of the Persian forces would be neutralized. The choice fell on the narrow pass of Thermopylae and the adjacent Euboean strait. While a select force of hoplites held the pass, the Greek fleet, following a strategy devised by Themistocles, harried the larger Persian one. Neither action produced a Greek victory, but none could have been expected.

At Thermopylae, the Greeks held firm for days against wave after wave of assaulting troops. Finally, Greek allies of the Persians showed them a narrow mountain track by which they were able to attack the Greek position from the rear. Seeing that all was lost, the Spartan king Leonidas (490–480 B.C.E.) sent most of his allies home. Then he and his three hundred Spartan equals faced certain death with a casual disdain characterized by the comment made by one Spartan equal.

Told that when the Persians shot their arrows, they were so numerous that they hid the sun, the Spartan replied, "Good. If the Persians hide the sun, we shall have our battle in the shade." The epitaph raised later by the Spartan state to Leonidas and his men read simply, "Go tell the Spartans, you who read: we took their orders, and are dead."

While the Persian troops were blocked at Thermopylae, their fleet was being battered by fierce storms in the Euboean straits and harassed by the heavier Greek ships. Here the Greeks learned that in close quarters, they could stand up to Xerxes' navy. This lesson proved vital a short time later. While the Persian army burned Athens and occupied Attica, Themistocles lured the fleet into the narrow strait between Salamis and the mainland. There the slower Greek vessels bottled up the larger and vastly more numerous enemy ships and cut them to pieces.

After Salamis, Xerxes lost his appetite for fighting Greeks. Without his fleet, he could not supply a vast army far from home in hostile territory. Leaving a force to do what damage it could, he led the bulk of his forces back to Persia. At Athenian urging, the Greek allies under Leonidas' kinsman Pausanias (d. ca. 470 B.C.E.) met the Persians at Plataea in 479 B.C.E. Once more hoplite discipline and Greek determination meant more than numerical superiority. That night the Spartan king dined in the splendor of the captured tent of the

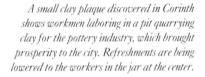

A small clay plaque discovered in Corinth shows workmen laboring in a pit quarrying clay for the pottery industry, which brought prosperity to the city. Refreshments are being lowered to the workers in the jar at the center.

defeated Persian commander. Athenian sea power and Spartan infantry had proven invincible. Soon the Athenians were taking the offensive, liberating the Ionian cities of Asia Minor and, in the process, laying the foundations of an Athenian empire every bit as threatening to their neighbors as that of Xerxes.

The Athenian Empire

Sparta, not Athens, should have emerged as the leader of the Greek world after 479 B.C.E. However, the constant threat of a helot revolt and the desire of the members of Sparta's Peloponnesian League to go their separate ways left Sparta too preoccupied with internal problems to fill the power vacuum left by the Persian defeat.

Athens, on the other hand, was only too ready to take the lead in freeing the Greek world from the Persian menace. With Sparta out of the picture, the Athenian fleet was the best hope of liberating the Aegean from Persians and pirates. In 478 B.C.E. Athens accepted control of what historians have come to call the Delian League, after the island of Delos where the league met. Athens and some of the states with navies provided ships; others contributed annual payments to the league. Initially, the league pursued the war against the Persians, driving them back along the Aegean and the Black seas. At the same time, Athens hurriedly rebuilt its defensive fortifications, a move correctly interpreted by Sparta and other states as directed more against them than against the Persians.

Athens' domination of the Delian League assured its prosperity. Attica, with its fragile agriculture, depended on Black Sea wheat, and the league kept these regions under Athenian control. Since Athens received not only cash "contributions" from league members but also one-half of the spoils taken in battle, the state's public coffers were filled. The new riches made possible the reconstruction of the city that was burned by the Persians into the most magnificent city of Greece.

The league was too vital to Athenian prosperity to stand and fall with the Persian threat. The drive against the Persian Empire began to falter after a league expedition to Egypt in 454 B.C.E. ended in total defeat. Discouraged by this and other setbacks, the league and the Persians concluded a treaty of peace in 449 B.C.E. For a brief moment it appeared that since Persia was no longer a threat, the Delian League might disband. But it was too late. The league had become an empire and Athens' allies were its subjects.

The Athenian empire was an economic, judicial, religious, and political union held together by military might. Athens controlled the flow of grain through the Hellespont to the Aegean, ensuring its own supply and heavily taxing cargoes to other cities. Athens controlled the law courts of member cities and used them to repress anti-Athenian groups. Athenian citizens—rich and poor alike—acquired territory throughout the empire. The rich took over vast estates confiscated from local opponents of Athenian dominance, while the poor replaced hostile populations in the colonies. Control over this empire depended on the Athenian fleet to enforce cooperation. Athenian garrisons were established in each city and "democratic" puppet governments ruled according to the wishes of the garrison commanders. Revolt, resignation from the league, or refusal to pay the annual tribute resulted in brutal suppression. Persian tyranny had hardly been worse than Athenian imperialism, and Sparta and its allies looked with growing fear upon this dangerous new imperial power.

Private and Public Life in Athens

During the second half of the fifth century B.C.E., Athens, enriched by tribute from its over 150 subject states, was a vital, crowded capital drawing merchants, artisans, and laborers from throughout the Greek world. At its height, the total population of Athens and surrounding Attica numbered perhaps 350,000. However, probably fewer than 60,000 were citizens, that is, adult males

Sixth-century B.C.E. Attic black figure vase showing women spinning and weaving wool.

qualified to own land and participate in Athenian politics. Over one-quarter of the total population were slaves. Great landowners, unable to force ordinary free men to work their estates, had turned to slave labor. Slaves were also vital in mining and other forms of craft and industrial work.

Greek slaves were not distinguished by race, ethnicity, or physical appearance. Anyone could become a slave. Prisoners of war, foreigners who failed to pay taxes, victims of pirate raids, could all end up on the auction blocks of the ancient world. Slaves were as much the property of their owners as their land, houses, cattle, and sheep. Many masters treated their slaves well, but beatings, tattooing, starvation, and shackling were all too common as a means of enforcing obedience.

Roughly half of Athens' free population were foreigners called metics. These were primarily Greek citizens of the tributary states of the empire, but they might also be peoples from Africa or from Asia Minor, such as Lydians. The number of metics increased after the middle of the fifth century B.C.E. both because of the flood of foreigners into the empire's capital and because Athenian citizenship was restricted to persons with two parents who were of citizen families. Metics could not own land in Attica nor could they participate directly in politics. They were required to have a citizen protector and to pay a small annual tax. Otherwise, they were free to engage in every form of activity. The highest concentration of metics was found in the port of Piraeus, where they participated in commerce, manufacturing, banking, and skilled crafts.

More than half of those born into citizen families were entirely excluded from public life. These were the women, who controlled and directed the vital sphere of the Athenian home, but who were considered citizens only for purposes of marriage, transfer of property, and procreation. From birth to death, every female citizen lived under the protection of a male guardian, either a close relative such as father or brother, or a husband or son. Women spent almost their entire lives in the inner recesses of the home. Fathers arranged marriages, the purposes of which are abundantly clear from the ritualized exchange of words sealing the betrothal:

> I give this woman for the procreation of legitimate children.
> I accept.
> And (I give a certain amount as) dowry.
> I am content.

A wife had no control over her dowry, which passed to her son. In the event of divorce or the death of her husband, the woman and her dowry returned to her father. An honorable Athenian woman stayed at home and managed her husband's household. Only the poorest citizens sent their wives and daughters to work in the marketplace or the fields. Even the most casual contact with other men without permission was strictly forbidden, although men were expected to engage in various sorts of extramarital affairs. In the words of one Athenian male, "Hetairai we have for our pleasure, mistresses for the refreshment of our bodies, but wives to bear us legitimate children and to look after the house faithfully." The household, as Athenians never tired of repeating, was the foundation of all society. Thus the role of women was indeed important, even though the public sphere was entirely closed to them.

Male control over women may have resulted in part from fear. Women were identified with the forces of nature, which included both positive forces such as fertility and life and negative forces such as chaotic irrationality, which threatened civilization. These two poles were epitomized by the cult of Dionysus. He was the god of wine, life blood, and fertility, but he was also the deity whose female devotees, the *maenads*, were portrayed as worshiping him in a state of frenzied savagery that could include tearing children and animals limb from limb.

The male citizens of fifth-century B.C.E. Athens were free to an extent previously unknown in the world. But Athenian freedom was freedom in community, not freedom from community. The essence of their freedom lay in their participation in public life, especially self-government, which was their passion. This participation was always within a complex network of familial, social, and religious connections and obligations, each of which placed different and even contradictory demands on its members. The impossibility of satisfying all of these demands, of responding to the special interests of each, forced citizens to make hard choices, to set priorities, and to balance conflicting obligations. The sum of these overlapping groupings was Athenian society, in which friends and opponents alike were united.

Unity did not imply equality. Even in fifth-century B.C.E. Athens, not all Athenians were socially or economically equal. Most were farmers who looked to military service as a means of increasing their meager income. Others engaged in trade or industry, although metics, with their commercial contacts in their cities of origin, dominated much of these activities in Athens. However, the aristocracy was still strong, and most of the popular leaders of the century came from the ranks of old wealth and influence. Still, sovereignty lay not with these aristocrats but with the demos, the people, who formed the assembly and large juries, always composed of several hundred citizens, who decided legal cases less on law than on the political merits of the case and the quality of the orators who pleaded for each side. Such large bodies were too unwieldy to deal with the daily tasks of government. Thus, control of these tasks fell to the council, composed of five hundred members selected by lot by the tribes; the magistrates, who were also chosen by lot; and ten military commanders or generals, the only major officeholders elected rather than chosen at random.

Paradoxically, the resolute determination of Athenian democrats to prevent individuals from acquiring too much power helped create a series of extraconstitutional power brokers. Since most offices were filled by lot and turned over frequently, real political leadership came not from officeholders but from generals and from popular leaders. These so-called demagogues, while at times holding high office, exercised their power through their speaking skills, informal networks, and knowledge of how to get things done. Demagogues tended to be wealthy aristocrats who could afford to put in the time demanded by these largely voluntary services.

Although many demagogues competed for power and attracted the support of the people, the Athenian demos was not kind to its heroes. Themistocles, the hero of Salamis, was ostracized in 470 B.C.E. So too was the person responsible for Themistocles' ostracism, Cimon (ca. 510–451 B.C.E.), after he led an army to assist Sparta in suppressing a revolt of its helots.

For the next thirty years, one individual dominated Athenian public life, the general Pericles (ca. 495–429 B.C.E.). Although not an original thinker, he was a great orator and a successful military commander, who proved to be the man most able to win the confidence of Athens and to lead it during the decades of its greatest glory. Athens' system of radical democracy reached its zenith under the leadership of Pericles, even while its imperial program drew it into a long and fatal war against Sparta, the only state powerful enough to resist it.

Pericles and Athens

Pericles was descended from the greatest aristocratic families of Athens. Nevertheless, as one ancient author put it, he "took his side, not with the rich and the few, but with the many and the poor." Pericles acquired intimate knowledge of government through long service on various public works projects, projects that provided lucrative income to poorer citizens. He was also presi-

dent of the commission responsible for constructing the great ivory and gold statue of Athena that stood in the Parthenon, the main temple in Athens. He served on the commission that built the Lyceum, or city exercise center, and the Parthenon itself. These enormous projects won him a great popular following while giving him an intimate knowledge of public finance and the details of Athenian government. He enhanced his position further through his great powers of persuasion.

Pericles led Athens, but he never ruled it. As a general he could only carry out the orders of the assembly and the council, and as a citizen he could only attempt to persuade his fellows. Still he was largely responsible for the extension of Athenian democracy to all free citizens. Under his influence Athens abolished the last property requirements for officeholding. He convinced the state to pay those who served on juries, thus making it possible for even the poorest citizens to participate in this important part of Athenian government. But he was also responsible for restricting citizenship to those whose mothers and fathers had been Athenians—a law that would have denied citizenship to many of the most illustrious Athenians of the sixth century B.C.E., including his own ancestors. The law also prevented citizens of Athens' subject states from developing a real stake in the fate of the empire.

Pericles' policies ultimately drew Athens into deadly conflict with Sparta. The source of the conflict was not a clash between democracy and oligarchy but rather the threat to Sparta and its allies posed by the growth of the Athenian empire. Pericles had disputed Cimon's foreign policy, which saw Athens and Sparta as "yoke mates" against Persia. With the disappearance of the Persian threat, Pericles saw Sparta and its allies as the only threat to Athens' domination of the Greek world. For their part, neutral cities and those allied with Sparta looked on Athens' mix of radical democracy at home and brutal imperialism abroad with growing fear.

Neither Athens with its prosperous trading empire nor Sparta with its internal problems wanted war, but so precarious was the balance of power between the two that the whole Greek world was a tinderbox ready to burst into flame. The spark came when Athens aided a breakaway colony of Corinth, a Spartan ally. This assistance infuriated Corinth, and in 432 B.C.E., the Corinthians convinced the Spartans that Athenian imperial ambitions were insatiable. In the words of the great historian of the war, Thucydides (d. ca. 401 B.C.E.), "What made war inevitable was the growth of Athenian power and the fear which this caused in Sparta." The

A bust of Pericles, the statesman and general who dominated Athenian public life in the mid-fifth century B.C.E.

next year, Sparta invaded Attica. The Peloponnesian War, which would destroy both great powers, had begun.

The Peloponnesian War

The Peloponnesian War was actually a series of wars and rebellions. Athens and Sparta waged two devastating ten-year wars, from 431 B.C.E. to 421 B.C.E. and then again from 414 B.C.E. to 404 B.C.E. At the same time, cities in each alliance took advantage of the wars to revolt against the great powers, eliciting terrible vengeance from both Athens and Sparta. Within many of the Greek city-states, oligarchs and democrats waged bloody civil wars for control of their governments. Moreover, between 415 and 413 B.C.E., Athens attempted to expand its empire in Sicily, an attempt that ended in disaster.

Before it was over, the Peloponnesian War had become an international war, with Persia, always interested in promoting disunity among the Greeks, entering the fray on the side of Sparta. In the end, there were no real victors, only victims.

Initially, Sparta and Athens both hoped for quick victory. Sparta's strength was its army, and its strategy was to invade Attica, devastate the countryside, and force the Athenians into an open battle. Pericles urged Athens to a strategy of conserving its hoplite forces while exploiting its naval strength. Athens was a naval power and, with its empire and control of Black Sea grain, could hold out for years behind its fortifications, the great walls linking Athens to its port of Piraeus. At the same time, the Athenian fleet could launch raids along the coast of the Peloponnesus, thus bringing the war home to the Spartans. Pericles hoped in this way to outlast the Spartans. In describing the war, Thucydides uses the same word for "survive" and "win."

The first phase of the war, called the Archidamian War after the Spartan king Archidamus (431–427 B.C.E.), was indecisive. Sparta pillaged Attica but could not breach the great wall nor starve Athens. In 430 B.C.E., the Spartans received unexpected help in the form of plague, which ravaged Athens for five years. By the time it ended in 426 B.C.E., as much as one-third of the Athenian population had died, including Pericles. Still Athens held out, establishing bases encircling the Peloponnesus and urging Spartan helots and allies to revolt. During this phase the Athenian commander, Thucydides, was ostracized for a military failure and retired to Spartan territory to write his great history of the war. Exhausted by a decade of death and destruction, the two sides contracted peace in 421 B.C.E. Although Athens was victorious in that its empire was intact, the peace changed nothing and tensions festered for five years.

After the peace of 421 B.C.E., Pericles' kinsman Alcibiades (ca. 450–404 B.C.E.) dominated the demos. Well-spoken, handsome, and brave, but also vain, dissolute, and ambitious, Alcibiades led the city into disaster. Although a demagogue who courted popular support, he despised the people and schemed to overturn the democracy. In 415 B.C.E., he urged Athens to expand its empire west by attacking Syracuse, the most prosperous Greek city of Sicily, which had largely escaped the devastation of the Archidamian War. The expedition went poorly and Alcibiades, accused at home of having profaned one of the most important Athenian religious cults, was ordered home. Instead, he fled to Sparta, where he began to assist the Spartans against Athens. The Sicilian expedition ended in disaster. Athens lost

THE TWO FACES OF ATHENIAN DEMOCRACY

■ *Early in the Peloponnesian War, Thucydides summarized the virtues of Athenian democracy in the speech he ascribes to Pericles in honor of those who died in the first year of the war. By 416 B.C.E., the sixteenth year of the Peloponnesian War, Athenian imperialism no longer even paid lip service to the ideals of democracy or freedom. Thucydides illustrates this in his reconstructed debate between representatives of the Spartan colony of Melos, which had attempted to remain neutral, and those of the Athenians, who demanded their surrender and enslavement.*

PERICLES' FUNERAL ORATION

Our constitution is called a democracy because power is in the hands not of a minority but of the whole people. When it is a question of settling private disputes, everyone is equal before the law; when it is a question of putting one person before another in positions of public responsibility, what counts is not membership of a particular class, but the actual ability which the man possesses. No one, so long as he has it in him to be of service to the state, is kept in political obscurity because of poverty. And, just as our political life is free and open, so is our day-to-day life in our relations with each other . . . We are free and tolerant in our private lives; but in public affairs we keep to the law. . . .

We make friends by doing good to others, not by receiving good from them. This makes our friendship all the more reliable, since we want to keep alive the gratitude of those who are in our debt by showing continued good will to them . . . In (Athens') case, and in her case alone, no invading enemy is ashamed at being defeated, and no subject can complain of being governed by people unfit for their responsibilities.

From Thucydides, *The Peloponnesian War*.

THE MELIAN DEBATE

Athenians: You know as well as we do that, when these matters are discussed by practical people, the standard of justice depends on the equality of power to compel and that in fact the strong do what they have the power to do and the weak accept what they have to accept . . .

Melians: And how could it be just as good for us to be the slaves as for you to be the masters?

Athenians: You, by giving in, would save yourselves from disaster; we by not destroying you, would be able to profit from you.

Melians: So you would not agree to our being neutral, friends instead of enemies, but allies of neither side?

Athenians: No, because it is not so much your hostility that injures us; it is rather the case that, if we were on friendly terms with you, our subjects would regard that as a sign of weakness in us, whereas your hatred is evidence of our power.

Ultimately the Melians rejected Athens' demands, and shortly after the Athenians captured the city, executed all of the men, and sold the women and children as slaves.

From Thucydides, *The Peloponnesian War*.

over two hundred ships and fifty thousand men. At the same time, Sparta resumed the war, this time with naval support provided by Persia.

Suddenly Athens was fighting for its life. Alcibiades soon abandoned Sparta for Persia and convinced the Athenians that if they would abandon their democracy for an oligarchy, Persia would withdraw its support of Sparta. In 411 B.C.E., the desperate Athenian assembly established a brutal oligarchy controlled by a small faction of antidemocratic conspirators. Alcibiades' promise proved

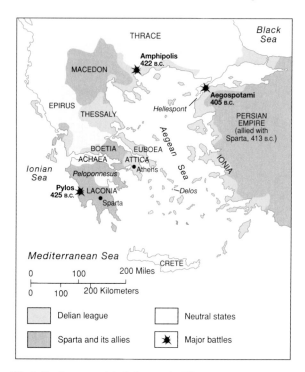

The Delian League and the Peloponnesian War

This statuette is a realistic portrait of the philosopher Socrates, who was celebrated for his mind rather than his physical endowments. Our verbal portraits of Socrates and his ideas come to us from Plato and Xenophon.

hollow and the war continued. Athens reestablished its democracy, but the brief oligarchy left the city bitterly divided. The Persian king renewed his support for Sparta, sending his son Cyrus (ca. 424–401 B.C.E.) to coordinate the war against Athens. Under the Spartan general Lysander (d. 395 B.C.E.), Sparta and its allies finally closed in on Athens. Lysander captured the Athenian fleet in the Hellespont, destroyed it, and severed Athens' vital grain supply. Within months Athens was entirely cut off from the outside world and starving. In 404 B.C.E., Sparta accepted Athens' unconditional surrender. Athens' fortifications came down, its empire vanished, and its fleet, except for a mere twelve ships, dissolved.

The Peloponnesian War showed not only the limitations of Athenian democracy but the potential brutality of oligarchy as well. More ominously, it demonstrated the catastrophic effects of disunity and rivalry among the Greek cities of the Mediterranean.

Athenian Culture in the Hellenic Age

Most of what we today call Greek is actually Athenian: throughout the Hellenic age (the fifth and early fourth centuries B.C.E., as distinct from the Hellenistic period of roughly the later fourth through second centuries), the turbulent issues of democracy and oligarchy, war and peace, hard choices and conflicting obligations found expression in Athenian culture even as the glory of the Athenian empire was manifested in art and architecture. The great dramatists Aeschylus, Sophocles, and Euripides were Athenian, as were the sculptor Phidias, the Parthenon architects Ictinus and Callicrates, the philosophers Socrates and Plato. To Athens came writers, thinkers, and artists from throughout the Greek world.

The Examined Life

A primary characteristic of Athenian culture was its critical and rational nature. In heated discussions in the assembly and the agora, the courtroom and the private symposium, Athenians and foreigners drawn to the city no longer looked for guidance to the myths and religion of the past. Secure in their identity and protected by the openness of their radical democracy, they began to examine past and present and to question the foundations of traditional values. From this climate of inquiry emerged the traditions of moral philosophy and its cousin, history.

Throughout the Hellenic age interest in natural philosophy, the explanation of the universe in rational terms, remained high. But philosophers also began to turn their attention to the human world, in particular to the powers and limitations of the individual's mind and the individual's relationship with society. The philosopher Heraclitus (see chapter 2, p. 59) examined the rational faculties themselves rather than what one could know with them. In part, this meant a search for personal, inner understanding that would lead to proper action within society, in other words, to the search for ethics based in reason. Moreover, such an inquiry led to a study of how to formulate arguments and persuade others through logic. This study of rhetoric, the art of persuasion, was particularly important in fifth-century Athens because it was the key to political influence. Teachers, called *sophists* ("wise people"), traveled throughout Greece offering to provide an advanced education for a fee. Sophist teachers such as Gorgias (ca. 485–ca. 380 B.C.E.) and Protagoras (ca. 490–421 B.C.E.) trained young men in the arts of rhetoric and in logic. By exercising their students' minds with logical puzzles and paradoxical statements, the sophists taught a generation of wealthy Greeks the powers and complexities of human reason.

Fragment of a vase from Tarentum showing an actor holding a mask. Greek dramas were presented in outdoor theaters. Men played women's roles and the actors wore masks to indicate the nature of the characters they played.

Socrates (ca. 470–399 B.C.E.) was considered a sophist by many of his contemporaries, but he himself reacted against what he saw as the amoral and superficial nature of sophistic education. As a young man he was interested in natural philosophy, but he abandoned this tradition in favor of the search for moral self-enlightenment urged by Heraclitus. "Know thyself" was Socrates' plea. An unexamined life, he argued, was not worth living. Socrates refused any pay for his teaching, arguing that he had nothing to teach. He knew nothing, he said, and was superior to the sophists only because he recognized his ignorance while they professed wisdom.

Socrates' method threatened and infuriated many of his contemporaries who prized their reputations for wisdom or skill. He engaged them in discussion and then, through a series of disarmingly simple questions, forced them to defend their beliefs. The inevitable result was that in their own words the outstanding sophists, politicians, and poets of the day demonstrated the inadequacy of their beliefs. Condemned to death in 399 B.C.E. on the trumped-up charges of corrupting the morals of the Athenian youth and introducing strange gods, he rejected the opportunity to

SOCRATES THE GADFLY

■ *In Plato's* Apology *he presents an account of Socrates' defense of his role in Athenian society, constantly driving his fellow citizens to examine their assumptions.*

And now, Athenians, I am not arguing in my own defense at all, as you might expect me to do, but rather in yours in order that you may not make a mistake about the gift of the god to you by condemning me. For if you put me to death, you will not easily find another who, if I may use a ludicrous comparison, clings to the state as a sort of gadfly to a horse that is large and well-bred but rather sluggish because of its size, so that it needs to be aroused. It seems to me that the god has attached me like that to the state, for I am constantly alighting upon you at every point to arouse, persuade, and reproach each of you all day long. You will not easily find anyone else, my friends, to fill my place; and if you are persuaded by me, you will spare my life. You are indignant, as drowsy persons are when they are awakened, and, of course, if you are persuaded by Anytus, you could easily kill me with a single blow, and then sleep on undisturbed for the rest of your lives, unless the god in his care for you sends another to arouse you.

From Plato, *Gorgias.*

escape into exile. Rather than reject Athens and its laws, he drank the fatal potion of hemlock given him by the executioner. Since Socrates refused to commit any of his teaching to writing, we have no direct knowledge of the content of his instruction. We know of him only from the conflicting reports of his former students and opponents. Two things about him are certain, however. Socrates never doubted the moral legitimacy of the Athenian state and he demanded that every aspect of life be investigated.

The philosophical interest in human choices and social constraints found echo in the historical writing of the age. Herodotus, a native of Halicarnassus (ca. 484–ca. 420 B.C.E.), found in Athens the intellectual climate and audience he needed to write an account of the Persian Wars of the preceding generation. His book of inquiries, or *historia*, into the origins and events of the conflict between Greeks and Persians is the first true history. Herodotus had traveled widely in the eastern Mediterranean, collecting local stories and visiting famous temples, palaces, and cities. In his study he presents a great panorama of the civilized world at the end of the sixth century B.C.E. Herodotus does not hesitate to report myths, legends, and outrageous tales. His faith in the gods is strong and he believes that the gods intervene in human affairs. Still, he is more than just a

good storyteller or a chronicler of legends. Often, after reporting conflicting accounts he will conclude, "Both stories are told and the reader may take his choice between them." In other cases, after recounting a particularly far-fetched account heard from local informants, he comments, "Personally, I think this story is nonsense."

As he explains in his introduction, Herodotus' purpose in writing was twofold. First, he sought to preserve the memory of the past by recording the achievements of both Greeks and non-Greeks. Second, he set out to show how the two came into conflict. It was this concern to explain, to go beyond mere storytelling, that earned Herodotus the designation of the "father of history." Like other Hellenic Greeks, Herodotus is less interested in the mythic dimensions of the conflict than in the human, and his primary concern is the action of individuals under the press of circumstances. Ultimately, the Persian Wars become for Herodotus the conflict between freedom and despotism, and he describes with passion how different Greek states chose between the two.

Thucydides, a different sort of historian, recorded the story of the Peloponnesian War. He focused more narrowly on the Greek world and on political power. Thucydides had been an Athenian general and a major

Man and Youth, a fifth-century B.C.E. drinking cup in terra-cotta from Attica in Greece. The cup is signed by Douris. Over two hundred extant vases are ascribed to him.

actor in the first part of the Peloponnesian War until his ostracism in 425 B.C.E. He began his account at the outbreak of the conflict, thus writing a contemporary record of the war rather than a history of it. As Herodotus is called the father of history, Thucydides might be called the first social scientist.

The central subject of his account is not myth nor religion nor morality but human society in action. Thucydides describes the Greek states acting out of rational self-interest. His favorite device for showing the development of such policies is the political set speech in which two opposing leaders attempt to persuade their fellow citizens on the proper course of action. Thucydides was seldom actually present at the events he describes. Even when he was, he could not have transcribed the speakers' exact words. Rather he

attempted to put into the mouths of the speakers "whatever seemed most appropriate to me for each speaker to say in the particular circumstances." Although fictitious by modern standards, these speeches penetrate to the heart of the tough political choices facing the opposing forces. This hard-nosed approach to political decisions continues to serve as a model to historians and practitioners of power politics.

Still, morality is always just below the surface of Thucydides' narrative. Even as he unflinchingly chronicles the collapse of morality and social order in the face of political expediency, he recognizes that this process will destroy his beloved Athens. The consequences of political self-interest, devoid of other considerations, follow their own natural course to disaster and ruin. In the later, unfinished chapters (Thucydides died shortly

GREEKS AND BARBARIANS

■ *Herodotus was unique among classical authors in his refusal to consider Greek customs superior to those of non-Greeks. In the following passage, he tells a story to prove his point.*

If it were proposed to all nations to choose which seemed best of all customs, each, after examination made, would place its own first; so well is each persuaded that its own are by far the best. It is not therefore to be supposed that any, save a madman, would turn such things to ridicule. I will give this one proof among many from which it may be inferred that all men hold this belief about their customs: When Darius was king, he summoned the Greeks who were with him and asked them what price would persuade them to eat their fathers' dead bodies. They answered that there was no price for which they would do it. Then he summoned those Indians who are called Callatiae, who eat their parents, and asked them (the Greeks being present and understanding by interpretation what was said) what would make them willing to burn their fathers at death. The Indians cried aloud, that he should not speak of so horrid an act. So firmly rooted are these beliefs; and it is, I think, rightly said in Pindar's poem that use and wont is lord of all.

From Herodotus, Book III.

after Athens' final defeat), the Peloponnesian War takes on the characteristics of a tragedy. Here Thucydides, the ultimate political historian, shows the deep influence of the dominant literary tradition of his day, Greek drama.

Athenian Drama

Since the time of its introduction by Peisistratus in the middle of the sixth century B.C.E., drama was popular, not only in Athens, but throughout the Greek world. Plays often dealt with mythic subject matter largely taken from the *Iliad* and the *Odyssey*. Three types of plays honored the annual Dionysian festival—tragedies, comedies, and satyr plays. Tragedies dealt with great men who failed because of flaws in their natures. Their purpose was, in the words of the philosopher Aristotle, to effect "through pity and terror the correction and refinement of passions." Comedies were more directly topical and political. They parodied real Athenians, often by name, and amused even while making serious points in defense of democracy. Somewhere between tragedies and comedies, satyr plays remained closest to the Dionysian cult. In them lecherous drunken satyrs, mythical half-man, half-goat creatures, interact with gods and men as they roam in search of Dionysus.

Only a handful survive today of the hundreds of Greek plays written in the Hellenic age. The first of the great Athenian tragedians whose plays we know is Aeschylus (525–456 B.C.E.), a veteran of Marathon and an eyewitness of the battle of Salamis. His one surviving trilogy, the *Oresteia*, traces the fate of the family of Agamemnon, the Greek commander at Troy. The three plays of the trilogy explore the conflicting obligations of filial respect and vengeance, which ultimately must be settled by rational yet divinely sanctioned law. Upon his return from Troy, the victorious Agamemnon is murdered by his unfaithful wife Clytemnestra. Orestes, his son, avenges his father's murder by murdering Clytemnestra, but in so doing incurs the wrath of the Furies, avenging spirits who pursue him for killing his mother. The conflict of duties and loyalties cannot be resolved by human means. Finally, Orestes arrives at the shrine of Apollo at Delphi, where the god purifies him from the pollution of the killing. Then at Athens, Athena rescues Orestes, creating the Athenian law court and transforming the Furies into the Eumenides, the kindly guardian spirits of Athens.

Aeschylus' younger contemporary Sophocles (496–406 B.C.E.) sought to express human character in his plays. He shows how humans make decisions and carry them out, constrained by their pasts, their weaknesses, and their vices, but free nonetheless. Sophocles'

The ruins of the Athenian Acropolis are dominated by the Parthenon. This temple of Athena was largely intact until 1687, when the Turks, attempting to conquer Athens, used it as a powder magazine. The powder exploded and devastated the building.

message is endurance, acceptance of both human re- sponsibility and the ways of the gods who overrule peo- ple's plans. The heroine of *Antigone* is the sister of Poly- neices, exiled son of King Oedipus of Thebes. Polyneices has died fighting his city and Creon, its new ruler, commands under penalty of death that Polyne- ices' body be left unburied. This would mean that his soul would never find rest, the ultimate punishment for a Greek. Antigone, with a determination and courage equal to her love for her brother, buries Polyneices and is entombed alive for her crime. Here the conflict be- tween the state, which claims the total obedience of its people, and the claims of familial love and religious piety meet in tragic conflict. Creon, warned by a prophet that he is offending heaven, orders Antigo- ne's release, but it is too late. Rather than wait for death, she has already hanged herself.

Euripides (485–406 B.C.E.), was far more original and daring in his subject matter and treatment of human emotions. Unlike the stately dramas of Aeschylus and the deliberate progressions of Sophocles, Euripides' plays abound in plot twists and unexpected, violent outbursts of passion. His characters are less recon- ciled to their fates and less ready to accept the tradi- tional gods:

> Does someone say that there are gods in heaven?
> There are not, there are not—unless one choose
> to follow old tradition like a fool.

Neither passion nor reason, but politics rules the world of Greek comedy. Rather than the timelessness of the human condition, Athenian comic playwrights fo- cused their biting satire on the political and social issues of the moment. Particularly the comic genius Aris- tophanes (ca. 450–ca. 388 B.C.E.) used wit, imagination, vulgarity, and great poetic sensitivity to attack every- thing that offended him in his city. In his plays he mocks and ridicules statesmen, philosophers, rival playwrights, and even the gods. His comedies are full of outrageous twists of plot, talking animals, obscene jokes and puns, and mocking asides. And yet Aristophanes was a deeply patriotic Athenian, dedicated to the democratic system and equally dedicated to the cause of peace. In his now-lost *Babylonians*, written around 426 B.C.E., as Athenians struggled to recover from the plague and Cleon continued to pursue the bloody war against Sparta, he mocks Cleon and the Athenian demagogues while portraying the cities of the Delian League as slaves forced to grind grain at a mill. In *Lysistrata*, written in 411 B.C.E., after Athens had once more renewed the war, the women of Greece force their men to make peace by conspiring to refuse them sex as long as war continues. Through the sharp satire and absurd plots of his plays, Aristophanes communicates his sympathy for ordinary people, who must match wits with the charlatans and pompous frauds who attempt to dominate Athens' public life.

The Human Image in Art and Architecture

Hellenic art and architecture reflected the same Greek emphasis on humanity found in Greek drama. In the late sixth century B.C.E., a reversal of the traditional black figure technique had revolutionized vase painting. Artists had begun to outline scenes on unfired clay and then fill in the background with black or brown glaze. The interior details of the figures were also added in black. The result was a much more lifelike art, a lighter, more natural coloring, and the possibility of more perspective, depth, and molding. Sculpture reflected the same development toward balance and realism contained within an ideal of human form. The finest bronzes and marbles of the fifth century B.C.E. show freestanding figures whose natural vigor and force, even when engaged in strenuous exertion, are balanced by the placidity of their faces and their lack of emotion. The tradition established by the Athenian sculptor Phidias (ca. 500–ca. 430 B.C.E.) sought a naturalism in the portrayal of the human figure, which remained ideal rather than individual.

The greatest artistic achievement of the Hellenic age was the Athenian acropolis, a magnificent complex of buildings and statues that towered over the city and, in a larger sense, over the ancient world. One entered the acropolis complex through the monumental *Propylaea*, or gateway, a T-shaped structure approached by a flight of steps. From the top of the steps, one could glimpse both Phidias' great bronze statue of Athena Promachos in the center of the acropolis and, to the right, the Parthenon. As visitors entered the acropolis itself, they passed on the right the small temple of Athena as Victory. Continuing on the Sacred Way, one saw on the left the delicate Erechtheum, which housed

the oldest Athenian cults. On the right, visitors were overawed by the Parthenon, a monument as much to Athens as to Athena. Even today, the ruined temple seems a rectangular embodiment of order, proportion, and balance, an effect achieved through irregularity, illusion, and variation. Every surface, from the floor to the columns to the horizontal beams, curves slightly. The spacing of the columns varies and each leans slightly inward. Those at the rear are larger than those at the front to compensate for the effect of viewing them from a greater distance.

An illusion, too, was the sense of overwhelming Athenian superiority and grandeur the acropolis was intended to convey. By the time the Erechtheum was completed in 406 B.C.E., the Athenian empire was all but destroyed, the city's population devastated, and its democracy imperiled. Two years later Athens surrendered unconditionally to Sparta.

The intellectual and artistic accomplishments of Athens were as enduring as its empire proved ephemeral. Writers and artists alike focused their creative energies on human existence, seeking a proper proportion, order, and meaning, a blend of practical and the ideal, which Athens' political leaders tragically lacked.

From City-States to Macedonian Empire, 404–323 B.C.E.

The Peloponnesian War touched every aspect of Greek life. The war brought changes to the social and political structures of Greece by creating an enduring bitterness between elites and populace and a distrust of both democracy and traditional oligarchy. The mutual exhaustion of Athens and Sparta left a vacuum of power in the Aegean. Finally, the war raised fundamental questions about the nature of politics and society throughout the Greek world.

Politics After the Peloponnesian War

Over the decades-long struggle, the conduct of war and the nature of politics had changed, bringing new problems for victor and vanquished alike. Lightly armed professional mercenaries willing to fight for anyone able to pay gradually replaced hoplite citizen soldiers as the backbone of the fighting forces. The rise of mercenary armies undermined democracies such as Athens as well as Sparta with its class of equals.

Victory left Sparta no more capable of assuming leadership in 404 B.C.E. than it had been in 478 B.C.E. Years of war had reduced the population of equals to less than three thousand. The Spartans proved extremely unpopular imperialists. As a reward for Persian assistance, Sparta returned the Ionian cities to Persian control. Elsewhere it established hated oligarchies to rule in a way favorable to Sparta's interests. In Athens, a brutal tyranny of thirty men took control in 404 B.C.E. With Spartan support, they executed fifteen hundred democratic leaders and forced five thousand more into exile. The Thirty Tyrants evoked enormous hatred and opposition. Within a year the exiles recaptured the city, restored democracy, and killed or expelled the tyrants.

Similar opposition to Spartan rule emerged throughout the Greek world, shattering the fragile peace created by Athens' defeat. For over seventy years the Greek world boiled in constant warfare. Mutual distrust, fear of any city that seemed about to establish a position of clear superiority, and the machinations of the Persian Empire to keep Greeks fighting each other produced a constantly shifting series of alliances.

Persia turned against its former ally in 401 B.C.E. when Sparta supported an unsuccessful attempt by Cyrus to unseat his brother Artaxerxes II. Soon the unlikely and unstable alliance of Athens, Corinth, Argos, Thebes, and Euboea, financed by Persia, entered a series of vicious wars against Sparta. The first round ended in Spartan victory, due to the shifting role of Persia, whose primary interest was as ever the disunity of the Greeks. By 377 B.C.E., however, Athens had reorganized its league and with Thebes as ally was able to break Spartan sea power. The decline of Sparta left a power vacuum soon filled by Thebes. Athens, concerned by this new threat, shifted alliances, making peace with its old enemy. However, Spartan military fortunes had so declined that when Sparta attacked Thebes in 371 B.C.E., its armies were destroyed and Spartan power broken. The next year Thebes invaded the Peloponnesus and freed Messenia, the foundation of Sparta's economic prosperity. Sparta never recovered. Deprived of its economic base, its body of equals reduced to a mere eight hundred, and its fleet gone, Sparta never regained its historic importance. Theban hegemony was short-lived. Before long the same process of greed, envy, and distrust that had devastated the other Greek powers destroyed Thebes. Athens' reconstituted league disintegrated as members opposed Athenian attempts once more to convert a free association of states into an empire. By the 330s, all of the Greek states had proven

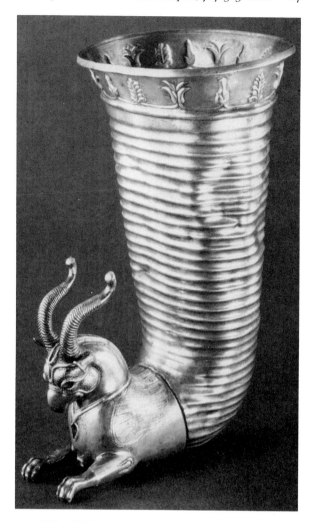

A partially guilded silver rhyton, or drinking vessel, is an example of Persian art. A horned griffin forms the base and lotus buds encircle the rim. Treasures such as this were looted from the Persians by Alexander's conquering army.

themselves incapable of creating stable political units larger than their immediate polis.

Philosophy and the Polis

The failure of Greek political forms, oligarchy and democracy alike, profoundly affected Athenian philosophers. Plato (ca. 428–347 B.C.E.), an aristocratic student of Socrates, grew up during the Peloponnesian War and had witnessed the collapse of the empire, the brutality of the Thirty Tyrants, the execution of Socrates, and the revival of the democracy and its imperialistic ambitions. From these experiences he developed a hatred for Athenian democracy and a profound distrust of ordinary people's ability to tell right from wrong. Disgusted with public life, Plato left Attica for a time and traveled in Sicily and Italy, where he encountered different forms of government and different philosophical schools. Around 387 B.C.E., he returned to Athens and opened the Academy, a school to provide Athenian youth with what he considered to be knowledge of what was true and good for the individual and the state.

For transmitting his teachings Plato chose a most unlikely literary form, the dialogue. He developed his ideas through discussions between his teacher, Socrates, and a variety of students and opponents. While Plato shared with his mentor the conviction that human actions must be grounded in self-knowledge, Plato's philosophy extended much further. His arguments about the inadequacy of all existing forms of government and the need to create a new form of government through the proper education of elite philosopher rulers were part of a complex understanding of the universe and the individual's place in it. (See Special Feature, "The First Utopia," pp. 90–91.)

Plato argued that true knowledge is impossible as long as it focuses on the constantly changing, imperfect world of everyday experience. Real knowledge consists of only that which is eternal, perfect, and beyond the experience of the senses, the realm of what Plato calls the Forms. When we judge that individuals or actions are true or good or beautiful, we do so not because these particular persons or events are truly virtuous, but because we recognize that they participate in some way in the Idea or Form of truth or goodness or beauty.

The evils of the world, and in particular the vices and failures of government and society, result from ignorance of the truth. Most people live as though chained in a cave in which all they can see are the shadows cast by a fire on the walls. In their ignorance, they mistake these flickering, imperfect images for reality. Their proper ruler must be a philosopher, one who is not deceived by the shadows. The philosopher's task is to break their chains and turn them toward the source of the light so that they can see the world as it really is.

Plato's idealist view of knowledge (so called because of his notion of Ideas or Forms) dominated much of ancient philosophy. His greatest student, Aristotle (384–322 B.C.E.), however, rejected this view in favor of a philosophy rooted in the natural world. Aristotle came from a medical family of northern Greece and, although a student in Plato's Academy for almost twenty years, he never abandoned observation for speculation. Systematic investigation and explanation characterize Aristotle's vast work, and his interests ranged from biology to statecraft to the most abstract

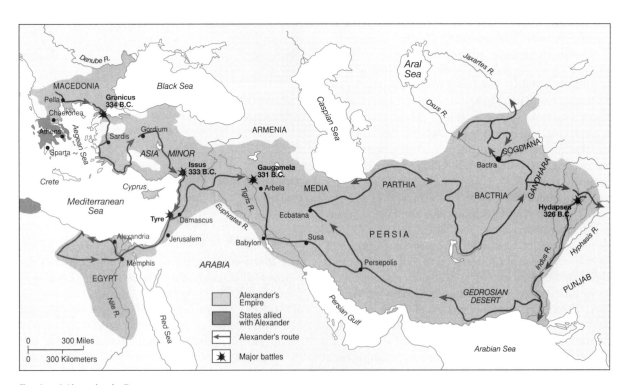

Empire of Alexander the Great

philosophy. In each field, he employed essentially the same method. He observed as many individual examples of the topic as possible and from these specific observations extracted general theories. His theories, whether on the nature of matter, the species of animals, the working of the human mind, ethics, or the proper form of the state, are distinguished by clarity of logical thinking, precision in the use of terminology, and respect for the world of experience.

Aristotle brought this empirical approach to the question of life in society. He defined humans as "political animals," that is, animals particularly characterized by life in the polis. Unlike Plato, he did not regard any particular form of government as ideal. Rather, he concluded that the type of government ultimately mattered less than the balance between narrow oligarchy and radical democracy. And yet, during the very years that Aristotle was teaching, the vacuum created by the failure of the Greek city-states was being filled by the dynamic growth of the Macedonian monarchy, which finally ended a century of Greek warfare and with it, the independence of the Greek city-states.

The Rise of Macedon

The polis had never been the only form of the Greek state. Alongside the city-states of Athens, Corinth, Syracuse, and Sparta were more decentralized ethne ruled by traditional hereditary chieftains and monarchs. Macedonia, in the northeast of the mainland, was one such ethnos. Its kings, chosen by the army from within a royal family, ruled in cooperation with nobles and clan leaders. The Macedonian people spoke a Greek dialect, and Macedonian kings and elite identified with Greek culture and tradition. Macedonia had long served as a buffer between the barbarians to the north and the Greek mainland, and its tough farmers and pastoralists were geared to constant warfare. As Athens, Sparta, and Thebes fought each other to mutual exhaustion, Macedonia under King Philip II (359–336 B.C.E.) moved into the resulting power vacuum. Philip showed a particular genius for rapidly organizing and leading armies and for conducting complex, multiple campaigns each year. He secured his borders against northern barbarians and captured the northern coast of the Aegean, including the

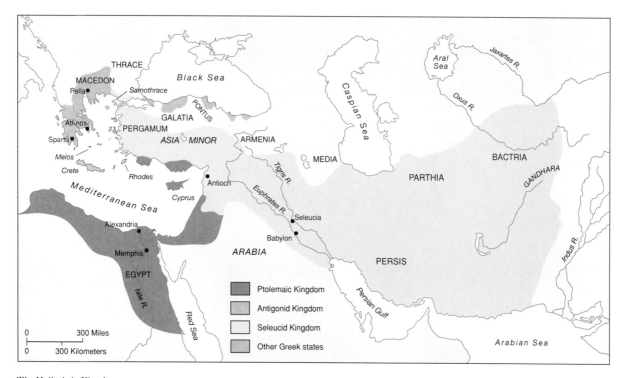

The Hellenistic Kingdoms

A mosaic showing Plato surrounded by his disciples.

The First Utopia

If the Greeks were fixated on good government, it might be because they had seen so many examples of bad. The bewildering variety of political forms that replaced the tyrants of the sixth century B.C.E. had proved no better than the evil they had sought to correct. By the end of the fourth century B.C.E., Lysander's brutal rule disillusioned many about the advantages of the Spartan mixture of monarchy, oligarchy, and democracy. The oligarchy of Corinth and the federalism of Thebes proved no better. And the radical democracy of Athens had brought disaster not only to the city but to all of Greece.

Aristotle and Plato tackled the problem, each according to his own philosophical inclinations. Aristotle, ever the empiricist, collected over 150 city constitutions, which he hoped to analyze in order to discover the best form of government. His teacher Plato would have thought such an exercise a waste of time. To Plato, all existing constitutions were bad. No place had the perfect form of government. He thus set about in his *Republic* to describe the constitution of "no place" (in Greek, *utopia*, a term coined over eighteen hundred years later), the ideal government.

In his description, Plato tackles the ultimate problem of politics: how should the state be ordered? His answer is a disturbing and fascinating image of a just society, created by a philosopher-king and ruled by a hand-picked body of Guardians.

Plato's ideal state resembles the Greek polis in size. A relatively small, territorially limited state is all that he can imagine. It is committed to equality of the sexes and populated by four groups of people: slaves, craftsmen, auxiliaries, and Guardians. The first group is implied but never discussed. Plato, like any other Greek, could not have imagined a society existing without slave labor. The bulk of the citizens are farmers, craft workers, and tradesmen, each specializing in that form of economic activity for which he or she is most suited. They are the only property owners in the republic, form the basis of its prosperity, and lead lives much like those of the ordinary citizens of a Greek polis, except that they have no role in defense or government.

The third group, in part self-perpetuating, in part recruited from the most promising children of the first, are the auxiliaries, who devote themselves exclusively to protecting the state from internal and external dangers. Auxiliaries are made, not born, and the program of education outlined by Plato is the critical ingredient in his ideal state. Boys and girls destined to be auxiliaries must be trained to know what is true and good and must be protected from lies and deception. Thus Plato bans poets and dramatists from his educational program. After all, Homer, Hesiod, Aeschylus, and Sophocles clothe fictions about the immorality of the gods and men in language of great beauty. Instead, the auxiliaries will be taught music and lyric poetry to instill in them a love of the harmony and order of the world. They also undertake physical training appropriate for soldiers, which not only prepares them for battle but, like music, develops the proper harmony of body and soul.

The auxiliaries must be free of private interests or ambitions, which would distract them from the needs of the state. Thus, they must live without private property or private family. Their needs are to be provided for by the craft worker class, making it unnecessary and impossible for the auxiliaries to amass anything of their own. Because family concerns might distract them from their duty, they must live in a garrison-like arrangement. Rulers would select appropriate male and female auxiliaries to mate and produce the best offspring. The children of such unions would be brought up together, regarding themselves and the adult auxiliaries as one large family identical with the state.

The best of these children, distinguished by their intellectual and moral ability, are to be selected as rulers, or Guardians. They undergo further education in the exact sciences and logic to train them to recognize the fundamental principles on which all truth depends. Finally, at the age of thirty-five, after years of study, a Guardian undertakes the hard task of governing, which Plato sees as a process of sharing with those less fortunate the enlightenment that education has given them.

Plato did not consider his republic an exercise in imagination. He firmly believed that it was practical and possible. The best person to establish it was a philosopher-king, a ruler in whom "political power and philosophy meet together."

Plato's contemporaries as well as subsequent generations have been at once fascinated and horrified by this ideal state. For many, the idea of total equality of the sexes was too absurd to consider. For others, the abolition of the family or the banning of poetry went beyond the realm of reason. Aristotle thought that the effects of such a system would be the opposite of what Plato intended, creating dissension and rebellion rather than reducing them. Modern readers praise or condemn Plato's republic because it smacks of communism, thought control, and totalitarianism. The modern social philosopher Karl Popper, for example, has termed Plato's political demands "purely totalitarian and antihumanitarian," and considers Plato the most determined enemy of freedom ever known. Goaded by Plato's challenge, political theorists ever since have taken up the task of devising their own image of the perfect society, seeking their own answer to Plato's challenge, "Where shall we find justice?"

gold and silver mines of Mount Pangaeus, which gave him a ready source of money for his campaigns. Then he turned his attention to the south.

Philip forced himself into the center of Greek affairs in 346 B.C.E. when he intervened to end the war between Thebes and Phocis. From then on he was relentless in his efforts to swallow up one Greek state after another. The Greek states had united against the Persians but resisted cooperating against Philip, and one by one they fell. In 338 B.C.E., Philip achieved a final victory at Chaeronea and established a new league, the League of Corinth. However, unlike all those that had preceded it, this league was no confederation of sovereign states. It was an empire ruled by a king and supported by wealthy citizens whose cooperation Philip rewarded well. This new model of government, a monarchy drawing its support from a wealthy elite, became a fixture of the Mediterranean world for the next two thousand years.

Philip's success was based on his powerful military machine, which combined both Macedonian military tradition and the new mercenary forces that had emerged over the past century in Greece. The heart of his army was the infantry, which was trained in the use of pikes some fourteen feet long, four feet longer than those of the Greek hoplites. Macedonian phalanxes moved forward in disciplined ranks, pushing back their foes, whose shorter lances could not reach the Macedonians. When the enemy were contained, the Macedonian cavalry charged from the flank and cut them to pieces. The cavalry, known as the Royal Companions, were the elite of Macedon and the greatest beneficiaries of Philip's conquests.

No sooner had Philip subdued Greece than he announced a campaign against Persia. He intended to lead a combined Greek force in a war of revenge and conquest to punish the great empire for its invasion of Greece 150 years earlier and its subsequent involvement in the Greek world. Before he could begin, however, he met the fate of his predecessors. At the age of forty-six he was cut down by an assassin's knife, leaving his twenty-year-old son, Alexander (336–323 B.C.E.), to lead the expedition. Within thirteen years Alexander conquered not only the Persians but western Asia as far as India.

The Empire of Alexander the Great

Alexander was less affected by his teacher, the philosopher Aristotle, than he was by the poet Homer. Envisioning himself a new Achilles, Alexander sought to imitate and surpass that legendary warrior and hero of the Iliad. Alexander's military genius, dedication to his troops, reckless disregard for his own safety, and ability to move both men and supplies across vast distances at great speed inspired the war machine developed by Philip and led it on an odyssey of conquest that stretched from Asia Minor to India. In 334 B.C.E., the first year of his campaign, Alexander captured the Greek cities of Asia Minor. Then he continued east. At Gordium, according to legend, he confronted an ancient puzzle, a complex knot tied to the chariot of the ancient king of that city. Whoever could loosen the knot, the legend said, would become master of Asia. Alexander solved that puzzle, as he did all of his others, with his sword. Two months later he defeated the Persian king Darius III at Issus and then headed south toward the Mediterranean coast and Egypt. After his victories there, he turned again to the north and entered Mesopotamia. At Gaugamela in 331 B.C.E., he defeated Darius a second, decisive time. Shortly after, Darius was murdered by the remnants of his followers. Alexander captured the Persian capital of Persepolis with its vast treasure and became the undisputed ruler of the vast empire.

The conquest of Persia was not enough. Alexander pushed on, intending to conquer the whole world. His armies marched east, subduing the rebellious Asian provinces of Bactria and Sogdiana. He negotiated the Khyber Pass from what is now Afghanistan into the Punjab, crossed the Indus River, and defeated the local Indian king. Everywhere he went he reorganized or founded cities on trade routes, entrusting them to loyal Macedonians and other Greeks, settling there veterans of his campaigns, and then pushed on toward the unknown. On the Hyphasis River in what is now Pakistan, his Macedonian warriors finally halted. Worn out by years of bloody conquest and exhausting travel, they refused to go further, and Alexander led his troops back to Persepolis in 324 B.C.E. No mortal had ever before accomplished such a feat. Even in his own lifetime, Alexander was venerated as a god.

Alexander is remembered as a greater conqueror than ruler, but his plans for his reign, had he lived to complete them, might have won him equal fame. Unlike his Macedonian followers, who were interested mainly in booty and power, he recognized that only by merging local and Greek peoples and traditions could he forge a lasting empire. Thus, even while founding cities on the Greek model throughout his empire, he carefully respected the local social and cultural traditions of the conquered peoples. Whether his program of cultural and

The Nike, or Winged Victory, was found in fragments on the island of Samothrace in the Aegean Sea in 1863. The head and arms were never discovered. The statue is now in the Louvre Museum in Paris.

social amalgamation could have succeeded is a moot point. In 323 B.C.E., less than two years after his return from India, he died at Babylon at the age of thirty-two.

The empire did not outlive the emperor. Vicious fighting soon broke out among his generals and his kin. Alexander's wife Roxana and son Alexander IV (323–317 B.C.E.) were killed, as were all other members of the royal family. The various units of the empire broke apart into separate kingdoms and autonomous cities in which each ruler attempted to continue the political and cultural tradition of Alexander in a smaller sphere. Alexander's empire became a shifting kaleidoscope of states, kingdoms, and cities, dominated by priest-kings, native princelings, and territorial rulers, all vying to enhance their positions while preserving a relative balance of power. By 275 B.C.E., three large kingdoms—Egypt, an expanded Persia, and a combination of Greece and Macedonia—dominated Alexander's former domain. The most stable was Egypt, acquired upon Alexander's death by Ptolemy I (323–285 B.C.E.), one of Alexander's closest followers, and ruled by Ptolemy and his descendants until 31 B.C.E., when Cleopatra VII (51–30 B.C.E.) was defeated by the Roman Octavian. In the east, the Macedonian general Seleucus (246–226 B.C.E.) captured Babylon in 312 B.C.E., and he and his descendants ruled a vast kingdom reaching from what is today western Turkey to Afghanistan. Gradually whittled away from all sides, the Seleucid kingdom gradually shrank to

ALEXANDER AT THE HYPHASIS

■ *The second century C.E. historian Arrian, drawing on earlier accounts and his own sense of Alexander, re-creates the exchange between Alexander and his trusted officer Coenus, which led Alexander at last to abandon his relentless easterly march of conquest.*

Alexander: I observe, gentlemen, that when I would lead you on a new venture you no longer follow me with your old spirit. I have asked you to meet me that we may come to a decision together: are we, upon my advice, to go forward, or, upon yours, to turn back? . . . With all that [has been] accomplished, why do you hesitate to extend the power of Macedon—*your* power—to the Hyphasis and the tribes on the other side? Are you afraid that a few natives who may still be left will offer opposition? . . .

For a man who *is* a man work, in my belief, if it is directed to noble ends, has no object beyond itself . . . Our ships will sail round from the Persian Gulf to Libya as far as the Pillars of Hercules, whence all Libya to the eastward will soon be ours, and all Asia too, and to this empire there will be no boundaries but what God Himself has made for the whole world.

Coenus: I judge it best to set some limit to further enterprise. You know the number of Greeks and Macedonians who started upon this campaign, and you can see how many of us are left today . . . Every man of them longs to see his parents again, if they yet survive, or his wife, or his children . . . Do not try to lead men who are unwilling to follow you; if their heart is not in it, you will never find the old spirit or the old courage. Consent rather yourself to return to your mother and your home. Once there, you may bring good government to Greece and enter your ancestral house with all the glory of the many victories won in this campaign, and then, should you so desire it, you may begin again and undertake a new expedition against these Indians of the East, or if you prefer, to the Black Sea or to Carthage and the Libyan territories beyond . . . Sir, if there is one thing above all others a successful man should know, it is *when to stop*.

From Arrian, *The Campaigns of Alexander*, Book V.

a small region of northern Syria before it fell to Rome in 64 B.C.E. The third kingdom, in Macedon and Greece, was secured by Antigonus II Gonatas (276–239 B.C.E.), the grandson of another of Alexander's commanders, after fifty years of conflict. His Antigonid successors ruled the kingdom until it fell to the Romans in 168 B.C.E.

Alexander's conquests transformed the political map of southern Europe, western Asia, and Egyptian Africa. They swept away or absorbed old traditions of government, brought Greek traditions of urban organization, and replaced indigenous ruling elites with Hellenized dynasties. Within this vast region, rulers encouraged commercial and cultural contact, enriching their treasuries and creating a new form of Greek culture. Still, Alexander's successors never developed the interest or ability to integrate this Greek culture and the more ancient indigenous cultures of their subjects. Ultimately, this failure proved fatal for the Hellenistic kingdoms.

The Hellenistic World

Although vastly different in geography, language, and custom, the Hellenistic kingdoms shared two common traditions, west Asian centralized government and Greek culture. First, great portions of the Hellenistic world, from Asia Minor to Bactria and south to Egypt, had been united at various times by the Assyrian and Persian empires. During these periods they had absorbed much of Mesopotamian civilization and in particular the administrative traditions begun by the Assyrian Tiglath-pileser. Thus the Hellenistic kings ruled kingdoms already accustomed to centralized government and could rely on the already existing machinery of tax collection and administration to control the countryside. For the most part, however, these kings had little interest in the native populations of their

Marble head of Epicurus from the third century B.C.E.

China came silks and spices. Syrian and Egyptian workshops produced luxury goods such as jewelry and glass. The Aegean world exported wine and oil, while the Black Sea territories, Egypt, and Sicily shipped wheat throughout the Mediterranean. Greek-speaking merchants dominated this trade, their language becoming the common means of communication in far-flung ports and caravan towns. Likewise, everywhere Hellenistic governments involved themselves directly in these commercial enterprises, especially in Egypt, where the Ptolemies used Greek colonists to rationalize and organize agriculture and trade for the benefit of the dynasty.

Urban Life and Culture

The Hellenistic kingdoms lived in a perpetual state of warfare with one another. Kings needed Greek soldiers, merchants, and administrators and competed with their rivals in offering Greeks all the comforts of

kingdoms beyond the amount of wealth that they could extract from them. Hellenistic monarchs remained Greek and lavished their attentions on the newly created Greek cities, which absorbed vast amounts of the kingdom's wealth.

The second unifying factor in the Hellenistic world was the spread of Greek culture and the establishment of cities on the Greek model. In the tradition of Alexander himself, the Ptolemys, Seleucids, and Antigonids cultivated Greek urban culture and recruited Greeks for the most important positions of responsibility. Alexander had founded over thirty-five cities during his conquests. The Seleucids established almost twice as many throughout their vast domain, even replacing the ancient city of Babylon with their capital, Seleucia, on the Tigris. In Egypt the Ptolemys replaced the ancient capital of Memphis with the new city of Alexandria. These cities became the centers of political control, economic consumption, and cultural diffusion throughout the Hellenistic world.

These two common traditions aided the creation, across the Hellenistic world, of a vastly expanded commercial network, resulting in greatly increased wealth for its elites. Caravans crossed the Seleucid Empire from Seleucia-on-the-Orontes to the Black Sea, Alexandria in Egypt became the port for trade up the Nile into Africa, and Rhodes served as a commercial center for trade throughout the Mediterranean. From India and

Classical Greece	
525–456 B.C.E.	Aeschylus
ca. 500–ca. 430 B.C.E.	Phidias
496–406 B.C.E.	Sophocles
490 B.C.E.	Battle of Marathon
485–406 B.C.E.	Euripides
ca. 484–ca. 420 B.C.E.	Herodotus
480 B.C.E.	Battles of Thermopylae and Salamis
478 B.C.E.	Athens assumes control of Delian League
ca. 470–399 B.C.E.	Socrates
ca. 460–430 B.C.E.	Pericles dominates Athens
ca. 450–ca. 388 B.C.E.	Aristophanes
431–421; 414–404 B.C.E.	Peloponnesian War
ca. 428–347 B.C.E.	Plato
384–322 B.C.E.	Aristotle
384–322 B.C.E.	Demosthenes
338 B.C.E.	Philip of Macedon defeats Athens
336–323 B.C.E.	Reign of Alexander the Great

home. Hellenistic cities were Greek in physical organization, constitution, and language. Each had an agora, or marketplace, that would not have been out of place in Attica. They boasted temples to the Greek gods and goddesses, theaters, baths, and most importantly, a *gymnasion*, or combination sports center and school. In the gymnasion young men competed in Greek sports and absorbed Greek poetry and philosophy just as did their cousins in the Peloponnesus. Sophocles' tragedies played to enthusiastic audiences in an enormous Greek theater in what is today Ai Khanoum on the Oxus River in Afghanistan, and the rites of Dionysus were celebrated in third-century B.C.E. Egypt with processions of satyrs, maenads, free wine for all, and a golden phallus 180 feet long. These Greeks were drawn from throughout the Greek-speaking world, and in time a universal Greek dialect, *koine*, became the common language of culture and business.

For all their Greek culture, Hellenistic cities differed fundamentally from Greek cities and colonies of the past. Not only were they far larger than any earlier Greek cities, but their government and culture were different from those of other cities or colonies. Colonies had been largely independent poleis, but the Hellenistic cities were never politically sovereign. The regional kings maintained firm control over the cities, even while working to attract Greeks from the mainland and the islands to them. This policy weakened the political significance of Greek life and culture. Theoretically, these cities were democracies, although kings firmly controlled city government, and participation in the city councils and magistracies was the province of the wealthy.

In the new cities of the east, Greeks from all over were welcomed as soldiers and administrators regardless of their city of origin. By the second century B.C.E., Greeks no longer identified themselves by their city of origin but as "Hellenes," that is, Greeks. The great social and geographical mobility possible in the new cities extended to women as well as men. No longer important simply as transmitters of citizenship, women began to assume a greater role in the family, in the economy, and in public life. Marriage contracts, particularly in Ptolemaic Egypt, emphasized the theoretical equality of husband and wife. In one such contract, the husband and wife were enjoined to take no concubines or male or female lovers. The penalty for the husband was loss of the wife's dowry; for the wife, the punishment was divorce.

Since women could control their own property, many engaged in business and some became wealthy. Wealth translated into civic influence and power. Phyle, a woman of the first century B.C.E. from Priene in Asia Minor, spent vast sums on a reservoir and aqueducts to bring water to her city. She was rewarded with high political office, as was a female archon in Histria on the Black Sea in the second century B.C.E.

The most powerful women in Hellenistic society were queens, especially in Egypt, where the Ptolemys adopted the Egyptian tradition of royal marriages between brothers and sisters. Arsinoë II (ca. 316–270 B.C.E.) ruled as an equal with her brother-husband Ptolemy II (285–246 B.C.E.). She inaugurated a tradition of powerful female monarchs that ended only with Cleopatra VII, the last independent ruler of Egypt, who successfully manipulated the Roman generals Julius Caesar (100–44 B.C.E.) and Mark Antony (81–30 B.C.E.) to maintain Egyptian autonomy.

Just as monarchs competed with one another in creating Greek cities, they vied in making their cities centers of Greek culture. Socially ambitious and newly wealthy citizens supported poets, philosophers, and artists and endowed gymnasia and libraries. The largest library was in Alexandria in Egypt. In time the library housed half a million book-rolls, including all of the great classics of Greek literature. Generations of poet-scholars edited and commented on the classics, in the process inventing literary criticism and preserving much of what is known about classical authors.

Hellenistic writers were not simply book collectors or critics. They developed new forms of literature, including the romance, which often recounted imaginary adventures of Alexander the Great, and the pastoral poem, which the Sicilian Theocritus (ca. 310–250 B.C.E.) developed out of popular shepherd songs.

Political rivalry also encouraged architectural and artistic rivalry, as kings competed for the most magnificent Hellenistic cities. Temples, porticoes, and public buildings grew in size and ornamentation. Hellenistic architects not only developed more elaborate and monumental buildings, they also combined these buildings in harmonious urban ensembles. In cities such as Rhodes and Pergamum, planners incorporated their constructions into the terrain, using natural hills and slopes to create elegant terraced vistas.

Freestanding statues and magnificent murals and mosaics adorned the public squares, temples, and private homes of Hellenistic cities. While artists continued the traditions of the Hellenic age, they displayed more freedom in portraying tension and restlessness as well as individuality in the human form. Sculptors demonstrated their skill in the portrayal of drapery tightly folded or falling naturally across the human form. The Nike (Victory) from Samothrace (ca. 200 B.C.E.) and the Aphrodite from Melos, known more commonly as the Venus de Milo (ca. 120 B.C.E.), are supreme examples of Hellenistic sculptural achievement.

Hellenistic Philosophy

Philosophy, too, flourished in the Hellenistic world, but in directions different from those initiated by Plato and Aristotle, who were both deeply committed to political involvement in the free polis. Instead, Cynics, Epicureans, and Stoics turned inward, advocating types of morality less directly tied to the state and society. These philosophies appealed to the rootless Greeks of the Hellenistic east no longer tied by bonds of religion or patriotism to any community. Each philosophy was as much a way of life as a way of thought and offered different answers to the question of how the individual, cut loose from the security of traditional social and political networks, should deal with the whims of fate.

The Cynic tradition, established by Antisthenes (ca. 445–ca. 365 B.C.E.), a pupil of Socrates, and Diogenes of Sinope (d. ca. 320 B.C.E.), taught that excessive attachment to the things of this world was the source of evil and unhappiness. An individual achieves freedom by renouncing material things, society, and pleasures. The more one has, the more one is vulnerable to the whims of fortune. The Cynics' goal was to reduce their possessions, connections, and pleasures to the absolute minimum. "I would rather go mad than enjoy myself," Antisthenes said.

Like the Cynics, the Epicureans sought freedom, but from pain rather than from the conventions of ordinary life. Epicurus (341–270 B.C.E.) and his disciples have often been attacked for their emphasis on pleasure. "You need only possess perception and be made of flesh, and you will see that pleasure is good," Epicurus wrote. But this search for pleasure was not a call to sensual indulgence. Pleasure must be pursued rationally. Today's pleasure can mean tomorrow's suffering. The real goal is to reduce desires to that which is simple and attainable. Thus Epicureans urged retirement from politics, retreat from public competition, and concentration instead on friendship and private enjoyment. For Epicurus, reason properly applied illuminates how best to pursue pleasure. The traditional image of the Epicurean as an indulgent sensualist is a gross caricature. As Epicurus advised one follower, an Epicurean "revels in the pleasure of the body—on a diet of bread and water."

The Stoics also followed nature, but rather than leading them to retire from public life, it led them to greater participation in it. Stoic virtue consists in applying reason to one's life in such a way that one knowingly lives in conformity to nature. Worldly pleasures, like worldly pain, have no particular value. Both are to be accepted and endured. Just as the universe is a system in which stars and planets move according to fixed laws, so too is human society ordered and unified. As the founder of Stoicism, Zeno (ca. 335–ca. 263 B.C.E.) expressed it, "All men should regard themselves as members of one city and people, having one life and order." Every person has a role in the divinely ordered universe, and all roles are of equal value. True happiness consists in freely accepting one's role, whatever it may be, while unhappiness and evil result from attempting to reject one's place in the divine plan.

Cynicism, Epicureanism, and Stoicism all emphasized the importance of reason and the proper understanding of nature. Hellenistic understanding of nature was one area in which Greek thinkers were influenced by the ancient Near Eastern traditions brought to them through the conquests of Alexander.

Mathematics and Science

Particularly for mathematics, astronomy, and engineering, the Hellenistic period was a golden age. Ptolemaic Egypt became the center of mathematical studies. It was the home of Euclid (fl. ca. 300 B.C.E.), whose *Elements* was the fundamental textbook of geometry until the twentieth century, and of his student Apollonius of Perga (ca. 262–ca. 190 B.C.E.), whose work on conic sections is one of the greatest monuments of geometry. Both Euclid and Apollonius were as influential for their method as for their conclusions. Their treatises follow rigorous logical proofs of mathematical theorems, which established the form of mathematical reasoning to the present day. Archimedes of Syracuse (ca. 287–212 B.C.E.) corresponded with the Egyptian mathematicians and made significant contributions to geometry, such as the calculation of the approximate value of π—as well as to mechanics with the invention of Archimedes' screw for raising water—and to arithmetic and engineering. Archimedes was famous for his practical applications of engineering, particularly to warfare, and legends quickly grew up about his marvelous machines, with which he helped Syracuse defend itself against Rome.

Many mathematicians, such as Archimedes and Apollonius, were also mathematical astronomers, and the application of their mathematical skills to the exact data collected by earlier Babylonian and Egyptian empirical astronomers greatly increased the understanding of the heavens and earth. Archimedes devised a means of measuring the diameter of the sun, and Eratosthenes of Cyrene (ca. 276–194 B.C.E.) calculated the circumference of the earth to within two hundred miles. Aristarchus of Samos (fl. ca. 270 B.C.E.) theorized that the sun and fixed stars were motionless and that the earth moves around the sun. His theory, unsupported by mathematical evidence and not taking into account the elliptical nature of planetary orbits or the planets' nonuniform speeds, was rejected by contemporaries.

Like astronomy, Hellenistic medicine combined theory and observation. In Alexandria, Herophilus of Chalcedon (ca. 335–ca. 280 B.C.E.) and Erasistratus of Ceos (fl. ca. 250 B.C.E.) conducted important studies in human anatomy. The Ptolemaic kings provided them with condemned prisoners whom they dissected alive and thus were able to observe the functioning of the organs of the body. The terrible agonies inflicted on their experimental subjects were considered to be justified by the argument that there was no cruelty in causing pain to guilty men to seek remedies for the innocent.

Hellenistic science and mathematics were, like other aspects of Hellenistic culture, blends of Greek reason and Near Eastern experience with a strong practical orientation. The same combination of indigenous and Greek traditions was largely lacking in other aspects of Hellenistic life, leaving Hellenistic culture an elite and fragile veneer.

The Limits of Hellenism

For all of the vitality of the Hellenistic civilization, these cities remained parasites on the local societies. No real efforts were made to integrate them into a new civilization. Some ambitious members of the indigenous elites tried to adopt the customs of the Greeks, while others plotted insurrection. The clearest example of these conflicting tensions was that of the Jewish community. Early in the second century B.C.E., a powerful Jewish faction in Jerusalem, which included the High Priest of Yahweh, supported Hellenization. With the assistance of the Seleucid king, this faction set up a gymnasion in Jerusalem where Jewish youths and even priests began to study Greek and participate in Greek culture. Some even underwent painful surgery to reverse the effects of circumcision so that they could

pass for Greeks in naked athletic contests. This rejection of tradition infuriated a large portion of the Jewish population. When the Seleucids finally attempted to introduce pagan cults into the temple in 167 B.C.E., open rebellion broke out and, under the leadership of the family of the Maccabees, continued intermittently until the Jews gained independence in 141 B.C.E.

Such violent opposition was repeated elsewhere from time to time, especially in Egypt and Persia, where, as in Judea, old traditions of religion and monarchy provided rallying points against the transplanted Greeks. In time the Hellenistic kingdoms' inability to bridge the gap between Greek and indigenous populations proved fatal. In the East, the non-Greek kingdom of Parthia replaced the Seleucids in much of the old Persian Empire. In the West, continuing hostility between kingdoms and within kingdoms prepared the way for their progressive absorption by the new power to the west: Rome.

In the fifth century B.C.E., the rugged slopes, fertile plains, and islands of the Greek world developed characteristic forms of social, political, and cultural organization that have reappeared in varying forms that have become an integral part of world civilization. In Athens, which emerged from the ruins of the Persian invasion as the most powerful and dynamic state in the Hellenic world, the give-and-take of a direct democracy challenged men to raise fundamental questions about the relationship between individual and society, freedom and absolutism, gods and mortals. At the same time, this society of free males excluded the majority of its inhabitants—women, foreigners, and slaves—from participation in government and fought a long and ultimately futile war to hold together an exploitative empire.

The interminable wars among Greek states ultimately left the Greek world open to conquest by a powerful, semi-Greek monarchy that went on to spread Athenian culture throughout the Mediterranean world and western Asia. Freed from the particularism of individual city-states, Hellenistic culture became a universal tradition emphasizing the individual rather than the community of family, tribe, or religious association. And yet, this universal Hellenistic cultural tradition remained a thin veneer, hardly assimilated into the masses of the ancient world. Its proponents, except for Alexander the Great, never sought a real synthesis of Greek and barbarian tradition. Such a synthesis would begin only with the coming of Rome.

SUGGESTIONS FOR FURTHER READING

GENERAL READING

John Boardman, Jasper Griffin, and Oswyn Murray, *Greece and the Hellenistic World* (New York: Oxford University Press, 1988). An excellent, up-to-date survey of Greek history by a series of experts.

* Michel M. Austin and Pierre Vidal-Naquet, *Economic and Social History of Ancient Greece* (Berkeley, CA: University of California Press, 1977). An excellent survey of Greek society.

Cambridge Ancient History, 2d ed., vols. 5 (1989) and 7 (1984). Contains essays on most aspects of Greek history.

* Simon Hornblower, *The Greek World, 479-323 B.C.* (New York: Routledge, Chapman & Hall, 1983). An up-to-date survey concentrating on political history.

WAR AND POLITICS IN THE FIFTH CENTURY

John Manuel Cook, *The Persian Empire* (New York: Schocken Books, 1983). The standard history of Persia from the perspective of history and archaeology.

R. Meiggs, *The Athenian Empire* (New York: Oxford University Press, 1979). The standard account.

P. J. Rhodes, *The Athenian Empire* (Oxford: The Clarendon Press, 1985). A short summary.

* A. H. M. Jones, *Athenian Democracy* (Baltimore, MD: Johns Hopkins University Press, 1957). A collection of essays by a major traditional historian.

* M. I. Finley, *Democracy Ancient and Modern*, 2d ed. (New Brunswick, NJ: Rutgers University Press, 1985). A valuable essay on Athenian democracy by a leading historian of antiquity.

W. R. O'Connor, *The New Politicians of Fifth-Century Athens* (Princeton, NJ: Princeton University Press, 1971). Reappraises the demagogues within the context of Athenian political life.

A. W. Gomme, *Historical Commentary on Thucydides*, 5 vols. (New York: Oxford University Press, 1945–80). The fundamental study of the sources.

G. E. M. de St. Croix, *The Origins of the Peloponnesian War* (Ithaca, NY: Cornell University Press, 1972). An interpretation of the Peloponnesian War broader than the title indicates.

* David M. Schaps, *Economic Rights of Women in Ancient Greece* (New York: Columbia University Press, 1979). An examination of the roles of women in Greek society, focusing on property rights.

* W. K. Lacey, *The Family in Classical Greece* (Ithaca, NY: Cornell University Press, 1984). Ordinary life in the Greek world.

* Renate Bridenthal and Claudia Koonz, eds., *Becoming Visible: Women in European History*, 2d ed. (Boston: Houghton Mifflin, 1988). Includes essays on women in classical Greece.

Eva C. Keuls, *The Reign of the Phallus: Sexual Politics in Ancient Athens* (New York: Harper & Row, 1985). A controversial history of sexual relations in Athens.

* Yvon Garlan, *Slavery in Ancient Greece* (Ithaca, NY: Cornell University Press, 1988). A recent study of Greek slavery.

ATHENIAN CULTURE IN THE HELLENIC AGE

* W. K. C. Guthrie, *History of Greek Philosophy*, Vol. 3 (New York: Cambridge University Press, 1971). Covers the Sophists.

I. Crombie, *An Examination of Plato's Doctrines*, 2 vols. (Atlantic Highlands, NJ: Humanities Press International, 1963). A safe guide into works on Plato.

* G. E. R. Lloyd, *Aristotle: The Growth and Structure of His Thought* (New York: Cambridge University Press, 1968). A developmental approach to Aristotle.

W. Burkert, *Greek Religion* (Cambridge, MA: Harvard University Press, 1985). General survey of the topic.

* J. Boardman, *Greek Art*, 3d ed. (New York: Thames & Hudson, 1985). A handbook introduction by period.

* Simon Goldhill, *Reading Greek Tragedy* (New York: Cambridge University Press, 1986). A general introduction to Athenian tragedy.

FROM CITY-STATES TO MACEDONIAN EMPIRE, 404–323 B.C.E.

G. Cawkwell, *Philip of Macedon* (Boston: Faber & Faber, 1978). A political biography of the Macedonian king.

* A. B. Bosworth, *Conquest and Empire* (New York: Cambridge University Press, 1988). A scholarly but readable account of Alexander the Great.

R. L. Fox, *Alexander the Great* (New York: Dial, 1973). Lively recent biography.

THE HELLENISTIC WORLD

* R. W. Walbank, *The Hellenistic World* (Cambridge, MA: Harvard University Press, 1981). General overview.

P. M. Fraser, *Ptolemaic Alexandria* (New York: Oxford University Press, 1972). Especially good on Hellenistic literature in Egypt.

A. A. Long, *Hellenistic Philosophy* (Wolfeboro, NH: Longman Publishing Group, 1974). On Hellenistic thought.

* J. J. Pollitt, *Art in the Hellenistic Age* (New York: Cambridge University Press, 1986). A recent survey.

J. Barnes et al., *Science and Speculation* (New York: Cambridge University Press, 1982). A collection of papers on Hellenistic science.

* Indicates paperback edition available.

QUEEN DRAUPADI'S REVENGE

Time has weathered the limestone, but it has not diminished the violence of the images. Draupadi, the figure second from left, prepares to wash her hair in the blood of Duhsasana, who is falling at her feet. At the far right is Bhima, who has opened Duhsasana's body with his bare hands. The figure at the left is probably Hidimba, the demon-wife of Bhima. This is but one episode in the Mahabharata war, a war between two groups of cousins, the Pandava (the side Bhima is on) and the Kaurava (the side Duhsasana is on), traditionally dated to 3102 B.C.E., but more probably belonging to the early first millennium B.C.E.

A long and complex chain of events brought our characters to this scene. Draupadi, the daughter of a king, was won by Arjuna in a competition for her hand. When he arrived home, he told his preoccupied mother about his victory. Unaware that he had won a bride, she told him that he must share his prize with his brothers. Even when she realizes that she has commanded that Arjuna share his wife with his brothers, she cannot retract her statement. So the brothers, known as the Pandava, share Draupadi. This is but one example of how words, once spoken, have in this epic a profound, sometimes almost magical, power.

In a story that is perhaps as old as kingship itself, the Kauravas, cousins of the Pandava, had become restive and wished to seize the throne for themselves. They happened upon a trick: they challenged Yudhisthira, the eldest of the Pandava, to a game of dice. The force of the challenge resembled a European challenge to a duel. Yudhisthira, who had no skill at dice, could not refuse the game. He lost the game and everything else: his kingdom, his brothers, himself, and finally, Draupadi. After Draupadi

has been lost, the Kaurava wish to humiliate her. It is a time-honored battle strategy: one hurts men by hurting their women. Draupadi was summoned to the assembly, and Duhsasana grabbed her by her hair. In the words of the epic:

> The hair that at the concluding bath
> Of the king's consecration had been sprinkled
> With pure-spelled water, Duhsasana
> Now caressed with force, unmanning the Pandus.

Then Duhsasana began to undress her. The epic continues: "when her skirt was stripped off, another similar skirt appeared every time. A terrible roar went up from all the kings, a shout of approval, as they watched that greatest wonder on earth." The miracle of the skirts was worked by the god Krishna: Draupadi's luminous body was not for the eyes of her enemies.

Draupadi swore that she would wear her hair unbound until revenge was wreaked on the Kaurava, and that she would wash her hair in Duhsasana's blood. That is the scene depicted here. Draupadi's hair, the symbol of her sensuality and her fertility, had been an instrument of her defilement, and the means by which her husbands were "unmanned." It is through a reconsecration of her hair in the blood of her enemy that she and her husbands obtain a measure of revenge.

After the fateful game of dice, the two sides had agreed that the Pandava are to go into exile in the forest for twelve years and into hiding for a thirteenth year, at the end of which time the throne will be returned to them. But when the time came, the Kauravas do not relinquish the throne and bloody war ensues. At the end of the war, only a handful of people survive. Arjuna's grandson, an infant still in his mother's womb, numbers among the dead. But the god Krishna revives the unborn child, and he survives and founds a line of kings. The epic is told at the court of King Janemejaya, the great-grandson of Arjuna, and it is simultaneously a story of human origins and political legitimacy. The *Mahabharata* is, like many epics, the story of rebirth from a scene of vast destruction. The war ushers in the Kali yuga, the cosmic era that has continued to the present day.

The *Mahabharata*, at 90,000 stanzas the longest poem in world literature, is not the product of a single author. Rather it is the product of a long and evolving oral tradition. The earliest portions of the text were written down about 400 B.C.E., the most recent about 400 C.E.. While the Vedas were sacred religious texts that were transmitted intact from master to pupil, the text of the *Mahabharata* epic underwent changes during its long oral transmission. And the written text did not fix the form of the epic; it is still alive and changing in Indian oral traditions today.

The text does not overstate its own importance when it says that a person who knows all the Vedas and Upanishads, the religious ritual texts, but does not know the *Mahabharata*, does not know anything at all. The epic and its characters have played an important role in Indian religion and politics from its inception down to the present day.

The epic, in its exploration of the divine and the heroic, touches on themes of connection between the world of gods and the world of humans. Yudhisthira is the son of Dharma, a deity who is the personification of the concept of *dharma. Dharma* means "law and duty," and in the broadest sense can be construed as the principles by which life must be lived. The god Krishna is a presence throughout the epic. Although he had promised neutrality in the war, he advised Arjuna, the Pandava warrior, on the eve of battle and drove his chariot in the battle. The weathered limestone image of the queen washing her hair in the blood of her enemy is a preview of the themes of this chapter: the question of how men and women in ancient India and China made ethical choices in times of political chaos. The world of the *Mahabharata* is the world of the epic and poetry, but the concerns expressed therein—how human life was to be lived, and how the seen world of ordinary life and the unseen world of the gods and spirits are connected—are concerns we shall see in many other texts.

In both China and India, the period from the sixth to the second centuries B.C.E. was a time of social change and intellectual ferment. Many of the ideas that have shaped Asian culture and world history—Buddhism, Hinduism, Confucianism, and Taoism—were the product of this era. But the differences between China and India during this period are as instructive as the similarities. In China, from the Zhou dynasty (eleventh century-256 B.C.E.) through the Han dynasty (206 B.C.E.–220 C.E.), the dominant story is one of political and cultural unification. Although profound regional differences remained, they existed in the context of a unified political entity. In India, despite the cultural commonality provided by the great religions, the political unity provided by the Mauryan Empire proved ephemeral.

The Golden Age of China

The Zhou (eleventh century-221 B.C.E.) dynasty has played a crucial role in the Chinese political and cultural imagination. In the eyes of thinkers since the time of Confucius (551–479 B.C.E.), the early Zhou was a golden era of good government that later ages could scarcely hope to emulate. Early Zhou rulers were remembered as sage kings who ruled through moral suasion. Their wise government and benevolent rule led to both economic and moral prosperity. The reality of early Zhou rule, of course, is considerably more complicated and less idyllic than the political mythology. The Zhou dynasty is conventionally divided into two periods, the Western and Eastern Zhou: the division is not geographical, as the names might suggest, but rather it is chronological. Because the capital was moved eastward in 771 B.C.E., historians refer to the period before that date as Western Zhou and the period from 771 to 221 B.C.E. as Eastern Zhou.

For much of the Western Zhou, there are no contemporary textual records. The historian must apply a combination of archaeological evidence and later textual accounts to piece together its history. But for the Eastern Zhou, there are contemporary textual records: works of poetry and philosophy as well as historical chronicles. As a result, our picture of Eastern Zhou society is much richer and more highly nuanced than that of the Western Zhou. The Eastern Zhou is divided into two periods, named after the most important historical chronicles that describe them. The earlier period (771–480 B.C.E.) is called the Spring and Autumn period, after the *Spring and Autumn Annals*, a text purportedly compiled by Confucius. The later period (480–221 B.C.E.) is called the Warring States period, after a text called the *Chronicles of the Warring States*.

The Early Zhou

Zhou mythology is concerned with the question of how human beings found their way out of a state of nature and into civilization. These myths describe how before civilization, human beings resided in a state of chaos. In this state of chaos, people knew who their mothers were but did not recognize their fathers. The sage King Yao granted surnames to people, bringing order to their social organization. Thus Chinese mythology establishes that the ability to trace patrilineal descent is a precondition of civilization. In addition to surnames, these sage kings taught humans other essentials of civiliza-

tion, such as agriculture and writing. The culture hero Shen Nong, also known as the Divine Plowman, was honored as the inventor of agriculture. And Cang Qie was credited with inventing writing by observing patterns of bird tracks on the ground. The demons in the forest wept when writing was invented, because then humankind had a weapon with which to control them. This myth expresses an awareness of the relationship between writing and power that would become even more evident in later Chinese history. Another of these early sages, a woman named Xian Can, the first sericulturist, introduced silk-raising techniques. The heroes and heroines of these myths are superhumans who teach ordinary men and women the skills necessary for civilized life.

Some aspects of Zhou mythology are more explicitly political. The Zhou conquest of the Shang is one of the pivotal episodes in the creation of Chinese political mythology. The *Book of Documents*, a historical text dating from the time of Confucius, describes the Shang decline in clear moralistic terms. The fault for the decline lay with the last Shang kings, who lived lives of luxury and

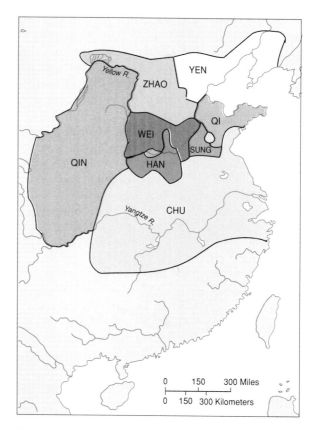

Pre-Imperial China

"had not heard of the hard labors of the common people." Because "they sought for nothing but excessive pleasure," their lives and their rule were both cut short. Until very recently, the *Book of Documents* was the oldest account of the conquest. But in 1976 archaeologists unearthed an inscribed bronze vessel cast eight days after the conquest. The inscription begins "King Wu [of the Zhou] vanquished Shang, it was in the morning, on the day *jiazi* . . ." It continues, extolling the virtues of king Wu: "Our king has indeed a virtuous character, compliant to heaven, an inspiring example to my own feebleness . . ." The Zhou attributed their victory to the king's virtue and his obedience to heaven.

The conquest of the Shang was begun by King Wen, the father of King Wu, and the two men are regarded as co-founders of the dynasty. *Wu* means "martial" and *Wen* means "civil" (or literary), and the names of these two men encompass the two poles of Chinese political virtue. After the death of King Wu, his young son, King Cheng, inherited the throne. The Duke of Zhou, the uncle of the new young king, acted as regent for his nephew. The Duke of Zhou consolidated the king's rule and put down a rebellion in the eastern provinces by remnants of the Shang ruling house. His significance in later political thought is equal to that of Kings Wen and Wu.

The key ideological problem facing the Zhou was political legitimacy, a particular problem for a regime that had overthrown its predecessor. Zhou approaches to the problem form the repertoire of theories of legitimacy for later generations.

One of the ways in which Zhou political theorists justified the conquest was to stress Shang depravity. The last king and his evil concubine were alleged to have committed all manner of atrocities. The bad last emperor, often deluded by an evil and beautiful woman, became a virtual stereotype in Chinese historiography, a stereotype that served to explain the fall of dynasties.

Another way in which Zhou theorists justified the conquest was through myths of their supernatural origins. The Zhou mythical ancestor Houji was conceived when his mother trod in a god's footprint. This pattern will be repeated; the details will vary, but the conception and the birth of founding emperors and other heroes is often marked by supernatural occurrences, both separating them from the past (they have no human father) and giving added legitimacy to their conquest and rule.

But the most important technique the Zhou used to secure their legitimacy is the concept of the Mandate of Heaven. In the discussion of a concept like "heaven,"

Bronze vessel from the late eleventh century B.C.E. The inscription relates the downfall of the Shang dynasty and glorifies the Zhou king.

we become acutely aware of the limitations of language and the problems of translation. *Tian*, the word translated as "heaven," can mean something as grand as all of nature, or something as mundane as the weather. In Zhou thought, it was the force of the cosmos, a force with will and intentions, mightily interested in the doings of mortals. One of the ways it expressed this interest was by approving or disapproving of a ruler. If a ruler met with heavenly approval, then weather was seasonable, crops prospered, and the people flourished. But if the mandate was revoked, then catastrophes of a natural or a political sort might result. A discussion of the mandate, reportedly by the Duke of Zhou himself and preserved in the *Book of Documents*, stresses the unpredictability of the mandate:

> Heaven has sent down ruin on the Shang. Shang has lost the mandate and Zhou has received it. Yet I do not dare say whether our foundations will always abide in prosperity . . . or whether they will end in misfortune. Heaven's mandate is not easily preserved. Heaven is not easy to rely on.

These two ideas—that the ruler has legitimacy because heaven has granted him a mandate, and that that mandate is infused with morality—represent new political notions. The emperor, though an autocrat, was accountable to heaven, who in turn, was vigilant on behalf of the people. The Mandate of Heaven remains absolutely crucial throughout Chinese history as the cornerstone of theories of dynastic legitimacy. The first rallying cry for many a rebel group has been that the ruling dynasty has lost the mandate.

Although the Zhou conquest marked the clear beginnings of a new kind of political mythology, it did not mark a sharp break in Chinese culture. The Zhou had probably lived alongside the Shang for some time before the conquest. They used the same written language, and were probably of the same ethnic group. Zhou culture maintained strong continuities with that of the Shang.

The Warring States Transformation

The Zhou king made no attempt to rule directly. Rather, he granted territories and ranks to members of the royal family and their allies. They were obliged to reciprocate with military service and with other forms of labor service and tribute. Title and territory were passed on to the eldest son, in a system called primogeniture. The Chinese term used to describe this system of granting land and territories, *fengjian*, is normally translated as "feudalism." The social system is of course not identical to the European system that is sometimes called feudalism, but it shares certain general features, including decentralized control and unified political and military authority. Early in this period a modicum of centralized control was retained because the Zhou king acknowledged the new heir at an investiture ceremony held at the Zhou capital. As time went on, the forces holding the Zhou together weakened and even the investiture ceremony became less and less significant. After 770 B.C.E., the investiture ceremonies ceased, but the Zhou king was not deposed. He retained a limited political charisma, though his actual power to enforce his will was no more than (and was often less than) that of other regional kings in what had become, in effect, a multistate system.

During the period roughly from the fifth century to 221 B.C.E., known as the Warring States period, China underwent a series of social transformations that destroyed the old Zhou aristocracy and prepared China for unification. Among these changes were the rise of private ownership of land, an increase in the population, the disappearance of the old aristocracy, and the rise of a bureaucracy in many states. Accompanying these changes was a revolution in social thought, which justified the new social order and paved the way for the unified China of the future.

During the Warring States period there was a rise in the private ownership of land. The actual workings of the early Zhou land system remain shrouded in obscu-

Mirror with five-mountain design, from the late Warring States period, ca. third century B.C.E.

rity. Later generations believed that land in the early Zhou was held collectively, in a system called the well-field system. The Chinese character for well (*jing*) is written like a tick-tack-toe board, with nine squares. In this land allotment system, each of the eight outer squares would be allotted to a different family. The central square would be tilled by all eight collectively, for the benefit of the common good. Scholars dispute the degree to which this land system was actually put into effect. It retained, however, an extremely important place in political mythology, and countless later reformers and rebels would call for a return of the collective ownership of the early Zhou land system.

During the Eastern (later) Zhou, a number of innovations in agricultural technology increased productivity, thereby making possible an increase in population. Iron came into use during the seventh and sixth centuries B.C.E. Using iron, farmers could fashion better plows. And, perhaps even more important in the Chinese agricultural context, they could use iron tools to dig larger and more efficient irrigation canals. Other innovations, like the wheelbarrow, aided agricultural productivity. The wheelbarrow may seem like a rather modest invention, but its low center of gravity makes it an extremely efficient way for a human being to transport heavy loads. Increasing the efficiency of human labor has an added significance in the Chinese case because Chinese agriculture during the Zhou, as in later

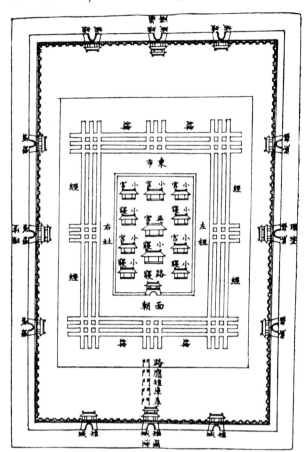

An idealized plan of the Zhou capital of Loyang shows an orderly layout of city walls and gates, with royal palaces, markets, and temples. Major avenues run at right angles.

times, is characterized by its relatively light reliance on animals, both as a source of labor and of food.

Farmers also began to use fertilizers more widely. In particular they used human waste, euphemistically called night soil. This was a highly efficient means of simultaneously disposing of waste and increasing agricultural productivity.

These changes did not lead to unqualified and universal prosperity. Li Kui, an advisor to the duke of Wei in the fourth century B.C.E., wrote that "farmers are constantly in want and have not the heart to exert themselves in plowing." It is entirely likely that these developments in agriculture led to an increase in the gulf between the rich and the poor.

The Warring States period, as the late Eastern Zhou is known, is aptly named. During this period, not only was warfare frequent, but also its nature was changing. During the Western Zhou, warfare had been an aristocratic activity, which somewhat limited its scope and

violence. Protracted sieges of towns were recorded for the first time in the Warring States period. In this period, military service began to be an avenue of social mobility. Hence warfare was instrumental in two changes: it destroyed the old aristocratic families and it provided mobility for a new category of people.

The increasingly competitive nature of Warring States politics meant that many rulers were more interested in an official's competence than they were in his pedigree. A class of officials with expertise in government arose as a result. These men were the forerunners of what was to develop into the Chinese bureaucracy. And the theoretical writings of the best of them were to form the foundations of Chinese political philosophy.

The warfare and social unrest of the period had clear social consequences. The families who were prominent in the Spring and Autumn period no longer played a role in the Warring States period. By the end of the period, social power was based less on heredity than on achievement. The old Zhou aristocracy had been destroyed, never to reemerge. New forms of social organization were evolving, forms that would culminate in the Qin unification of China in 221 B.C.E.

The growth of the small landholder, the changes in population, the destruction of the old Zhou aristocracy through warfare, the growth of a political class of experts and advisors, and the decline of the central authority of the Zhou royal house are the dominant features of the Warring States transformation.

The Flowering of Chinese Philosophy: Confucius, Mencius, and the Tao

This period of political unrest was an era of great cultural flowering. One of the oldest Chinese literary texts is the *Book of Odes*. The *Odes* is a collection of 305 songs, probably compiled about 600 B.C.E., although many of the songs are doubtless earlier. Confucius himself, according to one tradition, wandered among the people and collected their songs. The poems in the *Odes* vary in subject matter. Some of them are love poems, as the following:

> Cold is the north wind,
> The snow falls thick.
> If you are kind and love me,
> Take my hand and we will go together.
> You are modest, you are slow,
> But oh, we must hurry.

Other poems are epics of dynastic founding, or songs celebrating the agricultural cycle. The poems are written in a language that later became obscure. Beginning in the Han dynasty, scholars attached voluminous and often arcane commentary to the poems. The ability to interpret the *Odes*, originally folk songs, became the sign of an educated person.

Another collection of old poems, the *Songs of the South*, was put into its present form in the second century C.E., but again, the poems in it are much older. The poems are one of the most important documents of the tradition of the southern state of Chu, which had a venerable history and a flourishing culture distinctive from that of north China. The man to whom many of the poems is attributed is Qu Yuan, whose date of birth is conventionally reported as 343 B.C.E. Legend has it that he served as an unappreciated minister who drowned himself in the Milo River. The Dragon Boat Festival, still celebrated today in Chinese societies on the fifth day of the fifth lunar month, commemorates the death of Qu Yuan. In the poem "Encountering Sorrow," the poet laments that his ruler is ignoring his advice and casts himself as a spurned lover, using lush and erotic language to convey his disappointment.

Splendid as the poems are, the most noteworthy achievement of Zhou culture lay in the realm of philosophy. This was the classical age of Chinese philosophy, the age of Confucius, of Mencius, of Laozi and Zhuangzi. The political unrest of the age seems to have spawned a lively intellectual life. Contemporaries referred to a hundred different schools of thought. Later ages would pick and choose those aspects of Zhou philosophy and mythology that were most useful to them. In many important ways, the basic parameters of political discourse were set during this age. Zhou philosophy and mythology are cultural resources that will continue to be interpreted and reinterpreted throughout Chinese history.

"SUMMONS OF THE SOUL"

■ *One of the most dramatic of the poems in the collection* Songs of the South *is "Summons of the Soul," which was written in the third century B.C.E. in the southern Chinese state of Chu. The voice in the poem is that of a shaman, calling back the soul of a person recently dead, probably a king. The opening portions of the poem detail the horrors that await the soul if it ventures out in any one of the four directions, or if it climbs to heaven above or descends below to the Land of Darkness. All such departures from home (by which the poet doubtless means both the human body and the state of Chu) spell disaster. The final sections of the poem, not included here, regale the soul with the blandishments that await it, including beautiful women and fine food, if it returns to the body it has recently left. This poem is important evidence of the lively Chinese shamanistic tradition, a tradition in which both male and female shamans could, through incantations and other techniques, maintain contact with the spirit world.*
Summons of the Soul

O soul, come back! In the south you cannot stay. There the people have tattooed faces and blackened teeth; They sacrifice the flesh of men and pound their bones for meat paste.

There the venomous cobra abounds, and the great fox that can run a hundred leagues. And the great nine-headed serpent, who darts swiftly this way and that, And swallows men as a sweet relish.

O soul, come back! In the south you may not linger. O soul, come back! For the west holds many perils. The Moving Sands stretch on for many leagues.

You will be swept into the Thunder's Chasm, and dashed in pieces, unable to help yourself; And even should you chance to escape from that, beyond is the empty desert, And red ants as huge as elephants and wasps as big as gourds.

The five grains do not grow there; dry stalks are the only food; And the earth there scorches men up; there is nowhere to look for water

And you will drift there for ever, with nowhere to go in that vastness

O soul, come back! Lest you bring on yourself perdition.

From David Hawkes, trans. and ed., *The Songs of the South: An Ancient Chinese Anthology of Poems by Qu Yuan and Other Poets.*

Portrait of Confucius, cut in stone by Prince Kuo and dated 1734.

It is difficult to overestimate the significance of K'ung Ch'iu (551–479 B.C.E.), known in the West as Confucius, in Chinese culture, although it is perhaps equally difficult to agree on what that significance has been. Confucius was born in the state of Lu, a small and rather weak state whose rulers were direct lineal descendants of the Duke of Zhou. By the time of Confucius, the high traditions of the Zhou were in decline. Confucius's aim was to restore to contemporary politics the wisdom of antiquity and the luster of the early Zhou. Yet he met with limited success in finding a ruler to follow his advice, and his own political career was rather modest. But his successes as a teacher, both during his lifetime and after his death, have been phenomenal.

The sayings of Confucius, known in English as the *Analects*, were written down by his disciples after his death. The style of the *Analects* is the pithy aphorism, and many lines in it are subject to more than one interpretation. This circumstance has given rise to a rich and complex tradition of commentary and debate on the precise meanings of the master's words.

Confucius was primarily interested in how human beings can live harmoniously in society. In the Confucian view, harmony was facilitated by hierarchy, a social order where everyone knows his or her place. The hierarchy within a family was based on gender and generation: males and seniors were privileged over females and juniors. The centrality of both hierarchy and the family is demonstrated in the Five Relationships, which can be regarded as the building blocks of Confucian social theory. The Five Relationships are the relationship between ruler and minister, father and son, husband and wife, elder brother and younger brother, and friend and friend. The relationships, especially the first three, were often analogized one to another. The duty a child owes parents, known as filial piety, is one of the most characteristic virtues of Confucianism. It demanded that a child provide for the material needs of his or her parents. But more importantly, it demanded that a child serve parents with the proper attitude of reverence. Because this relationship was seen as the basis for political loyalty, it was often actively promoted by the state. Similarly, the sexual loyalty a wife owes her husband is seen as analogous to the political loyalty a minister owes his ruler. Thus family virtue and public virtue are seen as two aspects of the same ethical stance.

The fact that these central relationships were conceptualized as analogous did not mean that Confucians never felt any conflicts between family duty and political duty. A man might be simultaneously son and subject, and despite the fact that the virtue of loyalty and the virtue of filial piety are parallel, the demands posed by one's father and by the political order might conflict. The *Analects* recounts the story of a man so upright that he turned in his father for stealing a sheep. Confucius replied, "In my country the upright are different than this. A father will screen his son and a son will screen his father." Although acknowledging the possibility of conflict between demands of the father and demands of the state, Confucius values filial piety over political loyalty.

The promotion of virtue was at the center of the Confucian agenda, and chief among the virtues was *ren*, translated variously as "benevolence" or "humanity." Harmony was a primary Confucian goal, and education and ritual were both mechanisms whereby human society could be rendered more harmonious. But to Confucius education was not merely useful. It was a profound pleasure, as the opening sentence of the *Analects* demonstrates—"To learn and at appropriate times to repeat what one has learned—is that not a pleasure?" One studied the texts of the ancients in order to absorb their wisdom and apply it to the present day. The written word had an almost sacred power in Confucianism. Indeed, the word *wen* can mean both "writing" and "civilization."

Confucius was a demanding teacher. He instructed only those students who were, in his words, "bursting with eagerness." Confucius did not restrict his students to the sons of the nobility; he wrote that everyone had the capacity to learn. While Confucius clearly did advocate opening avenues of knowledge and power to a wider spectrum of people, we should not take his "everyone" too literally. He never directly addressed the question of female education, although he did make deprecating comments about the abilities of women and servants. But it is clear that Confucius's discussion of education is gendered: he is concerned with the education of men. In the Confucian view, education and power were closely connected. One educated one's sons so that they might rule. While daughters of the elite could be, and often were, quite learned, their education played no role in the transformative theories of Confucius.

One of the key concepts in Confucianism is *li*, a word usually translated as "ritual." Ritual in Confucianism could be simple, like the proper etiquette between host and guest, or it could be majestic, like the sacrifices offered to the spirits of the dead ancestors. In its broadest sense, li can be interpreted as behavior that furthers proper social order. But even in its more particular senses, ritual was not mere formalism: it was the profound expression of the inner self. There is a voluminous literature, beginning with the *Book of Rites*, that prescribes the correct ritual for every occasion. The sheer weight of the ritual could, and did, become oppressive. But it is important to remember that for the men who devised these systems, ritual was a cornerstone of civilized life, and its observance carried meaning as well as weight.

The writings of Confucius show clear evidence of the social transformation of his day. The Chinese term for "gentleman," *junzi*, underwent a transformation in meaning during this period—from a word indicating social status (literally meaning "sons of lords") to one indicating moral status. Confucius stresses that the ordinary human has the capacity to act virtuously. Virtue is no longer the preserve of the nobility. And because in the ideal Confucian world, virtue and power are intimately connected, power itself should not be the preserve of the nobility.

The central questions that concerned Confucius had to do with living life in the human world, rather than with the cosmos, the afterlife, or the spirit world. As he put it in the *Analects*, "If one does not know how to serve the living, how can one serve the dead?" The universe in the Confucian worldview is ultimately comprehensible; there are no profound mysteries at its center.

The Confucian point of view did not remain unchallenged. Mozi (480–390 B.C.E.) challenged Confucius on many points. He was a firm believer in the spirit world. In response to Confucius's agnosticism about the spirit world, Mozi countered: "To maintain that there are no spirits and to study the sacrificial rites is like studying the ceremonies for having guests without having any guests." Mozi was also a sharp critic of the family, which he regarded as the cause of many social problems. In his view, attachment to the particular diminishes people's attachment to the general. Mozi argues, for example, that robbers steal to support their families. To combat the pernicious effects of particular love, Mozi advocated universal love. One should love a stranger as much as one loves one's parents. Confucians found Mozi's views outrageous and unnatural. The ideas of Mozi remained very important for hundreds of years following his death, but then more or less disappeared from view until modern times.

Mengzi (372–289 B.C.E.), known in the West as Mencius, also entered into a dialogue with Confucius, but in a way that refined rather than challenged his basic premises. Mencius was a disciple of a disciple of Confucius's grandson. He was a native of the state of Zou, which was located near Lu. He too made his career as a political advisor and met with mixed success.

Confucius had not unequivocally stated his position on human nature, and later thinkers debated the question. Mencius argued that human nature is essentially good, using the anecdote of the child and the well (see "Mencius on Human Potential," p. 110). But, he argued, this essential goodness is easily deluded, often by the mind itself, and readily corrupted by the social environment. The ethical human being must always be attentive to the moral struggle to retain the initial goodness of the mind.

Mencius, like Confucius, drew connections between the ethical struggles of individual human beings and their sociopolitical contexts. He argued that a hungry man cannot think about virtue, and time and time again he advised rulers against making excessive demands on the people they governed. The *Mencius*, as the collection of Mencius's writings is known, did not enjoy prominence in the centuries immediately following its composition. It was rediscovered in the Tang dynasty (618–907, see chapter 8), and was made one of the fundamental texts of a revived Confucianism.

MENCIUS ON HUMAN POTENTIAL

■ *In this passage, Mencius argues that the potential for goodness is inherent in human nature. He argues by analogy, a mode of argument common in Chinese philosophy. He identifies four essential qualities of the human being, which he calls "germs," which are as natural as the four limbs of the human body. But the germs exist as potentialities, and must be developed. Thus in this passage an essential optimism about human nature is combined with an injunction to moral vigilance.*

My reason for saying that no man is devoid of a heart sensitive to the suffering of others is this. Suppose a man were, all of a sudden, to see a young child on the verge of falling into a well. He would certainly be moved to compassion, not because he wanted to get in the good graces of the parents, nor because he wished to win the praise of his fellow villagers or friends, nor yet because he disliked the cry of the child. From this it can be seen that whoever is devoid of the heart of compassion is not human, whoever is devoid of the heart of shame is not human, whoever is devoid of the heart of courtesy and modesty is not human, and whoever is devoid of the heart of right and wrong is not human. The heart of compassion is the germ of benevolence; the heart of shame, of dutifulness; the heart of courtesy and modesty, of observance of the rites; the heart of right and wrong, of wisdom. Man has these four germs just as he has four limbs. For a man possessing these four germs to deny his own potentialities is for him to cripple himself; for him to deny the potentialities of his prince is to cripple his prince. If a man is able to develop all these four germs that he possesses, it will be like a fire starting up or a spring coming through. When these are fully developed, he can take under his protection the whole realm within the Four Seas, but if he fails to develop them, he will not be able even to serve his parents.

From *Mencius.*

In contrast to Mencius, Xunzi (sometime between 340 and 245 B.C.E.) argued that human nature was evil. He challenged Mencian optimism by saying that if humans were truly virtuous, then there would be no need for ritual or the teachings of the sage kings. But even Xunzi remains optimistic. He argued that a person of true intelligence could mold himself to virtue. Ritual and education were ways in which one could master the anarchic forces in one's nature.

Another important group of thinkers, the Taoists, challenged Confucian views about the importance of social life, politics, and words themselves. The term *Taoism* (also spelled *Daoism*) is derived from the word *dao*, which literally means "the way," but implies the entirety of the cosmic order. The classical era produced two Taoist texts of fundamental importance, *The Way and Its Power*, attributed to Laozi, who may or may not have existed, and the *Zhuangzi*, attributed to Zhuang Zhou (ca. 370–300 B.C.E.).

The Way and Its Power is a book of mystical poetry; the *Zhuangzi* consists of anecdotes that are often paradoxical. Both works powerfully suggest ways in which hu-

man beings might find connections with the dao, the forces of the cosmos. Early Taoism exhibits a playful skepticism about words, which is ironic as Taoism develops into one of the world's great textual religions. Zhuangzi says it best: he compares words to a fishnet, and meaning to fish. Just as the net is useful only to get fish, words are useful only until you have grasped their meaning. Once you have grasped the meaning, you may dispense with words. The anecdote ends with the seemingly paradoxical line, "Show me a man who has forgotten words so that I may have a word with him." This irreverence about words is in stark contrast to Confucianism, which as we have seen came close to regarding words as the repository of civilization.

In further contrast to Confucianism, Taoism posits the possibility of a fruitful life outside human society. The hermit who devotes his life to the search for a mystical union with nature is one of the ideals of Taoism. Taoism asks the question of how human beings have become alienated from nature and how to reunite the human and the natural. Later Taoism became concerned with longevity techniques and a literal search for

This incense-burner sculpture from the Song dynasty (960-1276) is a portrait of Laozi riding on a water buffalo.

eternal life, including meditation, respiratory techniques, and drugs. Most of the practices developed by later Taoists have their roots in these classical texts.

Many emperors followed Taoism, and Taoist insights were useful in governing. Perhaps the most useful of these is a phrase that can be loosely translated as "nonaction" or "actionless action." Again, an anecdote from Zhuangzi can explain. Butcher Ding never sharpened his knife. He explained his technique: When carving up an ox, he always found the interstices between the joints. Therefore his knife never touched bone. Thus by understanding the natural structure of the ox, he never acted in opposition to it. That is what is meant by "nonaction."

If the Taoists were primarily concerned with the alienation of people from nature, the Legalists, another important school of thought, were concerned single-mindedly with state building. According to the Legalists, agriculture and war were the fundamental activities of the state, and all other activities should be banished. Legalists maintained that a strong state rests on institutions, and a harsh penal code, equally applied, was one of the key institutions.

The Legalists took positions on human nature and on virtue that ran directly counter to those of Confucians. In the Legalist view, human nature was evil. Furthermore, Confucian notions of virtue were abhorrent to the Legalists. Legalists believed persons convinced of their own virtue would not be docile subjects: they might make their own decisions about right and wrong. Likewise, Legalists were suspicious of education. They thought it was potentially subversive, because it teaches independent thinking. Legalism is a philosophy that has had a bad press in China for the last two thousand years because of its harshness, but as we shall soon see, key aspects of it were integrated into Confucianism under the Han dynasty.

Chinese thinkers in the Warring States period exhibited a diversity of opinion. This diversity is perhaps the most important characteristic of the thought of the age. But these diverse thinkers were addressing a common set of concerns: the nature of human nature, the relationship between the human world and the spirit world, and the proper constitution of human society.

The Unified Empire

When a king asked Mencius, "How can the world be settled?" Mencius replied, "By unification." One of the most remarkable aspects of Chinese history has been that for most of the period from 221 B.C.E. to 1911 C.E., it has been a unified empire. The basic outlines of the political system remained recognizable for two thousand years—an empire headed by a hereditary emperor aided by a bureaucracy selected, in theory at least, by merit. There were of course many changes during that period, but there remained profound consensus about what politics and government ought to be. Much of that consensus is derived from the powerful role Confucianism had in the education of the ruling elite. But some of the institutional aspects that facilitated unification

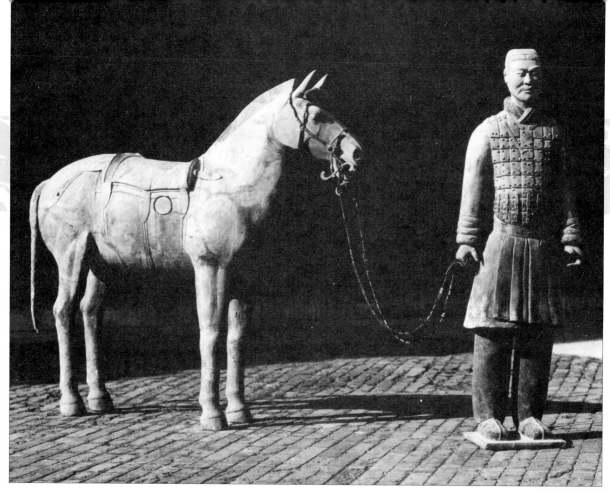

A soldier and his horse, unearthed near the tomb of Qin Shihuangdi.

*T*he Deathless Armies of Qin

One of the most remarkable archaeological finds of this century was made nearly twenty years ago in central China. An excavation twenty-five miles east of Xian revealed an army of 7500 life-size terra-cotta soldiers. The soldiers were positioned near the tomb of Qin Shihuangdi, the founding emperor of the Qin dynasty and the unifier of all of China. Historians had long known of the splendor of the tomb from the textual record.

According to *The Records of the Grand Historian of China:*

As soon as the first emperor became king of Qin, excavations and building were started at Mount Li, and after he won the empire, more than 700,000 conscripts from all parts of the country worked there. They dug through three subterranean streams and poured molten copper for an outer coffin. And the tomb was filled with models of palaces, pavilions, and offices, as well as fine vessels,

precious stones and rarities. Artisans were ordered to fix up crossbows so that any thief breaking in would be shot. All the country's streams, including the Yellow River and the Yangzi, were reproduced in quicksilver and by some mechanical means made to flow into a miniature ocean. The heavenly constellations were shown above and the regions of the earth below. The candles were made of whale oil to ensure their burning for the longest possible time. The second emperor decreed, "It is not right to send away those of my father's ladies who had no sons." Accordingly all of those were ordered to follow the first emperor to the grave. After the internment, someone pointed out that the artisans who had made the mechanical contrivances might disclose all of the treasure that was in the tomb. Thereafter, after the burial and the setting up of treasures, the middle gate was shut and the outer gate closed so to imprison the artisans and laborers so that no one came out. Trees and grass were planted over the mausoleum to make it look like a hill.

Despite the gruesome precautions taken by the emperor to preserve the secrets of his burial, the tomb had been looted a number of times. Excavations have not yet begun on the tomb itself. But the terra-cotta army buried with the emperor remained undisturbed until the late twentieth century. The soldiers and horses were found in three pits, standing in military formation. The torsos of the human figures were probably cast using a mold, but no two faces are identical. The figures show re-markable attention to detail. The technical achievement of the tomb and the sheer beauty of the figures are causes of wonder in themselves. But they lead to another question, a cause of even more wonder. Why did the first emperor commission such a splendid army to guard his tomb?

The tomb of Qin Shihuangdi is the most elaborate example of a tomb that reflects a particular kind of belief in the afterlife: the next world is a place very much like this one, where kings need armies and the sky is molded in mercury. The evidence of material culture from such tombs provides a countervailing view to Confucian agnosticism about the world of the spirits. Later emperors continued the practice of lavish burials.

The clay soldiers represent human ones, and the models are a substitute for human sacrifice. But there was no substitute for the consorts of Qin Shihuangdi. The death of the consorts represents one of the last recorded episodes of human sacrifice in Chinese history. The second emperor, Shihuangdi's son, did not wish to dismiss those consorts who had no sons, perhaps because he feared no one would protect their honor. Only their deaths could ensure their virtue.

Emperors were not the only ones who wanted to be well fitted in the next world. Much of what we know about daily life in early China comes from tomb figurines, clay models of people and of objects. These mortuary objects reflected the Han conviction that the afterlife resembled this world in its broad outlines. The tombs often were decorated with scenes from daily life, sometimes with murals painted on walls, sometimes with scenes incised on tiles. It is a splendid irony that much of our information on the world of the living comes from the realm of the dead.

were due to the Legalist program. During the Han dynasty both the general form of the Chinese state and of Confucianism as an ideology that supports that state were established. The Former Han (206 B.C.E.–9 C.E.) and the Latter Han (25–220 C.E.) are separated by the brief Xin dynasty.

The First Emperor

In 246 B.C.E. the boy who would become the emperor who unified China ascended the throne of the state of Qin. Aided by a series of able ministers, he put Legalist policies into practice. In a series of wars between 230 and 221 B.C.E., he defeated rival states. In 221 B.C.E. the unification was complete, and the emperor assumed the title Qin Shihuangdi, the first emperor of Qin.

After the unification, the emperor applied a centralized system of government to all the territories he conquered, rather than parcel them out to family members and allies, as the Zhou emperor had done. He divided China into thirty-six units he called commanderies, which were further divided into about a thousand districts. Each commandery was staffed by a civil governor, a military governor, and an overseeing official, who were responsible to, and paid by, the central

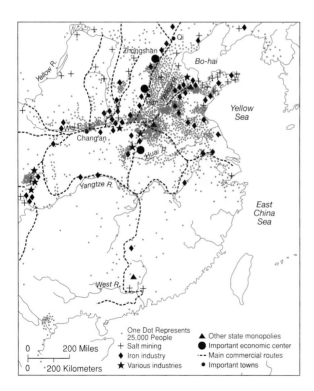

Population and Economic Centers, Early Han

government. Governors were not allowed to serve in their native areas, to prevent them from building strong local power bases. Leading provincial families, perhaps as many as 120,000 of them, were forcibly relocated to the capital to destroy their regional power bases. The administrative structure was set out in a clearly articulated legal code.

Qin policies enhanced the integration of the regions they had conquered. For example, they instituted policies to facilitate long-distance trade: They standardized weights and measures and issued standardized coinage. They regulated the lengths of cart axles to facilitate travel along the easily rutted roads of north China. Peasants, both male and female, were mobilized in an unprecedented way, to build both roads and defensive walls, including portions of the Great Wall. It has been estimated that the Qin built 4,250 miles of imperial highways. These policies served the economic interests of the state, but they also promoted economic unification which would long outlast the Qin dynasty.

Another Qin policy that furthered cultural integration was the standardization of writing. Chinese, then and now, is written with characters rather than with an alphabet. Each character represents one syllable, which in the classical language is one word. (Modern Chinese, by contrast, has many two-syllable words.) There are thousands upon thousands of characters in written Chinese. There are, and always have been, a number of distinct dialects of Chinese, which are often mutually unintelligible to native speakers. Modern Mandarin, the language spoken in the vicinity of Beijing, and Cantonese are no more closely related than are English and German. Words that have the same meaning are pronounced differently in different dialects, but still may be written with the same character. Thus people who cannot understand one another's speech—natives of Beijing and Canton, for example—could, if they were literate, write each other letters. Thus the common written language facilitated governing the large territorial expanse of China, and was a profound force for cultural unification among members of the literate elite.

Although there is no doubt that the unification of China was the culmination of a long and complex process, the man who completed the unification left his particular mark. (See Special Feature, "The Deathless Armies of Qin," pp. 112–113.) Qin Shihuangdi was a man of prodigious energy. Reportedly, he handled 120 pounds of documents a day. Even taking into account that documents during the third century B.C.E. were written on bamboo or wood rather than on paper, this still represents an enormous amount of work. And he

One of the standardized weights mandated by the Qin to regulate trade throughout China.

was not content with conquering the states of the Zhou heartland. The conquests of Qin extended southward into what is now northern Vietnam. There is even a legend that he sent a shipload of young men and women eastward in search of the Isles of the Immortals, and that they became the original inhabitants of Japan.

But the unification was not achieved without cost. In 213 B.C.E., officials criticized the emperor and his advisors for being insufficiently attentive to the models provided by antiquity. The government responded by ordering that all books be burned, except those on the history of the state of Qin or those with practical utility, such as handbooks of agriculture, divination, or medicine. The devastation was not total: the Imperial Library was spared. But the book burning has greatly complicated textual reconstruction of earlier Chinese history. The event is a symbolic ending of the period of intellectual diversity and debate that marked the Zhou period.

The Qin dynasty was short-lived; it scarcely lasted past the demise of the founding emperor. Later historians have attributed its fall to its harshness. The Han scholar Jia Yi (200–168 B.C.E.), for example, wrote a famous essay entitled "The Faults of Qin" in which he explained that the dynasty fell "because it failed to rule with humanity and righteousness, and did not realize that the power to attack and the power to retain what one has thereby won are not the same."

The Han Synthesis

The episode that brought down the Qin began simply enough. A group of peasants on their way to perform labor service for the emperor were delayed by heavy rains. The penalty for tardiness was execution: they had nothing to lose by rebelling. Once begun, the small rebellion spread quickly and the Qin was destroyed. One of the key players in the destruction of the Qin was Xiang Yu. After a brief but costly civil war—the *Han History* estimates that more than half the population died—a peasant named Liu Bang established the Han dynasty. Liu Bang, who ruled under the name of Han Gaozu, represented a firm break with the old aristocracy. He initially had no patience with scholars. There is a very old story, perhaps even true, that he once urinated into a scholar's hat to express his contempt. But as his reign progressed, he began to realize the utility of scholars in formulating a ruling ideology.

After Gaozu took the throne, he rewarded his followers by granting them territory—a decision he would regret. One of the major problems of his and subsequent reigns was reasserting control of those lands. It was not until the reign of the great emperor Wu (141–87 B.C.E.) that centralized control was regained.

The basic outlines of the political structure of the Han followed the Qin. The emperor was assisted by a bureaucracy, which during the Han was recruited primarily by recommendation. Although the sons of the rich and powerful had advantages in obtaining recommendations, official posts were not hereditary. As under the Qin, the empire was divided into commanderies and districts, and the officials who governed those areas were appointed from the center.

During the Han dynasty, political thinkers made an important synthesis of Legalism and Confucianism. This synthesis remained central to all later Chinese political philosophy. Classical Confucians had argued that because good men made good government, elaborate institutional arrangements should not be necessary. Legalists countered that because good men are hard to find, a sensible political policy rested on good laws. When Gaozu came to power, he promulgated a law code that was only ten Chinese words: anyone who kills anyone else shall be put to death; anyone who wounds another person or steals shall be punished according to the gravity of his offense, and all Qin laws are to be abolished. But under later reigns, there was an elaboration of law. The Han state adopted the humanitarian views of Confucianism with the institutional efficiency of Legalism.

Han Confucianism underwent other changes as well. One of the major figures in this Han synthesis was Dong Zhongshu (ca. 175–105 B.C.E.), who articulated a theory of correspondences, suggesting that activities occurring anywhere in the universe influence activities occurring anywhere else. It was at this time that the concepts of *yin* and *yang* were integrated into the Confucian worldview. Yin is the female principle: it is passive, moist, dark, and associated with the earth. Yang is the male principle: it is active, dry, light and associated with the sun. The two principles are mutually generating: when yang reaches its extreme, it generates yin. An excess of either yin or yang is unhealthy for the cosmos or for a human being. Yin-yang cosmology was later used to justify male dominance in society.

Another important aspect of Han Confucianism was the Five Elements theory. The Five Elements are water, fire, wood, earth, and metal. They are mutually interrelated: water subdues fire, which destroys wood, and so on. Theorists constructed elaborate charts, assigning to each of the elements a color, a planet, a compass direction, a number, an animal, and so forth. The theory of the succession of the elements provided an explanation for change and was used to legitimate dynastic ambitions.

Under the urging of Dong Zhongshu, Emperor Wu established this modified Confucianism as the state orthodoxy. Confucian orthodoxy was canonized in the form of the Five Classics. The Five Classics are: the *Book of Documents*, the *Book of Odes*, the *Book of Changes*, the *Spring and Autumn Annals*, and the *Book of Rites*. We have already discussed the *Documents*, *Odes*, and *Rites*. The *Book of Changes* originated as a divination text, then became broadly elaborated. It articulates a highly developed correlative cosmology, in which events in one part of the cosmos have clear repercussions in another part.

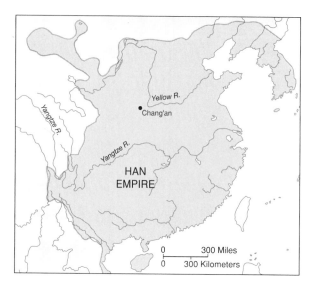

The Han Empire, 108 B.C.E.

The *Spring and Autumn Annals* is a history of the state of Lu. It is so terse as to be cryptic, and has generated much commentary. In 136 B.C.E., scholars proficient in the Five Classics were appointed to the government—an important step in transforming Confucianism from a political philosophy to a state ideology.

Education became a prerequisite for government service, and there is ample evidence that education was fairly widespread, at least among males of the elite class. Schools were established throughout the empire, even in remote rural villages. Children of the upper classes were often educated by tutors at home. A tutor whose

A Han stone relief tells of an unsuccessful attempt by Jing Ko to assassinate emperor Qin Shihuangdi. To the right of the pillar, the emperor holds aloft a jade disk as a symbol of his authority.

primary responsibility was to teach the sons of a family might also teach the daughters. The educational curriculum included, but was not restricted to, the Five Classics. The intellectual common ground provided by the classics was an important factor in promoting Chinese unity.

The intellectual common ground bound men of the elite together. But everyone in Han China did not read Confucius. Other belief systems also found followers. For example, in 3 B.C.E., a peasant cult devoted to the Queen Mother of the West, one of the chief deities of popular Taoism, staged an uprising. The cult followers roamed the streets barefoot, with disheveled hair, clutching talismans and amulets. They passed around a written message, saying "The Mother tells the people that those who wear this talisman will not die." This use of written messages by a peasant cult indicates the nearly magical power of the written word. Here too we see a strain that will be more highly developed in later Taoism: the gods communicate with human beings through written media.

Family and Society

The fundamental division of Chinese society was described by Mencius when he said that there were two categories of labor, mental and physical, and that it was the fate of those who labored with their hands to be governed by those who worked with their minds. This social stratification was further elaborated by other Confucian social theorists, who divided society into four groups, arranged hierarchically, beginning with scholars and moving through farmers, artisans, and merchants. Scholars ranked first—not surprising in a list drawn up by scholars. Farmers ranked second because they were primary producers. Artisans follow because they were secondary producers. Merchants rank last because Confucians regarded them as mere parasites who moved goods from one area to another, earning a living from the labor of others.

It is important not to confuse an idealized view of how society ought to function with how it actually functioned. As one official complained to Emperor Wen (180–157 B.C.E.), "At present merchants are rich and honored although they are humbled by the law; farmers are poor and lowly although they are respected by the law." Early in the Han, the typical agriculturalist was a small independent farmer. As time went on, land was concentrated into the hands of great families, and the small landholder of the early Han became a tenant. The normal unit of production was a family, which had on the average five or six members. A typical agricultural community was a hamlet, consisting of perhaps a hundred families. Already by the time of the Han, the peasant household was not entirely self-sufficient; many daily necessities were purchased at local markets. Markets in the cities were under the control of a bureaucrat known as the "market chief."

Although there was gendered division of labor, women worked in a variety of occupations. Mozi was among the first to articulate what later became a clichéd description of the gendered division of labor in China: men plow and women spin. But women worked at a variety of occupations. They worked as weavers, pearl peddlers, domestic servants, cinnabar merchants, sorceresses, courtesans, and prostitutes. We know that female laborers participated in the large public works projects, such as building the city walls of the capital of Chang'an, though it is possible that sources mention it because it was unusual.

The low ranking of merchants reflects clear ideological prejudice against them. But despite this prejudice, at many times and in many places Chinese merchants have done quite well. Indeed, from the repeated prohibitions on merchant office holding issued by the Han state we can see that they posed a threat to the political elite. Several of the most lucrative enterprises under the Han—salt, iron, and liquor—were run by merchants who were licensed under government monopoly.

Funeral tile from a Han tomb, found in Sichuan province. A hunting scene shows nobles shooting birds with bow and arrow while in the lower panel peasants are working in the fields.

Han cities were lively and crowded places. The census of 2 C.E., which placed the population of all of China at about 60 million, records the population of the city of Chang'an as 246,200; Loyang, 195,504; Chengdu, 282,147; and Pengcheng, 148,725. One Han poem describes dwellings packed "as closely as the teeth of a comb," and another describes markets so full of goods and people that there is scarcely space to turn one's head.

For all social classes, the family was not only the basic unit of production, but was also the fundamental social unit. Much of Chinese social thought is devoted to the family and its social role. According to prevailing Confucian ideas, the key to the harmonious functioning of the family was a hierarchy based on seniority and gender. Confucian ritual texts like the *Book of Rites* prescribe rituals for coming-of-age, marriage, funeral, and ancestral sacrifices. The family was thought of as a chain, in which the living were but a link between dead ancestors and as yet unborn descendants. The ancestors demanded sacrifices, in the form of food and other offerings. Those who had no descendants to make offerings to them would wander as unpropitiated hungry ghosts.

The gender-bound nature of Confucianism does not mean that Han dynasty Confucians ignored women. But the role of women in a well-ordered world was vastly different from that of men. Beginning in the Han dynasty, authors, both male and female, wrote texts offering examples and guidance to women. Ban Zhao, a woman who was a prominent historian, was the author of one such text in the first century C.E. An earlier text is the *Biographies of Exemplary Women*, attributed to a man named Liu Xiang (79–8 B.C.E.). There are a number of different kinds of virtue celebrated by this text. Military heroism, exceptional intelligence, and chastity all found their place. One of the most famous stories is that of the mother of Mencius. Her biography begins by explaining that Mencius and his mother lived near a cemetery. When the mother noticed the child playing at burial rituals, she decided to move. The family then moved near a marketplace, and Mencius began playing at buying and selling. Once again his mother decided that the neighborhood was exerting a bad influence on her child, and once again the family moved. Finally, they moved near a school, and Mencius played at ancestral sacrifices and "practiced the common courtesies between students and teachers." His mother decided that was the place she would remain. Illustrations from this text were engraved on stone a number of times during the Han dynasty and have been the subject of countless paintings.

This use of representational art is one way the ideas of the literate elite could be impressed upon nonliterate classes or genders.

Marriage was the foundation of the family, and as such it received much attention from ritual theorists. Ritual texts prescribed late ages at marriage: twenty for women and thirty for men. The actual ages at marriage seem to have been much earlier. Ban Zhao wrote that the average age at marriage was fourteen for women and sixteen for men. At marriage, the family of the bride provided her with a dowry, which would remain her property throughout the marriage. The family of the groom paid the family of the bride a bride-price. The relative value of dowry and bride-price varied greatly with time and place throughout China's history. After marriage, the young couple typically lived with the groom's parents and submitted to their authority.

During the Han, and later dynasties, divorce was possible, though not common, and it was the prerogative of men. There were seven conditions under which a man could divorce his wife: if she disobeyed his parents, if she was barren, if she committed adultery, if she was jealous, if she had an incurable disease, if she was too talkative or if she committed theft. But, more importantly, there were three conditions under which a man could not divorce his wife: if she had mourned the death of his parents for the full three years, if he had been poor when he married her but had subsequently become wealthy, and if she had no place to go. These limitations on when a man could divorce a woman were an important protection to wives.

A man who tired of a wife could simply install a concubine. A man could take as many concubines as he wished, but he might have only one wife. A concubine did not usually enter her husband's household with a dowry and had no guarantees that she would not be thrown out of the house. Her children were fully legitimate, and were not disadvantaged in relation to the offspring of the main wife in terms of inheritance of property. But there is ample evidence that the children of concubines were socially disadvantaged.

Property was collectively held by the family. At some point in the family cycle, usually but not always at the death of the father, the family would divide the estate. The property was divided equally among sons. Some stipulation might be made for the provision of dowry for unmarried daughters. Widows in the Zhou and Han seem to have remarried with relatively little stigma. A widow's children were, in theory, to remain with their father's family. It was more or less expected that a widowed man remarry.

Reading Han History

One of the great contributions of Han culture to Chinese civilization was the *Records of the Historian*, a great literary achievement that set the format for many later histories. The story of its author, Sima Qian (ca. 145–90 B.C.E.), is a poignant one. His father had been a historian, and on his deathbed charged his son to follow his profession, saying "you must make something of yourself, so that your name may go down in the ages to the glory of your father and mother." In 98 B.C.E. Sima Qian made a political error by defending a general the court believed had committed treason. Political errors were not taken lightly in those days, and Sima Qian was sentenced to death. But he was given a choice: if he submitted to castration, he might be allowed to stay alive just long enough to finish his history. He justifies this choice in a letter to a friend, saying "If my writings be handed down to those who will appreciate them, and be passed down to the villages and great cities, though I should suffer a thousand mutilations, what regret would I have?"

The *Records of the Historian* is divided into three sections: the annals, which are a year-by-year account of the activities of kings; the treatises, which are essays on topics such as ritual, music, astronomy, geography, administration, and the economy; and finally the biographies. Biographies are an extremely important part of the *Records of the Historian* and of later historical writing as well, reflecting a profound conviction that history is made up of the actions of individual men and the occasional woman.

Sima Qian gives graphic accounts of battles he never saw, and provides verbatim accounts of speeches he never heard. This lends to his work a vividness that remains almost unmatched in later Chinese historical writing. But it was not without its critics. Ban Gu wrote in the *Han History* in about 92 C.E. that Sima Qian is "careless and sketchy and takes improper liberty with his sources." Despite this charge, Ban Gu made ample use of Sima Qian. Vast portions of the *Han History* are copied verbatim from the *Records of the Historian*. The *Han History*, written in the Latter Han dynasty about the Former Han, set the precedent that each dynasty would undertake to compile an official history of its predecessors. The early dynastic histories can be quite lively and complex, but in time the narrative, though useful and usually reliable, becomes more predictable and routine. Chinese readers from the time of the Han saw history as a mirror to the present, a guide to ministers and kings about the wisdom of some policies and the follies of others.

Threats to Han Stability

The Han were not the only empire rising on the Asian continent in the third century B.C.E. The Xiongnu were a nomadic people who lived on the steppe of central Asia. Cattle herding was fundamental to their economy. They also depended on the sedentary societies of China for certain necessities, such as grain and metals. When conditions permitted, they traded with the Chinese. Otherwise, they obtained what they needed through plunder.

In 209 B.C.E., a Xiongnu leader named Maodun (d. 174 B.C.E.) took advantage of the temporary disarray accompanying the fall of the Qin dynasty and solidified a confederation of tribes that stretched from western Manchuria to Chinese Turkestan. The confederation unified a linguistically diverse group of nomads. It is no exaggeration to say that the Former Han dynasty was dominated by the problem of the steppe. The problem of the northern neighbors is a persistent one in Chinese history, as we shall see even more clearly in subsequent chapters.

The early Han policy toward the Xiongnu was one of appeasement. The Chinese sent gifts to the Xiongnu and forged marriage alliances with the Xiongnu rulers. The *Han History* records the lament of one princess who was sent northward in such an alliance:

> A yurt is my chamber,
> Felt my walls.
> Flesh my only food,
> Koumiss to drink.
> My thoughts are all of home,
> My heart aches within.
> O to be the yellow crane
> Winging home again!

The alien felt walls of the nomadic tent (the yurt) and strange diet of meat and fermented mare's milk (koumiss) intensified the princess's longing for home. And the tent and the diet also signify the difference between the Chinese and their steppe neighbors, in the eyes of the Chinese at least. Peoples of the steppe do not practice sedentary agriculture. In fact, an early Han advisor proposed that the Han establish a series of restaurants along the border, on the theory that once the Xiongnu became accustomed to Chinese food they would adopt the sedentary agricultural practices needed to produce it.

After 133 B.C.E., Han policy toward the Xiongnu became more aggressive. Emperor Wu's wars against the Xiongnu met with a certain amount of tactical success but they were very costly. A single expeditionary force might number 100,000 men. In addition to military efforts, during the reign of Emperor Wu there were major attempts to colonize the northwest. Perhaps as many as

Selection From *The Records* of the Grand Historian of China

■ *The excerpt below follows a long (36 pages in English translation) biography of Xiang Yu in which Sima Qian recounts his rise and fall. After each of the biographies in the* Records of the Grand Historian *Sima Qian includes commentary in which he gives an evaluation of the person's life and a commentary on reasons for his success or failure.*

After Xiang Yu met with success on the central plains of China (known as the area within the pass), he went back to Chu, saying "To become rich and famous and then not go back to your own home is like putting on an embroidered coat and going out walking at night. Who is to know about it?" He returned to Chu and deposed the Righteous Emperor, King Huai.

In the excerpt that follows, Sima Qian praises the capacity of Xiang Yu. But he must also account for his failure, which he does in moral terms.

The Grand Historian Remarks: How sudden was [Xiang Yu's] rise to power! When the rule of Qin floundered and Chen She led his revolt, local heroes and leaders arose like bees, struggling for power in numbers too great to be counted. Xiang Yu did not have an inch of territory to begin with, but by taking advantage of the times he raised himself in the space of three years from a commoner in the fields to the position of commander of feudal lords. He overthrew Qin, divided up the empire, and parceled it out in fiefs to various kings and marquises: but all power of government proceeded from Xiang Yu and he was hailed as king. Though he was not able to hold this position to his death, yet from there has never before been such a thing!

But when he went so far as to turn his back on the Pass and return to his native Chu, banishing the Righteous Emperor and setting himself up in his place, it was hardly surprising that the feudal lords revolted against him. He boasted and made a show of his own achievements. He was obstinate in his opinions and did not abide by established ways. He thought to make himself a dictator, hoping to attack and rule the empire by force. Yet within five days he was dead and his kingdom was lost. He met death at Dongcheng, but even at that time, he did not wake to or accept responsibility for his errors. "It is Heaven," he declared, "which has destroyed me, and no fault of mine in the use of arms!" Was he not indeed deluded?

From Sima Qian, *Records of the Grand Historian.*

two million people were resettled there. The Xiongnu problem came to an end when the Xiongnu confederation split in two groups. In 43 B.C.E., the Southern Xiongnu surrendered to the Han, and many of them did in fact take up sedentary agriculture. The Northern Xiongnu moved westward. The Xiongnu as an identifiable group had ceased to be an active player on the East Asian political scene. But groups of nomadic and semi-nomadic peoples from the steppe would continue to play a role in the history of China.

The most important transformations occurring during the course of the Han dynasty were not caused by external factors, but rather were internally motivated. There were profound changes in the social structure. At the beginning of the Han dynasty, the typical farmer was a smallholder. As the dynasty progressed, wealthy people began accumulating large estates. The peasant fell easily into debt, and was often forced to sell his land to a large landowner. As a result, the large families became more and more powerful. In 9 C.E. a rebel, a nephew of an empress of the Emperor Yuan (43–33 B.C.E.) named Wang Mang (45 B.C.E.–23 C.E.) overthrew the Han dynasty and established the Xin (New) dynasty. He tried to implement land reforms, which would have seriously damaged the great families. His policies met with little success, and after a very few years in power, he was overthrown and the Latter Han dynasty was established by Liu Xiu, a member of the Han imperial family. One of the major forces working for the overthrow of Wang Mang was the great families. The great families continued to grow in power throughout the Latter Han, and we shall hear more of them in chapter 8.

The Classical Age of China

11th century–771 B.C.E.	Western Zhou dynasty
771–480 B.C.E.	Eastern Zhou dynasty: Spring and Autumn period
559–479 B.C.E.	Confucius
480–221 B.C.E.	Eastern Zhou dynasty: Warring States period
4th century B.C.E.	Development of Taoism
221 B.C.E.	Unification of China and the establishment of the Qin dynasty
206 B.C.E.–9 C.E.	Former Han dynasty
9–25 C.E.	Xin dynasty
25–220 C.E.	Latter Han dynasty

The Han synthesis established an ideological and institutional pattern that was to remain important as a model for centuries to come. And problems that confronted the Han, including incursions by northern nomadic peoples and great families with the potential to threaten the throne, were problems later dynasties confronted as well.

The Classical Age in India

The long-term configurations of Indian political structure contrast rather starkly with those of China. From the seventh to the second century B.C.E., however, some similar patterns emerge. In India, as in China, the political scene is dominated by a number of small states. By the sixth century B.C.E., the competition among these states had created a climate of political instability. As it did in Zhou China, this competition and unrest in the political world fostered the development of new schools of thought, the most important of which are known as Buddhism and Jainism. And finally, in the fourth century B.C.E. north India unified for the first time under the Mauryan Empire. India during this period saw the growth of an upper-class cultural identity, primarily religious, which served to link Indians of diverse local cultures. But unlike China, where for most of history diverse local cultures were unified in one political entity, the unity provided in India by a commonality of religious culture remained amorphous. States like the Mauryan Empire, in which all of north India was unified into a strong political entity, are the exception rather than the rule.

The Age of the Small State

Beginning in about the seventh century B.C.E., a number of small states began forming in north India. The internal political structure of the states varied. The majority were monarchies, but some were republics. The republics were clustered in the foothills of the Himalayas, while the monarchies were concentrated in the plain of the Ganges.

The monarchies were ruled by hereditary kings. The king collected taxes, raised armies, and administered justice. A king was not, however, an ordinary human being with political power, as is shown by the royal consecration ceremony. The consecration ceremonies were rituals that, in their full form, took place over the course of more than a year. During the ceremony, the chief priest addressed the gods, saying, "Of mighty power is he who has been consecrated; now he has become one of yours; you must protect him." One of the most spectacular royal rituals in early India was the horse sacrifice. A white horse would be allowed to roam free for a year. Chieftains and kings on whose turf the horse wandered would be required to do homage to the horse's master or else fight him. At the end of the year the horse would be sacrificed. The horse sacrifice simultaneously demonstrated and expanded the power of the king.

Some republics were completely independent, but many were vassal states to kingdoms and exercised only internal autonomy. Some republics were governed by an aristocratic council. In others, the head or chief was elected by an assembly and could be replaced if he was unsatisfactory. Members of all free castes were eligible to attend the assembly meetings, but offices were reserved for members of the warrior caste. The *Arthasastra*, a political manual of the fourth century B.C.E. (discussed below), gives the king advice on how to conquer a republic: He should sow dissension among the members of the assembly so that they will not be able to achieve consensus. One may conclude that intellectual life in the republics was diverse and stimulating. It is indicative of this lively atmosphere that the founders of the two most important heterodox sects, the Buddha and Mahavira, the Jain founder, were from republics.

The roles of the two highest castes, the warriors *(kshatriyas)* and the priests *(brahmins)*, differed in the republics and the monarchies. In the monarchies, the status of the brahmins was higher than it was in the republics, while the kshatriyas had a dominant position in the republics. This difference reflects the underlying basis of political legitimacy in the two systems. Monarchs looked to gods to define their positions, while in republics political power rested on a more diffuse basis, including military might. Although in theory the priest ranked higher than the warrior, their actual social rankings might vary. As time went on in the republics, the position of head became hereditary, and the chiefdoms came to be more like monarchies. But some republics managed to survive until the fifth century C.E.

Religious Transformation

Political disunity among the states led to intellectual diversity. Brahmanism, as the Vedic religion was known, was characterized by ever more elaborate ritual, and was dominated by the priestly caste. Much of the core of what would later be called Hinduism developed during this period. Vedic texts retained their central importance in Hinduism. But Brahmanic religion, which had stressed elaborate rituals performed by a priestly caste, was gradually transformed into Hinduism, where the central act was an individual devotee's worship of a deity. During the period of small-state formation, in some areas the old priestly castes were losing their authority, and the secular nobility and a growing class of wealthy merchants were assuming positions of power. The old lineage relations were eroding, and were replaced in part by new religious orientations. A number of new sects arose, many of them urban and rooted in the republics. One text describes sixty-three schools of thought.

One of the most influential religious developments is manifested in a group of texts known as the Upanishads, which are the end portion of the Vedas. Not only are the Upanishads crucial in the formation of Hinduism, but they articulate a number of ideas important in both Buddhism and Jainism. For example, the notion of transmigration, that after death a being returns to existence in another form, appears in the Upanishads. Transmigration links all of life in a single system. The notion of *karma*, which literally means "deed," also appeared in these texts. Although various Indian religions attach different nuances to the concept of karma, it essentially means a deed and its consequences, which extend beyond a single lifetime.

The most avid proponents of the Upanishads were ascetics, people who subjected their bodies to rigorous discipline. Through practicing austerities they believed that they could gain magical powers, including the ability to see the past, present, and future. The idea that all of reality can be reduced to one fundamental unity, which forms an important role in later Hinduism, is fully articulated in the Upanishads.

The psychological uncertainty of the day is expressed by a king quoted in the Upanishads:

> The oceans have dried up, mountains have crumbled, the Pole Star is shaken, the earth founders, the gods perish. I am like a frog in a well.

From this sense of social and psychological crisis, the great religions of Buddhism and Jainism emerged. They never replaced the Vedic religion, which developed into what is today called Hinduism, but they continued to exist with it, side by side, providing an alternative.

The discussion of the four life stages, which began to appear in texts about this time, is probably a response to extreme asceticism. The first stage was that of student, followed by those of householder, forest-dweller, and finally wandering ascetic. It was necessary that the stages be lived in a proper order. At the end of the period of study, a man would receive the cord that marked him as a member of one of the twice-born castes. It was a marker both of social status and of male adulthood. A woman became an adult when she married. After a man's duties as a householder were completed, he was to leave home and live austerely in the seclusion of a forest. Sometimes a man and wife would enter this life stage together. Finally, one became a wandering ascetic, begging for one's food and meditating on the Upanishads. It is important to remember this life pattern as we look at Mahavira and Buddha.

The Jain religion arose in Vesali, a flourishing town in north India. Mahavira (whose date of death is traditionally given as 528 B.C.E.) is usually referred to as the Jain founder. According to Jain cosmology, he was preceded by twenty-three prophets, the earliest of whom lived literally millions of years ago. But Mahavira is the first of the prophets to have a fully elaborated biography. According to this biography, Trisala, Mahavira's mother, had an auspicious dream before his birth. But there is an unusual twist in some versions of the story of Mahavira's birth. According to Jain legend, prophets were always born to women of the warrior caste. The embryo that was to become Mahavira first descended in the womb of a woman from the priestly caste. It was thus necessary that he be removed from her womb and placed in the womb of Trisala, a woman of the warrior caste, who then gave birth to him.

Mahavira grew up, married, and had a daughter. At the age of thirty, he renounced his family and became an ascetic and wandered for twelve years before he finally found deliverance from the bonds of pleasure and pain. The method he used to obtain deliverance was extreme asceticism, denying his body even the most basic of physical comforts. His followers also adopted this path. Although there is a clear role for the layman in the Jain religion, ultimate deliverance is available only to the monk who has freed himself from all of the trammels of earthly existence.

The Jain teachings are briefly as follows: All nature, even seemingly inanimate objects, possesses life and the capacity for reanimation. Everything has a soul, and the purification of the soul is the purpose of life. When the purification of the soul is complete, it will leave the body and reside in a state of bliss. Jain philosophy is radically nonviolent: a Jain may not kill even an insect. Because of this, Jains refuse to practice agriculture; many make their living as merchants and businessmen.

The teachings of Jainism were transmitted in an oral tradition until about the third century B.C.E., when they

Transference of the Embryo. *In this painting the embryo of Mahavira, the Jain founder, is transferred to Trisala, his mother.*

were written down. They did not, however, reach their final form until the fifth century C.E. In the third century B.C.E., major sectarian divisions occurred within Jainism. One of the sects admitted women to monastic orders.

The historical Buddha was more or less a contemporary of Mahavira. He was a prince of the Shakya clan who lived in Magadha, a republic in north India. According to later legend, he was conceived when a white elephant entered his mother's side, and was later born through her side. He was raised in luxury within the palace and led a life sheltered from all knowledge of human suffering. Not until the age of thirty, after he had married and fathered a child, did he leave the palace and see an old man, a sick man, a corpse, and a religious beggar. The first three were his first indications that suffering was a part of human life, and the joyfulness of the fourth offered him some hope of release from suffering. The young prince left home and practiced extreme asceticism in an attempt to understand human suffering, but his austerities were to no avail. Then he had an enlightenment experience, in which he understood both the reason for human suffering and the way to eliminate it. The core of his enlightenment is called the Four Noble Truths, and, put simply, it consists of the following four propositions: All life is infused with suffering; suffering is caused by desire; one may eliminate suffering by eliminating desire; one may eliminate desire by following the Noble Eightfold Path. The Noble Eightfold Path consists of right outlook, right aims, right speech, right effort, right livelihood, right mindfulness, right action, and right concentration. It is a program of ethical action and moral discipline leading to freedom from desire.

The Buddha referred to his teachings as the Middle Way because they negotiated a middle ground between a life of pleasure and lust, which he described as "degrading, sensual, vulgar, ignoble and profitless," and a life of asceticism, which he described as "painful, ignoble and profitless."

There are several concepts that are crucial to an understanding of Buddhist worldview: karma, rebirth, and Nirvana. Buddhist karma, which is adopted from the Vedic concept, posits quite simply that for every action there is a response: good deeds are rewarded and bad deeds are punished. There need be no deity who distributes reward and punishment. The mechanism of karma works like a law of physics—for every action there is an equal and opposite reaction. But there is always the problem of good people who do not prosper and evildoers who thrive. Karmic theory takes this into account by explaining that reward and punishment do not necessarily take place in this life. One's status in the next life,

Schist seated Buddha from the second or third century C.E. Such representations of the Buddha are found throughout the Asian countries to which Buddhism had spread.

whether one is reborn as a human or a mosquito, is determined by one's action in this life and in past lives. Rebirth in the Hindu and Buddhist scheme of things should not be confused with immortality; it is not the rebirth of an individual. Buddhist teachers clarify this by using the analogy of a river: The river you see today is the "same" as the river you saw yesterday, yet there is not a single drop of water in the river today that was there yesterday.

The ordinary person lives out countless lives of birth, death, and rebirth, sometimes moving up on the karmic scale, sometimes down. The very fortunate would be reborn as human males; it was not a gender-blind cosmology. Enlightenment offered the path to Nirvana, which literally means "to blow out." Nirvana can best be understood as a release from the cycle of birth and death. Later Buddhist sects, especially those in East Asia, would postulate elaborate paradises that were in fact physical places. But Nirvana as taught by the Buddha was simple release. The Buddha himself did not speak of Nirvana in much detail, and indeed was rather dismissive when questioners pressed him on it. He responded to one persistent questioner by asking him where a fire goes when it is extinguished, suggesting

how difficult it is to conceive of nonexistence even at a rather mundane level.

This early Buddhism, commonly called Theravada Buddhism—*Theravada* means "the teaching of the elders"—was a monastic order. The attainment of Nirvana was something that required technical mental training, and was hence not available to ordinary people living at home with their families. The monastic community differentiated Buddhists from other sects, and became an extremely important form of social organization. Buddhist monks did not take a vow of obedience. Any issue that could not be resolved unanimously by the assembly was referred to a committee of elders for resolution. It is probable that the internal organization of Buddhist monastic institutions was derived from the north Indian republics where they evolved.

The role Buddhism allowed women is difficult to evaluate. Five years after the Buddha attained enlightenment, his disciple Ananda persuaded him to allow women to join special monastic orders. A collection of seventy-three hymns in praise of the Buddha by women devotees, called *Therigatha*, has been preserved. Women from all walks of life seem to have joined monastic orders. Women preached to other women, but they also preached to men. One story of a woman converted by the Buddha is the story of Kisa-Gotami, who was distraught over the death of her child. She went to the Buddha for comfort, and he asked her to bring him a mustard seed from a house untouched by death. She failed, and the knowledge she gained from this is recorded in a poem she wrote:

> No village law is this, no city law
> No law for this clan, nor for that alone;
> For the whole world—ay, for the gods in heaven,
> This is the Law: All is impermanent.

But women had impediments in their religious quest. The most learned nun was forced to be subservient to the youngest of monks. The egalitarianism of the monastic community did not obliterate gender hierarchy. And there was no consensus about the spiritual potential of women. The Buddha had thirty-two auspicious marks on his body, including a retractable penis. Many people argued that since women did not resemble the Buddha physically, they could not emulate him spiritually. Others countered by saying that if the body is but an illusion, then gender ought not to matter.

The doctrine of transmigration offers one solution to the problem of gender in Buddhism. A pious woman can simply be reborn a man, and then can attain enlightenment. (Buddhists are not alone in positing this solution.

FROM *QUESTIONS OF KING MILINDA*

■ *Milinda is the Sanskrit name of the Bactrian king known to the Greeks as Menander. He reigned from approximately 155 to 130 B.C.E. The text that bears his name is a dialogue between the king and Nagasena, a Buddhist monk. Milinda is a willing pupil, and the text ends with his conversion to Buddhism. The text remains one of the most accessible explications of Buddhist beliefs.*

In this passage, Nagasena explains to Milinda how Arhats, Buddhists who have attained a state of enlightenment that will exempt them from the cycle of rebirth, have freed themselves from mental pain. In the excerpt here, the king begins the dialogue. Dashes indicate when the speaker is changing.

The king asked, "For what reason does the common worldling suffer both physical and mental pain?"—"Because his thought is so undeveloped He is like a hungry and excited ox, who has been tied up with a weak, fragile and short piece of straw and who, when agitated, rushes off, taking his tether with him. So someone whose thought is undeveloped gets agitated in his mind when a pain arises in him, and his agitated mind bends and contorts his body and makes it writhe. Undeveloped in his mind he trembles, shrieks and cries in terror. This is the reason the common worldling suffers both physical and mental pain."—"And what is the reason Arhats feel only one kind of feelings, physical and not mental?"—"The thought of the Arhats is developed, it is obedient and disciplined. When invaded by a painful feeling, the Arhat firmly grasps at the idea of its impermanence, and ties his thought to the post of contemplation. And his thought remains steadfast and undisturbed. But the influence of pain makes his body writhe."

"That, Nagasena, is indeed a most wonderful thing in this world, that someone's mind should remain unshaken when his body is shaken. Tell me the reason for that!"—"Suppose, your majesty, that there is a gigantic tree, with trunk, branches and leaves. If that tree were hit by the force of the wind, its branches would shake, but would the trunk also shake?"—"No, Venerable Sir."—"Just so the thought of the Arhat does not tremble or shake, like the trunk of the gigantic tree."

From *Buddhist Scriptures*.

Jains did so as well.) Later Japanese Buddhists had a ceremony that they would perform on the deathbed of a pious woman, which would ritually transform her to a man, so that she could enter paradises forbidden her as a woman.

Buddhist salvation may be gender-bound, but the ethics of Buddhism are universalistic. This does not mean that it preaches social equality to a caste society, but it does advocate an equality of ethical responsibility. One Buddhist position on caste accepts that it is an appropriate distinction in social life, but not in religious life, "For dharma is a question of qualities, and qualities do not reflect caste." *Dharma* is a word laden with meaning: it is often translated "religious law," but it carries with it clear connotations of ethical responsibility and cosmic causality.

The new religions continued to co-exist with the older forms. Buddhists and Jains continued to rely on Vedic texts for life-cycle rituals. After the advent of

Buddhism and Jainism, the older Brahmanic religion began to incorporate more local cults, such as those to deities like Siva and Vishnu. Paradoxes are at the heart of Siva: he is an erotic ascetic, a cosmic dancer who both creates and destroys. Vishnu is imagined by his followers as a supreme being who appears in the human world in many forms. Two of the most important of these forms, or avatars, are Rama, the hero of the great epic *Ramayana*, and Krishna, who plays a key role in the *Mahabharata*.

Family and Society

Because India at this time was even more diverse than China, it is difficult to make blanket statements about social life. The areas to the south of the Vindhya mountains, a low range that cuts across peninsular India, had a culture distinct from that of the north. During this period, however, southerners began to use the Sanskrit language and religious rituals of the north. But the various areas of India retained their linguistic and cultural distinctiveness.

One of the main sources for information about everyday life in early India is the *Laws of Manu*, probably composed late in the first century B.C.E. *Manu* consists of 2,685 verses on a variety of aspects of life and how it should be lived. But it is also a legal text. Manu is very clear on the need for laws: if the king did not inflict punishments, "the stronger would roast the weaker, like a fish upon a spit."

The text begins with a number of sages asking Manu, the first legendary king, to tell them the duties of the four classes of people. Manu responds by telling them the Vedic story of the creation of the universe, in which the caste system is presented as a part of the creation of the universe, an artifact of nature. The beginnings of the caste system were already visible in Aryan India. During the period of small-state formation, the system underwent refinements. Subcastes proliferated, often based on occupational divisions. In general, people married within their caste. But during this early period the lines between castes seem to have been less rigid than they became later.

Manu is ambivalent about the implications of gender. Women clearly represent a threat to men. A priest, for example, would go to hell for having a sexual relationship with a servant girl. Elsewhere Manu writes, "Where women are not revered, all rites are fruitless." Men are obliged to have sexual relations with their wives during their fertile periods. Manu tirades against bride-price, saying that a man who accepts a bride-price for his daughter is no better than a pimp. His vehemence leads a reader to suspect that the practice was widespread.

There is contradictory information about the age at marriage during this period. Manu says that an ideal husband is three times the age of his wife and that a father must marry off a daughter by the time she reaches puberty. If he fails to marry her before she begins to menstruate, he is guilty of a crime equivalent to procuring an abortion for every month she remains unmarried. But contemporary medical wisdom cautioned that the healthiest children were born to mothers who were more than sixteen years old, a caution that may have tempered enthusiasm for child brides.

There was enormous regional and class variation regarding inheritance practices. Property was normally divided during the lifetime of the owner into more or less equal shares among his sons. Women could hold property, called *stridhana*, which included but was not restricted to dowry. A woman's stridhana might be inherited by her daughters. During these centuries, widow remarriage seems to have been possible.

The Mauryan Empire

The first great empire in north India was founded by Chandragupta Maurya (321–298 B.C.E.), who usurped the throne of Magadha in 321 B.C.E. In addition to the legitimating theories for Indian kings discussed above, Mauryan kings claimed to be Universal Emperors. According to this theory, Universal Emperors appear from time to time in the cosmic cycle. They rule all of the known world, and will rule it righteously. Under their rule, the world will prosper. Because the appearance of Universal Emperors was cosmically ordained, they had a kind of religious sanction. This notion of Universal Emperorship was adopted by Buddhist rulers and was employed by emperors in China as well as in other Buddhist countries. But even with the concept of Universal Emperor, the king remained a law-interpreter rather than a law-giver. The king was not above dharma.

One of the great Indian works of political theory, the *Arthasastra*, is attributed to a minister of Chandragupta Maurya named Kautilya. Although the text as presently constituted dates from after the reign of the Chandragupta, the *Arthasastra* remains an invaluable source of information on Mauryan politics. In the political world described by the *Arthasastra*, a council assists the king in ruling. The council had the authority to make decisions

Indian women bring offerings of rice to the Buddha at their village's sacred tree. The thatched roofs of their homes are shown in the background.

Gender and Culture

VENUS OF WILLENDORF

Figure 1

The portrayal of the human body in the visual arts is a telling study in gender. While the presence or absence of sexual characteristics may tag a figure man or woman, it is the handling of the whole form—its curves, its angles, its emphases—that transcends biological fact and reflects ideas about gender. This subtle but suggestive mode of representation can be traced to the dawn of time and tracked across diverse cultures. The most accessible of all visual languages, we read it through association, based on our own physical experience.

One of the earliest known representations of woman is the *Venus of Willendorf* (ca. 30,000–10,000 B.C.E., Germany; Figure 1). No records survive to explain the meaning of this figure, but its form and scale suggest an interpretation. The full, ripe modeling of the breasts and abdomen contrasts with the summary treatment of the arms, head, and legs. This selective emphasis tells us that this "Venus," so-called by the modern archeologists who unearthed it, embodies fertility rather than love or beauty. Similarly, the figure's diminutive scale, small enough to fit in the palm of a hand, suggests its function as a talisman, an object carried to ensure the perpetuation of the community. Rather than a portrait of a woman, the *Venus of Willendorf* portrays and celebrates woman's power to bear and nourish new life.

The voluptuous figures carved in relief on the facade of the *Chaitya Hall at Karle* (early second century B.C.E., India; Figure 2) reveal the aesthetic commonalities, rather than the functional differences, between men and women. While the couple represents the generos-

CHAITYA HALL AT KARLE

Figure 2

KING SHABAQO

Figure 3

ity of individual donors to the monument, their relaxed positions, muscular curves, and elegant proportions portray the canon of physical beauty of ancient Indian art. There is no denying the gendered differences in these figures, but their swelling contours and swaying stances echo a shared aesthetic. There is a natural intimacy in the way they rest their hands on one another; these are bodies of ease and pleasure. Here, the beauty of the curving form is neither masculine nor feminine in its code. It is human, and it is beautiful.

In western tradition the basic form of a figure is clearly gendered. Just as the curve encodes the female in form and function, the angle presents the descriptive structure for the male. The preference for the angular male body type can be traced back to the earliest dynasties of Egypt. The influence of this aesthetic traveled the length of the Nile Valley and the breadth of the ancient Mediterranean world. Even when Egypt's political power succumbed to foreign domination, its visual language survived.

The bronze statuette of *King Shabaqo*, kneeling in ritual offering (late eighth century B.C.E., Ancient Kush; Figure 3), was produced during the era of Kushite rule in Egypt (twenty-fifth dynasty; 747–656 B.C.E.). Shabaqo, identified by his name on his belt buckle, has a strongly sculptured face and his noble presence speaks of the pride associated with the traditions of the Nubian homeland. But his physique bears the Egyptian stamp in its proportions: broad shoulders, columnar arms, and a triangular torso that flares in the defined pectoral muscles and tapers to a narrow waist. The ramrod posture and the uplifted head on its trunk-like neck recall the ancient conventions of Pharaonic portraiture. The overall effect of these features is dignity, appropriate to the ruler of the twin nations of Egypt and Nubia, as symbolized by the two cobras poised on his cap.

PEPLOS KORE

Figure 4

Greek form incorporated the angle both for the male and the female physique. The traditional Greek aesthetic—a celebration of height, vitality, and athleticism—also had its impetus in an Egyptian influence, which was planted and reinforced by centuries of pan Aegean trade. Emerging as a distinct type in the seventh century B.C.E., ancient Greek free-standing sculpture took on a singular form and a preferred subject: the idealized, nude male, or *Kouras*. Less common, but equally characteristic, was the clothed, young female, the *Kore*. The *Peplos Kore* (ca. 530 B.C.E., Greece; Figure 4), named for her distinctive garment, is typical in her proportions and stance. Unlike the *Venus of Willendorf*, the *Peplos Kore* celebrates form rather than function, and her alert gaze and active gesture suggest the individual spirit within a human ideal.

WOMEN MUST BE HONORED

■ *The* Laws of Manu *consist of 2,685 verses on a variety of topics, covering a variety of aspects of life and offering guidance as to how it should be lived. It was probably composed late in the first century B.C.E. It is a text that retained enormous authority throughout Indian history.*

The passages here show the complexity of Manu's position on women. They are drawn from several sections of the text.

Women must be honored and adorned by their fathers, brothers, husbands, and brothers-in-law who desire great good fortune.

Where women are honored, there the gods rejoice; where, however, they are not honored, there all sacred rights prove fruitless.

Where the female relations live in grief—that family soon perished completely; where, however, they do not suffer from any grievance—that family always prospers . . .

Her father protects her in childhood, her husband protects her in youth, her sons protect her in old age—a woman does not deserve independence.

The father who does not give away his daughter in marriage at the proper time is censurable; censurable is the husband who does not approach his wife in due season; and after the husband is dead, the son is censurable who does not protect his mother.

Even against the slightest provocations should women be particularly guarded, for unguarded they would bring grief to both the families.

Regard this as the highest dharma of all four classes: Husbands, though weak, must strive to protect their wives.

The husband should engage his wife in the collection and expenditure of wealth, in cleanliness, in religious rites, in cooking food for the family, and in looking after the necessities of the household . . .

From *The Laws of Manu.*

on minor matters without consulting the king. Members of the council were, in theory, selected by the king on the basis of merit, though the positions eventually became more or less hereditary. The court chaplain could be a very important official. The *Arthasastra* suggests that the king consult with him before deciding important matters. Provincial officials, who were often members of the royal family, were appointed by the king. The governors of districts were then appointed by provincial governors. The structure of the Mauryan Empire was less centralized than that of Han China, and its institutional bases were less firmly grounded.

Although the *Arthasastra* gives the king rather cynical advice on how to manipulate others for his own gain, it very clearly states that the function of the king is to protect society. It gives a sample schedule of activities in the day of a king, which allows him only four and one-half hours of sleep. Kings who do not expedite justice suffer cosmic punishment. One king was reportedly reborn as a lizard because he kept litigants waiting.

Law was not applied equally in ancient India: one's punishment depended on one's social position. This system usually worked to the benefit of the upper classes, but not always: theft, for example, was punished more seriously for members of the upper classes than for members of the lower classes.

The invasions of Alexander the Great took place just before the reign of Chandragupta. Our best estimates about the population of the Indian subcontinent in the fourth century B.C.E. come from calculations based on Greek accounts of the size of the armies Alexander confronted; they range from between 100 and 181 million people. In a story that is probably apocryphal, the two great kings are said to have met in the Punjab. As we have seen earlier, Alexander's empire did not long outlast him. But his invasion of India was not without consequences, though most of them were probably unintended. Wars with the Greeks weakened the small states of north India, and thereby facilitated the Mauryan unification. Hellenistic artistic styles exerted a

This carving above a gate at the Great Stupa at Sanchi shows a jungle hermitage. It is crowded with figures of children, adults, and animals—a hunter with bow and arrow, an elephant bathing, and a woman gathering fruit.

permanent influence on Indian art. Hellenistic astronomy also had a profound influence on Indian science. And Greek use of writing may have influenced the development of the Brahmi script.

The connections with the Hellenistic world continued under the reign of Chandragupta's son Bindusara, who assumed the throne about 297 B.C.E. A charming story relates that Bindusara asked the Seleucid emperor Antiochus I to send him sweet wine, dried figs, and a sophist. Antiochus complied with the first two requests, but denied Bindusara the sophist, saying that Greek philosophers were not commodities for export.

Under the Mauryas, the state took a lively interest in economics. Some large-scale private manufacture took place during this period; for example, one man owned more than 500 potters' shops. But many lucrative large-scale enterprises, such as mines and pearl fisheries, were run by the state. The state also ran manufactories for spinning and weaving, typically staffed by poor women. This was not the only concern the Maurya state showed for public welfare: the *Arthasastra* prescribes a public well for every ten houses.

In addition to the monastic organizations, which helped order society as the old lineage structures broke down, another form of social organization prominent under the Mauryas was craft organizations. These organizations, loosely resembling European guilds, could be very powerful. They set rules of work, the level at which wages would be paid, the standards of production, and the prices of commodities. The guild rules were usually backed by the king and had the force of law. Guild

masters on occasion became the counselors of kings. Many guilds had their own courts, which mediated disputes, including domestic disputes of guild members. Other guilds patronized Buddhist monasteries. Buddhist monastic codes stipulated that a woman could not become a nun without the consent of her husband and his guild. Guilds took responsibility for the welfare of widows and orphans of their members. Usually, though not always, sons followed in the occupation of their father. The guild organizations have been regarded by some as the precursors to subcastes organized by occupation.

In spite of the lively commercial life, agriculture was the dominant form of economic activity in ancient India. The typical farmer in India was a small landholder. Although there were some large estates formed by tenants, large estates were not as prominent as they were in Latter Han China. There was considerable regional variation in the crops grown. Farmers in the north grew wheat and barley. In the plains formed by the Indus and Ganges rivers, farmers planted rice. In the far south they grew millet and the spices for which India became so famous. Everywhere farmers grew cotton. Early Greek accounts of the Indian landscape described cotton as wool growing on trees. In most places in India, farmers could grow two crops a year on the same plot of land, a process known as double cropping. In the far south, three or even four crops a year on the same field were possible.

Cattle were used for plowing, transport, and food. Manure was an important source of fertilizer. While later Indians observed strict taboos on the killing of cows, the evidence for the Maurya period is inconclusive. One of

The Great Stupa at Sanchi was originally dedicated by Asoka around 15 C.E.

the most important food products from cattle was *ghee*, butter clarified by heating, which will keep indefinitely in a hot climate.

The greatest of the Mauryan emperors was Asoka, the son of Bindusara and the grandson of Chandragupta. Asoka is an important historical figure, but the role he plays in legend is even greater. He is sketched as a vicious libertine, a man with a hundred brothers, who killed them all. But reportedly he sickened of bloodshed after a successful war against the people of Kalinga (modern coastal Orissa), and he converted to Buddhism. One of his most famous acts was the construction of 84,000 religious monuments, known as stupas, to honor relics of the Buddha. The figure of 84,000 is certainly an exaggeration, but there do remain in every part of the Indian subcontinent a large number of inscriptions made at the behest of Asoka. Even under Asoka, however, the Mauryan Empire was probably more a loose federation of rulers who acknowledged Maurya dominance than it was a true empire.

After Asoka, the Mauryas did not last very long. The last Mauryan king was murdered in 184 B.C.E. by Pushyamitra, who established a dynasty known as the Sungas. The power and authority of the Sungas was a pale reflection of their Mauryan predecessors. But disunity did not mean decay. Under the Sungas and later rulers, culture and trade with ports as distant as Rome continued to flourish.

The unity of Buddhism too was not long for this world. With the fall of the Mauryas, Buddhism lost important royal patronage in the north. Pushyamitra was a champion of a reaction against Buddhism, which reasserted Brahmanic religion. Buddhists began to differ among themselves about points of doctrine, and formed a number of sects. The most important of these new sects is called Mahayana, which means Greater Vehicle.

Mahayana Buddhism differed in several ways from Theravada Buddhism, which came to be called by some Hinayana, or Lesser Vehicle. It offered greater possibilities for salvation to lay believers, both male and female, than Theravada Buddhism had. Monastic life was no longer a prerequisite for salvation. The Buddha, who had been revered by early Buddhists as a great teacher, was now imagined as a divinity. And a new group of semidivine figures, called bodhisattvas, became prominent in Mahayana Buddhism. Bodhisattvas are beings who, when they are on the brink of attaining salvation, take a vow to remain in the world of mortals until all living beings have been saved. One version of the vow reads in part:

> I must bear the burden of all beings, for I have vowed to save all things living, to bring them safe through the forest of birth, age, disease, death and rebirth. I think not of my own salvation . . . So I take upon myself the sorrow of all beings.

A bodhisattva would accumulate merit through good deeds, which might then be transferred to an ordinary person. Thus a man or woman might pray to a bodhisattva for good health, offspring, or success. Individual bodhisattvas became associated with particular benefits— compassion or wisdom, for example. Bodhisattvas

The Classical Age of India

7th to 2nd centuries B.C.E.	The Age of the Small State
6th to 5th centuries B.C.E.	Development of Hinduism, Jainism, and Buddhism
326 B.C.E.	Invasion of India by Alexander the Great
321 B.C.E.	Founding of Mauryan Empire
321–298 B.C.E.	Reign of Chandragupta Maurya
ca. 269–232 B.C.E.	Reign of Asoka
184 B.C.E.	End of Mauryan Empire

played an important role in religious imagination as beings who would intercede on behalf of human beings.

Buddhism was a religion popular with merchants, and this doubtless facilitated its spread. Mahayana Buddhism made its way along trade routes to East Asia, where it would completely transform the cultures of China, Japan, and Korea.

In this chapter we have seen the formation of the classical ages of two great civilizations. Although the patterns of their subsequent histories differ greatly, during these formative years we see a common connection between political unrest and intellectual ferment. During these early years, Indians and Chinese both formulated philosophies that explained the meaning of human existence and that provided blueprints for social life, blueprints which would have an impact on ages to come.

SUGGESTIONS FOR FURTHER READING

GENERAL READING

Ainslie T. Embree, ed., *Encyclopedia of Asian History*, 4 vols. (New York: Charles Scribner's Sons, 1988). An authoritative and handy quick reference.

PRIMARY SOURCES

* William Theodore de Bary, ed., *Sources of Indian Tradition*, 2 vols. (New York: Columbia University Press, 1958), and his *Sources of Chinese Tradition* 2 vols. (New York: Columbia University Press, 1964) both have good selections of texts,

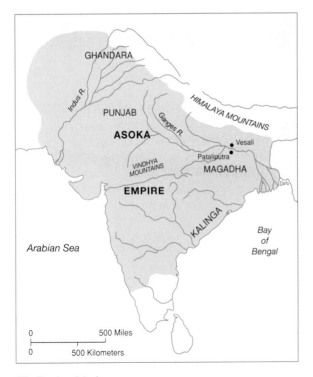

The Empire of Asoka

primarily philosophical. Translations of the *Mencius*, the *Analects*, the *Songs of the South* and the *Laws of Manu* are available in Penguin editions. *Buddhist Scriptures* (also published by Penguin) has an accessible collection of Buddhist texts. Burton Watson has translated sections of the *Records of the Historian*, *Tso chuan* (a commentary to the *Spring and Autumn Annals*), *Chuang tzu*, *Mo-tzu*, *Han Fei-tzu*, *Hsun-tzu*, all of which are available from Columbia University Press.

THE GOLDEN AGE OF CHINA

H. G. Creel, *The Origins of Statecraft in China* (Chicago: University of Chicago Press, 1970). Although it perhaps overstates the degree of centralization present in Zhou China, this work is a massive repository of information.

* Jacques Gernet, *A History of Chinese Civilization*, trans. by J. R. Foster (Cambridge: Cambridge University Press, 1985). An authoritative general history.

* David Hall and Roger Ames, *Thinking Through Confucius* (New York: SUNY Press, 1987). An exploration of the commonalities and disjunctures between Confucian and Western philosophies.

Mark Edward Lewis, *Sanctioned Violence in Early China* (Albany, NY: State University of New York Press, 1990). A provocative interpretation of the Warring States Transition that centers on the role of sanctioned violence.

* Frederic Mote, *The Intellectual Foundations of China*, 2d ed. (New York: McGraw Hill, 1989) An elegant introduction to the major issues in classical Chinese thought.

* Benjamin Schwartz, *The World of Thought in Ancient China* (Cambridge, MA: Harvard University Press, 1985). A thoughtful and sustained reappraisal of major thinkers of the late Zhou.

Edward L. Shaughnessy, *Sources of Western Zhou History: Inscribed Bronze Vessels* (Berkeley and Los Angeles: University of California Press, 1991). A technical yet accessible introduction to the study of bronze inscriptions.

THE UNIFIED EMPIRE

Derk Bodde, *Festivals in Classical China: New Year and Other Annual Observances During the Han Dynasty 206 B.C.-A.D.200* (Princeton, NJ: Princeton University Press, 1975). An encyclopedic account of textual references to festivals during the Han.

Ch'u T'ung-tsu (edited by Jack Dull) *Han Social Structure* (Seattle: University of Washington Press, 1972). Includes both primary sources and analysis of Han dynasty society.

Jean Levi, *The Chinese Emperor*, trans. Barbara Bray (New York: Vintage Books, 1989). A sinologist's novelistic account of the intrigues and power struggles in the first emperor's reign.

Michael Loewe, *Crisis and Conflict in Han China: 104 B.C. to A.D. 9* (London: Allen and Unwin, 1974). A collection of essays that discuss Han dynasty politics.

Michael Loewe, *Ways to Paradise: The Chinese Quest for Immortality* (London: Allen & Unwin, 1979). A survey of archaeological and textual materials on Han dynasty beliefs about immortality and other religious issues.

Denis Twitchett and Michael Loewe, eds., *The Cambridge History of China, Vol. I, The Ch'in and Han Empires 221 B.C.-A.D. 220* (Cambridge: Cambridge University Press, 1986). A collection of authoritative essays.

Wu Hung, *The Wu Liang Shrine: The Ideology of Early Chinese Pictorial Art* (Stanford, CA: Stanford University Press, 1989). A splendidly illustrated analysis of the engravings at a Han dynasty shrine.

THE CLASSICAL AGE IN INDIA

Jeannine Auboyer, *Daily Life in Ancient India (From Approximately 200 B.C. to A.D.700)*, trans. Simon Watson Taylor (London: Weidenfeld and Nicolson, 1965). Accessible and well-written.

* A. L. Basham, *The Wonder That Was India* (New York: Hawthorn Books, 1963). A classic account of Indian culture, engagingly written.

* Wendy Doniger, trans. and ed., *The Laws of Manu* (New York: Penguin, 1991). An eminently accessible translation of a rich and fascinating text.

* Wendy Doniger O'Flaherty, *Siva: The Erotic Ascetic* (New York: Oxford University Press, 1973). An analysis of the myths that surround Siva, accompanied by translations of relevant primary texts.

The Mahabharata, directed by Peter Brook (New York: Parabola Video Library, 1989). Part One: *The Game of Dice*; Part Two: *Exile in the Forest*; Part Three: *War*. A splendid modern western-movie interpretation of the ancient Indian epic.

* *The Mahabharata*, trans. and ed. by J. A. B. van Buitenen, 3 vols. (Chicago: University of Chicago Press, 1973–1978). A wonderful translation of the first portions of the epic.

Barbara Stoler Miller, *The Bhagavad Gita: Krishna's Counsel in Time of War* (New York: Columbia University Press, 1986). A translation and discussion of a crucial section of the *Mahabharata*.

John Strong, *The Legend of King Asoka: A Study and Translation of the Asokavadana* (Princeton, NJ: Princeton University Press, 1983). A lucid introduction to the legend of Asoka, followed by an elegant translation of a text.

* Romila Thapar, *A History of India*, Vol. 1 (New York: Penguin: 1969). A standard authoritative account of Indian history prior to the Mughals.

*Indicates paperback edition available.

CHAPTER 5

Early Rome and the Roman Republic, 800–31 B.C.E.

ETERNAL ROME

Five miles from its mouth, the Tiber River snakes in a lazy S around the first highlands that rise from the marshes of central Italy. These weathered cliffs, separated by tributary streams, look down on the river valley that broadens to over a mile and a half wide, the first and only natural ford for many miles. Only three promontories, the Capitoline, Palatine, and Aventine, are separate hills. The others, the Quirinal, Viminal, Caelian, Oppian, and Esquiline, are actually spurs of the distant Apennines. The history of Rome is etched into these hills and valleys, the story of how simple, pragmatic farmer-soldiers developed a military machine that conquered the known world and a political system in which victor and vanquished alike could share. But also written into this landscape is the story of how, having conquered the world, the conquerors were themselves conquered by the cultural and moral values of the vanquished and how in time the values of devotion and loyalty to Rome and its traditions eroded in the face of personal ambition, greed, and brutality.

The earliest Roman villages were found on the Palatine, from whose heights the photograph was taken. Here Latin shepherds and farmers first erected their crude huts. Later republican senators and then emperors built on its slopes their residences, so splendid that the term *palace* became synonymous with the seat of royalty. The Capitoline with its steep cliffs, which begin at the extreme left of the photograph, became the religious center of the community. Here were found not only temples but also the state archives and the city mint beside the temple of Juno the Admonisher, *Juno Moneta*, hence our word for money. As these farmer soldiers established colonies across Italy and throughout the Mediterranean, the colonies too had their hill temples, their so-called capitols.

The area shown in the center of the photograph between the Palatine and Capitol was originally a low, marshy burial ground. In the seventh century B.C.E., Etruscan kings, whose cultural and political traditions were decisive in early Roman civilization, drained the marshes, paved the area, and turned it into a public meeting place, or forum. The Forum became the heart of the city. Through it ran the Sacred Way, the road that cuts diagonally from left to right in the photograph. At the south end, to the right of the photograph, was the marketplace, which bustled with shops and businesses. To the north was the *Comitium*, the meeting place of the citizens' assembly. Here the king and, in republican times, the popular assembly conducted political business. Just below it still stands the *Curia*, the meeting place of the Roman Senate, which survived because it was converted into a Christian church in the seventh century C.E.

Here too temples and monuments rose to meet religious and public needs. Perhaps the most ancient structure was the circular temple of Vesta, the hearth goddess, the surviving columns of which can be seen in the lower center of the photograph. In this temple consecrated virgins, the most honored women of Rome, tended the sacred fire, the symbol of the life of Rome. The ruins of the virgins' magnificent residence fill the lower right of the photograph. Just above it stood the royal residence, the *Regia*, which during the republic became the quarters of one of Rome's chief priests, the *pontifex maximus*. To the lower right stood the temple to the twin gods, Castor and Pollux, who were credited with bringing victory in the early days of the republic against Rome's Latin neighbors. In time, still other temples joined these, for honoring the gods and honoring Rome were one.

As Rome grew from a simple city to an empire, Roman values changed, and the Forum reflected these changes. Simple Etruscan architecture gave way to the Greek style of building. Marble replaced brick and stucco. Near the Curia, the golden milestone marked the point from which all distances were measured and to which all roads of the empire led. The turmoil of the last years of the republic, when powerful individuals sought to take over the state, also left its mark. In the center of the photograph the semicircular brown stone ruin is all that remains of the temple of the Divine Julius, erected on the spot where Julius Caesar's remains were cremated after his murder on the Ides of March. After his death, Caesar received divine honors, the first Roman to be so treated by his city. Next to the temple stands all that remains of the monumental arch of Caesar's adopted son, Octavian, known to history as Augustus, the first and greatest of the Roman emperors.

By the time of Caesar and Augustus, Rome had replaced its Forum, just as it had replaced its republican constitution and the traditions that had been the foundation of Rome's greatness. Caesar had begun and Augustus completed new forums, known collectively as the Forum of the Caesars, which lay beyond the trees at the top of the picture. Their successor Trajan (98–117 C.E.) would build a still greater one just beyond it. Still, for centuries of Romans and for the societies that succeeded them, the narrow space encompassing the Capitoline, Palatine, and the Forum was the epicenter of the city and the world.

The Western Mediterranean to 509 B.C.E.

Early Romans were a mix of indigenous and migrant pastoralists and warriors whose villages stood between Greek and Phoenician merchant adventurers to the south and Etruscan cities to the north. Rome's formula for success lay in learning from all of these neighbors, then dominating and conquering them, and finally adapting and incorporating elements of their traditions into those of Rome itself.

Civilization came late to the western Mediterranean, carried in the ships of Greeks and Phoenicians. While the great floodplain civilizations of Mesopotamia and Egypt and the Greek communities of the eastern Mediterranean were developing sophisticated systems of urban life and political organization, western Europe and North Africa knew only the scattered villages of simple farmers and pastoralists. However, Europe was rich in metals, and an indigenous Bronze Age culture developed slowly between 1500 and 1000 B.C.E., spreading widely north of the Alps and south into Italy and Spain.

The western shores of the Mediterranean did not escape the widespread crisis of the twelfth century B.C.E., which transformed so profoundly the established civilizations of Mycenae and the Fertile Crescent, but its exact effects on southern Europe are unknown. Sometime around the year 1000 B.C.E., a new, distinctive iron-using civilization, termed Villanovan, appeared in northern Italy.

No one knows whether the Villanovans were new arrivals in Italy or simply the descendants of previous inhabitants. However, around this same time small groups of warrior peoples did begin to infiltrate Italy from the east and the north, occupying the mountainous terrain of the Apennines and pushing the indigenous society west. These new arrivals shared no common organization or identity, but all spoke related Indo-European languages we call Italic, including Latin. These newcomers were warriors. Like the Dark Age Greeks, they soon developed the art of making iron weapons, which gave them a decided advantage over the older inhabitants of the peninsula. By 800 B.C.E., they were in firm control of the mountainous region of central Italy and threatened the coastal societies of the west and south.

Mercantile Carthage

Also around 800 B.C.E., Phoenicians arrived in the west, first as traders and then as colonists. Setting out in warships from the regions of Tyre, Sidon, and Byblos, they ventured beyond the Strait of Gibraltar in search of supplies of silver and tin. They established a trading post at Cadiz (*Gadir*, "walled place" in Phoenician) at which they could trade with the local inhabitants for silver from the Sierra Morena and for tin, which the Spanish (Iberians) obtained from distant Britain and Ireland. The Phoenicians established a series of bases along the route to and from Spain on the coast and on the islands of Corsica, Sicily, Ibiza, and Motya in the Mediterranean and at Utica and Carthage on the coast

of North Africa. Carthage was initially no more than a small anchorage for ships. Gradually, its population grew as overcrowding forced emigration from Tyre. When, in the sixth century B.C.E., Tyre was conquered by Nebuchadnezzar and incorporated into the Babylonian Empire, Carthage became an independent city and soon established itself as the center of an expanding Phoenician presence in the western Mediterranean.

The city was perfectly situated to profit both from the land and the sea. Its excellent double harbor, which had attracted the Phoenicians initially, made it an ideal port. The city was equally protected on land, situated on a narrow isthmus and surrounded by massive walls. As long as Carthage controlled the sea, its commercial center was secure from any enemies. The wealth of Punic (from *Puni* or *Poeni*, the Roman name for the Carthaginians) commerce was supplemented by the agricultural riches of the surrounding region, which produced grain and fruits for export in abundance, while inland the subject native population engaged in cattle raising and sheepherding for their masters.

Although superficially similar to many Greek cities, the Punic state differed profoundly from them in its government. Ordinary citizens had little involvement and, apparently, little interest in government, which

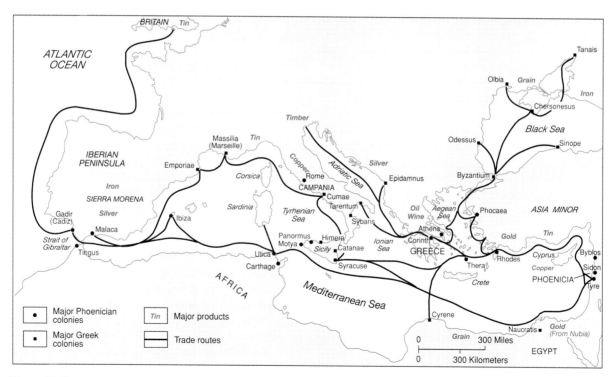

Western Mediterranean

was dominated by a merchant aristocracy. However, this aristocracy generously shared its commercial and imperial wealth with the rest of society, thus avoiding the class pressures that created tyrants in Greek cities.

By the middle of the sixth century B.C.E., Carthage was the center of a real empire. But in contrast with the Athenian empire of the following century, that of Carthage was much more successful at integrating other cities and peoples into its military and thus sharing the burden of warfare. As a society of merchants, Carthaginians mistrusted military leaders and carefully subordinated them to civil authority. Their choice was often based more on their trustworthiness than on military ability. These generals commanded mercenary armies consisting of Libyan light infantry, Numidian cavalry, Spanish hill people, Balearic sling throwers, Gallic infantry, Italians, and often Greeks. Only the fleet was composed primarily of Carthaginians. This multiethnic empire proved far more stable than any of those created by the Greeks, succeeding in victory and withstanding defeat to endure for over three centuries.

This traditional, conservative perspective of Carthaginian government was also evident in Carthaginian religion. The gods of Carthage were local variations of the Phoenician gods, especially Baal Hammon, the supreme god El of the Semitic world, and the goddess Tanit, a version of the Near Eastern goddess Asherat. Baal Hammon was an awesome figure. The Greeks equated him not with Zeus but with the more ancient supreme god, Kronos, a cruel tyrant who devoured his children. Tanit, goddess of fertility, assumed an importance equal to that of Baal Hammon, probably under the influence of the indigenous Libyan society.

Stable, prosperous, and devout, Carthage was the master of the western Mediterranean. But its dominion was not undisputed. From the sixth century B.C.E., the Punic empire felt the pressure of ambitious Greek cities eager to compete in the western Mediterranean.

The Western Greeks

The Greek arrival in the west was the result of a much more complex process than the trading policy of the Phoenicians. As explained in chapter 2, toward the end of the Dark Age, commerce, overpopulation, and civic tension sent Greek colonists out in all directions. In the eighth century B.C.E., Crete, Rhodes, Corinth, Argos, Chalcis, Eretria, and Naxos all established colonies in Sicily and southern Italy.

Both commercial rivalry and open warfare characterized the relationship between Greeks and Phoenicians in the western Mediterranean. In the sixth century B.C.E., Greeks in Sicily attempted to expel the Phoenicians from the island. In the fifth century B.C.E., Syracuse, under its tyrant Gelon (ca. 540–478 B.C.E.), threatened both Punic and Greek cities on the island. In an attempt to defend its colonies, in 480 B.C.E. Carthage launched an enormous force to support the Greeks against Gelon. At the battle of Himera, the Syracusans soundly defeated the Carthaginians.

Gelon's victory at Himera ushered in a period of prosperity and cultural achievement in Sicily only slightly less extraordinary than that which followed the victories of Marathon and Salamis in Greece. The tyrants of Syracuse, enriched with the spoils of victory, created a court whose magnificence, wealth, and generosity won admiration throughout the Greek world. This prosperity continued after the elimination of the tyranny in mid-century, and in 415 B.C.E., Syracuse was able to withstand Athens' attempt at conquest (see chapter 3, p. 78). Early in their struggle with the Sicilian Greeks, the Carthaginians found allies in the third major civilization of the West. These were the Etruscans, who in the seventh century B.C.E. dominated the western part of central Italy known as Etruria.

Etruscan Civilization

Etruscan civilization was the first great civilization to emerge in Italy. It coalesced slowly in Etruria over the course of the seventh century B.C.E. from diverse regional and political groups sharing a similar cultural and linguistic tradition. In the mid-sixth century B.C.E., in the face of Greek pressure from the south, twelve of these groups united in a religious and military confederation. Over the next one hundred years, the confederation expanded north into the Po Valley and south to Campania. Cities, including Rome, each initially ruled by a king, were the centers of Etruscan civilization, and everywhere the Etruscans spread they either improved upon existing towns or founded new ones. Still, the Etruscan confederation never developed into a centralized empire. Etruscan kings assumed power in conquered towns, but between the sixth and fifth centuries B.C.E., Etruscan kingship gave way to oligarchic governments, much as Greek monarchies did a bit earlier. In the place of kings, aristocratic assemblies selected magistrates, often paired together or combined into "colleges" to prevent individuals from seizing power. These oligarchic institutions provided the foundation for later Roman republican government.

The remnants of an ancient civilization, the Etruscans retained throughout their history social and cultural traditions long since vanished elsewhere in the Mediterranean. Society divided sharply into two classes, lords and servants. The lords' wealth was based on the rich agricultural regions of Etruria where grain grew in abundance and on the equally rich deposits of copper and iron. The vast majority of the population were actual slaves, working the lands and mines of the aristocracy.

The most striking aspect of Etruscan life to Greek contemporaries and to later Romans was the elevated status of Etruscan women. As in the much earlier Minoan civilization, women played an active, public role in society. Unlike elite Greek women, Etruscan women took part in banquets. They attended and even occasionally presided over dances, concerts, and sporting events. Women, as wives and mothers, were also active in political life. When a king died, his successor had to be designated and consecrated by the Etruscan queen to establish his legitimacy. Greeks such as Aristotle regarded the public behavior of Etruscan women as lewd. The great philosopher accused them of lying under the same cloak with men at banquets. The political role of women such as Tullia, wife of Tarquin the Proud (Lucius Tarquinius Superbus, d. ca. 510 B.C.E.), the last Etruscan king of Rome, also scandalized later Romans. The Roman historian Livy (59 B.C.E.–17 C.E.) writes that when Tullia was the first person to acknowledge her husband as the rightful king, he was so shocked that he sent her home. In truth, since kings needed the recognition of queens, he was surely grateful.

While the Etruscans were consolidating their hegemony in western Italy, they were also establishing their maritime power. From the seventh to the fifth centuries B.C.E., Etruscans controlled the Italian coast of the Tyrrhenian Sea as well as Sardinia, from which their ships could reach the coast of what is today France and Spain. Attempts to extend farther south into Greek southern Italy and toward the Greek colonies on the modern French coast brought the Etruscans and the Greeks into inevitable conflict. Etruscan cities fought sporadic sea battles against Greek cities in the waters of Sicily as well as off the coasts of Corsica and Etruria. Common hostility toward the Greeks as well as complementary economic interests soon brought the Etruscans into alliances with Carthage. Toward the end of the sixth century B.C.E., Etruscan cities including Rome signed a series of pacts with Carthage that created military

On the Etruscan sarcophagus of Larthia Scianti a matron reclines as at a banquet. Much of our knowledge of this first Italian civilization comes from the elaborate paintings and statuary found in Etruscan cemeteries.

alliances against Syracuse and other Greek rivals. Etruscan fleets scored some minor victories, but they were no match for Syracuse. In 474 B.C.E., shortly after the battle of Himera, the Syracusans destroyed the Etruscan fleet off Cumae. The defeat marked the beginning of Etruscan decline. Through the fifth century B.C.E., Etruscan cities lost control of the sea to the Greeks. Around the same time, Celts from north of the Alps invaded and conquered the Po Valley. And to the south, Etruscans saw their inland territories progressively slipping into the hands of their former subjects, the Romans, who had expelled their last king in 509 B.C.E.

These Romans had learned and profited from their domination by the Etruscans as well as from their dealings with Greek and Carthaginian civilizations. From these early civilizations on the western shores of the Mediterranean Sea, Rome had begun to acquire the commercial, political, and military expertise to begin its long development from a small city to a great empire.

From City to Empire, 509–146 B.C.E.

What manner of people were these who came from obscure origins to rule an empire? Their own answer would have been simple: They were farmers and soldiers, simple people accustomed to simple, straightforward actions. Throughout their long history, Romans liked to refer to the clear-cut models provided by their semi-legendary predecessors: Cincinnatus, the farmer, called away to the supreme office of dictator in time of danger, then returning to his plow; Horatius Cocles, the valiant warrior who held back an Etruscan army on the Tiber bridge until it could be demolished and then, despite his wounds, swam across the river to safety; Lucretia, the wife who chose death after dishonor. These were myths, but they were important myths to Romans, who preferred concrete models to abstract principles. They were indeed part of the Roman success formula: devotion to family and to the state, determination and steadfastness, a willingness to incorporate other peoples and their cultures into those of Rome, and a genius for organization and administration at home and abroad.

Latin Rome

Prior to the seventh century B.C.E., civilization in Italy meant Etruria to the north and Greater Greece to the south. In between lay Latium, a marshy region punctured by hills on which a sparse population could find protection from disease and enemies. This population was an amalgam of aboriginal Ligurians and the more recently arrived Latins and Sabines who lived a pastoral life in small scattered villages.

The Alban Hills south of the Tiber were a center of Latin population. Sometime in the eighth century B.C.E., roughly forty Latin villages formed a loose confederation, the Alban League, for military and religious purposes. Not long after, in the face of an expanding Etruscan confederation from the north and Sabine penetration from the east, the Albans established a village on the steep Palatine hill to the north. The Palatine was one of several hills overlooking a natural ford on the Tiber. This Alban village, called Roma Quadrata, was

soon joined by other Latin and Sabine settlements on nearby hills. By the end of the eighth century B.C.E., seven Latin villages along the route from the Tiber to Alba had formed a league for mutual defense and shared religious cults.

Early Roman society was composed of households; clans, or *gentes*; and village councils, or *curiae* (sing. *curia*). The male head of each household, the *paterfamilias*, had power of life and death over its members and was responsible for the proper worship of the spirits of the family's ancestors, on whom continued prosperity depended. Within some villages, these families were grouped into gentes, which claimed descent from a semimythical ancestor.

Male members of village families formed councils, which were essentially religious organizations but also provided a forum for public discussion. These curiae tended to be dominated by gentes, but all males could participate, including *plebeians*, those who belonged to the *plebs*, that is, families not organized into gentes. Later, the leaders of the gentes called themselves *patricians* ("descendants of fathers") and claimed superiority to the plebs.

Important plebeian and patrician families increased their power through a system of *clientage*, which remained a fundamental aspect of social and political organization throughout Roman history. Clients were free men who depended on the protection of a more powerful individual or family and who owed various services, including political support, in return for this protection.

Villages grouped together for military and voting purposes into ethnic *tribus*, or tribes, each composed of a number of curiae. Assemblies of all members of the curiae expressed approval of major decisions, especially declaration of war and the selection of new kings, and thus played a real if limited political role. More powerful although less formal was the role of the *senate* (assembly of elders), which was composed of heads of families. Kings served as religious leaders, the primary means of communication between gods and men. Through the early Latin period royal power remained fundamentally religious and limited by the senate, curiae, gentes, and families.

The seven villages that made up primitive Rome developed independently of their Etruscan and Greek neighbors. Initially, Romans lived in thatched huts, tended their flocks on the hillsides, and maintained their separate village identities. By the seventh century B.C.E., they had built fortifications and other structures indicating the beginnings of a dynamic civic life. This independent course of development changed in the middle of the seventh century B.C.E., when the Etruscans overwhelmed Latium and absorbed it into their civilization.

Etruscan Rome

The Etruscans introduced in Latium and especially in Rome their political, religious, and economic traditions. Etruscan kings and magistrates ruled Latin towns, increasing the power of traditional Latin kingship. The kings were not only religious leaders, directing the cults of their humanlike gods, but also led the army, served as judges, and held supreme political power. As Latium became an integral part of the Etruscan world, the Tiber became an important commercial route. For the first time, Rome began to enter the wider orbit of Mediterranean civilization. The town's population swelled with the arrival of merchants and craft workers.

As Rome's importance grew, so did its size. Surrounding villages were added to the original seven, as were the Sabine colonies on the Quirinal and Capitoline hills. Etruscan engineers drained the marshes into a great canal flowing to the Tiber, thus opening to settlement the lowlands between the hills. This improvement enabled them to create and pave the Forum, the center of civic, religious, and commercial life. The Etruscans were also builders, constructing a series of vast fortifications encircling the town. Under Etruscan influence, the fortified Capitoline hill, which served much like a Greek acropolis, became the cult center with the erection of the temple to Jupiter, the supreme god; Juno, his consort; and Minerva, an Etruscan goddess of craftwork similar to Athena. In its architecture, religion, commerce, and culture, Latin Rome was deeply indebted to its Etruscan conquerors.

As important as the physical and cultural changes brought by the Etruscans was their reorganization of the society. As in Greece, this restructuring was tied to changes in the military. The Etruscans had learned from the Greeks the importance of hoplite tactics, and King Servius Tullius (578–534 B.C.E.) introduced this system of warfare into Rome. This change led to the abolition of the earlier curia-based military and political system in favor of one based only on property holding. The king divided Roman society into two groups. Those landowners wealthy enough to provide armed military service were organized into five *classes* (from which the word *class* is derived), ranked according to the quality of their arms and hence their wealth. Each class was further divided into military units called centuries. Members of these centuries constituted the centuriate assembly, which replaced the older curial assemblies for such vital decisions as the election of magistrates and the declaration of war. The rest of the society was *infra classem* (literally "under class"). Owning no property, they were excluded from military and political activity.

With this military and political reorganization came a reconstruction of the tribal system. Servius Tullius abolished the old tribal organization in favor of geographically organized tribes into which newcomers could easily be incorporated. Henceforth, while the family remained powerful, involvement in public life was based on property and geography. Latins, Sabines, Ligurians, and Etruscans could all be active citizens of the growing city.

As the old tribal units and curiae declined, divisions between the patricians and the plebeians grew more distinct. During the monarchy the patricians became an upper stratum of wealthy nobles. They forbade marriage outside their own circle, forming a closed, self-perpetuating group that monopolized the senate, religious rites, and magisterial offices. Although partially protected by the kings, the plebeians, whether rich or poor, were pressed into a second-class status and denied access to political power.

In less than two centuries, the Etruscans transformed Rome into a prosperous, unified urban center

By the middle of the second century B.C.E., the Roman republic had evolved to the point where private citizens could cast private ballots. This Roman coin of 137 B.C.E. features a Roman voter dropping a stone tablet into a voting urn.

that played an important role in the economic and po-litical life of central Italy. They laid the foundations of a free citizenry, incorporating Greek models of military and social organization. The transformations brought about by the Etruscan kings became an enduring part of Rome. The Etruscans themselves did not. Around 509 B.C.E. the Roman patricians expelled the last king, Tar-quin the Proud, and established a republic—a term de-rived from the Latin *res publica*, public property, as op-posed to *res privata*, private property of the king.

Rome and Italy

Later Roman historians, always the moralizers, made the expulsion of King Tarquin the dramatic result of his son's lust. According to legend, Sextus, the son of Tar-quin, raped Lucretia, a virtuous Roman matron. She told her husband of the crime and then took her own life. Outraged, the Roman patricians were said to have driven the king and his family from the city. Actually, monarchy was giving way to oligarchic republics across Etruria in the sixth century B.C.E. Rome was hardly ex-ceptional. However, the establishment of the Roman republic coincided roughly with the beginning of the Etruscan decline, allowing Rome to assert itself and to develop its Latin and Etruscan traditions in unique ways. The patrician oligarchy had engineered the end of the monarchy and patricians dominated the new repub-lic at the expense of the plebs who, in losing the king, lost their only defender. Governmental institutions of the early republic developed within this context of pa-trician supremacy.

Characteristic of republican institutions was that at every level, power was shared by two or more equals elected for fixed terms. This practice of shared power was intended to ensure that magistrates would consult with each other before making decisions and that no individual could achieve supreme power at any level. Replacing the king were the two *consuls*, each elected by the assembly for a one-year term. Initially only the con-suls held the *imperium*, the supreme power to com-mand, to execute the law, and to impose the death penalty. Only in moments of grave crisis might a con-sul, with the approval of the senate, name a single *dictator* with extraordinary absolute power for a very brief period, never more than six months. In time other magistracies developed to perform specialized functions.

During the early republic, wealthy patricians, aided by their clients, monopolized the senate and the mag-istracies. Patricians also controlled the system of priest-hoods, which they held for life. With political and reli-gious power came economic power. The poorer plebs were increasingly indebted to wealthy patricians, losing their property, and with it the basis for military service and political participation.

The plebs began to organize in response to patrician control. On several occasions in the first half of the fifth century B.C.E., the whole plebeian order withdrew a short distance from the city, refusing to return or to serve in the military until conflicts with the patricians were resolved. In time the plebs created their own as-sembly, the Council of the Plebs, which enacted laws binding on all plebeians. This council founded its own temples and elected magistrates called *tribunes*, who protected the plebs from arbitrary patrician power. Any-one harming the tribunes, whether patrician or plebe-ian, could be killed by the plebs without trial. With their own assembly, magistracies, and religious cults, the plebeians were well on the way to creating a separate republic.

This conflict between the plebeians and the patri-cians, known as the Struggle of Orders, threatened to tear the Roman society apart at the same moment that pressure from hostile neighbors placed Rome on the defensive. Roman preeminence in Latium had ended with the expulsion of the last king and enemies both north and south began periodic attacks against Rome.

This military pressure, and the inability of the patri-cians to meet it alone, ultimately forced them to a com-promise with the plebeians. Around 450 B.C.E. the plebs won a victory with the codification of basic Roman law, the Law of the Twelve Tables, which announced publicly the basic rights of all free citi-zens. Around the same time, the state began to absorb the plebeian political and religious organizations intact. Gradually, priesthoods, magistracies, and thus the sen-ate were opened to plebeians. The consulship was the last prize finally won by the plebs in 367 B.C.E. In 287 B.C.E., as the result of a final secession of the plebs, the decisions of the plebeian assembly became bind-ing on all citizens, patrician and plebeian alike.

Bitter differences at home did not prevent patricians and plebs from presenting a united front against their enemies abroad. External conquest deflected internal hostility and profited both orders. By the beginning of the fourth century B.C.E., the united patrician-plebeian state had turned back its enemies and was expanding its rule both north and south. Roman legions, com-manded by patricians but formed of the whole spec-trum of property-owning Romans, reestablished Roman preeminence in Latium and then began a series of wars

THE TWELVE TABLES

■ The recording of the Twelve Tables in 449 B.C.E. was a great victory for the plebs both because it curbed the exercise of arbitrary power by patrician magistrates and because it established the principle of equality before the law.

TABLE I Preliminaries to and Rules for a Trial

If plaintiff summons defendant to court, he shall go. If he does not go, plaintiff shall call witness thereto. Then only shall he take defendant by force.

If defendant shirks or takes to his heels, plaintiff shall lay hands on him . . .

For a landowner, a landowner shall be surety; but for a proletarian person, let any one who is willing be his protector . . .

When parties make a settlement of the case, the judge shall announce it. If they do not reach a settlement, they shall state the outline of their case in the meeting place or Forum before noon . . .

TABLE III Execution; Law of Debt

When a debt has been acknowledged, or judgment about the matter has been pronounced in court, thirty days must be the legitimate time of grace. After that, the debtor may be arrested by laying on of hands. Bring him into court. If he does not satisfy the judgment, or no one in court offers himself as surety in his behalf, the creditor may take the defaulter with him. He may bind him either in stocks or in fetters . . . The debtor, if he wishes, may live on his own. If he does not live on his own, the person [who shall hold him in bonds] shall give him one pound of grits for each day . . .

TABLE IV Rights of Head of Family

Quickly kill . . . a dreadfully deformed child.

TABLE VI Guardianship; Succession

Females shall remain in guardianship even when they have attained their majority . . . except Vestal Virgins.

Conveyable possessions of a woman under guardianship of agnates cannot be rightfully acquired by [long-term possession], save such possessions as have been delivered up by her with a guardian's sanction . . .

TABLE IX Public Laws

Laws of personal exception [i.e., bills of attainder] must not be proposed; cases in which the penalty affects the person of a citizen must not be decided except through the greatest assembly and through those whom the censors have placed upon the register of citizens . . .

TABLE XI Supplementary Laws

Intermarriage shall not take place between plebeians and patricians.

---

that brought most of Italy under Roman control. By 265 B.C.E., Rome had absorbed the Etruscan cities of the north and the Hellenistic cities of the south.

The Roman conquest benefited patrician and plebeian alike. While the patricians acquired wealth and power, the plebeians received a prize of equal value: land. Since landowning was a prerequisite for military service, this distribution created still more peasant soldiers for further expeditions. Still, while the constant

supply of new land did much to diffuse the tensions between orders, it did not actually resolve them. Into the late third century B.C.E., debt and landlessness remained major problems creating tensions in Roman society. Probably not more than one-half of the citizen population owned land by 200 B.C.E.

The Roman manner of treating conquered populations was radically different from anything seen before, and contributed to Rome's success. In war, no one could

Terra-cotta statuette of one of Hannibal's elephants.

Hannibal's Elephants

Elephants were the most spectacular, extravagant, and unpredictable element in ancient warfare. Since the time of Alexander the Great, Hellenistic kings and commanders tried to use the great strength, size, and relative invulnerability of these animals to throw opposing infantry into confusion and flight.

Elephants' unusual smell and loud trumpeting also panicked horses not accustomed to these strange beasts, wreaking havoc with cavalry units. *Mahouts*, or drivers, who were usually Indians, controlled and directed the animal from a seat on the elephant's neck. Normally each elephant carried a small,

towerlike structure from which archers could shoot down on the massed infantry. However, like modern tanks, the primary importance of the beasts was the enormous shock effect created by a charge of massed war elephants. Still, they often created more problems than they solved.

Indian princes had used elephants in warfare for centuries. When Alexander the Great crossed the Indus in 326 B.C.E., the Indian king Porus came within an ace of defeating the Greek conqueror, thanks largely to his more than two hundred elephants. In 302 B.C.E., Seleucus I received 500 war elephants from an Indian king as part of a peace treaty. The next year these animals contributed greatly to Seleucus' victory over Antigonus at Ipsus, which made possible the creation of his separatist kingdom in Syria.

The Romans first experienced the terror of elephant charges in their war against the Greeks in the south of Italy. They next encountered them in the Punic wars. The Carthaginians had learned to use elephants around the middle of the third century B.C.E., capturing them in the Atlas Mountains of North Africa and putting them to good use in Spain. When Hannibal decided to invade Italy via the Alps, he naturally wanted to take along these formidable beasts.

This was easier said than done. In 217 B.C.E., Hannibal set out from New Carthage (now Cartagena) in Spain and some weeks later arrived at the Rhone River with an army that included roughly 38,000 infantry, 8,000 cavalry, and 37 elephants. Ferrying the pachyderms across the river was a major undertaking since the frightened animals refused to walk onto rafts.

Finally, the Carthaginians lashed together a series of rafts, the first two on dry land, the others forming a pontoon into the river. The sides were piled with earth so that the elephants could not see that they were not walking on dry land. Their Indian mahouts led them a few at a time to the end rafts, which were then cut free and towed across the river by boats. Most of the animals, seeing water on all sides, remained terrified but still. Others panicked, upsetting the rafts, falling into the river, and drowning their mahouts. Once in the water, however, most of the elephants were able to swim to the far shore.

As difficult as the river crossing was, it paled in comparison with the problems of crossing the Alps. As Hannibal moved slowly up the valley of the Arc, his troops were under constant harassment from the local Celtic tribes. From high up in the passes, the Celts showered down rocks, throwing the pack animals into confusion and causing them to hurl themselves off the narrow paths. Landslides carried away portions of the track and, as Hannibal's army advanced, the path became too narrow for elephants and, eventually, even for horses and mules. Engineers had to rebuild paths, taking up valuable time. At the top of the pass, new snow forced a three-day halt while

a new road wide enough for the elephants to descend was constructed down the more precipitous Italian side of the mountain. During this time the elephants were without fodder and suffered enormously. Finally, after fifteen days Hannibal's depleted troops reached the fertile plains of the Po Valley. He had lost almost half of his infantry and cavalry since reaching the Rhone and more than half of his elephants.

Was it worth it? In his first major encounter with the Romans at the Trebia River, Hannibal split his elephants into two groups to protect the wings of his infantry. The beasts were a major factor in the devastating defeat inflicted on the Romans. However, shortly after, the cold and snow killed all but one of the animals. This lone survivor became Hannibal's personal command post. The great Punic victories at Lake Trasimene and Cannae were won without the assistance of the pachyderm shock force. In 207 B.C.E., Hannibal's brother Hasdrubal (d. 207 B.C.E.) entered Italy with ten elephants, but at the battle of Metaurus they panicked, stampeded, and did more harm to the Carthaginians than to the Romans.

The next time that Hannibal faced a Roman army with his full

contingent of war elephants was at Zama. There his eighty animals proved a bitter disappointment. Ordered to charge, many of the elephants panicked at the sound of trumpets and horns, wheeled about, and went raging into the massed African cavalry arrayed on the Punic side. Others did charge, but with limited effect. The Romans had learned to take aim at the mahouts, killing them and leaving the animals without direction. The Romans also allowed the elephants to charge past, then attacked their flanks with javelins and their legs with swords. Finally, the Roman commander had taken the precaution of leaving wide paths between his formations. Many of the animals simply charged down these paths and disappeared into the open fields beyond the Roman lines.

The Romans themselves made little use of elephants in warfare. These exotic beasts better suited the inflated egos of kings than the practical minds of Roman generals. The Romans preferred the disciplined advance of a well-trained cohort of Roman legionnaires to the charge of a war elephant. It was with these steadfast and resolute infantrymen rather than with raging elephants that they conquered an empire.

match the Roman legions for ruthless, thorough destruction. Yet no conquerors had ever shown themselves so generous in victory. After crushing the Latin revolt of 338 B.C.E., The Romans incorporated virtually all of the Latins into the Roman citizenry. Later colonies founded outside Latium were given the same status as Latin cities. Other more-distant conquered peoples were considered allies and required to provide troops but no tribute to Rome. In time, they too might become citizens.

The implications of these measures were revolutionary. By extending citizenship to conquered neighbors and by offering the future possibility to allies, Rome tied their fate to its own. Rather than potentially subversive subjects, conquered populations became strong supporters. Thus, in contrast to the Hellenistic cities of the east where Greeks jealously guarded their status from the indigenous population, Rome's colonies acted as magnets, drawing local populations into the Roman cultural and political orbit. Greeks were scandalized by the Roman tradition of giving citizenship even to freed slaves. By the end of the fourth century B.C.E., some of the sons of these freedmen were finding a place in the senate. Finally, in all of its wars of conquest, Rome claimed a moral mandate. Romans went to great lengths to demonstrate that theirs were just wars, basing their claims on alleged acts of aggression by their enemies, on

the appeal to Rome by its allies, and, increasingly, by presenting themselves as the preservers and defenders of Greek traditions of freedom. Both these political and propagandistic measures proved successful. Between 265 B.C.E. and 91 B.C.E., few serious revolts shook the peace and security of Italy south of the Po.

Benevolent treatment of the conquered spurred further conquest. Since subject cities and peoples did not pay tribute, the only way for Rome to benefit from its conquests or to exercise its authority was to demand and use troops. By 264 B.C.E., all of Italy was united under Roman hegemony. Roman expansion finally brought Rome into conflict with the great Mediterranean power of the west, Carthage.

Rome and the Mediterranean

Since its earliest days, Rome had allied itself with Carthage against the Greek cities of Italy. The zones of interest of the two cities had been quite separate. Carthage was a sea empire, while Rome was a land-based power without a navy. The Greeks, aspiring to power on land and sea, posed a common threat to both Rome and Carthage. However, once Rome had conquered the Greek cities to the south, it became enmeshed in the affairs of neighboring Sicily, a region with well-established Carthaginian interests. There, in 265 B.C.E., a group of Italian mercenary pirates in Messana, threatened by Syracuse, requested Roman assistance. The senate refused but the plebeian assembly, eager for booty, exercised its newly won right to legislate for the republic and accepted. Shortly afterward the Romans invaded Sicily, and Syracuse turned to its old enemy, Carthage, for assistance. The First Punic War had begun.

The First Punic War, which lasted from 265 to 241 B.C.E., was a costly, brutal, and drawn-out affair, which Rome won by dint of persistence and methodical calculation rather than strategic brilliance. Rome invaded and concluded an alliance with Syracuse in 263 B.C.E. The war rapidly became a sea war. Rome had little previous naval experience but quickly learned the rules of the game and then rewrote them to its own advantage. Still, it took over 20 years before Rome forced the Carthaginian commander, Hamilcar Barca (ca. 270–229 B.C.E.), to surrender simply because the Romans could afford to build one more fleet than he. Carthage paid a huge indemnity and abandoned Sicily. Syracuse and Messana became allies of Rome. In a break with tradition, Rome obligated the rest of Sicily to pay a true tribute in the form of a tithe (one-tenth) of their crops.

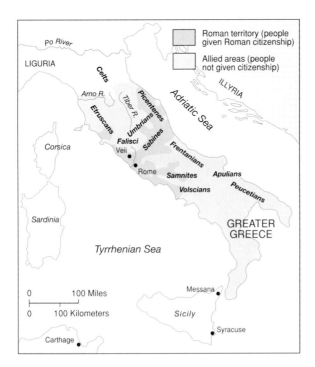

Rome in 264 B.C.E.

Shortly after that, Rome helped itself to Sardinia as well, from which it again demanded tribute, not simply troops. Rome had established an empire.

During the next two decades Roman legions defeated the Ligurians on the northwest coast, the Celtic Gauls south of the Alps, and the Illyrians along the Adriatic coast. At the same time, Carthage fought a bitter battle against its own mercenary armies, which it had been unable to pay off after its defeat. Carthage then began the systematic creation of an empire in Spain. Trade between Carthage and Rome reached the highest level in history, but trade did not create friendship. On both sides, powerful leaders saw the treaty of 241 B.C.E. as just a pause in a fight to the death. Fearful and greedy Romans insisted that Carthage had to be destroyed for the security of Rome.

Fear of Carthaginian successes in Spain, led after Hamilcar's death by his son-in-law Hasdrubal (d. 221 B.C.E.) and his son Hannibal (247–183 B.C.E.), provoked Rome to war in 218 B.C.E. As soon as this Second Punic War had begun, Hannibal began an epic march north out of Spain, along the Mediterranean coast, and across the Alps. In spite of great hardships, he was able to transport over 23,000 troops and approximately eighteen war elephants into the plains of northern Italy. Hannibal's brilliant generalship brought victory after victory to the Carthaginian forces. (See Special Feature, "Hannibal's Elephants," pp. 142–143.) Soon many of Rome's Gallic, Italian, Etruscan, and Greek allies turned against Rome, hoping to benefit from a Carthaginian victory.

Three things saved the Roman state. First, while some important allies and colonies defected, the

Relief of a Roman war galley. The deck is crowded with infantrymen. Galleys were usually rowed by slaves while the soldiers remained fresh for the task of subduing enemy ships.

majority held firm. Rome's traditions of sharing the fruits of victory with its allies, extending the rights of Roman citizenship, and protecting central and southern Italy against its enemies proved stronger than the appeals of Hannibal. The second reason for Rome's survival was the tremendous social solidarity all classes and factions of its population showed during these desperate years. In spite of the internal tensions between patricians and plebeians, their ultimate dedication to Rome never faltered. The final reason for Rome's ultimate success was Publius Cornelius Scipio (236–184 B.C.E.), also known as Scipio the Elder, a commander able to force Hannibal from Italy. Scipio, who earned the title Africanus for his victory, accomplished this not by attacking Hannibal directly, but by taking the war home to the enemy, first in Spain and then in Africa, where at Zama in 202

B.C.E. he defeated Hannibal and destroyed the Carthaginian army. Saddled with a huge indemnity and forced to abandon all of its territories and colonies to Rome, Carthage had become in effect a Roman subject.

But still this humiliating defeat was not enough for Rome. While some Roman senators favored allowing Carthage to survive as a means of keeping the Roman plebs under senatorial control, others demanded destruction. Ultimately trumped-up reasons were found to renew the war in 149 B.C.E. In contrast to the desperate, hard-fought campaigns of the Second Punic War, the Third was an unevenly matched slaughter. In 146 B.C.E., Scipio Aemilianus (184–129 B.C.E.), or Scipio the Younger, the adopted grandson of Scipio the Elder, overwhelmed Carthage and sold its few survivors into slavery. As a symbolic act of final destruction, he then

POLYBIUS DESCRIBES THE SACK OF NEW CARTHAGE

■ *In the following selection, the Greek historian Polybius, who was a close friend of the adopted grandson of Scipio Africanus, describes the Roman capture of New Carthage in Spain in 210 B.C. during the Second Punic War. Before a siege, Romans offered their enemies generous terms, but once the siege was begun, they offered no terms. The passage shows the combination of brutality and thoroughness with which the Romans liquidated those who defied them.*

Scipio, when he judged that a large enough number of troops had entered the town, let loose the majority of them against the inhabitants, according to the Roman custom; their orders were to exterminate every form of life they encountered, sparing none, but not to start pillaging until the word was given to do so. This practice is adopted to inspire terror, and so when cities are taken by the Romans you often see not only the corpses of human beings but dogs cut in half and the dismembered limbs of other animals, and on this occasion the carnage was especially frightful because of the large size of the population.

Scipio himself with about 1,000 men pressed on toward the citadel. Here the Carthaginian commander Margo at first put up some resistance, but as soon as he knew for certain that the city had been captured he sent a message to plead for his safety, and handed over the citadel. Once this had happened the signal was given to stop the slaughter and the troops then began to pillage the city. When darkness fell . . . Scipio . . . recalled the rest of his troops from the private houses of the city and ordered them through the military tribunes to collect all the spoils in the marketplace, each maniple bringing its own share . . . Next day all the booty . . . was collected in the marketplace, where the military tribunes divided it among their respective legions, according to the Roman custom . . . All those who have been detailed to collect the plunder then bring it back, each man to his own legion, and after it has been sold, the tribunes distribute the proceeds equally among all.

From Polybius, *The Rise of the Roman Empire.*

had the site razed, plowed, and cursed. Carthage's fertile hinterland became the property of wealthy Roman senators.

In the same year that Carthage was destroyed, Roman armies destroyed Corinth, a second great center of Mediterranean commerce. This victory marked the culmination of Roman imperialist expansion east into the Greek and Hellenistic world, which had begun with the conquest of Illyria. This expansion was not simply the result of Roman imperialist ambitions. The Hellenistic states, in their constant warring and bickering, had drawn Rome into their conflicts against their neighbors. Greek states asked the Roman senate to arbitrate their disputes. Pergamum requested military assistance against Macedonia. Appealing to Rome's claims as "liberator," cities pressed the senate to preserve their freedom in the face of aggressive expansion by their more powerful neighbors. In a series of intermittent, uncoordinated, and sporadic engagements, Rome did intervene, although its real focus was on its life-and-death struggle with Carthage. Roman intentions may not have been conquest, but Roman intervention upset the balance of power in the Hellenistic world. The price of Roman arbitration, intervention, and protection was loss of independence. Gradually the Roman shadow fell over the eastern Mediterranean.

The Roman Republic

509 B.C.E.	Expulsion of the last Etruscan king; beginning of Roman republic
295 B.C.E.	Rome extends rule north to Po Valley
265–241 B.C.E.	First Punic War
264 B.C.E.	All of Italy under Roman control
218–202 B.C.E.	Second Punic War
149–146 B.C.E.	Third Punic War; Carthage is destroyed
136–132 B.C.E.	First Sicilian slave war
133–121 B.C.E.	Gracchi reform programs
91–82 B.C.E.	Social War and civil war (Marius vs. Sulla)
79–27 B.C.E.	Era of civil wars
63 B.C.E.	Cicero elected consul; Pompey conquers eastern Mediterranean
60 B.C.E.	First Triumvirate (Pompey, Crassus, Caesar)
49–48 B.C.E.	Civil war (Caesar defeats Pompey)
44 B.C.E.	Caesar murdered
43–32 B.C.E.	Second Triumvirate (Antony, Lepidus, Octavian)
31 B.C.E.	Octavian defeats Antony and Cleopatra at Actium

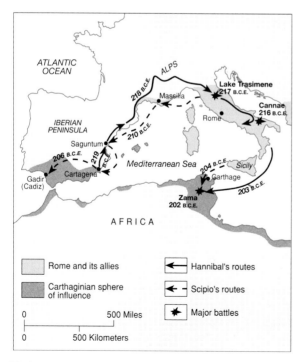

The Punic Wars

In the west, in northern Italy, Spain, and North Africa, Roman conquest had been direct and complete. Tribal structures had been replaced with Roman provinces governed by former magistrates or proconsuls. In the east, Rome preferred to work through the existing political hierarchies. Still, Rome cultivated its image as protector of Greek liberties against the Macedonian and Seleucid monarchies and preferred indirect control to annexation. Its power was no less real for being indirect.

By 146 B.C.E., the Roman republic controlled the whole rim of the Mediterranean from Rhodes in the east across Greece, Dalmatia, Italy, southern Gaul, Spain, and North Africa. Even Syria and Egypt, although nominally independent, bowed before Roman will. Roman perseverance and determination, its citizen army, republican government, and genius for adaptation and organization, had brought Rome from obscurity to the greatest power the West had ever known. The republic had endured great adversity. It would not survive prosperity.

Republican Civilization

Territorial conquest, the influx of unprecedented riches, and exposure to sophisticated Hellenistic civilization ultimately overwhelmed earlier Roman civilization. This civilization had been created by stubborn farmers and soldiers who valued above all else duty, simplicity, and piety and whose political and cultural institutions had been flexible and accommodating. This unique blend was the source of strength that led Rome to greatness, but its limitations prevented the republic from resolving its internal social tensions and the external problems caused by the burden of empire.

Farmers and Soldiers

Rome rose to world power on the strength of its military, composed neither of aristocrats nor professional soldiers but of farmers. The ideal Roman farmer was not the great estate owner of the Greek world, but the smallholder, the dirt farmer of central Italy. The most important crop of Roman farms was citizens. Nor was the ideal Roman soldier the gallant cavalryman but rather the solid foot soldier. Cavalry, composed of wealthy citizens who made up the elite equestrian order (from the Latin *equus*, horse), and especially allies, provided reconnaissance and protected Roman flanks. However, the main fighting force was the infantry. Sometime in the early republic the Greek phalanx was transformed into the Roman legion, a flexible unit composed of thirty companies of 120 men each.

Constant training, careful preparation, and painstaking execution characterized every aspect of Roman military expeditions. Wars were won as much by engineering feats as by feats of arms. Engineers constructed bridges, siege machines, and catapults. By the time of the late republic, Roman armies on the march could construct identical camps each night, quickly building a strong square fort 2,150 feet on a side. Within the camp, every unit had exactly the same location for its quarters, as did the commander and paymaster. The chain of command was rigidly maintained from the commander, a Roman consul, through military tribunes and centurions, two of whom commanded each company of 120 men.

These solid, methodical troops, the backbone of the republican armies that conquered the Mediterranean, were among the victims of that conquest. The pressures of constant international warfare were destroying the farmer-soldiers whom the traditionalists loved to praise. When the Roman sphere of interest had been confined to central Italy, farmers could do their planting in spring, serve in the army during the summer months, and return home to care for their farms in time for harvest. When Rome's wars became international expeditions lasting for years, many soldiers, unable to work their lands while doing military service, had to mortgage their farms in order to support their families. When they returned they often found that during their prolonged absences they had lost their farms to wealthy aristocratic moneylenders. Without land, they and their sons were excluded from further military service and sank into the growing mass of desperately poor, disenfranchised citizens.

The Roman Family

The family was the basic unit of society and of the state. In Roman tradition, the *paterfamilias* was the master of the family, which in theory included his wife, children, and slaves, over whom he exercised the power of life and death. This authority lasted as long as he lived. Only at his death did his sons, even if long grown and married, achieve legal and financial independence.

Roman women were not kept in seclusion as in Greece, but they rarely exercised independent power in this male-dominated world. Before marriage, a Roman girl was subject to the authority of her father. When she married, her father traditionally transferred legal guardianship to her husband, thus severing her bonds to her paternal family. A husband could divorce his wife at will, returning her and her dowry to her father. However, within the family, wives did exercise real though informal authority. Part of this authority came from their role in the moral education of their children and the direction of the household. Part also came from their control over their dowries. Widows might exercise even greater authority in the raising of their children.

Paternal authority over children was absolute. Not all children born into a marriage became members of the family. The Law of the Twelve Tables allowed defective children to be killed for the good of the family. Newborn infants were laid on the ground before the father, who decided whether the child should be raised. By picking up a son, he accepted the child into the family. Ordering that a daughter be nursed similarly signified acceptance. If there were too many mouths to feed or the child was simply unwanted, the father could command that the infant be killed or abandoned. Nor were all sons born into Roman families. Romans made use of adoption for many purposes. Families without heirs could adopt children. Powerful political and military figures might adopt promising young men as their political heirs. These adopted sons held the same legal rights as the natural offspring of the father and thus were integral members of his family.

Slaves, too, were members of the family. On the one hand, slaves were property without personal rights. On the other, they might live and work alongside the free members of the family, worship the family gods, and enjoy the protection and endure the authority of the paterfamilias. In fact, the authority of the paterfamilias was roughly the same over slave and free members of the family. If he desired, he could sell the free members of the family into slavery.

In the wake of imperial conquests, the Roman family and its environment began to change in ways disturbing to many of the oligarchy. Some women, perhaps in imitation of their more liberated Hellenistic sisters, began to take a more active role in public life. One example is Cornelia, a daughter of Scipio Africanus. After her husband's death in 154 B.C.E., she refused to remarry, devoting herself instead to raising her children, administering their inheritance, and directing their political careers.

Some married women, too, escaped the authority of their husbands. When fathers did not transfer authority over daughters to their husbands, these daughters remained under their father's authority as long as he lived. Upon his death, these women became independent persons, able to manage their own affairs without the consent of or interference from their husbands. Although as legal bonds loosened, the sentimental bonds of affection may have increased between many husbands and wives and parents and children, this also meant that the wife's relationship to her children was weakened. Roman mothers were not legally related to their children and wives and mothers were not legally part of their husband's families. Thus the wife's brothers, not her own children, were her natural heirs. Just as adoption created political bonds, marriage to daughters sealed alliances between men. However, when these alliances fell apart or more advantageous ones presented themselves, fathers could force their daughters to divorce their husbands and to marry someone else.

Not every Roman family could afford its own *domus* and in the aftermath of the imperial expansion, housing problems for the poor became acute. In Rome and other towns of Italy, shopkeepers lived in small houses attached to their shops or in rooms behind their workplaces. Peasants forced off their land and crowded into

The progress of a Roman son. At left the baby nurses while the proud father looks on. The toddler in his father's arms soon gives way to the young boy playing with a donkey and cart. The maturing youth is seen at right reciting his lessons.

A street in Herculaneum. This Roman town was buried in the eruption of Mt. Vesuvius in 79 C.E., along with the nearby city of Pompeii. A blanket of volcanic ash and pumice preserved the archeological treasures until the sites were rediscovered in modern times.

cities found shelter in multistory apartment buildings, an increasingly common sight in the cities of the empire. In these cramped structures, families crowded into small, low rooms about ten feet square. In Roman towns throughout Italy, simple dwellings, luxurious mansions, shops, and apartment buildings existed side by side. The rich and the poor rubbed shoulders every day, producing a friction that threatened to burst into flame.

Roman Religion

Romans worshiped many gods, and the list expanded with their empire's boundaries. Every aspect of daily life and work was the responsibility of individual powers, or *numina*. Every man had his *genius*, or personal *numen*, just as every woman had her *juno*. Each family had its household powers, the *lares familiares*, whose proper worship was the responsibility of the paterfamilias. *Vesta* was the spirit of the hearth fire. The *lares* were the deities of farmland, the *domus*, and the guardians of roads and travelers. The *penates* guarded the family larder or storage cupboard. These family spirits exercised a binding power, a *religio*, upon the Romans, and the pious Roman householder recognized these claims and undertook the *officia*, or duties, to which the spirits were entitled. These basic attitudes of religion, piety, and office lay at the heart of Roman reverence for order and authority. They extended to other traditional Roman and Latin gods such as Jupiter, the supreme god; Juno, his wife; Mars, the god of war; and the two-faced Janus, spirit of gates and new beginnings.

Outside the household, worship of the gods and the reading of the future in the entrails of sacrificed animals, the flight of birds, or changes in weather were the responsibilities of colleges of priests. Unlike those in Mesopotamia and Egypt, Roman priests did not form a special caste but rather were important members of the elite who held priesthoods in addition to other public offices. Religion was less a matter of personal relationship with the gods than a public, civic activity binding society together. State-supported cults with their colleges of priests, Etruscan- and Greek-style temples, and elaborate ceremonies were integral parts of the Roman state and society. The world of the gods reflected that of mortals. As the Roman mortal world expanded, so did the divine. Romans were quick to identify foreign gods with their own. Thus Zeus became Jupiter, Hera became Juno, and Aphrodite became Venus.

Still, the elasticity of Roman religion could stretch only just so far. With the empire not only the cults of Zeus, Apollo, and Aphrodite came to Rome but also that of Dionysus. Unlike the formal, public cults of the other Greek deities, which were firmly in the control of authorities, the cult of Dionysus was largely outside state control. Women, in the tradition of the maenads, controlled much of the ecstatic and overtly sexual rituals associated with the god. Following the Second Punic War, the cult of Dionysus, known in Latin as Bacchus, spread rapidly in Italy. It was rumored that at its secret rites, or *Bacchanalia*, men and women engaged in every kind of sexual act.

In 186 B.C.E., the senate decreed the cult of Bacchus a conspiracy and ordered an inquiry. The consul Spurius Postumius Albinus, acting on the spurious testimony of a former prostitute, began a brutal persecution. Rituals were banned, priests and adherents arrested, and rewards offered to informants who provided lurid and fanciful accounts of what had taken place at the Bacchanalia. Hundreds of people were imprisoned and greater numbers were executed. The senate banned Bacchanalia throughout Italy and ordered all shrines to Bacchus destroyed. Perhaps more than any other episode, the suppression of the Bacchic cult showed the fear that the oligarchy felt about the changes sweeping Roman civilization.

Republican Letters

As Rome absorbed foreign gods, it also absorbed foreign letters. From the Etruscans the Romans adopted and adapted the alphabet, the one in which most Western languages are written to this day. Early Latin inscriptions are largely funeral monuments and some public notices such as the Law of the Twelve Tables. The Roman high priest responsible for maintaining the calendar of annual feasts also prepared and updated annals, short accounts of important religious and secular events of each year. However, prior to the third century B.C.E., apart from extravagant funerary eulogies carefully preserved within families, Romans had no apparent interest in writing or literature as such. The birth of Latin letters began with Rome's exposure to Greek civilization.

Early in the third century B.C.E., Greek authors had begun to pay attention to expanding Rome. The first serious Greek historian to focus on this new western power was Timaeus (ca. 356–ca. 260 B.C.E.), who spent most of his productive life in Athens. There he wrote a history of Rome, interviewing Roman and Greek witnesses to Roman victories against Greeks in southern Italy. Polybius (ca. 200–ca. 118 B.C.E.), the greatest of the Greek historians to record Rome's rise to power, gathered his information firsthand. As one of a thousand eminent Greeks deported to Rome for political investigation, he became a close friend of Scipio Aemilianus and accompanied him on his Spanish and African campaigns. Polybius' history is both the culmination of the traditions of Greek historiography and its transformation, since it centers on the rise of a non-Greek power to rule "almost the whole inhabited world."

At the same time that Greeks began to take Rome seriously, Romans themselves became interested in

Relief of Roman comic actors at work. The action of many Roman comedies took place on a street. The back wall of the stage represented house fronts with doorways for entrances and exits.

Greece and in particular in the international Hellenistic culture of the eastern Mediterranean. The earliest Latin literary works were clearly adaptations if not translations of Hellenistic genres and texts. Already in 240 B.C.E., plays in the Greek tradition were said to have been performed in Rome. The earliest of these that survive are the plays of Plautus (ca. 254–184 B.C.E.) and Terence (186–159 B.C.E.), lightly adapted translations of Hellenistic comedies.

Determined soldier-farmers, disciplined by familial obligations and their piety toward the gods and the Roman state, spread Roman rule throughout the Mediterranean world. Confident of their military and governmental skills and lacking pretensions to great skill in arts, literature, and the like, they were eager to absorb the achievements of others, even while adapting them to their own needs.

The Price of Empire, 146–121 B.C.E.

Rome's rise to world power within less than a century profoundly affected every aspect of republican life and ultimately spelled the end of the republican system. Roman society could not withstand the tensions caused by the enrichment of the few, the impoverishment of the many, and the demands of the excluded populations of the empire to share in its benefits. Traditional Roman culture could not survive the attraction of Hellenistic civilization with its wealth, luxuries, and individualistic values. Finally, Roman government could not restrain the ambitions of its oligarchs or protect the interests of its ordinary citizens. The creation of a Mediterranean empire brought in its wake a century of revolutionary change before new, stable social, cultural, and political forms emerged in the Roman world.

Winners and Losers

Rome had emerged victorious in the Punic and Macedonian wars against Carthage and Macedon, but the real winners were the members of the oligarchy—the *optimates*, or the "best," as they called themselves—whose wealth and power had grown beyond all imagining. These optimates included roughly three hundred senators and magistrates, most of whom had inherited wealth, political connections, and long-established clientages. Since military command and government of the empire were entrusted to magistrates who were answerable only to the senate of which they were members, the empire was essentially their private domain.

But new circumstances created new opportunities for many others. Italian merchants, slave traders, entrepreneurs, and bankers, many of lowly origin, poured into the cities of the east in the wake of the Roman legions. These newly enriched Romans constituted a second elite and formed themselves into a separate order, that of the *equites*, or equestrians, distinguished by their wealth and honorific military service on horseback, but connected with the old military elite. Since the senate did not create a government bureaucracy to administer the empire, equestrian tax collectors became essential to provincial government. Companies of these tax farmers, or publicans, purchased the right to collect rents on public land, tribute, and customs duties from provincials. Whatever they collected beyond the amount contracted for by Roman officials was theirs to keep. Publicans regularly bribed governors and commanders to allow them to gouge the local populations with impunity and on occasion even obtained Roman troops to help them make their collections. Gradually, some of these "new men," their money "laundered" through investments in land, managed to achieve lower magistracies and even move into the senatorial order. Still, the upper reaches of office were closed to all but a tiny minority. By the end of the Punic wars, only some twenty-five families could hope to produce consuls.

The losers in the wars included the vanquished who were sold into slavery by the tens of thousands, the provincials who bore the Roman yoke, the Italian allies who had done so much for the Romans, and even the citizen farmers, small shopkeepers, and free craft workers of the republic. All four groups suffered from the effects of empire, and over the next century all resorted to violence against the optimates.

The slaves revolted first, beginning in 135 B.C.E. Thousands of them, captured in battle or taken after victory, flooded the Italian and Sicilian estates of the wealthy. Estimates vary, but in the first century B.C.E., the slave population of Italy was probably around two million, fully one-third of the total population. This vastly expanded slave world overwhelmed the traditional role of slaves within the Roman *familia*. Rural slaves on absentee estates enjoyed none of the protections afforded traditional Roman servants. Some Romans sold off their slaves who reached old age; others simply worked them to death. Many slaves, born free citizens of Hellenistic states, found such treatment unbearable. Revolts profoundly disturbed the Roman state, all the more because not just slaves revolted. In many cases poor free peasants and disgruntled provincials rose up against Rome.

Revolts by slaves and provincials were disturbing, but revolts by Rome's Italian allies were much more serious. After the Second Punic War, these allies, on whose loyalty Rome had depended for survival, found themselves badly treated and exploited. Government officials used state power to undermine the position of the Italian elites. At the same time Roman aristocrats used their economic power to drive the Italic peasants from their land, replacing them with slaves. Some reform-minded Romans attempted to diffuse tensions by extending citizenship to the allies, but failure of this effort led to a revolt at Fregellae south of Rome in 125 B.C.E. A broader and more serious revolt took place between 91 and 89 B.C.E. after the senate blocked an attempt to extend citizenship to the allies. During this so-called Social War (from *socii*, the Latin word for *allies*), almost all the Italian allies rose against Rome. These revolts differed from those in the provinces in that the Italian elites as well as the masses aligned themselves against the Roman oligarchy. Even some ordinary Roman citizens joined the rebel forces against the powerful elite.

Optimates and Populares

The despair that led ordinary Roman citizens to armed rebellion grew from the social and economic consequences of conquests. While aristocrats amassed vast landed estates worked by cheap slaves, ordinary Romans

Roman slaves sifting grain. Roman victories in the Punic and Macedonian wars brought in a huge influx of slaves from the conquered lands. Slaves were pressed into service on the estates and plantations of wealthy landowners.

often lacked even a family farm capable of supporting themselves and their families. Many found their way to Rome, where they swelled the ranks of the unemployed, huddled into shoddily constructed tenements, and lived off the public subsidies.

While many senators bemoaned the demise of the Roman farmer-soldier, few were willing to compromise their own privileged position to help. In the face of the oligarchy's unwillingness to deal with the problem, the tribune Tiberius Gracchus (ca. 163–133 B.C.E.) in 133 B.C.E. attempted to introduce a land-reform program that would return citizens to agriculture. Gracchus was the first of the *populares*, political leaders appealing to the masses. His motives were probably a mixture of compassion for the poor, concern over the dwindling number of citizens who qualified for military service, and personal ambition. Gracchus attempted to get around senatorial opposition to reform by using the plebeian assembly to acquire unprecedented powers. To his opponents, these measures smacked of an attempt to make himself sole ruler, a democratic tyrant on the Greek model. A group of senators and their clients, led by one of Gracchus' own cousins, broke into the assembly meeting at which the election was to take place and murdered the tribune and three hundred of his supporters.

The optimates in the senate could eliminate Tiberius Gracchus, but they could not so easily eliminate the movement he had led. In 123 B.C.E., his younger brother, Gaius Gracchus (153–121 B.C.E.), became tribune and during his two one-year terms initiated an even broader and more radical reform program. Tiberius had been concerned only about poor citizens. Gaius attempted to broaden the citizenry and shift the balance of power away from the senate. Alarmed by the revolts of the Latin allies, he sought to extend citizenship to all Latins and improve the status of Italian allies by extending to them the right to vote in the assembly. In order to check the power of senatorial magistrates in the provinces, he transferred to the equestrians the right to investigate provincial corruption. This move brought the wealthy equestrian order into politics as a counterbalance to the senate.

Gaius also improved the supply and distribution of grain in Rome and other Italian cities to benefit the urban poor. He reestablished his brother's land-distribution project, extended participation to Latins and Italians, and encouraged colonization as a means to provide citizens with land. Finally, in order to protect himself and his party from the anticipated reaction of the senate and to avenge his brother's death, he pushed

THE REFORMS OF TIBERIUS GRACCHUS

■ *In the following passage, the Romanized Greek Appian of Alexandria (ca. 95–ca. 165 C.E.), drawing on earlier but now lost records, describes the positions of the two factions in the dispute over the land reform Tiberius Gracchus introduced in 133 B.C.E.*

Tiberius Sempronius Gracchus, an illustrious man, eager for glory, a most powerful speaker, and for these reasons well known to all, delivered an eloquent discourse while serving as tribune, lamenting the fact that the Italians, a people so valiant in war and related in blood to the Romans, were declining little by little into pauperism and paucity of numbers without any hope of remedy. He inveighed against the multitude of slaves as useless in war and never faithful to their masters, and adduced the recent calamity brought upon the masters by their slaves in Sicily . . . After speaking thus he again brought forward the law providing that nobody should hold more than 500 *iugera* of public domain. But he added a provision to the former law, that (two) sons of the occupiers might each hold one-half that amount and that the remainder should be divided among the poor by three elected commissioners, who should be changed annually.

This was extremely disturbing to the rich because, on account of the commissioners, they could no longer disregard the law as they had done before; nor could they buy from those receiving allotments, because Gracchus had provided against this by forbidding such sales. They collected together in groups, and made lamentation, and accused the poor of appropriating their fields of long standing, their vineyards, and their buildings. Some said they had paid the price of the land to their neighbors. Were they to lose the money with the land? Others said the graves of their ancestors were in the ground, which had been allotted to them in the division of their fathers' estates. Others said that their wives' dowries had been expended on these estates, or that the land had been given to their own daughters as dowry . . . All kinds of wailing and expressions of indignation were heard at once. On the other side were heard the lamentations of the poor—that they were being reduced from competence to extreme poverty, and from that to childlessness, because they were unable to rear their offspring. They recounted the military services they had rendered, by which this very land had been acquired, and were angry that they should be robbed of their share of the common property . . . Emboldened by numbers and exasperated against each other they kindled incessant disturbances, and waited eagerly for the voting of the new law, some intending to prevent its enactment by all means, and others to enact it at all costs.

through a law stipulating that only the people could condemn a citizen to death.

Gaius' program was extraordinary for several reasons. In the first place, it was exactly that, a program, the first comprehensive attempt to deal with the problems facing Roman society. Secondly, it proposed a basic shift of power, for the first time drawing the equestrian order into the political arena opposite the senate and making the assembly rather than the senate the initiator of legislation. Finally, it offered a solution to the problem of the allies which, although rejected at the time, was finally adopted twenty years later. In the short run, however, Gaius' program was a failure. In 121 B.C.E., he failed to be reelected for a third term and thus lost the immunity of the tribunate. Recalling the fate of his brother, he armed his supporters. Once more the senate acted, ordering the consul to take whatever measures he deemed necessary. Gaius and some three thousand of his supporters died.

The deep inequalities within the Roman citizenry and the increasingly brutal treatment of slaves and allies flared into violence in the second and first centuries B.C.E. The only serious attempts to restructure the state to settle these conflicts ended with the deaths of Tiberius and Gaius Gracchus.

The End of the Republic, 121–27 B.C.E.

The murders of the Gracchi also marked a new beginning in Roman politics and provided a model for future attempts at reform. Henceforth reformers would look not to the senate or the aristocracy for their support but to the people, and competition for power would be settled by violence. In the following century, personal ambition replaced dedication to the state, and power as an end in itself replaced power in the service of Rome.

With the Gracchi dead and the core of their reforms dismantled, the senate appeared victorious against all challengers. At home, the masses of ordinary Roman citizens and their political leadership were in disarray. The conquered lands of North Africa and the Near East filled the public coffers as well as the private accounts of Roman senators and publicans.

In reality, Rome had solved neither the problem of internal conflict between rich and poor nor that of how to govern its enormous empire. The apparent calm ended when revolts in Africa and Italy exposed the fragility of the senate's control and ushered in an ever increasing spiral of violence and civil war.

The Crisis of Government

In 112 B.C.E., the senate declared war against Jugurtha (ca. 160–104 B.C.E.), the king of a North African client state who, in his war against a rival, had killed some Roman merchants. The war dragged on for five years amid accusations of corruption, incompetence, and treason. Finally in 107 B.C.E., the people elected as consul Gaius Marius (157–86 B.C.E.), a "new man" who had risen through the tribunate, and entrusted him with the conduct of the war. In order to raise an army, Marius ignored property qualifications and enlisted many impoverished Romans and armed them at public expense. Generals had recruited landless citizens before, but never in such an overt and massive manner. Senators looked on Marius' measure with great suspicion, but the poor citizen recruits, who had despaired of benefiting from the land reforms proposed by the Gracchi, looked forward to receiving a grant of land at the end of their military service.

Marius quickly defeated Jugurtha in 106 B.C.E. In the next year Celtic and Germanic barbarians crossed the Alps into Italy and, although technically disqualified from further terms, Marius was elected consul five times between 104 and 100 B.C.E. to meet the threat. During this period he continued to recruit soldiers from among the poor and on his own authority extended citizenship to allies. To his impoverished soldiers, Marius promised land but, after his victory in 101 B.C.E., the senate refused to provide veterans with farms. As a result, Marius' armies naturally shifted their allegiance away from the Roman state and to their popular commander. Soon this pattern of loyalty became the norm. Politicians forged close bonds with the soldiers of their armies. Individual commanders, not the state or the senate, ensured that their recruits received their pay, shared in the spoils of victory, and obtained land upon their retirement. In turn, the soldiers became fanatically devoted to their commanders. Republican armies had become personal armies, potent tools in the hands of ambitious politicians.

Portrait bust of Marcus Tullius Cicero. The famous statesman and orator fought throughout his career to save the dying Roman republic.

The outbreak of the Social War in 91 B.C.E. marked the first use of these armies in civil war. Both Marius and the consul Sulla (Lucius Cornelius Sulla, 138–78 B.C.E.) raised armies to fight the Italians, who were pacified only after Roman citizenship was extended to all Italians in 89 B.C.E. Soon, however, the two were fighting each other, with Marius leading the populares and Sulla the optimates. In the course of this war Rome was occupied three times, once by Marius, twice by Sulla. Each commander ordered mass executions of his opponents and confiscation of their property, which he then distributed to his supporters.

Ultimately Sulla emerged victorious and ruled as dictator from 82 to 79 B.C.E., using this time to shore up senatorial power. In 79 B.C.E., his reforms in place, Sulla stepped down to allow a return to oligarchic republican rule. Although his changes bought a decade of peace, they did not solve the fundamental problems dividing optimates and populares. If anything, his rule had proven that the only real political option was a dictatorship by a powerful individual with his own army. During the last generation of the republic, idealists continued their hopeless struggle to prop up the dying republican system while more forward-thinking generals fought among themselves for absolute power.

The Civil Wars

Marcus Tullius Cicero (106–43 B.C.E.) reflected the strengths and weaknesses of the republican tradition in the first century B.C.E. Although cultivated, humane, and dedicated to the republican constitution, he was also ambitious, blind to the failings of the optimates, a poor judge of character, and out of touch with the political realities of his time. He was a "new man," the son of a wealthy equestrian who provided his children with the best possible education both in Rome and in Athens and Rhodes. In Greece, Cicero developed a lifelong attachment to Stoic philosophy and developed the oratory skills necessary for a young Roman destined for public life. After returning to Rome he quickly earned a reputation for his skills as a courtroom orator. At the same time he began his climb up the political ladder by championing popular causes while protecting the interests of the wealthy and soliciting the assistance of young optimates. Cicero identified firmly with the elite, hoping that the republic could be saved through the harmonious cooperation of the equestrian and senatorial orders. Neither group was interested in following his program, but most considered him a safer figure than military strongmen like Sulla, who sought high office. In 63 B.C.E.

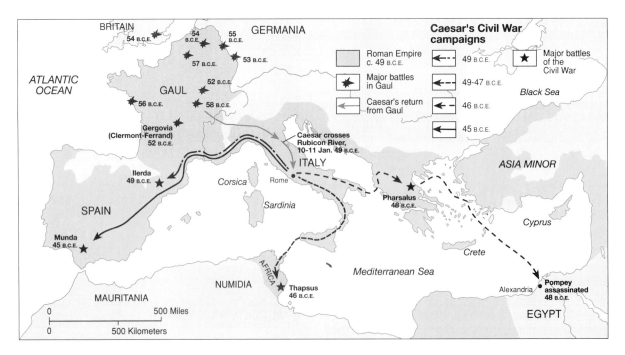

The Roman Empire and Career of Julius Caesar

Cicero was elected consul, the first "new man" to hold the office in over thirty years. The real threat to the existence of the republic was posed by the ambitions of powerful military commanders—Pompey (Gnaeus Pompeius Magnus, 106-48 B.C.E.), Crassus (Marcus Licinius Crassus, ca. 115-53 B.C.E.), and Julius Caesar (Gaius Julius Caesar, 100-44 B.C.E.).

Pompey and Crassus, both protégés of Sulla, rose rapidly and unconstitutionally through a series of special commands by judicious use of fraud, violence, and corruption. Pompey first won public acclaim by commanding a victorious army in Africa and Spain. Upon his return to Rome in 70 B.C.E., he united with Crassus, who had won popularity for suppressing a slave rebellion. Together they worked to dismantle the Sullan constitution to the benefit of the populares. In return, Pompey received an extraordinary command over all of the coasts of the Mediterranean, in theory to suppress piracy but actually to give him control over all of the provinces of the empire. His army conquered Armenia, Syria, and Palestine, acquired an impressive retinue of client kings and increased the income from the provinces by some 70 percent.

While Pompey was extending the frontiers of the empire to the Euphrates, Crassus, whose wealth was legendary—"no one should be called rich," he once observed, "who is not able to maintain an army on his income"—was consolidating his power in Rome. He allied himself with Julius Caesar, a young, well-connected orator from one of Rome's most ancient patrician families, who nevertheless promoted the cause of the populares. The senate feared the ambitious and ruthless Crassus, and it was to block the election of Crassus' candidate Catiline (Lucius Sergius Catilina, ca. 108-62 B.C.E.) to the consulate in 63 B.C.E. that the senate elected Cicero instead. Catiline soon joined a conspiracy of Sullan veterans and populares, but Cicero quickly uncovered and suppressed the conspiracy and ordered Catiline's execution.

When Pompey returned triumphant from Asia in 62 B.C.E., he expected to find Italy convulsed with the Catiline revolt and in need of a military savior in the

CICERO ON JUSTICE AND REASON

■ *In his* On the Laws, *Cicero recast the Stoic tradition of the universal laws of nature into a dialogue modeled on Plato's dialogue by the same name. In it, Cicero defends the belief that true justice must be based on reason, which, accessible to all persons, could be the solution to the evils facing the Roman republic and a guide in the governance of its empire.*

But the most foolish notion of all is the belief that everything is just which is found in the customs or laws of nations. Would that be true, even if these laws had been enacted by tyrants? . . . Justice is one; it binds all human society, and is based on one Law, which is right reason applied to command and prohibition . . . But if Justice is conformity to written laws and national customs, and if, as the same persons claim, everything is to be tested by the standard of utility, then anyone who thinks it will be profitable to him will, if he is able, disregard and violate the laws. It follows that Justice does not exist at all, if it does not exist in Nature, and if that form of it which is based on utility can be overthrown by that very utility itself. And if nature is not to be considered the foundation of Justice, that will mean destruction of the virtues on which human society depends, for where then will there be a place for generosity, or love of country, or loyalty, or the inclination to be of service to others or to show gratitude for favors received? For these virtues originate in our natural inclination to love our fellow-men, and this is the foundation of Justice . . . But if the principles of Justice were founded on the decrees of peoples, the edicts of princes, or the decisions of judges, then Justice would sanction robbery and adultery and forgery of wills, in case these acts were approved by the votes of decrees of the populace.

From Marcus Tullius Cicero, *De Legibus*.

tradition of Sulla. Instead, thanks to Cicero's quick action, all was in order. Although he never forgave Cicero for stealing his glory, Pompey disbanded his army and returned to private life, asking only that the senate approve his organization of the territories he had conquered and grant land to his veterans. The senate refused. In response Pompey formed an uneasy alliance with Crassus and Caesar. This alliance was known as the first triumvirate (from the Latin for "three men"). Caesar was elected consul in 59 B.C.E. and the following year received command of the province of Cisalpine Gaul in northern Italy.

Pompey and Crassus may have thought that this command would remove the ambitious young man from the political spotlight. Instead, Caesar, who has been called with only some exaggeration "the sole creative genius ever produced by Rome," used his province as a staging ground for the conquest of a vast area of western Europe to the mouth of the Rhine. His brilliant military skills beyond the Alps and his dedication to his troops made him immensely popular with his legions. His ability for self-promotion ensured that this popularity was matched at home, where the populares eagerly received news of his Gallic wars. In 53 B.C.E. Crassus died leading an army in Syria, leaving Pompey and the popular young Caesar to dispute supreme power. As word of Caesar's military successes increased his popularity in Rome, it also increased Pompey's suspicion of his younger associate. Finally, in 49 B.C.E., Pompey's supporters in the senate relieved Caesar of his command and ordered him to return to Italy.

Return he did, but not as commanded. Rather than leave his army on the far side of the Rubicon River, which marked the boundary between his province of Cisalpine Gaul and Italy, as ordered, he marched on Rome at the head of his legions. This meant civil war, a vicious bloodletting that convulsed the whole Mediterranean world. In 48 B.C.E., Caesar defeated Pompey in northern Greece, and Pompey was assassinated shortly after. Still the wars went on between Pompey's supporters and Caesar until 45 B.C.E., when with all his enemies defeated, Caesar returned to Rome. There, unlike Sulla, he showed his opponents clemency as he sought to heal the wounds of war and to undertake an unprecedented series of reforms. He enlarged the senate to nine hundred and widened its representation, appointing soldiers, freedmen, provincials, and above all wealthy men from the Italian towns. He increased the number of magistracies to broaden participation in government, founded colonies at Carthage and Corinth, and settled veterans in colonies elsewhere in Italy,

Greece, Asia, Africa, Spain, and Gaul. Still, he made no pretense of returning Rome to republican government. In early 44 B.C.E., although serving that year as consul together with his general Mark Antony (Marcus Antonius, ca. 81–30 B.C.E.), Caesar had himself declared perpetual dictator. This move was finally too much for some sixty diehard republican senators. On March 15, a group led by two enemies whom Caesar had pardoned, Cassius Longinus and Marcus Junius Brutus, assassinated him as he entered the senate chamber.

Cicero rejoiced when he heard of the assassination, clear evidence of his political naïveté. The republic was dead long before Caesar died, and the assassination simply returned Rome to civil war, a civil war that destroyed Cicero himself. Antony, Marcus Lepidus (Marcus Aemilius Lepidus, d. 12 B.C.E.), another of Caesar's generals, and Caesar's grandnephew and adopted son Octavian (Gaius Octavius, 63 B.C.E.–14 C.E.), who took the name of his great uncle, soon formed a second triumvirate to destroy Caesar's enemies. After a bloody purge of senatorial and equestrian opponents, including Cicero, Antony and Octavian set out after Cassius and Brutus, who had fled into Macedonia. At Philippi in 42 B.C.E. Octavian and Antony defeated the armies of the two assassins (or, as they called themselves, liberators), who chose suicide rather than capture.

After the defeat of the last republicans at Philippi, the members of the Second Triumvirate began to look suspiciously at one another. Antony took command of the east, protecting the provinces of Asia Minor and the Levant from the Parthians to the east and bleeding

This silver coin was struck to commemorate the assassination of Julius Caesar. Two daggers flank a cap symbolizing liberty. The legend reads "the Ides of March." On the other side is a profile of Brutus.

them dry in the process. Lepidus received Africa, and Octavian was left to deal with the problems of Italy and the west.

Initially Octavian had cut a weak and unimposing figure. Still, he had the magic of Caesar's name with which to inspire the army, he had a visceral instinct for politics and publicity, and he combined these with an absolute determination to succeed at all costs. Aided by more competent and experienced commanders, notably Marcus Agrippa (Marcus Vipsanius Agrippa, ca. 63–12 B.C.E.), and Gaius Maecenas (ca. 70–8 B.C.E.), he began to consolidate his power at the expense of his two colleagues. Lepidus attempted to gain a greater share in the empire but found that his troops would not fight against Octavian. He was forced out of his position and allowed to retire in obscurity, retaining only the honorific title of *pontifex maximus*.

Antony, to meet his ever growing demand for cash, became dependent on the Ptolemaic ruler of Egypt, the clever and competent Cleopatra. For her part, Cleopatra manipulated Antony in order to maintain the integrity and independence of her kingdom. Octavian seized the opportunity to portray Antony as a traitor to Rome, a weakling controlled by an alien woman who planned to move the capital of the empire to Alexandria. Antony's supporters replied with propaganda of their own, pointing to Octavian's humble parentage and his lack of military ability. The final break came in 32 B.C.E. Antony, for all his military might, could not attack Italy as long as the despised Cleopatra was with him. Nor could he abandon her without losing her essential financial support. Instead, he tried to lure Octavian to a showdown in Greece. His plan misfired. Agrippa forced him into a naval battle off Actium in 31 B.C.E. in which Antony was soundly defeated. He and Cleopatra committed suicide and Octavian ruled supreme in the Roman Empire.

The Good Life

Mere survival was a difficult and elusive goal through the last decades of the republic. Still, some members of the elite sought more. They tried to make sense of the turmoil around them and formulate a philosophy of life to provide themselves with a model of personal conduct. By now Rome's elite were in full command of Greek literature and philosophy, and they naturally turned to the Greek tradition to find their answers. However, they created from it a distinctive Latin cultural tradition. The most prominent figure in the late republic is

Cicero, who combined his active life as lawyer and politician with an abiding devotion to Stoic philosophy. In stoicism's belief in divine providence, morality, and duty to one's allotted role in the universe, he found a rational basis for his deeply committed public life. In a series of written dialogues, Cicero presented Stoic values in a form that created a Latin philosophical language freed from slavish imitation of Greek. He also wrote a number of works of political philosophy, particularly *The Republic* and *The Laws*, in conscious but creative imitation of Plato's concern for the proper order of society. For Cicero, humans and gods are bound together in a world governed not simply by might but by justice. The universe, while perhaps not fully intelligible, is nonetheless rational, and reason must be the basis for society and its laws.

These same concerns for virtue are evident in the writings of the great historians of the late republic, Sallust (Gaius Sallustius Crispus, 86–ca. 34 B.C.E.) and Livy (Titus Livius, 59 B.C.E.–17 C.E.). Sallust was a supporter of Julius Caesar, who had written his own stylistically powerful histories of the Gallic and Civil wars. For him as well as for his younger contemporary Livy, the chaos of civil war was the direct result of moral corruption and decline that followed the successes of the empire. For Sallust, the moral failing was largely that of the senate and its members, who trampled the plebs in their quest for power and personal glory. Livy, who was much more conservative, condemned plebeian demagogues as well as power-hungry senators. Only those aristocratic conservatives who had stood for the ancient Roman traditions merited praise. In the second century B.C.E. the Greek historian Polybius had been fascinated with the rise of the Roman republic to world supremacy. A century later the Roman historians were even more fascinated with its decline.

A different kind of morality dominated the work of Lucretius (Titus Lucretius Carus, ca. 100–55 B.C.E.), the greatest poet of the late republic. Just as Cicero had molded stoicism into a Roman civic philosophy, Lucretius presented Epicurean materialist philosophy as a Roman alternative to the hunger for power, wealth, and glory. In his great poem, *On the Nature of Things*, Lucretius presents the Epicurean's thoroughly physical understanding of the universe. He describes its atomic composition, the evolution of man from brutish beginnings to civilization, and the evil effects not only of greed and ambition but also of religion. All that exists is material reality. Religion, whether the state-supported cults of ancient Rome or the exotic cults introduced from the East, plays on mortal fear of death, a fear that is irrational and groundless. "Death is nothing to us," Lucretius writes. "It is only the natural fulfillment of life. A rational, proportional enjoyment of life is all that matters. Sorrow and anxiety come from but an ignorant emotionalism."

Emotion was precisely the goal of another poetic tradition of the late republic, that of the "neoteric" or new-style poets, especially Catullus (Gaius Valerius Catullus, ca. 84–ca. 54 B.C.E.). Avoiding politics or moralistic philosophy, these poets created short, striking lyric poems which, although inspired by Hellenistic poetry, combine polished craftsmanship with a direct realism that is without precedent. One of the most striking differences between this Latin poetry and its Greek antecedents is the reality and individuality of the persons and relationships expressed.

The same interest in the individual affected the way artists of the late republic borrowed from Greek art. Since Etruscan times, Romans had commemorated their ancestors in wax or wooden busts displayed in their homes. Hellenistic artists concentrated on the ideal, but Romans cherished the individual. The result was a portraiture that caught the personality of the individual's face, even while portraying him or her as one of a type. Statues of the ideal nude, the armored warrior, or the citizen in his simple toga followed the proportions and conventions of Hellenistic sculpture. The heads however, created in hard, dry style, are as unique and personal as the characters who live in Catullus' lyric poems. We see in them the strengths and weaknesses, the stresses and the privileges, that marked the last generation of the Roman republic.

Rome had come a long way since its origin as an outpost of the Alban League. At first overshadowed by its more civilized neighbors to the north and south, it had slowly and tenaciously achieved independence from and then domination over its more ancient neighbors. It is difficult to point to particular Roman ideas, institutions, or techniques that made this possible. Virtually all of these were absorbed or adapted from the Etruscans, Greeks, and others with whom Rome came into contact. Rome's great success was largely due to Roman authoritarianism as well as to its genius for creative adaptation, flexibility, and thoroughness, and its willingness to give those it conquered a stake in Roman victory. Until the middle of the second century B.C.E., this formula had served the republic well. After the final destruction of Carthage, however, an isolated and fearful oligarchy appeared unwilling or unable to broaden the base of those participating in the Roman achievement. The result was a

century and a half of intermittent violence and civil war before a new political and social order headed by an absolute monarch established a new equilibrium.

SUGGESTIONS FOR FURTHER READING

PRIMARY SOURCES

Many of the works of Polybius, Livy, Cato, Caesar, Cicero, and other Roman authors are available in English translation from Penguin Books. The first volume of *Naphtali Lewis and Meyer Reinhold, *Roman Civilization, Selected Readings, Vol I: The Republic* (1951) contains a wide selection of documents with useful introductions.

THE WESTERN MEDITERRANEAN TO 509 B.C.E.

*R. H. Warmington, *Carthage*, rev. ed. (New York: F. A. Praeger, 1969). A basic introduction.

Massimo Pallottino, *The Etruscans* (Bloomington, IN: Indiana University Press, 1975). A general introduction to Etruscan history, language, and civilization.

FROM CITY TO EMPIRE, 509–146 B.C.E.

Leon Homo, *Primitive Italy and the Beginnings of Roman Imperialism* (Philadelphia: Century Bookbindery, 1968). Classic introduction to early Italian history.

*Michael Crawford, *The Roman Republic* (Cambridge, MA: Harvard University Press, 1978). A modern survey of the Republican period, emphasizing political history.

*John Boardman, Jasper Griffin, and Oswyn Murray, *The Roman World* (New York: Oxford University Press, 1988). A balanced collection of essays on all aspects of Roman history and civilization.

*P. A. Brunt, *Social Conflicts in the Roman Republic* (New York: Norton, 1971). Analyzes the continuing struggle between patricians and plebeians until the end of the republic.

*Keith Hopkins, *Conquerors and Slaves* (New York: Cambridge University Press, 1978). A sociological study of the effects of slavery on imperial society and government.

*Mary Beard and Michael Crawford, *Rome in the Late Republic* (Ithaca, NY: Cornell University Press, 1985). A short interpretative essay on the crisis of the late republic.

REPUBLICAN CIVILIZATION

Suzanne Dixon, *The Roman Mother* (Norman, OK: University of Oklahoma Press, 1988). A balanced view of Roman mothers in law and in society.

*Erich S. Gruen, *The Hellenistic World and the Coming of Rome*, 2 vols. (Berkeley, CA: University of California Press, 1984). A detailed history of the Hellenistic world, presenting Rome's gradual and unintended rise to dominance in it.

*Géza Alfoldy, *The Social History of Rome* (Berlin: Walter de Gruyter, 1988). A survey of Rome that emphasizes the relationship between social structure and politics.

The Price of Empire, 146–121 B.C.E.

* Mary Beard and Michael Crawford, *Rome in the Late Republic* (Ithaca, NY: Cornell University Press, 1985). An analysis of the political processes of the last republic as part of the development of Roman society, not simply the decay of the republic.

* E. Badian, *Roman Imperialism in the Late Republic* (Ithaca, NY: Cornell University Press, 1968). A study of the contradictory forces leading to the development of the empire.

The End of the Republic, 121–27 B.C.E.

Ronald Syme, *The Roman Revolution*, 2d ed. (New York: Oxford University Press, 1960). A classic study of the social groups who made up the party of Augustus.

E. S. Gruen, *The Last Generation of the Roman Republic* (Berkeley: University of California Press, 1973). A recent and controversial analysis of the politics of the late republic.

D. Stockton, *Cicero: A Political Biography* (London: Oxford University Press, 1971). A biography of the great orator in the context of the end of the republic.

* Indicates paperback edition available.

CHAPTER 6

The Mediterranean World and the Roman Empire, 27 B.C.E.–500 C.E.

COIN OF THE REALM

The magnificent medallion shown here depicts on one side likenesses of the imperial brothers Valentinian I and Valens, who jointly ruled the Roman Empire from 364 to 375. On the obverse is pictured a mounted emperor, surrounded by a nimbus, the symbol of divinity, and the gods Tellus (earth) and Fortuna (good fortune). The inscription reads, "The glory of the Romans," and the AN indicates that the medallion was struck at the imperial mint at Antioch. Beneath these facts about the medallion, however, lies a much broader story. It is the story of the transformation of the Roman Empire.

The medallion fairly bristles with apparent contradictions and incongruities. Sole rule was the cornerstone of the empire created by Octavian. Now two emperors instead of one rule the empire. Rome had been founded on its piety to the gods. The two emperors, although they are surrounded by traditional pagan symbols and appear to be equated with the gods, are actually Christians. Finally, the inscription on the face, "King of the Romans," reveals the medallion for what it is: a counterfeit. The Roman emperors did not call themselves kings—that was the term the barbarian Goths, who struck this coin and who did not have kings themselves, used for the Roman emperors. Although the medallion is counterfeit, it is not worthless. Its gold is of higher purity than many genuine Roman coins of the period.

By the last quarter of the fourth century, the barbarian and Roman worlds were inextricably connected, like the two sides of the coin itself. The Goths had struck the coin to show their esteem for the Roman Empire and its rulers. Yet, only a few years after this coin was struck, the Emperor Valens and his army were destroyed by the very Goths who had produced it in his honor. This counterfeit medallion demonstrates the radical transformations of Rome and its barbarian neighbors under the Roman Empire.

The empire created on the ruins of the republic was sustained not only by its military force but on the power of its cultural traditions to draw into it Romans, provincials, and even barbarians outside its borders. Only after centuries did its economic weaknesses, institutional limitations, and social tensions combine with external pressure to transform the meaning of "Roman" as thoroughly as is seen in this medallion. Even then the new sense of Roman—fragmented, Christian, and detached from a specific political institution—remained the ideal of European peoples for over a millennium.

It took Octavian two years following his victory at Actium in 31 B.C.E. to eliminate remaining pockets of resistance and to reconcile his rule with Roman constitutional traditions without surrendering any power. That power rested on three factors: his immense wealth, which he used to secure support; his vast following among the surviving elites as well as among the populares; and his total command of the army. Octavian's power also rested on the exhaustion of the Roman people, who were eager, after decades of civil strife, to return to peace and stability. Remembering the fate of Julius Caesar, however, Octavian had no intention of rekindling opposition by establishing an overt monarchy. Instead, in 27 B.C.E., he returned the republic from his own charge to the senate and the people of Rome. In turn the senate decreed him the title of *Augustus*, meaning "exalted."

What this meant was that Augustus, as he was now called, continued to rule as strongly as before, but not through an autocratic office or title—he preferred to be called simply the "first citizen," or *princeps*. Thus he preserved the traditional Roman magistracies.

These formalities deceived no one. Augustus' power was absolute. However, by choosing not to exercise it in an absolutist manner, he forged a new constitutional system that worked well for himself and his successors. This system included a renewed senate, an equestrian order removed from politics, a professional army, and a cultural renewal with the emperor's cult at its center. So successful was this system that for two centuries the empire enjoyed stability and peace, the *Pax Romana*.

The Empire Renewed

Cicero had sought in vain a concord of the orders, a settlement of the social and political frictions of the empire through the voluntary efforts of a public-minded oligarchy. What could not happen voluntarily, Augustus imposed from above, reforming the Roman state, society, and culture.

Key to Augustus' program of renewal was the senate, which he made, if not a partner, then a useful subordinate in his reform. He gradually reduced the number of senators, which had grown to over a thousand, back down to six hundred. In the process he eliminated the unfit and incompetent as well as the impoverished and those who failed to show the appropriate reverence toward the emperor. At the same time he made senate membership hereditary, although he continued to appoint individuals of personal integrity, ability, and wealth to the body. Most conspicuous among the "new men" to enter the senate under Augustus were the wealthy leaders of Italian cities and colonies. These small-town notables formed the core of Augustus' supporters and worked closely with him to renew the Roman elite.

Augustus also shared with the senate the governance of the empire, although again not on an equal footing. The senate named governors to the peaceful provinces, while Augustus named commanders to those frontier "imperial" provinces where the bulk of the legions were stationed. Senators themselves served as provincial governors and military commanders. The senate also functioned as a court of law in important cases. Nonetheless, the senate remained a creature of the emperor, seldom asserting itself even when asked to do so by Augustus or his successors. Senators competed with each other to see who could be first to do the emperor's bidding.

Augustus undertook an even more fundamental reform of the equites, those wealthy businessmen, bankers, and tax collectors who had vied with the senatorial aristocracy since the reforms of Tiberius Gracchus. Equestrians formed the backbone of the officer corps of the army, of the treasury, and of the greatly expanded imperial administration. The equestrian order was open at both ends. Freedmen and soldiers who acquired sufficient wealth moved into the order, and the most successful and accomplished equestrians were promoted into the senate. However, the price for a renewed equestrian order was its removal from the political arena. No longer was provincial tax collection farmed out to companies of equestrian publicans nor were they allowed a role in executive or judicial deliberations. For most, these changes were a small price to pay for security, standing, and avenues to lucrative employment.

Augustus also addressed the land crisis that had provoked much of the unrest in the late republic. After Actium, he had to satisfy the need for land among the loyal soldiers of his sixty legions. Drawing on his immense wealth, acquired largely from the estates of his proscripted enemies, he pensioned off thirty-two legions, sending them to colonies he purchased for them throughout the empire. The remaining twenty-eight legions became a permanent professional army stationed in imperial provinces. In time the normal period of enlistment became fixed at twenty years, after which time Augustus provided the legionnaires with land and enough cash to settle in among the notables of their colonies. Augustus established a small, elite unit, the praetorian guard, in and around Rome as his personal military force.

acquired by arms. Likewise, ambitious provincials, through service as auxiliaries and later as citizens, acquired a stake in the destiny of Rome.

Divine Augustus

A cornerstone of Augustus' renewal was religious reform. He assumed the office of *pontifex maximus* and used it to direct a reinvigoration of Roman religion. In 17 B.C.E. he celebrated three days of sacrifices, processions, sacred games, and theater performances, known as the secular games. He restored numerous temples and revived ancient Roman cults. He established a series of public religious festivals, reformed priesthoods, and encouraged citizens to participate in the traditional cults of Rome. Augustus' goals in all these religious reforms were twofold. He was determined to restore the traditions of Roman piety, morality, sacred order, and faith in the relationship between the gods and Roman destiny. An equally important goal was Augustus' promotion of his own cult. His adoptive father, Julius Caesar, had been deified after his death, and Augustus benefited from this association with a divine ancestor. His own *genius*, or guiding spirit, received special devotion in temples throughout the western portion of the empire dedicated to "Rome and Augustus." In the eastern regions he was worshiped as a living god. In this manner the emperor became identical with the state and the state religion closely akin to emperor worship. After his death Augustus and virtually all of the emperors after him were worshiped as official deities in Rome.

Closely related to his fostering of traditional cults was Augustus' attempt to restore traditional Roman family virtues. Like the reformers of the late republic, he believed that the declining power of the paterfamilias was at the root of Rome's ills. To reverse the trend and to restore the declining population of free Italians, Augustus encouraged marriage, procreation, and the firm control of husbands over wives. He imposed penalties for those who chose not to marry and bestowed rewards on those who produced large families.

Augustus actively patronized those writers who shared his conservative religious and ethical values and who might be expected to glorify the *princeps*, and he used his power to censor and silence writers he considered immoral. Chief among the favored were the poets Virgil (70–19 B.C.E.) and Horace (65–8 B.C.E.). Both came from provincial and fairly modest origins, although both received excellent educations. Both lost property in the proscriptions and confiscations during the civil

An idealized marble portrait statue of the emperor Augustus addressing his army. Augustus ruled without benefit of any aristocratic office or title. He preferred to be called simply the "first citizen," or princeps.

These measures created a permanent solution to the problem of the citizen-soldier of the late republic. Veteran colonies—all built as model Roman towns with their central forum, baths, temples, arenas, and theaters as well as their outlying villas and farms—helped Romanize the far provinces of the empire. These colonies, unlike the independent colonies of Greece in an earlier age, remained an integral part of the Roman state. Thus Romanization and political integration went hand in hand, uniting through peaceful means an empire first

AUGUSTUS DESCRIBES HIS ACCOMPLISHMENTS

■ *Shortly before his death, Augustus ordered an account of his accomplishments inscribed on bronze pillars and set up before his mausoleum. The following are excerpts from a copy found inscribed on the walls of a temple in modern Ankara, Turkey.*

1. At the age of nineteen, on my own initiative and at my own expense, I raised an army by means of which I liberated the Republic, which was oppressed by the tyranny of a faction. For which reason the senate, with honorific decrees, made me a member of its order . . . giving me at the same time consular rank in voting, and granted me the imperium . . .

2. Those who assassinated my father I drove into exile, avenging their crime by due process of law; and afterwards when they waged war against the state, I conquered them twice on the battlefield.

3. I waged many wars throughout the whole world by land and by sea, both civil and foreign, and when victorious I spared all citizens who sought pardon. Foreign peoples who could safely be pardoned I preferred to spare rather than to extirpate . . .

8. . . . Three times I revised the roll of senators . . .

15. To the Roman plebs I paid 300 sesterces apiece in accordance with the will of my father; and in my fifth consulship I gave each 400 sesterces in my own name out of the spoils of war . . .

17. Four times I came to the assistance of the treasury with my own money, transferring to those in charge of the treasury 150,000,000 sesterces . . .

22. I gave a gladiatorial show three times in my own name, and five times in the names of my sons or grandsons; at these shows about 10,000 fought . . .

25. I brought peace to the sea by suppressing the pirates. In that way I turned over to their masters for punishment nearly 30,000 slaves who had run away from their owners and taken up arms against the state . . .

26. I extended the frontiers of all the provinces of the Roman people on whose boundaries were peoples subject to our empire. . .

28. I established colonies of soldiers in Africa, Sicily, Macedonia, in both Spanish provinces, in Achaea, Asia, Syria, Narbonese Gaul, and in Pisidia. . .

31. Royal embassies from India, never previously seen before by any Roman general, were often sent to me.

34. In my sixth and seventh consulships [28 and 27 B.C.E.] after I had put an end to the civil wars, having attained supreme power by universal consent, I transferred the state from my own power to the control of the Roman senate and people. For this service of mine I received the title of Augustus by decree of the senate.

wars, but their poetry eventually won them the favor of Augustus and with it estates and wealth. In return, through their poetry in praise of the emperor, Horace and Virgil conferred immortality on Augustus.

Horace celebrated Augustus' victory at Actium, his reform of the empire, and reestablishment of the ancient cults that had brought Rome divine favor. In Horace's poems, Augustus is almost a god, his deeds superior to those of the great heroes of Roman legend. Interspersed with the poems praising Augustus are poems of great beauty praising love and the enjoyment of wine and music.

Virgil began his poetic career with pastoral poems celebrating the joys of rural life and the bitterness of the loss of lands in the civil wars. Later, under the patronage of Augustus, Virgil turned directly to glorifying the *princeps* and the new age. The ultimate expression of this effort was the *Aeneid*, an epic consciously intended to serve for the Roman world the role of the Homeric poems in the Greek.

As Virgil reworked the legend of Aeneas—a Trojan hero who escaped the destruction of the city, wandered throughout the Mediterranean, and ultimately came to Latium—he presented a panoramic history of Rome and its destiny. In the midst of his wanderings, Aeneas (like Odysseus before him) enters the underworld to speak with his dead father. Here he sees a vision of Rome's future greatness. He sees the great heroes of Rome, including Augustus, "son of a god," and he is told of the particular mission of Rome:

> Let others fashion in bronze more lifelike, breathing images
> Let others (as I believe they will) draw living faces from marble
> Others shall plead cases better and others will better
> Track the course of the heavens and announce the rising stars.
> Remember, Romans, your task is to rule the peoples
> This will be your art: to teach the habit of peace
> To spare the defeated and to subdue the haughty.

The finest of the poets who felt the heavy hand of Augustus' disfavor was Ovid (43 B.C.E.-17 C.E.), the great Latin poet of erotic love. In *Art of Love* and *Amores*, he cheerfully preaches the art of seduction and adultery. He delights in poking irreverent fun at everything from the sanctity of Roman marriage to the serious business of warfare. In his great *Metamorphoses*, a series of artfully told myths, he parodies the heroic epic, mocking with grotesque humor the very material Virgil used to create the *Aeneid*. By 8 C.E. Augustus had had enough. He exiled the witty poet to Tomis, a miserable frontier post on the Black Sea. There Ovid spent the last nine years of his life, suffering from the harsh climate, the danger of nomadic attacks and, most of all, the pain of exile from the center of the civilization he loved.

Augustus' Successors

Through the poetry of Horace and Virgil, Augustus' fame was immortal. His flesh was not. The problem of succession occupied him throughout much of his long reign and was never satisfactorily solved. Unfortunately, Augustus outlived all of his first choices. His final choice, his stepson Tiberius (14-37 C.E.) proved to be a gloomy and unpopular successor but nevertheless a competent ruler under whom the machinery of the empire functioned smoothly. The continued smooth func-

tioning of the empire even under the subsequent members of Augustus' family—the mad Gaius, also known as Caligula (37-41), the bookish but competent Claudius (41-54), and initially under Nero (54-68)—is a tribute to the soundness of Augustus' constitutional changes.

The descendants of Augustus' military and aristocratic supporters had a vested interest in maintaining the stability that his reform had brought, but Nero was more than even they could bear. Although popular with the masses, he was also profligate, vicious, and paranoid, dividing his time between murdering his relatives and associates—including his mother, his aunt, his wife, his tutors, and eventually his most capable generals—and squandering his vast wealth on mad attempts to gain recognition as a great poet, actor, singer, and athlete. Then, in 68 C.E., the exasperated commanders in Gaul, Spain, and Africa revolted. Once more war swept the empire. Nero slit his own throat, and in the next year, the "Year of the Four Emperors," four men in quick succession won the office only to lose their lives just as quickly. Finally, in 70, Vespasian (69-79 C.E.), the son of a "new man" who had risen through the ranks to the command in Egypt, secured the principate and restored order.

The first emperors had rounded off the frontiers of the empire, transforming the client states of Cappadocia, Thrace, Commagene, and Judaea in the east and Mauritania in North Africa into provinces. Claudius (41-54 C.E.) presided over the conquest of Britain in 43 C.E. These emperors introduced efficient means of governing and protecting the empire, and tied together its inhabitants, roughly fifty million in the time of Augustus, in networks of mutual dependence and common interest.

Augustus established peaceful relations with the Parthians, the successors of the Seleucids, who ruled a vast empire from the Euphrates to the Indus River. The Parthian Empire was open to ancient Mesopotamian, Greek, and Indian religious, political, and cultural traditions. Peace with Parthia permitted unhampered trade between the Roman world and China and India.

In the western portions of the Roman Empire, after a disastrous attempt to expand the empire to the Elbe River ended in the loss of three legions in 9 C.E., the frontier was fixed at the Rhine. In the east, the northern border stopped at the Danube. The deserts of Africa, Nubia, and southern Arabia formed what in the first century C.E. many saw as the "natural" southern boundaries of the empire.

The emperors of the Flavian dynasty, Vespasian and his sons and successors Titus (79-81) and Domitian (81-96), were stern and unpretentious provincials who restored the authority and dignity of their office,

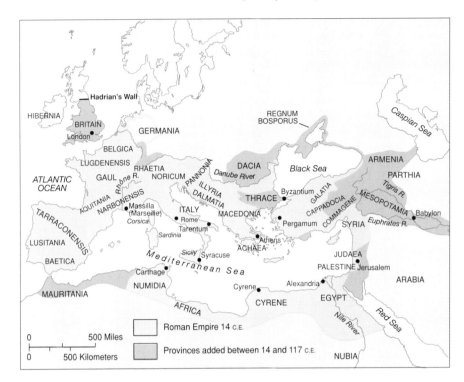

Roman Empire 14 and 117 C.E.

although they also did away with much of the trappings of republican legitimacy that Augustus and his immediate successors had used. They solidified the administrative system, returned the legions to their fairly permanent posts, and opened the highest reaches of power as never before to provincial elites. After the Flavian emperors, the Antonines (96–193), especially Trajan (98–117), Hadrian (117–138), and Antoninus Pius (138–161), ruled for what has been termed "the period in the history of the world, during which the human race was most happy and prosperous."

Augustus' concentration of all power in his own hands, combined with his reforms of the senate, equestrian order, and military, proved a formula that for over two centuries provided the empire, through good emperors and bad, with peace and stability.

The Pax Romana, 27 B.C.E.–180 C.E.

From 27 B.C.E. to 180 C.E., no major enemies appeared to challenge the Roman Empire. The imperial bureaucracy collected taxes, enforced law, and kept the peace.

Trade flourished and the standard of living rose. Within the vast empire, a system of military camps, towns, and rural estates constituted a remarkably homogeneous and prosperous civilization. Not only merchants but teachers circulated freely within the empire, spreading Greek philosophical ideas of universal harmony and Christian ideas of the kingdom of God.

Administering the Empire

The imperial government of this vast empire was as oppressive as it was primitive. Taxes, rents, forced labor service, military levies and requisitions, and outright extortion weighed heavily on its subjects. To a considerable extent, the inhabitants of the empire continued to be governed by the indigenous elites whose cooperation Rome won by giving them broad autonomy. In return for their participation in Roman rule, these elites received Roman citizenship, a prize that carried prestige, legal protection, and the promise of further advancement in the Roman world.

Finally, much of the governing of the empire was done by the vast households of the Roman elite, particularly that of the princeps. Freedmen and slaves from the emperor's household often governed vast regions, oversaw imperial estates, and managed imperial factories and mines. The descendants of the old Roman nobility might look down their noses at imperial freedmen, but they obeyed their orders.

The empire worked because it rewarded those who worked with it and left alone those who paid their taxes and kept quiet. Local elites, auxiliary soldiers, and freedmen could aspire to rise to the highest ranks of the power elite. As provincials were drawn into the Roman system, they were also drawn into the world of Roman culture. Proper education in Latin and Greek, the ability to hold one's own in philosophical discussion, the absorption of Roman styles of dress, recreation, and religious cults, all were essential for ambitious provincials. Thus, in the course of the first century C.E., the disparate portions of the empire competed, not to free themselves from the Roman yoke but to become Roman themselves.

The Rise of Christianity

The same openness that permitted the spread of Latin letters and Roman baths to distant Gaul and the shores of the Black Sea provided paths of dissemination for other, distinctly un-Roman, religious traditions. For many in the empire, the traditional rituals offered to the household gods and the state cults of Jupiter, Mars, and the other official deities were insufficient objects of religious devotion.

Since the second century B.C.E. the Roman world had been caught up in the emotional cult of Dionysus, an ecstatic, personal, and liberating religion entirely unlike the official Roman cults. Again in the first century C.E., so-called mystery cults, that is, religions promising immediate, personal contact with a deity that would bring immortality, spread throughout the empire. Some were officially introduced into Rome as part of its open polytheism. Generally, Rome tolerated these alien cults as long as they could be assimilated or at least reconciled in some way into the cult of the Roman gods and the genius of the emperor.

With one religious group this assimilation was impossible. The Jews of Palestine had long refused any accommodation with the polytheistic cults of the Hellenistic kingdoms or with Rome. Roman conquerors and emperors, aware of the problems of their Hellenistic predecessors, went to considerable lengths to avoid antagonizing this small group of people. When Pompey seized Jerusalem in 63 B.C.E., he was careful not to interfere in Jewish religion and even left Judaea (the Roman name for the old Kingdom of Judah) under the control of the Jewish high priest. Later, Judaea was made into a client kingdom under the puppet Herod. Jews were allowed to maintain their monotheistic cult and were excused from making sacrifices to the Roman gods.

Spoils From the Temple in Jerusalem, *a marble relief from the Arch of Titus. The arch was begun by Titus's father, the emperor Vespasian, to commemorate Titus's victory over the Jews in 78 C.E.*

A model of the ruins of a Roman apartment building near the Capitoline Hill. The ground-floor rooms facing the street were used as shops. The inset is a relief of a Roman butcher shop.

Urban Blight in the Eternal City

In spite of its magnificent temples, palaces, and forums, the Rome of the empire was a teeming city of narrow, twisted streets. The din of hawkers, animals, and shoppers; the stench of garbage and sewage; and above all, the teeming masses of the desperately poor made Rome a nightmare for those not rich enough to isolate themselves in the luxury of a Palatine mansion.

At its height in the second century, the population of Rome and Ostia, its port, numbered well over a million. Feeding, housing, employing, and maintaining even a minimum of sanitation for so many people were almost beyond the ability of the Roman state. The poor crowded together in dark, dank apartment buildings thrown up with little care and in constant danger of collapse. In his biting

satire on life in Rome, the poet Juvenal (ca. 55-after 127 C.E.) complained of the constant fear that Roman tenements would come crashing down on their inhabitants. Even if the buildings did not collapse, they were likely to catch fire from one of the many poorly protected fireplaces tended by each family. Fires were frequent, and the fire brigade organized under Augustus could do little to stop fire from racing through the crowded buildings. In 64 C.E., a disastrous fire (rumored to have been started by the Emperor Nero) swept from the area of the Circus Maximus near the Palatine hill through the city. Tacitus described the fire: "There were no residences fenced with masonry or temples surrounded by walls, or anything else to act as an obstacle. The blaze in its fury ran through the level portions of the city, rose to the hills, then again devastated the lower places." When it was over, of the fourteen districts of the city, only four remained undamaged. Three had been leveled; in seven there remained only a few shattered, half-burned relics of houses.

While catastrophes on so grand a scale were infrequent, daily life held sufficient terrors for most inhabitants. The city was filthy. Although the streets were mostly paved, they were thick with mud in rainy weather and with dust in dry weather. To this were added garbage, animal excrement, and human sewage illegally dumped from tenement windows. The *cloaca maxima*, or great sewer, could accommodate only a small portion of the city's wastes and in any case flowed into the Tiber, polluted with garbage, offal of slaughtered animals, and every sort of waste. By law, sewage was to be carried outside the city limits and dumped into foul-smelling pits that ringed

Rome, pushed back year to year as the suburban slums expanded with the city's growth.

During their short lives (urban men could hope to live to an average age of perhaps twenty-six, women to twenty-three), Rome's masses were constantly engaged in a desperate search for food. The bread of the famous "bread and circuses" provided by the emperors was too little and reached only a fraction of the urban poor. Only about one-third of Roman families received the monthly ration of thirty-three kilograms of wheat, hardly enough to sustain them. Even these had to find some sort of income with which to supplement their diet with oil, beans, cheese, fruits, and meat, as well as to pay for rent and clothing.

Since Rome had virtually no industry, the majority of the middle classes supported themselves by working to transport the vast quantities of foodstuffs and other necessities the city consumed each day. The poor, if they found work at all, did so in menial service positions, often in public enterprises such as baths.

Competition for even the most humble positions was keen and, in order to protect their jobs, Roman workers of all levels organized into colleges or guilds, trade associations with social and religious functions. These guilds protected members from unauthorized competition, set salaries, and at the same time provided the city government with a means of policing its vast population. Guilds ranged from teachers, physicians, scribes, and shippers, to sewer cleaners and muleteers. There were over twenty specialized guilds in the public baths, such as bath attendants, masseuses, and even armpit-hair pluckers.

Their meager incomes protected by their guilds, their precarious diets supplemented by the public dole, Rome's masses lived their short lives in a condition exceeded in wretchedness only by that of the worst slaves. When they died, not even a pauper's grave awaited them. Their remains were simply dumped into the sewage pits beyond the city's walls.

Still, the Jewish community remained deeply divided about its relationship with the wider world and with Rome. At one end of the spectrum were the Sadducees, a party composed largely of members of priestly families who enjoyed considerable influence with their foreign rulers. They were staunch defenders of the ancient Jewish law, or Torah, but not to the exclusion of other later religious and legal traditions. They were willing to work with Rome and even adopt some elements of Hellenism, as long as the services in the temple could continue.

At the other end of the spectrum were the Hasidim (meaning "the pious," "the loyal ones"), those who rejected all compromise with Hellenistic culture and collaboration with foreign powers. Many expected the arrival of a messiah, a liberator who would destroy the Romans and reestablish the kingdom of David. One party within the Hasidim were the Pharisees, who practiced strict dietary rules and rituals to maintain the separation of Jews and Gentiles (literally, "the peoples," that is, all non-Jews). The Pharisees accepted the writings of the Hebrew prophets along with the Torah and abided by a still larger body of orally transmitted law, the "tradition of the elders." The most prominent figure in this movement was Hillel (ca. 30 B.C.E.–10 C.E.), a Jewish scholar from Babylon who came to Jerusalem as a teacher of the law. He began a tradition of legal and scriptural interpretation which, in an expanded version centuries later, became the Talmud. Hillel was also a moral teacher who taught peace and love, not revolt. "Whatever is hateful to you, do not to your fellow man: this is the whole Law; the rest is mere commentary," he taught.

For all their insistence on purity and separation from other peoples, the Pharisees did not advocate violent revolt against Rome. They preferred to await divine intervention. Another group of Hasidim, the Zealots, were less willing to wait. After 6 C.E., when Judaea, Samaria, and Idumaea were annexed and combined into the province of Judaea administered by imperial procurators, the Zealots began to organize sporadic armed resistance to Roman rule. As ever, armed resistance was met with violent suppression. Through the first century C.E., clashes between Roman troops and Zealot revolutionaries grew more frequent and more widespread.

The already complex landscape of the Jewish religious world became further complicated by the brief career of Joshua ben Joseph (ca. 6 B.C.E.–30 C.E.), known to history as Jesus of Nazareth and to his followers as Jesus the Messiah or the Christ. Jesus came from Galilee, an area known as a Zealot stronghold. However, while Jesus preached the imminent coming of the kingdom of God, he did so in an entirely nonpolitical manner. He was, like many popular religious leaders, a miracle worker. When people flocked around him to see his wonders, he preached a message of peace and love of God and neighbor. His teachings were entirely within the Jewish tradition and closely resembled those of Hillel—with one major exception. While many contemporary religious leaders announced the imminent coming of the messiah, Jesus informed his closest followers, the apostles and disciples, that he himself was the messiah.

For roughly three years Jesus preached in Judaea and Galilee, drawing large, excited crowds. Many of his followers pressed him to lead a revolt against Roman authority and reestablish the kingdom of David, even though he insisted that the kingdom he would establish was not of this world. Other Jews saw his claims as blasphemy and his assertion that he was the king of Jews, even if a heavenly one, as a threat to the status quo. Jesus became more and more a figure of controversy, a catalyst for violence. Ultimately the Roman procurator (imperial representative), Pontius Pilate, decided that he posed a threat to law and order. Pilate, like other Roman magistrates, had no interest in the internal religious affairs of the Jews. However, he was troubled by anyone who caused political disturbances, no matter how unintentionally. Pilate ordered Jesus scourged and put to death by crucifixion, a common Roman form of execution for slaves, pirates, thieves, and noncitizen troublemakers.

The cruel death of this gentle man ended the popular agitation he had stirred up, but it did not deter his closest followers. They soon announced that three days after his death he had risen and had appeared to them numerous times over the next weeks. They took this resurrection as proof of his claims to be the messiah and confirmation of his promise of eternal life to those who believed in him. Soon a small group of his followers, led by Peter (d. ca. 64 C.E.), formed another Jewish sect, preaching and praying daily in the temple. New members were initiated into this sect, soon known as Christianity, through baptism, a purification rite in which the initiate was submerged briefly in flowing water. They also shared a ritual meal in which bread and wine were distributed to members. Otherwise, they remained entirely within the Jewish religious and cultural tradition, and Hellenized Jews and pagans who wished to join the sect had to observe strict Jewish law and custom.

Christianity spread beyond its origin as a Jewish sect because of the work of one man, Paul of Tarsus (ca. 5–ca. 67 C.E.). Although Paul was an observant Jew, he was part of the wider cosmopolitan world of the empire and from

Peter Announces the Good News

■ *The following passage, attributed to the Apostle Peter in the book of Christian scripture known as the* Acts of the Apostles, *is probably a close approximation of the earliest Christian preaching. In it, Jesus is presented as the new Moses.*

Men of Israel, why do you stare at us, as though by our own power or piety we had made him [a paralytic who has just been cured] walk? the God of Abraham and of Isaac and of Jacob, the God of our fathers, glorified his servant Jesus, whom you delivered up and denied in the presence of Pilate, when he had decided to release him. But you denied the Holy and Righteous One, and asked for a murderer to be granted to you, and killed the Author of life, whom God raised from the dead. To this we are witnesses. And his name, by faith in his name, has made this man strong whom you see and know; and the faith which is through Jesus has given the man this perfect health in the presence of you all.

And now, brethren, I know that you acted in ignorance, as did also your rulers. But what God foretold by the mouth of all the prophets, that his Christ should suffer, he thus fulfilled. Repent therefore, and turn again, that your sins may be blotted out, that times of refreshing may come from the presence of the Lord, and that he may send the Christ appointed for you, Jesus, whom heaven must receive until the time for establishing all that God spoke by the mouth of his holy prophets from of old.

Moses said, "The Lord God will raise up for you a prophet from your brethren as he raised me up. You shall listen to him in whatever he tells you. And it shall be that every soul that does not listen to that prophet shall be destroyed from the people." And all the prophets who have spoke, from Samuel and those who came afterwards, also proclaimed these days.

You are the sons of the prophets and of the covenant which God gave to your fathers, saying to Abraham, "And in your posterity shall all the families of the earth be blessed." God, having raised up his servant, sent him to you first, to bless you in turning every one of you from your wickedness.

From *Acts* 3, 17–26. *The Holy Bible, Revised Standard Version.*

---

birth enjoyed the privileges of Roman citizenship. He saw Christianity as a separate tradition, completing and perfecting Judaism but intended for the whole world.

Paul set out to spread his message, crisscrossing Asia Minor, Greece, and even traveling to Rome. Wherever he went, Paul won converts and established churches, called *ecclesiae*, or assemblies. Everywhere Paul and the other disciples went they worked wonders, cast out demons, cured illnesses, and preached. Paul's teachings, while firmly rooted in the Jewish historical tradition, were radically new. God had created the human race, he taught, in the image of God and destined it for eternal life. However, by deliberate sin of the first humans, Adam and Eve, humans had lost eternal life and introduced evil and death into the world. Even then God did not abandon his people but began, through the Jews, to prepare for their eventual redemption. That salvation

was accomplished by Jesus, the son of God, through his faith, a free and unmerited gift of God to his elect. Through faith, the Christian ritual of baptism, and participation in the church, men and women can share in the salvation offered by God.

How many conversions resulted from Paul's theological message and how many resulted from the miracles he and the other disciples worked will never be known, but another factor certainly played a part in the success of conversions. That was the courage Christians showed in the face of persecution.

Even the tolerance and elasticity of Rome for new religions could be stretched only to a point. Their stubborn refusal to acknowledge the existence of the other gods and to participate in the cult of the genius of the emperor was intolerable. Christianity was an aggressive and successful cult, attracting followers throughout the empire. This was not religion, it was subversion. Beginning during Nero's reign, Roman officials sporadically rounded up Christians, destroyed their sacred scriptures, and executed those who refused to sacrifice to the imperial genius. But instead of decreasing the cult's appeal, persecution only aided it. For those who believed that death was birth into a new and better life, martyrdom was a reward, not a penalty.

This new religious movement, strengthened by a message of salvation, a reputation for wonders, a decentralized network of churches, and an enthusiasm for martyrdom, soon reached every corner of the empire. Progressively, an ever greater percentage of the empire's population looked to it for answers to life's problems.

The Cultural Legacy of Imperial Rome

During the two centuries of the Pax Romana, both members of old Roman families and provincials cultivated Latin and Greek letters as the mark of their status. Writers sought to mold character as well as to entertain and inform. Rome's greatest historian, Cornelius Tacitus (ca. 56–ca. 120), wrote to instruct and to edify his generation and did so in a style characterized by irony and a sharp sense of the differences between public propaganda and the realities of power politics. His subject was not only Rome but the barbarian world. His picture of Germanic and British societies served as a warning to Rome against excessive self-confidence and laxity.

Tacitus' contemporaries, Plutarch (ca. 46-after 119 C.E.) and Suetonius (ca. 69-after 122 C.E.), were biographers rather than historians. Plutarch, who wrote in Greek, composed *Parallel Lives*, a series of character studies in which he compared an eminent Greek with an eminent Roman. Suetonius also wrote biographies, using anecdotes to portray character. He delighted in the rumors of private scandals that surrounded the emperors and used personal vice to explain public failings.

In the later second century, Romans in general preferred the study and writing of philosophy, particularly stoicism, over history. The most influential Stoic philosopher of the century was Epictetus (ca. 55–135 C.E.), a former slave who taught that man could be free by the control of his will and the cultivation of inner peace. Like the early Stoics, Epictetus taught the universal brotherhood of humankind and the identity of nature and divine providence. He urged his pupils to recognize that dependence on external things was the cause of unhappiness and therefore they should free themselves from reliance on material possessions and public esteem.

The slave's philosophy found its most eager pupil in an emperor. Marcus Aurelius (161–180 C.E.) reigned during a period when stresses on the Empire were beginning to show in an alarming manner. Once more the Parthians attacked the eastern frontier, while in Britain and Germany barbarians struck across the borders. In 166 a confederation of barbarians known as the Marcomanni crossed the Danube and raided as far south as northern Italy. A plague, brought west by troops returning from the Parthian front, ravaged the whole empire. Aurelius spent virtually the whole of his reign on the Danubian frontier, repelling the barbarians and shoring up the empire's defenses.

Throughout his reign Aurelius found consolation in the Stoic philosophy of Epictetus. In his soldier's tent at night he composed his *Meditations*, a volume of philosophical musings. Like the slave, the emperor sought freedom from the burden of his office in his will and in the proper understanding of his role in the divine order. He called himself to introspection, to a constant awareness, under the glories and honors heaped upon him by his entourage, of his true human nature: "A poor soul burdened with a corpse."

Aurelius' Stoic philosophy did not serve the empire well. For all his emphasis on understanding, he badly misjudged his son Commodus (180–192 C.E.), who

The emperor Marcus Aurelius performing a sacrifice in front of the temple of Jupiter, Juno, and Minerva. The relief captures Marcus Aurelius in the role of Stoic disciple rather than in his position as Roman emperor.

TACITUS ON THE GERMANS

■ *At the end of the first century C.E., Tacitus wrote a brief account of the Germanic peoples living beyond the frontiers, in part to inform Romans about this neighboring people and in part to criticize the morals and practices of Roman society. In general, his information, although selective and filtered through Roman culture, appears quite accurate.*

They pick their kings on the basis of noble birth, their generals on the basis of bravery. Nor do their kings have limitless or arbitrary power, and the generals win favor by the example they set if they are energetic, if they are distinguished, if they fight before the battle-line, rather than by the power they wield. But no one except the priests is allowed to inflict punishment with death, chains, or even flogging, and the priests act not, as it were, to penalize and at the command of the general, but, so to speak, at the order of the god, who they believe is at hand when they are waging war . . . The nobles make decisions about lesser matters, all freemen about things of greater significance, with this priviso, nonetheless, that those subjects, of which ultimate judgment is in the hands of the mass of people, receive preliminary consideration among the nobles . . . When the crowd thinks it opportune, they sit down fully armed. Silence is demanded by the priests, who then also have the right of compulsion. Soon the king or the chieftains are heard, in accordance with the age, nobility, glory in war, and eloquence of each, with the influence of persuasion being greater than the power to command. If a proposal has displeased them, they show their displeasure with a roar; but if it has won favor, the bang their *frameae* [spears] together; the most prestigious kind of approval is praise with arms . . . There is an obligation to undertake the personal feuds as well as the friendships of one's father or blood-relative; but the feuds do not continue without possibility of settlement, for even murder is atoned for by a specific number of cattle and sheep and the entire family accepts the settlement, with advantage to the community, since feuds are the most dangerous when joined with freedom.

From Tacitus, *Germany.*

succeeded him. Commodus, whose chief interest was in being a gladiator, saw himself the incarnation of the legendary hero Heracles, and appeared in public clad as a gladiator and as consul. As Commodus sank into insanity, Rome was once more convulsed with purges and proscriptions. Commodus' assassination in 192 did not end the violence. The Pax Romana was over.

During these two hundred years, Roman culture had put down deep roots from Britain to Mesopotamia, uniting provincial and Roman elites in a common Greco-Roman tradition of literature, philosophy, and governance. At the same time, non-Roman cultural traditions, especially Christianity, spread across this same vast area, beginning a new, internal transformation of the empire. The violence and unrest that once more convulsed the empire affected them both.

Crisis, Restoration, Division, 192–376 C.E.

From the reign of Septimius Severus (193–211) to the time of Diocletian (284–305), both internal and external challenges shook the Roman Empire. The empire survived these third-century crises but its social, political, and economic structures were radically transformed. Stabilization of the empire under Diocletian meant the creation of a new, autocratic constitution. Reform under his successor Constantine (306–337) meant the abandonment of its old gods for that of the Christians.

The reasons for the third-century crisis were both internal and external. The sheer size of the empire was a fundamental problem. Haphazard expansion in many regions overextended the frontiers. The manpower and resources needed to maintain this vast territory strained the economic system of the empire.

The economic system itself was part of the reason for this strain on resources. For all of its commercial networks, the economy of the empire remained tied to agriculture. To the aristocrats of the ancient world, agriculture was the only honorable source of wealth. The goal of the successful merchant was to liquidate his commercial assets, buy estates, and rise into the leisured landholding elite. As a result, liquid capital either for investment or taxation was always scarce.

Lack of sophistication in commercial and industrial business practice characterized the financial system of the empire as well. Government had always been conducted on the cheap. The tax system of the empire had never been very efficient at tapping into the real wealth of the aristocracy. Each individual city made its own collective assessments. Individuals eager to win the gratitude of their local communities were expected to provide essential services from their own pockets. Even with the vast wealth of the empire at its disposal, the government never developed a system of public debt— that is, a policy of borrowing against future revenues. As a result, the only way to solve short-term cash-flow problems was to debase the coinage by using more copper and less silver.

The failure of the empire to develop a stable political base complicated its economic problems. In times of emergency, imperial control relied on the personal presence and command of the emperor. As the empire grew, it became impossible for this presence to be felt everywhere. Moreover, the empire never developed a regular system of imperial succession. Control of the army, which was the ultimate source of imperial power, was possible only as long as the emperor was able to lead his armies to victory.

An Empire on the Defensive

Through much of the late second and third centuries, emperors failed dismally to lead their armies to victory. The barely Romanized provincials in the military bore the brunt of these attacks. When the emperors selected by the distant Roman senate failed to win victory, front-line armies unhesitatingly raised their own commanders to the imperial office. These commanders set about restructuring the empire in favor of the army. They opened important administrative posts to soldiers, ex-

panded the army's size, raised military pay, initiated expensive building programs in frontier settlements, and in general introduced authoritarian military discipline throughout society. To finance these costly measures, the new military government confiscated senatorial wealth, introduced new forms of taxation, and increasingly debased the coinage.

Soon, however, the military control of the empire turned into a nightmare even for the provinces and their armies. Exercising their newly discovered power, armies raised and then destroyed a succession of pretenders, offering support to whichever imperial candidate promised them the greatest riches. The army's incessant demands for higher pay led emperors to lower the amount of silver in the coins with which the soldiers were paid. But the less the coins were worth, the more of them were necessary to purchase goods. Such drastic inflation wrecked the economic stability of the empire and spurred the army on to greater and more impossible demands for raises.

The crisis of the third century did not result only from economic and political instability within the empire. Rome's internal crises coincided with increased attacks from outside the empire. In Africa, Berber tribes harassed the frontiers. The Sassanid dynasty in the new Persian Empire, which replaced the Parthians in 224, threatened Rome's eastern frontier. When the Emperor Valerian (253–260) attempted to prevent the Persian king of kings Shapur I from seizing Roman Mesopotamia and Armenia, he was captured and held prisoner for the rest of his life.

This cameo was made to the order of Shapur I after the capture of Valerian during the great battle near Antioch in 260 C.E. The symbolic scene has Shapur seizing Valerian simply by grasping his hand.

While Rome most feared this empire to the east, its greatest danger lay rather in the west. Along both the Rhine and the Danube, new barbarian peoples raided deep into the empire and harassed Roman commerce on sea and land. The central administration of the empire simply could not deal effectively with these barbarian attacks. Left on their own, regional provincial commanders at times even headed separatist movements. Provincial aristocrats who despaired of receiving any help from distant Rome often supported these pretenders.

Political and military instability had devastating effects on the lives of ordinary people. Citizenship had been extended to virtually all free inhabitants of the empire in 212, but that right was a formality given simply to enlarge the tax base, since only citizens paid inheritance taxes. Society became sharply divided into the privileged *honestiores*—senators, municipal gentry, and the military—and the increasingly burdened *humiliores*—everyone else. The *humiliores* suffered the most from the tax increases because unlike the *honestiores* they could neither bribe their way out of them nor intimidate tax collectors with private armies. They were also frequent targets of extortion by the military and of violence perpetrated by bandits.

Barbarians at the Gate

The external attacks of the barbarians compounded the internal violence that threatened to destroy the Roman Empire. Along the Rhine, various Germanic tribes known collectively as the Franks and the Alemanni began raiding expeditions into the empire. Along the lower Danube and in southern Russia, a barbarian confederation known as the Goths raided the Balkans and harassed Roman shipping on the Black Sea. These attacks reflected changes within the Germanic world as profound as those within the empire. Between the second and fifth centuries the Germanic world was transformed from a mosaic of small, decentralized, agricultural tribes into a number of powerful military tribal confederations capable of challenging Rome itself.

The Germanic peoples typically inhabited small villages organized into patriarchal households, integrated into clans, which in turn composed tribes. For the most part, clans governed themselves, and except in war tribal leaders had little authority over their followers. In the second century many tribes had kings, but they were religious rather than political leaders.

Germanic communities lived by farming, but cattle raising and especially warfare carried the highest social prestige. Women took care of agricultural chores and household duties. Like the number of cattle, the number of wives showed a man's social position.

Warfare defined social groupings and warriors dominated public life. Conflict took the form of feuds, and each act of aggression was repaid in kind. If an individual within a clan had a grievance with an individual within another clan, all his kinsmen were obliged to assist him.

This relief shows landowners collecting rents from peasants. The peasantry, displaced by slaves, congregated in the capital and formed a poverty-stricken urban underclass.

Thus a single incident could result in a continuous escalation of acts of revenge.

The practice of feuding, especially within the tribe, had enormous costs. Families were decimated and strong warriors who were needed to defend the tribe from outside attack faced constant danger from members of their own tribe. These feuds could in turn lead to the hiving off of irreconcilable factions, which might in time form their own tribes. Thus tribal leaders attempted to reduce hostilities by establishing payments called *wergeld* in place of the blood vengeance demanded in reparation for crimes.

In contrast to the familial structure of barbarian society stood another warrior group that cut across kindred and even tribal units. This was the warrior band, called in Latin the *comitatus*. Some young warriors formed personal bonds with particularly able leaders and pledged them absolute loyalty. In return the leaders were obligated to lead their warriors to victory and to share with them the spoils of war. These warrior societies were organized for their own plunder and fighting. Although nontribal, successful *comitatus* could form the nuclei of new tribes.

This intratribal and intertribal violence produced a rough equilibrium of power and wealth as long as small Germanic tribes lived in isolation. The presence of the Roman Empire, felt both directly and indirectly in the barbarian world, upset this equilibrium. Unintentionally, Rome itself helped transform the Germanic tribes into the major threat to the imperial system since the attraction of Roman luxury goods and the Romans' efforts to establish friendly Germanic buffer zones along the borders drew even distant tribes into the Roman imperial system.

In return for payments of gold and foodstuffs, chieftains of these "federated" tribes opposed tribes hostile to Rome and supplied warriors for the Roman army. Others even led their people into Roman service. By the late third century the Roman army included Franks, Goths, and Saxons serving as far away from their homes as Egypt. Greater wealth and Roman military backing led to increasingly powerful warrior leaders among the Germanic barbarians, who created new tribes and tribal confederations—the Marcomanni, the Alemanni, and the Franks. By the end of the second century this internal barbarian transformation spilled over into the empire in the form of the Marcomannian wars and the Saxon, Frankish, and Alemannic incursions into the western provinces.

Around the same time, along the Oder and Vistula rivers to the north, a group later known as the Goths

An ivory plaque portraying Stilicho, a Vandal by birth, who rose to be Master of Soldiers and Consul of Rome. He is shown here in the patrician robes of a consul and carrying the weapons of a soldier, suggesting his dual role.

began their slow consolidation around a royal family. The Goths were unique in that their kings exercised more military authority than was usual for a Germanic tribe. These kings formed the nucleus of a constantly changing barbarian group. Between the second and fourth centuries, the bearers of this Gothic royal tradition began to filter to the south and east, ultimately transferring their model of barbarian organization to the area of present-day Kiev in southern Russia. This move was not so much a physical migration of thousands of people across Europe as the gradual confederation under Gothic leadership of various Germanic, Slavic, and Scythian peoples living around the Black Sea. By the early third century this Gothic confederation was fighting Rome for supremacy in the region.

The tetrarchy was an attempt to regulate the succession. Here, the emperors Diocletian and Maximian are depicted with their caesars, Constantius of the West and Galerius of the East, who were their respective sons-in-law.

The Empire Restored

By the last decades of the third century, the empire seemed in danger of crumbling under combined internal and external pressure. That it did not was largely due to the efforts of the soldier-emperor Aurelian (270–275), who was able to repulse the barbarians, restore the unity of the empire, and then set about stabilizing the internal imperial structure.

Diocletian, a Dalmatian soldier who had risen through the ranks to become emperor, completed the process of stabilization and reorganization of the imperial system begun by Aurelian. The result was a regime that in some ways increased imperial power and in other ways simply did away with the pretenses that had previously masked the emperor's true position.

No longer was the emperor *princeps*, or "first citizen." Now he was *dominus*, or "lord," the term of respect used by slaves in addressing their masters. He also assumed the title of *Iovius*, or Jupiter, thus claiming divine status, and demanded adoration as a living god. Diocletian recognized that the empire was too large and complex for one man to rule. To solve the problem, he divided the empire into eastern and western parts, each part to be ruled by both an augustus and a junior emperor, or caesar. Diocletian was augustus in the east, supported by his caesar, Galerius. In the west the rulers were the augustus Maximian and his caesar, Constantius.

In theory this tetrarchy, or rule by four, provided for regular succession. The caesars, who were married to daughters of the augusti, were to succeed them. Although from time to time subsequent emperors would rule alone, Diocletian's innovation proved successful and enduring. The empire was divided administratively into eastern and western parts until the death of Julius Nepos, the last legitimate emperor in the west, in 480.

In addition to this constitutional reform, Diocletian enacted or consolidated a series of measures to improve the functioning of the imperial administration. He reorganized and expanded the army, approximately doubled the number of provinces, separated their military and civil administration, and greatly increased the number of bureaucrats to administer them. He attempted to stem runaway inflation by increasing the amount of silver in coins and fixing maximum prices and wages throughout the empire. He restructured the imperial tax system, basing it on payments in goods and produce in order to distribute the burden more equitably on all citizens and to avoid problems of currency debasement.

The pillar of Diocletian's success was his victorious military machine. He was effective because, like the barbarian chieftains who had turned their tribes into armies, he militarized society and led this military society to victory. Like Diocletian himself, his soldiers were drawn from provincial, marginal regions. They showed tremendous devotion to their god-emperor.

Some aspects of Diocletian's program, such as the improvement of the civil administration and the military, were successful. Others, such as the reform of silver currency and wage and price controls, were dismal failures. One effect of the fiscal reforms was to bind *colons*, or hereditary tenant farmers, to their lands, since they were forbidden to leave the villages where they were registered to pay their taxes. In this practice lay the origins of European serfdom. Another effect was the gradual destruction of the local city councils, since their members, the *decurions*, were held personally responsible for the payment of local assessments whether or not they could be collected from the other inhabitants. In time this led to the dissolution of local civil government.

All of these measures were designed to marshal the entire population in the monumental task of preserving Roman culture. Central to this task was the proper reverential attitude toward the divine emperors who directed it. One group seemed stubbornly opposed to this heroic effort: the Christians. Their opposition led to the beginning of the Great Persecution, which formally began in 303 and lasted sporadically until 313. It resulted in the death of hundreds of Christians who refused to sacrifice to the pagan gods.

Constantine the Emperor of God

In 305, in the midst of the Great Persecution, Diocletian and his co-augustus Maximian took the extraordinary step of abdicating in favor of their caesars, Galerius and Constantius. This abdication was intended to provide for an orderly succession. Instead, the sons of Constantius and Maximian, Constantine and Maxentius (306–312), drawing on the prejudice of the increasingly barbarian armies toward hereditary succession, set about wrecking the tetrarchy. In so doing they plunged the empire once more into civil war as they fought over the western half of the empire.

Victory in the west came to Constantine in 312, when he defeated and killed Maxentius in a battle at the Mulvian Bridge outside Rome. Constantine attributed his victory to a vision telling him to paint a ♀ on the shields of his soldiers. For pagans this symbol indicated the solar emblem of the cult of the Unconquered Sun. For Christians it was the Chi-Rho, ☧, formed from the first two letters of the Greek word for Christ. The next year in Milan Constantine and his co-emperor Licinius (308–324) rescinded the persecution of Christians and granted Christian clergy the same privileges enjoyed by pagan priests. Constantine himself was not baptized until near death, a common practice in antiquity. However, during his reign Christianity grew from a persecuted minority to the most favored cult in the empire.

Almost as important as Constantine's conversion to Christianity was his decision to establish his capital in Byzantium, a city founded by Greek colonists on the narrow neck of water connecting the Black Sea to the Mediterranean. He transformed and enriched this small town, calling it the New Rome. Later it was known as Constantinople, the city of Constantine. For the next eleven centuries Constantinople served as the heart of the Roman and then the Byzantine world. From his new city, Constantine began to transform the empire into a Christian state and Christianity into a Roman state religion.

The effects of Constantine's conversion on the empire and on Christianity were far-reaching. Constantine himself continued to maintain cordial relations with representatives of all cults and to use ambiguous language that would offend no one when talking about "the deity." His successors were less broad-minded. They quickly reversed the positions of Christianity and paganism.

While paganism was being disestablished, Christianity was rapidly becoming the established religion. Constantine made enormous financial contributions to Christian communities to repay them for their losses during persecutions. He erected rich churches on the model of Roman basilicas, or administrative buildings, and converted temples into Christian places of worship. He gave bishops the authority to act as magistrates within the Christian community. Constantine attempted to make himself the de facto head of the Church. He even presided at the Council of Nicaea in 325, at which the assembled bishops condemned the Arian teaching that Jesus as Son of God was not equal to God the Father, and established the doctrine of the Trinity (three divine persons, the Father, Son, and Spirit, in one God). Constantine and his successors, with the exception of his nephew Julian (361–363), who attempted unsuccessfully both to reestablish paganism and to promote traditional Hellenism, sought to use the cult of the one God to strengthen their control over the empire.

RELIGIOUS TOLERATION AND PERSECUTION

■ *In 313 Constantine and Licinius met at Milan and agreed on an empire-wide policy of religious toleration. The first selection is from the "Edict of Toleration" and the so-called "Edict of Milan" (actually a directive probably issued to eastern governors shortly after by Licinius). The second, from the* Theodosian Code, *published by Emperor Theodosius in 395, ends toleration, both of Arianism and of pagan practices, reversing the status of persecutor and persecuted.*

Observing that freedom of worship should not be denied, but that each one should be given the right in accordance with his conviction and will to adhere to the religion that suits his preference, we had already long since given orders both to the Christians . . . to maintain the faith of their own sect and worship . . .

When I, Constantine Augustus, and I, Licinius Augustus, met under happy auspices in Milan . . . we considered that first of all regulations should be drawn up to secure respect for divinity, to wit: to grant both to the Christians and to all men unrestricted right to follow the form of worship each desired, to the end that whatever divinity there be on the heavenly seat may be favorably disposed and propitious to us and all those placed under our authority. Accordingly, with salutary and most upright reasoning, we resolved on adopting this policy, namely that we should consider that no one whatsoever should be denied freedom to devote himself either to the cult of the Christians or to such religion as he deems best suited for himself, so that the highest divinity, to whose worship we pay allegiance with free minds, may grant us in all things his wonted favor and benevolence.

From Lewis and Reinhold, *Roman Civilization, Selected Readings*, Vol. II.

I, 2. It is Our will that all the peoples who are ruled by the administration of Our Clemency shall practice that religion which the divine Peter the Apostle transmitted to the Romans, as the religion which he introduced makes clear even unto this day . . . According to the apostolic discipline and the evangelic doctrine, we shall believe in the single Deity of the Father, the Son, and the Holy Spirit, under the concept of equal majesty and of the Holy Trinity.

We command that those persons who follow this rule shall embrace the name of Catholic Christians. The rest, however, whom We adjudge demented and insane, shall sustain the infamy of heretical dogmas, their meeting places shall not receive the name of churches, and they shall be smitten first by divine vengeance and secondly by the retribution of Our own initiative, which we shall assume in accordance with the divine judgment.

X, 2. Superstition shall cease, the madness of sacrifices shall be abolished. For if any man in violation of the law of the sainted Emperor, Our father, and in violation of this command of Our Clemency, should dare to perform sacrifices, he shall suffer the infliction of a suitable punishment and the effect of an immediate sentence.

From *The Theodosian Code.*

Over the course of the fourth century, the number of Christians rose from five to thirty million. Imperial support was essential to the spread of Christianity in the fourth century but other factors encouraged conversion as well. Christian miracles, particularly that of exorcism, or casting out of demons, made Christian preachers seem more competent than others to deal with these supernatural creatures whose existence no one doubted. Finally, persecution of polytheists by Constantine's successors and local Christian authorities played a large part as well.

During the third and fourth centuries, the empire endured crises from within and without. It survived by transforming itself from a decentralized civilian system

entire barbarian world into chaos once more. In the following century, the empire was profoundly changed. In the east, emperors ruled a shrinking and increasingly Hellenized empire, while in the west, barbarian kings replaced imperial governors as rulers of former Roman provinces. At the same time that the political traditions of the empire were being transformed, new and powerful forms of religious expression transformed its cultural traditions.

The Huns quickly destroyed the Gothic confederation and absorbed many of the peoples who had constituted the Goths. Others, such as the Visigoths, sought protection in the empire. But the Roman authorities treated them as brutally as had the Huns, forcing some to sell their children into slavery in return for morsels of dog flesh. In despair the Visigoths rose up against the Romans, and against all odds, annihilated an imperial army at Adrianople in 378, killing the emperor Valens himself. His successor, Theodosius (379–395), was forced to allow the Visigoths to settle along the Danube and to be governed by their own leaders.

Theodosius' treaty with the Visigoths set an ominous precedent. Never before had a barbarian people been allowed to settle as a political unit within the empire. Within a few years, the Visigoths were again on the move, traveling across the Balkans into Italy under the command of their chieftain Alaric (ca. 370–410). In 410 they captured Rome and sacked it for three days, an

Colossal head of Constantine with eyes upraised to show that the emperor thought of himself as close to God.

to an autocratic military one; from a Roman, Latin empire to an increasingly Greek, eastward-looking one; by enlisting its external enemies in its armies; and by making a persecuted sect its official religion. All of these measures were undertaken by powerful and ruthless emperors who sought, by whatever means, to bolster their position.

The Empire Transformed, 376–500 C.E.

The emperor and the empire needed bolstering in 376 when the Huns, a nomadic horse people from central Asia, swept into the Black Sea region and threw the

Painting of Christ from a catacomb ceiling. The catacombs were underground passages near Rome used by the early Christians as cemeteries, for funeral and memorial services, and as places of refuge during times of persecution.

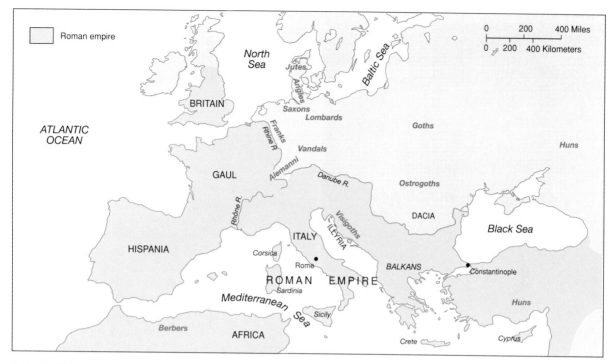

Barbarian Tribes

event that sent shock waves throughout the entire empire. Ultimately the Visigoths settled in Spain and southern Gaul with the approval of the emperor.

The Barbarization of the West

Rome did not fall. It was transformed. Romans participated in and even encouraged this transformation. Roman accommodation with the Visigoths set the pattern for subsequent settlement of barbarians in the western half of the empire. By this time, barbarians made up the bulk of the imperial army, and were frequently themselves its commanders. Indeed, these so-called imperial Germans had often proven even more loyal to Rome than the Roman provincial populations they were to protect. In the late fourth and fifth centuries, emperors accepted whole barbarian peoples as integral parts of the Roman army and settled them within the empire.

The Visigothic kingdom in southern Gaul and Spain was typical in this respect. Alaric's successor, Ataulf, was extremely eager to win the approval of the emperor. He married Galla Placidia, the daughter of the Emperor Theodosius and the sister of Emperor Honorius, in a Roman ceremony in Narbonne in 414. Soon afterward he

established a government at Bordeaux directed by Gallo-Roman aristocrats. Although his opponents soon assassinated him, his successors concluded a treaty with Constantinople in which the Visigoths were recognized as a legitimate, established political presence within the empire.

The Visigoths were not the only powerful barbarian people to challenge the empire. The Vandals, who had entered the empire in 406, crossed over into Africa, the richest region of the western empire, and quickly conquered it. In 455 they sacked Rome much more thoroughly than had the Goths forty-five years earlier.

Another threat appeared in the 430s, when the Huns, formerly Roman allies, invaded the empire under their charismatic leader Attila (ca. 406–453). Although defeated in Gaul by a combined army of barbarians in 451, they turned toward Italy and penetrated as far as Rome. There they were stopped not by the rapidly disintegrating imperial forces but by the bishop of Rome, Pope Leo I (c. 400–461), who met Attila before the city's gates. What transpired between the two is not known, but Attila's subsequent withdrawal from Italy vastly increased the prestige of the papacy. Now not only were popes successors of Saint Peter and bishops

On this medallion from Spain the emperor Theodosius is presented as a godlike figure detached from the struggles of ordinary people.

of the principal city of the west, but they were replacing the emperor as protector of the city. The foundations of the political power of the papacy were established.

The confederation of the Huns collapsed after the death of Attila in 453, but imperial power did not revive in Italy. A series of incompetent emperors and pretenders were pushed aside by barbarian generals, the last of these pretenders being Romulus Augustulus in 476. However, after the death of the last legitimate western emperor, Julius Nepos, in 480, Emperor Zeno (474–491) conferred the title of patrician on the Ostrogothic king Theodoric, who invaded Italy with imperial blessing and established himself as ruler. Imperial presence had ceased to exist in Italy.

In Gaul, between the Seine and the Loire, the Roman general Flavius Aëtius and, after his death, the general Syagrius continued to represent some imperial presence. But the armies that Aëtius and Syagrius commanded consisted entirely of barbarians, particularly of Visigoths and Franks, and they represented the interests of local aristocratic factions rather than those of Constantinople. So thoroughly barbarized had these last Roman commanders become in their military command and political control that the barbarians referred to Syagrius as "king of the Romans." Ultimately in 486 Syagrius was defeated and replaced by the Frank Clovis, son of his military commander Childeric, probably with the blessing of the emperor.

Britain met a similar fate. Abandoned by Roman legions around 407, the Romano-Celtic population in this province concluded a treaty with bands of Saxons and Angles to protect Britain from other barbarian raiders. As had happened elsewhere in the empire, the barbarians came as federated troops and stayed as rulers.

The establishment of barbarian kingdoms within the Roman world meant the end of the western empire as a political entity. However, the emperors continued to pretend that all these barbarian peoples, with the exception of the Vandals, were Roman troops commanded by loyal Roman officers who happened to be of barbarian origin. Occasionally emperors granted them portions of abandoned lands or existing estates. Local Roman elites considered these leaders rude and uncultured barbarians who nevertheless could be made to serve these elites' own interests more easily than better educated imperial bureaucrats.

Barbarian military leaders needed local ties by which to govern the large indigenous populations over whom they ruled. They found cooperation with these aristocrats both necessary and advantageous. Thus while individual landowners might have suffered in the transition from Roman to barbarian rule, for the most part this transition took place with less disturbance of the local social or political scene than was once thought. The one real source of friction between barbarians and provincial elites was religion. Many Goths had converted to Christianity around the time that the Huns had destroyed the Gothic confederation. However, they had chosen the Arian form of Christianity and had held to it long after it had been abandoned in the empire. Thus, wherever the barbarians settled, they were met with distrust and hostility from the orthodox clergy. In southern Gaul and

The Vandals crossed into North Africa from Spain and founded a state centered on Carthage. This mosaic of the late fifth or early sixth century shows a prosperous Vandal lord leaving his villa. His costume is typical of barbarians.

Italy this hostility created serious difficulties because during the fifth century bishops had assumed many of the traditional duties and powers held by provincial Roman administrators. Accommodation on the political plane was thus complicated by differences of belief, and continued to be elusive as long as barbarian kings and their armies remained Arian.

The Hellenization of the East

The eastern half of the empire, in contrast to the west, managed to survive and even to prosper in the fifth and sixth centuries. In the east, beginning in 400, the trends toward militarization and barbarization of the administration were reversed, the strength of the imperial government was reaffirmed, and the vitality and integrity of the empire were restored.

Several reasons account for the contrast between east and west. First, the east had always been more urbanized and civilized than the west. It had an old tradition of civil control that antedated the Roman Empire itself. When the decay of Roman traditions allowed regionalism and tribalism to arise in the west, the same decay brought in the east a return to Hellenistic traditions. Second, the east had never developed the tradition of public poverty and private wealth characteristic of the west. In the east tax revenues continued to support an administrative apparatus, which remained in the hands of civilians rather than barbarian military commanders. Moreover, the local aristocracies in the eastern provinces never achieved the wealth and independence of their western counterparts. Finally, Christian bishops, frequently divided over doctrinal issues, never managed to monopolize either sacred power, which was shared by itinerant holy men and monks, or secular power, which was wielded by imperial agents. Thus under the firm direction of its emperors, especially Theodosius and later Zeno, the eastern empire not only survived but prepared for a new expansionist phase under the emperor Justinian.

Everywhere, the patina of Latin culture began to wear thin as provincials began to rise to positions of prominence and power. In the east, this meant the reemergence of regional cultures and especially of Hellenistic traditions. It also meant that Christian and pagan thinkers would use these traditions to interpret the crises of their world.

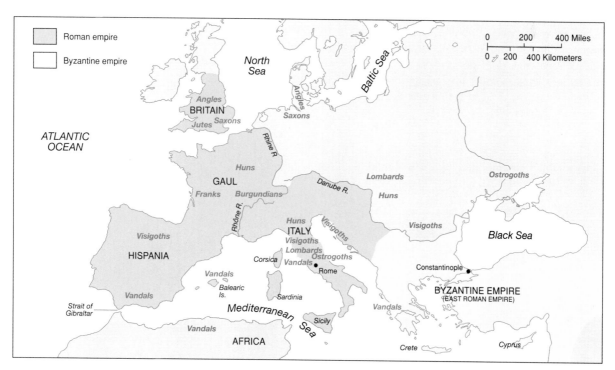

Barbarian Invasions

The Transformation of Elite Culture

The transformation of the classical world from a pagan empire, secure in its mastery over the civilized world, to a fragmented Christian one was as profoundly felt in the cultural sphere as it was in the political and social spheres. Crisis forces choice, and in the third through fifth centuries the choices faced by intellectuals were as profound as those faced by emperors. Where should one look for peace—within or without? Ought Christians to reject the intellectual tradition of the Greco-Roman world or recast it in Christian form? Finally, was the Roman political system in which Christianity had become so deeply embedded essential to its survival?

Three very different thinkers—Plotinus, Origen, and Augustine—set the stage for future European cultural developments.

During the crisis of the third century, Hellenistic culture reached its zenith in the life and work of the pagan Egyptian philosopher Plotinus (205–270), who recast Platonism into the form that was the foundation of Christian, Islamic, and Jewish thought through the Middle Ages. His contemporary and compatriot Origen (185–254) began to intellectualize the meaning of the Christian Scriptures and transformed pagan philosophy into a Christian intellectual tradition. As a result of his work Christian intellectuals could no longer be dismissed as "wool seekers, cobblers, laundry workers, and the most illiterate and rustic yokels." In the following century Augustine of Hippo (354–430) faced a new, internal challenge. Victory over paganism was quickly followed by serious disagreements over the proper rela-

tionship between the Christian community and the Christian empire. In the early period of Christianity the question was whether to be a Christian meant to be a Jew. Now Augustine had to decide whether to be a Christian meant to be a Roman.

Plotinus exemplified the vital Hellenistic high culture of late antiquity. He was born in a small provincial town in Upper Egypt, but his restless intellect led him first to dabble in Gnosticism and then to travel to Mesopotamia in the hope of studying Persian and Indian philosophy. The crucial event in his life was his introduction to Platonic philosophy as a student in Alexandria in his late twenties. The new, or Neoplatonic, tradition, which he studied and of which he became the principal spokesperson, was by the third century much more than a philosophy. It was a virtual religion, combining Platonic and Stoic thought and demanding withdrawal from the world and full-time dedication to the pursuit of wisdom.

Plotinus and his fellow Neoplatonists believed that through rational contemplation it was possible to see beyond material existence and to recognize the intimate connection between the invisible God and the visible world. Material and spiritual reality were thus intimately and properly associated. For those too ignorant or superstitious to see the beauty of this harmony, especially Christians, Plotinus and his followers had nothing but scorn. And yet the same Alexandrian teacher who instructed Plotinus had another, even more influential, student. He also taught Origen, who would reconcile Christianity and classical philosophy.

Origen was born into a Christian family in Alexandria, then the most cultivated city of the Hellenistic

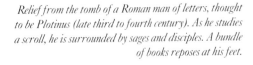

Relief from the tomb of a Roman man of letters, thought to be Plotinus (late third to fourth century). As he studies a scroll, he is surrounded by sages and disciples. A bundle of books reposes at his feet.

world, and grew up with an acute sense of the challenge of being a Christian. When Origen was seventeen his father was executed for his faith and his property was confiscated. Origen himself would perish in a subsequent persecution. To support his mother and six younger brothers, he began to teach rhetoric, that is, traditional pagan learning. Later he headed the Christian education program of Alexandria. Important Christians and pagans sought his advice.

Origen invented a new sort of Christian, the Christian intellectual. He moved Christian teaching from a literal to a symbolic understanding of Scripture, and he gave it a sound philosophical foundation by synthesizing it with Plotinus' Neoplatonism.

Initially, Origen interpreted Scripture literally, but eventually rejected literal interpretation when he realized the importance of symbolism. For Origen the Scriptures were a symbol of God's eternal teaching—incomprehensible to those who sought a literal meaning but apparent to those who looked for the hidden spiritual message. This allegorical tradition would dominate Christian biblical studies for over a thousand years. He also insisted that, since God endowed man with reason, he must have intended that humans reach true wisdom through reason. Origen's insistence that there was no contradiction between faith and reason established a continuing intellectual basis for Christianity.

Origen was the father of Christian philosophy. Augustine was the father of Christian political science. Born into a well-off North African family in the town of Tagaste, he was quickly drawn into the good life and upward mobility open to bright young provincials in the fourth century. His skills in rhetoric took him to the provincial capital of Carthage and then on to Rome and finally Milan, the western imperial residence, where he gained fame as one of the foremost rhetoricians of the empire.

Although his mother was a Christian, he was not baptized at birth, and while in Carthage he joined the Manichees, a materialist, dualist sect that rejected the notion of spiritual reality and taught that good and evil were caused by two different ultimate principles. As protégé of the Manichees, Augustine gained introductions to the leading pagan aristocrats of his day.

While in Milan, Augustine came into contact with kinds of people he had never encountered in Africa, particularly with Neoplatonists and Christians. The encounter with a spiritual philosophy and a Christianity compatible with it profoundly changed the young professor. After a period of agonized searching, Augustine converted to the new religion. Abandoning his Italian

life, he returned to the North African town of Hippo where he soon became bishop.

Augustine elaborated a new Christian understanding of human society and the individual's relationship to God, which dominated Western thought for the next fifteen centuries. He argued that the true members of God's elect necessarily coexisted in the world with sinners. No earthly community, not even the empire or the Church, was the true "city of God." Earthly society participated in the true "city of God" through Christian rituals and did so quite apart from the individual worthiness of the recipients or even of the ministers of these rites. Salvation came through the Church, but the saved were not identified solely with any particular group of Christians. In this way, Augustine argued for a distinction between the visible Christian empire and the Christian community, a vital distinction at a moment when barbarians were threatening the empire's very existence.

The Transformation of Popular Culture

The responses of Plotinus, Origen, and Augustine to the choices of late antiquity were fundamental for the subsequent intellectual development of Western civilization. On a more popular level a different sort of Christian had an equally profound influence on the future. This was the hermit, monk, or recluse, who taught less by words than life, a life often so unusual that even the most ignorant and worldly citizen of the late empire could recognize in it the power of God. Beneath the apparent eccentricity, however, lay a fundamental principle: the radical rejection of society's values in favor of absolute dedication to God's.

While Plotinus was teaching in the serenity of his Roman villa, and shortly after Origen had died fighting for the integrity of the Christian intellectual tradition, another Egyptian was undertaking a different path to enduring fame. Anthony (ca. 250–355), a well-to-do peasant, heard the same Biblical text that later converted Augustine, "Go, sell all you have and give to the poor and follow me." Anthony was uneducated; it was said that he had been too shy as a boy to attend school. This straightforward peasant did exactly what the text commanded. He disposed of all his goods and left his village for the Egyptian desert. There, for the next seventy years, he sought to follow Christ in a life of constant self-mortification and prayer.

This dropout from civilization deeply touched his fellow Christians, many of whom were disturbed by the

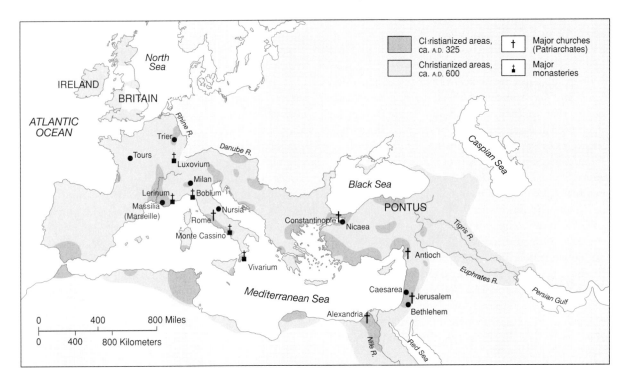

The Spread of Christianity

abrupt transformation of their religion from persecuted minority to privileged majority. By the time of his death this monk—the word comes from the Greek *monos*, alone—found himself the head of a large, loosely knit community of like-minded persons who looked to him as spiritual father, or abbot. These men and women sought spiritual perfection through physical self-mortification and through the subordination of their own wills to that of the abbot. Monks drank no wine, ate no meat, used no oil. They spent their days in prayer, either communal or individual. During the fourth century this monastic tradition spread east to Bethlehem, Jerusalem, and Constantinople and west to Rome and Gaul. In the following centuries it reached beyond the borders of the empire when Egyptian-style monasticism was introduced into Ireland. Over the next centuries thousands rejected the worldliness of civilization and the easy life of the average Christian to lead a monastic life in the wildernesses of the empire.

Monasticism took two forms, communal organization or solitary life. Basil the Great (ca. 329–379) in the east and Benedict of Nursia (ca. 480–547) in the west perfected the former. Basil outlined a form of monastic life in which a day of agriculture, craft work, and care for the sick and the poor was organized within an ordered progression of liturgical prayer. His emphasis on com-

munal life rather than on heroic acts of individual asceticism provided the model for eastern monasticism from his day to the present. Eastern monasteries provided the early religious training for most religious leaders. Monks and abbots often involved themselves wholeheartedly in the politics of the empire. Monks rioting in the streets of Constantinople over political issues was a familiar sight for over a thousand years.

In the west, Benedict of Nursia was as influential in structuring communal religious life as was Basil in the east. As abbot of a small community of monks at Monte Cassino, between Rome and Naples, Benedict drafted a rule that became the definitive statement of western monasticism. Benedict's rule encouraged moderation and flexibility while emphasizing a life of poverty, chastity, and obedience to an elected abbot. Monks were required to perform some physical labor, and the monastery was intended to be a self-sufficient community. However, the real task of the monk was the continuous praise of God. This consisted of gathering at regular intervals through the day and night for communal prayer. Although Benedict lived and died in obscurity, within two and one-half centuries his rule became the universal rule for western monasticism.

Western monasteries, too, provided their share of bishops, but unlike those in the east, western monks

The Roman Empire and the Transformation of the Classical World

27 B.C.E.–68 C.E.	Julio-Claudian period
27 B.C.E.–14 C.E.	Augustus
ca. 30 C.E.	Death of Jesus
54–68 C.E.	Nero
69	Year of the Four Emperors
69–96	Flavian period
96–193	Antonine period
161–180	Marcus Aurelius
193–211	Septimius Severus
224–636	Sassanid dynasty
284–305	Diocletian
303–313	Great Persecution
306–337	Constantine
313	Edict of Milan
364–378	Valens
378	Battle of Andrianople
410	Sack of Rome by Visigoths
430	Death of Augustine
480	Death of Julius Nepos

attention of their contemporaries by their lifestyles. The most famous of the hermits, Simeon Stylites (ca. 390–459), spent thirty-six years perched at the top of a pillar fifty feet high.

Their lack of ties to human society made such people of God the perfect arbitrators in the constant disputes that threatened to disrupt village life. They were "individuals of power," whose proven ability to cast out demons and work miracles made them ideal community patrons at a time when traditional power brokers of the village were being lured away to imperial service or provincial cities.

Unlike the eastern monks, the Syrian hermits of the fourth and fifth centuries had few parallels in the west and these exceptions did not establish themselves either as independent sources of religious power or as political power brokers. In the west, in spite of the creation of the barbarian kingdoms, cultural and political leadership remained firmly in the hands of the aristocracy. Aristocratic bishops, rather than hermits, monopolized the role of mediators of divine power just as their lay brothers, in cooperation with barbarian rulers, monopolized the role of mediators of secular power.

Gold plaque from a sixth-century Syrian reliquary. The subject is Simeon Stylites on his pillar. The snake represents the vanquished devil. Clients could consult the holy man by climbing up the ladder on the left.

remained more isolated from population centers and from direct involvement in public affairs. Western monasteries were not, however, peripheral to western society and religion. Rather, these rustic communities were centers of religious and economic activity as well as education and learning in the largely rural west. They remained under the authority of the local bishops, who were usually drawn from the lay aristocracy of the empire in the west. Also, western monasteries depended upon the political and economic support that they received from lay patrons.

Although Anthony had begun as a hermit, he and most Egyptian monks eventually settled into communal lives. Elsewhere, particularly in the desert of Syria, the model of the monk remained the individual hermit. Here Christian hermits were wild men and women who came down from the mountainsides and galvanized the

During the first and second centuries, a deeply Hellenized Roman civilization tied together the vast empire by incorporating the wealthy and powerful of the Western world into its fluid power structure while brutally crushing those who would not or could not conform. The binding force of the Roman Empire was great and survived the political crises of the third century, which were as serious as those that had brought down the republic three hundred years before.

Thereafter, the fundamental differences between east and west led to a divergent transformation of the two halves of the Roman Empire at the close of late antiquity. The east remained more firmly attached not only to Roman traditions of government but also to the much more ancient traditions of social complexity, urban life, and religious culture that stretched back to the dawn of civilization.

The west experienced a transformation even more profound than that of the east. The triple heritage of late Roman political and military forms, barbarian society, and Christian culture coalesced into a new civilization that was perhaps less the direct heir of antiquity than that of the east, but the more dynamic for its distinctiveness. In culture, politics, and patterns of urban and rural life, the west and the east had gone separate ways, and their paths diverged ever more in the centuries ahead.

SUGGESTIONS FOR FURTHER READING

PRIMARY SOURCES

Major selections of the works of Tacitus, Plutarch, Suetonius, and Marcus Aurelius are available in English translation from Penguin Books. The second volume, *Naphtali Lewis and Meyer Reinhold, Roman Civilization, Selected Readings, Vol. II: The Empire* (1951), contains a wide selection of documents with useful introductions.

THE AUGUSTAN AGE

G. W. Bowersock, *Augustus and the Greek World* (New York: Oxford University Press, 1965). A cultural history of the Augustan Age.

D. A. West and A. J. Woodman, *Poetry and Politics in the Age of Augustus* (New York: Cambridge University Press, 1984). The cultural program of Augustus.

J. B. Campbell, *The Emperor and the Roman Army* (New York: Oxford University Press, 1984). Essential for understanding the military's role in the Roman Empire.

Richard Duncan-Jones, *The Economy of the Roman Empire*, 2d ed. (New York: Cambridge University Press, 1982). A series of technical studies on Roman wealth and its economic context and social applications.

THE PAX ROMANA, 27 B.C.E.–180 C.E.

Fergus Millar, *The Roman Empire and Its Neighbors*, 2d ed. (New York: Holmes & Meier, 1981). A collection of essays surveying the diversity of the empire.

Peter Garnsey and Richard Saller, *The Roman Empire: Economy, Society, and Culture* (Berkeley: University of California Press, 1987). A topical study of imperial administration, economy, religion, and society, arguing the coercive and exploitative nature of Roman civilization on the agricultural societies of the Mediterranean world.

Fergus Millar, *The Emperor in the Roman World* (Ithaca, NY: Cornell University Press, 1977). A study of emperors, stressing their essential passivity, responding to initiatives from below.

Philippe Ariès and Georges Duby, eds., *History of Private Life., Vol. 1., From Pagan Rome to Byzantium* (Cambridge, MA: Harvard University Press, 1986). Essays on the interior, private life of Romans and Greeks by leading French and British historians.

* Judith P. Hallett, *Fathers and Daughters in Roman Society & the Elite Family* (Princeton, NJ: Princeton University Press, 1984). A study of indirect power exercised by elite women in the Roman world as daughters, mothers, and sisters.

* Ramsay MacMullen, *Paganism in the Roman Empire* (New Haven, CT: Yale University Press, 1981). A description of the varieties and levels of pagan religion in the Roman world.

Jane E. Gardner, *Women in Roman Law and Society* (Bloomington, IN: Indiana University Press, 1986). A study of the extent of freedom and power over property enjoyed by Roman women.

Edward Champlin, *Fronto and Antonine Rome* (Cambridge, MA: Harvard University Press, 1980). A cultural history of Antonine court life through the letters of the second century's greatest rhetorician.

*Joseph Jay Deiss, *Herculaneum: Italy's Buried Treasure* (New York: Harper and Row, 1985). A vividly written and well-illustrated introduction to Herculaneum for a general audience.

CRISIS, RESTORATION, DIVISION, 192–376 C.E.

* A. H. M. Jones, *The Later Roman Empire, 284–602: A Social, Economic and Administrative Survey*, 2 vols. (Baltimore: The Johns Hopkins University Press, 1986). The standard, detailed survey of late antiquity by an administrative historian.

* Peter Brown, *The World of Late Antiquity, A.D. 150–750* (New York: Harcourt Brace Jovanovich, 1971). A brilliant essay on the cultural transformation of the ancient world.

E. A. Thompson, *The Early Germans* (Oxford: Oxford University Press, 1965). An important social and economic view of Germanic society.

THE EMPIRE TRANSFORMED 376–500 C.E.

* Ramsay MacMullen, *Paganism in the Roman Empire* (New Haven, CT: Yale University Press, 1981). A sensible introduction to the varieties of Roman religion in the imperial period.

T. D. Barnes, *The New Empire of Diocletian and Constantine* (Cambridge, MA: Harvard University Press, 1982). A current examination of the transformations brought about under these two great emperors.

* Philip Willis Dixon, *Barbarian Europe* (Oxford: Elsevier Phaidon, 1976), an introduction to Germanic societies.

* Herwig Wolfram, *History of the Goths* (Berkeley, CA: University of California Press, 1988). An ethnologically sensitive history of the formation of the Gothic peoples.

* Ramsay MacMullen, *Christianizing the Roman Empire* (100–400) (New Haven, CT: Yale University Press, 1984). A view of Christianity's spread from the perspective of Roman history.

* Judith Herrin, *The Formation of Christendom* (Princeton, NJ: Princeton University Press, 1987). A history of early Christianity from the perspective of a noted Byzantinist.

* Karl E. Morrison, ed., *The Church in the Roman Empire* (Chicago: University of Chicago Press, 1986). Major documents of early Christianity.

Peter Brown, *Society and the Holy in Late Antiquity* (Berkeley, CA: University of California Press, 1982). Imaginative essays on religion and society, emphasizing the role of saints.

* David Knowles, *Christian Monasticism* (New York: McGraw-Hill, 1969). A very readable introduction by a great historian of monastic history.

* Indicates paperback edition available.

FROM DAMASCUS TO TIMBUKTU

The ancient Sankoré mosque, a mud and brick structure with its curved lines and sloping pyramid-like minaret, rises above the northern parts of the ancient city of Timbuktu—a world apart from the Great Mosque in Damascus, Syria. Yet both are enduring witnesses to the complexity and creativity of Byzantine, Islamic, and African civilizations.

The wealthy Tuareg merchants of Timbuktu, whose camel caravans linked Sudan and the Mediterranean coast, trading Saharan salt for Sudanese gold, raised the mosque some time in the twelfth century, five hundred years after the arrival of Islam in sub-Saharan Africa. Mosques, with their minarets, towers from which Muslim religious leaders call the faithful to prayer five times each day, are found throughout the Islamic world, although this most distinctive of Islamic structures has its origins in late Roman and Byzantine tradition. Many of the first mosques were Christian churches conquered from the Byzantine Empire in the seventh century, churches that were themselves often pagan temples rededicated to Christian worship. The Great Mosque of Damascus, shown at the right, for example, served as a temple dedicated to the Syriac god Hadad and then to the Roman Jupiter. It later became the Christian church of St. John before the caliph, or ruler, al-Walid (705–15), converted it into a mosque. The four bell towers at the corners of the porticoed courtyard, one of which appears in the photograph, became the first minarets, the direct ancestors of the tower seen at left.

Although the Tuareg converted to Islam and the Sankoré mosque became a brilliant center of Muslim intellectual life, sub-Saharan Africans adapted Islam to their cultural and social traditions just as Arabian Islam had adapted those of the Mediterranean world. Rather than attempting to build a mosque on a strict northern model, they used their traditional construction techniques, which were appropriate to the temperature extremes and lack of wood and stone for building materials in the West African savannah. The thick, curvilinear earthen walls store heat during the day and allow it to radiate at night into the curved open spaces. In the same way, they found room in Islam for their traditional social structure. Both Islamic and Byzantine traditions were strongly patriarchal. In both cultures, women normally held subordinate and nonpublic roles—the tradition of veiling women, common in some Islamic societies, was first taken over from Christian practice in Syria. In contrast, Tuareg society was matrilinear and known for its women scholars. Veiling is practiced by Tuareg, but the veils are worn by men, not women. According to local legend, the Sankoré mosque was built, not by some ancient patriarch or powerful ruler, but "by a woman, a great lady, very rich, very desirous of doing good work."

The same kind of accommodation, adaptation, and transformation characterized each of the three civilizations examined in this chapter. The Roman Empire in the east evolved into a distinctive, strongly hierarchical and culturally Greek polity that endured until the fifteenth century. Islam, which arose in the deserts of the Arabian Peninsula, absorbed and transformed the cultural and political traditions of both Byzantium and Persia as it united the world from India to Spain into a new religious and cultural system. Sub-Saharan Africans developed their own societies based on agriculture, pastoralism, and village life while participating in both of these wider worlds through commerce and religion.

The Byzantines

At the end of the fifth century, the eastern empire had escaped the fate that its western counterpart had suffered at the hands of the Germanic peoples. Wealthier and more urbanized than the west, its population had also been accustomed to centralized government for more than a thousand years. Still, the long-term survival of the eastern empire seemed far from certain. Little unified the empire of Constantinople. The population of the capital split into rival political factions, whose violent conflicts often threatened the stability of the government. Beyond Constantinople, the empire's population consisted of the more or less Hellenized peoples of Asia Minor, Armenians, Slavs, Arabs, Syrians, Egyptian Copts, and others. Unlike western Europe, the east was still a world of cities, which were centers of commerce, industry, and Hellenistic culture. But the importance of these urban centers began to decline in favor of the rural, peasant world, which not only fed the empire and was the source of its great wealth but also provided the generations of tough soldiers necessary to protect it from its enemies.

Finally, the eastern empire was more divided than unified by its Christianity. Rivalry among the great cities of Antioch, Alexandria, Jerusalem, Rome, and Constantinople was expressed in the competition among their bishops, or patriarchs. The official "right teaching," or orthodox, faith of Constantinople and its patriarch was bitterly opposed by "deviant," or heterodox, bishops of other religious traditions, around which developed separatist ethnic political movements. By the time of Justinian (527–65), emperors were obsessed with maintaining absolute authority and imposing uniformity on their empire.

Justinian and the Creation of the Byzantine State

Strong-willed, restless, and ambitious, Justinian is remembered as "the emperor who never slept." Although his goals were essentially conservative, he, his wife Theodora, and his able generals and advisors transformed the very foundations of the imperial state, its institutions, and its culture. He hoped to restore the territory, power, and prestige of the ancient Roman Empire, but his attempts to return to the past created a new world. First, he brutally suppressed the political factions in the capital, leaving 30,000 dead but

asserting his control over the city. His armies recaptured North Africa from the Vandals, Italy from the Ostrogoths, and part of Spain from the Visigoths, restoring for one last moment some of the geographical unity of the empire of Augustus and Constantine. His legal advisor Tribonian revised and organized the existing codes of Roman law into the *Justinian Code*, a great monument of Western jurisprudence that remains today the foundation of most of Europe's legal systems. His architects combined their knowledge of mathematics, geometry, kinetics, and physics to build the Church of the Holy Wisdom (Hagia Sophia) in Constantinople, one of the largest and most innovative churches ever constructed.

Ultimately, Justinian's spectacular achievements came at too high a price. He left his successors an empire virtually bankrupt by the costs of his wars and his building projects, bitterly divided by his attempts to settle religious controversies, and poorly protected on its eastern border, where the Sassanid Empire was a constant threat. Most of Italy and Spain soon returned to barbarian control. In 602 the Sassanid emperor Chosroes II (d. 628) invaded the empire, capturing Egypt, Palestine, and Syria, and threatening Constantinople itself. In a series of desperate campaigns, the emperor Heraclius (610–41) turned back the tide and crushed the Sassanids, but it was too late. A new power, Islam, had emerged in the deserts of Arabia. This new power was to challenge and ultimately absorb both the Sassanids and much of the eastern Roman Empire. As a result, the latter became increasingly less Roman and more Greek. This smaller, Hellenized survivor of the Roman Empire, although it continued to consider itself the Roman Empire, is today called Byzantine, a term derived from the original name of Constantinople, Byzantium.

For over eight hundred years the Byzantine Empire played a major role in world history. It protected western Europe from the expansion of Islam. To both the Latin west and the Islamic worlds it provided a model of a centralized, bureaucratic state ruled according to principles of Roman law and transmitted to them the heritage of classical philosophy, medicine, science, and art. When the Slavic north, caught between the Latin Christians and the Muslims, sought its cultural and religious orientation, it looked to the liturgical culture of Byzantine orthodoxy. Perhaps most importantly, when urban civilization had all but disappeared from the rest of Europe, Greeks, Latins, Slavs, and others could still look to "The City," *eis ten polin*, or as the Turks pronounced it, *Istanbul*.

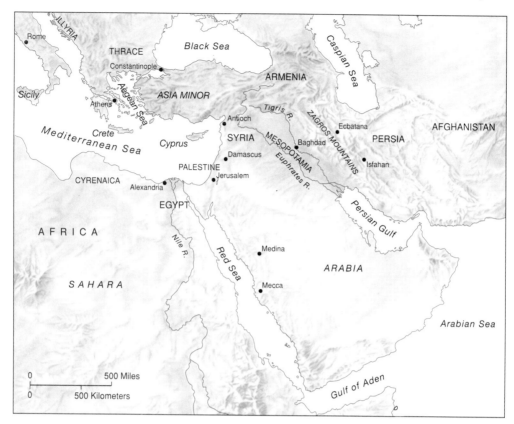

The Eastern Mediterranean

Emperors and Individuals

The classic age of Byzantine society, roughly from the eighth through the tenth centuries, has been described as "individualism without freedom." The Byzantine world was intensely individualistic, but Byzantine individualism did not lead to a great amount of individual initiative or creativity. Still less did it imply individual freedom of action within the political sphere. Instead Byzantine individualism meant that individuals and small family groups stood as isolated units in a society characterized, until the mid-eleventh century, by the direct relationship between an all-powerful emperor and citizens of all ranks.

As long as the empire remained a civilian autocracy, it was even possible for a woman to rule, either as regent for a minor son or as sovereign. Thus Irene (780–802), widow of Leo IV (725–80), ruled first as regent for her son Constantine VI (780–97) and then as emperor herself. In the eleventh century the empire was ruled at times by two sisters, Zoe (1028–34) and Theodora (1042–56).

While the emperor was the source of all authority, the actual administration of the empire was carried out by a vast bureaucracy composed of military and civilian officers. The empire was divided into roughly twenty-five provinces, or themes. The soldiers in each theme were also farmers, rather than full-time warriors. These farmer-soldiers were the backbone of both the imperial military and the economic system.

In contrast to the military command of the themes, the central administration, which focused on the emperor and the imperial family, was wholly civil. The most important positions at court were occupied by eunuchs, castrated men who offered a number of advantages to imperial administration. Eunuchs often directed imperial finance, served as prime ministers, directed the vast bureaucracy, and even undertook military commands. Because they could not have descendants, there was no danger that they would attempt to turn their offices into hereditary positions or that they would plot and scheme on behalf of their children.

A godlike emperor and a centralized bureaucracy left little room for the development of the hierarchies of

The interior of Hagia Sophia. The building was converted into a mosque after the Ottoman conquest of 1453. The magnificent mosaics were painted over to conform to Islamic religious dictates against representing human figures.

private patronage, lordship, and group action that were characteristic of western Europe. In the Byzantine Empire, aristocrat and peasant were equal in their political powerlessness. Against the emperor and the bureaucracy, no extended kin group or local political unit offered security or comfort. Thus Byzantine society tended to be organized at the lowest level, that of the nuclear family. Daily life focused on the protective enclosure of the private home, which served as both shelter and workplace. Professional and craft associations continued to exist as they had in antiquity. However, like everything else in Byzantium, these were not autonomous professional groups intended to protect the interests of their members. Instead, they were fostered and controlled by imperial officials to regulate and tax urban industry.

The countryside, which was the backbone of Byzantine prosperity into the eleventh century, was also a world with limited horizontal and vertical social bonds. Villages were the basic elements in the imperial system. The village court handled local affairs and tax assessments, but it in turn dealt directly with the imperial bureaucracy.

At the other extreme, because of its strategic location on the Bosporus, Constantinople was ideally situated to develop into the greatest commercial center of the Mediterranean. Commerce was in the hands of Italians and Syrians, but all of the products of the empire and those of the Slavic, Latin, and Islamic worlds, as well as Oriental goods arriving overland from central Asia, had to pass through the city. Silks, spices, and precious metals were loaded onto ships at Trebizond and then transported south to Constantinople. Baltic amber, slaves, and furs from the Slavic world were carried down the Dnepr River to the Black Sea and then to the capital. There, all goods passing north or south had to be unloaded, assessed, and subjected to a flat import-export tariff of 10 percent.

THE JUSTINIAN CODE

■ *In 533 the commission appointed by the Emperor Justinian completed the* Digest, *the most important section of his great* Code, *the most influential legal text in European history. In his preface, Justinian explains his reasons for ordering the codification and reveals the image of imperial power that would be the cornerstone of the Byzantine state for almost a thousand years.*

IN THE NAME OF OUR LORD JESUS CHRIST. THE EMPEROR CAESAR FLAVIUS JUSTINIANUS, CONQUEROR OF THE ALEMANNI, GOTHS, FRANKS, GERMANS, ANTES, ALANI, VANDALS, AND AFRICANS, PIOUS, HAPPY, AND GLORIOUS, CONQUEROR AND VANQUISHER, TO YOUNG MEN DESIROUS OF LEARNING THE LAW, GREETING.

Imperial majesty should not only be adorned with military might but also graced by laws, so that in times of peace and war alike the state may be governed aright and so that the Emperor of Rome may not only shine forth victorious on the battlefield, but may also by every legal means cast out the wickedness of the perverters of justice, and thus at one and the same time prove as assiduous in upholding the law as he is triumphant over his vanquished foes.

This double objective we have achieved with the blessing of God through our utmost watchfulness and foresight. The barbarian races brought under our yoke know well our military achievements; and Africa also and countless other provinces bear witness to our power having been after so long an interval restored to the dominion of Rome and to our Empire by our victories which we have gained through the inspiration of Divine guidance. Moreover, all these peoples are now also governed by laws which we ourselves have promulgated or compiled.

When we had elucidated and brought into perfect harmony the revered imperial constitutions which were previously in confusion, we turned our attention to the immense mass of ancient jurisprudence. Now, by the grace of Heaven, we have completed this work of which even we at one time despaired like sailors crossing the open sea.

From Justinian, *The Digest of Roman Law. Theft, Rapine, Damage and Insult.*

The empire's cities were centers for the manufacture of luxury goods in demand throughout the Islamic and Christian worlds. Imperial workshops in Constantinople and closely regulated workshops in Corinth and Thebes produced fine silks, brocades, carpets, and other luxury products marketed throughout the Mediterranean, again subject to the state's customary 10 percent tax.

A Foretaste of Heaven

The cultural cement that bound emperor and subjects together was Orthodox Christianity. The Islamic capture of Alexandria, Jerusalem, and Antioch had removed the centers of regional religious particularism from the empire. The barbarian domination of Italy had isolated Rome and reduced its influence. These two processes left Constantinople as the only remaining patriarchate in the empire and thus the undisputed center of Orthodox Christianity. However, like virtually every other aspect of Byzantine society and culture, the patriarch and the Orthodox faith he led were subordinated to the emperor. Although in theory patriarchs were elected, in reality emperors appointed them. Patriarchs in turn controlled the various levels of the Church hierarchy, which included metropolitans, bishops, and the local clergy. This ecclesiastical structure reflected the organization of the state bureaucracy, which it reinforced. Local priests were drawn from the peasant society of which they were a part. They were expected to be married and to live much like their neighbors. Bishops, metropolitans, and patriarchs were recruited from monasteries and remained celibate. They were, so to speak, spiritual eunuchs who represented the emperor.

The essence of Orthodox religion was the liturgy, or ceremonies, of the Church, which provided, it was said,

A tenth-century Greek manuscript of the gospels from Constantinople is decorated with a drawing of laborers in a vineyard. Such illustrated texts often recorded the daily activities of the ordinary people including plowing, fishing, farming, and sheep shearing.

a foretaste of heaven. Adoration of God and veneration of the emperor went hand in hand as the cornerstone of imperial propaganda. Ecclesiastical and court processions assured that everything and everyone was in the proper place, that order and stability reigned in this world as a reflection of the eternal order of the next. This confirmation, in churches and in court, of stability and permanence in the face of possible crisis and

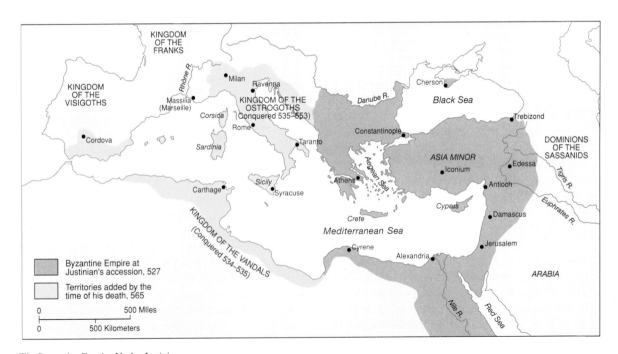

The Byzantine Empire Under Justinian

disruption calmed and reassured the liturgically oriented society. The effects of Byzantine ceremonial reached far beyond the Byzantines themselves. According to Russian sources, the prince of Kiev sent observers to report on the manners of worship in Islamic, Latin, and Greek societies. So strong was the impression made by the rituals of the Byzantine liturgy that the prince decided to invite Byzantine clergy to instruct his people.

The one aspect of religious life not entirely under imperial control was monasticism. Since the time of the desert fathers, monastic communities had been an essential part of Christianity. From the sixth century, numerous monastic communities were founded throughout the empire, and by the eleventh century there were at least three hundred monasteries within the walls of Constantinople alone. Monasteries were often wealthy and powerful. Moreover, their religious appeal, often based on the possession of miracle-working religious images, or icons, posed an independent source of religious authority at odds with the imperial centralization of all aspects of Byzantine life. To the faithful, icons were not simply representations or reminders of Jesus and the saints. They had a real if intermediary relationship with the person represented, and as such themselves merited veneration and, some argued, adoration. In the eighth century, a series of military emperors sought to curtail the independence of monastic culture and particularly the cult of icons. These so-called *icon-*

oclasts (literally, "breakers of images") destroyed icons, statues, and illustrated manuscripts, and painted over frescoes in churches. The defenders of icons, *iconodules*, or image venerators, were imprisoned, tortured, and even executed. Most bishops, the army, and much of the non-European population of the empire supported the iconoclast emperors, but monks, the lesser clergy, and the majority of the populace, particularly women, violently resisted the destruction of their beloved images. For over a century, the iconoclast dispute threatened to tear the empire apart. Finally, in 843, the Empress Theodora (842–58), who ruled during the minority of her son, ended the persecution and restored image worship.

Thus between the sixth and ninth centuries, the reduced but still vital Roman Empire in the east developed a distinctive political and cultural tradition based on imperial absolutism buttressed by a powerful religious tradition and an effective bureaucracy which dealt directly with individual subjects on behalf of the emperor.

The Rise of Islam

Recite: in the name of your Lord,
The Creator Who created man from clots of blood!
Recite: Your Lord is the Most Bounteous One, Who taught by the pen,
Taught mankind things they did not know.

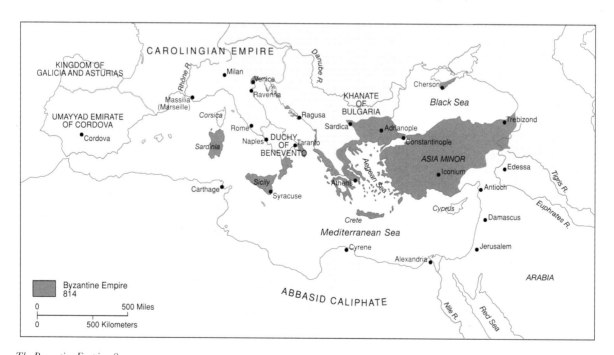

The Byzantine Empire, 814

This command to recite, to reveal God's will, communicated directly by God, launched an obscure merchant in the Arabian city of Mecca on a career that would transform the world. Through faith, Abu al-Qasim Muhammad ibn 'Abd Allah ibn 'Abd al-Muttalib ibn Hashim (ca. 570–632), or more simply Muhammad, united the tribes of the Arabian Peninsula and propelled them on an unprecedented mission of conquest. Within a century of Muhammad's death, the world of *Islam*—a word that means "submission to the will of God"—included all of the ancient Near East and extended from the Syr Darya River in Asia, south into the Indian subcontinent, west across the North African coast to the Atlantic, north through Spain, and along the Mediterranean coast to the Rhone River. Just as their faith combined elements of traditional Arab worship with Christianity and Judaism, the Arabian conquerors and their subject populations created a vital civilization from a mix of Arabian, Roman, Hellenistic, and Sassanid traditions, characterized from its inception by a multiplicity of forms in which these various elements were combined with the religious traditions of the prophet Muhammad.

Arabia Before the Prophet

Although Arabs did not appear in written sources as such before the ninth century B.C.E., their ancestors had played an important if supporting role in Near Eastern history for thousands of years. Already in the Egyptian Old Kingdom, the incense trees of southern Arabia had drawn Egyptians to the region, then known as the land of Punt. Trade routes between the Fertile Crescent and Egypt had crossed northern Arabia for just as long. By the sixth century C.E., Arabic-speaking peoples from the Arabian Peninsula had spread through the Syrian Desert as far north as the Euphrates.

Those who lived on the fringes of the Byzantine and Sassanid empires had been largely absorbed into the cultural and political spheres of these two great powers. The northern borders of Arabia along the Red Sea formed Roman provinces that even produced an emperor, Philip the Arab (244–49). Hira, to the south of the Euphrates, became a Sassanid puppet principality that, although largely Christian, often provided the Persians with auxiliaries. Within both empires, the distinction between Arab and non-Arab populations was blurred. Except for a common language and a hazy idea of common kinship, nothing differentiated Arabs from their neighbors.

Southern Arabia, with a relatively abundant rainfall and fertile soils, was an agricultural region long governed by monarchs. Here was the kingdom of Saba, the Sheba of the Bible, which had existed since the tenth century B.C.E. During the fifth century C.E. the kings of the Yemen had extended their influence north over the Bedouin tribes of central Arabia in order to control and protect the caravan trade between north and south. However, in the late sixth century Ethiopian and then Persian conquerors destroyed the Arabian kingdom of the Yemen and absorbed it into their empires. The result was a power vacuum that left central Arabia and its trade routes across the deserts in confusion.

The interior of the Arabian Peninsula was much less directly affected by the great empires to the north or the Arabian kingdoms to the south. Waterless steppes and seas of shifting sand dunes had long defeated Roman and Persian or Sassanid efforts to control the Arabic Bedouin. These nomads roamed the peninsula in search of pasturage for their flocks. Theirs was a life of independence, simplicity, and danger.

Although they acknowledged membership in various tribes, the Bedouin's real allegiance was to much more narrow circles of lineages and tenting groups. As in the Germanic tribes of Europe, kin relationships rather than formal governmental systems protected individuals through the obligation for vengeance and blood feud.

Some of the Arabs of the more settled south, as well as inhabitants of towns along caravan routes, were Christian or Jewish. As farmers or merchants, these groups were looked down upon by the nomadic Bedouin, most of whom remained pagan. Rivalry and feuding among tribes could be set aside at a mutually accepted neutral site, which might grow up around a religious sanctuary. A sanctuary, or *haram*, which was often on the border between tribal areas, was founded by a holy man not unlike the Christian holy men of the Syrian Desert.

Mecca was just such a sanctuary, around whose sacred black rock, or *Ka'bah*, a holy man named Qusayy established himself and his tribe, the Quraysh, as its guardians sometime early in the sixth century. In the next century Mecca grew into an important religious and commercial center under the patronage of the Quraysh. When Muhammad, a descendant of Qusayy, began to recite the monotheistic message of Allah, his preaching was seen as a threat to the survival of his tribe and his city.

Muhammad, Prophet of God

Muhammad was an orphan raised by relatives. At about age twenty he became the business manager for Khadijah, a wealthy widow whom he later married. This marriage gave him financial security among the middle

THE QUR'AN

■ *The following passages from the* Qur'an *express the central importance of the revelation of Allah, compassion for Jews and Christians as sharers in the belief in the one God, and the condemnation of polytheistic idolaters.*

In the Name of Allah, the Compassionate, the Merciful

This Book is not to be doubted. It is a guide to the righteous, who have faith in the unseen and are steadfast in prayer; who bestow in charity a part of what We give them; who trust what has been revealed to you [Muhammad] and to others before you, and firmly believe in the life to come. These are rightly guided by their Lord; these shall surely triumph.

As for the unbelievers, whether you forewarn them or not, they will not have faith. Allah has set a seal upon their hearts and ears; their sight is dimmed and a grievous punishment awaits them . . .

Men, serve your Lord, who has created you and those who have gone before you, so that you may guard yourselves against evil; who has made the earth a bed for you and the sky a dome, and has sent down water from heaven to bring forth fruits for your sustenance. Do not knowingly set up other gods besides Him . . .

Believers, Jews, Christians, and Sabaeans [ancient rulers of Yemen believed to be monotheists]— whoever believes in Allah and the Last Day and does what is right—shall be rewarded by their Lord; they have nothing to fear or to regret . . .

Yet there are some who worship idols, bestowing on them the adoration due to Allah (though the love of Allah is stronger in the faithful). But when they face their punishment the wrongdoers will know that might is His alone and that Allah is stern in retribution. When they face their punishment the leaders will disown their followers, and the bonds which now unite them will break asunder. Those who followed them will say: "Could we but live again, we would disown them as they have disowned us not."

Thus Allah will show them their own works. They shall sigh with remorse, but shall never come out of Hell.

From *The Koran.*

---

ranks of Meccan merchants. During this time he may have traveled to Syria on business and heard the preaching of Christian monks. He certainly became familiar with Judaism through contact with Jewish traders. In his thirties, he began to devote an increasing amount of time to meditation, retiring to the barren, arid mountains outside the city. There, in the month of Ramadan in the year 610, he reported a vision of a man, his feet astride the horizon. The figure commanded: "O Muhammad! Thou art the Messenger of God. Recite!"

His early teachings stressed the absolute unity of God, the evils of idolatry, and the threat of divine judgment. Further revelations to Muhammad were copied word for word in what came to be the *Qur'an*, or Koran. These messages offered Arabs a faith founded on a book.

In their eyes, this faith was both within the tradition of and superior to the Christianity and Judaism of their neighbors. The *Qur'an* was the final revelation and Muhammad the last and greatest prophet. To Muslims— the term means "true believers"—Muhammad is simply the Prophet.

Allah's revelation emphasized above all his power and transcendence. The duty of humans is worship. The prayers of Islam, in contrast with those of Christianity and Judaism, are essentially prayers of praise, seldom prayers of petition. This reverential attitude places little premium on scriptural interpretation or theological speculation. Muslims regard the whole *Qur'an* as the exact and complete revelation of God, literally true, and forming a unified whole, though revelations contained in it came at various times throughout the Prophet's life. It is the complete guide for secular and religious life, the fundamental law of conduct for Islamic society. The Prophet emphasized constantly that he was simply God's messenger and that he merited no special veneration or worship. For this reason Muslims have always rejected the label Muhammadan, which nonbelievers often apply to them. Muslims are not followers of Muhammad but of the God of Abraham and Jesus, who chose to make the final and complete revelation of his power and his judgment through the Prophet.

Initially, such revelations of divine power and judgment neither greatly bothered nor influenced Mecca's merchant elite. But soon Muhammad began to insist that those who did not accept Allah as the only God were damned, as were those who continued to venerate the sorts of idols on which Mecca's prosperity was founded. With this proclamation, toleration gave way to hostility. Muhammad and his followers were ostracized and even persecuted. On 24 September 622, Muhammad and one supporter secretly made their way from Mecca to Medina, a smaller trading community populated by rival pagan, Jewish, and Islamic clans. This short journey of less than three hundred miles, known as the *Hijra*, was destined to change the world. In Medina Muhammad organized his followers into the *Umma*, a community that transcended the old bonds of tribe and clan. He was God's messenger, and his authority was absolute. His goal was to extend this authority far beyond his adopted town of Medina to Mecca and ultimately to the whole Arab world.

First, he gained firm control of Medina at the expense of its Jewish clans. He then used this unified community to attack the Quraysh where they were most vulnerable—in their protection of camel caravans. In 629, Muhammad and 10,000 warriors marched on Mecca and captured the city in a swift and largely bloodless campaign.

During the three years between Muhammad's triumphant return to Mecca and his death, Islam moved steadily toward becoming the major force in the Arabian Peninsula. The divine revelations increasingly took on legal and practical dimensions as Muhammad was forced to serve, not just as Prophet, but as political leader of a major political and economic power. The

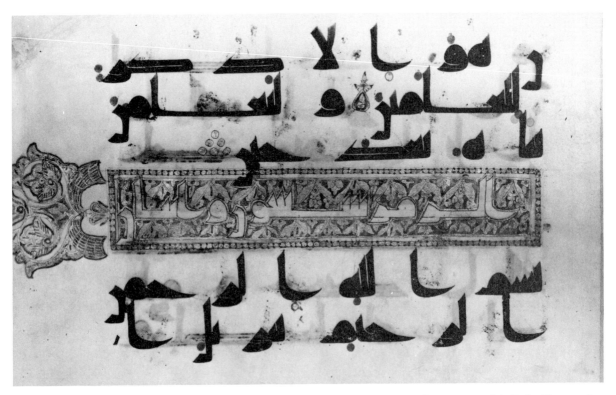

Arabic manuscripts were decorated with intricate geometric designs. This page from an eighth- or ninth-century copy of the Qur'an illustrates the elegance and formality of the Kufic form of Arabic calligraphy. Vowel marks appear as dots of various colors.

Umma had become a sort of supertribe, open to all individuals who would accept Allah and his Prophet. The invitation extended to women as well as to men who, although subordinate, had a status recognized and protected within the Umma.

The rapid spread of Islam within the Arab world can be explained by a number of religious and material factors. Islam promised an afterlife of refreshing streams and sensuous delights to the faithful and torments of eternal fire for nonbelievers. But as central as these otherworldly considerations were, the concrete attractions of Islam in this world were equally important. These included both economic prosperity and the opportunity to continue a lifestyle of raiding and warfare in the name of Allah.

Muhammad won over the leaders of the Quraysh by making Mecca the sacred city of Islam and by retaining the Ka'bah, cleansed of idols, as the center of Islamic pilgrimage. His message spread to other tribes through diplomatic and, occasionally, military means. Since the *Qur'an* commanded Muslims to destroy idol worship, conversion provided the occasion for holy wars (*jihads*) of conquest and profitable raids against their still-pagan neighbors. Converts showed their piety by sending part of their spoils as alms to Medina. The *Qur'an* permitted

Christians and Jews living under the authority of Islamic communities to continue to practice their faith, but they were forced to pay a head tax shared among members of the Umma.

The Spread of Islam

Muhammad died in the summer of 632 after a short illness, leaving no successor and no directions concerning the leadership of the Umma. Immediately his closest and most influential followers selected Abu Bakr (632–34), the fourth convert to Islam, to be caliph, or successor of the Prophet. Tensions developed between the early Medina followers of the Prophet and the Meccan elite, and at the same time the tribes that had accepted the Prophet's leadership believed that his death freed them from their treaty obligations.

To prevent the collapse of the Umma, Abu Bakr launched a war of reconversion. Purely by chance, this war developed into wars of conquest that reached far beyond the Arab world. Muslim forces defeated tribe after tribe and brought them back into the Umma. But long-term survival demanded expansion. Since Muslims were forbidden to raid fellow believers, and raids were an integral part of Bedouin life, the only way to

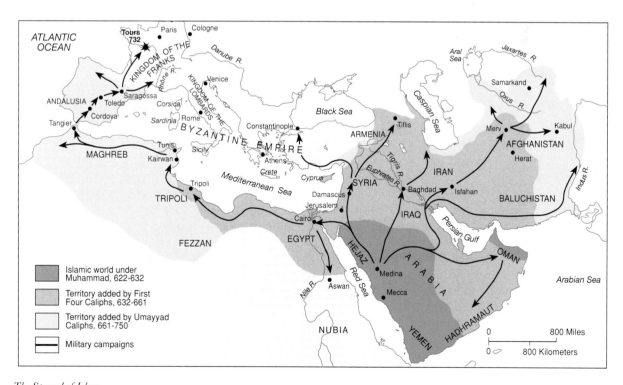

The Spread of Islam

The seven-tiered heaven of Islam. The Bedouin, in their harsh, dry land under the implacable sun, conceived of paradise as a cool, shaded garden full of lush, fruiting plants and washed by the waters of murmuring fountains.

keep recently converted Bedouin in line was to lead them on military expeditions against non-Muslims. Under Abu Bakr, Muslim expansion covered all of Arabia. Under his successor 'Umar (634–44), Islam profited from the mutual exhaustion of the Byzantine and Sassanid empires to conquer Iran, Iraq, Syria, and Egypt. By 650 Islam stretched from Egypt to Asia Minor, from the Mediterranean to the Indus River.

Because of their religious differences with Constantinople's form of Christianity, many Christians and Jews in Syria, Palestine, Egypt, and North Africa viewed this Muslim conquest as liberation rather than enslave-

ment. Jews and Christians may have been second-class citizens in the Islamic world, but at least they had a defined place.

During the reigns of Constantine IV (668–85) and Leo III (717–41), Constantinople itself fought for its own survival against besieging Muslim fleets. Each time it survived only through the use of a secret weapon, so-called Greek fire, an explosive liquid that burst into flame when sprayed by siphons onto enemy ships. Although the city itself survived, the Muslim conquests left the once-vast empire a small state reduced to little more than Greece, western Asia Minor, southern Italy, and the Balkans.

Authority and Government in Islam

Conquering the world for Islam proved easier than governing it. What had begun as a religious movement within Arabian society had created a vast, multinational empire in which Arabs were a tiny minority. Nothing in the *Qur'an*, nothing in Arabian experience, provided a blueprint for empire. Thus, the Muslims' ability to consolidate their conquests is even more remarkable than the conquests themselves. Within the first decades following the death of the Prophet, two models of governance emerged, models that continue to dominate Islamic politics to the present.

The first model was that of pre-Islamic tribal authority. The Umma could be considered a supertribe, governed by leaders whose authority came from their secular power as leaders of the superior military and economic elements within the community. This model appealed particularly to Quraysh and local tribal leaders who had exercised authority before Muhammad. The second model was that of the authority exercised by the Prophet. In this model, the Umma was more than a supertribe, and its unity and purity had to be preserved by a religiously sanctioned rule exercised by a member of the Prophet's own family. This model was preferred by many of the more recent converts to Islam, especially the poor. Governance under each of the two models was attempted successively in the seventh and eighth centuries.

Regardless of their disagreements on the basis of political authority, both groups adopted the administrative systems of their conquered lands. Byzantine and Sassanid bureaucracy and government, only slightly adjusted, became the models for government in the Islamic world until the twentieth century. In Syria and Egypt, Byzantine officials and even churchmen were incorporated into the government, much as had been the case in Europe following the Germanic conquests.

The terrifying weapon known as Greek fire is turned on an enemy during a naval battle. This early example of chemical warfare was a mixture of unknown ingredients that united and burned furiously when it came into contact with water. The sailors in the illustration are using it like a flamethrower.

Likewise, the Muslims left intact the social structures and economic systems of the empires they conquered. Lands remained in the hands of their previous owners. Only state property or, in the Sassanid Empire, that of the Zoroastrian priesthood, became common property of the Muslim community. The monastery of Saint Catherine on Mount Sinai, founded by the emperor Justinian around 540, for example, survived without serious harm and still shelters Orthodox monks today.

The division of the spoils of conquest badly divided the Umma and precipitated a crisis in the caliphate. The Meccan elite, especially the Umayyad family, clashed both with earliest followers of the Prophet and with more recent converts from the fringes of Arabia. The fourth caliph, Muhammad's beloved son-in-law and nephew 'Ali (656–61), encountered strong opposition from the Umayyad commander of Syria. To protect himself, 'Ali moved the caliphate from Arabia to Iraq. There he sought the support of underprivileged, recent converts by stressing the equality of all believers and the religious role of the caliph, who was to be less governor and tax collector than spiritual guide of Islam.

In 661 'Ali was murdered by supporters of his Umayyad rivals. Still, the memory of the "last orthodox caliph" remained alive in the Islamic world, especially in Iraq and Iran. Centuries later, a tradition developed in Baghdad that legitimate leadership of Islam could come only from the house of 'Ali. Adherents of this belief developed into a political and religious sect known as Shi'ism. Although frequently persecuted as heretical by the majority of Muslims, Shi'ism remains a potent minority movement within the Islamic world today.

The immediate effect of 'Ali's death, however, was the triumph of the old Quraysh and in particular the Umayyads, who established at Damascus in Syria a caliphate that lasted a century. The Umayyads made no attempt to base their rule on spiritual authority. Instead, they ruled as secular leaders, attempting to unite the Islamic empire through an appeal to Arab unity. Profits from this state went entirely to the Quraysh and members of Arabian tribes who formed the backbone of the early Umayyad army, monopolized high administration, and acquired rich estates throughout the empire.

The Umayyads extended the Islamic empire to its farthest reaches. In the north, armies from Syria marched into Anatolia and were stopped only in 677 by the Byzantine fleet before Constantinople itself. In the east, Umayyad armies pressed as far as the Syr Darya River on the edge of the Chinese Tang empire. In the south and southwest, Umayyad progress was even more successful, with the conquest in 711 of Spain, much of which remained part of the *Dar al-Harab* (the House of Islam) until 1492.

The Umayyad caliphate's external success in conquering failed to extend to its dealings with the internal tensions of the Umma. The Umayyads could not build a stable empire on the twin foundations of a tiny Arabian elite and a purely secular government taken over from their Byzantine predecessors. Not only were the numbers of Muslims increasing, so also was their fervor. Growing numbers of devout Muslims—Arabs and non-Arabs alike—were convinced that leadership had to be primarily spiritual, and that this spiritual mandate was the exclusive right of the family of the Prophet. Ultimately, a coalition of dissatisfied Persian Muslims and Arabian religious reformers united under the black banners of the descendants of Muhammad's paternal uncle, 'Abbas (566–ca. 653). In 750 this group overthrew the Umayyads everywhere but in Spain and established a new caliphate in favor of the 'Abbasids.

With the fall of the Umayyad caliphate, Arabs lost control of Islam forever. The 'Abbasids attempted to govern the empire according to religious principles. These were found in the *Qur'an* and in the *sunnah*, or practices established by the Prophet and preserved first orally and then in the *hadith*, or traditions, which were somewhat comparable to the Christian Gospels. This new empire was to be a universal Muslim commonwealth in which Arabs had no privileged position. "Whoever speaks Arabic is an Arab," ran a popular saying. The 'Abbasids had risen to power as "the group of the saved," and they hoped to make the moral community of Islam the cornerstone of their government, with obedience to 'Abbasid authority an integral part of Islamic belief.

The institutional foundations of the new caliphate, however, like those of the Umayyads, remained firmly in the ancient empires they had conquered. The great caliph Mansur (754–75) moved the capital from Damascus to Baghdad, an acknowledgment of the crucial role of Iraqi and Iranian military and economic strength. With their claims to divine sanction as members of the "holy family" and their firm control of the military, increasingly composed of slave armies known as Mamluks, the 'Abbasids governed the Islamic empire at its zenith.

Ultimately, however, the 'Abbasids were no more successful than the Umayyads in maintaining authority over the whole Muslim world. By the tenth century, local military commanders, termed *emirs*, took control of provincial governments in many areas while preserving the fiction that they were appointed by the 'Abbasid caliphs. The caliphs maintained the symbolic unity of Islam while the emirs went their separate ways. The majority of Muslims accepted this situation as a necessary compromise. In contrast to the Shi'ites, who continued to look for a leader from the family of 'Ali, the Sunnis, as they came to be known, who have remained to the present the majority group of Muslims, had no fixed theory of government or succession to the caliphate. Instead, they accepted the events of history in a practical manner, secure in the truth of the hadith, "My umma will never agree upon an error."

In the west the 'Abbasids could not maintain even a facade of unity. Supporters of 'Ali's family had never accepted the 'Abbasid claims to be the legitimate spiritual leaders of the Islamic community. These Shi'ites launched sporadic revolts and separatist movements. The most successful was that of 'Ubayd Allah the Fatimid (d. 934), who claimed to be the descendant of 'Ali and rightful leader of Islam. In 909, with the support of North African seminomadic Berbers, he declared himself caliph in defiance of the 'Abbasids at Baghdad. In 969 'Ubayd's Fatimid successors conquered Egypt and established a new city, Cairo, as the capital of their rival caliphate. By the middle of the eleventh century, the Fatimid caliphate controlled all of North Africa, Sicily, Syria, and western Arabia.

In Umayyad Spain, although the Muslim population remained firmly Sunni, the powerful emir 'Abd ar-Rahman III (891–961) took a similar step. In 929 he exchanged his title for that of caliph, thus making his position religious as well as secular. Everywhere the political and religious unity of Islam was being torn apart.

The arrival in all three caliphates of Muslim peoples not yet integrated into the civilization of the Mediterranean world accelerated this disintegration. From the east, Seljuq Turks, long used as slave troops, entered Iraq and in 1055 conquered Baghdad. Within a decade they had conquered Iran, Syria, and Palestine as well. Around the same time Moroccan Berbers conquered much of North Africa and Spain, while Bedouin raided freely in what are today Libya and Tunisia. These invasions by Muslims from the fringes of the Islamic commonwealth had catastrophic effects on the Islamic world. The Turks, unaccustomed to commerce and to the administrative traditions of the caliphate, divided their empire among their war leaders, displacing traditional landowners and disrupting commerce. The North African Berbers and Bedouins destroyed the agricultural and commercial systems that had survived successive Vandal, Byzantine, and Arabian invasions.

Islamic Civilization

The Islamic conquest of the seventh century brought peace to Iraq and Iran after generations of struggle and set the stage for a major agricultural recovery. In the tradition of their Persian predecessors, the caliphs organized vast irrigation systems, which made Mesopotamia the richest agricultural region west of China. Peasants and slaves raised dates and olives in addition to wheat, barley, and rice. Sophisticated hydraulics and scientific agriculture brought great regions of Mesopotamia and the Mediterranean coast into cultivation for the first time in centuries.

By uniting the Mediterranean world with Arabia and India, the 'Abbasid empire created the greatest trade network that had ever been seen. Muslim merchants met in busy, bustling ports on the Persian Gulf and the Red Sea. There they traded silks, paper, spices, and horses from China for silver and cotton from India. Gold from the Sudan was exchanged for iron from Persia. Carpets from Armenia and Tabaristan (what is today Iran) were traded; from western Europe came slaves. Much of these luxury goods found their way to Baghdad, known as the marketplace for the world.

The marketplace for ideas was as active as that for merchandise. Within a few generations, descendants of Bedouin established themselves in the great cities of the ancient Near East and absorbed the traditions of Persian, Roman, and Hellenistic civilization. However, unlike the Germanic peoples of western Europe, who quickly adopted the Latin language and Roman Christianity, the Muslims recast Persian and Hellenistic culture in an Arabic form. Even in Iran, where Farsi, or Persian, survived as the majority language, Arabic vocabulary and structure transformed the traditional language. While 'Abbasid political unity was falling apart, this new civilization was reaching its first great synthesis.

As desert conquerors, the Arabs might have been expected to destroy or ignore the heritage of Persian and Hellenistic culture. Instead, they became its protectors and preservers. As early as the eighth century, caliphs collected Persian, Greek, and Syriac scientific and philosophical works and had them translated into Arabic. Legal scholars concerned with the authenticity of hadith used Greek rationalist methods to distinguish genuine from spurious traditions. Religious mystics called *Sufis* blended Neoplatonic and Muslim traditions to create new forms of religious devotion. The medical writings of Hippocrates and Galen circulated widely in the Islamic world, and Muslim physicians were by far the most competent and respected in the West through the fifteenth century. Mathematics and astronomy were both practical and theoretical fields. Muslim intellectuals introduced the so-called Arabic numerals from India and by the tenth century had perfected the use of decimal fractions and algebra. Muslim astronomers absorbed

This engraved brass astrolabe was made by the Yemeni sultan al-Ashraf in 1291. Astrolabes such as this were used by seafarers from ancient times to measure the angles of celestial bodies above the horizon.

and continued the highly accurate traditions of Mesopotamian planetary observation. The tables they compiled were more accurate than those known in the Byzantine and Latin worlds.

Although most Islamic scientists were professional physicians, astronomers, or lawyers, they were also deeply concerned with abstract philosophical questions, particularly those raised by the works of Plato and Aristotle, which had been translated into Arabic. Many sought to reconcile Islam with this philosophical heritage in the same manner that Origen and Augustine had done for Christianity. Ya'qub al-Kindi (d. 873), the first Arab philosopher, noted that "The truth . . . must be taken wherever it is to be found, whether it be in the past or among strange peoples." The Persian physician Ibn Sina (980–1037), known in Christian Europe as Avicenna, wrote over a hundred works on all aspects of science and philosophy. He compiled a vast encyclopedia of knowledge in which he attempted to synthesize Aristotelian thought into a Neoplatonic view of the universe. In the next century the Cordoban philosopher Ibn Rushd (1126–98), called Averroës in Christian Europe, went still further, teaching an authentic Aristotelian philosophy stripped of Neoplatonic mystical trappings. His commentaries on Aristotle were enormously influential even outside the Islamic world. For Christian philosophers of the thirteenth century, Averroës was known simply as "the Commentator."

At the same time that Muslim thought and culture was at its most creative, Islam faced invasion from a new and unaccustomed quarter: Constantinople. In the tenth and early eleventh centuries, the Byzantines pressed the local rulers of northern Syria and Iraq in a series of raids, which reached as far as the border of Palestine. At the end of the eleventh century western Europeans, encouraged and supported by the Byzantines, captured Jerusalem and established a western-style kingdom in Palestine that survived for over a century. Once more, Constantinople was a power in the Mediterranean world.

The revelations to the prophet Muhammad led to one of the greatest transformations the world has ever known. Islam forged a united Arabian people who went on to conquer more of Asia, Africa, and Europe than had any military empire in history. This conquest in the name of Allah created a vast religious and commercial zone in which ideas and cultures flowed as freely as silks and spices. The Arabians soon lost political control of the Islamic movement, but their religious tradition and its emphasis on worship of the one God remains an enduring legacy in world civilization.

The Byzantine Apogee and Decline, 1000–1453

During the tenth and eleventh centuries, Byzantium dominated the Mediterranean world for the last time. Regions lost to Islam were reconquered, assistance from western Europe checked Islamic power on the eastern Mediterranean coast, and new areas to the north were brought under Byzantine hegemony. And yet these very successes planted the seeds of the ultimate decline of Byzantine civilization.

Imperial armies under the Macedonian dynasty (867–1059) began to recover some lands lost to Islam during the previous two centuries. Antioch was retaken in 969, and for over a century Byzantine armies operated in Syria and pushed to the border of Palestine. By the middle of the eleventh century Armenia and Georgia, which had formed independent principalities, had been reintegrated into the empire. To the west Sicily remained in Muslim hands, but southern Italy, which had been subject to Muslim raids and western barbarian occupation, was secured once more. Byzantine fleets recaptured Crete, cleared the Aegean of Muslim pirates, and reopened the vital commercial sea routes. To the north, missionaries spread not only the Christian religion but also Byzantine culture among the Slavic peoples beyond the frontiers of the empire. The most important missionaries were the brothers Cyril (ca. 827–69) and Methodius (ca. 825–84), who preached to the Khazars and the Moravians. They also invented the Cyrillic alphabet, which they used to translate the Bible and other Christian writings into Slavic. Their missionary activities laid the foundation for the conversion of Serbia, Bulgaria, and Russia. In 1018 Basil II (976–1025) destroyed the Bulgarian kingdom and brought peace to the Balkan Peninsula.

The conquests of the Macedonian dynasty laid the foundation for a short-lived economic prosperity and cultural renaissance. Conquered lands, particularly Anatolia, brought new agricultural wealth. Security of the sea fostered a resurgence of commerce, and customs duties enriched the imperial treasury. New wealth financed the flourishing of Byzantine art and literature. However, just as in the spheres of Byzantine liturgy and court ceremonial, the goal of Byzantine art was not to reflect the transient "reality" of this world but rather the permanent, classical values inherited from the past. Only in rare works such as the popular epic *Digenis Akrites* does something of the flavor of popular Byzantine life appear. The title of the work means roughly "the border defender born of two peoples," for the hero, Basil, was the son of a Muslim father and a Christian Greek mother. The descriptions of the hero's battles, his encounters with wild beasts and dragons, and his heroic death, as well as those of his intelligence, learning, and magnificent palace, are at once part of the epic tradition and a reflection of life on the edge of the empire.

The Disintegration of the Empire

In all domains, however, the successes of the Macedonian emperors set the stage for serious problems. Rapid military expansion and economic growth allowed new elites to establish themselves as autonomous powers and to position themselves between the imperial administration and the people. The constant demand for troops always exceeded the supply of traditional salaried soldiers. In the eleventh century, emperors began to grant imperial estates to great magnates in return for military service. These grants, termed *pronoia*, often included immunity from imperial taxation and the right to certain administrative activities traditionally carried out by the central government. The practice created in effect a largely independent, landed military aristocracy that stood between the peasantry and the imperial government. This policy weakened the centralized state and reduced its income from taxes.

As generals became dissatisfied with the civilian central administration, they began to turn their armies against the emperors, launching over thirty revolts in as many years. To defend itself against both the Muslims without and the generals within, the central government, composed of intellectuals, eunuchs, and urban aristocrats, had to spend vast sums on mercenary armies. These armies, composed largely of Armenians, Germans, and Normans, soon began to plunder the empire they were hired to protect. Further danger came from other, independent Normans who, under their commander Robert Guiscard (ca. 1015–85), conquered Byzantine Bari and southern Italy and then Muslim Sicily. Soon Guiscard was threatening the empire itself. The hostility between military aristocracy and imperial administration largely destroyed the tradition of civilian government.

Under increasing pressure from local magnates on the one hand and desperate imperial tax collectors on the other, villages began to make deals with powerful patrons who would represent them in return for the surrender of their independence. Through the eleventh and twelfth centuries, the Byzantine peasantry passed from the condition of individualism without freedom to collectivism without freedom. Through the same process landlords and patrons acquired the means to exercise a political role, which ended the state's monopoly on public power.

At the same time that civil war and external pressure were destroying the provincial administration, Byzantine disdain for commerce was weakening the empire's ability to control its income from customs duties. In the tenth and eleventh centuries, merchants of Amalfi, Bari, and then Venice came to dominate Byzantine commerce. Venetian merchant fleets could double as a powerful navy in times of need, and by the eleventh century the Venetians were the permanent military and commercial power in the Mediterranean. When Robert Guiscard and his Normans threatened the empire, the emperors had to turn to the Venetians for protection and were forced to cede them major economic privileges.

The Venetians acquired the right to maintain important self-governing communities in major ports throughout the empire and were allowed to pay lower tariffs than the Byzantines themselves.

In 1071, the year that Robert Guiscard captured the last Byzantine city in Italy, the empire suffered an even more disastrous defeat in the east. At Manzikert in Anatolia the emperor Romanus IV (1067–71) and his unreliable mercenary army fell to the Seljuq Turks, who captured Romanus himself. Manzikert sealed the fate of the empire. Anatolia was lost and the gradual erosion of the empire both west and east had begun.

The Conquests of Constantinople and Baghdad

At the end of the eleventh century the Comnenian dynasty (1081–1185) briefly halted the political and economic chaos of the empire. Rather than fighting the tendency of the centralized state to devolve into a decentralized aristocratic one, Alexius I Comnenus (1081–1118) tied the aristocracy to his family, thus making it an instrument of imperial government. In the short run the process was successful. He expanded the use of pronoia to strengthen loyal aristocrats and he granted them offices in the central administration that had been traditionally reserved for eunuchs. He stabilized Byzantine currency, which was the international exchange medium in the Islamic and Christian worlds and which had been dangerously devalued by his predecessors. Still, by the late twelfth century, the empire was a vulnerable second-rate power caught between Latin Europe and Islam.

Initially, the Christian west was a more deadly threat than the Islamic east. In the eleventh century, after more than five hundred years of economic and political weakness, western Europe was beginning to reach parity with Byzantium. Robert Guiscard and his Normans, who had conquered Sicily and southern Italy, were typical examples of the powerful, militaristic aristocracy developing in the remains of the old western empire. This military threat from the west was paralleled by a religious one. In the centuries that Rome had been largely cut off from Constantinople, western Christianity had developed a number of rituals and beliefs differing from Orthodox practice. This parting of the ways had already appeared during the iconoclastic controversies of the eighth and ninth centuries. In the eleventh, it was directed by an independent and self-assertive papacy in Rome, which claimed supreme authority throughout Christendom. Disagreements between the patriarchs of Constantinople and the popes of Rome

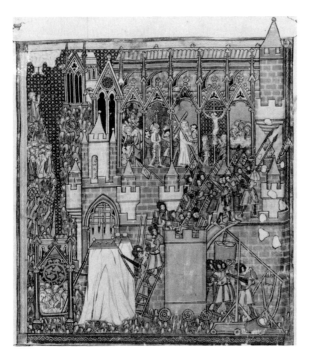

The battle of Jerusalem is illustrated in this twelfth-century manuscript. Events in the life of Christ are shown at the top as if in stained-glass windows. Crusaders storm the walls while siege engines hurl stones at the defenders.

prevented cooperation between the two Christian worlds and led to further deterioration of relationships between Greeks and Latins. These disagreements came to a head in 1054, when the papal representative, or legate, Cardinal Humbert (ca. 1000–61) met with the patriarch of Constantinople, Michael Cerularius (ca. 1000–59), to negotiate ecclesiastical control over southern Italy and Sicily. Humbert was arrogant and demanding, Michael Cerularius haughty and uncompromising. Acting beyond his authority, Humbert excommunicated the patriarch and all his followers. The patriarch responded in kind, excommunicating Humbert and all connected with him. This formal excommunication was lifted in the 1960s, but the schism, or split, between the churches of Rome and Constantinople continues to the present.

Excommunication was probably the least of the dangers the Byzantines faced from the west. The full fury of this western society reached the empire when, after the defeat at Manzikert, the emperor Alexius called on western Christians for support against the Muslims. To his horror, adventurers of every sort eager to conquer land and wealth in the name of the cross of Jesus flooded

the empire. In the penetrating and often cynical biography of her father, Alexius' daughter Anna (ca. 1083–1148) describes how, as quickly as possible, Alexius hurried these crusaders (from the Latin *cruciata*, "marked with a cross") on to Palestine before they could turn their violence against his empire. Despite enormous hardships, the First Crusade was able to take advantage of division in the Muslim world to conquer Palestine and establish a Latin kingdom in Jerusalem in 1099.

The crusaders' initial victories and the growth of Latin wealth and power created in Constantinople a temporary enthusiasm for western European styles and customs. The Byzantines soon realized, however, that the Latin kingdom posed a threat not only to Islam but to them as well. While crusaders threatened Byzantine territories, Venetian merchants acquired a monopoly on Byzantine trade. When emperors granted other Italian towns concessions equal to those of the Venetians, they found that they had simply amplified their problems. Anti-Latin sentiment reached the boiling point in 1183. In the riots that broke out in that year Italians and other westerners in Constantinople were murdered and their goods seized. Just twenty-one years later, in 1204, a wayward crusade, egged on by Venice, turned aside from its planned expedition to Palestine to capture a bigger prize: Constantinople. After pillaging the city for three days—the Byzantine survivors commented that even the Saracens would have been less cruel—the westerners established one of their own as emperor and installed a Venetian as patriarch.

The Byzantines did manage to hold on to a portion of their empire centering on Nicaea, and before long the Latins fell to bickering among themselves. In 1261 the ruler of Nicaea, Michael Palaeologus (ca. 1224–82), recaptured Constantinople with the assistance of the Genoese and had himself crowned emperor in the Hagia Sophia. Still, the empire was fatally shattered, its disintegration into autonomous lordships complete. The restored empire consisted of little more than the district around Constantinople, Thessalonica, and the Peloponneseus. Bulgarians and Serbs had expanded far into the Greek mainland. Most of the rich Anatolian regions had been lost to the Turks, and commercial revenues were in the hands of the Genoese allies. The restored empire's survival for almost two hundred years was due less to its own prerogative than to the internal problems of the Islamic world.

The caliphs of Baghdad, like the emperors of Constantinople, succumbed to invaders from the barbarous fringes of their empire. In 1219 the Mongol prince Temujin (ca. 1162–1227), better known to history as

The Byzantine Empire and the Rise of Islam

527–565	Reign of Justinian
610	Muhammad's vision
622	The Hijra, Muhammad's journey from Mecca to Medina
726–787	First phase of iconoclast dispute
732	Muslim advance halted by Franks
750	'Abbasids overthrow Umayyads; take control of Muslim world
802–843	Second phase of iconoclast dispute
843	Empress Theodora ends iconoclast persecution; restores image worship
867–1059	Macedonian dynasty rules Byzantine Empire; begins recovering lands from Muslims
1054	Schism splits churches of Rome and Constantinople.
1071	Robert Guiscard captures Sicily and southern Italy; battle of Manzikert; Seljuq Turks defeat Byzantines
1099	First Crusade establishes Latin kingdom in Jerusalem
1221	Genghis Khan leads Mongol army into Persia
1453	Constantinople falls to Ottomans

From the ruins of the Seljuq kingdom arose a variety of small Turkish principalities, or emirates. After the collapse of the Mongol empire, one of these, the Ottoman, began to expand at the expense of both the weakened Byzantine and the Mongol-Seljuq empires. In the next centuries the Ottomans expanded east, south, and west. Around 1350, they crossed into the Balkans as Byzantine allies but soon took over the region for themselves. By 1450 the Ottoman stranglehold on Constantinople was complete. The final scene of the conquest, long delayed but inevitable, occurred three years later.

For Greeks and for Italian intellectuals of the Renaissance, the conquest of Constantinople by the Ottomans was the end of an imperial tradition that reached back to Augustus. But Mehmed the Conqueror (1452–81) could as easily be seen as its restorer. Once more, Constantinople, for centuries a capital without a country, was the center of a great Mediterranean empire. In the following centuries, Ottoman rule stretched from the gates of Vienna to the Caspian Sea and from the Persian Gulf to the Strait of Gibraltar. The legacy of absolutism, of imperial government, and of cultural pluralism, inherited from Sassanid Persia and imperial Rome, survived until the beginning of the twentieth century.

Africa and the Impact of Islam

In sub-Saharan Africa, the perennial village-based communities of agriculturalists had worked out effective means of dealing with the peculiarities of African soil, weather, and environment. They were in contact with the Mediterranean and Indian worlds through commercial ties dominated by big men who used their economic position to expand political power. From the seventh century, two of these were greatly affected by the rise of Islam.

West African Trade, State Building, and the Spread of Islam

Although one could discuss many important African states, we shall concentrate on two groups that, although widely separated geographically, were both greatly affected by the rise and spread of Islam. These were the western Sudanic states of Ghana, Mali, and Songhai, and the Swahili city-states of the East African coast and the great state of Zimbabwe in the interior of southeast Africa.

Genghis Khan (Universal Ruler), led his conquering army into Persia from central Asia. From there, a portion of the Mongols went north, invading Russia in 1237 and dividing it into small principalities ruled by Slavic princes under Mongol control. In 1258 a Mongol army captured Baghdad and executed the last 'Abbasid caliph, ending a five-hundred-year tradition. The Mongol armies then moved west, shattering the Seljuq principalities in Iraq, Anatolia, and Syria and turning back only before the fierce resistance of the Egyptian Mamluks.

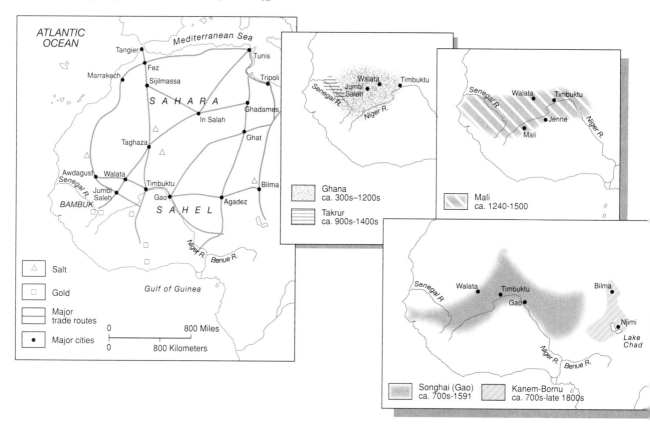

West African States

In the western Sudanic area, along the southern fringe of the Sahara, is the zone known as the Sahel. It was in this area that the drying out of the Sahara/Sudanic regions that had begun by around 3500 B.C.E. forced people to move gradually into oases, river valleys, and to the shores of lakes where, unlike the situation in much of Africa, there was enough water to sustain intensive agriculture. In the Sahel zone, people had established by the first millennium B.C.E. relatively dense communities that often numbered well over five thousand inhabitants. Such large settlements clearly transcended social organization based on families alone and appear to have served two purposes: to organize efficient intensive agricultural production based largely on rice and to provide defense against raids by nomadic Berbers from the Sahara.

Two later changes set the stage for the establishment of large states in the area. First, in the second century C.E., traders from the east introduced the camel to the Sahara. As camels were able to go without water for long periods of time and to carry up to a quarter of a ton of baggage across the desert's arid wastes, they were aptly known as the "ships of the desert." Berbers with

their horses had been restricted to the fringes of the desert, but after the introduction of the camel they began to live in the desert itself and, most importantly, to conduct caravan trade across it. Trade between the Roman settlements of North Africa and West Africa's Sudanic zone blossomed briefly, but when the Roman Empire declined in the fourth century C.E., the trade shriveled and atrophied.

In the late seventh century, however, Arab conquerors carried the new religion of Islam from Arabia into North Africa and Spain, incorporating these areas into a single political and economic zone that extended from India to Spain, and producing a remarkably sustained growth in the economy of the Mediterranean region and western Asia. This economic growth revived the trans-Saharan trade and provided the second stimulus to state building in the western Sudanic region. Traders from the north sought West African kola nuts, gums, cotton cloth, and hides for leather working as well as West African slaves. Of crucial importance, the burgeoning economy of the Islamic world also required unlimited amounts of West Africa's gold for coinage, jewelry, and ornamentation.

A fourteenth-century map of northwestern Africa, showing Mansa Musa of Mali receiving a caravan of traders while holding aloft a golden nugget.

Salt, a seemingly mundane commodity, was the basis of the complex trade that developed for all these commodities. In West Africa high-quality salt was found only in a few locations deep in the Sahara. The Berbers who controlled these places used slaves to mine the salt and traded it southward to the Sudan and the forest in exchange for gold and other goods. Salt was so rare south of the desert that it was claimed that a single ounce could be traded for an ounce of gold. At the height of the trade, an estimated five hundred thousand ounces of gold crossed the desert annually. With a trade of such magnitude, successful "big men" who controlled locations that allowed them to levy tolls on the caravans became important kings ruling over impressive states, eventually using the new learning and literacy associated with Islam to make their governments more efficient. Soon after the revival of the Islamic world's economy, therefore, a series of states began to develop across the western Sudanic area, straddling the trade routes between desert and forest and gaining widespread fame for their great wealth.

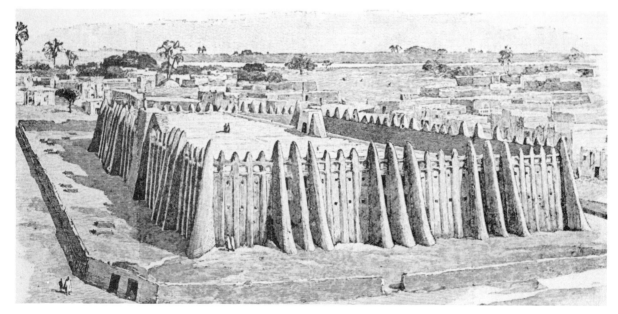

Reconstruction of the old mosque at Jenne, an intellectual center that rivalled Timbuktu. Jenne was destroyed in 1830 by a Muslim zealot who led a Fulani jihad against the perceived moral corruption of the inhabitants.

The first of these states, already old when Arab travelers began writing about it in the ninth century C.E., was Ghana, a Soninke-speaking state based on the trading town of Kumbi Saleh, an oasis in the desert inhabited by an estimated twenty thousand people. In effect, the king of Ghana was a middleman who controlled the trade between West Africa's Bambuk and Bure gold fields and the southern Moroccan trading city of Sijilmassa. Profiting from Ghana's geographical position, the Ghanaian elite developed a powerful cavalry and expanded its territory into the area between the upper Niger and Senegal rivers and over the Saharan salt mines. While its leaders welcomed Muslim traders and teachers and used Muslim learning for economic and administrative purposes, they themselves converted to Islam only late in Ghana's history. With its prosperity based on control over far-flung trade routes rather than the actual production of commodities at the center of the state, Ghana eventually weakened and declined. The Almoravids, a zealous Muslim sect established among the Berbers of the western Sahara in the mid-eleventh century, began to attack northern sections of the weakened empire, and toward the end of the century Ghana broke apart.

The trans-Saharan trade continued to grow, however, with its main routes gradually shifting eastward and providing the base upon which another great state, Mali, grew and prospered. The fertile valley of the upper Niger River was Mali's core area, and from there its leaders expanded their control over the trade from the gold fields of the White Volta and Akan areas of the forest zone to the south. Its profits allowed them to build a powerful cavalry that was used to extend their rule westward as far as the area between the Senegal and Gambia rivers. Its merchants journeyed far beyond the state's borders, enriching themselves and the state through their trading. Unlike Ghana's rulers, Mali's leaders also used slave labor to produce food for desert oases and major towns that included Gao, Jenne, and the fabled Timbuktu, thus helping to hold the empire together through networks of internal trade. And, again unlike Ghana's rulers, they enthusiastically converted to Islam and embraced Muslim juridical principles. By the thirteenth century, Mali, like Ghana before it, had become famous throughout the Muslim world for its wealth, splendor, and peace.

Mali's reputation in the Muslim world was greatly enhanced when its ruler, Mansa Musa (1312–37), made a pilgrimage to Mecca in 1324, accompanied by a huge retinue of servants and retainers. He gave away large amounts of gold to show his largesse and also spent large

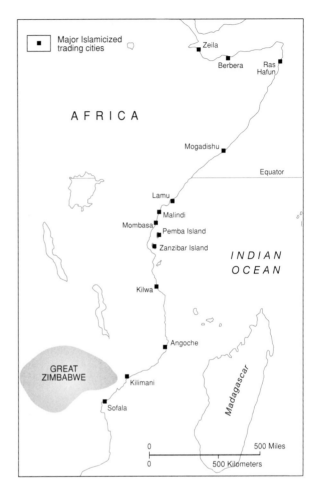

Swahili City-States

amounts for provisions. He put so much gold into circulation that it is said he caused a startling burst of inflation in Egypt. The trip's most enduring result, however, was the intensification of Islamic influence in the Sudanic zone itself. Muslim schools were established in the cities. The Mali elite patronized the arts and religion, sponsored the building of mosques, and encouraged people to convert to Islam. As a consequence of such patronage, even though some earlier African religious practices lived on, the area became predominantly Muslim.

Yet the tensions between central government and outlying provinces, between empire and village or town, remained, with local leaders always alert to the possibilities of secession. As the Almoravids had attacked Ghana earlier, in the mid-fourteenth century the nomadic Tuareg Berbers of the desert attacked the northern parts of the state and even seized Timbuktu. As time passed, localism gradually won out and the central

AN ASSESSMENT OF ISLAM IN MALI IN 1353

■ *In the western Sudan, as elsewhere, religious differences have been used to justify warfare. Differences among Muslims over specific practices have often led to wars of purification aimed at practices deemed "un-Islamic." In 1352–53, Ibn Battuta (1304–69), a Moroccan jurist who was one of the greatest travelers of his age, visited the great Sudanic state of Mali just thirty years after Mansa Musa's pilgrimage to Mecca intensified Islam's impact. In his writings he assessed the Islamic practices he witnessed. The deviations he mentions were precisely the type that prompted later purifiers of Islam to carry out holy wars in the region.*

Amongst their good qualities is the small amount of injustice amongst them, for of all people they are the furthest from it. Among these qualities there is also the prevalence of peace in their country, the traveller is not afraid in it nor is he who lives there in fear of the thief or of the robber by violence. Another of the good habits amongst them is the way they meticulously observe the times of the prayers and attendance at them, so also it is with regard to their congregational services and their beating of their children to instill these things in them. When it is Friday, if a man does not come early to the mosque he will not find a place to pray because of the numbers of the crowd. Among their good qualities is their putting on of good white clothes on Friday. If a man among them has nothing except a tattered shirt, he washes and cleans it and attends the Friday prayer in it. Another of their good qualities is their concern for learning the sublime Qur'an by heart. They make fetters for the children when they appear on their part to be falling short of learning it by heart.

Among the bad things which they do—their serving women, slave women and little daughters appear before people naked, exposing their private parts. Also among their bad customs is the way women will go into the presence of the sultan naked, without any covering; and the nakedness of the sultan's daughters. Another of their bad customs is their putting of dust and ashes on their heads as a sign of respect. And another is that many of them eat animals not ritually slaughtered, and dogs and donkeys.

From *Ibn Battuta in Black Africa*.

state was able to maintain control over less and less trade, less and less territory, and less and less wealth. By the 1370s, a mere fifty years after Mansa Musa's magnificent sojourn to Egypt and Arabia, Songhai, an important area in eastern Mali, seceded. It became the next— but by no means the last—great state of the Sudanic region based on the wealth of the trans-Saharan trade, and throughout the fifteenth century it continued to foster the expansion of Islam in West Africa.

The Growth of Swahili Culture and the Rise of Zimbabwe

As people converted to Islam along the trade routes of West Africa and while the revived economy of the wider Muslim world stimulated the growth of prosperous states along the southern fringe of the Sahara, a similar, though not identical, development was taking place along the coast of East Africa. The monsoon winds of the Indian Ocean blow steadily from the southwest in the warm part of the year and steadily from the northeast in the cool period. Although the actual months of the prevailing winds differ from place to place, sailors have been able to cross the ocean confident that the winds would last for four months and that they would not be unexpectedly stranded. Once the growing economy of the Islamic world had created a market hungry for African commodities, it was inevitable that merchants from Arabia and the Persian Gulf would set sail for East Africa to meet the demand.

By the time these merchants arrived on the coast in the ninth and tenth centuries C.E., it had already been populated by Bantu-speaking agriculturalists who spoke an early form of Swahili. In addition to growing millet, sorghum, and rice and raising chickens and some livestock, these people had begun to fish on the ocean. Using their boats, they had spread southward from their original

Great Zimbabwe was one of a number of stone complexes that existed in southeastern Africa. The soapstone bird statue in the inset was found there.

Great Zimbabwe, Racism, and Understanding African History

A traveler along the road through the scrubby, nondescript bush of southern Zimbabwe might be startled by the sudden appearance of a large fortress built atop a low hill. Its massive walls are some thirty feet high and are built of large rocks and boulders, some of which are fifteen feet across, connected by drywalls. It is honey-combed with narrow passages and large rooms. At the foot of the hill is an even more striking building, a gigantic walled enclosure that has been called "the largest prehistoric structure in sub-Saharan Africa." Its wall, constructed without any cement or mortar from exquisitely sculpted stone, is 270 yards long, over thirty feet high, and in places over fifteen feet thick. At one end of the enclosure stands a stone tower about thirty feet in height and eighteen feet in diameter. Outside the walls are remnants of other, less imposing buildings, now long abandoned. This site is Great Zimbabwe.

The first white person to see it was a prospector searching for gold in 1871. It amazed him, and, despite the lack of written inscriptions anywhere, he concluded that it was the site of the fabled King Solomon's Mines. Later, other whites attributed Great Zimbabwe variously to Phoenicians, to a lost tribe of Israel, to Arabians, and to Indians. To understand this white preoccupation with identifying the ruins with foreign builders, one must situate it in the intellectual context of the times. Anti-black racism and European imperialism characterized white attitudes toward Africa in the late nineteenth and early twentieth centuries. One core racist belief held that whites were the main force of human history because they alone were imaginative, innovative, and daring. On the other hand, because of their alleged mental deficiency, it was asserted that blacks repeated the same patterns of living generation after generation. Indeed, their very survival in a challenging universe required them to live in accordance with the wisdom of their unchanging customs. Therefore, whenever anything was discovered in Africa that demonstrated that radical change had occurred in the past, it was immediately attributed to white invaders from the north. Only they could have done something so striking!

The belief that Great Zimbabwe had been built by white outsiders persisted among most observers for almost a century. It was only in the 1960s, when imperialism was ending and racism weakening, that the obvious and simple truth that local Africans had built it began to displace the earlier myths. As archaeologists have explored the site, an accurate picture of Great Zimbabwe's purpose and history has begun to emerge. For one aware of the patterns of history in the western Sudanic region, the truth is not surprising.

What made it possible to support the leadership that would have been required to mobilize labor adequate to build the stone buildings of Great Zimbabwe in the thirteenth century was that it was the capital of a large state whose powerful leaders directed an important long-distance trade. Discoveries of Persian and Chinese porcelain, tens of thousands of glass beads from India, cowrie shells, and other items in the ruins attest to trade links with Asia. Its prosperity was based on the overseas gold and ivory trades. The presence of large amounts of copper shows that its trade also extended from Great Zimbabwe to copper-producing areas in the interior, probably in Zambia. Quite simply, Great Zimbabwe was the site of southern Africa's first large town, having a population of about 18,000, many of whom tended cattle and grew food crops, while many others were artisans and administrators.

Moreover, archaeologists have also uncovered something that suggests that Great Zimbabwe was also a religious shrine. Several carved statues of birdlike creatures positioned in key parts of the site suggest that worship of a spirit associated with the sky was carried out here, perhaps aimed at ensuring adequate rainfall in a part of Africa where rains are always uncertain.

Center of trade and commerce, administration, and worship, Great Zimbabwe clearly demonstrated the might of the powerful state that supported it. Yet, despite its glory, when the environment around it collapsed from overuse, it had to be abandoned. As in other parts of Africa, the soils of the plateau are fragile. Large numbers of people living here for centuries resulted in overhunting, overgrazing, and overcultivating the soil. The environment could no longer support the city, and so, perhaps stimulated by a sudden epidemic of cattle disease or a prolonged drought and famine, sometime in the early fifteenth century the elite withdrew to better locations. They left behind massive buildings, which became both a puzzle to later white explorers and settlers and a source of historical pride to the contemporary African people of Zimbabwe, which is itself named after the site.

The end of the occupation of Great Zimbabwe did not mean the end of the gold trade nor the end of commerce with the Indian Ocean basin, of course. In the succeeding centuries, other states followed in the pattern of growth that it had pioneered. Yet in none of these did the elite produce buildings of such magnificence as those at the little hill in the midst of the bush where travelers can still be startled and amazed.

source area in Kenya to Tanzania and the Comoro Islands. In subsequent centuries, migration continued, with settlers establishing themselves as far north as Mogadishu in Somalia and as far south as Mozambique. With the arrival of more merchants from overseas, the coastal areas enjoyed greater and greater prosperity.

Then, in the twelfth and thirteenth centuries, commercial activity in the Indian Ocean basin accelerated sharply, partly as a result of a revival of Egypt that had begun as early as the tenth century and partly because of the work of Salah ad-Din (1138–93), the great opponent of the European Christian crusaders and known by them as Saladin. He had cleared the Red Sea trade routes of Christian interference by 1174, opening them to the busy trade of the Indian Ocean basin. Shortly afterwards, Muslims expanded into India, establishing a state of great brilliance and prosperity, and then into Malaya and parts of Indonesia. These geopolitical changes increased demand for African products in both Europe and Asia, and trade with the coast grew still more.

Unlike the situation in West Africa, the increased trade did not produce a single large state like Ghana or Mali. Instead, some of the earlier small Swahili coastal settlements became city-states based on trade and ruled by a single ruler or an oligarchy. These included ports such as Mogadishu, Mombasa, Zanzibar, and Kilwa. Very much like the situation in West Africa, however, these new towns prospered as intermediaries in the trade that existed between the African interior and Asia. African traders brought ivory, rhinoceros horns, and slaves to coastal towns, where they exchanged them with the resident Swahili merchants for ironware, foodstuffs, and, most importantly, cloth and ornaments.

The development of Swahili culture after 1100 included an important Islamic dimension. Many of the Asian merchants brought with them not only their religion but also Islamic courts to adjudicate disputes over land and trade and Islamic schools for the education of their children. They also used Islamic architectural models to construct stone mosques, houses, and palaces. In effect, the Swahili towns became centers of an Islamic culture that existed alongside earlier African culture, with each adapting to the other. Large numbers of Africans also converted to Islam, beginning a process that continues today.

During the period of increased economic activity along the coast and the growth of Swahili culture between 1100 and 1500, another African state became important in the trade of the Indian Ocean basin. This state, situated on the highland plateau that is occupied by Shona-speakers today, was Zimbabwe.

As a result of three closely interrelated changes Zimbabwe had begun developing as early as the ninth century. First, the population had grown, apparently as a consequence of the beginning of large scale cattle keeping in areas free of the tsetse fly. Second—and probably because of the availability of cattle, which were considered the embodiment of wealth—an elite of big men had emerged, able to mobilize ever larger amounts of labor. Third, to feed the larger population in an area of uncertain rainfall, stone hillside terraces and large stone cattle enclosures (known as *zimbabwes*) had been built over the whole of the plateau. These supplied the growing labor force with food.

Swahili traders in search of ivory came to the port of Sofala, located on the southern coast of Mozambique, in the tenth century and soon made contact with Zimbabwe, an area rich in gold. Once connected with the Swahili trading system, the Zimbabwean elite used their labor force to mine outcroppings of gold to a depth of up to one hundred feet. With this additional source of revenue, the elite expanded public works projects, improved agriculture, and established a military force. Some time in the thirteenth century, the additional revenue also enabled the Zimbabwean elite to construct the monumental buildings of Great Zimbabwe, which became the capital of their state and the center for its trade and religion (See Special Feature, Great Zimbabwe, Racism, and Understanding African History," pp. 216–217.) Great Zimbabwe gradually declined, apparently because of overpopulation, and around 1450 it was finally abandoned. Its people, however, moved to other parts of the plateau and established new successor states based on cattle keeping and a continuation of trade with the Swahili coast.

By the fifteenth century, Africa had changed immensely. While the basic unit of production and politics remained the local village or town, great states had grown and died as a result of new patterns of trade, largely stimulated by economic growth in the Islamic world. As a consequence, through its links with the Islamic world, Africa was increasingly affected by what went on beyond its shores. In succeeding decades, the potent influences of Islam continued and were joined by another powerful external force that would fundamentally affect the trajectory of Africa's history. That new force was Europe.

Distinctive but interrelated cultures developed to the north, east, and south of the Mediterranean after the transformation of the Roman Empire. Although often deadly enemies, the Byzantine and Islamic worlds were both genuine heirs of the great eastern empires of antiquity. The traditions of the Assyrian, Alexandrian, Persian, and Roman empires lived on in their cities, their bureaucracies, their agricultural and commercial systems. Both also shared the monotheistic religious tradition that had emerged from Judaism. In their schools and libraries, they preserved and transmitted the literary and scientific heritage of antiquity. Through Islam, the legacy of the Mediterranean World reached the Far East. Through Byzantium, the peoples of the Slavic world became heirs of the caesars. Sub-Saharan Africa too shared in this heritage both through the spread of Islam and the commercial links brought by Islamic merchants. Still, all three regions adapted this heritage and transformed it in accord with its own unique physical environment and indigenous culture.

SUGGESTIONS FOR FURTHER READING

THE BYZANTINES

George Ostrogorsky, *History of the Byzantine State* (Rutgers, NJ: Rutgers University Press, 1969). The standard one-volume history of Byzantium.

Cyril Mango, *Byzantium: The Empire of New Rome* (New York: Scribners, 1980). An imaginative and provocative reevaluation of the Byzantine world.

Joan M. Hussey, *The Orthodox Church in the Byzantine Empire* (New York: Oxford University Press, 1986). An introduction to Orthodox Christianity.

* Dimitri Obolensky, *The Byzantine Commonwealth: Eastern Europe 500-1453* (Crestwood, NY: St. Vladimir's Seminary Press, 1983). Relates Byzantium to the Slavic world.

* J. W. Barker, *Justinian and the Later Roman Empire* (Madison, WI: University of Wisconsin Press, 1975). A survey of Justinian's reign intended for a general public.

Speros Vryonis, Jr., *Byzantium and Europe* (New York: Harcourt Brace Jovanovich, 1967). A survey of the relationship between Byzantium and the West.

A. A. Vasiliev, *History of the Byzantine Empire* (Madison, WI: University of Wisconsin Press, 1952). A classic survey of Byzantine history by a great Russian scholar.

Alexander Kazhdan and Giles Constable, *People and Power in Byzantium* (Washington, DC: Dumbarton Oaks, 1982). An imaginative and controversial analysis of Byzantine culture by a Russian Byzantinist and a western medievalist.

THE RISE OF ISLAM

* Bernard Lewis, *The Arabs in History* (New York: Harper & Row, 1966). A well-written general introduction by an authority.

* Hugh Kennedy, *The Prophet and the Age of the Caliphates* (White Plains, NY: Longman, 1986). A valuable summary of the early political history of Islam.

* John L. Esposito, *Women in Muslim Family Law* (Syracuse, NY: Syracuse University Press, 1982). A general introduction to the topic, with historical material in the first two chapters.

G. E. Von Grunebaum, *Classical Islam: A History 600-1258* (Chicago: Aldine, 1970). A general introduction to early Islamic history.

Aziz Al-Azmeh, *Arabic Thought and Islamic Societies* (London: Routledge, Chapman & Hall, 1986). A demanding but valuable introduction to Islamic intellectual history.

Roy P. Mottahedeh, *Loyalty and Leadership in an Early Islamic Society* (Princeton, NJ: Princeton University Press, 1980). An important introduction to the social values and structures of western Iran and southern Iraq in the tenth and eleventh centuries.

Bernard Lewis, ed., *Islam and the Arab World* (New York: Knopf, 1976). An illustrated collection of essays on Islamic history and culture.

* Bernard Lewis, *The Muslim Discovery of Europe* (New York: W.W. Norton, 1985). Views of the West by Muslim travelers.

THE BYZANTINE APOGEE AND DECLINE, 1000-1453

* Michael Agold, *The Byzantine Empire 1025-1204* (White Plains, NY: Longman, 1985). A solid recent survey of the Byzantine Empire prior to the capture of Constantinople by the Latins.

* P. M. Holt, *The Age of the Crusades: The Near East from the Eleventh Century to 1517* (White Plains, NY: Longman, 1986). An excellent up-to-date survey of the political history of the Near East in the later Middle Ages.

AFRICA AND THE IMPACT OF ISLAM

* Philip Curtin, Steven Feierman, Leonard Thompson, and Jan Vansina, *African History* (London: Longman, 1978). A standard text of African history that, though somewhat dated, is still useful.

Roland Oliver, *The African Experience* (New York: Harper-Collins, 1991). A highly stimulating overview of the main themes in all African history.

* J. F. Ade Ajayi and Michael Crowder, eds., *History of West Africa*, 3d ed., Vol. I (New York: Longman, 1985). An encyclopedic treatment of all West African history.

* Jan Vansina, *Paths in the Rainforests* (Madison, WI: University of Wisconsin Press, 1990). A difficult but important discussion of Bantu migrations into the Congo basin.

* Graham Connah, *African Civilizations* (New York: Cambridge University Press, 1987). A very useful general survey of precolonial African states.

E. W. Bovill, *The Golden Trade of the Moors*, 2d ed. (London: Oxford University Press, 1968). A highly readable account of the trans-Saharan trade through the nineteenth century.

* Mervyn Hiskett, *The Development of Islam in West Africa* (New York: Longman, 1984). A dense and erudite survey of Islam's impact on West African societies.

* Derek Nurse and Thomas Spear, *Reconstructing the History and Language of an African Society* (Philadelphia: University of Pennsylvania Press, 1985). Explores the complex origins of the Swahili people of East Africa.

David Beach, *The Shona and Zimbabwe, 900-1850* (London: Heinemann, 1980). A historian's synthesis of the history of Great Zimbabwe and the Shona people who constructed it.

* Indicates paperback edition available.

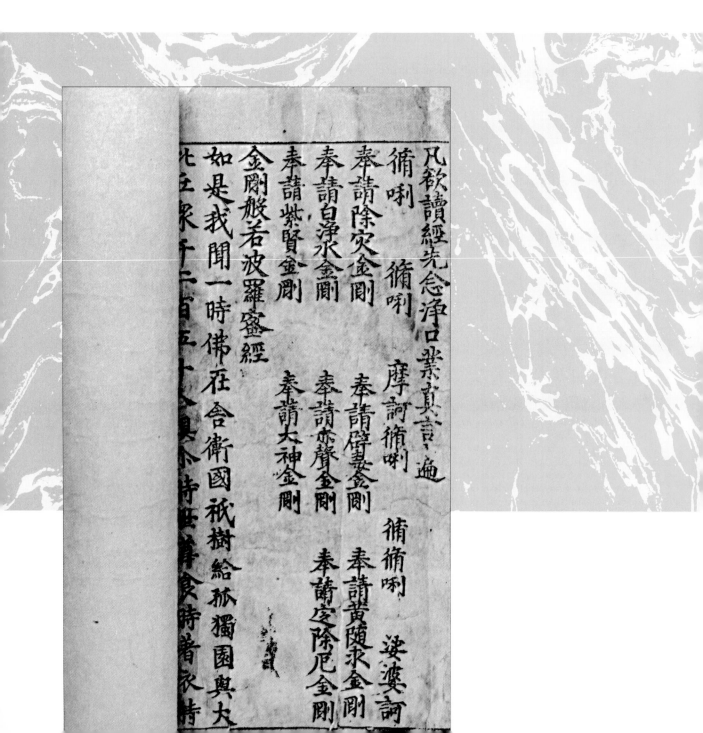

EARLY ASIAN PRINTING

It is hard for those of us who live in the late twentieth century, surrounded as we are by the printed word—newspapers, novels, magazines, even textbooks—to visualize a world without printing and to imagine the ways in which the development of printing transformed the cultural landscape. The mass production of texts meant that those texts had much wider circulation than had earlier hand-written texts. This transformation of the cultural landscape began in East Asia in the eighth century, hundreds of years before it began in the West. The earliest printing in East Asia was intimately connected with Buddhism, but the new technology soon spread to secular realms. Print spread the written word, and hence served as an agent of cultural diffusion.

The first two examples we have of printing, one from Korea and one from Japan, are *dharani*, brief texts possessing magical potency not unlike that of a charm. Reproducing *dharani* and other kinds of Buddhist texts was a means by which a man or woman could accumulate karmic merit.

But merit making alone is not a sufficient precondition for the development of printing. Certain technical prerequisites are also necessary. The Chinese had developed paper by the end of the Han dynasty. Seals and stamps, which make impressions on paper in much the same way woodblocks do, were in wide usage from the late Han. The earliest extant printed text we know of is a Buddhist *dharani* printed in Korea sometime before 751. It was found inside a Buddhist image in 1966.

The second earliest text we know of was motivated by the need to gain prodigious merit. In Japan, the Empress Shotoku, to appease the Buddhist clergy and to gain protection for herself, between 764 and 770 commissioned the manufacture of one million small pagodas. She had a *dharani* placed inside each of the pagodas, and she bestowed one hundred thousand of the pagodas to each of ten major temples. One might suspect that these are merely conventional large numbers, except that as of the early part of the twentieth century, the temple of Horyuji still possessed 43,930 of the pagodas. The printing of these *dharani* is rather crudely done, as if the craft were not yet very well developed. But it is hard to imagine that this effort at mass production was the first time Japanese had attempted to print.

The earliest Chinese printed text we have is an edition of the *Diamond Sutra*, found at the Tang desert outpost of Dunhuang, and dated at 868. This text is elegantly printed and elaborately illustrated, and seems to be the product of a long tradition of printing.

The chief technique of East Asian printing was woodblock printing. In early Japan, the most commonly used kind of wood was the catalpa, although the Japanese cypress was sometimes used. A calligrapher first wrote the text on a thin piece of paper, which was attached facedown to the wood with rice-starch paste. Then the printer rubbed the paper with hemp-seed oil to make it transparent so that the characters would emerge more clearly. He then carved the wood away from the characters to leave them in relief in reversed image. A worker removed the paper from the block and cleaned and dried it. Then the artisan applied ink to the block. He put on the block paper that had been soaked in water for several hours, and smoothed it until the ink adhered to the paper. The pages were left to dry, and then the pages were bound.

The blocks were kept and used for later printings of books. After they became worn, a craftsman recarved them to sharpen the lines of the characters and made another set of impressions, thus printing a second edition from the same set of blocks.

Some printing establishments, especially in later times, were quite large and elaborate. But the basic technical requirements were simple, and, especially for a short text, a single craftsman could perform all the necessary tasks. Moveable type makes a great deal of sense for an alphabetic language, like English, but for languages like Chinese and Japanese with thousands of characters, it hardly made sense to use moveable type in an era before mechanization. In the sixteenth century, Matteo Ricci (1552-1610), an Italian Jesuit missionary, commented that it took scarcely as much time for a Chinese craftsman to carve a block than it took a European craftsman to set a page of type.

Printing developed in East Asia in close conjunction with religion, specifically Buddhism. But it soon found other, secular uses. The early and sophisticated development of printing in East Asia facilitated the diffusion of aspects of culture among China, Japan, and Korea. The printed word became a powerful medium for the transmission and preservation of culture.

Cultures rarely exist in isolation, and Asia during the period 200-1000 is no exception. But the precise mechanisms whereby cultural diffusion occurs are complex. Pilgrims, missionaries, and merchants are often the transmitters of culture. But what of the receivers of foreign culture? What compels people to accept alien ideas, transform them, and make them their own? Why do people choose to accept certain ideas and reject others?

Asia during this period provides ample opportunity for exploring these questions. During the third century C.E., Buddhism began to spread from its home in north India throughout the rest of Asia. The spread of Buddhism was accompanied by other elements of culture, both Indian and Chinese. However, it is primarily Buddhism that allows us to speak of an Asian community during this period.

But the Asian community is marked by differences: it is not one Asian world. Language, social organization, political structures, and religion show pronounced differences. China and India, the two dominant forces in Asia during this period, are two worlds, vastly different. Among the key ways in which they differ are their concepts of kingship and community and the models of political integration they present.

China: The Durability of Empire

The situation in China at the fall of the Han dynasty was not unlike that of Europe at the fall of the Roman Empire. At the beginning of the third century, China was fragmented, her ruling ideology had been called into question, and a foreign religion was poised on the brink of taking over the hearts and minds of aristocrat and commoner alike. Parts of north China were under the rule of non-Chinese nomadic peoples, who several generations before they began to rule were sheepherders and horsemen. China after the fall of the Han might have developed as Europe did after the fall of the Roman Empire—into discrete states, each with its own language, culture, and political system. But it did not.

The remarkable thing about Chinese civilization in the face of these internal and external threats is its endurance as a unified empire. Even during long periods of disunion, the idea of the unified empire, and even

Gender and Culture

MAN AND HIS WIFE

Figure 1

The way a man or woman serves his or her society is often defined by gender. Throughout history and across cultural boundaries, certain roles in the family, in the community, or in the structures of power have been designated male or female. Although we currently challenge this separation, the tradition has been long practiced. This division is so much a part of our cultural vocabulary that we approach the study of these roles with a presupposition of their gender. For example, few readers would expect a story about a priest, a commander, or a warrior to feature a woman. Reversals of these roles, such as Deborah the Israelite Judge or Boadicea the ancient British warrior Queen, are rare in the annals of history. The traditional roles for women—helpmate, mother, lover—are more familiar and the way they appear in the visual arts of the ancient world reveals the origins of our assumptions about gender and society, and even challenges some of our beliefs.

The woman's place in the domestic setting marks a telling juxtaposition to that of the man in the public sphere. The ancient Roman portrait on the preceding page of a *Man and His Wife* (ca. 69 C.E., Pompeii; Figure 1), painted on the wall of a Pompeian house, appears to give them equal status. Dressed in upper class garments, both figures face the viewer with a calm, steady gaze. Although the woman stands in front of the man, neither dominates the space. They occupy it equally. But the objects they hold situate their powers and their concerns. The papyrus scroll with its red wax seal in the man's hand links him to public communication and official action. The stylus or writing stick that the woman presses to her lips, and the diptych, or double-leaved, wooden tablet that she holds in her hand, suggest household accounts. His record is permanent. Hers, scratched into the erasable wax surface inside the leaves of the tablet, can be changed when needed. They both perform a role within society, but his extends out to the community and hers is confined to the home.

YASHODA AND KRISHNA

Figure 2

BOOK OF KELLS   *Figure 3*

The most commonly depicted role for a woman is that of mother. It is a basic and
enduring subject in the arts shared by cultures throughout time. Tradition trusts the nurtur-
ing of a child to the woman and the bond between mother and child can be an intimate
expression of loving care. In the copper statue of *Yashoda and Krishna* (ca. 14th century C.E.,
India; Figure 2), the female instinct to nourish and protect is celebrated. *The Bhagavata
Purana*, the great Hindu epic of Krishna's life, records that the infant god was switched
with the daughter of a cowherd at birth to protect him from the wicked King Kamsa. Yashoda, the cowherd's wife, accepted Krishna as her foster child. Cradling the young god's
head in her hand, she holds him in her lap and feeds him as if he were her own. It matters
little that Krishna was not born of her body; the bond of mother and son is universal.

Hierarchy supplants intimacy in the eighth-century Hiberno-Saxon manuscript illumination from the *Book of Kells* (ca. 700 C.E., Ireland; Figure 3). The image depicts a traditional
Nativitas Domini, or "birth of our Lord." The Virgin Mother's stiff posture and impassive

gaze diminishes her human role as nurturer, but defines her importance as the selected agent for Christ's incarnation. Dressed as a queen, she presents Christ to the world. As angels surround her in tribute, she offers her divinely fathered son, both a present and a sacrifice for the earth's population. Here, woman's role is symbolic; her body functions as the vessel to bear the holy child. Her noble bearing and magnificent raiment suggest her child's reign over heaven, but on earth, she serves as his throne.

Female beauty has been celebrated in all the arts, and woman is often portrayed as the object of man's desire. But in the western world view, desire leads to temptation. *Eve*, the original temptress, carved by Giselbertus to flank a portal of the cathedral of Saint-Lazare at Autun (ca. 1120 C.E., France; Figure 4), is a vision of sensuous beauty. Her long, elegant limbs entwine with the branches of the trees that surround her and, as she gazes at the viewer, she calls attention to her lovely face, cupping it in her graceful right hand. But, in its Christian context, while the sculpture depicted desire, it warned against evil temptation. Eve's serpentine position, and the forbidden apple she plucks with her left hand, would remind the faithful of original sin as they entered the cathedral to pray for their own deliverance.

more importantly, the conviction among the elite that they all partook of one culture, never wavered. But continuity does not mean stagnation. During the Period of Disunion (206–581) and the Tang dynasty (617–907), China was remarkably open to outside influence. Buddhism, a foreign religion, swept through China during the Period of Disunion, ultimately having an impact on virtually every aspect of life. The cosmopolitanism of the Tang empire, represented by its territorial expansion, was also demonstrated by the vogue in the capital for foreign food and music.

The Collapse of the Old Order in China

The period from the fall of the Han in 220 to the Sui reunification in 589 is sometimes known as the Period of Disunion, or the Six Dynasties—after the six successive southern dynasties whose capital was located at Jiankang (present-day Nanking). Despite the political disunity, or perhaps because of it, the period was an immensely fruitful one for Chinese thought. Buddhism became firmly established during this period, and Taoism developed into an important popular religion. During the Period of Disunion, there were numerous interchanges between Chinese states and non-Chinese border peoples that had an important impact on the cultures of both.

The Period of Disunion is also known as the Northern and Southern dynasties. In the south non-Chinese aboriginal peoples occupied most of the lands. After the fall of the capital city of Loyang in 311, settlers from the central plains moved south. The original inhabitants were driven off the lowlands into mountainous areas, where the land was less productive. The aboriginal peoples gradually adopted aspects of Chinese culture. But this cultural interchange was not a one-way street. Aboriginal customs influenced those of the Chinese; vestiges of aboriginal customs can be seen today, for example, in marriage patterns in south China.

As wave after wave of invaders swept down from the north, many Chinese inhabitants of north China in turn moved south. The south of China at this time was thinly populated and relatively poor. In many ways it resembled a colonial society, with the ethnic Chinese from the north, known as Han Chinese, acting as the colonizing power. A relatively small number of aristocratic families dominated society. The power of these aristocratic families in the south was recognized by the rulers of the various southern states. These families were often granted tax exemptions, which facilitated their accumulation of large estates, further increasing their power. The southern dynasties were thus characterized by landholding aristocracies. The aristocracies in the south laid particular ethnic claims to being Chinese, with relatively little blending with the non-Chinese around them.

The situation in the north during the Period of Disunion was quite different. The northern nomadic peoples, who were from a variety of non-Han ethnic groups, increasingly took up the practice of sedentary agriculture. The northern states were strongly centralized, militarily expansionist, and often quite powerful. The contacts in the north between the Chinese and the non-Chinese people were much more extensive than they were in the south. As a result, the boundaries of what came to be called Chinese were much more indistinct.

The Toba Wei are an example of a northern nomadic people who adopted some elements of Chinese culture, a process known as sinicization. Originally an ethnic group from western Manchuria called Xianbei, in the fifth century they moved their capital to Loyang, one of the old Han capitals. The Toba emperor Xiao Wendi (471–99) forbade the use of Xianbei clothes, language, and surnames, and encouraged intermarriage with Chinese families. This tension between their ethnic origins and Chinese life produced rich cultural interaction and innovation. The ability of Chinese culture to absorb energy from the northern nomadic peoples doubtless contributed to the energetic rebirth of a unified China with the Sui dynasty.

The Birth of Chinese Buddhism and the Growth of Taoism

During this period of political turmoil Buddhism became significant as a Chinese religion. It was brought along trade routes, first along the overland route connecting the Amu Darya valley with the Kansu corridor, and later along maritime routes. Even more remarkable than the distance Buddhism traveled was the swift and dramatic impact it made on China. The first mention of Buddhism in China is of monks in the trading center of Pengcheng in 64 C.E. In 100 C.E., a Buddhist text was adapted into Chinese, the *Sutra in Forty-two Chapters*. During this early period, Buddhism was still primarily a religion of foreigners, but all that was soon to change.

China during the Period of Disunion was suffering from what might be termed a crisis of confidence. During the Han dynasty, Confucianism had become so closely identified with the political order that the fall of the political order challenged the intellectual order and

The Guanyin Bodhisattva (early twelfth century), a polychrome wooden sculpture from north China.

The Guanyin Bodhisattva

The deity sits on a pedestal, perhaps a rough-hewn lotus petal, one arm resting on a raised leg in a stance known as royal ease. Avalokitasvara, whose Chinese name is Guanyin and Japanese name is Kannon, is one of the most important of the bodhisattvas in Mahayana Buddhism, and this image shows the deity in full glory. But a closer look at the image may make the reader wonder: what is the gender of this Guanyin? The legs are heavily muscled; the torso offers no sure evidence of breasts, and the beauty of the face does not mark the image as female. The gender of this splendid image is purposefully ambiguous: An artist capable of creating the delicacy of fabric folds and serenity of facial expression of this image surely could have left clearer gender clues. But he did not.

The gender of Avalokitasvara has a complicated history. A bodhisattva, a being who has chosen to delay Nirvana until all sentient beings have attained salvation, should be beyond gender. If, as Buddhism suggests, the body itself is but an illusion, then gender is scarcely a category of any importance. But when sculptors and other image makers render images in solid anthropomorphic form, they cannot avoid the issue of gender. When a deity is imagined in human form, then the deity is imagined with a human gender. In Avalokitasvara's case, the gender is neither consistent nor unambiguous. As Avalokitasvara, in India, he is a male deity. Early representations of him, all over Asia, are clearly male. He is sometimes portrayed with a mustache. But with the transmission of Buddhism to East Asia, the deity undergoes a shift in gender. We increasingly see images like this one, where gender is ambiguous, and other images in which the deity is unambiguously female.

In China during the Song dynasty, Guanyin became associated with Miaoshan, a princess whose father went to great lengths to prevent her from becoming a nun. But Miaoshan not only triumphed over her father, she converted him to Buddhism. The identification of Miaoshan and Guanyin fixes Guanyin's career as a female in East Asia.

We can only speculate as to why the deity changed from male to female. But perhaps to the Chinese imagination, the qualities of Guanyin—such as compassion—and the particular interest the bodhisattva had in reproduction were feminine attributes. It may have been easier to change the gender of the bodhisattva than to revise notions about gender-linked virtues.

In the *Lotus Sutra*, the Buddha proclaimed the powers of Avalokitasvara:

If there is one who keeps the name of this bodhisattva, even if he should fall into a great fire, the fire would be unable to burn him, thanks to the imposing supernatural power of the bodhisattva. If he should be carried off by a great river and call upon this bodhisattva's name, then straightaway he would find a shallow place.

The bodhisattva is particularly concerned with procreation. the *Lotus Sutra* continues:

If there is a woman, and she is desirous and hopeful of having a son, making worshipful offerings to the bodhisattva she shall straightaway bear a son of happiness, excellence and wisdom. If she be desirous and hopeful of having a daughter, she shall straightaway bear a daughter, upright and endowed with proper marks, one who is loved and honored by a multitude of people.

Avalokitasvara is the bodhisattva of compassion, and is a bestower and protector of children.

The language in which a Chinese reader would have read the *Lotus Sutra* scarcely clarifies the gender issue. For all the attention to gender in Chinese societies, pronouns in the classical Chinese language are gender neutral. A Song dynasty reader could read the *Lotus Sutra* as if it were about a male bodhisattva or a female bodhisattva.

Seated Buddha from the Tang dynasty. The artist used the dry lacquer technique, in which layers of lacquer-soaked cloth were placed over a clay figure and allowed to dry and harden. When the clay was removed, a light, durable statue remained.

gave rise to a more pluralistic intellectual life, in some ways reminiscent of the earlier Warring States period. People were searching for new answers to old questions: even more importantly they were asking new questions. Buddhism dealt extensively with problems earlier Chinese philosophy had minimized, such as the origins of the cosmos and the consequences of death for the human spirit.

The most important southern Buddhist was Huiyuan (334–416), a Confucian man of letters who showed an early interest in Taoist texts. Influenced by the Buddhist Dao'an (312–85), Huiyuan converted to Buddhism. In 402 he assembled a group of 123 monks and laymen, who vowed to be reborn in the Western Paradise, also known as the Pure Land, and to help one another in that effort. This was the beginning in China of Pure Land Buddhism, which remained an important sect in China and was later transmitted to Japan, where it is known as Zen. The simple and direct beliefs of Pure Land Buddhism—that if one believed in the Buddha of Western Paradise, one would be reborn in paradise, and

that one demonstrated faith by chanting the name of the Buddha—facilitated the spread of Buddhism to ordinary people.

During this period the most important activity of northern Buddhists was translating Buddhist texts from Sanskrit into Chinese, a process that transformed many Buddhist ideas. In the search for Chinese terms for Buddhist ideas, many Taoist terms were used. For example, the concept of Nirvana was rendered into Chinese as *wu wei*, or nonaction. Many of the key translators were Central Asians. One of the greatest of these was Kumarajiva (350–413), who had studied in Kashmir and Khotan. Captured by the Chinese and imprisoned for seventeen years, he made good use of his time and became a master stylist at writing literary Chinese. In 401, he arrived at Chang'an, where he supervised a staff of hundreds of translators. The corpus of Buddhist sacred texts translated was enormous—a total of 1692 works, amounting to forty million Chinese characters. Many of the texts produced by this project are still regarded as standard translations. After Huiyuan and Kumarajiva, Buddhism developed into a Chinese religion of energy and influence among all levels of society.

In spite of the rapid spread and influence of Buddhism, it was not universally appreciated. Some Chinese objected to the celibate monastic lifestyle as a direct threat to filial piety. Buddhists countered by arguing that the salvation of a single person benefited the entire family, and converting one's parents to Buddhism was in fact the supreme act of filial piety. Other people objected to Buddhism on the grounds that it was foreign, pointing out that Confucius never talked about it. Buddhist apologists countered that the nature of Confucius' teachings was ad hoc: he discussed only those matters that arose in discussion.

Despite the opposition, Buddhism became an important source of secular power during this period. By the fifth century there were approximately 24,000 monks and nuns in China. Some people attached themselves to monasteries in the hope of avoiding taxation. Thus monasteries accumulated wealth, and many became important landlords.

Simultaneous with the growth of Buddhism was a growth in Taoism, which flourished among the southern aristocracy during the Period of Disunion. Important to the growth of Taoism during this time was the search for techniques of longevity and immortality. And one of the chief deities of religious Taoism was the immortal Queen Mother of the West. One story about her dates from the Period of Disunion and emphasizes central

Taoist themes. Emperor Wu of the Han dynasty was anxious to obtain the secrets of immortality. The Queen Mother of the West and her attendants came to earth to interview him, bringing heavenly texts and peaches of immortality. The immortal queen and the mortal emperor held a feast. But she decided not to give him the secrets of immortality for two reasons: he was lewd and ambitious; and, more poignantly, he was human and mortal and the worlds of the humans and the gods are separate. This story also illustrates the prominence of women in Taoism, especially as intermediaries between the world of mortals and immortals.

The Period of Disunion was also important for innovation in poetry and the development of Chinese poetic theory. A poem by Shen Yue (441–512) illustrates ways in which nature functioned in the literary imagination:

> The wanderer was in love with the spring of the year
> And the spring in love with the wanderer.
> Languid sunbeams in the morning draped their splendor,
> Gentle dew at dawn lay frozen by the ford.
> Seasonal bird songs lilted through the new-grown leaves
> While scented airs were stirring in the early duckweed.
> Then one morning found me far from my old home,
> Ten thousand miles had come between me and that
> dawn.

Not until the end of the poem does the reader learn that the young wanderer is Shen Yue, who has grown old and alienated from the languid sunbeams of the dawn of his youth.

The Achievements of Sui Reunification

After three centuries of disunity, the Sui dynasty reconstituted China in the late sixth century. Yang Jian, the man who was to reunify China, was born in 541 to a prominent family in the Northern Zhou. Marriage politics combined with royal lust and revenge to place him in a precarious position. Yang Jian's daughter was married to the Northern Zhou king. A crisis at court was precipitated when the king raped a woman, made her his consort, and killed her husband. When Yang Jian's daughter comforted the woman, the king interpreted her act as disloyalty, and the entire Yang family was imperiled. Yang Jian's wife encouraged him to stage a coup, saying, "When you are on a tiger and can't get off, the only thing to do is to spur him on." Yang Jian not only staged the coup but also reunified the empire. He ruled from 581 to 604 under the name of Emperor Wen.

At the time of the conquest, the most important state in the south was the Chen, which Yang Jian over-

came through propaganda. His propagandists wrote an edict scornful of the Chen ruler and distributed 300,000 hand-written copies throughout the south. Implicit in Yan Jian's strategy is his confidence that everyone who mattered could read! However, even the cleverest propaganda did not eliminate the need for war. The conquest of the south was greatly facilitated by a woman known as the Lady Chiaoguo, an aboriginal woman who had married into the Chen ruling house. In return for wide latitude in governing Chen territories, she surrendered to the Sui, ensuring a relatively smooth transition from Chen to Sui.

Of the many forces facilitating the reunification of China, the common written language shared by all Chinese was one of the most important. Recall that a Chinese character might be pronounced differently according to the native dialect of the speaker, yet usually retained the same meaning. The tension between locally divergent spoken languages and one common written language facilitated the growth of distinct regional cultures under the umbrella of one China-wide culture. By the sixth century, virtually every male member of the upper classes—regardless of his ethnic origin—could read Chinese. Unity was present in popular culture as well as high culture. Underlying proverbs as well as classics was a common body of values. Buddhism also acted as a unifying force. But perhaps the most important factor leading to the reunification of China was simply that the idea of unification never died.

The Sui founder, Emperor Wen, was a skillful manipulator of all of the ideological tools at his disposal, Buddhist and Taoist as well as Confucian. He built Buddhist temples at the foot of Confucian sacred mountains. His Buddhist building plan was modeled on that of the Mauryan king Asoka, who it will be remembered, built 84,000 stupas. Emperor Wen built a Taoist temple at the capital not only to honor Taoism but also to bring it under official control. He recognized that ordaining monks and nuns was one way the state could control them, and during his reign two thousand Taoists and 230,000 Buddhists were officially ordained.

Regionalism was a major problem facing the newly unified empire. The court had to win over the loyalty of the southern aristocratic clans. One strategy was to integrate the agricultural economies of China by improving transportation. To this end, the Grand Canal connecting Hangzhou and Chang'an to Beijing was built. The canal was 130 feet wide, with a royal road running by its side. Sources tell us that so much labor was needed to construct the Grand Canal that even women worked on it. Water transport is usually cheaper than land transport; in the China of this period, the ratio of cost of land transport to water transport was about 16:1. Huge granaries were built along the canal, to facilitate the collection of taxes, which were normally collected in grain, and to facilitate the shipment of grain to the north.

Another technique for controlling the aristocracy was an ambitious land reform program, the equal field system, which granted a fixed amount of land to every adult. The allotment depended on the quality of the land as well as on the social status of the recipient, but it seems to have been ample. An average farmer in north China in the sixth century was allotted an amount of land seven times greater than the size of an average farm

in the same area in the early twentieth century. Women were granted land, but a lesser amount than men. When the landholder died or reached the age of sixty, most of the land reverted to the state. Only a certain amount of land, called "mulberry land," could be transmitted to heirs. "Mulberry land" encouraged holders to make long-term investments by planting orchards, vineyards, or mulberry trees.

The Sui had—ironically, it turns out—modeled themselves on the Qin. And like the Qin, they were short-lived. A combination of military overextension and natural disasters created a climate ripe for rebellion. From 612 to 614 the Sui mounted three expensive and disastrous campaigns to bring Koreans under Sui control. On the northern frontier, Turks were beginning to

"THE OLD CHARCOAL SELLER"

■ *Bo Zhuyi (772–846) is one of the best-loved of all Chinese poets. This poem is an example of the way a poet might use literary craft to make veiled criticism of contemporary society.*

The issue is not simply that the charcoal seller must work hard for his livelihood. He is put in the ironic position of hoping for cold weather so that he might sell more charcoal. When the weather does turn cold, an official comes and buys the whole cart. Although the official pays for what he takes, he pays the peasant in luxury cloth, which was a common medium of exchange in Tang China. The image of the damask and lace draped over the ox shows the social distance between the officials and the peasantry of the Tang dynasty.

An old charcoal seller
Cuts firewood, burns coal by the southern mountains
His face, all covered with dust and ash, the color of smoke.
The money he makes selling coal, what is it for?
To put food on his back and clothes in his mouth.
The rags on his poor body are thin and threadbare;
Distressed at the low price of coal, he hopes for colder weather.
Night comes, an inch of snow has fallen on the city,
In the morning, he rides his cart along the icy ruts.
His ox weary, he hungry, and the sun already high.
In the mud by the south gate, outside the market, he stops to rest,
All of a sudden, two dashing riders appear;
An imperial envoy, garbed in yellow (his attendant in white),
Holding an official dispatch, he reads a proclamation.
Then turns the cart around, curses the ox, and leads it north.
One cartload of coal—a thousand or more catties!
No use appealing to the official spiriting the cart away:
Half a length of red lace, a slip of damask
Dropped on the ox—is payment in full.

From *Sunflower Splendor*.

cause problems. In 611 the Yellow River flooded. In 613, Li Shimin (598–649), a general responsible for defense against the Turks, made an alliance with them, and with the aid of his father Li Yuan (565–635), marched on Chang'an. Li Yuan's posthumous name was Tang Gaozu (612–26); he was succeeded by Li Shimin, who is known to history as Tang Taizong. The dynasty they founded is known as the Tang.

Bureaucrat and Merchant, Urban and Rural in the Tang

In the early years, Tang rulers were primarily concerned with continuing the Sui consolidation of the empire. During this period, the structure of the Chinese government developed into a full-scale bureaucracy that was the pattern of Chinese government for a millennium. There were four major institutions of the central government. The Department of State Affairs consolidated public administration; the Imperial Chancellery issued imperial decrees; the Grand Secretariat produced official texts; and the Council of State consisted of the emperor and important civil officials. A final arm of the government existed outside the other four. The Censorate served as the eyes and ears of the emperor, and at its worst could act as a kind of secret police. One of the tasks of the censors was to criticize the emperor, although the emperor did not always take kindly to criticism. During the Tang, merit became an important criterion for selection for office. The beginnings of the civil service examination system, which played such an important role in the recruitment of later bureaucracies, dates from this time.

Provincial affairs were of great interest to the central government. China was divided into provinces, which were further divided into prefectures, subprefectures, and districts. As under the Han dynasty, these administrative divisions were staffed by officials appointed

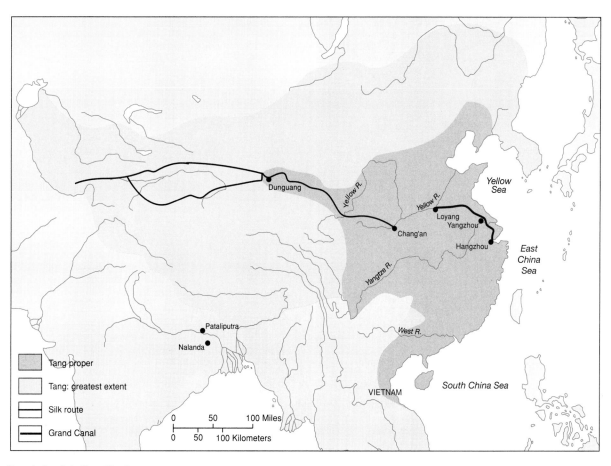

Boundaries of the Tang Empire

and paid by the central government. These officials were not natives of the areas they served, and as a consequence might not even be able to understand the spoken language of the area, although most of their staffs were locals. Officials rotated periodically, so they scarcely became intimately acquainted with local customs. In these ways, the central government assured loyalty to the center and prevented officials from building local power bases. But there were disadvantages to the system—local officials were often at the mercy of locally prominent families for even the most basic information about the areas they were governing.

The capital of China during the Tang was Chang'an, a splendid place. During part of the dynasty Loyang served as a secondary capital. At its height one million

people lived inside the city walls of Chang'an, and another million lived just outside. Chang'an was cosmologically oriented on a north-south direction to take proper advantage of geomancy, the energy that traditional Chinese thinkers believed resided within the hills and streams of the earth. As the poet Du Fu observed, Chang'an was like a chessboard; the streets were laid out in a regular fashion. Tang cities were walled and were subdivided into wards, which were also walled and gated. Each night the city and the wards were locked, which facilitated control of the population.

Despite their splendor, Tang cities have left no monumental architecture, since their buildings were mostly of wood. Although monumental architectural styles are in evidence in the great Buddhist cave temples, Tang

Terra-cotta figures of Tang court ladies playing polo. These women participated in strenuous outdoor games, unlike the women of later dynasties.

Tang wall painting of a farmer seeding a newly plowed field with an ox-drawn seeder. His military dress marks him as one of the soldier-farmers who settled newly occupied areas.

people perpetuated themselves more with their words than with their buildings. The Tang was a golden age of Chinese poetry.

In Tang China and later, temples were used as public spaces and were the sites of many social functions we would regard as secular, such as markets, fairs, and theatrical entertainments. During the Tang, Buddhist philanthropy began to assume an important social role. The state was not particularly involved in public welfare (no premodern state was), and so Buddhist monastic organizations played a key role. They operated dispensaries, pawnshops, lodgings, and the first public baths. Under contract with the state, monasteries operated hospitals that received bonuses if fewer than 20 percent of the patients died.

The chief economic goal of the Tang state was the maintenance of a stable, secure peasantry. Because trade was seen as disruptive of a stable agrarian order, merchants were considered a threat. Sui and Tang merchants were subject to certain legal restrictions; for example, the Sui required merchants as well as butchers and members of certain other degraded professions to wear black. These regulations, consistent with the traditional Confucian antipathy toward merchants, were relaxed by the late Tang, and many merchants seem to have done quite well.

Urban markets were tightly controlled, under the direction of a market director, who was responsible for registering shops and certifying the quality of goods and money and the accuracy of weights and measures. Merchants had to obtain licenses to trade in the cities. Rural markets were less tightly controlled. Usually established at road junctions, bridges, or wherever peasants congregated, most of these markets were periodic. By Tang times some rural markets had permanent buildings. Another avenue for commercial activity was the fair, often held at temples, perhaps in conjunction with a religious festival.

During the Tang, farmers improved rice agriculture. They developed better tools and became more sophisticated in transplanting techniques. The Grand Canal built by the Sui took rice north. During this period rice first became a part of the diet of the upper classes in north China. As rice agriculture in the south developed, more people immigrated there from north China. The agrarian prosperity of south China begun in this period precipitated a shift in the center of Chinese culture from the area around Loyang and Chang'an, the Han and Tang capitals, to the Yangzi River valley.

Tang society was governed by a legal code, compiled in 624 and periodically revised. It is the earliest complete Chinese legal code that has been preserved. Deeply embedded in the Tang legal code are principles of hierarchy. For example, the punishment inflicted for a crime depends on the relationship between the perpetrator and the victim. Killing one's father was a more

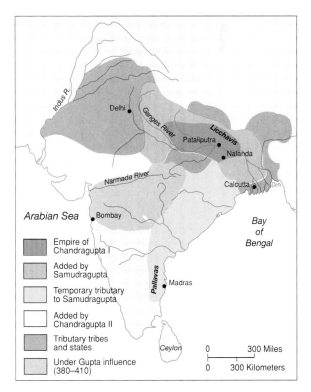

The Gupta Empire

Seventeenth-century scroll showing foreigners bringing exotic tribute for the Tang emperor—elephant tusks, peacock feathers, birds, and petrified wood for decorating Chinese gardens.

serious crime than killing a stranger, reflecting the crucial importance of filial piety in the Chinese ethical system. But stealing from a father was a lesser crime than stealing from a stranger, because one would have a greater claim to his property. A person awaiting trial was held in a prison, but imprisonment was not inflicted as a punishment. Tang punishments included beating, exile, and execution. The death penalty was not enacted lightly; all death sentences required the approval of a bureau in the capital.

The Tang and the World

The Tang empire was not only splendid, it was the most cosmopolitan empire that China has ever known. The Tang state dealt with foreign powers in two ways: by diplomacy and by warfare. The diplomatic method was the tribute system, which had also been used by earlier Chinese dynasties. A foreign power would acknowledge that the emperor of China was the son of heaven; that China was the center of the world; and that the Chinese calendar represented the only true reading of the movements of the sun, moon, stars, and planets. The state paying tribute would send goods, often exotic regional products—rare animals, strange plants, local handicrafts—to the Chinese court. In return, the Chinese court would send gifts to the tributary state. The transactions could involve enormous economic exchanges, but they were conceptualized political, diplomatic, or even ritual exchanges. Indeed the importance of the ritual aspect of the exchange is demonstrated by the fact that foreign relations were carried out by the Board of Rites.

But of course diplomacy does not always solve foreign relations problems, and the tributary system was more useful in dealing with the states of Southeast Asia than with the central Asian kingdoms. The extensive Tang northern frontier was defended by a militia system. Each militia unit consisted of 800 to 1200 men, usually soldier-farmers who had received allotments of land. They were of varying social origins: some were peasants, others aristocrats. The Tang military expansion was quite remarkable: a distance of 3100 miles separated the northwestern outpost at Kashgar from the capital at Chang'an. By 660 Manchuria and all of the Korean peninsula were under Tang control. But in time, the military colony system deteriorated and more and more power fell into the hands of regional military commanders.

One of these regional commanders was An Lushan, a man who became a court favorite. The emperor Xuanzong, by this time an old man, had become infatuated with Yang Guifei, a young beauty who used her wiles to gain powerful positions for men in her family. When An Lushan rebelled in 755, imperial troops refused to defend the emperor unless he agreed to have Yang Guifei executed. Reluctantly, he agreed. The rebellion was suppressed, but the Tang never regained its former glory. The power of the regional military governors was established, and the borders never were really secure again. In 751 Chinese troops under the leadership of the Korean general Gao Xianzhi were defeated by Arab forces at the battle of Talas. As a result of that defeat, Chinese influence in Central Asia declined.

After suppression of the An Lushan rebellion, the Tang continued to decline under the pressures of political and fiscal decentralization. The decline and despair were exacerbated by a financial crisis and a lack of revenue for the central government. In 780, in response to the crisis, the equal field system was recognized as a failure and was replaced with a new system of taxation, called the two-tax system because the tax was levied twice a year. Under this new system, people registered the amount of land they actually owned and the size of their dwelling; on the basis of this information they were put into a tax bracket.

With the change in the tax system, land became alienable, meaning that people could buy and sell it and transmit it to their heirs. This system remained intact for approximately 700 years. But the change in the tax system did not solve the revenue problems of the Tang state, and new methods of generating revenue were sought, including the sale of Buddhist and Taoist ordination certificates and the reinstitution of monopolies, especially those on salt and tea. During this period tea drinking became widespread in China, and the tea tax became an important source of revenue. Tea merchants were instrumental in generating new forms of credit, including negotiable certificates of deposit called flying cash, which were a prototype for paper money.

The sense of malaise during the late Tang is captured in this poem by Du Fu (712–70), from the sequence "Autumn Meditations":

> Well said Chang'an looks like a chessboard:
> A hundred years of the saddest news.
> The houses of princes and nobles all have new lords:
> Another breed is capped and robed for office.
> Due north on the mountain passes the gongs and drums shake,
> To the chariots and horses campaigning in the northwest the winged dispatches hasten
> While the fish and the dragons fall asleep and the autumn river turns cold
> My native country, untroubled times, are always in my thoughts.

Even the natural world, the fishes and dragons, are affected by the calamities that trouble the poet.

Another great Tang poet, Li Shangyin (ca. 812–58), is known for love poetry. The poem "Written on a Monastery Wall" shows an appreciation of Buddhism from the perspective of an outsider.

> They rejected life to seek the Way. Their footprints are before us.
> They offered up their brains, ripped up their bodies; so firm was their resolution.
> See it as large, and a millet-grain cheats us of the universe:
> See it as small and the world can hide in a pinpoint.
> The oyster before its womb fills thinks of the new cassia;
> The amber, when it first sets, remembers a former pine.
> If we trust the true and sure words written on Indian leaves
> We hear all past and future in one stroke of the temple bell.

Li Shangyin begins the poem by describing in vivid and compelling language sacrifices made by Buddhists. But he ends with an insight into what enlightenment entails: the ability to hear the past and the future in the sound of a temple bell.

During Li Shangyin's lifetime Buddhism was severely persecuted. During the period 843–45, 260,000 monks and nuns as well as 150,000 other monastery dependents were returned to secular life, which meant that they were liable for taxation and labor service. Four thousand, six hundred monasteries were destroyed or converted to secular buildings, and 40,000 small shrines were destroyed or converted to other use. Although in subsequent years a number of the defrocked monks and

China, 200-1000 C.E.

206-581	Period of Disunion
311	Fall of Loyang
581	Sui reunification of China
617-907	Tang dynasty
755	Rebellion of An Lushan

The Guptas and North India

After the fall of the Mauryan Empire in 185 B.C.E., north India was invaded by a series of foreigners from the northwest, including Bactrians and Kushans. The period was one of political chaos and fragmentation, and is sometimes called India's "Dark Ages." But during this period, trade between India and the civilizations of the Mediterranean on the one hand and Southeast Asia on the other developed to an unprecedented degree. These contacts between India and Southeast Asia played a crucial role in the development of both regions.

In the fourth century, the Gupta Empire rose to prominence in north India. This empire was less centralized than the Mauryan Empire had been. The Gupta emperor controlled the central core of his territory, but tributary princes controlled the outlying areas. These princes owed only minimal loyalty to the Gupta emperor, and were not even compelled to join him in war. This decentralization permeated all levels of society: Villages and towns had a great deal more autonomy than they had under the Mauryas. The Gupta model of local communities loosely integrated into a central empire was followed by most subsequent kingdoms in both north and south India.

The Gupta rulers used political strategies such as marriage alliances to form connections with other important states. When Chandragupta I (320-35) married Kumaradevi, a princess from a neighboring state, he incorporated the territory of that state into the Gupta Empire. The importance of this marriage is illustrated by the fact that Kumaradevi is featured on coins issued during the reign of Chandragupta. Samudragupta, the

nuns were allowed to return to religious life, the persecutions had a devastating effect on institutionalized Buddhism in China. The forms of Buddhism that remained important in later Chinese history were Pure Land and Chan, a meditational sect in which the key institution was the transmission between master and disciple. Buddhism in China would never again play an important role in court politics.

Much of the rhetoric justifying the persecutions spoke of restoring Chinese cultural purity. But the economic power of the monastic institutions also made them prime targets for a state desperate for both funds and legitimacy.

The persistent and durable unity of China is one of the remarkable aspects of its long history. But the durability of tradition during the Period of Disunion and the Tang reflects not a static society but a society that is rich, dynamic, and cosmopolitan.

India: The Strength of Regional Cultures

If the major theme in Chinese history during this period was the restoration and maintenance of a unified empire that encompassed diverse regional cultures, the dominant theme in India was the development of regional kingdoms. These local cultures existed, however, in a context that remained identifiably and distinctively Indian. Religion and an elite educated in Sanskrit form the core of this Indian cultural identity. This cultural identity existed independent of political institutions and thereby survived the vagaries of the political history of this complex period.

An Indian gold coin from the reign of Samudragupta commemorates a horse sacrifice.

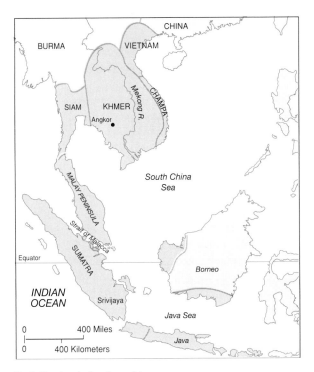

Early Empires in Southeast Asia

son of this couple, ascended the throne sometime between 340 and 350 and lay claim to royal blood through both his mother and his father.

The rather loose structure of the empire did not prevent the growth of an elaborate imperial ideology. For example, Samudragupta revived the classical horse sacrifice, and had coins cast commemorating it. It may be an exaggeration to describe Samudragupta as a god-king, but the connection between royalty and divinity was clear in the following inscription describing him:

> He was a mortal only on celebrating the rites of the observances of mankind, but otherwise was a god, dwelling on earth.

This royal propaganda influenced not only the successor states to the Guptas in north India but also later royal ideology in Southeast Asia. The divine stature of the king reinforced his legitimacy in the mundane world.

Under the Guptas, India's overall international trade declined, and its direction shifted. After the fall of Rome, western markets deteriorated, causing Indian merchants to turn their interest toward Southeast Asia. This shift produced lasting effects. As Indians plied their trade, they also transmitted their culture. Many of the merchants were Buddhist and carried their beliefs

along trade routes. Buddhism, Hinduism, and other aspects of Indian culture were spread along trade routes to Southeast Asia.

The Gupta period was a golden age of Indian culture, and both arts and sciences flourished. The court of Chandragupta II (380–415) was particularly noted for its cultural splendor. The most important of the "nine jewels," as the poets at Chandragupta's court were known, was Kalidasa, who wrote epic poetry as well as drama. Theater played a lively role in cultural life and as popular entertainment in Gupta India. Kalidasa and his contemporaries refined the Sanskrit drama during this period. Kalidasa's play *Shakuntala* describes in passages of lyric grace the love between a king and a hermit girl. Another important form of literature that developed during this period is the Puranas. These texts are compendia of myths, philosophical dialogues, and ritual prescriptions, which are coupled with genealogies of the dynasties that preceded the Guptas in both north and central India. The Puranas are revered by Hindus as sacred texts. They also have great significance as literary works and historical documents.

The Gupta achievements in the visual arts are also noteworthy. Gupta sculptors portrayed figures from Hinduism and Buddhism in images of startling beauty. One of the artistic forms particularly characteristic of India in this period is the cave temple. In these temple complexes, whole monasteries were cut into the faces of mountains. These monasteries consisted of chapels for worship as well as residential halls for monks and nuns. Important cave temples at Ajanta (located in Maharashastra) were begun in the mid-second century B.C.E. and completed in the late fifth century C.E.

India, 200–1200 C.E.

ca. 320–540	Gupta rule
ca. 376–415	Reign of Chandragupta II
515	Hun attack on north India
606–647	Reign of Harsha
600–1200	Development of regional states
849–1279	Chola domination of the south

At Ellora (another important site, also in Maharashastra) there are thirty-four temples cut in rock, constructed from the mid-sixth to the mid-tenth centuries. At Ellora, Buddhist, Hindu, and Jain temples are intermixed.

Natural science also played an important role in Gupta culture. In 499, Aryabhata calculated *pi*, the relationship of the radius of a circle to its circumference, to 3.1416; he also calculated the length of the solar year at 365.358605 days. He recognized that the earth was a sphere, that it rotated on its axis, and that lunar eclipses were caused by the shadow of the earth falling on the moon. Perhaps the most important university in the world during the sixth century was at Nalanda, near the Gupta capital of Pataliputra, which attracted students from as far away as China and Southeast Asia. The curriculum at Nalanda included grammar, rhetoric, prose, logic, metaphysics, and medicine.

The Gupta rulers were Hindus who patronized the cult of Vishnu. Deprived of royal patronage, Buddhism began to decline, imperceptibly at first. By the seventh century, Chinese pilgrims were reporting that Buddhism in India had declined. During the Gupta period, Buddhism gradually was reabsorbed into Hinduism. Buddhism had always been profoundly influenced by Hindu worldviews, and in many senses had never really departed from them. The worldview shared by both Hinduism and Buddhism assumes the following: All creatures go through cycles of birth and rebirth; the goal of religious cultivation is to gain release from the cycle; karma accumulated from good and bad deeds follows one from one life to another; the phenomenal world—the world of things—is illusory. Buddhism and Hinduism differed chiefly in the ways in which one might find release from the cycle of birth and rebirth. For Buddhists, the path was clear—the teachings of the Buddha were the way to release and salvation. For Hindus, devotion to Hindu deities was the primary means of release from the world of suffering. The relation between the two religions might be seen as analogous to the relation between Judaism and Christianity, which also share worldviews but have differing conceptions of salvation.

In the fifth century, a bitter war of succession sapped the vitality of the Gupta Empire, leaving it vulnerable to attack. The Guptas under Kumaragupta (415–54) were successful in repelling attacks from the Huns. (Part of what fuelled the Huns' attacks on Europe may have been the early failures of their attempts in India.) But in 515 north India was briefly incorporated into the Hun empire. Although Hun domination did not last long, it effectively destroyed both Gupta rule and north Indian urban culture.

The last emperor to rule all of north India was Harsha (606–47), who reasserted Indian rule after the Hun conquests. He is known as a just and capable ruler. Although Harsha ruled a territory nearly as great as that of the Guptas, his means of control were even less direct than theirs had been. Territories that Harsha conquered were left under the control of tributary princes, who retained a great deal of autonomy. Under Harsha, officials were no longer paid in cash: the decline in trade with Rome had diminished the flow of cash into India. Rather than being paid a salary, officials were assigned villages, from which they could then extract revenue. This model of decentralized fiscal administration developed under Harsha was followed by many kingdoms in medieval India. But Harsha had rivals, and after his death, his empire fragmented and the political situation in India was dominated by smaller kingdoms.

Indian statue of a woman writing, dating from the tenth or eleventh century C.E.

We can reconstruct something of the life of women in India during this period. Gupta period texts refer occasionally to female philosophers and teachers. A visiting Chinese Buddhist monk observed in the seventh century that women in India seemed to move about more freely than women in China. An eighth-century Indian woman wrote a midwifery text: her name in Arabic is Rusa. There was no gender equality in ancient India. Far from it. However, female gender seems to have been no hindrance to a business career. One of the more troubling aspects of Indian culture from a modern point of view is the practice of *sati*. The term, which literally means "virtuous woman," refers to the practice of a widow burning herself to death on her husband's funeral pyre. Although both epic literature and historical accounts mentioned the practice of widows committing suicide, the practice does not seem to have been common during the classical era. By the sixth century, however, the custom seems to have been widespread. Still, according to most contemporary writers, the preferred choice for a widow remained a life of asceticism. The poet Bana, writing in the seventh century at the court of Harsha, called *sati* "a foolish mistake of stupendous magnitude, committed under the reckless impulse of despair and infatuation," and suggested that a woman who immolated herself on her husband's funeral pyre would go straight to hell.

A widow's life was difficult, and by the sixth century, remarriage of a woman of the upper classes was frowned upon. From the seventh to the eleventh centuries, Indian jurists debated the question of whether a widow had rights to her husband's property. Not until 1300 was the right of a widow to inherit clear throughout all of the Indian subcontinent.

But the practice of sati was not simply escape from a harsh life. A widow who burned herself in her husband's funeral pyre was expunging her own sins and those of her husband. As a result of her heroic devotion, the couple would live blissfully together in paradise for thirty-five million years. A few moments of agony among burning twigs and flesh was the price to be paid for long-term, if not eternal, bliss. But this obligation of a woman to her husband was not reciprocal. A man whose wife predeceased him was not expected to die to procure the happiness of the couple. Indeed, because a wife was central to the carrying out of domestic religious duties, not to mention other domestic duties, a man was expected to remarry. Sati is an extreme example of a cultural practice that demands female sacrifice for the ultimate benefit of the couple as a corporate unit.

Hinduism, Temples, and Regional Identities

From the death of Harsha, no single power dominated all of north India until the Moghul conquest almost a thousand years later. During the period from roughly 600 to 1200, distinctive local cultures developed. For most of that time, competing kingdoms maintained rough regional balances of power. During the latter part of the period, the Cholas (849–1279), a southern power, dominated the Indian subcontinent and extended their influence through Southeast Asia.

During this time, the religion we now call Hinduism—the word was first widely used by Arabs in the eighth century—was fully developed as a popular devotional religion. Hinduism has no well-defined ecclesiastical organization. The Vedas were the most important sacred texts, and the caste system was the defining mode of social organization. Three changes in Hinduism occurred during the Gupta era. First, sacred images became the center of worship. Many of the splendid Gupta images remaining today were originally crafted as holy images. Second, worship came to consist of welcoming the deity as if he or she were a distinguished guest. Rituals of worship were rituals of hospitality. And third, social law came to be conceptualized as sacred law.

Religion and popular culture were deeply intertwined. One example of this is the *Ramayana*, one of the great Indian epics. The hero, Rama, is the son of a king who has gone into exile because of a succession dispute. He takes with him his beautiful wife, Sita. But demons abduct Sita, and try to win her love. The epic has a happy ending: Rama wins back his wife and his throne. The story is seen as the triumph of virtue over vice, and Rama became the object of a devotional cult in the first several centuries C.E. The story was repeated in both words and images, and became widespread throughout Southeast Asia as well as in India. With the propagation of stories like this, Hinduism became a dynamic mass movement.

With the rise of Hinduism as a religion of popular devotion, temples assumed an increasing importance, an importance that was not restricted to the religious realm. Especially in the kingdoms of southern India, temples played a multiple role. The model of political control exercised by the southern states was one in which a king exercised a degree of central power within a fragmentary political system, and temple networks were central to political integration. Local notables made donations to temples as acts of religious piety. The temples then served as redistribution centers for

BHARATA'S TREATISE ON DRAMATURGY

■ *Drama in ancient India reached a high form. Theatrical performances were generally held in conjunction with religious festivals. Performances of plays often began at dawn, to the accompaniment of clashing cymbals.*

Bharata was the premier theorist of Sanskrit drama. As the following excerpt shows, he also had theories about who formed the ideal audience for drama. Note from his description of the diversity of the audience that people of all ages, both male and female, and of a variety of social classes composed the audience. We can also read into Bharata's description of the ideal audience his ideas of what qualities an ideal man would possess.

They should be men of character and pedigree; endowed with composure, conduct and learning; intent on good name and virtue; unbiased; of proper age; well versed in drama and its constituent elements; vigilant, pure, and impartial; experts in instruments and make-up; conversant with dialects; adepts in arts and crafts—such men are to be made spectators for witnessing a drama. He who is satisfied when the feeling of satisfaction is portrayed, himself becomes sorrow-stricken when sorrow is shown, and attains the state of helplessness when helplessness is enacted—he is the proper spectator in a drama.

It is not expected that all these qualities will be present in a single spectator . . . Those in youth will be pleased with the love portrayed, the connoisseurs with the technical elements, those devoted to mundane things with the material activities presented, and the dispassionate ones with the efforts toward spiritual liberation depicted; of varied character are those figuring in a play, and the play rests on such variety of character. The valorous ones will delight in themes of violence, fights and battles, and the elders will always revel in tales of virtue and mythological themes. The young, the common folk, the women would always like burlesque and striking make-up. Thus he who is, by virtue of the response of the corresponding feeling or situation, able to enter into a particular theme is considered a fit spectator for that kind of theme, being endowed with those qualities needed for a proper spectator.

economic resources. Although there were forms of direct taxation practiced by many of these regional states, the economic role of the temple was crucial.

The social and cultural role of the temple was also important. Village assemblies, which continued to have a great deal of autonomy, often met at the local temple. Although irrigation was often the most important issue on the agenda of the local assembly, other matters of government might also be handled.

Temples and temple lore were also important in the building of regional and national identity. Temple chronicles, which recounted the histories of the various deities enshrined in a particular temple, were originally in Sanskrit or Pali, another classical language. But gradually people began telling these stories, and eventually recording them, in local languages. In the period from 1000 to 1300, vernacular languages such as Marathi, Ben-gali, Assamese, and Oriya developed. Moreover, during this period kings increasingly used local languages, rather than Sanskrit, for their proclamations and inscriptions.

The practice of pilgrimage enhanced the development of regional and national identities. The belief that worshiping particular divine images would enable one to gain release from the cycle of birth and death was a powerful impetus to go on a pilgrimage. Devout Hindus made long pilgrimages to important temples where particularly potent images were housed. Many Puranas, as well as later additions to the *Mahabharata*, provide details of pilgrimage routes. Pilgrims who traveled from holy site to holy site provided a network linking local, regional, and national holy sites. Pilgrimage routes cut across all of India, providing for regional integration. Pilgrims came back with stories about other parts of

In this bronze statue of Siva as King of Dancers, the god tramples the demon of ignorance and forgetfulness. The flaming circle is symbolic of the legend of the pillar of fire in which Siva revealed himself as creator of the universe.

India. A pilgrim would have a sense that he or she belonged to a cultural world whose boundaries extended far beyond the borders of the village.

Despite this integration, distinctive local cultures remained. One of the splendid cultural achievements of south India during this period was poetry written in Tamil. One poem, from a collection called the *Eight Anthologies*, probably dating from the sixth century, provides a vivid picture of a popular festival:

> The farmers who harvest rice in the hot sun
> now leap into the waves of the clear sea.
> The sailors, captains of stout craft,
> drink strong liquor and dance for joy,
> as they clasp the bright-bangled hands of women . . .
> In the cool woods, where the bees seek flowers,
> women, bright bangled and garlanded, drink
> the sap of the palm and the pale sugar cane,
> and the juice of the coconut which grows in the sand,
> then running they plunge into the sea.

Other Tamil poems are explicitly religious. They are the product of devotional cults that stressed love between the devotee and the god. One such poem, "Guide to the Lord Murugan," probably from the seventh century, describes the Tamil deity as having "the form of a young man, fragrant and beautiful" and as speaking tenderly to his devotees, telling them "Don't be afraid—I knew you were coming." While most of the Tamil poets were male, there were a few female poets such as Antal, who wrote poems as the lover of Vishnu. While men and women in other religious traditions, including Christianity, have used sexual metaphors to describe the mystical union with the divine, none have expressed it in terms as lush as the Hindu traditions.

India during this period presents something of a paradox. After the fall of the Guptas, political decentralization fostered the development of distinctive regional cultures. At the same time, the Hindu religion and an elite educated in Sanskrit provided for a sense of Indian identity that transcended localities. The mechanisms of integration operating in India were much more informal than the centralizing bureaucracy of China.

Southeast Asia:
A World Between Two Cultures

The various societies of Southeast Asia, positioned as they are between India and China, have been profoundly influenced by both civilizations, but have retained clear indigenous cultures. Chinese influence on Vietnam was direct and brutal: the Han dynasty Chinese conquered Vietnam in the second century B.C.E., and it remained a Chinese colony for a thousand years. Even after the Vietnamese gained their independence in the tenth century, they continued to feel the impact of Chinese culture and politics. Indian contact with Southeast Asia is more amorphous. There is no evidence of Indian colonization or conquest in the region. And yet the influence of Indian culture on parts of Southeast Asia was as profound as the influence of the Chinese in Vietnam. Khmer civilization, located in what is now Cambodia, was strongly influenced by Indian culture. Chinese and Indian political and religious theories and institutions provided potent tools in the hands of local monarchs. When a Vietnamese ruler talked about the Mandate of Heaven or a Khmer ruler said he was an incarnation of a Hindu deity, that ruler was clearly manipulating foreign ideas he found to be useful in a local context.

The kingdoms of Southeast Asia were not centralized empires. Political control was maintained through a variety of mechanisms that more closely resemble strategies used by Indian kings than they do those of the Chinese empire.

A Durable Indigenous Culture in Vietnam

Our knowledge of Vietnam before the Chinese conquest is fragmentary and comes primarily from archaeology. The Chinese conquered Vietnam in 111 B.C.E. and incorporated much of what is now Vietnam into the Han dynasty Chinese empire as the province of Tonkin. The Chinese census of 2 C.E. reports that in the three Vietnamese prefectures there were 143,643 households, containing a total of 981,755 persons. At the turn of the first century, during the troubles at the time of Wang Mang (see chapter 4), an influx of scholar-official families migrated from China to Vietnam. The Han Chinese administration attempted to transform Vietnamese culture to make it more "civilized," that is to say, more like that of China. They introduced schools and Chinese-

style plows and encouraged local people to marry according to Confucian rituals. Despite numerous rebellions, China retained control of Vietnam until the tenth century. Notable among these rebellions was that of the Trung sisters in 40 C.E. Trung Trac and Trung Nhi succeeded in driving the Han out of northern Vietnam and part of southern China. Their rule lasted for two years. But the rebellion was ultimately defeated and the Trung sisters were beheaded in 43 by the Chinese general Ma Yuan. The sisters became important cult figures. The fact that women were patriotic heroes was noted in this poignant fifteenth-century poem:

> All the male heroes bowed their heads in submission
> Only the two sisters proudly stood up to avenge the country.

But despite the rebellions, Chinese culture was not rejected out of hand. Ma Yuan, the Chinese general who suppressed the rebellion, also became a culture hero of sorts. Credited with introducing walled cities and the well-field system (see chapter 4) to Vietnam, he was posthumously venerated by local people as a water spirit. Following the failure of the Trung sisters' rebellion, Chinese immigration into Vietnam increased. Interaction among and intermarriage between the Chinese and the indigenous peoples increased. Beginning in the first century, intermarriage between Chinese and Vietnamese created a new Sino-Vietnamese elite.

Another celebrated rebellion took place in 284 C.E. Key players in this rebellion were the newly sinicized Vietnamese aristocracy. Now even Chinese immigrants sided with the rebels against the Chinese. This rebellion too was led by a woman, the lady Trieu, who rode

Elephant figure from a Vietnamese ceramic jar, dated to the eleventh or twelfth century C.E. The animal is wearing a harness, indicating that the Vietnamese of this period used domesticated elephants.

into battle astride an elephant. She became the focus of a cult, which may have exaggerated her actual significance. Nonetheless, the continuation of the identification of patriotic themes and female heroines is worthy of note.

The position of women in early Vietnamese society seems to have been rather high. Property was transmitted from both mothers and fathers to sons and daughters. Moreover, it may well be that prior to the Chinese conquest Vietnamese society was matrilineal and matriarchal. Chinese officials during the Han displayed perplexity and dismay at the marriage customs of the Vietnamese. According to one such official, "men and women joined at random." He sought to remedy the situation by ordering people to select proper mates, and he performed mass weddings, on one occasion marrying a thousand couples. He encouraged local officials to help people obtain betrothal gifts, according to Chinese rituals. But the persistence of indigenous customs was something that Chinese administrators were to continue to bewail.

Despite the failure of Chinese officials to impose Chinese values on the Vietnamese, the impact of Chinese culture was significant. The Vietnamese used Chinese characters in their writing. Tombs in Vietnam from the Han era reveal Chinese objects as grave goods, demonstrating that Chinese culture was important to the Vietnamese elite. Vietnamese education was centered on the Confucian classics. Nor was the impact limited to elite culture. The Chinese taught the Vietnamese agricultural techniques, such as the use of night soil, manure, and irrigation, which perhaps gave Vietnam a productive advantage over her Southeast Asian neighbors. The most far-reaching import from China was Buddhism, which was to play a crucial role in Vietnamese history. The first Buddhists to reach Vietnam were Chinese who arrived in the third century.

Despite a millennium of colonization, Vietnam never became Chinese. And once the Chinese were expelled, the Vietnamese began asserting their cultural independence. A tenth-century Vietnamese patriotic hero named Dinh Bo Linh was a buffalo herder who became emperor and established the Ly dynasty. His legitimacy was recognized by the Chinese in 970. The legends that surrounded him—that his father was an otter, and that dragons protected him—drew on indigenous non-Chinese lore to authenticate royal legitimacy.

This new-found cultural autonomy was evidenced in the sphere of writing as well. In the tenth and eleventh centuries the Vietnamese developed a writing system based on but not identical to Chinese characters. It was

used for private documents, deeds, and contracts. In later times, it was used to write popular literature as well. Official documents continued to be written in Chinese.

One assertion of autonomy and patriotism is a poem written, ironically enough, in classical Chinese. Its author, Ly Thuong Kiet (1019–1105), was an important general and statesman. Legend has it that he read the poem to his troops on the eve of a successful battle with the Chinese in 1076. The poem reads:

> The Southern emperor rules the southern land.
> Our destiny is writ in Heaven's Book.
> How dare you bandits trespass on our soil?
> You shall meet your undoing at our hands.

The rulers of the Ly dynasty found certain aspects of Chinese ruling ideology useful, but retained other indigenous elements, such as oaths of blood loyalty to the ruler, which had other sources. The proximity of Vietnam to other cultures, such as the Khmer, may have provided yet other models to its rulers.

Khmer Civilization in Cambodia

One of the most important states of Southeast Asia was the Khmer kingdom of Angkor (802–1432). Angkor's rulers achieved political integration by controlling people rather than land. Indeed, the kingdom had no precise geographical borders. At its height, the Khmer state controlled about a million people, ruling with a combination of political, religious, and economic institutions. The ruler was seen as the human agent of the gods, and the networks provided by temples were central to Khmer integration.

In the Khmer state, much as in south India, temples were the center of social and economic interaction. They were linked through an elaborate network. Local temples gained legitimacy and prestige by paying a percentage of the yield of their lands to a central temple, which gave the local priest ritual privileges in the central temple. These local temples were subsidized by the patronage of the local elite, who gained ritual prestige from their affiliation with the temple.

Angkor civilization was also integrated physically by a network of canals, which were used for both transport and irrigation. Most of the great Angkor monuments were built along the canal system, which greatly facilitated the transportation of the massive amounts of stone required for their construction. Vast reservoirs enabled the Khmer people to gain a measure of control over a monsoon climate in which most of the rain fell in a single season. The largest of these reservoirs had a capacity of 30 million gallons, and perhaps doubled the productive capacity of the Khmer lands. This enhanced productive capacity made possible the economic surplus that resulted in the construction of the splendid city of Angkor and the magnificent temple complex at Angkor Wat. Angkor Wat was built by the emperor Suryavarman II (ca. 1113–50) in the early twelfth century to celebrate the Hindu deity Vishnu, and to embody the identification between emperor and god. Its ruins are still the largest religious structure ever built anywhere in the world.

Tracing the relationship between indigenous Khmer cults and imported Indian ones is complicated by the fact that indigenous deities were often given names in Sanskrit, which was the language adopted by the Khmer court. Local cults and imported ones might exist side by side, at the same site, as they did at Mount Mahendra. It had been sacred in indigenous traditions. Under the reign of Jayavarman II (ca. 790–850), it became the center of a cult that incorporated the worship of Siva, the imperial ancestors, and the local gods. Siva and the Khmer ancestors resided together in multicultural harmony at Mount Mahendra. In a similar vein, the Bayon, one of the splendid monuments at Angkor, has been described as a monument that gathers together all of the spirits of the realm, Khmer and Buddhist, as well as deities from the Hindu pantheon. Royal edicts and inscriptions from throughout the Khmer period reveal tolerance of a wide variety of religious practices.

Although a number of aspects of Indian civilization became integrated into the Khmer way of life, others seem to have made no impact whatsoever. The caste system that pervaded Indian life, for example, does not appear in Khmer society. The greater political significance of women in Khmer society seems to have continued undiminished despite Indian influence. Certain of the Khmer kings, notably Indravarman II (ca. 1243) and Suryavarman I (1002–50), staked their claims to legitimacy to the throne by their maternal rather than their paternal pedigrees. In the Angkor state, women served as officials and judges. Unlike the Indians, Khmer commoners seem to have practiced neolocal

ZHOU DAGUAN'S RECOLLECTIONS OF THE CUSTOMS OF CAMBODIA

■ *Zhou Daguan wrote extensively on his travels in Southeast Asia. In this excerpt he remarks upon the agricultural customs of the Cambodians. Note that the rice he mentions is a type of aquatic rice that does in fact float to the surface of the water no matter how rapidly and high the water rises. Notice also how he uses Chinese agriculture as the standard for comparison.*

Generally, the Cambodians harvest three or four crops a year. Their whole year is like our summer months for they have neither frost nor snow. Half the year it rains every afternoon, the other half not a drop of rain falls. In the late summer and fall it rains every afternoon and the waters of the Great Lake flood until the mighty trees are drowned and only their very tops show. Those who live near the lake take to the mountains. When the rains stop—and not a drop falls in spring—the Great Lake is accessible only by means of little boats, for the deepest parts are only some three to five feet deep. Then the lake dwellers return.

The cultivators calculate the exact time when the rice is ripe, the time of the flood crest, how much land it will cover, and, following the location of their fields, they sow. They do not use buffalo to plow. Their plows, sickles, and hoes are the same kind as ours but made differently. They also have fields where the harvest comes without sowing, where, as the waters rise, the rice plants also grow. I think it is a special variety.

To fertilize their fields, they plant legumes; they do not use animal manure, disdaining it as impure. The Chinese who live there do not talk to them about this, and I think the Cambodians consider the Chinese method of fertilizing disgusting. Two or three families dig a ditch into which they throw grasses; when the ditch is filled with mulch, they cover it up and scoop out another.

Northeast Asia: Korea and Japan

Cultural diffusion is as prominent a theme in the history of northeastern Asia as it is in Southeast Asia, but its dynamics differ. In northeastern Asia, that is to say, in present-day Korea and Japan, indigenous peoples strategically adopted certain aspects of Chinese culture while rejecting others. Chinese religious ideas and political philosophies played an important role in the development of both Korean and Japanese culture. Chinese systems of thought—Confucianism, Buddhism, and, to a lesser degree, Taoism—coexisted alongside indigenous systems, such as Korean shamanism and Japanese Shinto. But family forms and social structures in northeastern Asia proved more resistant to outside influence than thought systems.

The relationship among these cultures is made more complex by the fact that Korea played a central role in the diffusion of mainland culture to Japan. In the earliest periods, the histories of the Japanese islands and the Korean peninsula are deeply intertwined. Indeed, for this period, "Japan" and "Korea" scarcely exist as separate entities.

marriage, where the newly married couple would set up their own residence. Bride price was relatively unimportant, and divorce was relatively easy. Chinese observers noted that much trade was carried on by Khmer women. These same observers showed their acute discomfort with gender norms that differed from the Chinese.

Thus Khmer culture adopted aspects of Indian culture that seemed useful, yet retained a distinctive core. Vietnam's relationship to China took a different form, largely due to the colonial experience. The distinctive core is there marked by a fierce independence. In both cases, gender norms and family patterns retained their local forms. And religious and political influences from outside were intertwined with local cults and ideologies in ways that are hard to disentangle.

Korea: The Three Kingdoms

Archaeological evidence is crucial to our understanding of early Korea. In the eighth and ninth centuries B.C.E., the societies on the Korean peninsula entered the

Angkor Wat is covered with bas-relief sculptures representing Hindu myths. Originally dedicated to Vishnu, the temple represents a fusion of Hinduism and Buddhism—after the fall of the Khmer dynasty in the sixteenth century it became a Buddhist shrine.

bronze age. During this time, Korean farmers began cultivating rice, probably introduced from China. These early Koreans lived in large settlements, many of which were walled. Some scholars have speculated that early Korean society was divided into two groups: aristocrats who lived within walled cities and commoners who dwelled outside the city walls. These cities and their hinterlands formed primitive yet powerful tribal communities.

The Han dynasty Chinese had imperial ambitions in Korea, and in 108 B.C.E. they established the command-ery of Lelang on the northern part of the Korean penin-sula. The Chinese commandery in Lelang lasted until the fourth century C.E., and its cultural influence was profound. Korean political ideas, burial customs, writ-ing, and agricultural technology were all influenced by Han Chinese models. Yet indigenous religious forms, particularly shamanism, persisted. Furthermore, Kore-ans continued to celebrate the harvest in the tenth lunar month and hold fertility festivals in the spring.

From the third century C.E., political life on the Ko-rean peninsula was dominated by the Three Kingdoms of Koguryo, Silla, and Paekche. Silla was located in the south, Koguryo in the north, and Paekche in the south-west. Under the Three Kingdoms, Korean society was dominated by an aristocracy. Government was in the hands of a king, who was aided by a bureaucracy staffed by aristocrats. Most Koreans were free peas-ants who paid taxes to the central government. Vil-lages were governed by a headman, who was recruited locally, but who derived his authority from the central government.

Buddhism was first introduced to Korea from China in the Three Kingdoms period, to Koguryo and Paekche in the fourth centuries, and to Silla in the sixth. In all three kingdoms, Buddhism was welcomed by the royal family, sometimes over the initial opposition of the ar-istocracy. But gradually, aristocrats too became adher-ents of the new religion, which was used to justify royal rule and aristocratic privilege. Buddhist monks were frequently important advisors to kings. The significance of Buddhism in Korea during this period is demon-strated by the Miruk monastery in Koguryo. Estab-lished in 634, it was the largest monastery in East Asia of its time.

The Buddhist sacred texts that Koreans read were written in Chinese. Korean students of Buddhism thus became by necessity students of Chinese as well. The spread of Buddhism in Three Kingdoms Korea was ac-companied by the spread of literacy in classical Chinese. The court of Paekche in the fourth century, for example,

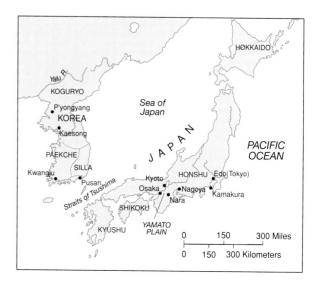

Korea and Japan

kept its records in Chinese. It was not until the sixth century that Koreans began to write the Korean language, using Chinese characters to represent Korean sounds.

The nature of early contacts beween Korea and Japan are controversial, and our understanding of them is com-plicated by the often difficult political relationship be-tween the two countries in the twentieth century. A controversial theory asserts that in the fourth century people from Korea invaded the Japanese islands and established the early Japanese state of Yamato. Begin-ning in the fourth century, people in Japan were placing new kinds of objects in graves. Tombs from this period contain more weapons, more armor, and more horse-riding equipment. These perhaps indicate an influx of immigrants from the mainland. Furthermore, recent tomb excavations in Japan, such as one in Nara prefec-ture in 1972, show murals and artifacts that bear a striking resemblance to those found in mainland tombs, providing evidence that the earliest Japanese elites had close ties with the mainland, and suggest-ing to some scholars that they were in fact immigrants from Korea.

Evidence of later contacts between the cultures of the Korean peninsula and Japan is clear. Buddhism and the Chinese language were both introduced to Japan not by Chinese but by Koreans. In 584 the first monk from Koguryo went to Japan, and in subsequent decades, many more followed his example. In 588 several nuns came to Korea from Japan to study and on their return they were instrumental in shaping the direction of early

Japanese Buddhism. In 655 a nun from Paekche went to Japan. Her ability to heal illness by chanting Buddhist scripture won her fame and a popular following. Her skills and popularity indicate the ways in which Buddhism, regarded by elites as a useful political tool, might have different meanings altogether among ordinary people.

The Three Kingdoms period in Korea coincided with the Period of Disunion in China. The reunification of China under the Sui and Tang dynasties posed a threat to the Korean kingdoms. The expansionist Tang empire mounted military campaigns against Korea in the seventh century. Silla, the southernmost Korean kingdom, allied with the Tang against the other two Korean kingdoms, and succeeded in unifying Korea in 668. The kingdom thus created is known by the name Unified Silla. The dislocations caused by the subsequent warfare resulted in the flight of a large number of refugees to Japan.

Unified Silla was a dynamic player in East Asian politics. Much of the trade between China and Japan was in Silla's hands. Its capital, located at modern Kyongju, in the eighth century had a population of 700,000 people. Silla imported administrative techniques and the Tang equal field system from China. It is not clear to what degree the Tang land system was implemented. The curriculum at the royal academy at Kyongju was the Confucian classics.

Silla politics was marked by a strong aristocracy that frequently asserted its power at the imperial court. Chinese administrative techniques were applied by the throne in a society that was firmly aristocratic. Social position depended on lineage, and the lineages of one's mother and one's father were equally important. And those principles remained unchallenged by Chinese influence.

Early Japan and Divine Imperial Power

Although the early histories of Japan and Korea are closely intertwined, after about the fourth century C.E., they undertook paths of separated development. Japan was strongly influenced by mainland culture. The writing system, certain aspects of political philosophy, Buddhism, Confucianism—all were profoundly influenced by the Chinese model, which was often filtered through Korea. But even at times when the infatuation of the Japanese elite with China was at its most intense, Japanese culture retained its distinctive forms.

One of these distinctive forms is the imperial institution. The Japanese state revolved around an emperor who was revered as the direct lineal descendant of the Sun Goddess. Thus imperial legitimacy was not problematic. But political authority did not always reside with the emperor, and the relationships between various forms of power and authority in Japan's long imperial history form a complex mosaic.

Shinto and the Founding of the Japanese State. The earliest period of Japanese history about which we know very much is called Yamato, and extends approximately from the third to the seventh centuries C.E. During this period, the imperial house consolidated its power. The Yamato state was a confederation of groups called *uji* that were bound by ties of both kinship and territory. In early Japan, political and social status came from belonging to a powerful uji. The position of uji chief was hereditary, and by the late seventh century, it was quite powerful. Early in the Yamato period, the imperial house was simply the most powerful of these uji. Attached to the uji were corporate subordinate groups called *be*, who provided for the material needs of the uji. Mosty be engaged in agricultural work, but they also performed other kinds of labor. Occupational categories were hereditary.

The uji was also the chief religious unit in early Japan. The uji leader acted as a mediator between the deities and the uji, and the be worshiped the same deities as the uji to which they were attached. The indigenous religion of early Japan is called *Shinto*, which literally "means the way of the gods." Practice of Shinto involves veneration of deities, known as *kami*, and purification rituals. A kami is anything that exhibits awesome potency—trees, rocks, dead heroes, the emperor—all are kami. A kami is characterized by its power, not by its goodness. Indeed, questions of good and evil are of little interest to early Shinto. Acts that harm other people are condemned because they are polluting. But other acts, which involve no malice or wrongdoing, such as childbirth, sex, and death, are also regarded as polluting. Pollution can be eliminated by ritual purification, often involving water, symbolically washing away the pollution. Shinto, especially early Shinto, does not have the elaborate doctrines that Buddhism or Taoism does. The founding myths of Shinto are the founding myths of the Japanese state. The land itself was formed by the gods and therefore contains the god-spirit. Therefore in a cultural—even spatial—sense Shinto is ultimately Japanese.

The founding myths of Japanese culture are recorded in the earliest Japanese written histories, the *Kojiki* from 712 and the *Nihongi* from 720. According to these accounts, Japan was created when Izanagi and Izanami,

Sixth-century terra-cotta haniwa *warrior figure from Japan. These figures of houses, warriors, and animals were not buried like the tomb figures of China but were placed around the grave as guardians.*

brother and sister, stood on a floating bridge and plunged a sword into the sea. They fished islands out of the sea, creating Japan. Izanami, who was Izanagi's spouse as well as his sister, subsequently gave birth to a series of deities, including the Fire God. She was burned giving birth to him and died. Izanagi, grief-stricken, went to the Land of Darkness to seek her, but all he found there was a mass of putrefied flesh. On his return to the land of the living, he purified himself in a stream. This purification ritual developed into an important part of early Japanese religion. From the various parts of Izanagi's body and clothing were born the next generation of deities, the most important of which are Amaterasu, the sun goddess, and Susa-no-o, the storm god. These two exhibited sibling rivalry on a cosmic scale. The storm god destroyed the irrigation on his sister's rice fields, he defecated in the palace, and so on. His sister retreated into a cave, and did not emerge until the other deities made her laugh by their lewd dancing.

The chronicles continue with an explanation of the Japanese royal line. Amaterasu sent her grandson to earth with the imperial regalia—mirror, sword, and jewels. Thus he is the ancestor of the Japanese imperial line. These myths make a universalistic claim to divine imperial power and articulate a close connection between emperor and sun goddess, a connection so close that even the empress and the heir apparent are normally not allowed to worship the sun goddess without the permission of the emperor.

Chinese chronicles also describe Japan's early history, in which female rulers were prominent—an aspect of Japanese politics that especially impressed the Chinese. One such ruler was a princess named Pimiko. According to a Chinese account, after her death a man succeeded to the throne, but people would not obey his authority. Order was restored only when a thirteen-year-old girl was put on the throne. Whether Pimiko was an actual historical personage is uncertain. But it is true than a significant number of the early rulers of Japan were female.

Contacts with the Mainland. During the seventh and eighth centuries the imperial house manipulated a variety of techniques to bolster its position as the most powerful of the uji. The mythology of descent from the sun goddess was one such technique. The ruling house also adopted administrative techniques and ideology from the mainland to further their effort.

Contacts between Japan and the mainland were probably begun by the fourth century. One of the most enduring legacies of that contact was the writing system. When the first mainlanders arrived in Japan, the Japanese had not yet devised a writing system, and they adapted the Chinese written language to write Japanese. The Japanese and Chinese languages are structurally unrelated: Chinese is structurally very simple, whereas Japanese is a highly inflected language. Chinese characters—where one symbol stands for one syllable—are not well suited to write the complex intricacies of the Japanese language. To accommodate the intricacies and inflections of their spoken language, the Japanese devised another writing system, called *kana*. Some texts were written entirely in kana. Most texts were (and continue to be) written in a mixture of Chinese characters, which the Japanese call *kanji*, and kana. Chinese also influenced the vocabulary of Japanese. According to one dictionary compiled in the nineteenth century, approximately 13,000 Japanese words were originally of Chinese derivation, while 22,000 were originally of Japanese derivation.

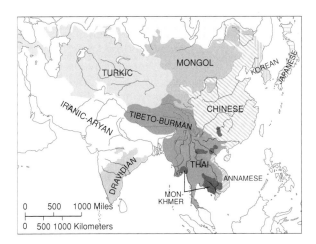

Ethnic Groups and Language Families

Buddhism is another of the elements of mainland culture that had a profound effect on Japanese culture. In 552 C.E., the king of Paekche in Korea sent the emperor of Japan a Buddhist image and a memorial lauding Buddhism. Some people at the Japanese court advocated adopting the new religion. But others feared that the Shinto deities would be enraged if Buddhism were adopted. In 587, the Soga family, who had been strong advocates of Buddhism, crushed the Mononobe family, who had opposed it, and Buddhism was adopted. It did not replace Shinto; it was merely added to the religious repertoire of the Japanese people. In the early days, the appeal of Buddhism was limited to court aristocrats, who were attracted to Buddhism because it promised powerful magic, magic associated with the power and prestige of China. Buddhist temples fulfilled much the same function as had the tombs of an earlier era; as physical representations of sacred power, they were a way for the ruling house to manifest its legitimacy.

Associated with this period of cultural borrowing was a series of administrative reforms known as the Taika Reforms. These reforms began in 646 and continued for the next century. The emperor and his courtiers hoped that by utilizing Chinese administrative techniques they could better centralize power. The goal of these reforms was to replace the aristocratic uji with administrators who were selected by, and owed their allegiance to, the central government. One means of achieving this goal was a reform of the land system, under which uji holdings were to be confiscated and redistributed along lines suggested by the Tang equal field system. The

Japanese system assigned each adult man two *tan* (a *tan* is three-tenths of an acre) of land; it assigned a woman two-thirds of that amount. The land tax was light—only two or three percent of what the land produced—but other taxes were also levied. An adult male would owe a fixed amount of tax payable in silk or other goods. He would also be obligated for labor service to the central government, which would normally be for ten days per year, but might be extended for as long as forty days. He would also be responsible for up to sixty days of labor service to the provincial government. Labor service was not required of women.

The land reform was not easy to implement. Powerful uji were able to prevent the central government from confiscating their land. The system was further complicated by the fact that the land allotments were often not large enough to support a family. The amount of record keeping required to maintain such a system was staggering. The problems facing land reformers in Japan were not unlike those facing administrators in Tang China. By the end of the eighth century, the Japanese system had fallen into decline.

Another aspect of Chinese influence can be seen in the establishment of the capital at Nara in 710, instituting a period called the Nara period (710–94). Prior to 710, there had been no fixed capital. Each emperor had set up the seat of government in a new location, probably because the death of the former emperor had, in Shinto terms, polluted the previous capital. But the Chinese-style capital, a symbolic center of the realm, was too large and too expensive to move constantly. Nara was the first Japanese city, and it was laid out on a grid that resembled that of Tang Chang'an. At its height in the eighth century, the population of Nara was about two hundred thousand people.

But the rulers of Japan were selective with regard to the Chinese political system, adopting some aspects and discarding others. The key element of Chinese ruling ideology that the Japanese did not adopt was the notion of a mandate of heaven that might leave the ruling house. In Japan, dynastic legitimacy rested with members of the ruling house because they were the direct lineal descendants of the sun goddess. One consequence of this belief was that an astonishing array of regents and military commanders assumed control of the central government, without usurping the throne. These regents and military strongmen used the emperor and the charisma of the imperial position rather than usurping it. Although the forms and names of Chinese-style administration were adopted, real power remained with the aristocrats.

Heian Politics: Emperors, Regents, and the Land. In 794 the court moved the capital from Nara to Heian-kyo, present-day Kyoto. During the next several centuries, known as the Heian period (794–1185), real political control lay in the hands of the Fujiwara family, regents for the emperors. In addition, all important ministers of state from the period 850 to 1167 were members of the Fujiwara family. The Fujiwara were, furthermore, masters at marriage politics, frequently arranging for the emperor to marry Fujiwara daughters, who then gave birth to future emperors. Of the emperors who ascended the throne from 806 to 1155, only three were not born of Fujiwara women. Because it was the custom for the empress to go home to her natal family to give birth, the young emperors-to-be were often raised in the Fujiwara household. Fujiwara Michinaga (966–1027) is reported as saying, "a man's wife makes him what he is," an extraordinary statement considering that four of Michinaga's daughters married emperors. Even if a man's wife did not make him what he was, his mother might.

Nonetheless, even when the emperor's mother was a Fujiwara, his wife was a Fujiwara, and his chief ministers were Fujiwara, the Fujiwara did not usurp the throne. As Fujiwara Michinaga himself said,

> Great as are our power and prestige, nevertheless they are those of the sovereign, for we derive them from the majesty of the throne.

The Fujiwara assumed the charisma of the emperor to grant them legitimacy. The emperor's legitimacy was beyond question; it did not depend on factors like the mere exercise of political power for its maintenance.

In Heian Japan political control meant control of land, and control of land was a constant problem. The land reform had been one attempt to solve the problem, but by the eighth century it had failed. The system that evolved to replace it is known as the *shoen* system. A shoen was a privately held estate, often tax-exempt. By the tenth century most of the land in Japan was divided into these largely tax-free estates. The imperial family controlled some estates, but the Fujiwara controlled more. During the height of Fujiwara power, it was said that "all the land in the country belongs to the regent's house. There is not even enough public land to stand upon. What a lamentable world!" The development of the shoen was fueled by a vicious circle. The more shoen there were, the less revenue the imperial government had, so the lower the stipends they were able to pay their courtiers. Courtiers who were strapped for cash then needed shoen, which the emperor granted, making the situation worse. As the amount of taxable land decreased, the burden on taxpaying peasants grew greater. More and more peasants would leave their lands and place themselves under the protection of a large estate.

The emperor Go-Sanjo (1068–72), whose mother was not a Fujiwara, attempted to rule directly and to revoke tax exemptions on shoen lands. He met with almost no success. His son, Shirakawa, continued the effort to assert direct imperial control. In 1089 Shirakawa abdicated, but continued to maintain control over governmental affairs from his palace, even though there was a reigning emperor and a regent. This system of rule by abdicated emperors, called *insei*, continued for the next century. The power of the Fujiwara began to wane, in part because they ceased to produce marriageable daughters.

By the late Heian, central control of the provinces had grown more tenuous. Provincial governors had begun to reside in the capital, partly because of the lure of the elegant life there, but also because they were concurrently holding positions in the central government. By about 1100, the control of the countryside was in the hands of a warrior aristocracy. Two of the most important groups in the warrior aristocracy are the Taira and the Minamoto, collateral branches of the imperial house, descendants of younger sons who were made commoners and sent to the provinces to make their fortunes. They would loom large in centuries to come.

Heian Religion and Japanese Buddhism. During the Heian period Buddhism developed in its complexity and began to spread beyond the narrow circles of aristocracy that had been its domain during the Nara period. The great temple of Todaiji was begun at Nara by the emperor Shomu (724–49), who asked that every Japanese contribute something to the enterprise, even if only a twig or a handful of dirt. The size of the temple staff exceeded all other government offices in the eighth century. Indeed, scholars have speculated that one of the reasons the capital was moved from Nara was so that the court could escape the pervasive influence of the Buddhist establishment.

During the Nara period Buddhism was in its essence a court religion. But from a very early period another strain of Japanese Buddhism was represented by the *ubasoku*, charismatic mountain men. They ministered to the needs of ordinary people; outside the normal channels of control both of state and church, they were a threat to both. During the eighth century, the government repeatedly issued edicts demanding that monks and nuns submit to monastic discipline as a means of bringing ubasoku under control. One of the most important of the ubasoku was Gyogi Bosatsu (645–749). According to legend, he carried a Buddhist relic to the shrine of the sun goddess at Ise to ask the goddess if she approved of the great Buddhist temple at Todaiji. She responded that she did approve. Gyogi henceforth argued that Shinto *kami* were localized manifestations of the Buddha. This began a long tradition in Japan of identifying particular Buddhist bodhisattvas with Shinto deities. Gyogi ended his career with the aura of respectability, as an advisor to the emperor Shomu.

In the early Heian, two men made important innovations in Japanese Buddhism. A monk named Saicho (767–822) founded the Tendai sect, and a monk named Kukai (773–835) founded the Shingon sect. Subsequent developments in Japanese Buddhism were by and large outgrowths of these two sects. Saicho, the son of a Chinese immigrant family, had been a monk in one of the Nara Buddhist sects. He left because of what he regarded as the excessive formalism, and went to China.

There he studied Tiantai Buddhism, a syncretic and tolerant school of Buddhism; then he returned to Japan. According to Saicho, all forms of Buddhism are true, but some are more true than others. Saicho held that the *Lotus Sutra* represented the highest form of truth. Tendai, as the Japanese form of Tientai is known, stressed moral precepts, monastic discipline, and meditation. Tendai continued the tradition of Buddhism as a nation-protecting religion. Saicho said, "To cause the *dharma* to abide eternally is to protect the nation." A universalistic religion of foreign origin was thus put to the service of the Japanese nation.

The second important early Heian Buddhist figure is Kukai, the founder of Shingon (or True Word) Buddhism. Kukai is an important literary as well as religious figure. He is credited with developing *kana*, the syllabic writing system discussed earlier. The basic premise of Shingon is that the entire universe is a manifestation of the Vairocana Buddha. Vairocana was associated with the sun god, facilitating his identification with the Japanese

OBSERVATIONS ON THE HEIAN CAPITAL, 982

■ *The first thing that strikes the reader of this segment is how crowded the capital is. Elsewhere in this passage, the author, Yoshishige no Yasutane (d. 1002), laments how stupid people are that they will not move. He points out social tensions that can result when rich and poor live in close proximity. The responsibility for the tension is laid squarely on the hawklike rich. But it is not only the unvirtuous rich who have made life miserable for ordinary people. Incompetent bureaucrats who have not made adequate provisions for flood control also come in for their share of blame.*

The eastern section from the Fourth Avenue northward, especially the northwestern and northeastern areas, is congested with people from all walks of life. The gates and buildings of great mansions follow one another. Smaller buildings are erected so closely that their eaves touch one another. If the neighbor to the east suffers a fire, the western neighbor cannot escape a similar fate. If the neighbor to the south is invaded by armed bandits, the northern neighbor can expect to be affected similarly . . . The rich are not necessarily endowed with virtue, while the poor still retain the sense of shame. Thus those poor people who live close to great families do not enjoy freedom of movement and behave continuously with trepidation. They do not dare replace their torn roofs or rebuild their broken fences. They are unable to laugh when happy or cry loudly when sorrowful. They are no different from sparrows who come near a flock of hawks.

By the river Kamo and on the northern fields, people not only build houses and dwellings but also cultivate fields and gardens. Old farmers toil on the land to create ridges between rice fields and dam up the river to irrigate their fields. But last year there was a flood and the river crested over the dike. The officials in charge of flood control used to boast of their accomplishment, but today they take no action to remedy the situation. Must people in the capital be consigned to a fate similar to that of fish?

sun goddess Amaterasu. If all the universe is the Buddha, everything that is beautiful partakes of the Buddha. Thus in Shingon, art is the primary medium for conveying the truth of Buddhism. Spells and charms, such as the *dharani* (see Special Feature, "The Guanyin Bodhisattva," pp. 224–225), were important components of Shingon worship.

Late in the Heian period, Buddhism became permeated with a sense of profound anxiety. Buddhist cosmologists calculated that in a year corresponding to 1052 in the western calendar, an era called *mappo*, the end of dharma, would begin. Buddhist law would wane, society would decline, and the scriptures would disappear. Consciousness of the transitory nature of life, already pervasive in Heian culture, was compounded by the prediction of impending mappo.

Heian Society: Peasant and Elite Families. Japanese families in the Heian period were organized very differently from those in later periods. Furthermore, peasant and elite families looked very different one from another. In eighth-century Japan, the average peasant household size seems to have been about ten people. The most convincing explanation for this large size is that a married couple would often live apart, each in their family of birth. Although children were normally registered with their fathers, they lived with their mothers. Thus these large households often consisted of several adult women and their children. Several kinds of marriage systems existed simultaneously in Heian Japan. Many couples lived apart for the duration of the marriage. In other marriages, the wife came to live with her husband, in a system called virilocal marriage. Another form of marriage, called uxorilocal, where the young couple lives with the bride's family, predominated among the elite of Heian Japan. Even in cases where the new couple did not reside with the wife's parents, it was her parents' responsibility to provide them with their first house. Houses would be passed from mother to daughter. The practical facts of the marriage system were reinforced by a folkloric belief that it was bad luck for the household deity of a mother-in-law and daughter-in-law to reside under the same roof. But by the twelfth century, marriages in which the couple lived with the wife's parents had all but disappeared. Male monogamy was not a requisite of the Heian marriage system. The plight of a divorced or widowed woman could be bitter, economically as well as emotionally. The Fujiwara family recognized this when they established a home for destitute women of their own family. By the end of the Heian period, as land became more important, there was a tendency for couples to reside in the household of the husband's family.

Grounds for divorce included mutual consent, as well as the seven grounds prescribed by Confucianism (see chapter 4). A woman whose husband disappeared in a foreign country might obtain a divorce. A man wanting a divorce had to get the consent of his parents and grandparents, and submit a written report. If he was illiterate, and he might well be, he would need to get someone to write the report for him.

Prior to the tenth century, a woman might control business enterprises. Moneylending, sake brewing, sericulture, and the storing of rice and currency were all enterprises in which early Heian women were prominent. The property a woman brought with her into her marriage remained under her control—a circumstance virtually necessitated by the ease of divorce. Divorce in Heian Japan might be very informal: a man's visits might simply cease. When the husband owned the house, divorce seems to have been less frequent, probably because of the greater economic dependence of the wife.

The vast majority of Japanese during the Heian period engaged in agriculture. During the course of the Heian period, improved agricultural techniques were introduced from the Asian mainland. One of the most significant of these was a better and heavier animal-drawn plow, which significantly improved agricultural productivity. But oxen, the draft animals most commonly used in Japan, remained expensive and beyond the reach of ordinary peasants. The presence of a technology that only some people could afford intensified social stratification. The plowmen grew to be a well-off provincial class that would become the warriors of the later Kamakura period (1185–1330).

Northeast Asia: Korea and Japan

3rd century C.E.	Three Kingdoms established on Korean Peninsula
646	Taika reforms begin in Japan
688	Silla unifies Korean Peninsula
710–794	Nara period in Japan
794–1185	Heian period in Japan

There are well-documented accounts of peasant protest in Heian Japan. Protest took distinctive forms: peasants absconded and then wrote memorials explaining their actions. One of the earliest recorded cases occurred in 988, when the district officials and peasants of Owari province filed a petition accusing the provincial governor of tax fraud, nepotism, extortion, and if that were not bad enough, murder. As a result of the petition, he was removed from office. Thus there is clear evidence that peasants could and did mobilize and act on their own behalf.

A great social gulf separated peasant and courtier in Heian Japan. The elite culture in that period was the epitome of refinement. The portrait of elite life drawn from literary works reveals an aristocracy preoccupied with aesthetics and beauty in all of its manifestations. People, particularly lovers, communicated with one another through poetry, written in exquisite calligraphy on elegant notepaper. The character of a man or woman was revealed by the choice of colors in a kimono, or the choice of perfume.

Literacy in classical Chinese was the mark of an educated man, and was regarded as an attainment unsuited for women. Nonetheless women played a prominent role in the literary life of Heian Japan. Japanese, written in the kana syllabary rather than Chinese characters, was the literary language of women. Indeed, Chinese characters were called "men's writing," and the Japanese kana was called "women's hand." Perhaps because of this gendered division of literary labor, a significant corpus of literary work by women from Heian Japan survives. Much of the work is literary diaries, which chronicle the daily life of elegant aristocrats. Indeed, diary writing was so female-dominated that when the celebrated male poet Ki no Tsurayuki wrote the *Tosa Diary*, he presented the text as if it had been written by a woman. Among the literary outpouring of Heian women is the world's first novel, Lady Murasaki's *Tale of Genji*. Lady Murasaki was the daughter of a minor official and a lady in waiting to the empress Shoshi (988–1074). The *Tale of Genji* is a meditation on the evanescence of human life and passion, which centers on the amorous escapades of Genji, a beautiful young prince.

Men and women of the Heian also used poetry to express themselves. The importance of poetry is demonstrated by the fact that it was anthologized in imperial collections. The following poem, written in the ninth century by a woman named Ono no Komachi, illustrates the refined state of the poetic art:

> Thinking about him
> I slept, only to have him
> Appear before me—
> Had I known it was a dream,
> I should never have wakened.

Her romantic longings are paired with a meditation on the reality of the dream world.

Heian Japan was in many ways profoundly influenced by Tang China. Buddhism, the writing system, and various administrative structures were consciously adopted from China. But marriage systems, the Japanese language itself, and a fundamentally aristocratic social structure remained distinctive. The Japanese imperial institution remained rather impervious to Chinese political ideas, especially the Mandate of Heaven. And Heian aesthetic sensibilities and literary achievements remain unique.

The history of Asia during the period from about 200 to 1000 is dominated by the theme of cultural diffusion. The most prominent example of this theme is the spread of Buddhism from its home in north India through all of Asia. In fact, it is chiefly Buddhism that enables us to speak of an Asian community at this period

An illustration from a twelfth-century scroll of the Tale of Genji *shows Prince Genji holding a newborn baby. The novel was written in the kana writing system.*

of history. However, Indian Buddhism was not simply transplanted into the various cultures of Asia. As it spread and transformed these cultures, it was itself transformed. Tenth-century Japanese Buddhism would probably have been recognizable to the historical Buddha, but some of its concerns would have seemed very odd indeed.

Chinese and Indian civilizations profoundly affected their neighbors. Local cultures appropriated elements of these civilizations and transformed them into locally distinctive cultural forms. But local cultures were not obliterated; religious cults, family forms, and gender roles seemed especially impervious to outside transformation. In Southeast Asia, Chinese and Indian culture both played a role. The dominance of these two cultures is the reason why the region has sometimes been called Indochina. In northeastern Asia—Korea and Japan—Chinese culture was the dominant outside influence during this period.

Despite the power of Chinese influence in shaping Vietnam, Korea, and Japan, those three cultures used Chinese influences to different ends. They were as different one from another a thousand years ago as they are today. Although one may be struck by the cultural commonalities of countries within the Chinese or Indian cultural sphere, even more remarkable are their differences. What has been striking about the cultures we have examined in this chapter is the diverse ways in which they approach political organization, religious life, and family structure. What we have seen in this chapter is the development of multiple Asian worlds.

SUGGESTIONS FOR FURTHER READING

CHINA: THE DURABILITY OF EMPIRE

* Patricia Buckley Ebrey, ed., *Chinese Civilization and Society: A Sourcebook* (New York: The Free Press, 1981). A rich collection of documents on Chinese social history.

Joseph Needham, *Science and Civilization in China* (New York: Cambridge University Press, 1954–). A multivolume magisterial survey of Chinese science and technology, painstakingly documented and lavishly illustrated.

* Arthur Wright, *Buddhism in Chinese History* (Stanford, CA: Stanford University Press, 1959). A classic account of the Chinese transformation of Buddhism.

Henri Maspero, *China in Antiquity*, trans. Frank Kierman (Amherst, MA: University of Massachusetts Press, 1978). Important studies of Taoism.

* Arthur Wright, *The Sui Dynasty* (New York: Alfred Knopf, 1978). A lucid account of the Sui.

Audrey Spiro, *Contemplating the Ancients: Aesthetic and Social Issues in Early Chinese Portraiture* (Berkeley and Los Angeles: University of California Press, 1990). An examination of portraiture of the Period of Disunion in its social context.

* Thomas Barfield, *The Perilous Frontier: Nomadic Empires and China 221 B.C. to A.D. 1757* (Cambridge, MA: Blackwell, 1989). A provocative interpretation of Chinese-nomad relations, designed for the general reader.

Glen Dudbridge, *The Legend of Miao-shan* (London: Ithaca Press, 1978). A detailed study of the legend of a young woman who is identified with the bodhisattva Guanyin.

Stephen F. Teiser, *The Ghost Festival in Medieval China* (Princeton, NJ: Princeton University Press, 1988). A detailed study of the Chinese festival of the dead.

Howard Wechsler, *Offerings of Jade and Silk: Ritual and Symbol in the Legitimation the Tang Dynasty* (New Haven, CT: Yale University Press, 1985). A political analysis that takes ritual seriously.

Denis Twitchett, *The Writing of Official History Under the T'ang* (New York: Cambridge University Press, 1992). A discussion of the politics and mechanics of history under the Tang.

INDIA: THE STRENGTH OF REGIONAL CULTURES

Hermann Kulke and Dietmar Rothermund, *A History of India* (New York: Dorset Press, 1986). A readable account incorporating much recent scholarship.

Joanna Gottfried Williams, *The Art of Gupta India: Empire and Province* (Princeton, NJ: Princeton University Press, 1982). Integrates analysis of aspects of Gupta style with political and social developments.

Three Sanskrit Plays (New York: Penguin, 1981). Translations of *Sakuntala*, *Visakhadatta*, and *Bhavabhuti*, each with a brief analytical introduction.

SOUTHEAST ASIA: A WORLD BETWEEN TWO CULTURES

Bernard Philippe Groslier, *The Art of Indochina, Including Thailand, Vietnam and Cambodia*, trans. George Lawrence (New York: Crown Publishers, 1962). A beautifully illustrated book that provides social and historical context for the objects it illustrates.

Kenneth R. Hall and J. K. Whitmore, eds., *Explorations in Early Southeast Asian History: The Origins of Southeast Asian Statecraft* (Ann Arbor, MI: Michigan Papers on South and Southeast Asia, No. 11, 1976). A collection of essays.

Kenneth R. Hall, *Maritime Trade and State Development in Early Southeast Asia* (Honolulu: University of Hawaii Press, 1985). A subtle and systematic attempt to analyze the development of the region as a whole.

David G. Marr and A. C. Milner, eds., *Southeast Asia in the Ninth to Fourteenth Centuries* (Singapore: Institute of Southeast Asian Studies, 1986). Essays on particular aspects of Southeast Asian culture and history.

Keith Weller Taylor, *The Birth of Vietnam* (Berkeley and Los Angeles: University of California Press, 1983). Treats the period from 111 B.C.E. until the Vietnamese assert their independence from China in the eleventh century.

NORTHEAST ASIA: KOREA AND JAPAN

Ki-baik Lee, *A New History of Korea*, trans. Edward W. Wagner with Edward J. Shultz (Cambridge, MA: Harvard University Press, 1984). An authoritative general history by a leading Korean scholar, including an extensive annotated bibliography.

Peter Lee, ed., *Anthology of Korean Literature from Early Times to the Nineteenth Century* (Honolulu: University of Hawaii Press, 1981). An anthology of poetry and prose, intelligently introduced.

* Mikiso Hane, *Premodern Japan: A Historical Survey* (Boulder, CO: Westview Press, 1991). A textbook account attentive to social and cultural issues.

* William Theodore de Bary, *Sources of Japanese Tradition*, 2 vols. (New York: Columbia, 1964). An anthology of primary sources concentrating on intellectual history.

David John Lu, *Sources of Japanese History*, vol. 1 (New York: McGraw Hill, 1974). An anthology of primary sources concentrating on social history.

Edward Seidensticker, translator *The Tale of Genji* (New York: Knopf, 1976). A translation of the world's first novel.

Ivan Morris, *The World of the Shining Prince: Court Life in Ancient Japan* (New York: Knopf, 1964). An elegantly written description of life at the Heian court.

Karl F. Friday, *Hired Swords: The Rise of Private Warrior Power in Early Japan* (Stanford, CA: Stanford University Press, 1992). A readable revisionist account of the relationship of warrior and court in Heian history.

Richard Bowring, *Murasaki Shikibu, The Tale of Genji* (Cambridge, MA: Cambridge University Press, 1988). A discussion of the plot and context of the tenth-century novel and the woman who wrote it.

Norma Field, *The Splendor of Longing in the Tale of Genji* (Princeton, NJ: Princeton University Press, 1987).

Haruo Shirane, *The Bridge of Dreams: A Poetics of the Tale of Genji* (Stanford, CA: Stanford University Press, 1987).

* Indicates paperback edition available.

EFFECTUSQUE PIIS DAT STUDIIS HOMINUM QUOR

THE CHAPEL AT THE WATERS

The Palatine Chapel in Aachen, now a small German city near the Belgian border, brings together a fascination with the traditions of the Roman past with the creativity of a new epoch. These two strands describe Europe during the Middle Ages, generally the period between 500 and 1000. Aachen was a favorite residence of the Frankish king Charles the Great, or Charlemagne (768–814), who often came there to enjoy its natural hot springs. In time it came to be his primary residence, the capital of his vast kingdom, which stretched from central Italy to the mouth of the Rhine River. Around 792 Charlemagne, a descendant of barbarian warriors, commissioned an architect to design a palace complex as his residence, one that would rival the great Roman and Byzantine buildings of Italy and Constantinople.

Royal agents scoured Europe for Roman ruins from which columns, precious marble, and ornaments could be salvaged and reused. From these ancient stones masons raised a complex of audience rooms, royal apartments, baths, and quarters for court officials. The whole ensemble was intentionally reminiscent of the Lateran Palace in Rome, which had been the residence of the emperors before being given to the popes.

The central building of Charlemagne's palace complex was the chapel, a symmetrical octagon three hundred feet on its principal axes, modeled on San Vitale in Ravenna. The choice of model was significant. Ravenna had been the former capital of Roman Italy and of Theodoric the Great, the Ostrogothic king whom Charlemagne greatly admired. But although modeled on Roman buildings, the Palatine Chapel was admirably suited to the glorification of Charlemagne.

The building was divided into three tiers. The first tier on the ground floor held the sanctuary, where priest and people met for worship. The topmost tier, supported by ancient Roman pillars shipped to Aachen from Rome and Ravenna, represented the heavens. Between the two was a gallery connected by a passage to the royal residence. On this gallery sat the king's throne. From his seat, Charlemagne could look down upon the religious services being conducted below. Looking up to where he sat, worshipers were constantly reminded of the king's intermediary position between ordinary mortals and God. This architectural design boldly asserted that Charlemagne was more than a barbarian king. By 805 when the chapel was dedicated, he had made good this assertion. As a contemporary chronicler wrote, while in Rome in the year 800

> On the most holy day of Christmas, when the king rose from prayer in front of the shrine of the blessed apostle Peter to take part in the Mass, Pope Leo placed a crown on his head, and he was hailed by the whole Roman people . . . He was now called Emperor and Augustus.

Thus, to Charlemagne and to his supporters, this coronation ceremony revived the Roman Empire in the west. Charlemagne, with his vast empire and his imperial palace, was a true successor of the ancient Roman emperors. Like his chapel in Aachen (long after known as Aix-la-Chapelle, the chapel at the waters), this empire was built on the remains of Roman traditions grafted onto a vigorous tradition of Germanic kinship and society. According to the Byzantines, who looked on Charlemagne and his imperial coronation with alarm, the western empire could not be revived because it had never really ended. According to them, the death of the last western emperor Julius Nepos in 480 had ended the division of the empire. Since then, the Byzantine emperors had pretended that they ruled both east and west. Charlemagne's claims, made through the cere- mony in Rome and more subtly in the imperial architecture of his palace, represented to them not a revival of the empire but a threat to its existence.

The Making of the Barbarian Kingdoms

The existence of a united empire had long been only a dream. In the year 500, Emperor Anastasius I (491–518) could delude himself that, through appointed agents, he ruled the whole empire of Augustus, Diocletian, and Constantine, both east and west. This imperial unity was more apparent than real. The Italian governor was the Ostrogothic king Theodoric the Great (493–526), whose Roman title meant less than his Ostrogothic army. The imperial representative in the Rhone Valley was the Burgundian king Gondebaud (480–516). The Roman officer in Aquitaine and Spain was the Visigothic king Alaric II (485–507), and the Gallic consul was the Frankish king Clovis (482–511). Each of these rulers courted imperial titles and recognition, but none regarded Anastasius as his sovereign.

The Goths: From Success to Extinction

In the early sixth century all of the Germanic peoples within the old Roman Empire acknowledged the Goths as the most successful of the barbarian peoples. The Ostrogoths had created an Italian kingdom in which Romans and barbarians lived side by side. The Visigoths ruled Spain and southern Gaul by combining traditions of Roman law and barbarian military might. Yet neither Gothic kingdom endured more than two centuries.

Theodoric the Ostrogoth was the most cultivated, capable, and sophisticated barbarian ruler. He was also the most powerful. Burgundians, Visigoths, and Alemanni looked to him for leadership and protection.

Even Clovis, the ambitious Frankish king, usually bowed to his wishes. Theodoric had spent his teenage years as a pampered hostage in Constantinople. There he had learned to understand and admire Roman ways. Later, after he had conquered Italy at the head of his Gothic army, he established a dual government, which respected both the remains of Roman civil administration and Gothic military organization. Following Theodoric's death in 526, internal conflict over the succession paved the way for a protracted and devastating invasion by the Byzantines, which destroyed not only the Ostrogothic kingdom but also much of what remained of Roman Italy.

Italy was simply too close to Constantinople and too important for the ambitious Byzantine emperor Justinian I (527–65) to ignore. Encouraged by his easy victory over the Vandals, he sent an army into Italy, where he anticipated an easy reconquest of the peninsula. He got instead almost twenty years of vicious warfare. Not only were the Goths more formidable foes than he had expected, but when Roman tax collectors arrived with the Roman armies, Justinian found that the Italian people did not greet their "liberators" with open arms. In addition, in the midst of the reconquest a new and terrible disease appeared throughout the Mediterranean world. Over the next two centuries, the plague cut down as much as one-third of Europe's population.

The destruction of Italy by war and disease paved the way for its conquest by the Lombards. As allies in Justinian's army, some members of this Germanic tribe from along the Danube had learned first-hand of the riches of Italy. In 568 the whole Lombard people left the Carpathian basin to their neighbors, the Avars, and invaded the exhausted and war-torn Italian peninsula. By the end of the sixth century the Ostrogoths had

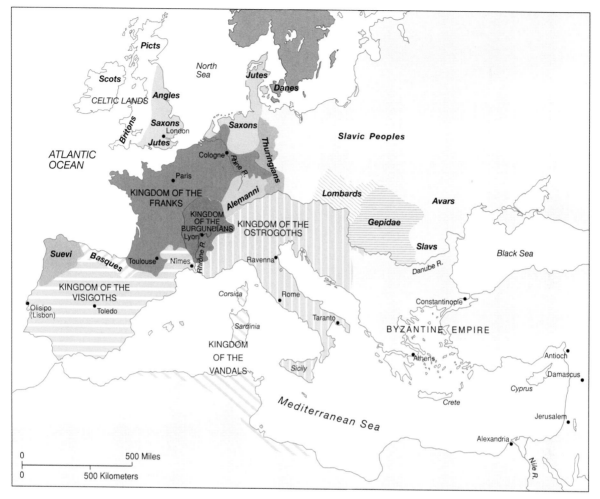

Barbarian Kingdoms

disappeared and the Byzantines retained only the heel and toe of the Italian boot and a narrow strip stretching from Ravenna to Rome. The Byzantine presence in Rome was weak and by default the popes, especially Gregory the Great (590–604), became the defenders and governors of the city. Gregory organized the resistance to the Lombards, fed the population during famines, and comforted them through the dark years of plague and warfare. A vigorous political as well as spiritual leader, he laid the foundations of the medieval papacy.

The Lombards largely eliminated the Roman tax system under which Italians had long suffered. They were less concerned with preserving their own cultural traditions than were the Ostrogoths, even in the sphere of religion. Initially many Lombards were Arians, but in the early seventh century the Lombard kings and their

followers accepted orthodox Christianity. This conversion paved the way for the unification of the society.

Rather than accepting a divided society as did the Ostrogoths or merging into an orthodox Roman culture as did the Lombards, the Visigoths of Gaul and Spain sought to unify the indigenous population of their kingdom through law and religion. Roman law deeply influenced Visigothic law codes and formed an enduring legal heritage to western Europe. Religious unity was a more difficult goal. The king's repeated attempts to force conversion to Arianism failed and created tension and mistrust. This mistrust proved fatal. In 507 Gallo-Roman aristocrats supported the Frankish king Clovis in his successful conquest of the Visigothic kingdom of Toulouse. Defeat drove the Visigoths deeper into Spain, where they gradually forged a unified kingdom

הַסּוֹחֵר רִיבָּנוֹ אָסַר תִּכְתּוֹב עַל הַכִּיס אוֹתוֹתַי אֶת שְׁמִי וְאֶת שֵׁם אֲבוֹתַי
... הַמָּעוֹת הֵים יָלְוְיִנ וּמִרְדָּם וַיֹּאמֶר הַנֵּע מַי חָפֵץ עַתָּה

A medieval manuscript showing Jews counting coins.

The Jews in the Early Middle Ages

The intolerance and persecution of Jews by the Visigoths was the exception rather than the rule in early medieval Europe. Since the diaspora, Jews had settled throughout Europe, primarily in towns. In Italy, Rome, Ravenna, and Pavia had important communities. In the Frankish kingdom Jews were particularly numerous in the southern cities of Lyons, Vienne, Arles, Marseille, and Narbonne, although Jewish communities could be found in more northern towns such as Orléans, Soissons, Nantes, Aachen and Frankfurt. In contrast with later practice, Jews appeared no different from their Christian neighbors. They spoke the same language, wore no distinctive clothing and occupied no designated section of town, or ghetto. Although they worshiped in their synagogues and studied in their yeshivas, they otherwise were very much integrated into the fabric of society.

Some Jews owned rural estates, where they cultivated vineyards and farms alongside their Christian neighbors. Jewish farmers and landowners were particularly common in the areas of Vienne, Mâcon, and Arles, where they appear in records of land transactions, buying selling and exchanging property with individuals and Christian churches. However, most Jews were merchants or practiced other urban professions such as goldsmithing or medicine. Some acted as tax collectors and emissaries for lay and ecclesiastical lords. The reasons for these specializations were obvious. First, Jewish communities in the west maintained ties with other Jews in the Byzantine and Muslim worlds, exchanging letters on religious and legal affairs and traveling back and forth. Second, while not frequent, sporadic attacks on Jews did occur. In the sixth century, for example, the Frankish king Chilperic (561–84) attempted to force Jews in his kingdom to be baptized. Thus Jews concentrated in occupations that allowed them to move easily and quickly in time of danger. Finally, the lack of interest in trade on the part of their Christian neighbors and the disappearance of Syriac and Greek merchants in the seventh century left long-distance commerce almost entirely in the hands of Jews. Royal documents speak frequently of "Jews and other merchants," implying that Gentile merchants were an unimportant minority.

Jewish merchants traveled widely, from Scandinavia to Iran, India, and even as far as China, exporting slaves, furs, and weapons and returning with such exotic luxuries as spices and silks. This trade was important to monarchs not only for supplies of luxuries, but also for the tariff income it provided. In the ninth century Jewish merchants were so vital to the empire of Louis the Pious that he granted them special privileges and took them under his royal protection. A palace official, the master of the Jews, was responsible for protecting them throughout the empire and appeals against them to the king usually were settled in the Jews' favor.

Not everyone was equally pleased with the tolerance shown this non-Christian minority. Bishop Agobard of Lyons (799–840) complained bitterly to Louis about his policy of tolerance. The bishop was particularly disturbed by the fact that, while few Jews could be persuaded to convert, in the area of Lyons many Christians found the sermons of rabbis preferable to those of their priests and that conversions to Judaism were becoming frequent.

The most celebrated conversion was that of Bodo, a young Frankish aristocrat raised in Louis' palace and educated in his school. In 838, while on what he had pretended to be a pilgrimage to Rome, he converted to Judaism, sold his entourage into slavery, married a young Jewish woman, and fled to Saragossa in Muslim Spain. From there he wrote scathing attacks on the immorality and doctrinal ignorance of the Christian clergy he had known in Aachen. Fourteen clerics there, he claimed, had held fourteen different opinions on their faith. Disgusted by what he considered to be the ignorance and idolatry of Christianity, he saw his conversion as a return to the worship of the one true God.

Christian churchmen were scandalized by Bodo and embarrassed by their inability to convert Jews through peaceful persuasion, but they were powerless to do anything about the situation. Traditional Christian doctrine asserted that the conversion of the Jews would be one of the signs of the end of the world. Until then, they had the right to toleration. Moreover, the early medieval world was one of many peoples, laws, and traditions. In a society in which different people in the same towns and even households might live according to Roman, Frankish, Gothic, or Burgundian law, Jews were but one more group with a distinct identity. Kings refused to limit the civil and religious rights of their Jewish subjects, forbade Christians to baptize Jewish slaves, and in general protected them as valued members of society. Only in the twelfth and thirteenth centuries, when monarchs began to centralize and unify the peoples they ruled, did systematic persecution and expulsion of Jews become the rule in western Europe.

TWO MISSIONARIES

■ *Bede (ca. 672–735) described in detail the two missionary movements in England. The first, led by Augustine of Canterbury, represented Roman traditions to which Bede himself was firmly attached. The second, led by Aidan (d. 651), represented the Irish traditions Bede opposed. And yet, he wrote vivid and contrasting descriptions of the character and styles of the two men.*

Those [British bishops] summoned [by Augustine] to this council first visited a wise and prudent hermit and enquired of him whether they should abandon their own Traditions and Augustine's demand. He answered: "If he is a man of God, follow him." "But how can we be sure of this?" they asked. "Our Lord says, Take my yoke upon you and learn of Me, for I am meek and lowly of heart," he replied. "Therefore if Augustine is meek and lowly in heart, it shows that he bears the yoke of Christ himself, and offers it to you. But if he is haughty and unbending, then he is not of God, and we should not listen to him. Arrange that he and his followers arrive first at the place appointed for the conference. If he rises courteously as you approach, rest assured that he is the servant of Christ and do as he asks. But if he ignores you and does not rise, then, since you are in the majority, do not comply with his demands."

The Bishops carried out his suggestion, and it happened that Augustine remained seated in his chair. Seeing this, they became angry, accusing him of pride and taking pains to contradict all that he said, . . . saying among themselves that if he would not rise to greet them in the first instance, he would have even less regard for them once they submitted to his authority.

Later, Bede describes Aidan's approach to spreading the word of God:

He never sought or cared for any worldly possessions, and loved to give away to the poor who chanced to meet him whatever he received from kings or wealthy folk. Whether in town or country, he always travelled on foot unless compelled by necessity to ride; and whatever people he met on his walks, whether high or low, he stopped and spoke to them. If they were heathen, he urged them to be baptized; and if they were Christians, he strengthened their faith, and inspired them by word and deed to live a good life and to be generous to others . . . He cultivated peace and love, purity and humility; he was above anger and greed, and despised pride and conceit; he set himself to keep as well as to teach the laws of God, and was diligent in study and prayer. He used his priestly authority to check the proud and powerful.

From Bede, *A History of the English Church and People.*

---

based on Roman administrative tradition and Visigothic kingship.

The long-sought-after religious unity was finally achieved when King Recared (586–601) and along with him the Gothic aristocracy embraced orthodox Christianity. This conversion further blurred the differences between Visigoths and Roman provincials in the kingdom. It also initiated an unprecedented use of the Church and its ideology to strengthen the monarchy. Visigothic kings modeled themselves after the Byzantine emperors, proclaimed themselves new Constantines, and used Church councils, held regularly at Toledo, as governing assemblies. Still, rivalry within the aristocracy weakened the kingdom and left it vulnerable

to attack from without. In 711 Muslims from North Africa invaded and quickly conquered the Visigothic kingdom. Jews rejoiced in the religious toleration brought by Islam, and many members of the Christian elite converted to Islam and retained their positions of authority under the new regime. (See Special Feature, "The Jews in the Early Middle Ages," pp. 258–259.)

The Anglo-Saxons: From Pagan Conquerors to Christian Missionaries

The motley collection of Saxons, Angles, Jutes, Frisians, Suebians, and others who came to Britain as federated troops and stayed on as rulers did not coalesce into a united kingdom until almost the eleventh century. Instead, these Germanic warriors carved out small kingdoms for themselves, enslaving or absorbing most of the Romanized Britons and driving others into Wales. Unlike the Goths, none of these peoples had previously been integrated into the Roman world. Thus rather than fusing Roman and Germanic traditions, they largely eradicated the former. Urban life disappeared and with it the Roman traditions of administration, taxation, and culture.

In their place developed a world whose central values were honor and glory, whose primary occupation was fighting, and whose economic system was based on plunder and the open-handed distribution of riches. This was a society dominated by petty kings and their aristocratic war leaders. These invaders were not, like

FROM SLAVE TO QUEEN

■ *Queen Balthild (d. ca. 680), an Anglo-Saxon woman captured and sold into slavery in Francia, became the wife of Clovis II, king of Neustria and Burgundy (639–657). Her career, including her regency for her son Clothar III and eventual forced retirement to the monastery she had founded at Chelles is typical of the complex role and reputation early medieval queens enjoyed. This laudatory account, which was probably written by a nun at Chelles, hints that she was forced into the convent by opposition to her political role.*

Divine Providence called her from across the seas. She, who came here as God's most precious and lofty pearl, was sold at a cheap price. Erchinoald, a Frankish magnate and most illustrious man, acquired her and in his service the girl behaved most honorably. She gained such happy fame that, when the said lord Erchinoald's wife died, he hoped to unite himself to Balthild, that faultless virgin, in a matronal bed. But when she heard this, she fled and most swiftly took herself out of his sight. Thereafter it happened, with God's approval, that Balthild, the maid who escaped marriage with a lord, came to be espoused to Clovis, son of the former king Dagobert. Thus by virtue of her humility she was raised to a higher rank.

She acted as a mother to the princes, as a daughter to priests, and as a most pious nurse to children and adolescents. She distributed generous alms to every one. She guarded the princes' honor by keeping their intimate counsels secret. In accordance with God's will, her husband King Clovis migrated from the body and left his sons with their mother. Immediately after him her son Clothar took up the kingdom of the Franks, maintaining peace in the realm. Then, to promote peace, by command of Lady Balthild with the advice of the other elders, the people of Austrasia accepted her son Childeric as their king and the Burgundians were united with the Franks. And we believe, under God's ordinance, that these three realms then held peace and concord among themselves because of Lady Balthild's great faith. She proclaimed that no payment could be exacted for receipt of a sacred rank. Moreover, she ordained that yet another evil custom should cease, namely that many people determined to kill their children rather than nurture them, for they feared to incur the public exactions which were heaped upon them by custom, which caused great damage to their affairs.

It was her holy intention to enter the monastery of religious women which she had built at Chelles. But the Franks delayed much for love of her and would not have permitted this to happen except that there was a commotion made by the wretched Bishop Sigobrand whose pride among the Franks, earned him his mortal ruin. Indeed, they formed a plan to kill him against her will. Fearing that the lady would act heavily against them, and wish to avenge him, they suddenly relented and permitted her to enter the monastery.

From the *Life of the Blessed Queen Balthild*.

the Goths, just a military elite. They also included free farmers who absorbed the Romanized British peasantry, introducing their language, agricultural techniques, social organization, and folkloric traditions to the southeastern part of the island. These ordinary settlers, much more than the kings and aristocrats, were responsible for the gradual transformation of Britain into England.

The Anglo-Saxons were pagans, and although Christianity survived, the relationship between conquered and conquerors did not provide a climate conducive to conversion. Christianity came largely from without. The conversion of England resulted from a two-part effort. The first originated in Ireland, the most western society of Europe, little touched by Greco-Roman civilization. Ireland had never formed part of the Roman Empire and thus had never adopted the forms of urban life and centralized, hierarchal government or religion characteristic of Britain and the Continent. In the fifth century merchants and missionaries introduced an eastern, monastic form of Christianity to Ireland, which adapted easily to the rural, tribal organization of Irish society. Although Irish Christianity was entirely orthodox in its beliefs, the isolation of Ireland led to the development of numerous practices at odds with those common to Constantinople and Rome. Thus, although Ireland had important bishops, the most influential churchmen were powerful abbots of strict, ascetic monasteries, closely connected with tribal chieftains, who directed the religious life of their regions. Around 565 the Irish monk Columba (521–97) established a monastery on the island of Iona off the coast of Scotland. From there wandering Irish monks began to convert northern Britain.

The second effort at Christianizing Britain began with Pope Gregory the Great. In 596 he sent the missionary Augustine (known as Augustine of Canterbury to distinguish him from the bishop of Hippo) to attempt to convert the English. Augustine laid the foundations for a hierarchal, bishop-centered church based on the Roman model. In time the pagan king Ethelbert (560–616) and much of his southwest kingdom of Kent accepted Christianity, and Augustine was named Archbishop of Canterbury by the pope.

As Irish missionaries spread south from Iona and Roman missionaries moved north from Canterbury, their efforts created in England two opposing forms of orthodox Christianity. One was Roman, episcopal, and hierarchal. The other was Irish, monastic, and decentralized. King Oswy of Northumbria (d. 670) called an episcopal meeting, or *synod*, in 664 at Whitby to settle the issue. After hearing arguments from both sides, Oswy accepted the customs of the Roman Church, thus allying himself and ultimately all of Anglo-Saxon England with the centralized, hierarchal form of Christianity, which could be used to strengthen his monarchy.

During the century and a half following the Synod of Whitby, Anglo-Saxon Christian civilization blossomed. Contact with the European mainland and especially with Rome increased. The monasteries of Monkwearmouth and Jarrow became centers of learning, culminating in the writings of Bede (673–735), the greatest scholar of his century. His history of the English church and people is the finest historical work of the early Middle Ages.

The Franks: An Enduring Legacy

In the fourth century various small Germanic tribes along the Rhine coalesced into a loose confederation known as the Franks. A significant group of them, the Salians, made the mistake of attacking Roman garrisons

A portrait of Bede, known as The Venerable. This illustration is from a manuscript of his Vita Sancti Cuthberti. *Bede's* Ecclesiastical History of the English Nation *earned him the title Father of English History.*

and were totally defeated. The Romans resettled the Salians in a largely abandoned region of what is now Belgium and Holland. There they formed a buffer to protect Roman colonists from other Germanic tribes and provided a ready supply of recruits for the Roman army. During the fourth and fifth centuries, these Salian Franks and their neighbors assumed an increasingly important role in the military defense of Gaul and began to spread out of their "reservation" into more settled parts of the province. Although many high-ranking Roman officers of the fourth century were Franks, most were neither conquerors nor members of the military elite. They were rather soldier-farmers who settled beside the local Roman peoples they protected.

In 486 Clovis, leader of the Salian Franks and commander of the barbarized Roman army, staged a successful coup (possibly with the approval of the Byzantine emperor), defeating and killing Syagrius, the last Roman commander in the west. Although Clovis ruled the Franks as king, he worked closely with the existing Gallo-Roman aristocracy as he consolidated his control over various Frankish factions and over portions of Gaul and Germany held by other barbarian kingdoms. Clovis's early conversion to orthodox Christianity paved the way for assimilation of Franks and Romans into a new society.

The mix of Frankish warriors and Roman aristocrats spread rapidly across western Europe. Clovis and his successors absorbed the Visigothic kingdom of Toulouse, the Thuringians, and the kingdom of the Burgundians, and expanded Frankish hegemony through modern Bavaria and south of the Alps into northern Italy. Unlike other barbarian kingdoms such as those of the Huns or Ostrogoths, which evaporated almost as soon as their great founders died, the Frankish synthesis was enduring. Although the dynasty established by Clovis, called the Merovingian after a legendary ancestor, lasted only until the mid-eighth century, the Frankish kingdom was the direct ancestor of both France and Germany.

With the establishment of the barbarian kingdoms, the theoretical unity of the western empire was forever destroyed. Within each of these smaller polities, rulers and ruled began forging from their complex Roman and Germanic traditions a new cultural synthesis.

Europe Transformed

The substitution of Germanic kings for imperial officials made few obvious differences in the lives of most inhabitants of Italy, Gaul, and Spain. The vast majority of Europeans were poor farmers whose lives centered on their fields and villages. For them the seasons in the agricultural year, the burdens of rent and taxation, and the frequent poor harvests, food shortages, famines, and epidemics were more important than empires and kingdoms. Nevertheless, fundamental if imperceptible changes were transforming ordinary life. These changes took place at every level of society. The slaves and semi-free peasants of Rome gradually began to form new kinds of social groups and to practice new forms of agriculture as they merged with the Germanic warrior-peasants. Elite Gallo-Roman landowners came to terms with their Frankish conquerors, and these two groups began to coalesce into a single, unified aristocracy. In the same way that Germanic and Roman society began to merge, Germanic and Roman traditions of governance united between the sixth and eighth centuries to create a powerful new kind of medieval kingdom.

Creating the European Peasantry

Three fundamental changes transformed rural society during the early Middle Ages. First, Roman slavery virtually disappeared. Next, the household emerged as the primary unit of social and economic organization. Finally, Christianity spread throughout the rural world. Economics, not ethics, destroyed Roman slavery. In the kind of slavery typical of the Roman world, large gangs of slaves were housed in dormitories and directed in large-scale operations by overseers. This form of slavery demanded a highly organized form of estate management and could be quite costly, since slaves had to be fed and housed year-round. Since slaves did not always reproduce at a rate sufficient to replace themselves, the supply had to be replenished from without. However, as the empire ceased to expand, the supply of fresh captives dwindled. As cities shrank, many markets for agricultural produce disappeared, making market-oriented, large-scale agriculture less profitable.

As a result, from the sixth through the ninth centuries, owners abandoned the practice of keeping gang slaves in favor of the less complicated practice of establishing slave families on individual plots of land. The slaves and their descendants cultivated these plots, made annual payments to their owners, and also cultivated the undivided portions of the estate, the fruits of which went directly to the owner. Thus slaves became something akin to sharecroppers. Gradually they began to intermarry with colons and others who, though nominally free, faced an economic situation much like that of slaves. By the tenth and eleventh centuries, peasant farmers throughout much of Europe were subject to the private justice of their landlords, regardless of whether their ancestors had been slave or free.

The division of estates into separate peasant holdings contributed to the second fundamental transformation of European peasant society: the formation of the household. Neither the Roman tradition of slave agriculture nor the Germanic tradition of clan organization had fostered the household as the basic unit of society. Now individual slaves and their spouses were placed on manses, which they and their children were expected to cultivate. The household had become the basic unit of western European economy.

The household was, however, more than an economic unit. It was also the first level of government. The head of the household, whether slave or free, male or female—women, particularly widows, were often heads of households—exercised authority over its other members. This authority made the householder a link in the chain of the social order, which stretched from the peasant hovel to the royal court. Households became the basic form of peasant life, but not all peasants could expect to establish their own household. The number of manses was limited, a factor that condemned many men and women to life within the household of a more fortunate relative or neighbor.

Peasant culture, like peasant society, experienced a fundamental transformation during the early Middle Ages: the peasantry became Christian. Christianity penetrated deeply into rural society with the systematic establishment of parishes, or rural churches. By the ninth century this parish system began to cover Europe. Bishops founded parish churches in the villages of large estates, and owners were obligated to set aside one-tenth of the produce of their estates for the maintenance of the parish church. The priests who staffed these churches came from the local peasantry and received a basic education in Latin and in Christian ritual from their predecessors and from their bishops. Through the village priests and the parish system, European folklife began to take on Christian values and beliefs.

"The labors of the months" was a popular motif in medieval art. This illustration from the Astronomical Notices *was found in Salzburg. The annual round of agricultural tasks, such as sowing, reaping, and threshing, vine dressing and grape picking, and the autumn slaughter of pigs are depicted along with scenes of hunting and hawking.*

Creating the European Aristocracy

At the same time that a homogeneous peasantry was emerging from the blend of slaves and free farmers, a homogeneous aristocracy was evolving out of the mix of Germanic and Roman traditions. In Germanic society, the elite had owed its position to a combination of inherited status and wealth, perpetuated through military command. Families who produced great military commanders were thought to have a special war-luck granted by the gods. The war-luck bestowed on men and women of these families a near-sacred legitimacy. This legitimacy made the aristocrats largely independent of their kings. In times of war kings might command, but otherwise the extent to which they could be said to govern aristocrats was minimal.

The Roman aristocracy was also based on inheritance, but of land rather than leadership. During the third and fourth centuries Roman aristocrats' control of land extended over the persons who worked that land. At the same time, great landowners were able to free themselves from provincial government. Like their Germanic counterparts, Roman aristocrats acquired a sacred legitimacy, but within the Christian tradition. They monopolized the office of bishop and became identified with the sacred and political traditions associated with the Church. Between the sixth and tenth centuries these two traditions merged.

This scene is from the lid of the Franks Casket, a whalebone box that was made in the north of England at the beginning of the eighth century. The carving depicts Egil the Archer defending his home. The other sides of the box are carved with a mixture of Christian and pagan scenes.

The aristocratic lifestyle focused on feasting, on hospitality, and on the male activities of hunting and warfare. During the fall and winter, aristocratic men spent much of their time hunting deer and wild boar in their forests. In March, aristocrats gathered their retainers, who had enjoyed their winter hospitality, and marched to war. The enemy varied. It might be rival families with whom feuds were nursed for generations. It might be raiding parties from a neighboring region. Or the warriors might join a royal expedition led by the king and directed against a rival kingdom. Whoever the enemy, warfare brought the promise of booty and, equally important, glory.

Within this aristocratic society women played a wider and more active role than had been the case in either Roman or barbarian antiquity. In part women's new role was due to the influence of Christianity, which recognized the distinct—though always inferior—rights of women, fought against the barbarian tradition of allowing chieftains numerous wives, and recognized women's right to lead a cloistered religious life. In addition, the combination of Germanic and Roman familial traditions permitted women to participate in court proceedings, to inherit and dispose of property, and, if widowed, to serve as tutors and guardians for their minor children. Finally, the long absence of men at the hunt, at the royal court, or on military expeditions left wives in charge of the domestic scene for months or years at a time. The religious life in particular opened to aristocratic women possibilities of autonomy and authority previously unknown in Europe.

Governing Europe

The combination in the early Middle Ages of the extremes of centralized Roman power and fragmented barbarian organization produced a wide variety of governmental systems. At one end of the spectrum were the politically fragmented Celtic and Slavic societies. At the other end were the Frankish kingdoms, in which descendants of Clovis, drawing on the twin heritages of Roman institutions and Frankish tradition, attempted not simply to reign but to rule.

Rulers and aristocrats both needed and feared each other. Kings had emerged out of the Germanic aristocracy and could rule only in cooperation with aristocrats. Aristocrats were primarily concerned with maintaining and expanding their own spheres of control and independence. They perceived royal authority over them or their dependents as a threat. Still, they needed kings. Strong kings brought victory against external foes and thus maintained the flow of booty to the aristocracy. Aristocrats in turn redistributed the spoils of war among their followers to preserve the bonds of warrior society. Thus under capable kings aristocrats were ready to cooperate, not as subjects but as partners.

As heirs of Roman governmental tradition, kings sought to incorporate these traditions into their roles. By absorbing the remains of local administration and taxation, kings acquired nascent governmental systems. Through the use of written documents, Roman scribes expanded royal authority beyond the king's household and personal following. Tax collectors continued to fill royal coffers with duties collected in markets and ports.

Finally, by assuming the role of protector of the Church, kings acquired the support of educated and experienced ecclesiastical advisors and the right to intervene in disputes involving clergy and laity. Further, as defenders of the Church, kings could claim a responsibility for the preservation of peace and the administration of justice—two fundamental Christian (but also Roman) tasks.

Early medieval kings had no fixed capitals from which they governed. Instead they were constantly on the move, supervising their kingdoms and consuming the produce of their estates. Since kings could not be everywhere at once, they were represented locally by aristocrats who enjoyed royal favor. In the Frankish world these favorites were called *counts* and their districts *counties*. In England royal representatives were termed *ealdormen* and their regions were known as *shires*. Whether counts or ealdormen, these representatives were military commanders and judicial officers drawn from aristocratic families close to the king. Under competent and effective kings, partnership with these aristocratic families worked well. Under less competent rulers and during the reigns of minors, these families often managed to turn their districts into hereditary, almost autonomous regions.

Thus at both ends of the social spectrum, Germanic and Roman traditions and institutions were combining to create a new society, organized not by nationality or ethnicity but by status and united by shared religious values and political leadership.

The Carolingians and the New Europe

The Merovingian dynasty initiated by Clovis presided over the synthesis of Roman and Germanic society. It was left to the Carolingians who followed to forge a new Europe. In the seventh century, members of the new aristocracy were able to take advantage of royal minorities and dynastic rivalries to make themselves into virtual rulers of their small territories. By the end of the century the kings had become little more than symbolic figures in the Frankish kingdoms. The real power was held by regional strongmen called dukes. The most successful of these aristocratic factions was led by Charles Martel (ca. 688–741) and his heirs, known as the Carolingians.

Charles Martel was ruthless, ambitious, and successful. He crushed rivals in his own family, subdued competing dukes, and united the Frankish realm. He was

successful in part because he molded the Frankish cavalry into the most effective military force of the time. His mounted, heavily armored warriors were extremely effective but extremely costly. He financed them with property confiscated from his enemies.

Charles Martel looked beyond military power to the control of religious and cultural institutions. He supported Anglo-Saxon missionaries such as Boniface (ca. 680–755), who were trying to introduce on the mainland the Roman form of Christianity they knew in England. This hierarchal style of Christianity served Carolingian interests in centralization, especially since Charles appointed his loyal supporters as bishops and abbots. Missionaries and Frankish armies worked hand in hand to consolidate Carolingian rule.

The ecclesiastical policy that proved most crucial to later Carolingians was Charles's support of the Roman papacy. Charles caught the attention of Pope Gregory III (731–41) in 732, when he defeated a Muslim raiding party near Tours, which had appeared to threaten the northward expansion of Islam. A few years later, when the pope needed protection from the Lombards to maintain his central Italian territories, he sought and obtained help from the Frankish leader.

The alliance with the papacy solidified during the lifetime of Charles's son Pippin (ca. 714–68). Pippin inherited his father's power. However, since he was not of the royal Merovingian family, he had no more right to supreme authority than any other powerful aristocrat. Pippin needed more than the power of a king: he needed the title. No Frankish tradition provided a precedent by which a rival family might displace the Merovingians. Pippin turned instead to the pope. With the cooperation of Pope Zacharias (741–52) Pippin deposed the last Merovingian and in 751 a representative of the pope anointed Pippin king of the Franks. The alliance between the new dynasty and the papacy marked the first union of royal legitimacy and ecclesiastical sanction in European history.

Charlemagne and the Renewal of the Western Empire

Pippin's son Charlemagne was the heir of the political, religious, and social revolutions begun by his grandfather and father. He was a conqueror, but he was also a religious reformer, a state builder, and a patron of the arts. As the leader of a powerful, united Frankish kingdom for over forty years, Charlemagne changed western Europe more profoundly than anyone since Augustus.

He subdued the Aquitainians and Bavarians, conquered the kingdom of the Lombards and assumed the title of King of the Lombards, crushed the Saxons, annexed the Spanish region of Catalonia, and destroyed the vast Pannonian kingdom of the Avars. In wars of aggression, his armies were invincible. Not only were they better armed and mounted, but their ability to transport men and material great distances was unmatched.

War booty fueled Charlemagne's renewal of European culture. As a Christian king he considered it his duty to reform the spiritual life of his kingdom and to bring it into line with his concept of the divinely willed order. To achieve this goal, he needed a dedicated and educated clergy. Most of the native clergy were poorly educated and indifferent in their observance of the rules of religious life. Charlemagne recruited leading intellectuals from England, Spain, Ireland, and Italy to the royal court to lead a thorough educational program. He supported schools in great monasteries such as Fulda and St. Gall for the training of young clerics and laymen. Schools needed books, and Charlemagne's educational reformers scoured Italy for fading copies of works by Virgil, Horace, and Tacitus.

The reformers of this era laid the necessary foundation for what has been called the Carolingian renaissance. Their successors in the ninth century built on this foundation to make creative contributions in theology, philosophy, and historiography, and to some extent in literature. The pursuit of learning was not a purely clerical affair. In the later ninth century, great aristocrats both male and female were highly literate and collected their own personal libraries.

Educational reform went hand in hand with reform of ecclesiastical institutions. Charlemagne and his son Louis the Pious (814–40) worked to establish the Benedictine rule as the norm for monastic life and to reform the parish clergy. The goal was a purified and organized clergy performing its essential role of celebrating Christian ritual and praying for the Frankish king. At the same time, the monasteries were to provide competent clerics to serve the royal administration at every level. These reforms were expensive, and the fiscal reorganization of ecclesiastical institutions was as far-reaching as their cultural reform. For the first time, Frankish synods or councils made tithing mandatory, specifying that one-tenth of all agricultural harvests were to go to the Church. Reform took on new life in 909 with the foundation of the monastery of Cluny in eastern France. Inspired by the monastic program of Louis the Pious and granted immunity from secular interference, Cluny became the center of the expansion of Benedictine monasticism throughout western Europe.

Carolingian Government

Charlemagne recognized that conquest alone could not unify his enormous kingdom with its vast differences in languages, laws, customs, and peoples. The glue that held it together was loyalty to him and to the Roman Church. He appointed as counts throughout Europe members of the great Frankish families who had been loyal to his family for generations. Thus he created what might be termed an "imperial aristocracy" truly international in scope. In addition to supervising the royal estates in their counties, each spring these counts led the local military contingent, which included all the free men of the county. Counts also presided over local courts,

The Carolingian Empire, ca. 800.

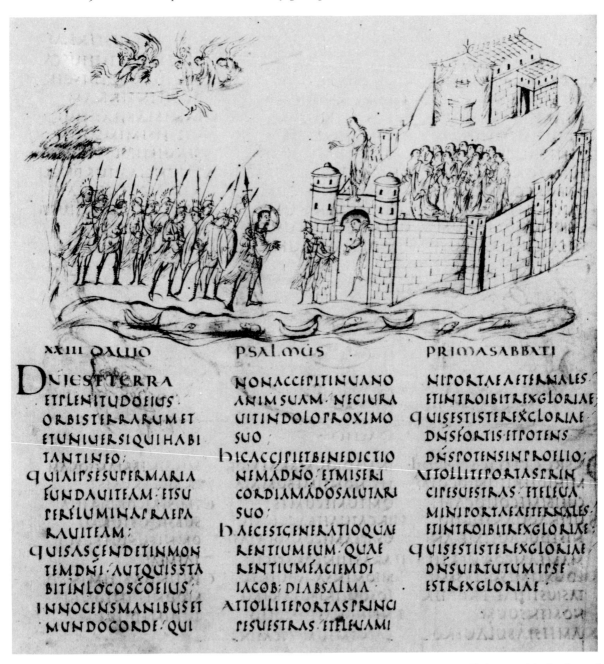

The Twenty-fourth Psalm (Twenty-third in the Vulgate), from the Utrecht Psalter, Reims, *made in about 820. The imagery of the drawings and the arrangement of the script on the page recall models from late antiquity.*

which exercised jurisdiction over the free persons of the county. The king maintained his control over the counts by sending teams of emissaries, or *missi dominici*, composed of bishops and counts to examine the state of each county.

Charlemagne recognized that while his representatives might be drawn from Frankish families, he could not impose Frankish legal and cultural traditions on all his subjects. The only universal system that might unify the kingdom was Roman Christianity. Unity of religious practices, directed by the reformed and educated clergy, would provide spiritual unity.

Carolingian government was no modern bureaucracy or state system. The laymen and clerics who served the

CHARLEMAGNE AND THE ARTS

■ *According to Charlemagne's biographer, Einhard, the emperor not only fostered education in others but he himself took an active interest in studies. In the following passage, Einhard describes the king's own educational program, the breadth of his interests, and his mixed results. The description should be taken with some caution, however. For example, his interest in astronomy and his practice of keeping writing materials in his bed (presumably to record his dreams) may indicate more his interest in astrology and divination than in the study of the liberal arts.*

Charles had the gift of ready and fluent speech, and could express whatever he had to say with the utmost clearness. He was not satisfied with command of his native language merely, but gave attention to the study of foreign ones, and in particular was such a master of Latin that he could speak it as well as his native tongue; but he could understand Greek better than he could speak it. He was so eloquent, indeed, that he might have passed for a teacher of eloquence. He most zealously cultivated the liberal arts, held those who taught them in great esteem, and conferred great honors upon them. He took lessons in grammar of the deacon Peter of Pisa, at that time an aged man. Another deacon, Albin of Britain, surnamed Alcuin, a man of Saxon extraction, who was the greatest scholar of the day, was his teacher in other branches of learning. The King spent much time and labor with him studying rhetoric, dialectics, and especially astronomy; he learned to reckon, and used to investigate the motions of the heavenly bodies most curiously, with an intelligent scrutiny. He also tried to write, and used to keep tablets and blanks in bed under his pillow, that at leisure hours he might accustom his hand to form the letters; however, as he did not begin his efforts in due season, but late in life, they met with ill success.

From Einhard, *The Life of Charlemagne.*

---

king were tied to him by personal oaths of loyalty rather than by any sense of dedication to a state or nation. Still, the attempts at governmental organization were far more sophisticated than anything that western Europe had seen for four centuries or would see again for another four. The system of counts and missi provided the most effective system of government prior to the thirteenth century and served as the model for subsequent medieval rulers.

The size of Charlemagne's empire approached that of the old Roman Empire in the west. Only Britain, southern Italy, and parts of Spain remained outside Frankish control. With the reunification of most of western Europe and the creative adaptation of Roman traditions of culture and government, it is not surprising that Charlemagne's advisors began to compare his empire to that of Constantine. This comparison was accentuated by Charlemagne's conquest of Lombard Italy and his protection of Pope Leo III—a role traditionally played by the Byzantine emperors. By the end of the eighth century the throne in Constantinople was held by a woman. Irene (752–802) was powerful and capable, but male leaders in the Frankish kingdom considered her unfit for such an office by reason of her sex. All these factors finally converged in one of the most momentous events in Western political history: Charlemagne's imperial coronation on Christmas Day in the year 800.

Historians debate the precise meaning of this event, particularly since Charlemagne was said to have remarked afterward that he would never have entered St. Peter's Basilica in Rome had he known what was going to happen. Presumably he meant that he wished to be proclaimed emperor by his Frankish people rather than by the pope, since this is how he had his son Louis the Pious acclaimed emperor in 813. Nevertheless, the imperial coronation of 800 subsequently took on great significance. Louis attempted to make his imperial title the sole basis for his rule, and for centuries Germanic kings traveled to Rome to receive the imperial diadem and title from the pope. In so doing they inadvertently strengthened papal claims to enthrone—and at times to dethrone—emperors.

After the Carolingians: From Empire to Lordships

Charlemagne, despite his imperial title, had remained dependent on his traditional power base, the Frankish aristocracy. For them, learned concepts of imperial renovation meant little. They wanted wealth and power. Under Charlemagne, the empire's prosperity and relative internal peace had resulted largely from continued, successful expansion at the expense of neighbors. Its economy had been based on the redistribution of war booty among the aristocracy and wealthy churches. But in the ninth and tenth centuries, new threats to the security of western Europe arose with the advent of the Vikings and the Magyars. The Vikings, or Northmen, burst out of Scandinavia to terrorize coastal areas all around the shores of Europe and the British Isles. They established settlements in Ireland, Britain, Normandy, and in what is today Russia and Ukraine. The Magyars, or Hungarians, came from the eastern steppes. They took over part of Pannonia and raided into the Carolingian empire, while Saracen Muslims from Spain and North Africa raided the northern Mediterranean coast. As wars of conquest under Charlemagne gave place to defensive actions against Magyars, Vikings, and Saracens, the supply of wealth dried up. Aristocratic supporters were rewarded with estates within the empire and thus became enormously wealthy and powerful.

Competition among Charlemagne's descendants as well as grants to the aristocracy weakened central authority. By fate rather than by design, Charlemagne had bequeathed a united empire to his son Louis the Pious (814–40). Charlemagne had intended to follow Frankish custom and divide his estate among all his sons but only Louis survived him. Louis's three sons, in contrast, fought one another over their inheritance, and in 843 they divided the empire among them. The eldest son, Lothair (840–55), who inherited his father's imperial title, received an unwieldy middle portion that stretched from the Rhine south through Italy. Louis the German (840–876) received the eastern portions of the empire. The youngest son, Charles the Bald (840–77), was allotted the western portions. In time this West Frankish kingdom became France, and the eastern Frankish kingdom became the core of Germany. The middle kingdom, which included modern Holland, Belgium, Luxembourg, Lorraine, Switzerland, and northern Italy, remained a disputed region into the twentieth century.

The disintegration of the empire meant much more than its division among Charlemagne's heirs. In no region were his successors able to provide the degree of

Division of Charlemagne's Empire

peace and public control that he had established. The Frankish armies, designed for offensive wars, were too clumsy and slow to defend against the lightning raids of Northmen, Magyars, and Saracens. The constant need to please aristocratic supporters made it impossible for kings to prevent aristocrats from absorbing free peasants and churches into their economic and political spheres. Increasingly, these magnates were able to transform the offices of count and bishop into inherited familial positions. They also determined who would reign in their kingdoms and sought kings who posed no threat to themselves.

Most aristocrats saw this greater autonomy as their just due. Only dukes, counts, and other local lords could organize resistance to internal and external foes at the local level. They needed both economic means and political authority to provide protection and maintain peace. These resources could be acquired only at the expense of royal power. Thus during the late ninth and tenth centuries, much of Europe found its equilibrium at the local level as public powers, judicial courts, and military authority became the private possession of wealthy families.

Ultimately, new royal families emerged from among these local leaders. The family of the counts of Paris, for example, gained enormous prestige from the fact that

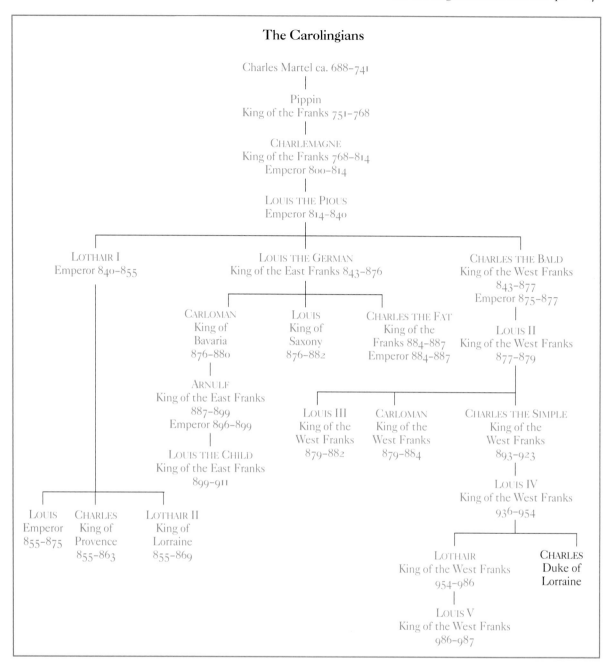

they had led the successful defense of the city against the Vikings in 885–86. For a time they alternated with Carolingians as kings of the West Franks. After the ascension of Hugh Capet in 987, they entirely replaced the Carolingians.

In a similar manner, the eastern Frankish kingdom, which was divided into five great duchies, began to elect non-Carolingians as kings. In 919 the dukes of this region elected as their king Duke Henry of Saxony (919–36), who had proven his abilities fighting the Danes and Magyars. Henry's son, Otto the Great (936–73), proved to be a strong ruler who subdued the other dukes and definitively crushed the Magyars. In 962 Otto was crowned emperor by Pope John XII (955–64), thus reviving the empire of Charlemagne, although only in its eastern half. However, the dukes of this eastern kingdom chafed constantly at the strong control the Ottonians attempted to exercise at their expense. Although the empire Otto reestablished endured until 1806 as the Holy Roman Empire, he and his successors never matched the political or cultural achievements of the Carolingians. It remained a loosely united amalgam of Germanic, Slavic, and Italian territories and principalities, and imperial authority seldom proved effective outside the power base of the current emperor's own family.

By the tenth century, the early medieval kingdoms, based on inherited Roman notions of universal states and barbarian traditions of charismatic military leadership, had all ended in failure. However, although western Europe was not united politically, the separate regions shared the cultural and institutional heritage of the Carolingians. After the demise of the Carolingian empire, western Europe began to develop this common heritage to create stability at a more local but also more permanent level.

Society and Culture in the High Middle Ages

The economic, social, and cultural transformations of Europe during the centuries that followed the collapse of the Carolingian empire were as profound as the political transformations of that period. The demographic upsurge of the tenth and eleventh centuries, the revolution redirecting agriculture toward markets rather than subsistence, the rebirth of towns and the development of complex commercial networks transformed the lives of Europeans everywhere. As peasants emerged from servitude and established autonomous social and cultural traditions, aristocrats wove together strands of Christianity and the warrior ethos to create an enduring social stratum whose values dominated elite ideology until the twentieth century. The increase in literacy and in the institutions of higher learning contributed to new visions of the relationship among people and between people and God.

The Peasantry: Serfs and Free

From the tenth through the thirteenth centuries enormous transformations re-created the rural landscape of Europe. The most significant of these changes concerned the peasantry, but they are difficult to chronicle since until the nineteenth century the majority of the common people left no record of their lives.

By the tenth century the population of Europe was growing, and with this population growth came new forms of social organization and economic activity. Between the years 1000 and 1300 Europe's population almost doubled, from approximately 38 million to 74 million. Various reasons have been proposed for this growth. Perhaps the end of the Viking, Magyar, and Saracen raids left rural society in relative peace to live and reproduce. The decline of slavery meant that individual peasant families could grow and reproduce themselves without constraints imposed by masters. Gradually improving agricultural techniques and equipment lessened somewhat the constant danger of famine. Possibly, too, a slowly improving climate increased agricultural yields. None of these explanations are entirely satisfactory. Whatever the cause of the population growth, it changed the face of Europe.

During the tenth century the great forests that had covered most of Europe began to be cut back as population spread out from the islands of cultivation. The peasants who engaged in the opening of this internal frontier were the descendants of the slaves, unfree farmers, and petty free persons of the early Middle Ages. In the east along the frontier of the Germanic empire, in the Slavic world, in Scandinavia, in southern Gaul, in northern Italy, and in the reconquered portions of Christian Spain, they

In this medieval farmstead newly cut from the forest, men beat acorns out of the trees for the pigs to eat while horses wearing collars pull the plow. Note the fenced-in vegetable garden at the right.

were free persons who owned land, entered into contracts with magnates, and remained responsible for their own fates. Across much of northwestern Europe, and in particular in France in the course of the eleventh century, the various gradations in status disappeared, and the peasantry formed a homogeneous social category termed "serfs." Their degraded status, their limited or nonexistent access to public courts of law, and their enormous dependency on their lords left them in a situation similar to that of those Carolingian slaves settled on individual farmsteads in the ninth century. Each year, peasants had to hand over to their lords certain fixed portions of their meager harvests. In addition, they were obligated to work a certain number of days on the *demesne,* or reserve of the lord, the produce of which went directly to him for his use or sale. Finally, they were required to make ritual payments symbolizing their subordination.

The expansion of arable land offered new hope and opportunities to peasants. As rapid as it was, between the tenth and twelfth centuries population growth did not keep up with the demand for laborers in newly settled areas of Europe. Thus labor was increasingly in demand and lords were often willing to make special arrangements with groups of peasants to encourage them to bring new land under cultivation. From the beginning of the twelfth century peasant villages acquired from their lord the privilege to deal with him and his representatives collectively rather than individually. But gradually during the late twelfth and thirteenth centuries, the labor market stagnated. Europe's population, particularly in France, England, Italy, and western Germany, began to reach a saturation point. As a result, lay and ecclesiastical lords found that they could profit more by hiring cheap laborers than by demanding customary services and payments from their serfs. They also found that their serfs were willing to pay for increasing privileges.

Peasants could purchase the right to marry without the lord's consent, to move to neighboring manors or to nearby towns, and to inherit. They acquired personal freedom from their lord's jurisdiction, transformed their servile payments into payments of rent for their manses, purchased their own land, and commuted their labor services into annual or even one-time payments. In other words, they began to purchase their freedom. This free peasantry benefited the emerging states of western Europe, since kings and towns could extend their legal and fiscal jurisdictions over these persons and their lands at the expense of the nobility. Governments thus encouraged the extension of freedom and protected peasants from their former masters. By the fourteenth century, serfs were a rarity in many parts of western Europe.

Even as western serfs were acquiring a precious though fragile freedom, the free peasantry in much of eastern Europe and Spain were losing it. In much of the Slavic world, through the eleventh century, peasants lived in large, roughly territorial communes of free families. Gradually, however, princes, churches, and aristocrats began to build great landed estates. By the thirteenth century, under the influences of western and Byzantine models and of the Mongols, who dominated much of the Slavic world from 1240, lords began to acquire political and economic control over the peasantry. A similar process took place in parts of Spain. In all of these regions, the decline of the free peasantry accompanied the decline of public authority to the benefit of independent nobles. The aristocracy rose on the backs of the peasantry.

The Aristocracy: Fighters and Breeders

Beginning in the late tenth century, writers of legal documents began to employ an old term in a novel manner to designate certain powerful free persons who belonged neither to the old aristocracy nor to the peasantry. The term was *miles.* In classical Latin *miles* meant "soldier." As used in the Middle Ages, we would translate it as "knight."

The center of the knightly lifestyle was northern France. From there, the ideals of knighthood, or chivalry, spread out across Europe, influencing aristocrats as far east as Byzantium. The essence of this lifestyle was fighting. Through warfare this aristocracy had maintained or acquired its freedom and through warfare it justified its privileges. The origins of this small elite (probably nowhere more than 2 percent of the population) were diverse. Many were descended from the old aristocracy of the Carolingian age. They traced descent through the male line, inheritance was usually limited to the eldest sons, and daughters were given a dowry but did not share in inheritance. Younger sons had to find service with some great lord or live in the household of their older brothers.

Such noble families, proud of their independence and ancestry, maintained their position through complex kin networks, mutual defense pacts with other nobles, and control of castles, from which they could dominate the surrounding countryside. Safe behind the castle walls, they were by the twelfth century often independent even of the local counts, dukes, and kings. This lesser nobility absorbed control of such traditionally public powers as justice, peace, and taxation.

For the sons of such nobles preparation for a life of warfare began early, often in the entourage of a maternal uncle or a powerful lord. There boys learned to ride, to handle a heavy sword and shield, to manage a lance on horseback, to swing an axe with deadly accuracy. They also learned more subtle but equally important lessons about honor, pride, and family tradition. The feats of ancestors or heroes, sung by traveling minstrels at the banqueting table on long winter nights, provided models of knightly action. The culmination of this education for English and French nobles came in a ceremony of knighting. An adolescent of age sixteen to eighteen received a sword from an older, experienced warrior. No longer a "boy," he now became a "youth," ready to enter the world of fighting for which he had trained.

A "youth" was a noble who had been knighted but who had not married or acquired land either through inheritance or as a reward from a lord for service, and thus had not yet established his own "house." During this time the knight led the life of a warrior, joining in promising military expeditions and amusing himself with tournaments—mock battles that often proved as deadly as the real thing—in which one could win an opponent's horses and armor as well as renown. Drinking, gambling, and lechery were other common activities. This was an extraordinarily dangerous lifestyle, and many youths did not survive to the next stage in a knight's life, that of acquiring land, wife, honor, and his own following of youths.

The period between childhood and maturity was no less dangerous for noblewomen than for men. Marriages were the primary forms of alliances between noble houses, and the production of children was essential to the continued prosperity of the family. Thus daughters were raised as breeders, married at around age sixteen to cement family alliances, and then expected to produce as many children as possible. Many noblewomen died in childbirth, often literally exhausted by frequent successive births. Although occasionally practiced, contraception was condemned both by the Church and by husbands eager for offspring.

In this martial society, the political and economic status of women declined considerably. Because they were considered unable to participate in warfare, in northern Europe women were also frequently excluded from inheritance, estate management, courts, and public deliberations. Although a growing tradition of "courtliness" glorified the status of aristocratic women in literature, women were actually losing ground in the real world. Some noblewomen did control property and manage estates, but usually such roles were possible

A knight and lady in a fifteenth-century garden. The ideals of chivalry and courtly love glorified women in literature and song, but in real life the subordinate status of women reflected the values of a martial society.

only for widows who had borne sons and who could play a major part in raising them. Both secular tradition and Christian teaching portrayed women as devious, sexually demanding temptresses often responsible for the corruption and downfall of men. Many men felt threatened by this aggressive sexual stereotype. They resented the power wielded by wealthy widows and abbesses.

To maintain a lifestyle of conspicuous consumption required wealth, and wealth meant land. The nobility was essentially a society of heirs who had inherited not only land but also the serfs who worked their manors. Lesser nobles acquired additional property from great nobles and from ecclesiastical institutions in return for binding contracts of mutual assistance. This tradition was at least as old as the Carolingians, who granted their followers land in return for military service and demanded that free warriors swear oaths of fealty to them. In later centuries, counts and lesser lords continued this tradition, exchanging land for support. Individual knights became *vassals* of lay or ecclesiastical magnates, that is, they swore fealty or loyalty to the magnate and promised to defend and aid him. In return the magnate swore to protect his vassal and granted him a means of support by which the vassal could maintain himself while serving his lord. Usually this grant, termed a fief, was a parcel of productive land and the serfs and privileges attached to it, over which the vassal exercised economic and judicial control. The vassal did not actually own the land but simply had the use of it as long as he and his descendants provided the service to his feudal lord (so called from the Latin word for fief) for which it has been granted. In addition the vassal owed his lord certain specific duties and payments and was subject to the lord's court in matters directly concerning his fief and his relationship with his lord.

Individual lords often had considerable numbers of vassals, who might also be the vassals of other lay and secular lords. The networks thus established formed vital social and political structures. However, these bonds were personal, not public. A feudal lord was a superior, a first among equals, but not a sovereign. In some unusual situations, such as in England immediately after the Norman Conquest and in the Latin Kingdom of Jerusalem founded following the First Crusade in 1099, these structures of lords and vassals constituted systems of hierarchical government culminating in the king. Elsewhere, while kings were feudal lords of many of the great aristocrats in their kingdoms, individuals often held fiefs from and owed service to more than one lord, and not all of the individuals in a given county or duchy owed their primary obligation to the count or duke. Likewise, often most of a noble's land was owned outright rather than held in fief, thus making the feudal bond less central to his status. As a result these bonds, anachronistically called *feudalism* by French lawyers of the sixteenth and seventeenth centuries, constituted just one more element of a social system tied together by kinship, regional alliances, personal bonds of fealty, and the surviving elements of Carolingian administration inherited by counts and dukes.

The Church: Saints and Monks

The religious needs of the peasantry remained those that their pre-Christian ancestors had known: fertility of land, animals, and women; protection from the ravages of climate and the warrior elite; supernatural cures for the ailments and disabilities of their harsh life. The cultural values of the nobility retained the essentials of the Germanic warrior ethos, including family honor, battle, and display of status. The rural Church of the High Middle Ages met the needs of both, although it subtly changed them in the process.

Most medieval people, whether peasants or lords, lived in a world of face-to-face encounters, a world in which abstract creeds counted for little and in which interior state and external appearance were rarely distinguished. In this world, religion meant primarily action, and the essential religious actions were the liturgical celebrations performed by the clergy, many of whom had received only rudimentary instruction from their predecessors and whose knowledge of Latin and theology was minimal. But these intellectual factors would become significant only centuries later. Ordinary lay people wanted priests who would not extort them by selling the sacraments and would not seduce their wives and daughters. They wanted priests who would not leave the village for months or years at a time to seek clerical advancement elsewhere rather than remaining in the village performing the rituals necessary to keep the supernatural powers well disposed toward men and women in the community.

The most important of these supernatural powers was not some distant divinity but the saints—local, personal, even idiosyncratic persons. During their lives saintly men and women had shown that they enjoyed special favor with God. After their deaths, they continued to be the link between the divine and the earthly spheres. Through their bodies, preserved as relics in the monasteries of Europe, they continued to live among mortals even while participating in the heavenly court. Thus they could be approached just like local earthly lords and like them be won over through offerings, bribes, oaths, and rituals of supplication and submission.

Monasteries did more than orchestrate the cult of the saints. They were also responsible for the cult of the ordinary dead, for praying for the souls of ordinary mortals. In particular, monastic communities commemorated and prayed for those members of noble families who, through donations of land, had become especially associated with the monastic community. Across Europe noble families founded monasteries on their own lands or invited famous abbots to reorganize existing monasteries. These monasteries continued the ritual remembrance of the family, providing it with a history and forming an important part of its material as well as spiritual prestige.

Supported by both peasants and nobles, Benedictine monasteries reached their height in the eleventh and twelfth centuries. Within their walls developed a religious culture that was one of the greatest achievements of the Middle Ages. The essence of the monastic life was the passionate pursuit of God. The goal was not simply salvation but perfection, and this required discipline of the body through a life of voluntary chastity and poverty and discipline of the spirit through obedience and learning.

Monasteries were communities of professional prayers that found in this role their social justification. They were also enormously rich and powerful social and political institutions. The monastery of Cluny, in saving souls through prayer, became the first international organization of monastic centers, with abbeys and dependent communities, called priories, throughout Europe. The abbots of Cluny were among the most powerful and influential people of the eleventh and twelfth centuries, dealing as equals with kings, popes, and emperors.

The Cluniac monks' comparative luxury and concentration on liturgy to the neglect of other spiritual activities led some monastic reformers to call for a return to simplicity, separation from the rest of society, and a deeper internal spirituality. Chief among these groups were the Cistercians, who under the dynamic leadership of Bernard of Clairvaux (1090–1153), spread a rigorous, ascetic form of monasticism from England to the Vienna Woods.

Although monks and bishops were spiritual warriors, most abhorred bloodshed among Christians and sought to limit the violence of aristocratic life. This attitude combined altruistic and selfish motives, since Church property was often the focus of aristocratic greed. The decline of public power and the rise of aristocratic autonomy and violence were particularly marked in southern France. There, beginning in the tenth century, churchmen organized the Peace of God and the Truce of God, movements that attempted to protect peasants, merchants, and clerics from aristocratic violence and to limit the times when warfare was allowed. During the eleventh century, the goals of warfare were shifted from attacks against other Christians to the defense of Christian society. This redirection produced the Crusades, those religious wars of conquest directed against Europe's non-Christian neighbors.

In order to direct noble violence away from Christendom, Pope Urban II (1088–99) in 1095 urged Western knights to use their arms to free the Holy Land from Muslim occupation. In return he promised to absolve them from all of the punishment due for their sins in this life or the next. The First Crusade was remarkably successful. The crusaders took Jerusalem in 1099 and estab-

lished a Latin kingdom in Palestine. For over two centuries bands of Western warriors went on armed pilgrimage to defend this precarious kingdom and, after the reconquest of Jerusalem by the Muslim commander Salah ad-Din (known to the Latins as Saladin) in 1187, to attempt to recapture it. Other such holy wars were directed against the Muslims in Spain, the Slavs in eastern Europe, and even against heretics and political opponents in France and Italy. By the end of the thirteenth century the military failure of the Crusades, the immorality of many of the participants, and doubts about the spiritual significance of such wars contributed to their decline.

Until the twelfth century, peasants, lords, and monks made up the great majority of Europe's population and lived together in mutual dependence, sharing involvement with the rhythm of the agrarian life. From the later part of the twelfth century, however, this rural world became increasingly aware of a different society, that of the growing cities and towns of Europe, whose citizens moved to a different rhythm, that of commerce and manufacture.

Medieval Towns

Monastic preachers liked to remind their listeners that according to the Bible, Cain had founded the first town

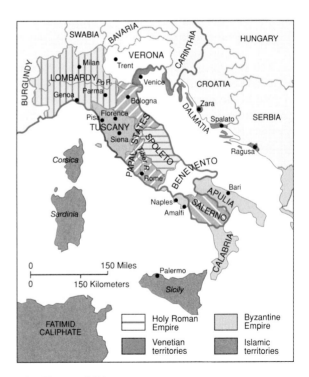

Italian Towns and Cities

after killing his brother Abel. Towns seemed somehow immoral and perverse but at the same time fascinating. Still, as rude warriors were transformed into courtly nobles, these nobles were drawn to the luxuries provided by urban merchants and became indebted to urban moneylenders in order to maintain their "gracious" lifestyles. For many peasants, towns were refuges from the hopelessness of their normal lives. "Town air makes one free," they believed, and many serfs fled the land to try their fortunes in the nearby towns. Clearly, something was very different about the urban communities that emerged, first in Italy, then in the Low Countries and across Europe in the later eleventh and twelfth centuries. These were centers of manufacture, commerce, and administration, structured less by the traditional relationships of vassalage and lordship than by the more fluid possibilities of wealth and patronage.

Italian Communes. Through the early Middle Ages the coastal cities of Amalfi, Bari, Genoa, and especially Venice had continued to play important roles in commerce both with the Byzantines and with the new Muslim societies. For Venice, this role was facilitated by its official status as a part of the Byzantine Empire, which gave it access to Byzantine markets. In order to protect their merchant ships, Italian coastal cities developed their own fleets, and by the eleventh century they were major military forces in the Mediterranean. Venice's fleet became the primary protector of the Byzantine Empire and Venice was thereby able to win more favorable commercial rights than those enjoyed by Greek merchants. As the merchants of the Italian towns penetrated the markets at the western end of the great overland spice routes connecting China, India, and central Asia with the Mediterranean, they established permanent merchant colonies in the East. They did not hesitate to use military force to win concessions.

The Crusades, armed pilgrimages for pious northern nobles, were primarily economic opportunities for the Italians, who had no scruples about trading with Muslims. Furthermore, only the Italians had the ships and the expertise to transport the crusaders by sea, the only option that offered hope of success, since every Crusade but the first that had followed an overland route had ended in failure. Moreover, the ships of the Italian cities were the only means of supplying the crusading armies once they were in Palestine. Crusaders paid the Italian merchants handsomely for their assistance and also granted them economic and political rights in the Palestinian port cities such as Tyre and Acre. The culmination of this relationship between northern crusaders and Italians was the Fourth Crusade. In 1204 a renegade

Crusade short on funds was sidetracked by the Venetians into capturing and sacking Constantinople.

By the thirteenth century, Italian merchants had spread far beyond the Mediterranean. The great merchant banking houses of Venice, Florence, and Genoa had established offices around the Mediterranean and Black seas; south along the Atlantic coast of Morocco; east into Armenia and Persia; west to London, Bruges, and Ghent; and north to Scandinavia. Some individual merchants, the Venetian Marco Polo (1254–1324) for example, traded as far east as China.

These international commercial operations required more sophisticated systems of commercial law and credit than Europe had ever known. Italian merchants developed the practices of double-entry bookkeeping, limited-liability partnership, commercial insurance, and international letters of exchange. Complex commercial affairs also required the development of a system of credit and interest-bearing loans, an idea abhorrent to traditional rural societies.

During the twelfth and thirteenth centuries Italy played host to a bewildering variety of experiments in self-government as urban populations banded together in communes of citizens who sought to govern themselves. These relatively small communities of citizens (the largest was approximately one hundred thousand adults) developed a keen sense of patriotism, local pride, and fierce independence reminiscent of the ancient Greek city-states. They manifested this pride in

An illustration from a fourteenth-century manuscript. The Venetian merchant Marco Polo (1254–1324), with his father and uncle, is seen departing from Venice for points east in 1271. Marco traveled as far as China and did not return home to Venice until twenty-four years later.

artistic and architectural competition as individual cities and their citizens sought to surpass each other in the construction of beautiful plazas, town halls, and sumptuous urban palaces.

The unity and patriotism that the Italian cities showed the rest of the world was matched in intensity by the violence of their internal disputes. Every adult male was expected to participate in government, usually in his free time and at the expense of his private business activities. This involvement was intensely partisan as magnates disputed among themselves and with the ordinary populace for control of the town. These conflicts frequently turned violent as citizens took sides on wider issues of Italian and European politics.

Within many towns, the magnates formed their own corporation, the society of knights, to protect their privileged position. Families of nobles and magnates, whose cultural values were similar to those of the rural aristocracy, competed with each other for honor and power. Opposing the magnates were popular corporations, the society of the people, which sought to rein in the violent and independent-minded nobles. These popular organizations were dominated by the prominent leaders of craft and trade associations, or guilds.

In order to tip the scales in their favor, differing parties frequently invited outside powers into local affairs. The greatest outside contenders for power in the Italian cities were the Empire and the papacy. Most towns had an imperial faction (named Ghibelline after a castle that belonged to the family of Emperor Frederick II), bitterly opposed by a papal faction (in time called Guelph after a family opposed to Frederick). In time, the issues separating Guelphs and Ghibellines changed, and the Guelphs became the party of the wealthy eager to preserve the status quo while those out of power rallied to the Ghibelline cause.

In order to maintain civic life in spite of these conflicts, cities established complex systems of government in which officers were selected by series of elections and lotteries designed to prevent any one faction from seizing control. Sovereignty lay with the *arengo*, or assembly, which comprised all adult male citizens. Except in very small communes this body was too large to function efficiently, so most communes selected a series of working councils. The great council might be as large as 400; an inner council had perhaps 24 to 40 members. Generally, executive authority was vested in consuls, whose numbers varied widely and who were chosen from various factions and classes. When these consuls proved unable to overcome the partisan politics of the factions, many towns turned to hiring *podestàs*,

nonpolitical, professional city managers from outside the community. These were normally magnates from other communes who had received legal educations and who served for relatively short periods.

Northern Towns. The Baltic and North seas and the English Channel tied together the peoples of Scandinavia, Lithuania, northern Germany, Flanders, and England. Scandinavian fish and timber, Baltic grain, English wool, and Flemish cloth circulated around the edges of these lands, linking them in a common economic network. Here, as in the south, there developed urban merchant and manufacturing communities linked by sea routes, distinguished from the surrounding countryside by the formation of a distinctly urban, commercial mentality.

The earliest of these interrelated communities were the cloth towns of Flanders, Brabant, and northern France. Chief among them were Ghent, Bruges, and Ypres, and the wool-exporting towns of England, particularly London. In the eleventh century Flanders, lacking the land for large-scale sheep grazing and facing a growing population, began to specialize in the production of high-quality cloth made from English wool. At the same time England, which experienced an economic and population decline following the Norman Conquest, began to export the greater part of its wool to Flanders to be worked. The production of wool cloth began to develop from a cottage occupation into Europe's first major industry. Wool cloth was a necessity of life across Europe, and the growing population provided the first large-scale market for manufactured goods since the disintegration of the Roman Empire.

Concentration of capital, specialization of labor, and increase of urban population created vibrant, exciting cities essentially composed of three social orders. At the top were wealthy patricians, the merchant-drapiers. Their agents traveled to England and purchased raw wool, which they then distributed to weavers and other master craftsmen. These craftsmen, often using equipment rented from the patricians, carded, dyed, spun, and wove the wool into cloth. Finally, the finished cloth was returned to the patricians, whose agents then marketed it throughout Europe. Through their control of raw materials, equipment, capital, and distribution, the merchant-drapiers controlled the cloth trade and thus the economic and political life of the Flemish wool towns. Through their closed associations, or guilds, they controlled production and set standards, prices, and wages. They also controlled communal government by monopolizing urban councils.

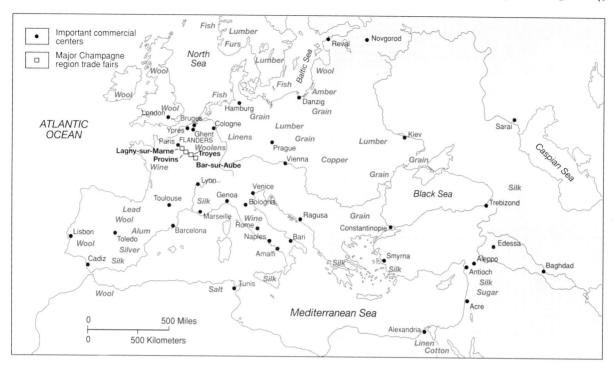

Medieval Trade

At the bottom of urban society were the unskilled and semiskilled artisans, called "blue nails," because constant work with dye left their fingers permanently stained. These workers led an existence more precarious than that of most peasants. Small wonder that from the thirteenth century on, "blue nails" were increasingly hostile to patricians. Sporadic rebellions and strikes spread across Flanders, Brabant, and northern France. Everywhere they were ruthlessly suppressed.

Between the patricians and the workers stood the masters—the skilled craftsmen who controlled the day-to-day production of cloth and lesser crafts. Masters organized into guilds with which they both regulated every aspect of their trades and protected them from competition. The masters often leased their looms or other equipment from the merchant-drapiers and from them received raw materials and wages to be distributed to their workers.

Tying together the northern and southern commercial worlds were the great fairs of Champagne. Six times during the year the towns of Champagne swelled with exotic crowds of merchants from Flanders, England, Scandinavia, Germany, Brabant, Spain, and Italy. Southern merchants brought silks, sugar, salt, alum (a chemical essential in cloth manufacture), and, most importantly, spices to trade at the fairs. These great inter-national exchanges connected the financial and marketing centers of the south with the manufacturing and trading communities of the north, tying the northern world to the south more effectively than had any system since the political institutions of the Roman Empire.

Urban Culture

In the late eleventh and early twelfth centuries, the pace of urban intellectual life quickened. The combination of population growth, improved agricultural productivity, political stability, and educational interest culminated in what has been called the "renaissance of the twelfth century." Bologna and Paris became the undisputed centers of the new educational movements. Bologna specialized in the study of law. There from the eleventh century a number of important teachers began to make detailed, authoritative commentaries on the Justinian Code (*Corpus iuris civilis*), the sixth-century compilation of law prepared on the order of the Roman emperor Justinian. In the next century the same systematic study was applied to Church law, culminating in the *Decretum Gratiani*, or "Concord of Discordant Canons," prepared around 1140 in Bologna by the monk Gratian. The growing importance of legal knowledge in politics, international trade, and

As towns grew, the numbers and types of jobs grew as well. In this fifteenth-century Flemish manuscript illumination, a guild master of the dyer's guild supervises as men of the guild dye cloth.

Church administration drew students from across Europe to Bologna, where they organized a *universitas*, or guild of students, the first true university. Professors and administrators were controlled by the guild and were fined if they broke any of the regulations.

North of the Alps, Paris became the center for study of the liberal arts and of theology during the twelfth century. The city's emergence as the leading educational center of Europe resulted from a convergence of factors. Paris was the center of an important cathedral school as well as of a monastic school. In the twelfth century it became the capital of the French kings, who needed educated clerics, or clerks, for their administration.

By 1200 education had become so important in the city that the universitas, or corporation of professors, was granted a charter by King Philip Augustus, who guaranteed its rights and immunities from the control of the city. Unlike that at Bologna, the University of Paris remained a corporation of masters rather than of students. It was organized like other guilds into masters; bachelors, who were similar to journeymen in other trades; and students, who were analogous to apprentices.

Students began their studies at around age fourteen or fifteen in the faculty of arts. After approximately six years, they received a bachelor of arts degree, which was a prerequisite to enter the higher faculties of theology,

medicine, or law. After additional years of reading and commenting on specific texts under the supervision of a master, they received the title of master of arts, which gave them the license to teach anywhere within Christian Europe.

Through the thirteenth and fourteenth centuries the intellectual life of the universities was dominated by a pagan philosopher already dead for a thousand years. The introduction of the works of Aristotle into western Europe between 1150 and 1250 created an intellectual crisis every bit as profound as that of the Newtonian revolution of the seventeenth or the Einsteinian revolution of the twentieth century. For centuries, European thinkers had depended on the Christianized Neoplatonic philosophy of Origen and Augustine. Aristotle was known in western Europe only through his basic logical treatises, which in the twelfth century had become the foundation of intellectual work. Logic, or dialectic, was seen as the universal key to knowledge, and the university system was based on its rigorous application to traditional texts of law, philosophy, and Scripture.

Beginning in the late twelfth century, Christian and Jewish scholars began translating into Latin Aristotle's treatises on natural philosophy, ethics, and metaphysics. Suddenly Christian intellectuals who had already accepted the Aristotelian method were brought face to face with Aristotle's conclusions: a world without an active, conscious God; a world in which everything from the functioning of the mind to the nature of matter could be understood without reference to a divine creator. Further complicating matters, the texts arrived not from the original Greek, but normally through Latin translations of Arabic translations accompanied by learned commentaries by Muslim and Jewish scholars, especially by Ibn Rushd (Averroës), the greatest Aristotelian philosopher of the twelfth century.

As the full impact of Aristotelian philosophy began to reach churchmen and scholars, reactions varied from condemnation to wholehearted acceptance. To many, it appeared that there were two irreconcilable kinds of truth, one knowable through divine revelation, the other through human reason.

One Parisian scholar who refused to accept this dichotomy was Thomas Aquinas (1225–74), a professor of theology and the most brilliant intellect of the High Middle Ages. Although an Aristotelian who recognized the genius of Averroës, Aquinas refused to accept the possibility that human reason, which was a gift from God, led necessarily to contradictions with divine revelation. Properly applied, the principles of Aristotelian philosophy could not lead to error, he argued. However, human reason unaided by revelation could not always lead to certain conclusions. Questions about such matters as the nature of God, creation, and the human soul could not be resolved by reason alone. In developing his thesis, Aquinas recast Christian doctrine and philosophy, replacing their Neoplatonic foundation with an Aristotelian base. Although not universally accepted in the thirteenth century (in 1277 the bishop of Paris condemned many of Aquinas's teachings as heretical), his synthesis came to dominate Christian intellectual life for centuries.

Aquinas was a member of a new religious order, the Dominicans, who along with the Franciscans appeared in response to the social and cultural needs of the new urbanized, monetized European culture. Benedictine monasticism was ideally suited to a rural, aristocratic world but had little place in the bustling cities of Italy, Flanders, and Germany. In these urban, commercial environments, Christians were more concerned with the problems of living in the world than escape from it. Lay persons and clerics alike were concerned with the growing wealth of ecclesiastical institutions, and across southern Europe especially individual reformers attacked the wealthy lifestyles of monks and secular clergy as unchristian. Torn between their own involvement in a commercial world and an inherited

SAINT FRANCIS OF ASSISI ON HUMILITY AND POVERTY

■ *By 1223 Francis of Assisi's desire to lead a life of radical poverty and simplicity in conformity with the life of Jesus in the Gospels had inspired thousands to follow his example, and he was obligated to prepare a rule by which his order of Friars Minor would be governed. This simple rule emphasizes his fundamental concerns of humility and poverty.*

1. This is the rule and way of living of the minorite brothers: namely to observe the holy Gospel of our Lord Jesus Christ, living in obedience, without personal possessions, and in chastity. Brother Francis promises obedience and reverence to our lord pope Honorius, and to his successors who canonically enter upon their office and to the Roman Church. And the other brothers shall be bound to obey brother Francis and his successors.

2. If any persons shall wish to adopt this form of living and shall come to our brothers, they shall send them to their provincial ministers . . . The ministers shall say unto them the word of the holy Gospel, to the effect that they shall go and sell all that they have and strive to give it to the poor. But if they shall not be able to do this, their good will is enough . . . And those who have now promised obedience shall have one gown with a cowl, and another, if they wish it, without a cowl. And those who are compelled by necessity, may wear shoes . . .

4. I firmly command all the brothers by no means to receive coin or money, of themselves or through an intervening person. But for the needs of the sick and for clothing the other brothers, the ministers alone and the guardians shall provide through spiritual friends, as it may seem to them that necessity demands.

5. Those brothers to whom God has given the ability to labor, shall labor faithfully and devoutly . . . As a reward, they may receive for themselves and their brothers the necessaries of life, but not coin or money, and this humbly, as becomes the servants of God and the followers of most holy poverty.

6. The brothers shall appropriate nothing to themselves, neither a house, nor a place, nor anything; but as pilgrims and strangers in this world, in poverty and humility, serving God, they shall confidently go seeking for alms. Nor need they be ashamed, for the Lord made Himself poor for us in this world . . .

11. I firmly command all the brothers not to have suspicious relations or to take counsel with women. And, with the exception of those whom special permission has been given by the Apostolic Chair, let them not enter nunneries. Neither may they become fellow god-parents with men or women, lest from this cause a scandal may arise among the brothers or concerning brothers.

In an imaginary meeting between Thomas Aquinas and Averroës by the Siennese painter Giovanni di Paolo, the great Arab philosopher is shown to be confounded by Aquinas, symbolizing the triumph of Scholasticism over the teachings of Averroës.

Christian-Roman tradition that looked upon commerce and capital as degrading, reformers called for a return to what they imagined to have been the life of the primitive Church, one that emphasized both individual and collective poverty. The poverty movement attracted great numbers of followers, many of whom added to their criticisms of traditional clergy a concern over clerical morality and challenges about the value of sacraments and the priesthood. Although many reformers were condemned as heretics and sporadically persecuted, the reform movement continued to grow and threatened to destroy the unity of western Christendom.

The people who preserved the Church's unity were inspired by the same impulses, but they channeled their enthusiasm into reforming the Church from within. Francis of Assisi (1182–1226), the son of a prosperous Italian merchant, rejected his luxurious life in favor of one of radical poverty, simplicity, and service to others. He was a man of extraordinary simplicity, humility, and joy, and his piety was in keeping with his character. As he wandered about preaching repentance he drew great numbers of followers from all ranks, especially from the urban communities of Italy. The Order of Friars Minor, or Franciscans, grew by thousands, drawing members from as far away as England and Hungary.

Francis insisted that his followers observe strict poverty, both individually and collectively. The order could not own property, nor could its members even touch money. They were expected to beg food each day for their sustenance. They were to travel from town to town, preaching, performing manual labor, and serving the poor. In time the expansion of the order and its involvement in preaching against heresy and in education brought about compromises with Francis's original ideals. The Franciscans needed churches in which to preach, books with which to study, and protection from local bishops. Most of the friars accepted these changes. These, the so-called Conventuals, were bitterly opposed by the Spirituals, or rigorists, who sought to maintain the radical poverty of their founder. In the fourteenth century this conflict led to a major split in the order and ultimately to the condemnation of the Spirituals as heretics.

The order of friars founded by Dominic (1170–1221) also adopted a rule of strict poverty approved by Innocent III, but the primary focus of the Dominicans was on preaching to the society of the thirteenth century. This order, which emphasized intellectual activity, concentrated on preaching against heresies and on higher education. Thus the Dominicans too gravitated toward the cities of western Europe and especially toward its great universities. These new orders of preachers, highly educated, enthusiastic, and eloquent, began to formulate for the urban laity of Europe a new vision of Christian society, a society not only of peasants, lords, and monks, but also of merchants, craftsmen, and professionals. Also, their central organizations and their lack of ties to the rural aristocracies made them the favorite religious orders of the increasingly powerful centralized monarchies.

The Romano-barbarian chieftains who inherited political power in the western Roman Empire experimented with a variety of ways to combine the political heritage of Rome and the military traditions of their peoples into enduring polities. The most successful were the Franks, whose early acceptance of orthodox Christianity made possible an amalgam of Roman and barbarian peoples. Under their kings, especially Charlemagne, they brought most of the old western empire under their control and introduced throughout it their synthesis of Frankish and Roman culture and institutions. The Frankish model proved enduring. The cultural renaissance laid the foundation of all subsequent European intellectual activities, and the alliance between Church and monarchy provided the formula for European kings for almost a thousand years. The idea of the Carolingian empire, the symbol of European unity, has never entirely disappeared from western Europe.

By 1300 Europe had achieved a level of population density, economic prosperity, cultural sophistication, and political organization greater than at any time since the Roman Empire. Across Europe, a largely free peasantry cultivated a wide variety of crops both for local consumption and for growing commercial markets, while landlords sought increasingly rational approaches to estate management and investment. In cities and ports, merchants, manufacturers, and bankers presided over an international commercial and manufacturing economy that connected Scandinavia to the Mediterranean Sea. In schools and universities, students learned the skills of logical thinking and disputation while absorbing the traditions of Greece and Rome to prepare themselves for careers in law, medicine, and government.

SUGGESTIONS FOR FURTHER READING

THE MAKING OF THE BARBARIAN KINGDOMS

Roger Collins, *Early Medieval Europe 300-1000* (New York: St. Martin's Press, 1991). A judicious and comprehensive survey of the early medieval kingdoms with an emphasis on politics and institutions.

* Herwig Wolfram, *History of the Goths* (Berkeley, CA: University of California Press, 1987). An outstanding study of the formation of the Goths in late antiquity.

* Patrick J. Geary, *Before France and Germany: The Origins and Transformation of the Merovingian World* (New York: Oxford University Press, 1988). A study of the Merovingians from the perspective of late Roman traditions.

* James Campbell, ed., *The Anglo-Saxons* (Oxford: Phaidon, 1982). A collection of essays on Anglo-Saxon England by an outstanding group of archaeologists and historians.

EUROPE TRANSFORMED

Suzanne Fonay Wemple, *Women in Frankish Society: Marriage and the Cloister 500-900* (Philadelphia: University of Pennsylvania Press, 1981). A pioneering study of women in the early Middle Ages.

* David Herlihy, *Medieval Households* (Cambridge, MA: Harvard University Press, 1985). An important survey of medieval peasant society.

THE CAROLINGIANS AND THE NEW EUROPE

* Rosamond McKitterick, *The Frankish Kingdoms Under the Carolingians, 751-987* (New York: Longmans, 1983). A very detailed study of Carolingian history with an emphasis on intellectual developments.

* Peter Sawyer, *The Age of the Vikings* (New York: St. Martins Press, 1971). A good introduction to Scandinavian history.

* Geoffrey Barraclough, ed., *Eastern and Western Europe in the Middle Ages* (New York: Harcourt Brace Jovanovich, 1970). Essays by specialists on eastern Europe and its relationship to the west.

* Heinrich Fichtenau, *Living in the Tenth Century: Studies in Mentalities and Social Orders* (Chicago: University of Chicago Press, 1990). A brilliant evocation of the quest for order on the Continent following the dissolution of the Carolingian empire.

SOCIETY AND CULTURE IN THE HIGH MIDDLE AGES

* Georges Duby, *Rural Economy and Country Life in the Medieval West* (Columbia, SC: University of South Carolina Press, 1968). An authoritative survey of medieval agriculture and society.

* Lynn White, Jr., *Medieval Technology and Social Change* (New York: Oxford University Press, 1966). Imaginative essays on the social impact of technology in the Middle Ages.

Georges Duby, *The Knight, the Lady, and the Priest: The Making of Modern Marriage in Medieval France* (New York: Pantheon Books, 1984). A short study of the conflict between lay and religious social values in medieval France.

Ronald C. Finucane, *Soldiers of the Faith: Crusaders and Moslems at War* (New York: St. Martin's Press, 1984). A critical reappraisal of the Crusades for general readers.

* Robert S. Lopez, *The Commercial Revolution of the Middle Ages, 950-1350* (New York: Cambridge University Press, 1971). An excellent survey of medieval commercial history.

* Daniel Waley, *The Italian City-Republics* (New York: McGraw-Hill, 1969). A brief and highly readable account of Italian towns.

* Helene Wieruszowski, *The Medieval University* (Princeton, NJ: Van Nostrand, 1966). A short history of medieval universities.

* R. W. Southern, *Western Society and the Church in the Middle Ages* (New York: Penguin Books, 1990). A well-written account of the medieval Church for a general public.

* Indicates paperback edition available.

HAROLD, KING OF THE ENGLISH

A few decades after William the Conqueror's victory at Hastings in 1066, his half brother, Bishop Odo of Bayeux (ca. 1036–97), commissioned a great tapestry recording the Norman version of the conquest. An unknown Anglo-Saxon artist sketched the cartoon, drawing on models taken from Anglo-Saxon and Carolingian manuscript illumination. Anglo-Saxon women then embroidered the tapestry, a strip of linen 230 feet long and 20 inches high, a masterful piece of art.

Using such techniques familiar to modern moviemakers as jump cuts, flashbacks, close-ups, panoramas, and decomposing movement into freeze-frames, the artist and embroiderers vividly present life in eleventh-century warrior society. It is almost exclusively masculine. Of the 623 people represented, only six are women. We see peasants working the fields, craftsmen felling trees and building ships for William's Channel crossing. We see cities, palaces, and churches. We see cooking and banqueting, hunting, traveling, and of course we see fighting and dying. The artists accurately render clothing, armor, and even hairstyles. But the tapestry is not simply a naive piece of artistry, it is a masterpiece of propaganda.

When King Edward the Confessor (1042–66) died, three claimants disputed the succession. Anglo-Saxon sources insist that Edward and his nobles choose Earl Harold Godwinson (ca. 1022–66) over William and the Norwegian king Harold III (1045–66). William insisted that Edward had designated him and that years before, when Earl Harold had been shipwrecked on the Norman coast and befriended by the duke, he had sworn an oath to assist William in gaining the crown. This is the scene presented in the top panel on the opposite page. Harold's death, portrayed in the bottom panel, suggests divine vengeance for his perjury. The message seems clear. William was the rightful heir and Harold, by his perfidy, merited his tragic fate. And yet the Anglo-Saxon artists who executed the tapestry for their Norman lord may have subtly introduced a different reading into the story of Earl Harold. Nothing in the tapestry itself specifically labels him a perjurer or usurper. In the critical scene following his coronation, shown in the middle panel, the legend declares him unambiguously the legitimate king: "Here sits Harold, King of the English." Moreover, in this scene he is acknowledged by representatives of the whole of society, that is, the workers, represented by the unarmed man at far left; the fighters, represented by the man holding the sword; and the prayers, present in the person of Stigand, the Archbishop of Canterbury.

In its vividness, its political subtlety, and its essential ambiguity, the Bayeux Tapestry is a fitting introduction to the world of the High Middle Ages, that is, the period from about 1000 to 1300. It was a world of workers, fighters, and prayers, but also one of cities, merchants, and scholars. Its culture and religion combined, like the tapestry, the extremes of brutal warfare and subtle artistry.

The disintegration of the Carolingian empire in the tenth century left political power fragmented among a wide variety of political entities. In general these were of two types. The first, the papacy and the empire, were elective, traditional structures that claimed universal sovereignty over the Christian world, based on a sacred view of political power. The universality of these two claims brought popes and emperors into direct confrontation, ultimately weakening both. The second, largely hereditary and less extravagant in their religious and political pretensions, were the limited kingdoms that arose within the old Carolingian world or on its borders. These kingdoms, especially France and England, built on less ambitious traditions of royal prerogative as well as on the feudal bonds of lord and vassal to create new and lasting forms of political organization.

The Universal States: Empire and Papacy

The Frankish world east of the Rhine had been less affected than the kingdom of the west Franks by the onslaught of Vikings, Magyars, and Saracens. The eastern Frankish kingdom, a loose confederacy of five great duchies—Saxony, Lorraine, Franconia, Swabia, and Bavaria—had preserved much of the Carolingian religious, cultural, and institutional traditions. In 919 Duke Henry I of Saxony (919–36) was elected king, and his son Otto I (936–73) laid the foundation for the revival of the empire. In 955 Otto inflicted a devastating defeat on the Magyars, subdued the other dukes, and tightened his control over the kingdom. He accomplished this largely through the extensive use of bishops and abbots, whom he appointed as his agents and sources of loyal support. In 951, in order to prevent a southern German prince from establishing himself in northern Italy, Otto invaded and conquered Lombardy. Eleven years later he entered Rome, where he was crowned emperor by the pope.

Otto, known to history as "the Great," had established the character and content of German imperial policy for the next three hundred years. It involved conflict with the German aristocracy, reliance on bishops and abbots as imperial agents, and preoccupation with Italy. His successors, both in his own Saxon dy-

nasty (919–1024) and in the succeeding dynasties, the Salians (1024–1125) and the Staufens (1138–1254), continued this tradition. The German Dukes and other aristocrats or magnates elected the German kings who were then consecrated as emperors by the pope. Generally, kings were able to bring about the election of their sons, and in this manner they attempted to turn the kingship into a hereditary office. However, the royal families did not manage to produce male heirs in each generation, and thus the magnates continued to exercise real power in royal elections. The magnates' ability to expand their own power and autonomy at the expense of their Slavic neighbors to the east also contributed to the weakness of the German monarchy.

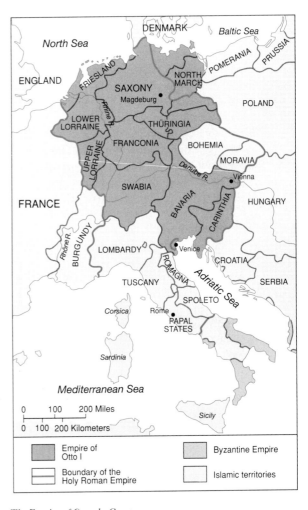

The Empire of Otto the Great

The second cornerstone of imperial power was the appointment of bishops and abbots. In order to counter aristocratic power, emperors looked to the Church both for the development of the religious cult of the emperor as "The Anointed of the Lord" and as a source of reliable military and political support. While the offices of count and duke had become hereditary within the great aristocracy, the offices of bishop and abbot remained public charges to which the emperor could appoint loyal supporters.

In addition to churchmen, emperors used their own trusted household serfs as their agents. Although unfree, these ministerials were entrusted with important military commands and given strategic castles throughout the empire. Despised by the free-born nobility, they tended at first to be loyal supporters of the emperor. In the twelfth century, they took on the chivalric ideals of their aristocratic neighbors and benefited from conflicts between emperor and pope to acquire autonomy. As old noble families died out, ministerial families replaced them as a new hereditary aristocracy.

The third keystone of imperial power was control of Italy. The empire was never considered merely a German kingdom, and Otto the Great and his successors considered Italy vital to their interests. As emperors, they had to be crowned by the pope. This was possible only if they controlled Rome. Moreover, the growing wealth of northern Italian towns was an important source of financial support if Lombardy could be controlled. Thus the emperors found themselves drawn into papal and Italian politics, frequently with disastrous results. Germany became merely a source of men and material with which to fight the Lombard towns and the pope. From the eleventh through the thirteenth centuries emperors granted German princes autonomy in return for this support.

The early successes of this imperial program created the seeds of its own destruction. Imperial efforts to reform the Church resulted in a second, competing claimant to universal authority, the papacy. In the later tenth and early eleventh centuries, emperors had intervened in papal elections, deposed and replaced corrupt popes, and worked to ensure that bishops and abbots would be educated, competent churchmen. The most effective reformer was Emperor Henry III (1039–56), who took seriously his role as the anointed of the Lord to reform the Church both in Germany and in Rome. When three rivals claimed the papacy, Henry called a synod, or meeting of bishops, which deposed all three and installed the first of a series of German popes.

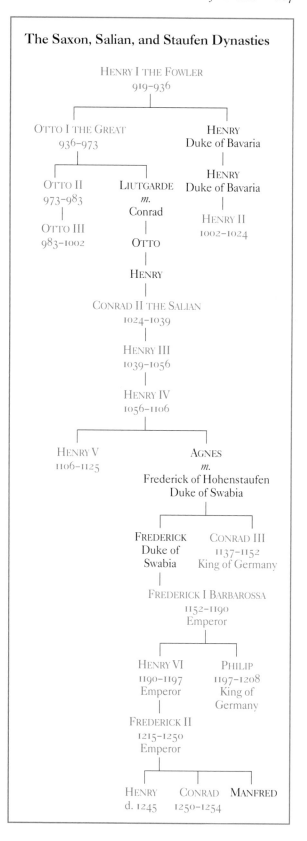

The Saxon, Salian, and Staufen Dynasties

HENRY I THE FOWLER
919–936

OTTO I THE GREAT
936–973

HENRY
Duke of Bavaria

OTTO II
973–983

LIUTGARDE
m.
Conrad

HENRY
Duke of Bavaria

OTTO III
983–1002

OTTO

HENRY II
1002–1024

HENRY

CONRAD II THE SALIAN
1024–1039

HENRY III
1039–1056

HENRY IV
1056–1106

HENRY V
1106–1125

AGNES
m.
Frederick of Hohenstaufen
Duke of Swabia

FREDERICK
Duke of
Swabia

CONRAD III
1137–1152
King of Germany

FREDERICK I BARBAROSSA
1152–1190
Emperor

HENRY VI
1190–1197
Emperor

PHILIP
1197–1208
King of
Germany

FREDERICK II
1215–1250
Emperor

HENRY
d. 1245

CONRAD
1250–1254

MANFRED

The most effective was Henry's own cousin who, as Leo IX (1049–54), traveled widely in France, Germany, and Italy. He condemned simony, that is, the practice of buying Church offices, and fostered monastic reforms such as that of Cluny. He also encouraged the efforts of a group of young reformers drawn from across Europe.

In the next decades, these new, more radical reformers began to advocate a widespread renewal of the Christian world, led not by emperors but by popes. These reformers pursued an ambitious set of goals. They sought to reform the morals of the clergy and in particular to eliminate married priests. They tried to free churches and monasteries from lay control both by forbidding lay men and women from owning churches and monasteries and by eliminating simony. They particularly condemned "lay investiture," that is, the practice by which kings and emperors appointed bishops and invested them with the symbols of their office. Finally, they insisted that the pope, not the emperor, was the supreme representative of God on earth and as such had the right to exercise a universal sovereignty.

Scenes from the investiture controversy. In the top panel at right Pope Gregory VII is seen being expelled from his throne, while at the left, Henry IV sits with Bishop Guibert of Ravenna, his choice for pope. At the bottom, Gregory dies in exile.

Every aspect of the reform movement met with strong opposition throughout Europe. However, its effects were most dramatic in the empire because of the central importance there of the imperial church system. Henry III's son Henry IV (1056–1106) clashed head-on with the leading radical reformer and former protege of Leo IX, Pope Gregory VII (1073–85), over the emperor's right to appoint and to install or invest bishops in their offices. This investiture controversy changed the face of European political history. Legal scholars for both sides searched Roman and Church law for arguments to bolster their claims, thus encouraging the revival of legal studies at Bologna. For the first time, public opinion played a crucial role in politics, and both sides composed carefully worded propaganda tracts aimed at secular and religious audiences. Gradually, the idea of the separate spheres of church and state emerged for the first time in European political theory. The conflict ended only in 1122, when Emperor Henry V (1106–25) and Pope Calixtus II (1119–24) reached an agreement known as the Concordat of Worms, which differentiated between the royal and the spiritual spheres of authority and allowed the emperors a limited role in episcopal election and investiture. This compromise changed the nature of royal rule in the empire, weakening the emperors and contributing to the long-term decline of royal government in Germany.

The decline that began with the investiture controversy continued as emperors abandoned political power north of the Alps in order to pursue their ambitions in Italy. Frederick I Barbarossa (1152–90) spent much of his reign attempting to reimpose imperial authority in northern Italy and to collect imperial incomes from its rich towns. For this he needed the support of the German aristocrats, and he granted them extraordinary privileges in return for their cooperation south of the Alps. Still, the combined efforts of the Lombard towns and the papacy were too much for Frederick and his armies to win a decisive victory. By the time of Frederick's death in 1190 in Germany the emperor was more a feudal lord with strictly limited, contractual rights than he was a sovereign; and in Italy his authority was disputed by the papacy and the towns. Frederick's successors continued his policy of focusing on Italy with no better success. In 1230 Frederick II (1215–50) conceded to each German prince sovereign rights in his own territory. From the thirteenth to the nineteenth century these princes ruled their territories as independent states, leaving the office of emperor a hollow title.

The investiture controversy ultimately compromised the authority of the pope as well as that of the emperor. First, the series of compromises beginning with the Concordat of Worms established a novel and potent tradition in Western political thought: the definition of separate spheres of authority for secular and religious government. Secondly, while in the short run popes were able to exercise enormous political influence, after the thirteenth century they were increasingly unable to make good their claims to absolute authority.

Papal power was based on more than Scripture. Over the centuries, the popes had acquired large amounts of land in central Italy and in the Rhone Valley, which formed the nucleus of the Papal States. Moreover, in every corner of Europe bishops and clergy were at least in theory agents of papal programs. The elaboration of systematic canon law, encouraged by the papal reformers as a weapon in the investiture controversy, created a system of courts and legal institutions more sophisticated than that of any secular monarch. Church courts claimed jurisdiction over all clerics regardless of the nature of the legal problem and over all baptized Christians in such fundamental issues as legitimacy of marriages, inheritances, and oaths. During the pontificate of Innocent III (1198–1216) the papacy reached the height of its powers. Innocent made and deposed emperors, excommunicated kings, summoned a crusade against heretics in the south of France, and placed whole countries such as England and France under interdict, that is, the suspension of all religious services, when rulers dared to contradict him. Still, he found time to support religious reformers such as Francis of Assisi, and in 1215 to call the Fourth Lateran Council, which culminated the reforms of the past century and had a lasting effect on the spiritual life of clergy and laity alike. At the council, more than twelve hundred assembled bishops and abbots, joined by great nobles from across Europe, defined fundamental doctrines such as the nature of the eucharist, ordered annual confession of sins, and detailed procedures for the election of bishops. They also mandated a strict lifestyle for clergy and forbade their participation in judicial procedures in which accused persons had to undergo painful ordeals, such as grasping a piece of red-hot iron and carrying it a prescribed distance, to prove their innocence. More ominously, the council also mandated that Jews wear special identifying markings on their clothing—a sign of the increasing hostility Christians felt toward the Jews in their midst.

During the thirteenth century the papacy continued to perfect its legal system and its control over clergy throughout Europe. However, politically the popes were unable to assert their claims to universal supremacy. This was true both in Italy, where the communes in the north and the kingdom of Naples in the south resisted direct papal control, and in the emerging kingdoms north of the Alps, where monarchs successfully intervened in Church affairs. The old claims of papal authority rang increasingly hollow. When Pope Boniface VIII (1294–1303) attempted to prevent the French king Philip IV (1285–1314) from taxing the French clergy, boasting that he could depose kings "like servants" if necessary, Philip proved him wrong. Philip's agents hired a gang of adventurers who kidnaped the pope, plundered his treasury, and released him a broken, humiliated wreck. The French king who had engineered Boniface's humiliation represented a new political tradition much more limited but ultimately more successful than either the empire or the papacy—the medieval nation-state.

The Nation-States: France and England

King was a less pretentious and more familiar office than that of emperor. As the Carolingian world disintegrated, a variety of kingdoms had appeared in France, Italy, Burgundy, and Provence. Beyond the confines of the old Carolingian world, kingship was well established in England and northern Spain. In Scandinavia, Poland, Bohemia, and Hungary powerful chieftains were consolidating royal power at the expense of their aristocracies. The claims of kings were much more modest than those of emperors or popes. Kings lay claim to a limited territory and, while the king was anointed, and thus a "Christus" (from the Greek word for sacred oil), kings were only one of many representatives of God on earth. Finally, kings were far from absolute rulers. Much of their real power derived, like that of other lords, from the feudal bonds uniting them with their vassals. Still, between the tenth and fourteenth centuries some monarchies, especially those of France and England, developed into powerful, centralized, and vigorous kingdoms. In the process they gave birth to what has become the modern state.

In 987, when Hugh Capet was elected king of the west Franks, no one suspected that his successors would become the most powerful rulers of Europe, for they were relatively weak magnates whose only real power lay in the region between Paris and Orléans. The dukes of Normandy, descendants of Vikings whose settlement

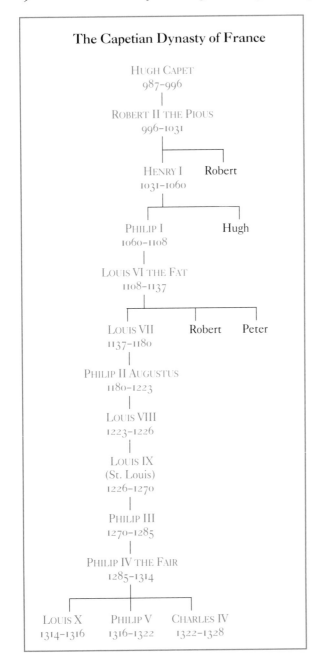

The Capetian Dynasty of France

HUGH CAPET
987–996

ROBERT II THE PIOUS
996–1031

HENRY I   Robert
1031–1060

PHILIP I   Hugh
1060–1108

LOUIS VI THE FAT
1108–1137

LOUIS VII   Robert   Peter
1137–1180

PHILIP II AUGUSTUS
1180–1223

LOUIS VIII
1223–1226

LOUIS IX
(St. Louis)
1226–1270

PHILIP III
1270–1285

PHILIP IV THE FAIR
1285–1314

LOUIS X   PHILIP V   CHARLES IV
1314–1316   1316–1322   1322–1328

sides of the English Channel termed the "Angevin Empire," territories much richer than those ruled by the French king. The counts of Flanders, too, ruled a prosperous region much better unified than the French king's small territory in the Parisian area. In the south, the counts of Poitou, who were also dukes of Aquitaine, were building up a powerful territorial principality in this most Romanized region of the kingdom, while in Anjou an ambitious aristocratic family was consolidating its territory as a virtually independent principality.

Biology and bureaucracy created the medieval French monarchy. Between 987 and 1314, every royal descendant of Hugh Capet (after whom the dynasty was called the Capetian) left a male heir—an extraordinary record for a medieval family. During the same period, by comparison, the office of emperor was occupied by men from no less than nine families. By simply outlasting the families of their great barons, the Capetian kings were able to absorb lands when other families became extinct. This success was not just the result of luck. Kings risked excommunication in order to divorce wives who had not produced male heirs. The Capetians also wisely used their position as consecrated sovereign to build a power base in the Ile de France (the region around Paris) and among the bishops and abbots of the kingdom, and then to insist on their feudal rights as the lords of the great dukes and counts of France. It was this foundation that Louis VII's son Philip II (1180–1223) used to create the French monarchy.

Philip II was known to posterity as Augustus or the aggrandizer, because through his ruthless political intrigue and brilliant organizational sense he more than doubled the territory he controlled and more than quadrupled the revenue of the French crown. (See Special Feature, "The Paris of Philip Augustus, pp. 292–293.) Philip's greatest coup was the confiscation of all the Continental possessions of the English king John (1199–1216). Although sovereign in England, as lord of Normandy, Anjou, Maine, and Touraine, John was technically a vassal of King Philip. When John married the fiancée of one of his Continental vassals, the outraged vassal appealed to Philip in his capacity as John's lord. Philip summoned John to appear before his court, and when he refused to do so, Philip ordered him to surrender all of his Continental fiefs. This meant war, and one by one John's Continental possessions fell to the French king. Philip's victory over John's ally the emperor Otto IV (1198–1215) at Bouvines in 1214 sealed the English loss of Normandy, Maine, Anjou, Poitou, and Touraine.

had been recognized by Frankish kings, ruled their duchy with an authority of which the kings could only dream. Less than a century later Duke William of Normandy expanded his power even more by conquering England. In the twelfth century, the English kings ruled a vast collection of hereditary lands on both

As important as the absorption of these vast regions was the administrative system Philip organized to govern them. Using members of families from the old royal demesne, he set up administrative officials called *baillis* and *seneschals*, salaried agents who collected his revenues and represented his interests. The baillis in particular, who were drawn from nonnoble families and who often had received their education at the University of Paris, were the foundation of the French bureaucracy, which grew in strength and importance through the thirteenth century. By governing the regions of France according to local traditions but always with an eye to the king's interests, these bureaucrats did more than anyone else to create a stable, enduring political system.

Philip's grandson Louis IX (1226–70) fine-tuned this administrative machine and endowed it with the aura of sanctity. Louis was as perfect an embodiment of medieval Christian virtue as Saint Francis of Assisi, who died in the year of Louis's coronation. Generous and pious, but also brave and capable, Louis took seriously his obligation to provide justice for the poor and protection for the weak. A disastrous Crusade in 1248, which ended in his capture and ransom in Egypt, convinced Louis that his failure was punishment for his sins and those of his government. When he returned to France, he dispatched investigators to correct abuses by baillis and

other royal officials and restored property unjustly confiscated by his father's agents during the Albigensian Crusade, directed against heretics in the south of France. In addition he established a permanent central court in Paris to hear appeals from throughout the kingdom. Although much of the work was handled by a growing staff of professional jurists, Louis often became involved personally. In 1270, Louis attempted another crusade and died in an epidemic in Tunis. The good will and devotion that Louis won from his subjects was a precious heritage that his successors were able to exploit for centuries. When his grandson Philip the Fair (1285–1314) faced the threat of Boniface VIII (see p. 308), he could rely on subjects and agents for whom the king of France and not the pope was sovereign.

By a quite different path the English monarchy reached a level of power similar to that of the French kings by the end of the thirteenth century. France was made by a family and its bureaucracy. The kingdom originally forged by Alfred and his descendants was transformed by the successors of William the Conqueror, using its judges and its people, often in spite of themselves.

In 1066 the Norman conquerors of England acquired a small insular kingdom that had been united by Viking raids little more than a century before. Hostile Celtic societies bordered it to the north and west. Still, it had important strengths. First, the king of the English was not simply a feudal lord—he was a sovereign. Secondly, Anglo-Saxon government had been participatory, with the free men of each shire taking part in court sessions and sharing the responsibilities of government. Finally, the king had agents, or *reeves*, in each shire (shire reeves, or sheriffs) who were responsible for representing the king's interests, presiding over the local court, and collecting royal taxes and incomes.

William preserved English government while replacing Anglo-Saxon officers with his Continental vassals, chiefly Normans and Flemings. He rewarded his supporters with land confiscated from the defeated Anglo-Saxons, but he was careful to give out land only in fief. In contrast to Continental practice, where many lords owned vast estates outright, in England all land was held directly or indirectly of the king. Because he wanted to know the extent of his new kingdom and its wealth, William ordered a comprehensive survey of all royal rights. The recorded account, known as the Domesday Book, was the most extensive investigation of economic rights since the late Roman tax rolls had been abandoned by the Merovingians.

Almost two decades of warfare over the succession in the first half of the twelfth century greatly weakened

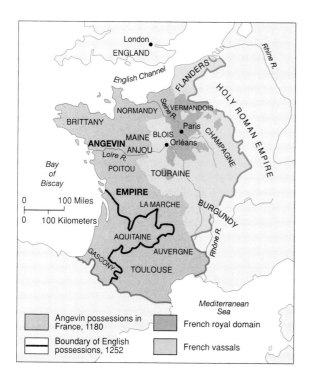

England and France in the Mid 1200s

"October," from the Duc de Berry's Trés Riches Heures, *an illuminated French manuscript of the 1400s by the Limbourg brothers. The peasants are sowing grain on the banks of the Seine. Across the river is the Louvre as it appeared in the time of Philip II.*

*T*he Paris of Philip Augustus

Returning to Paris after his victory over the emperor Otto IV at Bou-vines in July 1214, Philip Augustus was met before the city walls by crowds of townspeople, who spread flowers in his path and led him in triumph into his city. The people danced, clergy and students chanted, bells rang, and the homes and churches of the city overflowed with flowers. The rejoicing, which continued for seven days and nights, was a celebration of the king and the city that he had created.

Prior to his reign, Paris had been just one of several royal residences; Philip made it his capital, enriched it, and trans-formed it. During his reign the population of the city doubled, from approximately 25,000 to over 50,000 inhabitants, making it the most populous city north of the Alps. Philip paved the city's princi-pal streets and built aqueducts to replace those built by the Romans, which were long in ruins. Shortly before leaving on crusade in 1192, he ordered construction of a new city wall, protected by seventy-six towers and pierced by fourteen gates. To guard against the English down the river, Philip also con-structed a fortification, the Louvre, just outside the new walls. Within these walls, which eventually enclosed some 618 acres, devel-oped a complex combination of commercial, political, and cultural life unique in Europe.

Paris was actually three cities in 1214: the ancient island of the *cité* with its royal and episcopal functions; the *ville*, the commer-cial center of Paris on the right bank; and the *université*, the intellectual center of Europe, on the left bank. Philip left his mark on each.

The cité continued its ancient function as the religious and political center of Paris. The island was divided between the two lords of the city, the king and the bishop. At the eastern end, surrounded by a rabbit warren of smaller churches and clerical residences, stood the cathedral. Notre Dame had been in the process of reconstruction since 1163, its soaring Gothic vaulting rising from its older Romanesque pillars. By the first quarter of the thirteenth century, work had begun on the west facade, and the great rose window was under way. Across the entire facade stretched the gallery of the kings—twenty-eight imposing statues of biblical rulers who looked across the cathedral square to the western end of the island and the palace of the king of France.

The palace itself consisted of a round stone tower and a chapel dedicated to Saint Nicholas, both of which dated to the early eleventh century. Here Philip had established the royal court and permanently fixed his archives and accounting office. Here he resided when in Paris, and here he housed his family, retainers, chaplains, and chancery personnel. To the palace came Philip's baillis to report on their annual activities. For the first time, the French monarchy had a fixed seat of government.

The royal precincts on the cité were linked with the ville on the right bank by the Grand-Pont, a bridge covered with the houses of money changers. At the end of the bridge stood a small tower, or *Châtelet*, protecting access to the cité. It was in the ville that in 1183 Philip constructed the first permanent Paris market, *Les Halles,* which remained the principal Paris market until the 1960s. The buildings consisted of two large sheds surrounded by walls pierced with great doors out of which merchants and craftsmen sold their products. Around Les Halles rose the residences and workshops of the tailors, blacksmiths, goldsmiths, shoemakers, coopers, tanners, cartwrights, furriers, potters, carpenters, and other tradespeople. With few exceptions these craft workers occupied post-and-beam structures, crowded together so

closely that often their upper stories touched, forming arches over the narrow, twisting streets. Near Les Halles was the great cemetery of the Saints-Innocents, the most squalid and bizarre quarter of Paris. The primary cemetery of Paris for centuries, the site was used as an informal market, the favorite meeting place for thieves, charlatans, and prostitutes. Here dogs tore at half-buried corpses while lovers met for a few moments of pleasure. Philip had walled the cemetery in 1187, but the walls had accomplished little more than providing security for clandestine activities.

The episcopal quarter of the cité was connected to the predominantly clerical left bank by the Petit-Pont. At the end of this bridge stood another *Châtelet*, which protected access to the cité and which also served as a prison. In the previous century the left bank had become the intellectual center of Europe. Its schools, those of the monasteries of Saint-Germain-des-Prés and Saint-Victor, and especially the school established on Mont Sainte Geneviève, attracted students from as far away as Germany, England, Italy, Hungary, and Scandinavia. Philip's new wall enclosed only Mont Sainte Geneviève, which had become the nucleus of the corporation of masters that formed the University of Paris. Students and masters, reassured by the physical security of the new walls and the political security afforded by Philip's charters for the university, flocked to the area. By 1219 they were so numerous that they grouped themselves into four "nations," divisions of the university popula-

tion according to their countries of origin.

The crowding jostling atmosphere in the university was similar to that in the ville, but on the left bank the crowds consisted of students, teachers, their servants (the latter "nearly all thieves" as one alumnus later recalled), and wandering clerics, or goliards, who lived by their wits on the fringe of the university. Prosperous students rented rooms from local landlords and amused themselves in the numerous taverns. Generous benefactors were beginning to establish charitable foundations, or colleges in which poor clerics might find room and board. Already in existence were the colleges of *Dix-huit*, Saint-Honoré, and Saint-Thomas du Louvre. The most famous, founded by Louis IX's chaplain Robert de Sorbonne, would not be established until 1257.

A great and vibrant capital, Philip's Paris was also dangerous, filthy, and smelly. Twice during Philip's reign flooding destroyed both the Grand-Pont and the Petit-Pont. In 1196 Philip had had to seek refuge from rising water on Mount Saint Geneviève. Although Philip had paved the principal streets, the others remained virtually open sewers. Crowded conditions were ideal breeding grounds for infectious diseases of all sorts, and hospitals such as the Hotel Dieu probably did more to incubate and spread disease than to contain it.

Despite its dangers, crime, and lack of sanitation, Paris was alive, exciting, teeming with new people and new ideas. In the thirteenth century Paris became what it would continue to be—the vibrant heart of the French nation.

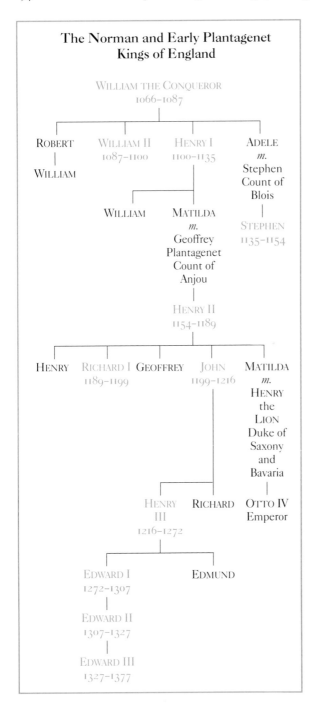

The Norman and Early Plantagenet Kings of England

WILLIAM THE CONQUEROR
1066–1087

ROBERT

WILLIAM

WILLIAM II
1087–1100

HENRY I
1100–1135

ADELE
m.
Stephen
Count of
Blois

WILLIAM

MATILDA
m.
Geoffrey
Plantagenet
Count of
Anjou

STEPHEN
1135–1154

HENRY II
1154–1189

HENRY

RICHARD I
1189–1199

GEOFFREY

JOHN
1199–1216

MATILDA
m.
HENRY
the
LION
Duke of
Saxony
and
Bavaria

HENRY
III
1216–1272

RICHARD

OTTO IV
Emperor

EDWARD I
1272–1307

EDMUND

EDWARD II
1307–1327

EDWARD III
1327–1377

royal courts by expanding royal jurisdiction at the expense of Church tribunals and of the courts of feudal lords.

Henry's program to assert royal courts over local and feudal ones was even more successful, laying the foundation for a system of uniform judicial procedures through which royal justice reached throughout the kingdom—the common law. In France, royal agents observed local legal traditions but sought always to turn them to the king's advantage. In contrast, Henry's legal system simplified and cut through the complex tangle of local and feudal jurisdictions concerning land law. Any free person could purchase, for a modest price, a letter, or *writ*, from the king ordering the local sheriff to impanel a jury to determine if that person had been recently dispossessed of an estate, regardless of that person's legal right to the property. The procedure was swift and efficient. If the jury found for the plaintiff, the sheriff immediately restored the property, by force if necessary. While juries may not have meted out justice, they did resolve conflicts, and they did so in a way that protected landholders. These writs became enormously successful and expanded the jurisdiction of royal courts into areas previously outside royal jurisdiction.

Henry's son John may have made the greatest contribution to the development of the English state by losing Normandy and most of his other Continental lands. Loss of these territories forced English kings to concentrate on ruling England, not on their Continental territories. Moreover, John's financial difficulties, brought about by his unsuccessful wars to recover his Continental holdings, led him to such extremes of fiscal extortion that his barons, prelates, and the townspeople of London revolted. In June 1215 he was forced to accept the "great charter of liberties," or *Magna Carta*, a conservative, feudal document demanding that he respect the rights of his vassals and of the burghers of London. The great significance of the document was its acknowledgment that the king was not above the law.

John and his weak, ineffective son Henry III (1216–72), although ably served by royal judges, were forced by their failures to cede considerable influence to the great barons of the realm. Henry's son Edward I (1272–1307), a strong and effective king who conquered Wales, defended the remaining Continental possessions against France, and expanded the common law, found that he could turn baronial involvement in government to his own advantage. By summoning his barons, bishops, and representatives of the towns and shires to participate in a "parley" or "parliament," he could raise more funds

royal authority, but Henry II (1154–89), reestablished central power by reasserting his authority over the nobility and through his legal reforms. Using his Continental wealth and armies, he brought the English barons into line, destroyed private castles, and reasserted his rights to traditional royal incomes. He strengthened

THE GREAT CHARTER

■ *Faced with defeat at the hands of the French King Philip Augustus abroad and baronial revolt at home, in 1215 King John was forced to sign* Magna Carta, *the "great charter" guaranteeing the traditional rights of the English nobility. Although a conservative document, in time it was interpreted as the guarantee of the fundamental rights of the English.*

John, by the grace of God king of England, lord of Ireland, duke of Normandy and of Aquitaine, and count of Anjou, to his archbishops, bishops, abbots, earls, barons, justiciars, foresters, sheriffs, reeves, ministers, and all his bailiffs and faithful men, greeting. Know that, through the inspiration of God, for the health of our soul and [the souls] of all our ancestors and heirs, for the honour of God and the exaltation of Holy Church, and for the betterment of our realm, by the counsel of our venerable fathers . . . of our nobles . . . and of our other faithful men—

1. We have in the first place granted to God and by this our present charter have confirmed, for us and our heirs forever, that the English Church shall be free and shall have its rights entire and its liberties inviolate . . . We have also granted to all freemen of our kingdom, for us and our heirs forever, all the liberties hereinunder written, to be had and held by them and their heirs of us and our heirs.

2. If any one of our earls or barons or other men holding of us in chief dies, and if when he dies his heir is of full age and owes relief [that heir] shall have his inheritance for the ancient relief . . .

6. Heirs shall be married without disparagement.

7. A widow shall have her marriage portion and inheritance immediately after the death of her husband and without difficulty; nor shall she give anything for her dowry or for her marriage portion or for her inheritance—which inheritance she and her husband were holding on the day of that husband's death . . .

8. No widow shall be forced to marry so long as she wishes to live without a husband; yet so that she shall give security against marring without our consent if she holds of us, or without the consent of her lord if she holds of another.

12. Scutage or aid shall be levied in our kingdom only by the common counsel of our kingdom, except for ransoming our body, for knighting our eldest son, and for once marrying our eldest daughter; and for these [purposes] only a reasonable aid shall be taken. The same provision shall hold with regard to the aids of the city of London.

17. Common pleas shall not follow our court, but shall be held in some definite place.

20. A freeman shall be amerced for a small offence only according to the degree of the offence; and for a grave offence he shall be amerced fined according to the gravity of the offence, saving his contenement [sufficient property to guarantee sustenance for himself and his family]. And a merchant shall be amerced in the same way, saving his merchandise; and a villein in the same way, saving his wainage [harvested crops necessary for seed and upkeep of his farm].

39. No freeman shall be captured or imprisoned or disseised [dispossessed of his estates] or outlawed or exiled or in any way destroyed, nor will we go against him or send against him, except by the lawful judgment of his peers or by the law or the land.

54. No one shall be seized or imprisoned on the appeal of a woman for the death of any one but her husband.

for his wars. Like similar Spanish, Hungarian, and German assemblies of the thirteenth century, these assemblies were occasions to consult, to present royal programs, and to extract extraordinary taxes for specific projects. They were also opportunities for those summoned to petition the king for redress of grievances. Initially, representatives of the shires and towns attended only sporadically. However, since the growing wealth of the towns and countryside made their financial support essential, these groups came to anticipate that they had a right to be consulted and to consent to taxation. This forced self-government through a system of royal courts and justices employing local juries and through a tradition of representative parliaments, coupled with an exacting system of accounting, increased the power of the English monarchy. By 1300, France with its powerful royal bureaucracy and England with its courts and accountants, were the most powerful states in the West.

Between the eleventh and the fourteenth centuries, western European societies experimented with a variety of forms in which political power was wielded. The Germanic emperors claimed the legacy of the Carolingians, but found it increasingly difficult to enforce any public authority over the great aristocrats and independent-minded towns of their empire. Likewise the popes, relying on a universal divine mandate, found it increasingly difficult to command obedience in areas increasingly seen as outside the religious sphere. At the same time, kings in France and England, by manipulating traditions of feudalism, justice, and personal allegiance, extended their authority over ever widening spheres of life in constantly expanding kingdoms.

Edward I presides over a session of Parliament. Edward expanded the institution to include representatives of the boroughs and shires.

War and Politics in the Later Middle Ages

In the fourteenth and fifteenth centuries, royal power continued to face challenges from traditions of private lordship and family ambitions which, for aristocrats across Europe, still took precedence over royal pretensions. Familial rivalries engulfed the feudal monarchies of France and England in the Hundred Years' War, which threatened to overwhelm them at the same time that weakening economic climates and demographic catastrophe exacerbated dynastic crises. In the empire, regionalism and dynastic concerns took precedence over imperial tradition. At the same time, new directions in elite and popular culture encouraged a flowering of a fragmented but vibrant intellectual life.

One Hundred Years of War

Territorial and dynastic rivalry were the triggers that set off the Hundred Years' War between France and England. The English king Edward III (1327–77), a grandson of the French king Philip the Fair, claimed the throne that had passed to Philip VI (1328–50) after the death of the last Capetian. This question of succession, combined with disputes over the remaining possessions of the English king on the Continent, led Edward to declare war in 1337. But if these rivalries were the triggers, the deeper cause of the war was chivalry, a code of

The battle of Agincourt (1415), was one of the great battles of the Hundred Years' War. The heavily armored French cavalry met defeat at the hands of a much smaller force of disciplined English pikemen and longbowmen.

conduct that required the elites of Europe not only to maintain their honor by violence but also to cultivate violence to increase that honor.

Edward III of England and his rival Philip VI of France both epitomized the chivalrous knight. Both gloried in luxurious living and conspicuous consumption. For a ruler like Edward, practical when it came to organizing and financing his campaigns but obsessed with knightly glory, war with France was the ideal way to win honor and fame.

Philip shared Edward's ideals but lacked his rival's practicality and self-assurance. As the first French king

in centuries elected rather than born into the right of succession, he treated with excessive deference the magnates from whose ranks he had come. He hesitated to press them for funds and deferred to them on matters of policy even while missing opportunities to raise other revenue from towns and merchants. Finally, although a competent warrior, Philip was no match in strategy or tactics for his English cousin.

In spite of chivalrous ideals, nobles no longer fought as vassals of the king but as highly paid mercenaries. The nature of this service differed greatly on the two sides of the Channel. In France, the tactics

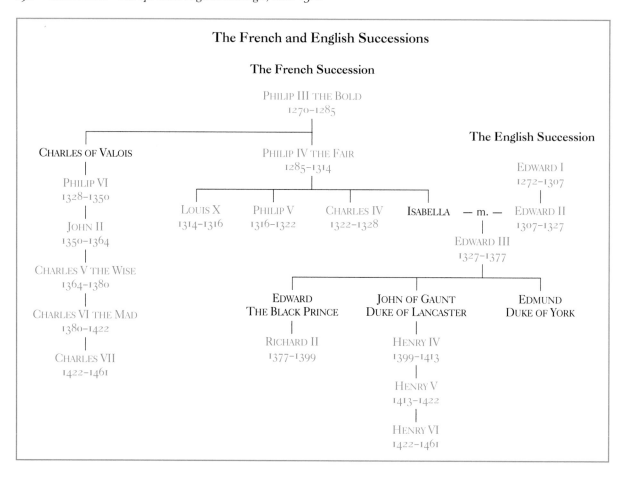

The French and English Successions

The French Succession

PHILIP III THE BOLD
1270–1285

CHARLES OF VALOIS

PHILIP IV THE FAIR
1285–1314

The English Succession

EDWARD I
1272–1307

PHILIP VI
1328–1350

LOUIS X
1314–1316

PHILIP V
1316–1322

CHARLES IV
1322–1328

ISABELLA   — m. —   EDWARD II
1307–1327

JOHN II
1350–1364

EDWARD III
1327–1377

CHARLES V THE WISE
1364–1380

CHARLES VI THE MAD
1380–1422

EDWARD
THE BLACK PRINCE

JOHN OF GAUNT
DUKE OF LANCASTER

EDMUND
DUKE OF YORK

CHARLES VII
1422–1461

RICHARD II
1377–1399

HENRY IV
1399–1413

HENRY V
1413–1422

HENRY VI
1422–1461

and personnel had changed little since the twelfth century. The core of any army was the body of heavily armored nobles who rode into battle with their lords, supported by lightly armored knights. Behind them marched infantrymen recruited from towns and armed with pikes. Although the French also hired mercenary Italian crossbowmen, the nobles despised them and never used them effectively.

In contrast, centuries of fighting against Welsh and Scottish enemies had transformed and modernized the English armies and their tactics. The great nobles continued to serve as heavily armored horsemen, but professional companies of pikemen and longbowmen made up the bulk of the army. Time and again the antiquated French cavalry lost pitched battles against numerically inferior English armies. But pitched battles were not the worst defeats for the French. More devastating were the constant raiding and systematic destruction of the French countryside by the English companies. Raiding and pillaging continued for decades, even during long truces between the French and English kings. During

periods of truce unemployed free companies of French and English mercenaries roamed the countryside, supporting themselves by banditry while awaiting the renewal of more-formal hostilities. Never had the ideals of chivalric conduct been so far distant from the brutal realities of warfare.

The French kings were powerless to prevent such destruction, just as they were unable to defeat the enemy in open battle. Since the kings were incapable of protecting their subjects or of leading their armies to victory, the "silken thread binding together the kingdom of France," as one observer put it, began to unravel, and the kingdom so painstakingly constructed by the Capetian monarchs began to fall apart. Not only did the English make significant territorial conquests, but the French nobles began carving out autonomous lordships. Private warfare and castle building, never entirely eradicated even by Louis IX and Philip IV, increased as royal government lost its ability to control the nobility. Whole regions of the kingdom slipped entirely from royal authority. Duke Philip the Good of Burgundy

(1396–1467) allied himself with England against France and profited from the war to form a far-flung lordship that included Flanders, Brabant, Luxembourg, and Hainaut. By the time of his death, he was the most powerful ruler in Europe. Much of the so-called Hundred Years' War was actually a French civil war.

During this century of war the French economy suffered even more than the French state. Trade routes were broken and commerce declined as credit disappeared. French kings repeatedly seized the assets of Italian merchant bankers in order to finance the war. Such actions made the Italians, who had been the backbone of French commercial credit, extremely wary about extending loans in the kingdom. The kings then turned to French and Flemish merchants, extorting from them forced loans that dried up capital that might otherwise have been returned to commerce and industry. Politically and economically, France seemed doomed.

The flower of French chivalry did not save France. Instead, at the darkest moment of the long and bloody struggle, salvation came at the hands of a simple peasant girl from the county of Champagne. By 1429 the English and their Burgundian allies held virtually all of northern France including Paris. Now they were besieging Orléans, the key to the south. The heir to the French throne, the dauphin, was the weak-willed and uncrowned Charles VII (1422–61). To him came Joan of Arc (1412–

A fifteenth-century portrait of Joan of Arc. The Maid of Orléans was tried for heresy and executed in 1431. Later, in 1456, Pope Calixtus III pronounced her innocent. Pope Benedict XV formally declared her a saint in 1920.

31), a simple, illiterate but deeply religious girl who bore an incredible message of hope. She claimed to have heard the voices of saints ordering her to save Orléans and have the dauphin crowned according to tradition at Reims.

Charles and his advisers were more than skeptical about this brash peasant girl who announced her divinely ordained mission to save France. Finally convinced of her sincerity if not of her ability, Charles allowed her to accompany a relief force to Orléans. The French army, its spirit buoyed by the belief that Joan's simple faith was the work of God, defeated the English and ended the siege. This victory led to others, and on 16 July 1429 Charles was crowned king at Reims.

After the coronation, Joan's luck began to fade. She failed to take Paris, and in 1431 she was captured by the Burgundians, who sold her to the English. Eager to get rid of this troublesome peasant girl, the English had her tried as a heretic. Charles did nothing to save his savior. After all, the code of chivalry did not demand that a king intervene on behalf of a mere peasant girl, even if she had saved his kingdom. She was burned at the stake in Rouen on 30 May 1431.

Despite Joan's inglorious end, the tide had turned. The French pushed the English back toward the coast. In the final major battle of the war, fought at Formigny

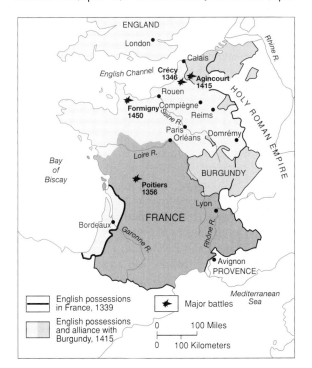

The Hundred Years' War

in 1450, the French used a new and telling weapon to defeat the English—gunpowder. Rather than charging the English directly as they had done so often before, they mounted cannon and pounded the English to bits. Gunpowder completed the destruction of the chivalric traditions of warfare begun by archers and pikemen. By 1452 English Continental holdings had been reduced to the town of Calais. The Continental warfare of more than a century was over.

Though war on the Continent had ended, warfare in England was just beginning. In some ways, the English monarchy had suffered even more from the Hundred Years' War than had the French. At the outset, English royal administration had been more advanced than the French. The system of royal agents, courts, and parliaments had created the expectation that the king could preserve peace and provide justice at home while waging successful and profitable wars abroad. As the decades dragged on without a decisive victory, the king came to rely on the aristocracy, enlisting its financial assistance by granting these magnates greater power at home. War created powerful and autonomous aristocratic families with their own armies. Under a series of weak kings these families fought among themselves. Ultimately they took sides in a civil war to determine the royal succession. For thirty years, from 1455 to 1485, supporters of the house of York, whose badge was the white rose, fought the rival house of Lancaster, whose symbol was the red rose, in the sort of dynastic struggle that would not have seemed out of place in the disintegrating German empire. The English Wars of the Roses, as the conflict came to be called, finally ended in 1485, when Henry Tudor of the Lancastrian faction defeated his opponents. He inaugurated a new era as Henry VII (1485–1509), the first king of the Tudor dynasty.

The Struggle for Central Europe

Fragmented and shifting territorial bases were as typical of the great families in the empire of the fourteenth and fifteenth centuries as they were in France and England. Everywhere, family politics threatened the fragile institutional developments of the thirteenth century. What mattered was neither territorial boundaries nor political divisions but marriage alliances, kinship, and dynastic ambitions.

Within the Holy Roman Empire, five great families competed for dominance. These were the Luxemburgs, originally from the Rhineland; the Bavarian Wittelsbachs; the Habsburgs from the Black Forest; the Bohemian Premysls; and the house of Anjou, descended from the younger brother of the French king Louis IX. All of these families spread their influence throughout the eastern portions of the empire through marriage alliances and feuds.

For over a century, not only great princes but also monks, adventurers, and simple peasants streamed into the kingdoms and principalities of eastern Europe. Since the early thirteenth century the Teutonic orders had used the sword to spread Christianity along the Baltic coast. By the early fourteenth century these knight-monks had conquered Prussia and the coast as far east as the Narva River, now well within Russia, where they reached the borders of the Christian principality of Novgorod. Long wagon trains of pioneers snaked their way across Germany from the Rhineland, Westphalia, and Saxony to this new frontier. There they were able to negotiate advantageous contracts with their new lords, guaranteeing them greater freedom than they had known at home.

By the fifteenth century religious and secular German lords had established a new agrarian economy, modeled on western European estates, in regions previously unoccupied or sparsely settled by the indigenous Slavic peoples. This economy specialized in the cultivation of grain for export to the west. Each fall fleets of hundreds of ships sailed from Gdansk and Riga to the ports of the Netherlands, England, and France. Returning flotillas carried Flemish cloth and tons of salt for preserving food as far as Novgorod. The influx of Baltic grain into Europe caused a decline in domestic grain prices and a corresponding economic slump for landlords throughout the fourteenth and fifteenth centuries.

Farther south, the Christian kingdoms of Poland, Bohemia, and Hungary beckoned different sorts of colonists from the west. Newly opened silver and copper mines in Bohemia, Silesia, southern Poland, and Hungarian Transylvania needed skilled miners, smelters, and artisans. Many were recruited from the overpopulated regions of western Germany. East-west trade routes developed to export these metals, giving new life to the Bohemian towns of Prague and Brno, the Polish cities of Kraków and Lwów, and Hungarian Buda and Bratislava. Trade networks reached south to the Mediterranean via Vienna, the Brenner Pass, and Venice. To the north, trade routes extended to the Elbe River and the trading towns of Lübeck and Bremen. The Bavarian towns of Augsburg, Rothenburg, and Nuremberg flourished at the western end of this network. To the east, Lwów became a trading center connecting southern Russia with the west.

Responses to the plague were equally varied. In many German towns terrified Christian citizens looked for outside scapegoats and slaughtered the Jewish community. Cities, aware of the risk of infection although ignorant of its process, closed their gates and turned away outsiders. Individuals with means fled to country houses or locked themselves in their homes to avoid contact with others. Nothing worked. As devastating as the first outbreak of the plague was, its aftershocks were even more catastrophic. Once established in Europe, the disease continued to return roughly once each generation. The last outbreak of the plague in Europe was the 1771 epidemic in Moscow that killed 60,000.

The Black Death, along with other epidemics, famines, and war-induced shortages, affected western much more than eastern Europe. The culminating effect of these disasters was a darker, more somber vision of life than that of the previous centuries. This vision found its expression in the Dance of Death, an increasingly popular image in art. Naked, rotting corpses dance with great animation before the living. The latter, depicted in the dress of all social orders, are immobile, surprised by death, reluctant but resigned.

The Black Death was the greatest disaster ever to befall Europe. It touched every aspect of life, hastening a process of social, economic, and cultural transformation already under way. Nothing had prepared Europe for this catastrophe, no teaching of the Church or its leaders could adequately explain it, and in spite of desperate attempts to fix the blame on Jews or strangers, no one but God could be held responsible. Survivors stood alone and uncertain before a new world. Across Europe, moralists reported a general lapse in traditional ethics, a breakdown in the moral codes. The most troubling aspect of this breakdown was what one defender of the old order termed "the plague of insurrection" that spread across Europe.

A page from the fourteenth-century psalter and prayer book of Bonne of Luxembourg, Duchess of Normandy. The three figures of the dead shown here contrast with three living figures on the facing page of the psalter to illustrate a moral fable.

The Plague of Insurrection

Initially, even this darkest cloud had a silver lining. Lucky survivors of the plague soon found other reasons to rejoice. Property owners, when they finished burying their dead, discovered that they were far richer in land and goods. At the other end of the social spectrum, the plague had eliminated the labor surplus. Peasants were suddenly in great demand. For a time at least, they were able to negotiate substantially higher wages and an improved relationship with landlords.

These hopes were short-lived. The rise in expectations produced by the redistribution of wealth and the labor shortage created new tensions. Landlords sought laws forcing peasants to accept preplague wages and tightened their control over serfs in order to prevent them from fleeing to cities or other lords. At the same time governments attempted to benefit from laborers' greater prosperity by imposing new taxes. In cities, where the plague had been particularly devastating, the demographic decline sharply lowered demand for goods and thus lowered the need for manufacturing and production of all kinds. Like rural landowners, master craftsmen sought legislation to protect their incomes. New laws reduced production by restricting access to trades and increased masters' control over the surviving urban laborers. Social mobility, once a characteristic of urban life, slowed to a halt. Membership in guilds became hereditary, and young apprentices or journeymen had little hope of ever rising to the level of independent master craftsmen.

These new tensions led to violence when kings added their demands for new war taxes to the landlords' and masters' attempts to erase the peasants' and workers' recent gains. The first revolts took place in France, where peasants and townspeople, disgusted with the incompetence of the nobility in their conduct of the war against England, feared that their new wealth would be stolen from them by corrupt and incompetent aristocrats.

In 1358 the French government attempted to increase taxes on the peasantry. Peasants in the north of France rebelled against their landlords. The revolt, known as the Jacquerie, was a spontaneous outburst directed against the nobility, whom the peasants saw as responsible for all their ills. Without real leadership or program, peasants attacked as many nobles as they could find, killing them along with their wives and children and burning their homes and castles. The peasants' brutality deeply shocked the upper classes, whose own violence was constrained within the bounds of the chivalric code. Because the Church largely supported the power structure, the uprising was also strongly anticlerical. Success bred further attacks, and the disorganized army of peasants began to march south toward Paris, killing, looting, and burning everything associated with the despised nobility.

In the midst of this peasant revolt, Etienne Marcel (ca. 1316–58), a wealthy Parisian cloth merchant, led an uprising of Parisian merchants, which sought to take control of royal finances and force fiscal reforms on the dauphin, the future Charles V. Although initially the rebels were primarily members of the merchant and guild elite, Marcel soon enlisted the support of the radical townspeople against the aristocracy. He even made overtures to the leaders of the Jacquerie to join forces. For a brief time it appeared that the aristocratic order in France might succumb. However, in the end peasant and merchant rebels were no match for professional armies. The Jacquerie met its end outside Paris, where an aristocratic force cut the peasants to pieces. The Parisian revolt met a similar fate. Aristocratic armies surrounded the city and cut off its food supply. Marcel was assassinated and the dauphin Charles regained the city.

The French revolts set the pattern for similar uprisings across Europe. Rebels were usually relatively prosperous peasants or townspeople whose economic situations were threatened by aristocratic attempts to turn back the clock to the period before the Black Death. In 1381 English peasants, reacting to new and hated taxes, rose in a less violent but more coordinated revolt known as the Great Rebellion. Peasant revolts took place in the northern Spanish region of Catalonia in 1395 and in Germany throughout the fourteenth and fifteenth centuries. The largest was the great Peasant's Revolt of 1524. Although always ruthlessly suppressed, European

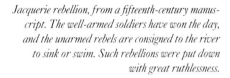

Jacquerie rebellion, from a fifteenth-century manuscript. The well-armed soldiers have won the day, and the unarmed rebels are consigned to the river to sink or swim. Such rebellions were put down with great ruthlessness.

peasant uprisings continued until the peasant rebellion of 1626 in upper Austria. These outbursts indicated not necessarily the desperation of Europe's peasantry, but the new belief that they could change their lives for the better through united action.

Urban artisans imitated the example of their rural cousins. Although there had been some uprisings in the Flemish towns before the Black Death, revolts of townspeople picked up momentum in the second half of the fourteenth century. In general the town rebels were not the destitute urban poor any more than the peasant rebels had been the landless rural poor. Instead they were generally independent artisans and small tradesmen who wanted to break the control of the powerful guilds. In spite of the brutal suppression and ultimate failure of popular revolts, they became permanent if intermittent features on the European social landscape.

Urban Life in the Later Middle Ages

In France and the Low Countries, population decline, war, and class conflict fatally weakened the vitality of the commercial and manufacturing system. These same events reduced the market for Italian goods and undermined the economic strength of the great Italian cities. The Hundred Years' War bankrupted many of Florence's greatest banking houses who lent to both French and English kings. Commercial activity declined as well. While Italians did not disappear from northern cities, they no longer held a near monopoly on northern trade.

These setbacks for the Italians worked to the advantage of German towns. Along the Baltic Sea, in Scandinavia, and in northern Germany, towns such as Lübeck, Lüneburg, Visby, Bremen, and Cologne formed a commercial and political alliance to control northern trade. During the second half of the fourteenth century, this Hanseatic League—the word *Hansa* means "company"—monopolized the northern grain trade and forced Denmark to grant its members exclusive rights to export Scandinavian fish throughout Europe. Hanseatic merchants established colonies from Novgorod to London to Bruges and even in Venice. They carried dried and salted fish to Prague and supplied grain from Riga to England and France.

English towns also profited from the decline of Flanders and France. The population decline of the fourteenth century led many English landowners to switch from traditional farming to sheep raising, since pasturing sheep required few workers and promised cash profits. While surviving peasants were driven off the land and forced to beg for a living, lords produced more wool than ever before. However, because the Hundred Years' War hampered the exportation of wool to Flanders, the English began to make cloth themselves. Protected by high tariffs on imports and low duties on exports, by the middle of the fifteenth century, England became a major exporter of finished cloth.

Some made fortunes from the new circumstances, many others fell into hopeless poverty. Driven both by mounting compassion for the urban poor and by a growing fear of the violent potential of this ever increasing population, medieval towns developed novel systems to deal with poverty. The first was public assistance, the second social control and repression.

Traditionally, charity had been a religious act that focused more on the soul of the giver than on the effect on the life of the recipient. The same had been true of charitable organizations such as confraternities and hospitals. Confraternities were pious religious organizations of lay people and clergy who ministered to the poor and sick. Hospitals were all-purpose religious institutions providing lodging for pilgrims, the elderly, and the ill. By the fourteenth century, such pious institutions had become inadequate to deal with the growing numbers of poor and ill. Towns began to assume control over a centralized system of public assistance.

One consequence of poverty was increased crime. Fear of the poor led to repressive measures and harsh punishments. During the later Middle Ages, gruesome forms of mutilation and execution became common for a long list of offenses. Petty larceny was punished with whipping, cutting off ears or thumbs, branding, or expulsion. In some towns, robbery of an amount over three pence was punished with death.

The later Middle Ages was a time of stark contrasts, of famine, pestilence, and revolt as well as of aristocratic opulence and royal pageantry. The streets and markets of fifteenth-century towns bustled with the sights and sounds of rich Hanseatic merchants, Italian bankers, and prosperous local tradesmen. The back alleys on the edges of these towns teemed with a growing mass of desperate and despairing workers and their families.

The Spirit of the Later Middle Ages

The Dance of Death and the gallows were not the only images of later medieval life. The constant presence of death made life more precious. Europeans celebrated life with a vigor and creativity characterized by a growing sense of individuality, independence, and variety. During the fourteenth century, the Church failed to provide unified spiritual and cultural leadership to Europe. The institutional division of the Church was paralleled by divisions over how to lead the proper Christian life. Many devout Christians developed independent lifestyles intended to bring them closer to God without reliance on the Church hierarchy. They elaborated beliefs branded by the Church as heresy. Others called into question the philosophical bases of theological speculation developed since the time of Aquinas. Finally, the increasing pluralism of European culture gave rise to new literary traditions that both celebrated and criticized the medieval legacy of Christianity, chivalry, and social order.

Christendom Divided

The universal empire as well as its traditional competitor, the universal Church, declined in the later Middle Ages. The papacy never recovered from the humiliating defeat Pope Boniface VIII suffered at the hands of King Philip the Fair in 1303. The ecclesiastical edifice created by the thirteenth-century popes was shaken to its foundations, first by becoming a virtual appendage of the French monarchy, and then by a dispute that for over forty years gave European Christians a choice between two, and finally three, claimants to the chair of Saint Peter.

In 1305 the College of Cardinals elected as pope the bishop of Bordeaux. The pope took up residence not in Rome but in the papal city of Avignon on the east bank of the Rhone River. Technically, Avignon was a papal estate within the Holy Roman Empire. Actually, with France just across the river, the pope at Avignon was under French control. For the next seventy years French popes and French cardinals ruled the Church. The traditional enemies of France as well as religious reformers who expected leadership from the papacy looked on this situation with disgust.

The popes of Avignon were more successful in achieving their financial goals than in winning political power. Although they attempted to follow an independent course in international affairs, their French orientation eroded their influence in European politics, especially in the Holy Roman Empire. No longer could the popes exert any direct influence in the internal affairs of Europe's states. Frustrated politically, the Avignon popes concentrated on perfecting the legal and fiscal system of the Church and were enormously successful in concentrating the vast financial and legal power of the Church in the papal office. From the papal court, or curia, they created a vast and efficient central bureaucracy whose primary role was to increase papal revenues.

The Great Schism

Revenues came from two main sources. The less lucrative but ultimately more critical source was the sale of indulgences, payments in place of penance due after the absolution of sins by the Church. Papal "pardoners" working on commission used high-pressure sales pitches to sell indulgences across Europe.

The second and major source of papal income was the sale of Church offices, or benefices. Popes claimed the right to appoint bishops and abbots to all benefices and to collect a hefty tax for the appointment. Papal appointees often acquired numerous offices and viewed them merely as sources of income, leaving pastoral duties, when they were performed at all, to hired local clergy.

In 1377 Pope Gregory XI (1370–78) returned from Avignon to Rome but died almost immediately upon arrival. Thousands of Italians, afraid that the cardinals would elect another Frenchman, surrounded the church where they were meeting and demanded an Italian pope. The terrified cardinals elected an Italian, who took the name of Urban VI (1378–89). Once elected,

Urban attempted to reform the curia, but he did so in a most undiplomatic way, insulting the cardinals and threatening to appoint sufficient non-French bishops to their number to end French control of the curia. The cardinals soon left Rome and announced that because the election had been made under duress it was invalid and that Urban should resign. When he refused they held a second election and chose a Frenchman, Clement VII (1378–94), who took up residence in Avignon. The Church now had two heads, both with reasonable claims to the office.

The chaos created by this so-called Great Schism divided western Christendom. Nothing in Church law or tradition offered a solution to this crisis. Nor did unilateral efforts to settle the crisis succeed. Twice France invaded Italy in an attempt to eliminate Urban but failed both times. The situation perpetuated itself. When Urban and Clement died, cardinals on both sides elected successors. By the end of the fourteenth century, France and the empire were exasperated with their popes and even the cardinals were determined to end the stalemate.

Church lawyers argued that a general council alone could end the schism. Both popes opposed this "conciliarist" argument because it suggested that an assembly of the Church rather than the pope held supreme authority. However, in 1408 cardinals from both sides summoned a council in the Italian city of Pisa. The council deposed both rivals and elected a new pope. But this solution only made matters worse, since neither pope accepted the decision of the council. Europe now had to contend with not two but three popes, each claiming to be the true successor of Saint Peter.

Six years later the Council of Constance managed a final solution. There under the patronage of the emperor-elect Sigismund (1410–37), cardinals, bishops, abbots, and theologians from across Europe met to resolve the crisis. Their goal was not only to settle the schism but also to reform the Church to prevent a recurrence of such a scandal. The participants at Constance hoped to restructure the Church as a limited monarchy in which the powers of the pope would be controlled through frequent councils. The Pisan and Avignon popes were deposed. The Roman pope, abandoned by all of his supporters, abdicated. Before doing so, however, he formally convoked the council in order to preserve the tradition that a general council had to be called by the pope. Finally, the council elected as pope an Italian cardinal not aligned with any of the claimants. The election of the cardinal, who took the name Martin V (1417–31), ended the schism.

The relief at the end of the Great Schism could not hide the very real problems left by over a century of papal weakness. The prestige of the papacy had been permanently compromised. Everywhere the Church had become more national in character. The conciliarist demand for control of the Church, which had ended the schism, lessened the power of the pope. Finally, during the century between Boniface VIII and Martin V, new religious movements had taken root across Europe, movements that the political creatures who had occupied the papal office could neither understand nor control. The Council of Constance, which brought an end to the schism, also condemned Jan Hus, the leader of the Czech reform movement and the spiritual founder of the Protestant reformation of the sixteenth century. The disintegration of the Church loomed ever closer as pious individuals turned away from the organized Church and sought divine help in personal piety, mysticism, or even magic.

Discerning the Spirit of God

When Joan of Arc first appeared before the dauphin in 1429, he feared that she was a witch. Only a physical examination by matrons, which determined that she was a virgin, persuaded him otherwise—witches were believed to have had intercourse with the devil. Everyone in the late Middle Ages was familiar with witches, saints, and heretics. Distinguishing among them was often a matter of perspective.

Accusations of witchcraft were relatively rare in the Middle Ages. The age of witch-hunts occurred in the sixteenth and seventeenth centuries. During the Middle Ages magic existed in a wide variety of forms, but its definition was fluid and its practitioners were not always considered witches. Alchemists and astrologers held honored places in society, while simple practitioners of folk religion and medicine were condemned, particularly when they were poor women. Witches, believed to have made a contract with the devil, were condemned as one type of heretic, that is, a Christian who persisted in a belief contrary to Church teaching, and were persecuted like other heretics. Only at the end of the fifteenth century, with the publication of the *Witches' Hammer*, a great handbook for inquisitors, did the European witch craze begin in earnest. Earlier, authorities feared more those people who sought their own pacts not with the devil but with God.

Even as Europeans were losing respect for the institutional Church, people everywhere were seeking

A WOMAN BEFORE THE INQUISITION

■ *In 1320 Jacques Fournier (ca. 1280–1342), bishop of Pamiers in France and the future pope Benedict XII, interrogated the villagers of Montaillou in southern France about their involvement in the Cathar heresy, a dualist religion present in the region since the eleventh century, whose members were called "the good Christians." The following excerpt is from the testimony of Béatrice de Planissoles, a member of the lower nobility and a prominent inhabitant of the village.*

Twenty-six years ago during the month of August, I was the wife of the late knight Bérenger de Roquefort, castellan of Montaillou. The late Raimond Roussel was the intendant and the stewart of our household which we held at the castle of Montaillou. He often asked me to leave with him and to go to Lombardy with the good Christians who are there, telling me that the Lord had said that man must quit his father, mother, wife, husband, son and daughter and follow him, and that he would give him the kingdom of heaven. When I asked him, "How could I quit my husband and my sons?" he replied that the Lord had ordered it and that it was better to leave a husband and sons whose eyes rot than to abandon him who lives for eternity and who gives the kingdom of heaven.

When I asked him "How is it possible that God created so many men and women if many of them are not saved?" he answered that only the good Christians will be saved and no others, neither religious nor priests, nor anyone except these good Christians. Because, he said, just as it is impossible for a camel to pass through the eye of a needle, it is impossible for those who are rich to be saved. This is why the kings and princes, prelates and religious, and all those who have wealth, cannot be saved, but only the good Christians . . . He also told me that all spirits sinned at the beginning with the sin of pride, believing that they could know more and be worth more than God, and for that they fell to earth. These spirits later take on bodies, and the world will not end before all of them have been incarnated into the bodies of men and women. Thus it is that the soul of a new born child is as old as that of an old man.

He also said that the souls of men and women who were not good Christians, after leaving their bodies, enter the bodies of other men and women a total of nine times. If in these nine bodies they do not find the body of a good Christian, the soul is damned. If on the contrary, they find the body of a good Christian, the soul is saved.

I asked him how the spirit of a dead man or woman could enter the mouth of a pregnant woman and from there into the mouth of the fruit that she carries in her womb. He answered that the spirit could enter the fruit of the woman's womb by any part of her body.

Thus he urged me to leave with him so that we could go together to the good Christians, mentioning various noble women who had gone there. Alesta and Serena, women of Châteauverdun, painted themselves with colors which made them appear foreign, so that they could not be recognized and went to Toulouse. When they arrived at an inn, the hostess wanted to know if they were heretics and gave them live chickens, telling them to prepare them because she had things to do in town, and left the house. [Cathars avoided killing and eating animals.] When she had returned she found the chickens still alive and asked them why they had not prepared them. They responded that if the hostess would kill them, they would prepare them but that they would not kill them. The hostess heard that and went to tell the inquisitors that two heretics were in her establishment. They were arrested and burned. When it was time to go to the stake, they asked for water to wash their faces, saying that they would not go to God painted thusly.

I told Raimond that they would have done better to abandon their heresy than to allow themselves to be burned, and he told me that the good Christians did not feel fire because fire with which they are burned cannot hurt them.

closer and more intimate relationships with God. Distrusting the formal institutions of the Church, lay persons and clerics turned to private devotions and to mysticism to achieve union with the divine. Most of these stayed within the Church. Others, among them many female mystics, maintained an ambiguous relationship with the traditional institutions of Christianity. A few broke sharply with it.

Christians of the later Middle Ages sought to imitate Christ and venerated the Eucharist, or communion wafer, which the Church taught was the actual body of Jesus. Male mystics focused on imitating Jesus in his poverty, suffering, and humility. Women developed their own form of piety, which focused not on wealth and power but on spiritual nourishment, particularly as provided by the Eucharist. For women mystics, radical fasting became preparation for the reception of the Eucharist, often described in highly emotional and erotic terms.

Only a thin line separated the saint's heroic search for union with God from the heretic's identification with God. The radical Brethren of the Free Spirit believed that God was all things and that all things would return to God. Such pantheism denied the possibility of sin, punishment, and the need for salvation. Members of the sect were hunted down and many were burned as heretics. The specter of the Inquisition, the ecclesiastical court system charged with ferreting out heretics, hung over all such communities.

When unorthodox Christians were protected by secular lords, the ecclesiastical courts were powerless. This was the case with John Wycliffe (ca. 1330–84), an Oxford theologian who attacked the doctrinal and political bases of the Church. He taught that the value of the sacraments depended on the worthiness of the priest administering them, that Jesus was present in the Eucharist only in spirit, that indulgences were useless, and that salvation depended on divine predestination rather than individual merit. Normally these teachings would have led him to the stake. But he had also attacked the Church's right to wealth and luxury, an idea whose political implications pleased the English monarchy and nobility. Thus he was allowed to live and teach in peace. Only under Henry V (1413–22) were Wycliffe's followers, known as Lollards, vigorously suppressed by the state. Before this condemnation took place, however, Wycliffe's teachings reached the kingdom of Bohemia through the marriage of Charles IV's daughter Anne of Bohemia to the English king Richard II. Anne took with her to England a number of Bohemian clerics, some of whom studied at Oxford and absorbed the political and religious teachings of Wycliffe, which they then took back to Bohemia.

In Prague some of Wycliffe's less radical teachings took root among the theology faculty of the new university, where the leading proponent of Wycliffe's teachings was Jan Hus (1373–1415), an immensely popular young master and preacher. Although Hus rejected Wycliffe's ideas about the priesthood and the sacraments, he and other Czech preachers attacked indulgences and demanded a reform of Church liturgy and morals. They grafted these religious demands onto an attack on German dominance of the Bohemian kingdom. These attacks outraged both the Pisan pope John XXIII (1410–15) and the Bohemian king Wenceslas IV (1378–1419), who favored the German faction. The pope excommunicated Hus, and the king expelled the Czech faculty from the university. Hus was convinced that he was no heretic and that a fair hearing would clear him. He therefore agreed to travel to the Council of Constance under promise of safe conduct from the emperor-elect Sigismund to defend his position. There he was tried on a charge of heresy, convicted, and burned at the stake.

News of Hus's execution touched off a revolt in Bohemia. Unlike the peasant revolts of the past, however, this revolt had broad popular support throughout all

The Later Middle Ages, 1300–1500

1305–1377	Avignon papacy
1337–1452	Hundred Years' War
1347–1352	Black Death spreads through Europe
1358	Jacquerie revolt of French peasants; Etienne Marcel leads revolt of Parisian merchants
1378–1417	Great Schism divides Roman Christianity
1381	Great Rebellion of English peasants
1414–1417	Council of Constance ends Great Schism
1415	Jan Hus executed
1455–1485	English Wars of the Roses

Illustration from the sixteenth-century Bohemian *Gradual of Malá Strana. Jan Hus, wearing the traditional heretic's cap adorned with devils, is burned at the stake.*

levels of Czech society. Peasants, nobles, and townspeople saw the attack on Hus and his followers as an attack on Czech independence and national interest by a Church and an empire controlled by Germans. Soon a radical faction known as the Taborites was demanding the abolition of private property and the institution of a communal state. Although moderate Hussites and Bohemian Catholics combined to defeat the radicals in 1434, most of Bohemia remained Hussite through the fifteenth century. The sixteenth-century reformer Martin Luther declared himself a follower of Jan Hus.

William of Ockham and the Spirit of Truth

The critical and individualistic approach that characterized religion during the later Middle Ages was also typical of the philosophical thought of the period. The delicate balance between faith and reason taught by Aquinas and other intellectuals in the thirteenth century disintegrated in the fourteenth. As in other areas of life, intellectuals questioned the basic suppositions of their predecessors, directing intellectual activity away from general speculations and toward particular, observable reality.

The person primarily responsible for this new intellectual climate was the English Franciscan William of Ockham (ca. 1300-49). Ockham developed a truly radical political philosophy. Imperial power, he argued, derived not from the pope but from the people. People are free to determine their own form of government and to elect rulers. They can make their choice directly, as in the election of the emperor by electors who represent the people, or implicitly, through continuing forms of government. In either case, government is entirely secular. He also denied the absolute authority of the pope,

even in spiritual matters. Rather, Ockham argued, parishes, religious orders, and monasteries should send representatives to regional synods, which in turn would elect representatives to general councils.

As radical as Ockham's political ideas were, his philosophical outlook was even more extreme and exerted a more direct and lasting influence. The Christian Aristotelianism that developed in the thirteenth century had depended on the validity of general concepts called universals, which could be analyzed through the use of logic. Aquinas and others who studied the eternity of the world, the existence of God, the nature of the soul, and other philosophical questions believed that people could reach general truths by abstracting universals from particular, individual cases. Ockham argued that universals were merely names, no more than convenient tags for discussing individual things. Universals had no connection with reality and could not be used to reason from particular observations to general truths. This radical nominalism (from the Latin *nomen*, "name") thus denied that human reason could aspire to certain truth.

Ockham's ideas on Church governance by a general council representing the whole Christian community offered the one hope for a solution to the Great Schism that erupted shortly after his death. Conciliarists drew on Ockham's attack on papal absolutism to propose an alternative church. The Council of Constance, which ended the schism, was the fruit of Ockham's political theory.

Just as Ockham's political theory dominated the later fourteenth century, his nominalist philosophy won over the philosophical faculties of Europe. Since he had discredited the value of Aristotelian logic to increase knowledge, the result was, on the one hand, a decline in abstract speculation and on the other, a greater interest in scientific observation of individual phenomena. In the next generation Parisian professors, trained in the tradition of Ockham, laid the foundation for scientific studies of motion and the universe that led to the scientific discoveries of the sixteenth and seventeenth centuries.

Vernacular Literature and the Individual

Just as the religious and philosophical concerns of the later Middle Ages developed within national frameworks and criticized accepted authority from the perspective of individual experience, so too did the literature, increasingly written in the many languages spoken by Europeans rather than in learned Latin, begin to explore the place of the individual within an increasingly complex society. Poets used their native tongues to express a spectrum of sentiments and to describe a spectrum of emotions and values. The themes and ideas expressed ranged from the polished, traditional values of the aristocracy trying to maintain the ideals of chivalry in a new and changed world to the views of ordinary people, by turns reverent or sarcastic, joyful or despondent.

In Italy, a trio of Tuscan poets, Dante Alighieri (1265-1321), Petrarch (1304-74), and Boccaccio (1313-75), not only made Italian a literary language but composed in it some of the greatest literature of all time. Dante, the first and greatest of the three, wrote philosophical treatises and literary works, which culminated in his *Divine Comedy*, written during the last years of his life.

The *Divine Comedy* is a view of the whole Christian universe, populated with people from antiquity and from Dante's own day. The poem is both a sophisticated summary of philosophical and theological thought at the beginning of the fourteenth century and an astute political commentary on his times.

English literature emerged from over two centuries of French cultural domination with the writings of William Langland (ca. 1330-95) and Geoffrey Chaucer (ca. 1343-1400). Both presented images of contemporary society with a critical and often ironic view. In *Piers Plowman* Langland presents society from the perspective of the peasantry. In Chaucer's great poem, *Canterbury Tales*, pilgrims traveling together to Canterbury represent every walk of life and spectrum of society. Chaucer uses them and the stories they tell to comment in subtle and complex ways on the literary, religious, and cultural traditions of which they are a part.

Christine of Pisan presenting a manuscript of her poems to Isabeau of Bavaria, the wife of King Charles VI of France.

Much of Italian and English literature drew material and inspiration from French, which into the fifteenth century was the language of courtly romance. In France, most literature continued to project an unreal world of allegory and nostalgia for a glorious if imaginary past. Popular literature, developed largely in the towns, often dealt with courtly themes, but with a critical and more realistic eye.

In this literary world appeared a new and extraordinary type of poet, a woman who earned her living with her pen, Christine de Pisan (1364-ca. 1430). As a professional woman of letters, de Pisan fought the stereotypical medieval image of women as weak, sexually aggressive temptresses. In her *Hymn to Joan of Arc*, she saluted her famous contemporary for her accomplishments, bringing dignity to women, striving for justice, and working for peace in France. De Pisan's life and writing epitomized the new possibilities and new interests of the fifteenth century. They included an acute sense of individuality, a willingness to look for truth not in the clichés of the past but in actual experience, and a readiness to defend one's views with tenacity.

The third literary tradition in fifteenth-century France was that of realist poetry. Around 1453, just as the English troops were enduring a final battering from the French artillery, Duke Charles of Orléans (1394-1465) organized a poetry contest. Each contestant was to write a ballad that began with the contradictory line, "I die of thirst beside the fountain." The duke, himself an outstanding poet, wrote an entry that embodied the traditional courtly themes of love and fortune:

> I die of thirst beside the fountain,
> Shaking from cold and the fire of love;
> I am blind and yet guide the others;
> I am weak of mind, a man of wisdom;
> Too negligent, often cautious in vain,
> I have been made a spirit,
> Led by fortune for better or for worse.

An unexpected and very different entry came from the duke's prison. The prisoner-poet, François Villon (1432–ca. 1464), was a child of the Paris streets, an impoverished student, a barroom brawler, a killer, and a thief who spent much of his life trying to escape the gallows. He was also the greatest realist poet of the Middle Ages. His entry read:

> I die of thirst beside the fountain,
> Hot as fire, my teeth clattering,
> At home I am in an alien land;
> I shudder beside a glowing brazier,
> Naked as a worm, gloriously dressed,
> I laugh and cry and wait without hope,
> I take comfort and sad despair,
> I rejoice and have no joy,
> Powerful, I have no force and no strength,
> Well received, I am expelled by all.

The duke focused on the sufferings of love; the thief on the physical sufferings of the downtrodden. The two poets represent the contradictory tendencies of literature in the later Middle Ages.

In the centuries that followed the disintegration of the Carolingian empire, the eastern half of the Carolingian world continued the imperial universalist tradition of the Carolingians until its conflicts with the other universalist tradition, that of the papacy, contributed to its disintegration into small autonomous principalities. In western Europe, public order was for a time largely replaced by numerous individual principalities. Gradually, however, first in France and in England, and then in the Iberian Peninsula, a new type of kingship emerged. Less ambitious than that in the east, it proved more enduring, surviving the centrifugal forces of the fourteenth and fifteenth centuries to emerge as the foundation of the nation-state.

The fourteenth and fifteenth centuries, with their demographic collapse, warfare, and dissension, placed enormous strains on these emerging forms of social and cultural organization. Individuals sought their own answers to the problems of life and death, using the legacy of the past, but using it in novel and creative ways. Mystics and heretics sought God without benefit of traditional religious hierarchies, and poets and philosophers sought personal expression outside the confines of inherited tradition.

The legacy of the Middle Ages was a complex and ambiguous one. The thousand-year synthesis of classical, barbarian, and Christian traditions did not disappear. The bonds holding this world together were not yet broken, but the last centuries of the Middle Ages bequeathed a critical detachment from this heritage, expressed in the revolts of peasants and workers, the preaching of radical religious reformers, and the poems of mystics and visionaries.

Suggestions for Further Reading

General Reading

Daniel Waley, *Later Medieval Europe* (London: Longman, 1975). A brief introduction with a focus on Italy.

* Johan Huizinga, *The Waning of the Middle Ages* (New York: St. Martins Press, 1954). An old but still powerful interpretation of culture and society in the Burgundian court in the late Middle Ages.

The Invention of the State

* Joseph R. Strayer, *On the Medieval Origins of the Modern State* (Princeton, NJ: Princeton University Press, 1970). A very brief but imaginative account of medieval statecraft by a leading French institutional historian.

John W. Baldwin, *The Government of Philip Augustus: Foundations of French Royal Power in the Middle Ages* (Berkeley, CA: University of California Press, 1986). A detailed but important study of the crucial reign of Philip II.

* Horst Fuhrmann, *Germany in the High Middle Ages, c. 1050–1200* (New York: Cambridge University Press, 1986). A fresh synthesis of German history by a leading German historian.

M. T. Clanchy, *England and Its Rulers, 1066–1272* (New York: B & N Imports, 1983). A good, recent survey of English political history.

War and Politics in the Later Middle Ages

* C. T. Allmand, *The Hundred Years War: England and France at War c. 1300–c. 1450* (New York: Cambridge University Press, 1988). A recent, brief introduction to the Hundred Years' War by a British historian.

* Joachim Leuschner, *Germany in the Late Middle Ages* (Amsterdam: Elsevier, 1980). An introduction to late medieval German history.

Richard W. Kaeuper, *War, Justice and Public Order: England and France in the Later Middle Ages* (Oxford: Oxford University Press, 1988). A fine analysis of the effects of war on England and France.

LIFE AND DEATH IN THE LATER MIDDLE AGES

* Philip Zieger, *The Black Death* (New York: Harper & Row, 1969). A reliable introduction to the plague in the fourteenth century.

H. A. Miskimin, *The Economy of Early Renaissance Europe, 1300-1460* (New York: Cambridge University Press, 1975). An accessible introduction to the economic history of the later Middle Ages.

* Edith Ennen, *The Medieval Town* (New York: North-Holland Publishing Co., 1979). A brief history of medieval cities by a German specialist.

Georges Duby, ed., *A History of Private Life Volume 2. Revelations of the Medieval World* (Cambridge, MA: Harvard University Press, 1988). A series of provocative essays on the origins of privacy and the individual.

Bronislaw Geremek, *Power or Pity: Europe and the Poor From the Middle Ages to the Present* (forthcoming). A history of the origins of public welfare, focusing on the late Middle Ages.

* Michel Mollat and Philippe Wolff, *The Popular Revolutions of the Late Middle Ages* (London: Allen and Unwin, 1973). An accessible history of late medieval revolts, focusing on those of medieval cities.

THE SPIRIT OF THE LATER MIDDLE AGES

* Geoffrey Barraclough, *The Medieval Papacy* (New York: W. W. Norton, 1968). A brief overview of the papacy.

*Emmanuel Le Roy Ladurie, *Montaillou: the Promised Land of Error* (New York: G. Braziller, 1978). A brilliant if contro-versial view of a medieval village as revealed through testimony given the Inquisition.

* Heiko A. Oberman, *The Harvest of Medieval Theology* (Cambridge, MA: Labyrinth Press, 1963). A technical but rewarding account of late medieval theology.

Howard Kaminsky, *A History of the Hussite Revolution* (Berkeley, CA: University of California Press, 1967). The best account of the Hussite movement.

Gordon Leff, *Heresy in the Later Middle Ages* (Manchester: Manchester University Press, 1967). A survey of heretical movements in the fourteenth and fifteenth centuries.

* Caroline Walker Bynum, *Holy Feast and Holy Fast: The Religious Significance of Food to Medieval Women* (Berkeley, CA: University of California Press, 1987). An imaginative and scholarly examination of the role of food in the spirituality of medieval women.

E. F. Chaney, *François Villon in His Environment* (Oxford: Oxford University Press, 1946). An old but still valuable study of Villon and his world.

H. S. Bennett, *Chaucer and the Fifteenth Century* (Oxford: Oxford University Press, 1961). An accessible historical introduction to Chaucer.

John Freccero, *Dante and the Poetics of Conversion* (Cambridge, MA: Harvard University Press, 1986). A serious and rewarding study of Dante by an acknowledged master.

* Indicates paperback edition available.

SENTIMENTALIZING PEASANT LIFE

They are idyllic images, men leaning against a shaded railing as they operate a waterwheel, watching one of their fellows as he fills a bucket with irrigation water from the stream below, and women sitting in the shade of a spreading tree as they do their mending and spinning. Both paintings, Song dynasty images, are literati representations of peasant life. The seals and calligraphic inscriptions on the illustration of the irrigators were placed there by successive owners of the piece, and attest to its value as a collector's item. The style of the inscription to the far right mimics the writing found on antique bronzes, a style which would have been utterly incomprehensible to the men in the painting, or most men and women, for that matter.

Let us look more closely at the way these images represent Chinese agrarian life. Much agriculture in south China was flooded-field rice cultivation, which demanded ingenious technology and constant vigilance on the part of villagers. The government did not intervene in matters such as the irrigation project we see under way here: villagers themselves, perhaps under the direction of local gentry, took the responsibility for maintaining the irrigation works.

Women's work in traditional China was conventionally defined as textile work, although in fact women engaged in a wide variety of labor. Here we see four women, open to our view but concealed from the public gaze by a thatched fence. The fence solves a thorny problem: How is a respectable woman to take advantage of summer breezes without exposing herself to public view? And how is an artist to represent her doing so?

This painting, which is part of a scroll illustrating an instructional text for women, entitled the *Lady's Classic of Filial Piety*, is labeled as depicting "common people." Perhaps they are common, but they are not inelegant. And, in keeping with the tenor of the instructional text in which they appear, they are concerned with modesty and propriety. And "common" seems to be a relative term: The woman second from the left seems to be a servant, presenting cloth to the seated woman for her attention. In the eyes of this painter, even ordinary people have servants.

These paintings are the product of an elite culture and were designed for an elite audience. They portray contented, aesthetically pleasing, productive peasants. (The men in the picture at the left may appear to be idling, but the rice is flourishing. Someone has been hard at work.)

The images of modest and industrious peasant women were perhaps also intended to serve as models for elite women, to urge them to greater frugality, diligence, and chastity. The images valorize hard work, but they have sentimentalized peasant life. These images are far removed from any social problems peasants may have faced. They are pretty peasants, at peace with themselves and their world.

The literati who painted these images imagined a world that was whole and harmonious, and in which women and peasants were content with their roles. It is true that in both China and Japan during this period cultures became more inclusive. Literacy expanded, and commerce linked regions and social classes to a greater degree than ever before.

But do not be deluded by the literati visions of a unified society. Peasants did not always conceptualize their interest in a way which meshed with literati notions. During this period, peasants on occasion rebelled. The most serious of these rebellions brought down the Yuan dynasty (1279–1368) in China and put a peasant on the throne.

Tang China and Heian Japan, for all their differences, were both aristocratic societies. In the years 1000 to 1300, the aristocratic society in both countries collapsed. In Song dynasty China (960–1276) the old aristocracy was replaced by a literati elite, and in Kamakura Japan (1185–1333) the warrior elite became the most politically powerful class. Changes in access to political power characterized this period in Asian history.

These changes were accompanied by other changes. In both China and Japan during this period towns grew, and in Japan merchants began to play a more active role in the development of culture. In both China and Japan, the social and political roles of women became more circumscribed. Men attained their elite status by passing civil service exams in China or by demonstrating their prowess on the battlefield in Japan. The battlefield and the examination hall were both gendered arenas, restricted to men.

In this chapter we discuss the diffusion of culture among various elements within China and within Japan. It would be misleading to suggest that by 1600 the culture of either China or Japan was homogeneous. But expanding literacy, the growth of vernacular literature, and the proliferation of forms of entertainment like the theater, which could be enjoyed by people from a wide variety of backgrounds, led to a more cohesive culture in both China and Japan than had existed in the past. At the same time, regional differences remained profound.

The Glories of Civilian Society Under the Song

Several seemingly paradoxical themes stand out in the history of the Song dynasty. First, the international situation was characterized by constant difficulties between the Song and the peoples on China's northern frontier, problems that culminated in the northern peoples' invading Chinese territory. The Jin took north China in 1126 and the Mongols conquered all of China in 1276. But in spite of these problems, the Song in many ways flourished. Not only was the Song dynasty a great age of commercial expansion and urban prosperity, but the Song state was remarkably effective at capturing commercial revenues to finance its activities. The Song state was an activist, effective state. Many Song institutional arrangements, such as the civil service examinations, proved durable. But in other ways, later dynasties were not able to equal the performance of the Song.

The foreign insecurity and the domestic prosperity contributed to intellectual changes that led to the development of a revised Confucianism, commonly known as neo-Confucianism, which was to have an important impact on Chinese life.

The Border Issue

From early in the dynasty, northern neighbors were a problem for the Song. In 1004, anxious to establish peaceful relations with the Liao, the Song concluded a treaty in which they agreed to pay tribute to the Liao. That the Chinese paid tribute to a neighboring state had more than an economic significance. In the traditional Chinese world order, states on China's periphery would send tribute to China as an acknowledgment of China's cultural superiority. In the early eleventh century, the Liao were able to turn the tables on the Song. In 1042, because the Liao had allied with the Chinese against the Tangut state of Western Xia, they were able to extract even more tribute from the Chinese. Both the

Gender and Culture

THE FALL OF MAN

Figure 1

In the late medieval era, the European world view shifted. For more than a millennium, earthly experience had been overshadowed by the promise of heavenly salvation. However, by the thirteenth century, with the rise of the cities, the new, cosmopolitan attitudes gained through trade and travel, and the emergence of powerful monarchs balancing the power of clergy, this focus began to change. The visual arts reflected this shift, adding images of individuals and scenes from daily life to the reigning repertoire of biblical heroes and narratives. Every aspect of men and women's lives offered subjects for the visual record, and marriage, previously a neglected subject in the arts, drew unprecedented attention.

In Judeo-Christian societies, Adam and Eve forged the prototype for all marriages. Tradition held that Eve was created to heal Adam of his loneliness. After their defiance of divine order and their expulsion from the garden, they lived a life together. The punishments imposed upon them for disobedience—that Eve would bear children in pain and that Adam would live by the sweat of his brow—cast a gendered matrix for matrimonial roles. Images of Adam and Eve after the expulsion are rare in western art. More typical is the depiction of their moment of temptation, as seen on the preceding page in Hugo Van Der Goes's *The Fall of Man* (ca. 1486–70, Flanders; Figure 1). As was common in this period, this panel was originally paired with a scene of the lamentation over Christ. The message to the faithful was clear: Follow the pattern ordained before the fall and redeem the sin with sacrifice.

The union of man and woman served the secular society as well as the sacred. The importance of marriage to the civic structure is illustrated in an unusual sculpture ensemble in the Romanesque cathedral in Naumburg. Six pairs of figures, natural in scale and detail, stand in tabernacles of the choir. These portray six married couples—the original benefactors of the church—each a descendant from the reigning houses of Billung and Wettin. *Ekkehard and Uta* (ca. 1250–60, Germany; Figure 2) are a striking pair. Their portraits seem real, a record of actual appearance. But this couple, like the others, died long before the

EKKEHARD AND UTA   Figure 2

GIOVANNI ARNOLFINI AND HIS BRIDE   Figure 3

 Figure 4

sculptures were carved. Their individuality reflects the ancient theory of the four humors, a discourse on personality based on the proportions of bodily fluids. Ekkehard, with his firm stance and self confident gaze, represents the sanguine type, dominated by blood. Uta is phlegmatic. Her timid nature and the constant chill caused by the excess of cold phlegm in her system prompts her to retreat from view in the folds of her voluminous cloak. These idealized portraits may be based on an outdated biology, but they suggest a modern cliche. In male and female relationships we still believe that opposites attract.

Jan Van Eyck's painting of *Giovanni Arnolfini and His Bride* (1434, Flanders; Figure 3), seen on the preceding page, is more than a matrimonial portrait. The symbols in the painting read as a wedding certificate. Arnolfini, an agent for the Medici, takes the hand of his Florentine bride and pledges his faith. Both have removed their shoes, suggesting that the bed chamber is transformed into sacred ground through the sacrament of marriage. There are signs of divine presence—the eye-like mirror, the single candle burning in the chandelier—and references to the fruits of matrimony—the whiskbroom for domesticity, the bride calling attention to the fullness of her skirt, indicating pregnancy. Even the little dog plays a role; it embodies fidelity. The officiating priest is seen in the mirror, as is the artist, whose signature, "Jan Van Eyck Was Here" bears witness to the ceremony.

Botticelli's *Venus and Mars* (ca. 1480, Italian; Figure 4) also celebrates a wedding, but its message is a metaphor. Commissioned for the marriage of Guiliano de'Medici to Simonetta Vespucci, the presentation of a slumbering Mars and an alert Venus corresponds with a Neo-Platonic discourse written by Marsilio Ficino. The chaste Venus of Neo-Platonism tames Mars, balancing his excessive and violent temperament. Ficino writes that Venus may master Mars, but Mars will never master Venus. In Botticelli's painting, Venus has vanquished her languid lover. The painting was seen by some contemporaries as an insult to the bridegroom. This may have been Botticelli's intention, for he based his vision of Venus on the bride Simonetta, and he positioned the Vespucci symbol of the wasp prominently in the background.

Western Xia and the Liao used these Chinese goods to trade with other Central Asian countries.

The Song policy of buying peace met with only temporary success. In the twelfth century the Song met with adversaries who were more interested in conquest than in commodities. In 1114, a people known as the Jurched had proclaimed the Jin dynasty, and rose to power with meteoric speed. In 1120 they allied with the Chinese against the Liao, but shortly thereafter they attacked China. In 1126, they took the Song capital Kaifeng and all of north China. After the fall of Kaifeng, the Song government fled south and in 1135 established a new capital at Lin'an, the city now called Hangzhou.

The year 1126 marks an important division in the history of the Song dynasty. The period prior to 1126 is known as the Northern Song, the period after, as the Southern Song. The Southern Song controlled a much smaller territory than did the Northern Song, and faced an ever present threat of further incursions from northern neighbors. The threat became reality in 1276 when the Mongols, invaders from the north, finally destroyed the dynasty.

The Triumph of Domestic Politics

The loss of the north not only divided the political history of the Song dynasty but also created a poignant sense of loss that pervaded all aspects of Southern Song culture. But it would be a mistake to read the history of the Song as the history of loss. The Song dynasty made permanent and far-reaching contributions to Chinese political culture. One of the most important contributions was the large-scale implementation of civil service examinations as the primary means of recruiting the bureaucracy. The civil service examination system had been used earlier, but not until the Song did it become the dominant means of recruiting the bureaucracy. Although the details of the curriculum varied to some extent, the core was unwavering: Students were tested on their knowledge of the Confucian classics. In general, practical knowledge, such as knowledge of the legal codes, was not subject to examination. Confucian political theory rested on the premise that the best training for a political career was a thorough grounding in the classics. The details of political administration—law, tax collection, agricultural management—could be learned on the job or entrusted to specialist assistants.

A job in the bureaucracy was not merely a job. It conferred political power and social prestige not only on the man who held it but on his family. His wife, his parents, and his grandparents were granted official titles. A man from a well-to-do family of scholars would clearly stand a better chance of doing well on the examinations than would a man from a more modest family background, but a young man from a prominent family still had to pass the examinations. Although failure would not doom him to poverty, or even necessarily to obscurity, it would preclude a career in government. There were several levels of examination a young man had to pass: first at the provincial level, then at the national level, and finally a palace examination. The entire cycle of examinations was repeated every three

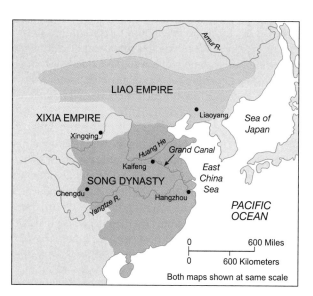

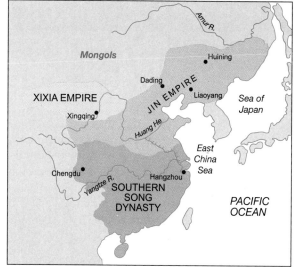

China in the Song and Southern Song Dynasties

Statue of an early Northern Song civil official holding a hu, *a tablet that symbolizes high office.*

years. Failure was the rule rather than the exception, but a candidate who failed the examinations might take them again. In the Song, one out of every five candidates would pass the palace exams, and the successful candidate was often in his mid-thirties.

This test upon which so much rested was fraught with anxiety. Chinese literature is full of stories of vulnerable young men on their way to take civil service examinations who are seduced by beautiful young women. These beauties, it often turns out, were often not human beings at all, but fox-fairies or some other kind of demon who have come to distract the young man from the serious business of study.

The examination system shaped Chinese political culture in several ways. Because most Chinese men were eligible to take the examinations, the system fostered a great deal of social mobility among the upper strata of society. An ambitious man need not oppose the political elite; by dint of hard work he could hope to enter it. In this way, the myth of social mobility may have served as a safety valve for social tensions. The examination system also promoted cultural cohesion in traditional China. Because young men of the upper classes in all parts of China aspired to take the same tests, they studied the same curriculum. As a result, there was a broad consensus about social values, about human nature, and about what government could and could not do. The civil service examination system was not abolished until 1905. It is true that during the course of this long history, the examinations occasionally had a stultifying effect on political life. But they also enriched that political life and provided it with rare cohesion.

The close connection between education and politics made the education of daughters problematic. On the one hand, a daughter would never take the civil service exam, so the elaborate classical education required for sons of the elite class was wasted on a daughter. On the other hand, mothers were by and large in charge of early childhood education. When an elite family was selecting a wife for a son, they looked for a woman who was well enough educated to teach the rudiments of reading to their grandsons. And when that same family was making decisions about whether or not to invest in educating a daughter, they would be attentive to the demands of the marriage market. Although during this time there was a well-developed system of academies and private schools, many elite families preferred to call in tutors to teach their sons. There is no way of knowing how many daughters picked up scraps of classical knowledge from a brother's tutor. Indeed, such exposure to the classics might well have been involuntary. One of the most important ways in which a boy would learn texts was by reciting them aloud. One can imagine that everyone in the household would learn the texts along with him, whether they wanted to or not.

The examination system is perhaps the most distinctive aspect of Chinese political culture in the Song and later periods. But, while it was crucial in shaping the national political elite, that elite was only a small portion of the total population. Elite status on the local level was conferred by other means: One became a member of the elite through education, through wealth, and through landholding. During the Song, a local elite that was more or less independent of the national government developed. This local elite proved crucial in providing stability and continuity during the period of Mongol rule during the Yuan dynasty (1279–1368), and would remain a powerful force throughout the Ming dynasty (1368–1644).

Commercial and Agricultural Productivity

Commerce flourished during the Song dynasty. The growing prosperity of the landed class provided a market for luxury goods, which stimulated economic growth. Long-distance trade, both domestic and international, prospered. Because water transport was the most efficient way of moving goods, an elaborate system of rivers and canals was developed for water traffic. The Song also participated in maritime trade. By the tenth or eleventh century, boats capable of high-seas navigation had been perfected, and the compass had been in use since the late eleventh century.

The prominence of long-distance trade led to technical innovations such as paper money. The first Chinese paper money was printed in 1024 in Sichuan province, supplementing the copper and silver coins that had been in circulation for more than a millennium. The amount of paper money in circulation under the Song was substantial: At its height it amounted to the equivalent of 400 million strings of copper cash (a string was a thousand coins). Paper money was a success during the Song. In later dynasties, however, governments under financial duress succumbed to the temptation to print more money, and inflation became a serious problem.

During the Song dynasty agricultural productivity increased modestly. Part of this increase was due to an increase in the amount of land under cultivation. Some of the new land was hills that were terraced. But much of it was wetlands around lakes, which were drained for agriculture. New strains of rice were also introduced. Sometime after 1012 Champa rice from Southeast Asia was introduced to China. This new strain had several advantages. It was quick-ripening and disease resistant. Champa rice enabled more Chinese farmers to grow two crops of rice a year on the same field. The Song government took an active role in agricultural development. Government officials systematically distributed the new seeds, along with information about other agricultural techniques, such as improved irrigation and

Painting of a knickknack peddler by Southern Song artist Li Sung. A woman and her children look over the hundreds of items on display.

soil preparation. Agricultural handbooks detailing the latest in farming techniques began to be widespread during the Song. Because most peasants were illiterate, landlords or county magistrates read these books and conveyed the techniques to peasants under their supervision.

Rural markets held on a periodic basis linked communities commercially and to some extent socially. Traveling peddlers would go from town to town, on a fixed route, carrying gossip and other news with their wares as they went from market to market. Parents sent matchmakers to a nearby market town to find spouses for their children. Marriage networks thus formed another way of linking these communities.

Mining played an important role in the Song economy, as did the production of cast iron. Porcelain was perfected in the twelfth century, and both government and private merchants sponsored its manufacture.

The cities that emerged during the Song represented a new kind of urban growth. The Tang dynasty capital of Chang'an, for all its splendor, had been principally an administrative center. The Song capital of Kaifeng, however, was dominated by commercial life and amusements. The wards within the cities were no longer walled, and some entertainment shops were open all night. The state no longer controlled markets as it had during the Tang. Various informal organizations, such as mutual aid societies and guilds, arose.

These informal organizations were important in promoting regional integration.

Even more remarkable than the degree of commercial development under the Song was the degree to which the Song government was able to exploit commercial wealth as a source of revenue. In the eleventh century, revenues from commercial taxes and monopolies equaled those produced by the land tax. By the thirteenth century they had exceeded it. The Song was, to an extent remarkable in a premodern state, based on commercial rather than agrarian wealth.

New Ways of Looking at the World

During the Song dynasty, social and economic change was accompanied by intellectual change. During the Period of Disunion (206–589) and the Tang dynasty, Confucianism had been eclipsed to some degree by Buddhism and Taoism. Buddhism had been introduced into China from India in the third century C.E., and it became an important religion remarkably rapidly. During the same period, Taoism also became prominent. Buddhism and Taoism had raised questions that were not central to classical Confucianism, questions dealing with how the universe was created, the generation of human life, and so forth. In the Song, a transformed Confucianism reasserted itself on the intellectual and social scene. In the classical era, Confucianism had been concerned primarily with questions of order in human society. Neo-Confucianism, as the revived Song Confucianism is called in the West, was much more involved in metaphysical speculation than classical Confucianism had been. In addition to being a political philosophy, it became a religion of personal salvation.

Neo-Confucianism described the universe as being made up of two components, *li* and *chi*. The root meaning of *li* is "pattern," and what the neo-Confucians meant by it was an ordering principle. *Chi* is the material of the universe, which li orders. The li that structures a bamboo leaf is the same as the li that structures

ZHU XI ON MIND, NATURE, AND FEELINGS

■ *In this excerpt, the neo-Confucian master is explaining the thorny relationship among feelings, nature, and the mind. Zhu Xi does not condemn feelings, as that would be Buddhist, and he is ever careful to distinguish himself from Buddhism. He offers a qualified endorsement of emotions here. Even anger, when appropriate, has a place in a balanced life.*

Nature is the state before activity begins, feelings are the state when activity has started, and the mind includes both of these states. As the saying goes: "the mind unites and commands one's nature and feelings." Desire emanates from feelings. The mind is like the flow of water, and the desire is like its waves. Just as there are good and bad waves, so there are good desires, such as "I desire to be humane," and bad desires which rush out like violent waves. When bad desires are substantial, they destroy the principle of Heaven, as water bursts a dam. When Mencius said that "feelings enable people to do good," he meant that the feelings flowing from our nature are originally all good.

Question: Is it correct to suppose that sages never show anger?

Answer: How can they never show anger? When they ought to be angry, they will show it . . . When one becomes angry at the right time, he will be acting to the proper degree. When the matter is over, anger disappears, and none of it will be retained.

Question: How can desires be checked?

Answer: Simply by thought. In learning there is nothing more important than thought. Only thought can check desires.

Someone said: If thought is not correct, it will not be adequate to check desires. Instead, it will create trouble. How about the saying: "Have no depraved thoughts"?

Answer: Thoughts that are not correct are merely desires. If we think through the right and wrong of a thing in accordance with its principle, then our thought will surely be correct.

the cosmos. Thus studying and understanding a bamboo leaf will lead to an understanding of the cosmos, and an understanding of the cosmos implies an understanding of one's place in it.

There are two primary ways in which knowledge can be acquired in the neo-Confucian program. The first is through the study of books, especially the classics and history. The second is through quiet-sitting, which is derived from Chan Buddhist meditational techniques. The public, political aspects of Confucianism that were so important in the classical era remain, but added to them is an element of personal enlightenment. The mastery of the self, known as self-cultivation, was central to the neo-Confucian program. In the document cited on page 322, Zhu Xi (1130–1200), one of the most important of the Song neo-Confucian thinkers, describes the proper role emotions should play in a well-balanced life.

Women's Place in the New World

Associated with the many changes occurring in the Song dynasty was a decline in the status of women. Chinese women had gained fame as poets in preceding centuries, and they were not necessarily confined to domestic roles. But the growing prosperity of the Song economy, coupled with the moral seriousness of the neo-Confucians, combined to restrict the role of women in China.

Palace Ladies Bathing Children, *a Song dynasty painting.*

Most symptomatic of the change in the status of women is foot binding. Tang women did not bind their feet. The origins of the custom are unclear—legend suggests that a dancer at the Tang court had extraordinarily tiny feet and that other women bound their feet to imitate her. A wife with bound feet became a symbol of conspicuous consumption. A man announced to the world that he was well off by marrying someone whose capacity for productive labor was literally hobbled. Furthermore, bound feet restricted a woman's physical ability to move about at the same time moralists were suggesting that her mobility ought to be restricted. Whatever the origins of the custom, its durability lies in the dark recesses of the erotic imagination. Chinese women bound their daughters' feet because tiny lotus-like feet made them more attractive on the marriage market.

The extent to which foot binding was prevalent among all the classes of Chinese society is unclear. It was widespread among the upper classes, though more so after the Song than during it. Parents who were planning for their daughters' futures might well have hoped that the girl would grow up and marry (or be a concubine) in a social stratum where bound feet were expected. As a result of such parental pretensions, countless peasant women labored in the fields with bound feet.

The most important unit in Chinese local society was the family. It was an economic unit, as well as a biological and moral one. Moreover, it was the fundamental unit of production and consumption among peasants. Marriage was almost universal for women, but was less so for men. Because upper-class men might marry several women as concubines, there were simply not enough women to go around. Women married relatively young, in their late teens or early twenties. In the most common form of marriage, known as virilocal marriage, the young woman lived with her new husband's family, which was frequently in another village. She was subject to the authority of her in-laws, particularly her mother-in-law. Her visits to her home village were restricted to ceremonial occasions.

Concubinage, always legal, became more widespread in the Song. A man might have only one legal wife, but he might have as many concubines as he could afford. A wife had certain protections against divorce, but a concubine had none.

The ideal household size was large, but its actual size was quite modest. Although the size varied with time, with class, and with region, it seems to have averaged five or six people. It was unusual for married brothers to continue living together in an undivided household.

Although marriage was arranged, an ideal marriage was not devoid of romance. One of the most celebrated poets of the Song dynasty, a woman named Li Qingzhao (1084–1141), wrote erotic poems to her husband. The following may serve as an example:

> How many evenings in the arbor by the river,
> when flushed with wine we'd lose our way back.
> The mood passed away, returning late by boat
> we'd stray off into a spot thick with lotus
>   and thrashing through
>   and thrashing through
> startle a shoreful of herons by the lake.

Servants played an important role in the households of the elite. Children were often nursed by wet nurses, who usually lived with the families of their young charges. Such nurses might remain for life with the children they had nursed, and retain significant influence in their lives. The fact that women of the lower classes had such a profound role in raising children of the upper classes probably fostered cultural integration among various levels of society. The stories servant women told their young masters became transformed into part of the culture of the elite.

Song Religion and Popular Culture

Chinese religion during the Song and later periods differs in many ways from Western religion. Chinese religion tended to be characterized by pragmatism rather than doctrinaire approaches. Although there were a number of different religions—Buddhism, Taoism, and Confucianism—which did not always approach problems in the same way, these different religions coexisted quite harmoniously. Not only did individual people subscribe to more than one, temples often housed images from all three traditions. Furthermore, there was no strong separation between secular and sacred. Neither Buddhism nor Taoism had weekly services that the faithful were expected to attend. Services were held to celebrate particular rituals; otherwise, believers entered temples to worship as it seemed appropriate to them to do so.

Temples, whether they were Buddhist, Taoist, or shrines to local gods, were always community centers. With the possible exception of the capital, Chinese cities and towns in general did not have public civic space the way European towns did. Temples served as public spaces. Markets and theatrical performances often took place at temples.

In addition to being entertainment centers, Buddhist temples were important sources of social welfare.

They functioned as orphanages, hospitals, soup kitchens, and schools. This function was even more important after the Song, when the state spent fewer resources on welfare.

Festivals were important components of local religion. Some festivals were calendrical, that is, they marked off seasonal changes. Calendrical festivals celebrated the passing of the seasons, such as the coming of spring. They sought to ensure the fertility of the land and of the people. At the root of this is a belief in correspondences between the world (and the actions) of humans and the cosmos. The lunar New Year, which falls on a date in the Western calendar sometime between mid-January and mid-February, marks the beginning of spring. It is the biggest festival of the year, and marks a new beginning. Celebrations last for much of the first lunar month. On the fifteenth of the first lunar month, there is a lantern festival, which is described in this poem by Xin Chiji (1140–1207):

> One night's east wind made a thousand trees burst into flowers
>   And breathe down still more
>   Showers of fallen stars.
> Splendid horses, carved carriages, fragrance filled the road
>   Music resounded from paired flutes,
>   Light swirled on the water-clock towers.
> All night long, the fabled fish-dragons danced.
> Gold-threaded jacket, moth or willow-shaped hair ornaments
> Melted into the throng, giggling, a trail of scents.
> In the crowd I looked for her a thousand and one times;
>   And all at once, as I turned my head,
>   I was startled to find her
> Among the lanterns where candles were growing dim.

Festivals such as the lantern festival were one of the rare occasions when women of the upper classes went out and mingled with crowds. The poet is strolling amid the festive splendor, looking for a particular woman, whom he in fact finds. This poem indicates the erotic overtones to festival life.

Another sort of festival is life-cycle rituals. Funerals are the only one of these rituals that required the assistance of a priest. Weddings were not religious ceremonies. They were solemn, they were much written about in ritual texts, but they did not require the intervention of a priest. The transition between life and death is dangerous, and a ritual expert was needed both to guide the dead person on his or her journey and to console the living.

Two major festivals to propitiate the dead were held in late traditional China. The first is called *Qingming*, which means "clear and bright." Qingming did not belong to Buddhism or Taoism or Confucianism, but rather was part of a culture common to all three religions. It was held in mid-spring, on a day calculated by the solar calendar, falling in the Western month of April. On this day, families would gather and sweep the graves of the dead. The festival, perhaps analogous to our Memorial Day, was a celebration of the lives of those no longer living. The dead were not threatening on Qingming.

But the dead were threatening at the ghost festival, which was celebrated on the fifteenth of the seventh lunar month. This festival had as its core a Taoist ghost festival, and was marked by danger. On that day the boundaries between the dead and the living were fluid; normally the gates of heaven and hell are guarded by tigers and leopards, and the boundaries between the living and the dead are fixed. Added to the Taoist festival was a Buddhist festival called Ulambana.

The story behind Ulambana illustrates several important points about Chinese Buddhism. A young monk named Mulian left some money with his mother so that she could give alms to wandering monks. She spent the money on herself. The money that should have gone to feed monks went for food, wine and musicians. When she dies she goes to hell. When Mulian discovers that she is suffering dreadful punishments in hell, he undertakes a horrendous journey to find her and save her. She can neither eat nor drink. The Buddha tells Mulian that he can save his mother by offering food and drink to monks and to "hungry ghosts" on the fifteenth of the seventh lunar month. Hungry ghosts are people whose descendants do not sacrifice to them, or people who died untimely or violent deaths.

In many senses the story of Mulian is a myth that reconciles Buddhism and filial piety. Its hero quite literally goes to hell to save a parent. It is worth noting that the filial tie honored here is not the father-son tie, but rather the mother-son tie.

The Chinese spirit world, especially the world of Taoism, resembled the world of the mundane bureaucracy. For example, when a person had a request to make of a Taoist divinity—for health, long life, prosperity—he or she would write a petition using the same form that would be used to petition the emperor. The believer would then burn the petition. If the deity did not grant the petition, the believer might then appeal to a higher deity.

In the Song, Yuan, and Ming dynasties, Taoism was articulated into a complex textual religion, with numerous rituals, meditation techniques, and other

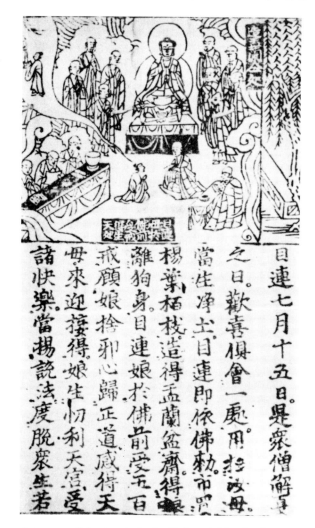

Japanese scroll dated 1346, showing Mulian administering the precepts to his mother. They kneel in the presence of the Buddha and an assembly of monks.

practices. It had a large following among the elite, and was particularly attractive to several of the late Ming emperors.

Buddhism in China survived the late Tang persecutions. But the forms that survived with the most vitality were Chan, which could be studied with a teacher, and Pure Land, in which the simple recitation of the name of the Amida Buddha would ensure salvation. The three religions in China usually had an easy coexistence. Individuals might believe that their own religious orientation was superior to that of their neighbor, but they had enough respect for the reality of the spirit world not to scorn their neighbor. Chinese religion was pragmatic rather than doctrinaire. If prayers to a Buddhist deity failed, then the sensible thing to do would be to pray to a Taoist or Confucian one.

A number of local deities who are neither Buddhist nor Taoist played an important role in Chinese religious life. One of these is the city god, who might well be a deity of local significance, or might be one with broader appeal. What often happened with these local deities was that the state incorporated them into the official orthodox pantheon. They became the representatives of the state cult at the local level, just like the magistrate is the representative of the emperor at the local level.

During the Song dynasty, cities prospered and trade flourished. The civil service examination system became the primary means of recruitment into the bureaucratic elite. Neo-Confucianism suggested new ways of looking at the interaction between human beings and the cosmos, and a wide variety of rituals and festivals were practiced among various social groupings.

Mongols and the Yuan Dynasty

The world of the Mongols was very different from the world of the Chinese, and the story of how they conquered and ruled China is a remarkable one. Equally remarkable is the way in which Chinese local society emerged from a century of Mongol domination essentially unscathed. While it might be an exaggeration to assert, as generations of Chinese historians have done, that Mongol domination exerted no influence on Chinese life, it is true that Chinese religion, family structures, and even political philosophy remained remarkably durable through the years of conquest.

Conquering from Horseback

The Mongols' homeland was on the steppe lands of northern Asia, land that was arid and inhospitable to sedentary agriculture. Their economy was based on raising sheep and horses, and they engaged in a minimal trade with the settled agricultural people of northern China in order to obtain commodities like grain, tea, textiles, and metals. They engaged in seasonal migrations—in the summer they pastured their animals on open plains, but in the winter they moved to more sheltered pastures. As befitted a nomadic people, they made their homes in felt tents called yurts.

Not only did the Mongol economy differ from the Chinese, their society was constructed along fundamentally different lines. The most important social unit of the Mongols was the clan, which was headed by a chieftain. Although the chief might be the eldest man in the clan, he was chosen primarily on the basis of his abilities rather than on seniority. Women held relatively high positions in Mongol society. A daughter might inherit her father's property if there were no sons, and a woman had the right to divorce her husband.

In the late eleventh and twelfth centuries, the Mongol clans began to consolidate and turn their attention to their neighbors to the south. The man who united the Mongol clans was Temujin (1167-1227), better known by his title of Genghis Khan. By invoking ties of personal loyalty, he forged a formidable military and political empire. In 1206 he was named Genghis Khan, a title meaning "universal ruler," of the Mongol tribes. In 1215 the Mongols captured the Jin capital, and by 1233 they had defeated the remnants of the Jin state. From the conquest of the Jin, the Mongols continued their southern expansion and by 1276, all of China was in their hands. Kublai Khan (1216-94) became the emperor of all China. He ruled the vast multicultural Mongol empire not from the traditional capital of Karakorum in Mongolia, but rather from Khanbaliq, near modern Beijing.

The success of the Mongols can be explained partly in terms of their military superiority. The military might of the Mongols was legendary, as was their battle prowess. But despite their military advantages, the Mongols were severely outnumbered by the Chinese. There were perhaps 1.5 million Mongols at the time of the conquest of China, and only one hundred thousand or so of them were in China. The total population of China at that time was about 60 million. Superior horsemanship might account for the conquest, but it does not explain nearly a century of Mongol rule of China. Chinese advisers were fond of quoting an old proverb to the Mongols: "One can conquer the world on horseback, but one cannot govern it on horseback." The story goes that Ogodai (1229-41), Genghis's successor, had imagined turning north China into pastureland, but was persuaded that it would be more profitable to leave the splendid cities and lush farmlands intact and extract wealth from them. Consequently, when the Mongols proclaimed the Yuan dynasty, they left more or less intact the bureaucratic structure of China.

Nor did they try to convert the Chinese to a Mongol way of life. The Mongol language, Mongol religion—a

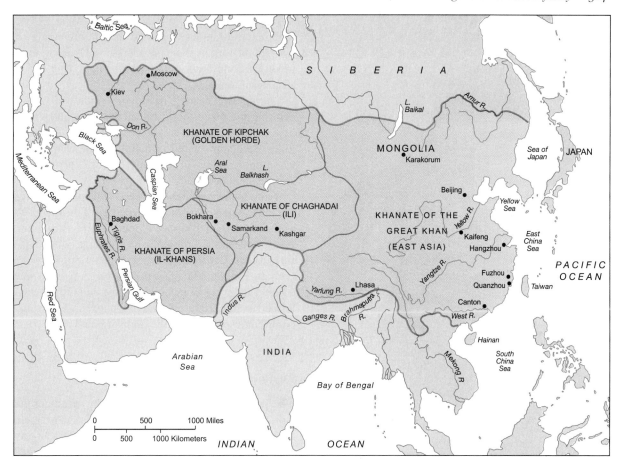

The Mongol Empire

form of Tibetan Buddhism known as lamaism—and even the Mongol law code remained restricted to Mongols.

Yuan Achievements

After the conquest of China was complete, the Yuan allowed the large estates in the south to remain more or less intact. The rich agricultural lands of south China continued to prosper. During the Yuan dynasty, cotton became a significant Chinese crop for the first time. The policy of leaving south China alone contrasted with Mongol policies elsewhere in the world, and won for the Yuan the neutrality, if not the support, of the large landowners there.

The Mongols were astute traders, and under their rule trade prospered. The sheer size of the Mongol empire facilitated contact between east and west, which enhanced trade. They improved the commercial infrastructure in China. Their most famous innovation was a

postal system with couriers who could travel 250 miles in a day, set up in 1236. The Yuan dynasty continued using paper currency, but the Chinese did not necessarily benefit from Yuan dynasty trade. Much of the trade under the Yuan was in the hands of non-Chinese middlemen, and hence much of the profit also went into non-Chinese hands.

China may have been a glittering prize the Mongols desperately desired, but Mongol ambitions extended well beyond China's boundaries. The Mongol empire stretched over much of the Eurasian continent. Much of the Mongol success in governing in fact lay with their strategy of leaving local societies and institutions more or less intact.

But that does not mean that the Mongol conquest was not brutal. The Koreans resisted the Mongol attacks, which began in 1231, with every resource at their disposal. They attempted to elicit divine aid as well by carving woodblocks to print the entire body of Buddhist scripture (known as the Tripitika). The project,

Pottery figurine of a dancing actor, Yuan dynasty, found in 1963 in Hunan province.

completed in 1236, required 81,000 woodblocks, which are still extant. But it was to no avail; the Mongols devastated Korea. A Korean dynastic history records the devastation of those years:

> Those who died of starvation were multitudinous, the corpses of the old and weak clogged ravines, and in the end some even left babies tied in trees.

The Mongols used Korea as a staging ground for their attempts to invade Japan in the late thirteenth century (see discussion below). The Mongols, believing that Vietnam had been a part of China, attempted to gain control of it in the 1280s, but failed.

Despite the fact that the preconquest Mongols lacked a written language, they were interested in cultural matters. Kublai Khan sent envoys to south India to bring back doctors and craftworkers. He established an

imperial library in Beijing in 1238. The Mongols even followed the Chinese practice of commissioning the dynastic history of their predecessors. Dynastic histories of the Song, Liao, and Jin were compiled under Yuan auspices in 1344–45.

During the Yuan dynasty, the traditional arts of painting and poetry both thrived in China, and a major new art form, the drama, evolved. While the older art forms were appreciated primarily by the connoisseurs who were members of the educated elite, drama found a wider audience.

Yuan drama was highly stylized and combined singing and the spoken word. The language of the drama was a mixture of Yuan dynasty colloquial and classical forms. It featured familiar stories, historical heroes, and romantic heroines. Earthy humor and poignant romance were both prominent. The plays may be categorized as comedies: the genre demanded a happy ending. Drama formed an important cultural link between literate and nonliterate segments of the population.

Downfall of the Yuan

The Yuan dynasty was brought down by rebellions precipitated by a combination of administrative inefficiency and natural disasters. The late Yuan dynasty was plagued by natural catastrophes, which in the Chinese political context were apt to be interpreted as signaling the loss of the Mandate of Heaven. In the 1330s, famine hit north China hard. Making matters worse, the Yellow River flooded repeatedly. The Yellow River is heavily laden with silt, hence its name. Because it has been dredged and diked for countless centuries, in many places the riverbed is higher than the surrounding land. Dikes must be maintained with absolute vigilance or the river will burst from its dikes and flood the surrounding land. In 1344, dikes downriver from Kaifeng broke, and they were not repaired for five years. Many catastrophes, like floods, which we are in the habit of calling natural, are often precipitated by human negligence. The fourteenth-century flooding of the Yellow River is an example of nature and humanity working in tandem to create calamity.

In the waning years of the dynasty, the Yuan court was plagued by factional disputes. In the years between 1320 and 1329 four different emperors occupied the throne. In 1328, a virtual civil war broke out among the princes. These problems both weakened the technical capacity of the government to govern and lessened its credibility among the populace.

A regime threatened by natural catastrophe and factional dissent might still survive if it has the support of the political elite. But the Yuan had never completely won over the Chinese literati. When the political situation began to decay in the fourteenth century, the elite were quick to throw their support behind rebels with whom they may in fact have had very little in common.

This combination of factors left the Yuan vulnerable to rebellion. Among the rebel groups that arose in the late Yuan was a group known as the White Lotus, a heterodox offshoot of Buddhism. The White Lotus sect was founded in 1133 by a man named Mao Ziyuan in Suzhou. It attracted a following among salt workers and boatmen in the lower Yangzi River area. White Lotus religion was millenarian, messianic, and salvational. It held that the coming of the Buddha of the Future, Maitreya, was imminent. In the coming age, Maitreya would save those who believed in him. Although many White Lotus groups were communities of law-abiding peasants, others rose in rebellion to destroy the existing society and prepare for the new order. Orthodox Buddhism regarded sectarian cults like the White Lotus with a great deal of skepticism. Moreover, the government was hostile to these sects and proscribed them whether or not they were rebellious. For example, laws that prohibited the mingling of men and women together after dark to eat vegetables were clearly aimed at vegetarian egalitarian sects. The state sought to proscribe these cults because they represented a challenge to its authority. White Lotus religion appealed to an authority structure outside the realm of the state, indeed even outside this world. In addition to invoking the Maitreya Buddha, some of these groups claimed descent from the Song ruling house, hence hearkening back to a pre-Mongol era of Chinese political legitimacy.

Mongol rule over China did not last a full century. The Chinese model of government was powerful enough that even conquerors adopted it. The Yuan dynasty was a time of political complexity and cultural innovation, especially in the arenas of painting and drama.

The Restoration of Chinese Power Under the Ming

After a century of Mongol rule, the Chinese Ming dynasty reasserted indigenous rule. The man who succeeded in establishing the Ming dynasty, Ming Taizu

(1368–98) was the son of an itinerant agricultural worker and the grandson of a master sorcerer. He rose to power through the ranks of a White Lotus sect. Taizu was the second peasant rebel to found a Chinese dynasty—Liu Bang, the Han founder, had been the first. When he became emperor, he made sectarian religion illegal, not because he underestimated it but because he knew how powerful it could be. Ming emperors were much more autocratic than previous rulers had been. Early rulers, were energetic men who had a clear vision of what Chinese society ought to be. But later emperors were often ineffective.

Chinese society under the Ming dynasty continued to function, even thrive. The local elites that began forming in the Song continued to prosper in the Ming. Indeed, they provided a center of gravity that provided for continuity. The growth of printing, which underwent a veritable explosion in the sixteenth century, meant that all kinds of texts could be printed and circulated like never before. Popular art forms like the drama served to link all classes of society.

Ming Continuity and Change

Ming Taizu was a man with a vision who had the political authority and will to enforce that vision. At the center of his vision was the establishment of a stable agrarian society, a society radically different from the vibrant commercial economy of the Song and early Yuan dynasties. But he was not a simple reactionary: The agrarian economy of north China had been ravaged during the Yuan by natural catastrophes and civil wars. Revitalizing the agrarian economy of the north was a pressing need. One aspect of the revitalization was a reforestation project, in which one hundred million trees were planted.

The administrative structure of the Ming dynasty resembled that of the Song, but the political reality was very different. Most Song emperors consulted on a regular basis with their ministers. It is perhaps an exaggeration to say that the Song emperor had a collegial relationship with his ministers of state—he was, after all, the Son of Heaven—but the emperor was not the sole and central focus of authority. The Ming emperor, however, was a supreme autocrat.

Comparisons between Song and Ming politics do not redound to the advantage of the Ming. Ming government was simultaneously more despotic and less efficient than Song government had been. The concentration of political power in the person of the emperor led to these seemingly conflicting trends. In a system where power is concentrated in the emperor, should the emperor choose not to exercise power—and some late Ming emperors were more interested in carpentry than they were in affairs of state—or should he exercise power badly, then the system is in trouble.

The autocratic tendencies of the early Ming were reinforced by some institutional changes. A crisis was precipitated in 1380 when Hu Weiyong, the prime minister, was charged with treason. He was executed along with thousands of his family members, friends, and supporters. Moreover, the position of prime minister was abolished. Hence, there was no one bureaucrat in the early Ming who had an institutional position that might have enabled him to provide a counterbalance to despotic or incompetent imperial power.

The third Ming emperor, commonly referred to by his reign name as Yongle (1403–24), was a powerful and energetic ruler. Under his reign, Ming rule was further consolidated and expanded. The Ming attempted to reincorporate Vietnam into the Chinese empire, but failed after twenty years of occupation. Ironically, after their expulsion in 1427, Chinese cultural influence in Vietnam, especially neo-Confucianism, experienced a resurgence.

The early Ming was a great maritime power, as had been the Song. But under the Ming, maritime expansion reached a new scale. Zheng He (1371–1433), a Moslem eunuch from Yunnan province, led seven expeditions. The voyages were massive: There were more than twenty thousand men on each trip. The overt purpose of the voyages was neither trade nor colonization. Rather, they aimed at securing recognition of the power and prestige of the Ming empire, and they were by and large successful. The tribute missions sent to the Ming court by Mamluk Egypt, for example, were probably prompted by the voyages. Another measure of the success of these voyages is the fact that in places in Southeast Asia, Zheng He was later deified as a popular god.

Zheng He returned from his last voyage in 1433, bringing the era of Chinese exploration to a close. After the death of the Yongle emperor, no one else at court seems to have been particularly interested in continuing the voyages. The voyages of Zheng He seem to have satisfied the curiosity of his imperial patrons about the outside world. This attitude is in marked contrast to that of Europeans later in the same century, who would embark upon an era of exploration and colonization. The Chinese in the early fifteenth century had technical navigational skills that were superior to those of the Europeans, but they chose not to continue to use them.

The retreat from expansionism can also be seen in policies toward the steppe peoples. Ming problems in dealing with the frontier can be seen in the Tumu incident in 1449, when Mongols captured the Ming emperor. The capture of the emperor created a profound political crisis, but it did not bring down the dynasty. The emperor was succeeded by his brother, who reigned until 1457, when the captive emperor was released.

Another aspect of Ming politics worthy of note is the growing power of eunuchs. Eunuchs had access to the Forbidden City, the residence of the emperor and his consorts. Men who were sexually intact were denied entrance into the emperor's private quarters because of an obsessive concern with the sexual purity of the emperor's consorts. But the imperial household was immense, and the system used to run it amounted to a shadow bureaucracy. In the Song, many of the positions were staffed by women. But under the Ming, most of those positions were held by eunuchs.

Eunuchs also controlled access to the emperor, since civil service bureaucrats were forbidden entry into the Forbidden City. It was easy for unscrupulous eunuchs to abuse power, especially if the emperor was indolent, as so many of the later Ming emperors were. Taizu had recognized the potential danger posed by the eunuchs, and had forbidden them to learn to read. But in the Chinese bureaucracy, knowledge was power and literacy was one of the most precious tools of the powerful. Recognizing this fact, eunuchs learned to read. After they gained control of the secret police, they became a truly formidable force.

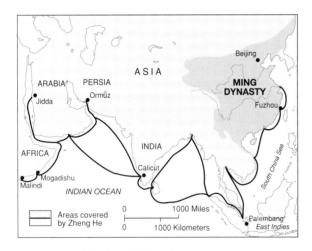

Ming China and the Zheng He Expeditions

Ming Commerce, Culture, and Corruption

The Ming vision of an ideal society was a stable agrarian order, and early Ming society reflected that vision. By the thirteenth century, cotton was grown widely in China. Hemp, another textile fiber, and mulberry, used to feed silkworms, were also widely grown. Chinese silk continued to be a luxury commodity prized on the international market. Cotton and mulberry had important implications for the gendered division of labor in the areas where they were important crops, such as the lower Yangzi valley. Textile production was lucrative, and it was women's work. By the sixteenth century in this area a woman spinning could produce as much income as a man working in the fields. The prominence of cash crops, which of course varied from place to place and even from time to time within the same place, implied a commercialized economy: a peasant family who grew cotton, for example, had cash to buy their grain.

Beginning in the sixteenth century, crops from the New World began to be introduced into China—corn, peanuts, potatoes, and sweet potatoes. The new crops gradually and profoundly transformed the Chinese agricultural economy. They had high nutritional value and could be grown on land that was marginal for rice. They fueled a population growth that would loom large in eighteenth-century China.

During the Yuan and early Ming dynasties, cities and commerce had been less important and less highly developed than they had been in the Song. But by the sixteenth century, Chinese cities were flourishing once again. Along with urban growth at this time, a distinctive urban culture developed. Printing increased dramatically, and—for the first time—fiction began to appear in the vernacular language. Some collections of fiction were printed with illustrations running across the top of each page, as if the pictures were for the benefit of the marginally literate. Novels printed in this way were found in the grave of a fifteenth-century official's wife, indicating not only that she read but that novels were treasured.

Several important popular novels were first published in the sixteenth century. *Journey to the West* is a comic novel about salvation. In it, a monkey, a monk, a pig, and a sand demon leave China for India on a quest for Buddhist scriptures. The novel, one hundred chapters long, is filled with their misadventures and their gradual awakening to the reality that all is illusion. *Jin ping mei* is a domestic tragedy, chronicling the life of Ximen Qing, a wealthy merchant, and his six wives. It is a bitter tale of jealousy, greed, and sexual excess, told by a master storyteller. The world in the novel is a far cry from that of the Confucian moralist.

For all the strength of the new urban cultural forms, they did not replace older literati forms. Indeed they never gained the cultural prestige held by the great literati artistic triad of painting, poetry, and calligraphy. Because the brush was used both to paint and to write, there was a close connection between painting and calligraphy in traditional China. Poems might be inscribed on a painting, either by the painter or by a later collector. If the inscription was done by the painter, the positioning of the words on the page would be an integral part of the spatial composition of the painting. If the inscription, or colophon, was written by a later collector, it would alter the spatial relationships in the painting. This was not regarded by painter or collector as an act defacing the painting. A work of art existed in dynamic interaction with later generations of viewers. It was only fitting that a collector who felt moved to inscribe a poem on the painting do so, provided of course that he had an elegant hand and a strong sense of space.

A splendid example of this is a poem and painting, both done by the fifteenth-century painter Shen Zhou:

> White clouds like a scarf enfold the mountain's waist,
> stone steps hang in space—a long, narrow path.
> Alone, leaning on my cane, I gaze intently at the scene,
> and feel like answering the murmuring brook with the
> music of my flute.

The poem inscribed on this painting is an integral part of the work of art. Besides describing the scene, the poem serves to locate the painter in it. The poem makes explicit the resonances between the world of the human and the natural world that are implied in the painting and makes the work function on a scale both human and grandiose. The placing of the poem on the painting is not accidental: the small human figure seems to be speaking the words.

In other matters, however, values were less humane. During the Song, attitudes about widow remarriage had begun to harden. Zheng Yi, the neo-Confucian philosopher, said that it was a small thing to starve to death but a large thing to lose one's chastity. In the early fourteenth century the government first established memorial arches for widows who had been widowed before they were thirty and had remained chaste until their fiftieth birthday. Such virtue had practical consequences; for example, the families of such women were granted tax exemptions. Political loyalty was analogous

Poet on a Mountain Top. *Leaf from an album with a poem and an ink drawing on paper by Shen Zhou (1427–1509).*

to sexual loyalty: by promoting the latter, the government doubtless hoped to promote the former. During the Ming and Qing (1644–1912) dynasties, the cult of widow chastity became widespread. At the same time, there were practical reasons for a woman to remarry, and she might be under pressure to do so. There was a sad and shocking proliferation of women who, under pressure from family members to remarry, committed suicide rather than do so.

Philosophy also flourished in sixteenth-century Ming culture. The most important philosopher of the Ming dynasty was Wang Yangming (1472–1529), who believed everyone had the innate capacity to know good, and that the point of moral cultivation was to extend that capacity. He asserted that external sources of authority, both texts and teachers, had only secondary significance. As he put it, "If words are examined in the mind and found to be wrong, even though they come from the mouth of Confucius, I dare not accept them as correct." Wang Yangming also articulated another position implicit in earlier Confucian thought when he asserted the unity of knowledge and action. For example, a person who does not treat his or her parents with filial piety cannot be said to understand filial piety. Real understanding of the concept would mandate action.

Although Wang Yangming asserted that everyone had the potential for sagehood, he by no means implied that the attaining of sagehood would be easy. But some of his followers did. The most radical of these thinkers, called the Taizhou school after the place where the school originated, took the precept that every person was a sage literally. The most important of these thinkers was Wang Gen (1483–1541). When Wang Gen preached, so

the story goes, thousands of people would flock to hear him—so many that shouters would stand in the audience and convey his words, as a kind of low-technology sound system. Influenced by these philosophical developments, as well as by the growth in urban commercial wealth and the growing importance of literacy, was a literary genre called Ledgers of Merit and Demerit. These texts provided a kind of popularized moral handbook for society.

Paradoxically, this period of great flourishing of Ming society in the sixteenth century also had serious social problems. One of the consequences of the Ming vision of an ideal society as a stable agrarian order was that when commerce began to flourish in the sixteenth century, the state was not able to capture revenues from the new prosperity. Ming taxes were consistently lower than taxes had been in the Song, and as a result the number of services the state could provide was much lower. Functions such as poor relief, which the Song state had shown some interest in financing, were funded entirely by local elites or religious organizations during the Ming dynasty. Moreover, this was a period of stunning imperial incompetence and corruption. Zhang Zhuzheng (1525–82), who held the extremely important and powerful position of Senior Grand Secretary, implemented a number of financial reforms. But what is most remembered about him is not the reforms but the fact that at his death his estate was lavish beyond even the Ming imagination. He has become emblematic of late Ming corruption. The reasons for the fall of the Ming are complex, but the problems of cumbersome and incompetent government play a significant role.

Japan: Aristocrats into Warriors

In Japan during the period from the twelfth to the seventeenth centuries, central power disintegrated and was reconstituted along new lines. The aristocratic culture of early Japan was replaced by a culture dominated by warriors, monks, and merchants. The Kamakura (1185–1338) and Ashikaga (1338–1573) periods are characterized by a growing trend toward political decentralization. The Ashikaga is marked by frequent warfare, and by its end, central power was completely meaningless. Yet, ironically, this period was also a time of economic growth and cultural flourishing. Much of what

MERITORIOUS DEEDS AT NO COST

■ *This work is typical of the genre of morality books, which flourished in the sixteenth and seventeenth centuries. These texts reflect a popularized notion of the possibilities for enlightenment.*

The moral precepts in this particular text are categorized by social status. Here are excerpts from what is expected of the local gentry, the peasantry, and finally of people in general. Note the ways in which one can infer social tensions by which kinds of behavior are prohibited.

LOCAL GENTRY

Take the lead in charitable donations. Rectify your own conduct and transform the common people. Do not make remarks about women's sexiness. Do not be arrogant, because of your own power and wealth, toward relatives who are poor or of low status. Do not ignore your own relatives and treat others as if they are of your kin. Persuade others to settle lawsuits through conciliation. Do not keep too many concubines.

PEASANTS

Do not miss proper times for farm work. Do not steal and sell your master's grain in connivance with his servants. In plowing, do not infringe on graves or make them hard to find.

PEOPLE IN GENERAL

Do not divulge your parents' faults to others. Respect women's chastity. Do not put curses on those from whom you have become estranged. When you meet fishermen, hunters, or butchers, try to have them change their occupations. Disseminate morality books which teach retribution and reward. Take good care of paper on which characters are written. Make peace between husbands and wives who are about to separate. Do not speak ill of Buddhist or Taoist monks. Do not listen to your wife or concubines if they should encourage you to neglect or abandon your parents. When helping to put out a fire, do not take advantage of it to steal others' belongings. Even if you see bad men prosper, do not lose faith in ultimate recompense.

From Tadao Sakai, "Confucianism and Popular Educational Works."

---

we think of as representing traditional Japanese culture—the tea ceremony, warrior ethics, Noh drama—had its beginnings during the Kamakura or Ashikaga period.

One of the clearest contrasts between China and Japan is in the nature of the imperial institution. In China, imperial legitimacy was conferred by the Confucian concept of the Mandate of Heaven, a mandate that did not rest permanently with any one ruling family. The mechanism for legitimating dynastic change is described as a change in mandate. By contrast, Japanese political theory does not allow for a changeable mandate. The legitimacy of the Japanese imperial house rested upon the mythology of its descent from the sun goddess. This made the emperor of Japan quasi-divine. Because of the charisma of the authority surrounding him, the emperor was not overthrown. But this did not

mean that the authority of the emperor could not be usurped. In the Kamakura period, a family named Minamoto established themselves as shoguns. Although the shogun was originally a military official, in fact shoguns held civil as well as military power. For example, they had the authority to appoint provincial officials. The emperor appointed the shogun, and granted him legitimacy. The shogun ruled in the name of the emperor, using his charisma rather than usurping it.

Kamakura: Warrior Rule

The first shogun was Minamoto Yoritomo (1147–99), who established his power base in the fishing village of Kamakura, which then gave its name to an era. During the Kamakura period, the emperor remained on the

Wooden sculpture of Minamoto Yoritomo, the first shogun of Japan, from the thirteenth century.

throne in Kyoto and the shogun ruled from Kamakura—a situation that created an uneasy balance of authority between the two centers of power.

Many of the early Kamakura policies were designed to give the shogun better control of the land and the revenues it produced. By the tenth century most of the land in Japan was divided into estates called *shoen*. A shoen was a privately held estate that was often tax-exempt. Yoritomo placed a steward on each shoen, who collected rent and dues from it. In return the stewards were granted military and judicial powers and a portion of the income from the estate. The shogun also appointed an official called the *shugo*, in each province, who oversaw the stewards. Yoritomo also offered protection and rights to land to his followers in return for their promise of military allegiance to him. In several important respects this resembles the feudalism of the European Middle Ages: Military and civil functions were fused into a single authority, and the vertical bond between lord (*daimyo* in the Japanese case) and vassal was the primary bond that tied society together. This system, whether or not we choose to call it feudalism, enabled the Kamakura to govern localities and provide for defense with minimal central government expenditures. But there were also negative consequences: Kamakura central control was very fragile.

After Yoritomo's death, his widow Hojo Masako (1157–1225) retained a position of power. Moreover, she manipulated her own family into positions of authority, and the Hojo became hereditary regents for the Minamoto shoguns, dominating the politics of the Kamakura shogunate until its demise in 1333. Thus another layer was added to the complicated picture of central authority in Kamakura Japan.

One consequence of the decentralization of Japan under the Kamakura was the fragmentation of legal authority. Neither the imperial government nor the shogunal government had the authority to promulgate a legal code that had force throughout the land. The important daimyo would have house codes, which would govern the behavior not only of members of the family but also of the peasants who resided on their estates. In order to bring about some uniformity in the legal structure for samurai (the warrior aristocracy), the Hojo regents to the shogun promulgated a legal code, the Joei code, in 1232. The Joei code was the first codification of feudal customary law in Japan. The main author, a man named Hojo Yasutoki (1183–1242), wrote that "the ancient codes and regulations are like complicated Chinese characters, understood only by a very few people. They are rendered useless to those who understand only the Japanese syllabary. This code is presented in such a way that the great majority of people can take comfort in it, just as there are many people who can understand the Japanese syllabary, so must this code be uniformly known." The code is at pains to assure vassals that they will be treated equally. It also demonstrates a clear concern with public order—it exhorts samurai to obey shoen law. It enshrined warrior values, such as loyalty, honor, and frugality, and celebrated aspects of warrior culture, such as horsemanship, archery, and swordsmanship. Despite the pretensions of the code to universality, its provisions pertained only to samurai. Justice for peasants remained a local matter, to be decided under local codes promulgated at the shoen level.

Important families, such as the Hojo regents, produced family instructions to regulate the behavior of family members. The Hojo instructions, written in 1247, reflect the ethical aura of the period. Some of the instructions advocate a person fear the gods and the Buddhas, and that he obey his lord. A person is cautioned to be aware of the Buddhist law of *karma* and the effect his or her actions will have on future generations. Bravery is a virtue that is celebrated—not surprising in a warrior society. The instructions also contain detailed rules of etiquette that reveal a highly elaborated social structure. Other exhortations resemble those that one might find in instruction books in any society. For example, the Hojo instructions tell the reader that one should obey one's parents and be generous and diligent.

This painting depicts Kublai Khan's massive seaborne invasion of Japan in 1274. The Mongol fleet has landed in northern Kyushu, and the ships are attacked by samurai armed with long swords.

Perhaps the most serious threat to face the Kamakura regime came from the Mongols, who had already conquered China and much of the rest of the world. In November of 1274 a force of 30,000 Mongols, Chinese, and Koreans sailed from Korean ports to Japan. They took the islands of Tsushima and Iki and landed at Hakata Bay. On the night of November 19, a violent storm came up, and the bulk of the Mongol army retreated. Later Japanese referred to this propitious storm as a *kamikaze*, or "divine wind." To prevent further attacks, the shogun ordered the building of a long defensive wall around all of Hakata Bay. But the Mongols were dissuaded neither by the weather nor by the wall. In 1281 Kublai Khan dispatched another force from China and Korea, this one of 140,000 men. After about two months of brutal fighting, once again the kamikaze intervened and forced the Mongol forces to retreat to Korea. The attempted Mongol invasions of Japan were the largest maritime expeditions in history prior to modern times. The expenses of defense sapped the resources of the central government, and the anxiety produced by the threat of Mongol conquest had a profound effect on Kamakura culture, especially religious culture.

Kamakura Culture: The Peasant, the Monk, the Warrior, and the Merchant

Although the economy of Kamakura Japan remained predominantly agrarian, towns and cities grew and prospered. In the late Kamakura period, peasants increased the productivity of their land by using more night soil (a

Tokugawa Japan

euphemism for human excrement) and animal manure. Farms were worked more intensively than they had been in earlier periods. Ordinary peasants in the Kamakura increasingly used metal plows and hoes and owned their own draft animals. All of these changes worked together to promote an increase in agricultural output. As villages became more prosperous, rural commerce became more highly developed. Markets held in villages became more frequent, meeting between three and six times a month. Goods produced in villages were also sold at regional markets, as well as in the growing cities.

Kamakura culture was dominated by Buddhism. In the Kamakura, we begin to see warrior values replace the aristocratic values of earlier Japanese history. And merchants begin to play a role as cultural patrons.

Three forms of Buddhism were important in Kamakura Japan—Zen, Pure Land, and Nichiren. Zen and Pure Land were imported from China, but the particular cast of Kamakura society influenced their development. Nichiren Buddhism, named after its founder, Nichiren (1222–82), on the other hand, was an indigenous development in Japanese Buddhism. Changes in the social order, such as the growth of a class of merchants and warriors, coupled with the anxieties of the age, had a transformative impact on Buddhism. In earlier periods, Japanese Buddhism had been elite in its appeal and abstract in its theology. During the Kamakura, it became a popular religion.

Zen Buddhism was extremely important in Kamakura Japan. Its influence extended beyond religion into the realm of aesthetics and politics. The Zen monk Dogen (1200–53) reminded his audience that the Buddha was not born enlightened, but rather attained enlightenment through meditation. For Dogen, this implied that even ordinary humans could attain enlightenment the same way. Zen Buddhists stressed that meditation had a value separate from and superior to intellectual thinking. Dogen advised:

> Do not study the words and letters of the sutras intellectually but rather reflect upon your self-nature inwardly. Thus, your body and mind will be cast off naturally and your original nature will be revealed. If you wish to do this, be diligent in meditation.

A Zen practitioner might meditate on a *koan*, a spiritual riddle, a question with no answer, as an aid to enlightenment. A famous koan asks what is the sound of one

"DEDICATION TO THE LOTUS" BY NICHIREN

■ *This excerpt, reflecting the beautiful cadences of Kamakura Buddhist preaching, reveals the profound reverence Nichiren holds for the* Lotus Sutra.

If you desire to attain Buddhahood immediately, lay down the banner of pride, cast away the club of resentment, and trust yourselves to the unique Truth. Fame and profit are nothing more than vanity of this life; pride and obstinacy are simply fetters to the coming life . . . When you fall into an abyss and some one has lowered a rope to pull you out, should you hesitate to grasp the rope because you doubt the power of the helper? Has not Buddha declared, "I alone am the protector and savior"? There is the power! Is it not taught that faith is the only entrance [to salvation]? There is the rope! One who hesitates to seize it, and will not utter the Sacred Truth, will never be able to climb the precipice of Bodhi (Enlightenment) . . . Our hearts ache and our sleeves are wet [with tears], until we see face to face the tender figure of the One, who says to us, "I am thy Father." At this thought our hearts beat, even as when we behold the brilliant clouds in the evening sky or the pale moonlight of the fast-falling night . . . Should any season be passed without thinking of the compassionate promise, "Constantly I am thinking of you"? Should any month or day be spent without revering the teaching that there is none who cannot attain Buddhahood? . . . Devote yourself wholeheartedly to the "Adoration to the Lotus of the Perfect Truth," and utter it yourself as well as admonish others to do the same. Such is your task in this human life.

hand clapping. Because ultimate spiritual reality differs from ordinary physical and social reality (which is but an illusion), techniques like koan were needed to startle the practitioner out of the frame of reference of ordinary reality. Dogen also preached on the capacity of women for salvation:

> When we speak of the wicked, there are certainly some men among them. When we talk of the noble, these surely include women. Learning the Law of the Buddha and achieving release from illusion have nothing to do with whether one happens to be a man or a woman.

Zen also valued manual labor and taught a rigid discipline. Its spare aesthetics had a profound influence on Kamakura and later Japanese art. As secular society became more and more the preserve of the warrior, Zen monasteries became more and more sanctuaries of learning. It was not uncommon for a warrior to retire to a Zen monastery after his career in battle was over. But it would be a mistake to regard Zen as an alternative to the life of the warrior. It was the religion of choice of the warrior aristocracy. Many shoguns were important patrons of Zen.

If Zen was characterized by monastic retreat, other forms of Kamakura Buddhism were taught by street preachers, who used parables and anecdotes featuring vivid portrayals of heaven and hell to entice and convert their listeners. A Heian monk named Genshin (942–1017) wrote a very popular text called the *Essentials of Salvation*, which characterized hell as the realm of the hungry spirits who were constantly thwarted in their attempts to obtain even the most basic essentials:

> When they happen to come to an orchard the various fruits suddenly disappear, and when they approach a pure stream of water this quickly dries up.

The hungry spirits were constantly tormented by mirages of satiation and salvation. According to Genshin, faith in the Amida Buddha could save hungry spirits, and by extension all of humankind. This faith would be made manifest by chanting his name, a practice called *nembutsu*. Faith in Amida was sufficient to cause a believer to be reborn in the Pure Land.

Honen (1133–1212) and Shinran (1173–1262) were both deeply influenced by the *Essentials of Salvation*, and further developed Pure Land Buddhism. Honen took Genshin's position one step further and argued that human beings cannot attain salvation on their own merits, no matter how hard they labor. In order to obtain salvation, it was necessary to invoke the power and grace of the Amida Buddha. Honen further asserted the equality of all in the eyes of the Buddha. Shinran, who

was married to the nun Eshin (1182–1270), made Pure Land Buddhism more appealing by arguing that there was no need for clerical celibacy.

But it was Nichiren (1222–82) who developed what was to be the most characteristically Japanese of all the varieties of Kamakura Buddhism. Nichiren based his teachings on the *Lotus Sutra*, an Indian Buddhist scripture that had enormous influence in both China and Japan. The *Lotus Sutra* portrays the Buddha as eternal, ever present, and existing in many forms. According to the *Lotus Sutra*, the historical Buddha had not been a human being, but was rather a manifestation of all-pervading Buddha nature. The *Lotus Sutra* stressed that everyone has the potential for salvation.

Nichiren lived during dangerous times, and his vision of human life and history was apocalyptic. The mid-thirteenth century saw widespread famine, and the Mongol invasions began in 1274. But Nichiren's vision of the apocalypse was not conditioned merely by secular catastrophe. Buddhist cosmologists calculated that in a year corresponding to 1052 in the Western calendar, an era called *mappo*, the end of Buddhist law, had begun. Mappo meant a precipitous decline in all aspects of life and society. Buddhists interpreted the social chaos of the Kamakura era as indicative of the degeneracy of the law (mappo). The opening of one of Nichiren's tracts gives the flavor of his apocalyptic vision:

> During recent years cosmic cataclysms, natural disasters, famines and epidemics have filled the world. Oxen and horses collapse at the crossroads; skeletons fill the lanes. Already more than one-half of the population has died; no one is unafflicted.

At the end of the degenerate age, Nichiren predicted, the period of the true law would come, and it would be ushered in by an ideal ruler, a Buddhist-Confucian sage-king.

The religion Nichiren founded was a national religion, and he declared the *Lotus Sutra* to be a nation-protecting sutra. When a believer invoked the text, he or she was performing an act that had implications for both personal and national salvation. But Nichiren was also universalistic: He advocated missionary work to spread the truth of the *Lotus Sutra* abroad. Japanese Buddhists, like their Chinese counterparts, were generally fairly tolerant of dissent. Here, too, Nichiren was exceptional. He was intolerant of Pure Land practitioners, and they reciprocated. He advocated suppressing them, and they burned his house to the ground.

Buddhism played an important role in Kamakura arts. Among the great achievements of the early

THE CONFESSIONS OF LADY NIJO

■ *This passage opens with the lament of the lady Nijo that the retired emperor is no longer an attentive lover. This exposes the cost of a relaxed marriage system.*
The text then moves to a description of the empress giving birth. Note how the shamanistic rituals are central to the procedure. The lady Nijo is operating in a realm where medicine and shamanism are not separate.

I was in no position to complain about the Retired Emperor's failure to visit me at night, but it was very disappointing to wait in vain time after time. Nor could I very well grumble like my companions about the women who visited him from outside the palace, but I rebelled inwardly against the conventions whenever I had to escort one of them. Was the time likely to come when I would recall this period in my life with nostalgia? The days went by and autumn arrived.

The approach of Higashinijoin's confinement, which was to take place in the Corner Palace, was causing concern because of the Imperial Lady's relatively advanced age and history of difficult births. I believe the time was around the Eighth Month. Every conceivable large ritual and secret ritual had been commissioned—prayers to the Seven Healing Buddhas and the Five Mystic Kings, prayers to Fugen for the prolongation of life, prayers to Kongo Doji and the Mystic King Aizen, and so on. At Father's special request, he assumed responsibility for the prayers to Kongo Doji this time, in addition to the ones to Kundali, which had always been supported by Owari Province in the past. The exorcist was the Jojuin bishop.

Kamakura period are lifelike wooden sculptured images of monks, such as those made by Unkei (ca. 1163–1233). The influence of Buddhism can be seen in the written word as well. The *Tales of Uji* are simple and powerful tales of Buddhist morality. The *Confessions of Lady Nijo*, written in the late fourteenth century by a court lady, portray life at the imperial court. But in the final two chapters, the lady Nijo abandons the court and becomes a wandering Buddhist nun.

Another important genre of Kamakura literature is the military romance. Perhaps the most famous of these is the *Tale of the Heike*, in which the Buddhist values of the warrior culture are made clear. The famous opening of the tale can be taken as emblematic of the period:

> The sound of the bell of the Gion temple echoes the impermanence of all things. The pale hue of the flowers of the teak-tree show the truth that they who prosper must fall. The proud do not last long, but vanish like a spring-night's dream. And the mighty ones will perish in the end, like dust before the wind.

Thus we see reflected in Kamakura culture the combination of a concern with Buddhist impermanence and the beginnings of a new society infused with warrior values and merchant wealth. These are trends that will develop more fully in the centuries to follow.

Ashikaga: Politics with No Center

If politics in Kamakura Japan was decentralized, in the Ashikaga (also known as Muromachi) period, the center ceased to hold entirely. From the Onin War (1467–77) until the Tokugawa reunification at the beginning of the seventeenth century, there was no effective central government in Japan. And yet, as we saw in the Kamakura period, these periods of political chaos do not preclude an era of cultural and economic flourishing.

In 1333, in what is known as the Kemmu restoration, an alliance between the forces of the Ashikaga family and the emperor Go-Daigo (1318–39) overthrew the Hojo regents to the Kamakura shoguns. But the alliance soon broke down, and the emperor Go-Daigo fled south and established his court at Yoshino. Although Go-Daigo insisted that he remained the only legitimate emperor, Ashikaga Takauji (1305–58) established on the throne his puppet, a man from a collateral line of the imperial house. Takauji declared himself shogun

THE DEATH OF ATSUMORI

■ *The* Tale of the Heike *is a chronicle that recounts the rise of the Ashikaga shoguns. The portion excerpted here is a famous exposition of the warrior ethos. Naozane is overcome by grief and remorse at the fact that duty compels him to kill the handsome young Atsumori, who is, we are told in a portion of the text not reproduced here, the age of Naozane's son. But Naozane is a warrior and Atsumori must die. The poignant discovery of the flute on the body of the dead youth leads Naozane to contemplate renouncing war and assuming the religious life of a monk.*

At the beginning of the passage excerpted here, Naozane is speaking to Atsumori.

"I would like to spare you," he said, restraining his tears, "but there are warriors everywhere. You cannot possibly escape. It will be better if I kill you than if someone else does it, because I will offer prayers on your behalf."

"Just take my head and be quick about it."

Overwhelmed by compassion, Naozane could not find a place to strike. His senses reeled, his wits forsook him, and he was scarcely conscious of his surroundings. But matters could not go on like that forever: in tears, he took the head.

"Alas! No lot is as hard as a warrior's. I would never have suffered such a dreadful experience if I had not been born into a military house. How cruel I was to kill him!" He pressed his sleeve to his face and shed a flood of tears.

He removed the youth's armor so that he might wrap it around the head. A brocade bag containing a flute was tucked in at the waist. "Ah, how pitiful! He must be one of the people I heard making music just before dawn. There are tens of thousands of riders in our eastern armies, but none of them has brought a flute to the battlefield. Those court nobles are refined men!"

When Naozane's trophies were presented for Yoshitsune's inspection, they drew tears from the eyes of all the beholders. It was learned later that the slain youth was Atsumori.

After that, Naozane thought increasingly of becoming a monk. It is deeply moving that music, a profane entertainment, should have led a warrior to the religious life.

---

in 1338, and moved the seat of the shogun's power from Kamakura to Kyoto. Thus began the period we call Ashikaga.

Until 1392, two emperors remained on the throne, one located at the southern court at Yoshino and the other at the northern court at Kyoto. The split was the occasion for sporadic but debilitating civil war. Contemporaries debated the competing claims of the two courts. One of the strongest proponents of the southern court was the historian Kitabatake Chikafusa (1293–1354), who said that the emperor's direct lineal descent from the sun goddess precluded any changes in the imperial line. The idea of direct lineal descent from the sun goddess first appeared in eighth-century texts, and Kitabatake Chikafusa's invoking it here shows how politics could summon both history and legend to its aid.

Early Ashikaga shogunal attempts to reassert central power met with some temporary success, but the de-

cline in central power proved irreversible. Several of the early fifteenth-century shoguns, such as Yoshimitsu (1353–1408) and Yoshinori (1428–41), were strong leaders. Some of the institutional arrangements made by these leaders to consolidate central control backfired. For example, Yoshimitsu attempted to restrict the power of the *shugo*, military leaders whose lands often included more than one province. He required each shugo to maintain a residence in Kyoto in addition to his provincial residence. This eroded their local power base, as well as making it easier for the shogun to supervise them. The shugo were forbidden to return to their provincial base without official permission, and returning without prior permission constituted treason.

However, these policies did not, in the end, strengthen the central government. The absence of the shugo from the land precipitated the rise of a new group of locally powerful warrior families, called *kokujin.*

During the early years of the fifteenth century the shugo lost control of the provinces to the kokujin and political power became even more decentralized.

During the course of the Ashikaga period, there was a change in Japanese inheritance practices. In earlier Japanese history, property was shared among sons and daughters. Women could hold property, and indeed, during the Heian period, houses were in general held by women. But during the Ashikaga, a system known as primogeniture—where one son, usually the eldest, inherits all property—became the norm. As a consequence, women lost rights to hold property. In general in the warrior society of Kamakura and Ashikaga Japan, women played a much more restricted role than they had in earlier Japanese history.

The effective end of Ashikaga control was marked by the Onin War (1467–77), though Ashikaga power continued in name only for another century. The war was caused by a succession dispute in the Ashikaga ruling house, a struggle that was entwined with a power struggle among shugo. By the end of the war, the splendid city of Kyoto lay in ruins, the power of the shugo was exhausted, and the Ashikaga was a government in name only.

But, ironically enough, the political chaos was not socially debilitating. Agricultural productivity continued the rise begun in the Kamakura period. Early-ripening Champa rice from Southeast Asia facilitated double cropping. Furthermore, other new crops such as soybeans and tea were introduced during the Ashikaga. The use of the water wheel and increased use of draft animals also stimulated agricultural productivity. Technical progress in mining, paper production, and sake brewing also stimulated economic growth.

Local villages became even more autonomous during the Ashikaga than they had been during the Kamakura. These villages were governed by assemblies of male residents. According to a fifteenth-century set of rules, male peasants who did not attend village assemblies would be fined. But village autonomy does not translate into peasant contentment. During the course of the fifteenth century, peasants rebelled with increasing frequency. Often peasants demanded that their debts be canceled, and on several occasions they met with success. Because the pawnbrokers to whom the peasants were in debt were often city dwellers, these uprisings on occasion took on the cast of a conflict between city and countryside.

Urban areas, like their rural counterparts, had a striking degree of autonomy during the Ashikaga period. During this period the tendency toward the develop-

A Japanese painting celebrates communal agriculture. To the tune of special "music of the fields," men in rush skirts carry rice plants to kimono-clad women, who set them out in the rice paddies.

ment of town culture we saw during the Kamakura increased. Not only did cities grow, but residents were increasingly identifying themselves as townsfolk of the city in which they lived. Confucian disdain for merchants, which often surfaced in both China and Japan, seemed absent during this period: Merchants were referred to as "men of virtue." By the beginning of the Ashikaga period, warriors and merchants were playing a significant role in the creation of an urban culture, which featured drama and other forms of popular entertainment. (See Special Feature, "The Flowering of Noh Drama," pp. 342–343.)

Ashikaga towns were subdivided into units called *machi*, which began to take on responsibility for important functions such as protection against fire and the maintenance of law and order. As the central power of the shogunal government declined, these local organizations became more and more important.

Another social organization that was gaining in importance was the guild. Guilds were formed by merchants and artisans to protect their rights over the production of particular goods or services. They often sought the protection of great families or great monasteries. For example, the pawnbrokers of Kyoto were protected by the famous Tendai monastery on Mt. Hiei, located just outside the city. The protection they sought was not just spiritual; on more than one occasion armed monks from Mt. Hiei fought on behalf of their clients.

From the middle of the fifteenth century, tension between urban and rural areas became more clearly expressed. Armed peasants attacked the city of Kyoto several times. Their specific targets varied: They targeted wealth, specific proprietors, or moneylenders and pawnbrokers. But when they attacked, the whole machi was subject to risk, and the machi fought back as a unit. Thus the crucial fault line in these uprisings seems not to lie on occupational or class lines, but rather between rural and urban society.

Under the Ashikaga, two new commercial groups rose to prominence—moneylenders and sake brewers. In fact, the groups overlapped to a considerable degree because sake brewing required a significant amount of capital. During the Ashikaga, the use of money had become more widespread, and bills of exchange were introduced. The moneylenders' power stemmed from the fact that everyone, including the shogun, owed them money. The shogunal government periodically issued edicts that wiped out all debts, but this proved only a temporary solution.

International trade played a significant role in the Ashikaga economy. The threat of Mongol invasions in the late Kamakura had stimulated Japanese shipbuilding. Prior to the Mongol invasions, most trade between Japan and the mainland had been carried by Chinese or Korean ships. But this began to change in the fourteenth century with the rise of Japanese shipbuilding, and with the fifteenth-century decline of China as a sea power.

During the early Ashikaga period, international trade in East Asia was not regularized, and it was often hard to tell the difference between piracy and trade. About 1350, Korea began to complain about Japanese pirates raiding the Korean coast, and in 1373 two monks traveling as envoys of the emperor of China asked that the raids against the Chinese coast be stopped. Between 1376 and 1384, Japanese pirates staged an average of forty raids a year. These raids could be substantial, the largest of them consisting of 400 ships with 3,000 men. The main objectives of the raids seem to have been the acquisition of grain and slaves. The impact of the raids

was serious. The disorder they produced contributed to the fall of the Korean Koryo dynasty in 1392. So-called Japanese pirates remained a problem for the rest of early modern East Asian history, though as time went on, more and more of the pirates were actually Chinese or Korean.

A regulated and restricted trade between China and Japan, known as the tally trade, was set up in 1404. When a merchant was granted permission to carry on the trade, he would receive a tally signifying his authority, hence the name of the trade. This trade was initially carried out under the rubric of tribute trade. In 1401, the shogun Yoshimitsu, using the title "king of Japan" sent tribute to the Chinese, and promised that the pirate raids would stop. The tally trade was profitable, but limited in scope. Only seventy or eighty of these trips were made before the system broke down in 1551. The Japanese exported copper, sulfur, folding fans, painted screens, and steel swords. Much to the consternation of the Ming government, tens of thousands of high-quality swords found their way to China from Japan. The Chinese exported silk, porcelain, paintings, medicine, books, and coins. During the fifteenth century, objects from China enjoyed resurgent prestige in Japan, especially among Buddhist monks.

In the early Ashikaga, trade with China was a monopoly of the shoguns. Later, the trade was carried out as joint ventures between the shogun, temples, and important daimyo. By the early sixteenth century, important warrior families, notably the Ouchi and the Hosokawa, monopolized the China trade, and the shogun was not even a participant. This is indicative of his declining general significance. Japanese merchants also conducted important trade with Korea, which was regulated by the So family from Tsushima. Textiles, especially cotton, were the chief commodity involved.

The period following the Onin War is known as the Warring States period, and it lasted until the Tokugawa reunification in 1600. In the late fifteenth century, a new group of locally powerful military leaders, called warring states daimyo, emerged. With few exceptions, they are new families, often descended from the kokujin. Of 142 major daimyo families existing in 1563, only 32 were descended from shugo families. Indeed, the old shugo had been destroyed as a class, and no longer played a role in the political arena. The great social upheavals of this era were often described by contemporaries with the phase "the lowly are overturning the mighty."

The warring states daimyo were even more independent of central authority than the shugo had been. In

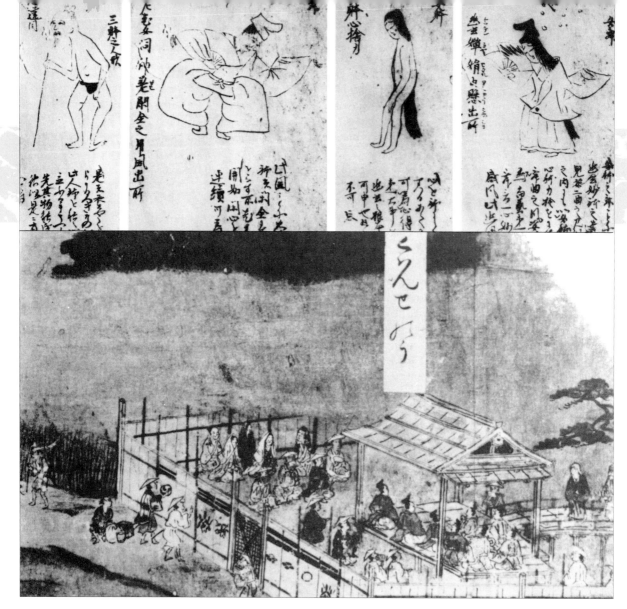

The figure at the top presents details of illustrations for Nikyoku Santai no Ezu *("Dance and Music"), a work of criticism by Zeami, the Japanese drama theorist. The human figures show how the body should be held in the performance of Noh drama. The bottom figure shows "Scenes Within and Without the Capital Screen," a painting from the early seventeenth century, which depicts the forms of popular entertainment available in Tokyo, including this Noh drama.*

The Flowering of Noh Drama

The story goes that in 1374 the shogun, the great Yoshimitsu, was out on the town and happened upon a performance of a play called "The Old Man." The performers were Kan'ami (1333–84) and his captivating twelve-year-old son Zeami (1363–1443). Yoshimitsu was taken by the performance, and perhaps smitten by the boy as well. He took the father and son back to the palace and became their patrons. The result of this happy meeting of artist and patron was the flowering of Noh drama.

Noh drama had its roots in peasant performances. One of its precursors was *dengaku*, field music, which had originated as songs that Japanese farmers sang when they did their fieldwork. These songs attracted the attention of the elite, already in the Heian period, dengaku was popular with members of the court. The *Taiheike*, a fourteenth-century text, tells us of the dance:

Around that time in the capital, men made much of the dance called field music, and high or low there was none that did not seek after it eagerly. Hearing of this a lay monk called down the New Troupe and the Original Troupe to Kamakura, where he amused himself with them day and night and morning and evening, with no other thought in his mind. When those dancers danced at a feast, the monk and all his kinsmen and captains took off their robes and trousers and tossed them out, none willing to be outdone.

Now drinking on a certain night, the monk grew merry with wine, so that he rose up and danced. (His dancing was only the vain dancing of a drunken old monk of more than forty years.) Suddenly from nowhere there came more than ten field music dancers of the New and Original Troupes, who lined up in the room dancing and singing with surpassing skill.

There was a lady-in-waiting who looked through a crack in the sliding door, irresistibly diverted by the sound of those voices. And she saw that of those who had seemed to be dancers, not one was a human being, but all were specters of divers kinds and shapes who had changed themselves into humans.

Sorely affrighted, the lady sent a man running to a castle lay monk, who made haste to go toward the room, sword in hand. But when his footsteps advanced violently through the middle gate, the phantoms vanished. And all the while the other monk slept drunkenly, knowing nothing of it.

The plays of Noh drama are divided into five categories by subject matter: plays about gods, warriors, women, demons, and miscellaneous subject matter. The stage was simple, open on three sides, with no curtain and no background scenery. The actors were often masked, and mime was one of the most important dramatic techniques employed.

After Noh became a palace art, it became less realistic and more abstracted and refined. These abstractions appealed to the taste of sophisticated connoisseurs. History is full of examples of elite culture being used on the popular level. But Noh drama is a clear example of the reverse: peasant work songs transformed into austere art forms for the court and the aristocracy.

1482, the shogun Yoshimasa (1435–90) lamented that "The daimyo do as they please and do not follow orders. This means there can be no government." Indeed, after the Onin War the shogun was a puppet of the most powerful daimyo. These powerful daimyo governed their lands more or less as independent principalities, and sixteenth-century European visitors often called them kings.

During the Warring States period, daimyo built splendid castles. Towns to serve the needs of these lords arose in the shadow of the castles. To be sure, the primary purpose of these castles was as defensive strongholds, but they were also strong expressions of cultural identity. Most of the Warring States castles have been destroyed, but the castles of Himeji in Hyogo Prefecture and Matsumoto in Nagano Prefecture are still extant. Castle towns were extremely important in promoting urban growth in Japan.

The warfare of the Warring States period does not seem to have had a negative impact on economic development. Warfare was bloody and protracted, and doubtless had locally negative economic consequences. But it stimulated demand, especially in the burgeoning castle towns.

Around 1550, the old order had completely disintegrated, and ambitious men imagined the reunification of Japan into a more strongly centralized state. The reunification of Japan was accomplished by three men: Oda Nobunaga (1534–82), Toyotomi Hideyoshi (1536–98) and Tokugawa Ieyasu (1542–1616). In 1573 Oda Nobunaga sent the last Ashikaga shogun into permanent exile. Through a combination of diplomacy and military skill, cooperation and treachery, these three men forged a unified country. The new state was called the Tokugawa, and will be discussed in chapter 23.

Ashikaga Culture: Temple and Ceremony

Despite the political chaos of this era, culture flourished. Merchants and warriors were crucial players in Ashikaga culture, but so were monks and nuns. In this era, Buddhism became an important part of lay life, and the monastic life was an attractive option for both men and women. Especially as civil society became war-torn during the Warring States period, the monastery became a repository of learning, Confucian as well as Buddhist. As an anonymous seventeenth-century author said, describing the situation during the civil wars in the fifteenth and sixteenth centuries,

If you wanted a cure for an illness, a horoscope read, a picture painted or a document written, it was to a temple that you went. All the arts became the monopoly of priests.

In this respect they fulfilled a role not unlike that played by monasteries in Europe during the Middle Ages.

The Kamakura cults that were discussed earlier all persisted, and Zen became even more important than it had been. As warrior values permeated society, Zen monasteries were used by the Ashikaga as the literate branch of government. In Kyoto a temple named Shokokuji, which had been established by the shogun Yoshimitsu, served as a center of foreign relations. Monks there drafted communications in Chinese for the Ming court.

Ashikaga merchants and monks showed a keen interest in Chinese objects. They eagerly studied Chinese religion, arts, and technology. For example, Song dynasty monochrome paintings became fashionable, and exerted an influence on Japanese art. These paintings, rendered in ink on silk with a minimum of color, were described as "transcending color."

The tea ceremony was an Ashikaga cultural form that occupied a ground somewhere between religious ritual and performance art. Often sponsored by, and even performed by, merchants, it flourished in the fifteenth and sixteenth centuries. The tea ceremony consisted of the preparation and serving of tea in a carefully arranged setting. The most highly regarded tea ceremonies were carried out in austere settings; the ascetic surroundings of the ceremony were symbolic of Buddhist renunciation. The aesthetics of the tea ceremony influenced secular architecture. The straw *tatami* mats covering the entire surface of the floor and the sliding paper *shoji* screens that we think of as characteristic of traditional Japanese architecture became popular as a result of their association with the tea ceremony.

The most famous tea master in all of Japan was not a warrior or a monk but a merchant from Sakai named Sen no Rikyu (1522–91). He founded a school of tea ceremony which stressed the utmost simplicity. Despite this, he became the tea master to both Oda Nobunaga and Hideyoshi, two of the men who played a prominent role in the unification of Japan. The fact that these sturdy warriors had a tea master indicates both the pervasiveness of the aesthetic sensibility reflected in the tea ceremony, and the ways in which the ceremony could be used for cultural legitimation. For reasons that remain obscure, Sen no Rikyu incurred Hideyoshi's displeasure and in 1591 was forced to commit suicide by disemboweling himself.

"The Four Seasons" by the Japanese painter Sesshu (1420-1506). He adapted Chinese models to Japanese artistic ideas.

The aesthetics of the tea ceremony propounded by Sen no Rikyu profoundly influenced the potter Chojiro (1576-92), the originator of a style of pottery known as Raku ware. While earlier ceramics were delicate and refined, Raku brings out the quality of the clay, and looks very modern to our eyes.

Literary forms remained important in this period, and one of the most important was a verse forms known as *renga*, or linked verse. These poems were often composed at social occasions. "Three Poets as Minase," composed in 1488 by Sogi and his disciples Shohaku and Socho, is one of the most famous. It opens with the following verses.

> *Sogi:* Snow clinging to slope,
> On mist-enshrouded mountains
> At eveningtime
> *Shohaku:* In the distance water flows
> Through plum-scented villages.
> *Socho:* Willows cluster
> In the river breeze
> As spring appears.
> *Sogi:* The sound of a boat being poled
> In the clearness of dawn.

Shohaku: Still the moon lingers
As fog o'er spreads
The night.
Socho: A frost covered meadow;
Autumn has drawn to a close.
Sogi: Against the wishes
Of droning insects
The grasses wither.

The various voices of this poem link the landscape and the passage of time. The poem is not dominated by a single authorial voice, rather, there are three voices drawing on a common tradition and writing by common rules. Renga melds multiple voices into a single poem without denying their multivocality.

Linked verse had a great comic capacity as well. Comic renga might be posed as answers to a riddle, as in the following sixteenth-century example:

It is dangerous
But also makes us joyful.
The log bridge
We cross in the evening
To welcome the groom.

The first two lines are anonymous, the final three are by Arakida Moritake (1473–1549). The danger represented by the log bridge might well be literally that. But the poem also invokes the dangerous moment at which a new member joins the family. Note that the wedding here is effected when the groom joins the bride's house, probably in a uxorilocal marriage.

China and Japan both underwent dramatic changes during the period covered by this chapter. The two societies were, if anything, even more different one from another by the end of the period. The most pronounced difference is of course in the way the elite was constituted; in China it was a literati elite recruited through civil service examinations, while in Japan it was a warrior elite recruited through battle.

Should we need any proof that history is not the story of progress, the fate of women in China and Japan during this period should suffice. Women, who in China had once played polo, now had their feet bound. Women, who in Japan had been the primary producers of what still ranks as one of the world's great literatures, lost the right to inherit property.

Both China and Japan saw the growth of splendid cities during this period. In Japan during the Ashikaga, a distinctive urban culture began to evolve. Townsfolk, people who were neither warriors nor aristocrats, began to identify themselves with their cities and began producing a culture that was distinctively urban. This was

much more pronounced in Japan than it was in China. A Chinese merchant could always aspire for his son to take the civil service exam. The possibility of joining the literati was a potent lure, and was significant in inhibiting the formation of an independent merchant culture.

SUGGESTIONS FOR FURTHER READING

THE GLORIES OF CHINA UNDER THE SONG

*Jacques Gernet, *Daily Life in China on the Eve of the Mongol Invasion* (New York: MacMillan, 1962). A lively and readable account of daily life in the Song capital.

Valerie Hansen, *Changing Gods in Medieval China. 1127–1276* (Princeton, NJ: Princeton University Press, 1990). A splendid study of the transmission and transformation of popular religion in Song dynasty China.

Patricia Ebrey, *Chu Hsi's Family Rituals: A Twelfth Century Manual for the Performance of Cappings, Weddings, Funerals and Ancestral Rites* (Princeton, NJ: Princeton University Press, 1991). A translation of a crucial ritual text.

Robert Hymes, *Statesmen and Gentlemen: The Elite of Fu-chou, Chiang-hsi, in Northern and Southern Sung* (Cambridge, MA: Cambridge University Press, 1986). An analysis in changes in elite status and society from the Northern to the Southern Song.

John Chaffee, *The Thorny Gates of Learning in Sung China: A Social History of Examinations* (Cambridge, MA: Cambridge University Press, 1985). An account of the examination system and its implications.

MONGOLS AND THE YUAN DYNASTY

Morris Rossabi, *Khubilai Khan: His Life and Times* (Berkeley and Los Angeles: University of California Press, 1988). A highly readable account of the man who ruled most of Eurasia in the thirteenth century.

Thomas Allsen, *Mongol Imperialism: The Politics of the Grand Oan Mongke in China, Russia and the Islamic Lands 1251–1259* (Berkeley and Los Angeles: University of California Press, 1987). The Mongol empire in world perspective.

Elizabeth Endicott-West, *Mongolian Rule in China: Local Administration in the Yuan Dynasty* (Cambridge, MA: Harvard University Press, 1989). A careful study of Yuan local administration.

*John Langlois, ed., *China under Mongol Rule* (Princeton, NJ: Princeton University Press, 1981). A collection of essays treating various aspects of Yuan history.

THE RESTORATION OF CHINESE POWERS UNDER THE MING

*Ray Huang, *1587, A Year of No Significance: The Ming Dynasty in Decline* (New Haven, CT: Yale University Press, 1981). A collection of biographies of key players in late Ming politics and society.

*John Dardess, *Confucianism and Autocracy: Professional Elites and the Founding of the Ming Dynasty* (Berkeley and Los Angeles:

University of California Press, 1983). An analysis of the role of the Confucian literati in the formation of the Ming state.

Craig Clunas, *Superfluous Things: Material Culture and Social Status in Early Modern China* (Urbana, IL: University of Illinois Press, 1991). A study of elite consumption with suggestive comparisons to early modern Europe.

Cynthia J. Brokaw, *The Ledgers of Merit and Demerit: Social Change and Moral Order in Late Imperial China* (Princeton, NJ: Princeton University Press, 1991). A study of popular morality books and the ways in which they are rooted in changing social contexts.

JAPAN: ARISTOCRATS INTO WARRIORS

Hitomi Tonomura, *Community and Commerce in Late Medieval Japan: The Corporate Villages of Tokuchin-ho* (Stanford, CA: Stanford University Press, 1992). A local study of the peasant economy in the sixteenth century.

Thomas Keirstead, *The Geography of Power in Medieval Japan* (Princeton, NJ: Princeton University Press, 1992). An examination of the shoen as a cultural system, with particular attention to how power is negotiated within that system.

Thomas Rimer and Masaku Yamazaki, *On the Art of the No Drama: The Major Treatises of Zeami* (Princeton, NJ: Princeton University Press, 1984). An informative and readable introduction followed by translations of nine treatises on the No drama.

Peter Arneson, *The Medieval Japanese Daimyo: The Ouchi Family's Rule in Suo and Nagato* (New Haven, CT: Yale University Press, 1979). A good, detailed discussion of the rise of the Ashikaga. It assumes an intelligent reader with some background knowledge of the subject.

Martin Collcutt, *Five Mountains: The Rinzai Zen Monastic Institution in Medieval Japan* (Cambridge, MA: Harvard University Press, 1981). An institutional study of Zen monasticism in Japan.

Kenneth A. Grossberg, *Japan's Renaissance: The Politics of the Muromachi Bakufu* (Cambridge, MA: Harvard University Press, 1981). A readable political history of the Muromachi era.

Janet Goff, *Noh Drama and the Tale of Genji: The Art of Allusion in Fifteen Classical Plays* (Princeton, NJ: Princeton University Press, 1991). A cogent analysis of Noh plays based on the novel *Tale of Genji*, coupled with a translation of selected texts.

Helen Craig McCullough, compiler and editor, *Classical Japanese Prose: An Anthology* (Stanford, CA: Stanford University Press, 1990). An easily readable accessible anthology of prose.

Jacob Raz, *Audience and Actors: A Study of their Interaction in the Japanese Theater* (Leiden, Netherlands: E.J. Brill, 1983). A survey beginning with the earliest theaters and continuing to modern times.

Mary Elizabeth Berry, *Hideyoshi* (Cambridge, MA: Harvard University Press, 1982). A look at political culture in the late sixteenth century through a biography of one of the unifiers.

Michael Cooper, *They Came to Japan: An Anthology of European Reports on Japan, 1543-1640* (Berkeley and Los Angeles: University of California Press, 1965). A collection of missionary and other travel accounts, arranged topically.

*Indicates paperback edition available.

CHAPTER 12

The Italian Renaissance, 1350–1525

A Civic Procession

It is 25 April 1444. On this day each year the city of Venice celebrates its patron, Saint Mark, with a procession around the square that bears his name. Processions are a common form of civic ritual through which a community defines itself. The special features that identify Venice for its citizens are all on display. Flags and emblems of the city are mounted on poles, and clothes bear the insignia of various orders and groups. The procession re-creates all forms of communal life. Here are the religious orders (the white-clad brothers of the Confraternity of Saint John are passing before us now), and the civic leaders can be seen just behind them. Musicians entertain both marchers and onlookers. An entire band files by on the right. The procession is orderly, but it is by no means contrived. It is not staged, as would be a modern ceremony, and this difference is evident in the relaxed attitude of the ordinary citizens who stand in groups in the middle of the square. There is no apparent drama to observe, and they walk and talk quite naturally. So, too, do the participants. In the lower left-hand corner, some friars are reading music; at the lower right, members of the confraternity carry their candles negligently.

Yet the painting, *The Procession of the Relic of the Holy Cross* (1496) by Gentile Bellini (ca. 1429–1507), was commissioned to commemorate a miracle rather than a civic procession. On the evening before Saint Mark's day, a visiting merchant and his son were touring the square when the boy accidentally fell and cracked his skull. The doctors who were called to treat him regarded the case as hopeless and advised the father to prepare for his son's death. The next morning, the Brothers of the Confraternity of Saint John carried the relic of a piece of the true cross beneath an embroidered canopy. The merchant approached the golden altarpiece that contained the relic, dropped to his knees, and prayed that Saint Mark would miraculously cure his son. He is the figure kneeling just to the right of center where the line of brothers breaks. The next day, the boy revived and his injury healed.

The Brothers of Saint John commissioned Bellini to commemorate this event. Bellini came from the most distinguished family of painters in Venice. His father Jacopo had studied in Florence and had brought both of his sons into his workshop when they were young boys. Until the age of thirty Gentile and his younger and more famous brother, Giovanni, worked on their father's commissions, learning the difficult craft of painting. Art was very much a family business in fifteenth-century Italy. The large workshops with their master and hordes of apprentices turned out vast canvasses with almost assembly-line precision. The master created the composition and sketched it out; his skilled assistants, like the Bellini brothers, worked on the more complex parts; and young apprentices painted backgrounds and indistinct faces. The master was first and foremost a businessman, gaining commissions to sustain his family and his workers. The Bellinis were well connected to the Confraternity of Saint John, and it was only natural that Gentile would receive this lucrative contract.

Though *The Procession of the Relic of the Holy Cross* was designed to re-create a central moment in the history of the confraternity, it is not the confraternity that dominates the picture. Miracles were part of civic life, and each town took pride in the special manifestations of heavenly care that had taken place within it.

And it is very much Venice that is the centerpiece of Bellini's canvas. Dominating the painting is the Basilica of San Marco, with its four great horses over the center portico and the winged lion, the city's symbol, on the canopy above the horses. The procession emanates from the duke's palace to the right of the church, and the great flags of the city are seen everywhere. By the end of the fifteenth century, Venice was one of the greatest powers on earth, the center for international trade and finance. Home to the largest concentration of wealthy families anywhere in Europe, it could well afford the pomp and splendor of its processions. The achievements of God and the achievements of humans blend together in this painting as they blended together in that era of remarkable accomplishments that historians call the Renaissance.

Renaissance Society

Perhaps the most surprising result of the Black Death was the way in which European society revived itself in the succeeding centuries. Even at the height of the plague a spirit of revitalization was evident in the works of artists and writers. Petrarch (1304–74), the great humanist poet and scholar, was among the first to differentiate the new age in which he was living from two earlier ones: the classical world of Greece and Rome, which he admired, and the subsequent Dark Ages, which he detested. This spirit of self-awareness is one of the defining characteristics of the Renaissance. "It is but in our own day that men dare boast that they see the dawn of better things," wrote Matteo Palmieri (1406–75). The Renaissance was a new age by self-assertion. In that self-assertion wave after wave of artistic celebration of the human spirit found its wellspring and created a legacy that is still vibrant five hundred years later.

What was the Renaissance? A French word for an Italian phenomenon, *Renaissance* literally means "rebirth." The word captures both the emphasis on humanity that characterized Renaissance thinking and the renewed fascination with the classical world. But the Renaissance was an age rather than an event. There is no moment at which the Middle Ages ended. Late medieval society was artistically creative, socially well developed, and economically diverse. Yet eventually the pace of change accelerated, and it is best to think of the Renaissance as an era of rapid transitions. Encompassing the two centuries between 1350 and 1550, it passed through three distinct phases. The first, from 1350 to 1400, was characterized by a declining population, the uncovering of classical texts, and experimentation in a variety of art forms. The second phase, from 1400 to 1500, was distinguished by the creation of a set of cultural values and by artistic and literary achievements that defined Renaissance style. The large Italian city-states developed stable and coherent forms of government and the warfare between them gradually ended. In the final period, from 1500 to 1550, invasions from France and Spain transformed Italian political life, and the ideas and techniques of Italian writers and artists radiated to all points of the Continent. Though Renaissance ideas and achievements did spread throughout western Europe, they are best studied where they first developed, on the Italian peninsula.

Cities and Countryside

The Italian peninsula differed sharply from other areas of Europe in the extent to which it was urban. By the late Middle Ages nearly one in four Italians lived in a town, in contrast to one in ten elsewhere. There were more Italian cities and more people in them. By 1500 seven of the ten largest cities in Europe were in Italy.

The streets of Florence were narrow and dark, with an incredible jumble of buildings in all sizes, shapes, and states of repair. All public inns were on a single street, and their management was strictly regulated.

Naples, Venice, and Milan, each with a population of more than one hundred thousand, led the rest. But it was the numerous smaller towns, with populations nearer to one thousand, that gave the Italian peninsula its urban character. Cities were still the wonder of the world, dominating their regions economically, politically, and culturally. The diversified economic activities in which the inhabitants engaged created vast concentrations of wealth. Cities also served as convenient centers of judicial and ecclesiastical power, and Italy was the banking capital of the world.

Cities acted as central places around which a cluster of large and small villages was organized. Urban areas, especially the small towns, provided markets for the agricultural produce of the countryside and for the manufactured goods of the urban craftsmen. This allowed for the specialization in agricultural and industrial life that increased both productivity and wages. Cities also

caught the runoff of rural population, especially the shower of younger sons and daughters who could not be accommodated on the farms. Thus the areas surrounding a city were critical to its prosperity and survival. Florence, the dominant city in the region of Tuscany, exemplifies this relationship. Though it possessed two-thirds of its region's wealth, Florence contained only 14 percent of the regional population. The surrounding countryside was agriculturally rich, for marketing costs were low and demand for foodstuffs high. Smaller cities like Prato and Pistoia to the north and Pisa to the west channeled their local produce and trade to Florence.

Though cities may have dominated Renaissance Italy, by present standards they were small in both area and population. A person could walk across fifteenth-century Florence in less than half an hour. In 1427 its population was thirty-seven thousand, only half its preplague size. Most Italian cities contained large fields for agricultural production, and within the outer walls of Florence were gardens and grain fields. Inside the inner city walls the people crowded together into tightly packed quarters. The intensity of the stench from raw sewage, rotting foodstuffs, and slaughtered animals was equaled only by the din made by hoofs and wooden cartwheels on paving stones.

Urban populations were organized far differently from rural ones. On the farms the central distinctions involved ownership of land. Some farmers owned their estates outright and left them intact to their heirs. Others were involved in a sharecropping system by which absentee owners of land supplied working capital in return for half of the farm's produce. A great gulf in wealth separated owners from sharecroppers. But within the groups the gaps were not as great. There were gradations, but these were ordinarily temporary conditions that bad harvests, generous dowries, or divided inheritances balanced out over time.

In the city, however, distinctions were based first on occupation, which largely corresponded to social position and wealth. Cities began as markets and it was the privilege to participate in the market that defined citizens. City governments provided protection for consumers and producers by creating monopolies through which standards for craftsmanship were maintained and profits for craftsmen were guaranteed. These monopolies were called guilds or companies. Each large city had its own hierarchy of guilds. At the top were the important manufacturing groups—clothiers, metalworkers, and the like. Just below them were bankers, merchants, and the administrators of civic and Church holdings. At the bottom were grocers, masons, and other skilled workers. Roughly speaking, all of those within the guild structure, from bottom to top, lived comfortably. Yet the majority of urban inhabitants were not members of guilds. Many managed to eke out a living as wage laborers; many more were simply destitute. As a group these poor constituted as much as half of the entire population. Most were dependent upon civic and private charity for their very survival.

The disparities between rich and poor were overwhelming. The concentration of wealth in the hands of an ever narrowing group of families and favored guilds characterized every large city. One reason for this was the extreme instability of economic life. Prices and wages fluctuated wildly in response to local circumstance. After an epidemic of plague, wages climbed and the prices of consumer goods tumbled. A bad harvest sent food prices skyrocketing. Only those able to even

out these extreme swings by stockpiling goods in times of plenty and consuming them in times of want were safe. Capital, however initially accumulated, was the key to continued wealth. Monopolies ensured the profitability of trade and manufacturing, but only those with sufficient capital could engage in either. In Florence, for example, 10 percent of the families controlled 90 percent of the wealth, with an even more extreme concentration at the top.

Production and Consumption

This concentration of wealth and the way in which it was used defined Renaissance economy. Economic life is bound up in the relationship between resources and desires, or, as economists would have it, supply and demand. The late medieval economy, despite the development of international banking and long-distance trade, was still an economy of primary producers: between 70 and 90 percent of Europe's population was involved in subsistence agriculture, only producing enough each year for survival. Even in Italy, which contained the greatest concentration of urban areas in the world, agriculture predominated. The manufacture of clothing was the only other significant economic activity, and it was dwarfed in comparison to farming. Moreover, most of what was produced was for local consumption rather than for the marketplace. The relationship between supply and demand was precisely measured by the full or empty stomach. Even in good times more than 80 percent of the population lived at subsistence level with food, clothing, and shelter their only expenses. Thus when we discuss the market economy of the Renaissance, we are discussing the circumstances of the few rather than the many.

The defining characteristic of the early Renaissance economy was change in population. Recurring waves of plague kept population levels low for more than a century. In the century between 1350 and 1450 one in every six years was characterized by an unusually high mortality rate. At the end of this period Florence's population was only a quarter of what it had been at the beginning. This dramatic reduction in population depressed economic growth. The general economy did not revive until the sustained population increase toward the end of the fifteenth century. Until then, in both agriculture and manufacturing supply outstripped demand. On the farms overabundance resulted from two related developments, the concentration of surviving farmers on the luxury became more alluring than ever. It was not merely the perceived shortage in profitable investments that brought on the increase in conspicuous consumption during the fifteenth century. In the psychological atmosphere created by unpredictable, swift, and deadly epidemics, people became more concerned with the present than the future. Secondly, in order to pay for wars, both offensive and defensive, rates of taxation increased. Since both houses and personal property were normally exempt from the calculations of wealth upon which taxation was based, the richest members of the community could escape this additional burden by purchasing luxury goods.

For whatever reasons, the production and consumption of luxuries soared. By the middle of the fourteenth century Florence was known for its silks and jewelry as much as for its cloth. Venice became a European center for the glass industry, especially for the finely ground glass that was used in eyeglasses. Production of specialty crops like sugar, saffron, fruits, and high-quality wine expanded. International trade increasingly centered on acquiring Eastern specialties, resulting in the serious outflow of gold and silver that enriched first the Byzantine and then the Ottoman emperors. Both public and private building projects increased, spurring the demand for architects, sculptors, and painters. The rise in the consumption of luxuries was everywhere apparent, taken by some as a sign of the vitality of the age, by others as an indication of its decay.

Cloth making was a major contributor to European economic growth during the Middle Ages. In this 1470 portrait of Cloth Merchants' Street, Bologna, a tailor (center) measures a prospective client.

The Experience of Life

Luxury helped improve a life that for rich and poor alike was short and uncertain. Nature was still people's most potent enemy. Renaissance children who survived infancy found their lives governed by parentage and by sex. In parentage the great divide was between those who lived with surplus and those who lived at subsistence. The first category encompassed the wealthiest bankers and merchants down to those who owned their own farms or engaged in small urban crafts. The vast majority of urban and rural dwellers comprised the second category. About the children of the poor we know very little other than that their survival was unlikely. If they did not die at birth or shortly afterward, they might be abandoned—especially if female—to the growing number of orphanages in the cities, waste away from lack of nutrition, or fall prey to ordinary childhood diseases. Eldest sons were favored, younger daughters were disadvantaged. But in poor families this favoritism meant

best land and the enlargement of their holdings. In the shops finished products outnumbered the consumers who survived the epidemics. Overproduction meant lower prices for basic commodities, and the decline in population meant higher wages for labor. At the lowest levels of society survivors found it easier to earn their living and even to create a surplus than had their parents. For a time the lot of the masses improved.

But for investors, such economic conditions meant that neither agriculture nor cloth making were particularly lucrative. Expensive investments in land or equipment for sharecropping were paid off in inexpensive grain; high wages for the few surviving skilled workers brought a return in cheap cloth. In such circumstances, consumption was more attractive than investment and

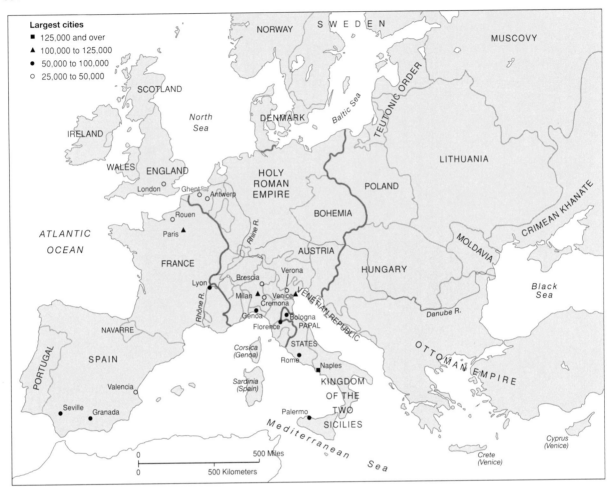

Europe, ca. 1500

little more than early apprenticeship to day labor in the city or farm labor in the countryside. Girls were frequently sent out as domestic servants far from the family home.

Children of the wealthy had better chances for survival than did children of the poor. For the better off, childhood might begin with "milk parents," life in the home of the family of a wet nurse who breast-fed the baby through infancy. Only the very wealthy could afford a live-in wet nurse, which increased the child's chances of survival. Again, daughters were more likely to be sent far from home and least likely to have their nursing supervised. The use of wet nurses not only emancipated parents from the daily care of infants, it also allowed them to resume sexual relations. Nursing

women refrained from sex in the belief that it affected their milk.

During the period between weaning and apprenticeship Renaissance children lived with their families. There was no typical Renaissance family. Nuclear families—that is, parents and their children under one roof—were probably more common than extended families, which might include grandparents and other relatives. But the composition of the family changed over the course of the life cycle and included times in which married children or grandparents were present and others when a single parent and small children were the only members. Moreover, even nuclear families commonly contained stepparents and stepchildren as well as domestic servants or apprentices.

Thus a child returning to the parental household was as likely to form emotional bonds with older siblings as with parents.

The family was an economic unit as well as a grouping of relatives. Decisions to abandon children, to send them away from the household when very young, or to take in domestic servants were based on economic calculations. In the competition for scarce resources, the way in which children were managed might determine the survival of the family unit. Sons could expect to be apprenticed to a trade probably between the ages of ten and thirteen. Most, of course, learned the crafts of their fathers, but not necessarily in their father's shop. Sons inherited the family business and its most important possessions, tools of the trade or beasts of labor for the farm. Inheritance customs varied. In some places only the eldest son received the equipment of the family occupation; in others, like Tuscany, all the sons shared it. Still, in the first fifteen years of life, these most

Ginevra de'Benci *by Leonardo da Vinci, painted around 1481. With its serenity and mystery, this portrait brings to mind the artist's more famous* Mona Lisa.

Old Man With a Child *by the Florentine painter Domenico del Ghirlandaio (1449–94).*

favored children spent between one-third and one-half of their time outside the household in which they had been born.

Expectations for daughters centered on their chances of marriage. For a girl, dowry was everything. If a girl's father could provide a handsome one, her future was secure; if not, the alternatives were a convent, which would take a small bequest, or a match lower down the social scale, where the quality of life deteriorated rapidly. Daughters of poor families entered domestic service in order to have a dowry provided by their masters. The dowry was taken to the household of their husband. There the couple resided until they established their own separate family. If the husband died, it was to his parental household that the widow returned.

Women married in late adolescence, usually around the age of twenty. Among the wealthy, marriages were perceived as familial alliances and business transactions rather than love matches. The dowry was an investment on which fathers expected a return, and while the bride might have some choice, it was severely limited. Compatibility was not a priority in matchmaking. Husbands

ALBERTI, *ON THE FAMILY*

■ *Leon Battista Alberti wrote a number of important tracts that set out the general principles of a subject, including* On Architecture, *which was considered the basic text for three hundred years. His writings on the family bring insight into the nature of a male-dominated, patriarchal institution.*

They say that in choosing a wife one looks for beauty, parentage, and riches . . . Among the most essential criteria of beauty in a woman is an honorable manner. Even a wild, prodigal, greasy, drunken woman may be beautiful of feature, but no one would call her a beautiful wife. A woman worthy of praise must show first of all in her conduct, modesty, and purity. Marius, the illustrious Roman, said in that first speech of his to the Roman people: "Of women we require purity, of men labor." And I certainly agree. There is nothing more disgusting than a coarse and dirty woman. Who is stupid enough not to see clearly that a woman who does not care for neatness and cleanliness in her appearance, not only in her dress and body but in all her behavior and language, is by no means well mannered? How can it be anything but obvious that a bad mannered woman is also rarely virtuous? We shall consider elsewhere the harm that comes to a family from women who lack virtue, but I myself do not know which is the worse fate for a family, total celibacy or a single dishonored woman. In a bride, therefore, a man must first seek beauty of mind, that is, good conduct and virtue.

In her body he must seek not only loveliness, grace, and charm but must also choose a woman who is well made for bearing children, with the kind of constitution that promises to make them strong and big. There's an old proverb, "When you pick your wife, you choose your children." All her virtues will in fact shine brighter still in beautiful children. It is a well-known saying among poets: "Beautiful character dwells in a beautiful body." The natural philosophers require that a woman be neither thin nor very fat. Those laden with fat are subject to coldness and constipation and slow to conceive. They say that a woman should have a joyful nature, fresh and lively in her blood and her whole being. They have no objections to a dark girl. They do reject girls with a frowning black visage, however. They have no liking for either the undersized or the overlarge and lean. They find that a woman is most suited to bear children if she is fairly big and has limbs of ample length. They always have a preference for youth, based on a number of arguments which I need not expound here, but particularly on the point that a young girl has a more adaptable mind. Young girls are pure by virtue of their age and have not developed any spitefulness. They are by nature modest and free of vice. They quickly learn to accept affectionately and unresistingly the habits and wishes of their husbands.

were, on average, ten years older than their wives and likely to leave them widows. In the early fifteenth century about one-fourth of all adult women in Florence were widows.

Married women lived in a state of nearly constant pregnancy. Alessandra Strozzi, whose father was one of the wealthiest citizens of Florence, married at the age of sixteen, gave birth to eight children in ten years, and was widowed at the age of twenty-five. Not all pregnan-

cies produced children. The rates of miscarriages and stillbirths were very high, and abortions and infanticide were not unknown. Only among the families who hovered between surplus and subsistence is there any evidence of attempts to control pregnancies. These efforts, which relied upon techniques like the rhythm method and withdrawal, were not particularly effective. The rhythm method was especially futile because of the misunderstanding of the role of women in conception. It was not yet known that the woman contained an egg that was fertilized during conception. Without this knowledge it was impossible to understand the cycle of ovulation. Practically speaking, family size was limited on the one end by late marriages and on the other by early deaths.

Life experiences differed for males. Men married later, near the age of twenty-five on the farms, nearer thirty in the cities because of the cost of setting up in trade or on the land. Late marriage meant long supervision under the watchful eye of father or master, an extended period between adolescence and adulthood. The reputation that Renaissance cities gained for homosexuality and licentiousness must be viewed in light of the advanced age at which males married. The level of sexual frustration was high and its outlet in ritual violence and rape was also high.

The establishment of one's own household through marriage was a late rite of passage considering the expectations of early death. Many men, even with families, never succeeded in setting up separately from their fathers or elder brothers. Men came of age at thirty but were thought to be old by fifty. Thus for men marriage and parenthood took place in middle age rather than in youth. Valued all their lives more highly than their sisters, male heads of households were the source of all power in their domicile, in their shops, and in the state. They were responsible for overseeing every aspect of the upbringing of their children. But their wives were essential partners who governed domestic life. Women labored not only at the hearth, but in the fields and shops as well. Their economic contribution to the well-being of the family was critical, both in the dowry they brought at marriage and in the labor they contributed to the household. If their wives died, men with young children remarried quickly. While there were many bachelors in Renaissance society, there were few widowers.

In most cases death came suddenly. Epidemic diseases, of which plague was the most virulent, struck with fearful regularity. Even in the absence of a serious outbreak, there were always deaths in town and country attributable to the plague. Epidemics struck harder at the young—children and adolescents who were the majority of the population—and hardest in the summer months when other viruses and bacteria weakened the population. Medical treatment was more likely to hasten death than to prolong life. Lorenzo de Medici's physician prescribed powdered pearls for the Florentine ruler's gout. After that Lorenzo complained more of stomach pains than of gout. Such remedies revealed a belief in the harmony of nature and the healing power of rare substances. They were not silly or superstitious, but they were not effective either. Starvation was rare, less because of food shortage than because the seriously undernourished were more likely to succumb to disease than to famine. In urban areas, the government would intervene to provide grain from public storehouses at times of extreme shortage; in the countryside large landholders commonly exercised the same function.

The Quality of Life

Though life may have been difficult during the Renaissance, it was not unfulfilling. Despite constant toil and frequent hardship, people of the Renaissance had reason to believe that their lives were better than those of their ancestors and that their children's lives would be better still. On the most basic level, health improved and, for those who survived plague, life expectancy increased. Better health was related to better diet. Improvement came from two sources, the relative surplus of grain throughout the fifteenth century and the wider variety of foods consumed. At the upper levels of society, sweet wine and citrus fruits helped offset the lack of vegetables. This diversification of diet resulted from improvements in transportation and communication, which brought more goods and services to a growing number of towns in the chain that linked the regional centers to the rural countryside.

But the towns and cities contributed more than consumer goods to Renaissance society. They also introduced a new sense of social and political cohesiveness. The city was something to which people belonged. In urban areas they could join social groups of their own choosing and develop networks of support not possible in rural environments. Blood relations remained the primary social group. Kin were the most likely source of aid in times of need, and charity began at home. Kin groups extended well beyond the immediate family, with both cousins and in-laws laying claim to the privileges of blood. The urban family could also depend upon the connections of neighborhood. In some Italian cities wealth or occupation determined housing patterns. In others, like Florence, rich and poor lived side by side and identified themselves with their small administrative unit and with their local church. Thus they could participate in relationships with others both above and below them in the social scale. From their superiors they gained connections that helped their families; from their inferiors they gained devoted clients.

As in the Middle Ages, the Church remained the spatial, spiritual, and social center of people's lives. Though the Renaissance is singled out as a time when people became more worldly in their outlook, this worldliness took place within the context of an absorbing devotional life. There was not yet any separation between faith and reason. The Church provided explanations for both the mysterious and the mundane. In it were performed the rituals of baptism, marriage, and burial that measured the passage of life. The Church was also the source of the key symbols of urban society. The flags of militia troops, the emblems of guilds, the regalia of the city itself were all adorned by recognizably religious symbols. The Church preserved holy relics that were venerated for their power to protect the city or to endow it with particular skills and resources. Through its holy days, as much as through its rituals, the Church helped channel leisure activities into community celebrations.

A growing sense of civic pride and individual accomplishment were underlying characteristics of the Italian Renaissance, enhanced by the development of social cohesion and community solidarity that both Church and city-state fostered. It is commonly held that the Renaissance was both elitist and male dominated, that it was an experience separate from that of the society at large. There can be no question that it was the rich who commissioned works of art or that it was the highly skilled male craftsmen who executed them. But neither lived in a social vacuum. The Renaissance was not an event whose causes were the result of the efforts of the few or whose consequences were limited to the privileged. In fact, the Renaissance was not an event at all. Family values that permitted early apprenticeships in surrogate households and that emphasized the continuity of crafts from one generation to the next made possible the skilled artists of the Renaissance cities. The stress on the production of luxury goods placed higher value upon individual skills and therefore upon excellence in workmanship. Church and state sought to express social values through representational art. One of the chief purposes of wall murals was to instruct the unlettered in religion, to help them visualize the central episodes in Christian history. The grandiose architecture and statuary that adorned central places were designed to enhance civic pride, nurture loyalty, and communicate the protective power of public institutions.

For ordinary people the world of the Renaissance was not much different from the world of the Middle Ages.

Though urban areas grew, providing a wider variety of occupations and a varied material life, most people continued to scratch a meager living from the soil. The crucial difference from generation to generation was the degree of infectious diseases or the rate of rising or falling population. For the lucky ones there was surplus; for the unfortunate there was dearth. Within these confines men were privileged over women, having greater security and status and monopolizing power. But the tightly knit organization of family life protected the weak and the poor while the Church provided faith, hope, and charity.

Renaissance Art

In every age, artistic achievement represents a combination of individual talent and predominant social ideals. Artists may be at the leading edge of the society in which they live, but it is the spirit of that society that they capture in word or song or image. Artistic disciplines also have their own technical development. Individually, Renaissance artists were attempting to solve problems about perspective and three-dimensionality that had defeated their predecessors. But the particular techniques or experiments that interested them owed as much to the social context as they did to the artistic one. For example, the urban character of Italian government led to the need for civic architecture, public buildings on a grand scale. The celebration of individual achievement led to the explosive growth of portraiture. Not surprisingly, major technological breakthroughs were achieved in both areas.

This relationship between artist and social context was all the more important in the Renaissance, when artists were closely tied to the crafts and trades of urban society and to the demands of clients who commissioned their work. Although it was the elite who patronized art, it was skilled tradesmen who produced it. Artists normally followed the pattern of any craftsman, an apprenticeship begun as a teenager and a long period of training and work in a master's shop. This form of education gave the aspiring artist a practical rather than a theoretical bent and a keen appreciation for the business side of art. Studios were identified with particular styles and competed for commissions from clients, especially the Church. Wealthy individuals commissioned art as investments, as marks of personal distinction, and as displays of public piety. Isabella d'Este (1474–1539), one of the great patrons of Renaissance artists, wrote hundreds of letters specifying the details of the works she commissioned. She once sent an artist a thread of the exact dimensions of the pictures she had ordered. Demand for art was high. The vast public-works projects needed buildings, the new piazzas (public squares) and palazzos (private houses) needed statuary, and the long walls of churches needed murals.

The survival of so many Renaissance masterpieces allows us to reconstruct the stages by which the remarkable artistic achievements of this era took place. Although advances were made in a variety of fields during the Renaissance, the three outstanding areas were architecture, sculpture, and painting. While modern artists would consider each a separate discipline, Renaissance artists crossed their boundaries without hesitation. Not only could these artists work with a variety of materials, their intensive and varied apprenticeships taught them to apply the technical solutions of one field to the problems of another. Few Renaissance artists confined themselves to one area of artistic expression, and many created works of enduring beauty in more than one medium. Was the greatest achievement of Michelangelo his sculpture of David, his paintings on the ceiling of the Sistine Chapel, or his design for the dome of Saint Peter's? Only a century of interdisciplinary cross-fertilization could have prepared the artistic world for such a feat.

An Architect, a Sculptor, and a Painter

The century that culminated in Michelangelo's extraordinary achievements began with the work of three Florentine masters who deeply influenced one another's development—Brunelleschi (1377–1446), Donatello (1386–1466), and Masaccio (1401–28). In the Renaissance the dominant artistic discipline was architecture. Buildings were the most expensive investment patrons could make and the technical knowledge necessary for their successful construction was immense. The architect not only designed a building, he served as its general contractor, its construction supervisor, and its inspector. Moreover, the architect's design determined the amount and the scale of the statuary and decorative paintings to be incorporated. By 1400 the Gothic style of building had dominated western Europe for over two centuries. Its characteristic pointed arches, vaulted ceilings, and slender spires had simplified building by

removing the heavy walls formerly thought necessary to support great structures. Gothic construction permitted greater height, a characteristic especially desirable in cathedrals, which stretched toward the heavens. But though the buildings themselves were simplified, the techniques for erecting them became more complex. By the fifteenth century architects had turned their techniques into an intricate style. They became obsessed by angular arches, elaborate vaultings and buttresses, and long, pointed spires.

It was Brunelleschi who decisively challenged the principles of Gothic architecture by recombining its basic elements with those of classical structures. Basing his designs on geometric principles, Brunelleschi reintroduced planes and spheres as dominant motifs. His greatest work was the dome on the cathedral in Florence, begun in 1420. His design for the dome was simple but bold. The circular windows are set inside a square of panels, which in turn are set inside a rectangle. Brunelleschi is generally credited with

Florence Cathedral was begun by Arnolfo di Cambio in 1296. The nave was finished about 1350, and the dome, designed by Brunelleschi, was added in the 1420s. This view shows the dome and the apse end of the cathedral.

having been the first Renaissance artist to have understood and made use of perspective, though it was immediately put to more dramatic effect in sculpture and painting.

The sculptor's study was the human form in all of its three-dimensional complexity. The survival of Roman and Hellenistic pieces, mostly bold and muscular torsos, meant that the influence of classical art was most direct in sculpture. Donatello translated these classical styles into more naturalistic forms. His technique is evident in the long flowing robes in most of his works, sculpted in the natural fashion in which cloth hung. Donatello revived the free-standing statue, which demanded greater attention to human anatomy because it was viewed from many angles. He also led the revival of the equestrian statue, sculpting the Venetian captain-general *Gattamelata* (1445–50) for a public square in Padua. This enormous bronze horse and rider relied upon the standpoint of the viewer to achieve its overpowering effect. This use of linear perspective is also seen in Donatello's breathtaking altar scenes of the miracles of Saint Anthony in Padua, which resemble nothing so much as a canvas cast in bronze.

These altar scenes clearly evince the unmistakable influence of the paintings of Masaccio. His frescoes in the Brancacci Chapel in Florence were studied and sketched by all of the great artists of the next generation, who unreservedly praised his naturalism. What most claims the attention of the modern viewer is Masaccio's shading of light and shadow and his brilliant use of linear perspective to create the illusion that a flat surface has three dimensions. Masaccio's work was on standard Christian themes, but he brought an entirely novel approach to them all. In an adoration scene he portrayed a middle-aged Madonna and a dwarfish baby Jesus; in a painting of Saint Peter paying tribute money, he used his own likeness as the face of one of the Apostles. His two best-known works are the *Holy Trinity* (1425) and the *Expulsion of Adam and Eve* (ca. 1427). In the *Holy Trinity* Masaccio provides the classic example of the use of linear perspective. In the painting, the ceiling of a Brunelleschi-designed temple recedes to a vanishing point beyond the head of God, creating the simultaneous illusion of height and depth.

Gattamelata, *Donatello's equestrian statue of the Venetian captain-general Erasmo da Narni stands in a square in Padua.*

Renaissance Style

By the middle of the fifteenth century a recognizable Renaissance style had triumphed. The outstanding architect of this period was Leon Battista Alberti (1404–72), whose treatise *On Building* (1452) remained the most influential work on the subject until the eighteenth century. Alberti consecrated the geometric principles laid down by Brunelleschi and infused them with a humanist spirit. He revived the classical dictum that a building, like a body, should have an even number of supports and, like a head, an odd number of openings. This furthered precise geometric calculations in scale and design.

No sculptor challenged the preeminence of Donatello for another fifty years, but in painting there were many contenders for the garlands worn by Masaccio. The first was Piero della Francesca (ca. 1420–92) who, though trained in the tradition of Masaccio, broke new ground in his concern for the visual unity of his paintings. From portraits to processions to his stunning fresco *The Resurrection* (ca. 1463) Piero concentrated upon the most technical aspects of composition. Another challenger was Sandro Botticelli (1445–1510), whose classical themes, sensitive portraits, and bright colors set him apart from the line of Florentine painters with whom he studied. His mythologies of the *Birth of Venus* and *Spring* (ca. 1478) depart markedly from the naturalism inspired by Masaccio.

This concern with beauty and personality is also seen in the paintings of Leonardo da Vinci (1452–1519), whose creative genius embodied the Renaissance ideal of the "universal man." Leonardo's achievements in scientific, technical, and artistic endeavors read like a list of all of the subjects known during the Renaissance. His detailed anatomical drawings and the method he devised for rendering them, his botanical observations, and his engineering inventions (including models for a tank and an airplane) testify to his unrestrained curiosity. His paintings reveal a continuation of the scientific application of mathematics to matters of proportion and perspective. Leonardo's psychological portrait *La Gioconda* (1503–06), popularly called the Mona Lisa, is quite possibly the best-known picture in the world.

From Brunelleschi to Alberti, from Masaccio to Leonardo da Vinci, Renaissance artists placed a unique stamp upon visual culture. By reviving classical themes, geometric principles, and a spirit of human vitality, they broke decisively from the dominant medieval traditions. Art became a source of individual and collective pride, produced by masters but consumed by all. Cities and wealthy patrons commissioned great works of art for public display. New buildings rose everywhere, adorned with the statues and murals that still stand as a testimony to generations of artists.

Michelangelo

The artistic achievements of the Renaissance culminated in the creative outpourings of Michelangelo Buonarroti (1475–1564). Poet, sculptor, painter, and architect, Michelangelo imparted his genius to everything he touched. Uncharacteristically, Michelangelo came from a family of standing in Florentine society. At the age of fourteen, over the opposition of his father, he was apprenticed to a leading painter and spent his spare time in Florentine churches copying the works of Masaccio among others.

In 1490 Michelangelo gained a place in the household of Lorenzo de' Medici. During this two-year period he claimed to have taught himself sculpturing, a remarkable feat considering the skills required. In fact, what was unusual about Michelangelo's early development was that he avoided the long years of apprenticeship

In The Expulsion of Adam and Eve, *Masaccio's mastery of perspective helps create the illusion of movement. Eve's anguish is shown in her deep eyes and hollow mouth, which are accentuated by casting the source of light downward and shading what otherwise would be lit.*

THE LIFE OF LEONARDO

■ *Giorgio Vasari celebrated the creativity of the artists who made Italy the center of cultural activity in the late Middle Ages. His commemoration of their achievements through the medium of biography helped to create the aura that still surrounds Renaissance art.*

The most heavenly gifts seem to be showered on certain human beings. Sometimes supernaturally, marvelously, they all congregate in one individual. Beauty, grace, and talent are combined in such bounty that in whatever that man undertakes, he outdistances all other men and proves himself to be specially endowed by the hand of God. He owes his pre-eminence not to human teaching or human power. This was seen and acknowledged by all men in the case of Leonardo da Vinci, who had, besides the beauty of his person (which was such that it has never been sufficiently extolled), and indescribable grace in every effortless act and deed. His talent was so rare that he mastered any subject to which he turned his attention. Extraordinary strength and remarkable facility were here combined. He had a mind of regal boldness and magnanimous daring. His gifts were such that his celebrity was worldwide, not only in his own day, but even more after his death, and so will continue until the end of time.

Leonardo was frequently occupied in the preparation of plans to remove mountains or to pierce them with tunnels from plain to plain. By means of levers, cranes, and screws, he showed how to lift or move great weights. Designing dredging machines and inventing the means of drawing water from the greatest depths were among the speculations from which he never rested. Many drawings of these projects exist which are cherished by those who practice our arts.

Leonardo, with his profound comprehension of art, began many things that he never completed, because it seemed to him that perfection must elude him. He frequently formed in his imagination enterprises so difficult and so subtle that they could not be entirely realized and worthily executed by human hands. His conceptions were varied to infinity. In natural philosophy, among other things, he examined plants and observed the stars—the movements of the planets, the variations of the moon, and the course of the sun.

From Giorgio Vasari, *The Life of Leonardo Da Vinci.*

during which someone else's style was implanted upon the young artist. In the Medici household he came into contact with leading Neoplatonists, who taught that man was on an ascending journey of perfectibility toward God. These ideas can be seen as one source of the heroic concept of humanity that Michelangelo brought to his work.

In 1496 Michelangelo moved to Rome. There his abilities as a sculptor quickly brought him to the attention of Jacopo Galli, a Roman banker who was interested in art and learning. Galli commissioned a classical work for himself and procured another for a French cardinal, which became the *Pietà*. Although this was Michelangelo's first attempt at sculpting a work of religious art, it was a masterpiece in beauty and composition. The *Pietà* created a sensation in Rome and by the time that

Michelangelo returned to Florence in 1501, at the age of twenty-six, he was already acknowledged as one of the great sculptors of his day. He was immediately commissioned to work on an enormous block of marble that had been quarried nearly a half-century before and had defeated the talents of a series of carvers. He worked continuously for three years on his *David* (1501–04), a piece that completed the union between classical and Renaissance styles.

Though Michelangelo always believed himself to be primarily a sculptor, his next outstanding work was in the field of painting. In 1508 Pope Julius II summoned Michelangelo to Rome and commissioned him to decorate the ceiling of the small ceremonial chapel that had been built next to the new papal residence. Michelangelo's plan was to portray, in an extended narrative, man's

Botticelli's Primavera (Spring), *also called* Garden of Venus. *Venus, in the center, is attended by the three Graces and by Cupid, Flora, Chloris, and Zephyr. Botticelli's figures have a dreamlike quality, an unreality highlighted by the beautiful faces and lithe figures of his characters.*

creation and those Old Testament events that foreshadowed the birth of the Savior. First Michelangelo framed his scenes within the architecture of a massive classical temple. In this way he was able to give the impression of having flattened the rounded surface on which he worked. Within the center panels came his fresco scenes of the events of the creation and of human history from the Fall to the Flood. His representations were simple and compelling: the fingers of God and Adam nearly touching; Eve with one leg still emerging from Adam's side; the half-human snake in the temptation are all majestically evocative.

The *Pietà*, the *David*, and the paintings of the Sistine Chapel were the work of youth. Michelangelo's crowning achievement, the building of Saint Peter's basilica in Rome, was the work of age. The intervening years saw the production of masterpiece after masterpiece, enough completed and unfinished work to have established his genius. The basework of St. Peter's had already been laid and drawings for its completion had been made thirty years earlier by Bramante. Michelan-

gelo altered these plans in an effort to bring more light within the church and provide a more majestic facade outside. His main contribution, however, was the design of the great dome, which centered the interior of the church on Saint Peter's grave. More than the height, it is the harmony of Michelangelo's design that creates the sense of the building thrusting upward like a Gothic cathedral of old. Michelangelo did not live to see the dome of Saint Peter's completed.

Renaissance art served Renaissance society. It reflected both its concrete achievements and its visionary ideals. It was a synthesis of old and new, building upon classical models, particularly in sculpture and architecture, but adding newly discovered techniques and skills. When Giorgio Vasari (1511–74) came to write his *Lives of the Great Painters, Sculptors, and Architects* (1550) he found over two hundred artists worthy of distinction. But Renaissance artists did more than construct and adorn buildings or celebrate and beautify spiritual life. Inevitably their work expressed the ideals and aspirations of the society in which they lived, the new

The creation of Adam and Eve. Detail from Michelangelo's frescoes on the ceiling of the Sistine Chapel. The Sistine frescoes had become obscured by dirt and layers of varnish and glue applied at various times over the years. In the 1980s they were cleaned to reveal their original colors.

emphasis upon learning and knowledge; upon the here and now rather than the hereafter; and most importantly upon humanity and its capacity for growth and perfection.

Renaissance Ideals

Renaissance thought went hand in glove with Renaissance art. Scholars and philosophers searched the works of the ancients to find the principles on which to build a better life. They scoured monastic libraries for forgotten manuscripts, discovering among other things, Greek poetry, history, the works of Homer and Plato, and Aristotle's *Poetics*. Their rigorous application of scholarly procedures for the collection and collation of these texts was one of the most important contributions of those Renaissance intellectuals who came to be known as humanists. Humanism developed in reaction to an intellectual world that was centered on the Church and dominated by otherworldly concerns. Humanism was by no means antireligious, but it was thoroughly secular in outlook.

Humanists celebrated worldly achievements. Pico della Mirandola's *Oration on the Dignity of Man* (1486) is the best known of a multitude of Renaissance writings influenced by the discovery of the works of Plato. Pico believed that people could perfect their existence on earth because humans were divinely endowed with the capacity to determine their own fate. This emphasis on human potential found expression in the celebration of human achievement.

Thus humanists studied and taught the humanities, the skills of disciplines like philology, the art of language, and rhetoric, the art of expression. Though they were mostly laymen, humanists applied their learning to both religious and secular studies. Humanists were not antireligious. Although most reacted strongly against Scholasticism (see chapter 13), they were heavily indebted to the work of medieval churchmen and most were devoutly religious. Nor were they hostile to the Church. Petrarch, Bruni, and Alberti were all employed by the papal court at some time in their careers, as was Lorenzo Valla, the most influential of the humanists. Their interest in human achievement and human potential must be set beside their religious beliefs. As Petrarch stated quite succinctly: "Christ is my God; Cicero is the prince of the language I use."

Humanists and the Liberal Arts

The most important achievements of humanist scholars centered upon ancient texts. It was the humanists' goal to discover as much as had survived from the ancient world and to provide texts of classical authors that were as full and accurate as possible. Though much was already known of the Latin classics, few of the central works of ancient Greece had been recovered. Humanists preserved this heritage by reviving the study of the Greek language and by translating Greek authors into Latin, the language of the Church. After the fall of Constantinople in 1453, Italy became the center for Greek studies as Byzantine scholars fled the Ottoman conquerors. Humanists also introduced historical methods in studying and evaluating texts, establishing principles for determining which of many manuscript copies of an ancient text was the oldest, the most accurate, and the least corrupted by their copyists. This was of immense importance in studying the writings of the ancient Fathers of the Church, many of whose manuscripts had not been examined for centuries. Their emphasis upon the humanistic disciplines fostered new educational ideals. Along with the study of theology, logic, and natural philosophy, which had dominated the medieval university, humanist scholars stressed the importance of grammar, rhetoric, moral philosophy, and history. They believed that the study of these "liberal arts" should be undertaken for its own sake. This emphasis gave a powerful boost to the ideal of the perfectibility of the individual that appeared in so many other aspects of Renaissance culture.

Humanists furthered the secularization of Renaissance society through their emphasis on the study of the classical world. Philology became one of the most celebrated humanist skills and the study of ancient manuscripts one of the most common humanist activities. The rediscovery of Latin texts during the late Middle Ages spurred interest in all things ancient. Petrarch, who is rightly called the father of humanism, revered the great Roman rhetorician Cicero above all others. Leonardo Bruni (1370–1444) was reputed to be the greatest Greek scholar of his day. He translated Plato and Aristotle and did much to advance mastery of classical Greek and foster the ideas of Plato in the late fifteenth century.

The study of the origins of words, their meaning, and their proper grammatical usage may seem an unusual foundation for one of the most vital of all European intellectual movements. But philology was the human-

A miniature portrait of Petrarch is seen within the illuminated initial a *in a manuscript of the poet's treatise* De remediis utriusque fortunae *("Remedies Against Fortune").*

ists' chief concern. This can best be illustrated by the work of Lorenzo Valla (1407–57). Valla was brought up in Rome, where he was largely self-educated, though according to the prescriptions of the Florentine humanists. Valla entered the service of Alfonso I, king of Naples, and applied his humanistic training to affairs of state. The kingdom of Naples bordered on the Papal States, and its kings were in continual conflict with the papacy. The pope asserted the right to withhold recognition of the king, a right that was based upon the jurisdictional authority supposedly ceded to the papacy by the Emperor Constantine in the fourth century—the so-called Donation of Constantine. Valla settled the matter definitively. Applying historical and philological critiques to the text of the Donation, Valla proved that it could not have been written earlier than the eighth century, four hundred years after Constantine's death. He mercilessly exposed words and terms that had not existed in Roman times, like *fief* and *satrap*, and thus proved beyond doubt that the Donation was a forgery and papal claims based upon it were without merit.

Valla's career demonstrates the impact of humanist values on practical affairs. Although humanists were scholars, they made no distinction between an active and a contemplative life. A life of scholarship was a life of public service. This civic humanism is best expressed in the writings of Leon Battista Alberti (1404-72), whose treatise *On the Family* (1443) is a classic study of the new urban values, especially prudence and thrift. Alberti extolled the virtues of "the fatherland, the public good, and the benefit of all citizens." An architect, a mathematician, a poet, a playwright, a musician, and an inventor, Alberti was one of the great virtuosi of the Renaissance.

Alberti's own life might have served as a model for the most influential of all Renaissance tracts, Castiglione's *The Courtier* (1528). Baldesar Castiglione (1478-1529) directed his lessons to the public life of the aspiring elite. It was his purpose to prescribe those characteristics that would make the ideal courtier, who was as much born as made. He prescribed every detail of the education necessary for the ideal state servant from table manners to artistic attainments. Castiglione's perfect courtier was an amalgam of all that the elite of Renaissance society held dear. He was to be educated as a scholar, he was to be occupied as a soldier, and he was to serve his state as an advisor.

Machiavelli and Politics

At the same time that Castiglione was drafting a blueprint for the idealized courtier, Niccolò Machiavelli (1469-1527) was laying the foundation for the realistic sixteenth-century ruler. No Renaissance work has been more important or more controversial than Machiavelli's *The Prince* (1513). Its vivid prose, its epigrammatic advice—"men must either be pampered or crushed"—and its clinical dissection of power politics have attracted generation after generation of readers. With Machiavelli, for better or worse, begins the science of politics in Europe.

Machiavelli came from an established Florentine family. He entered state service as an assistant to one of his teachers and unexpectedly rode those coattails into the relatively important office of secretary to the Council of Ten, the organ of Florentine government that had responsibility for war and diplomacy. Here Machiavelli

received his education in practical affairs. He was an emissary to Cesare Borgia during his consolidation of the Papal States at the turn of the century and carefully studied Borgia's methods. Machiavelli was a tireless correspondent and he began to collect materials for various tracts on military matters.

But as suddenly as he rose to his position of power and influence, he fell from it. The militia that he had advocated and in part organized was soundly defeated by the Spaniards, and the Florentine republic fell. Machiavelli was summarily dismissed from office in 1512 and was imprisoned and tortured the following year. Released and banished from the city, he retired to a small country estate. Immediately he began writing what became his two greatest works, *The Prince* (1513) and *The Discourses on Livy* (1519).

Machiavelli has left a haunting portrait of his life in exile, and it is important to understand how intertwined his studies of ancient and modern politics were.

> On the coming of evening, I return to my house and enter my study; and at the door I take off the day's clothing covered with mud and dust, and put on garments regal and courtly; and reclothed appropriately, I enter the ancient courts of ancient men, where, received by them with affection, I feed on that food which only is mine and which I was born for.

The Prince is a handbook for a ruler who would establish a lasting government. It attempts to set down principles culled from historical examples and contemporary events to aid the prince in attaining and maintaining power. By the study of these precepts and by their swift and forceful application, Machiavelli believed that the prince might even control fortune itself. What made *The Prince* so remarkable in its day, and what continues to enliven debate over it, is that Machiavelli was able to separate all ethical considerations from his analysis. Whether this resulted from cynicism or from his own expressed desire for realism, Machiavelli uncompromisingly instructed the would-be ruler to be half man and half beast—to conquer neighbors, to murder enemies, and to deceive friends. Steeped in the humanist ideals of fame and virtù—a combination of virtue and virtuosity, of valor, character, and ability—he sought to reestablish Italian rule and place government upon a stable, scientific basis that would end the perpetual conflict among the Italian city-states.

The careers of Lorenzo Valla and Niccolò Machiavelli both illustrate how humanists were able to bring the study of the liberal arts into the service of the state. Valla's philological studies had a vital impact on

Terra-cotta bust of Niccolò Machiavelli by an unknown artist. Because of the ideas set forth in The Prince, *Machiavellianism has passed into the language as a label for the ruthless, amoral pursuit of power.*

governing societies. By the beginning of the fifteenth century the Italian city-states were the center of power, wealth, and culture in the Christian world.

This dominion rested on several conditions. First, their geographical position favored the exchange of resources and goods between east and west. Until the fifteenth century, and despite the crusading efforts of medieval popes, east and west fortified each other. A great circular trade had developed, encompassing the Byzantine Empire, the North African coastal states, and the Mediterranean nations of western Europe. The Italian peninsula dominated the circumference of that circle. Its port cities, Genoa and Venice especially, became great maritime powers through their trade in spices and minerals. Second, just beyond the peninsula to the north lay the vast and populous territories of the Holy Roman Empire. There the continuous need for manufactured goods, especially cloth and metals, was filled by long caravans that traveled from Italy through the Alps. Milan specialized in metal crafts. Florence was a financial capital as well as a center for the manufacture of fine luxury goods. Finally, the city-states and their surrounding areas were agriculturally self-sufficient.

Because of their accomplishments we tend to think of these Italian city-states as small nations. Even the term *city-state* implies national identity. Each city-state governed itself according to its own rules and customs, and each defined itself in isolation from the larger regional or tribal associations that once prevailed. Italy was neither a nation nor a people.

diplomacy, and Machiavelli's historical studies were directly applicable to warfare. Humanists created a demand for learning that helps account for the growth of universities, the spread of literacy, and the rise of printing. They also created a hunger for knowledge that characterized intellectual life for nearly two centuries.

The Politics of the Italian City-States

Like studs on a leather boot, city-states dotted the Italian peninsula. They differed in size, shape, and form. Some were large seaports, others small inland villages; some cut wide swaths across the plains, others were tiny islands. The absence of a unifying central authority in Italy, resulting from the collapse of the Holy Roman Empire and the papal schism, allowed ancient guilds and confraternities to transform themselves into self-

The Five Powers

Although there were dozens of Italian city-states, by the early fifteenth century five had emerged to dominate the politics of the peninsula: Naples, the Papal States, Florence, Milan, and Venice. Among them developed the principle of the balance of power that governed Italian politics. In the south was the kingdom of Naples, the only city-state governed by a hereditary monarchy. Its politics were mired by conflicts over its succession. During the fourteenth century Naples was successively ruled by French and Hungarian princes. The fifteenth century began with civil warfare between rival claimants of both nations and it was not until the Spaniard Alfonso I of Aragon (1442–58) secured the throne in 1443 that peace was restored and Naples and Sicily were reunited. Bordering Naples were the Papal States, whose capital was Rome but whose territories

FROM *THE PRINCE*

■ *Niccolò Machiavelli wrote* The Prince *in 1513 while he was under house arrest. It is one of the classics of Western political theory, in which the author separates the political from the moral.*

Every one understands how praiseworthy it is in a prince to keep faith, and to live uprightly and not craftily. Nevertheless we see, from what has taken place in our own days, that princes who have set little store by their word, but have known how to overreach men by their cunning, have accomplished great things, and in the end got the better of those who trusted to honest dealing.

Be it known, then, that there are two ways of contending,—one in accordance with the laws, the other by force; the first of which is proper to men, the second to beasts. But since the first method is often ineffectual, it becomes necessary to resort to the second. A prince should, therefore, understand how to use well both the man and the beast . . . But inasmuch as a prince should know how to use the beast's nature wisely, he ought of beasts to choose both the lion and the fox; for the lion cannot guard himself from the toils, nor the fox from wolves. He must therefore be a fox to discern toils, and a lion to drive off wolves.

To rely wholly on the lion is unwise; and for this reason a prudent prince neither can nor ought to keep his word when to keep it is hurtful to him and the causes which led him to pledge it are removed. If all men were good, this would not be good advice, but since they are dishonest and do not keep faith with you, you in return need not keep faith with them.

From Niccolò Machiavelli, *The Prince*.

stretched far to the north and lay on both sides of the spiny Apennine mountain chain that extends down the center of the peninsula. Throughout the fourteenth and early fifteenth centuries, the territories under the nominal control of the Church were largely independent and included such thriving city-states as Bologna, Ferrara, and Urbino. Even in Rome the weakened papacy had to contend with noble families for control of the city.

The three remaining dominant city-states were bunched together in the north. Florence, center of Renaissance culture, was one of the wealthiest cities of Europe before the devastations of the plague and the sustained economic downturn of the late fourteenth century. The city itself was inland and its main waterway, the Arno, ran to the sea through Pisa, whose subjugation in 1406 was a turning point in Florentine history. Nominally Florence was a republic, but during the fifteenth century it was ruled in effect by its principal banking family, the Medici.

To the north of Florence was the duchy of Milan, the major city in Lombardy. It too was landlocked, cut off from the sea by Genoa. But Milan's economic life was oriented northward to the Swiss and German towns beyond the Alps, and its major concern was preventing foreign invasions. The most warlike of the Italian cities, Milan was a despotism, ruled for nearly two centuries by the Visconti family.

The last of the five powers was the republic of Venice. Ideally situated at the head of the Adriatic Sea, Venice became the leading maritime power of the age. Until the fifteenth century, Venice was less interested in securing a landed empire than in dominating a seaborne one. The republic was ruled by a hereditary elite, headed by an elected doge, who was the chief magistrate of Venice, and a variety of small elected councils.

The political history of the peninsula during the late fourteenth and early fifteenth centuries is one of unrelieved turmoil. Wherever we look, the governments of the city-states were threatened by foreign invaders, internal conspiracies, or popular revolts. In the 1370s the Genoese and Venetians fought their fourth war in little more than a century, this one so bitter that the Genoese risked much of their fleet in an unsuccessful effort to conquer Venice itself. At the turn of the century, the Hungarian occupant of the throne of Naples invaded both Rome and Florence. Florence and Milan were constantly at war with each other. Nor were foreign threats the only dangers. In Milan three Visconti brothers inherited power. Two murdered the third, and then the son of one murdered the other to reunite the inheritance. The Venetians executed one of their military leaders who was plotting treachery. One or another Florentine family usually faced exile when governments there changed hands. Popular revolts channeled social and economic discontent against the ruling elites in Rome, Milan, and Florence. The revolt of the "Ciompi" (the wooden shoes) in Florence in 1378 was an attempt by poorly paid wool workers to reform the city's exclusive guild system and give guild protection to the wage laborers lower down the social scale. In Milan an abortive republic was established in reaction against strong-arm Visconti rule.

By the middle of the fifteenth century, however, two trends were apparent amid this political chaos. The first was the consolidation of strong centralized governments within the large city-states. These took different forms but yielded a similar result—internal political stability. The return of the popes to Rome after the Great Schism restored the pope to the head of his temporal estates and began a long period of papal dominance over Rome and its satellite territories. In Milan, one of the great military leaders of the day, Francesco Sforza (1401–66), seized the reins of power after the failure of the Visconti line. The succession of King Alfonso I in Naples ended a half-century of civil war. In both Florence and Venice the grip that the political elite held over high offices was tightened by placing greater power in small advisory councils and, in Florence, by the ascent to power of the Medici family. In sum, this process is known as the rise of signorial rule. The rise of the signories—whether individual families or small councils—made possible the second development of this period, the establishment of a balance of power within the peninsula.

It was the leaders of the Italian city-states who first perfected the art of diplomacy. Constant warfare necessitated continual alliances, and by the end of the fourteenth century the large city-states had begun the practice of keeping resident ambassadors at the major seats of power. This provided leaders with accurate information about the conditions of potential allies and enemies. Diplomacy was both an offensive and defensive weapon. This was especially so because the city-states hired their soldiers as contract labor. These mercenary armies, whose leaders were known as *condottieri* from the name of their contract, were both expensive and dangerous to maintain. If they did not bankrupt their employers, they might desert them or, even worse, turn on them. Thus Francesco Sforza, the greatest *condottiere* of the fifteenth century, gained power in Milan. Sforza's consolidation of power in Milan initially led to warfare, but ultimately it formed the basis of the Peace of Lodi (1454). This established two balanced alliances, one between Florence and Milan, the other between Venice and Naples. These states, along with the papacy, pledged mutual nonaggression, a policy that lasted for nearly forty years.

The Peace of Lodi did not bring peace. It only halted the long period in which the major city-states struggled against one another. Under cover of the peace, the large states continued the process of swallowing up their smaller neighbors and creating quasi-empires. This was a policy of imperialism as aggressive as that of any in the modern era. Civilian populations were overrun, local leaders exiled or exterminated, tribute money taken, and taxes levied. Each of the five states either increased its mainland territories or strengthened its hold upon them. Venice and Florence especially prospered.

Venice: A Seaborne Empire

Water was the source of the prosperity of Venice. Located at the head of the Adriatic Sea, the city is formed by a web of lagoons. Through its center snakes the Grand Canal, whose banks were lined with large and small buildings that celebrated its civic and mercantile power. At the Piazza San Marco stood the vast palace of the doge, elected leader of the republic, and the Basilica of Saint Mark, a domed church built in the Byzantine style. At the Rialto were the stalls of the bankers and moneylenders, less grand perhaps but no less important. Here, too, were the auction blocks for the profitable trade in European slaves, east European serfs, and battlefield captives who were sold into service to Egypt or Byzantium.

Its prosperity based on trade rather than conquest, Venice enjoyed many natural advantages. Its position at the head of the Adriatic permitted access to the raw

Woodcut illustration of Venice, from Breydenbach's Peregrinations *(1486).*

materials of both east and west. The rich Alpine timberland behind the city provided the hardwoods necessary for shipbuilding. The hinterland population were steady consumers of grain, cloth, and the new manufactured goods—glass, silk, jewelry, and cottons—that came pouring onto the market in the late Middle Ages.

But the success of Venice was owed more to its own achievements than to these rich inheritances. The triumph of the Venetian state was the triumph of dedicated efficiency. The heart of its success lay in the way in which it organized its trade and its government. The key to Venetian trade was its privileged position with the Byzantine Empire. Venice had exchanged with the Byzantines military support for tax concessions that gave Venetian traders a competitive edge in the spice trade with the East. The spice trade was so lucrative that special ships were built to accommodate it. These galleys were constructed at public expense and doubled as the Venetian navy in times of war. By controlling these ships, the government strictly regulated the spice trade. Rather than allow the wealthiest merchants to dominate it, as

they did in other cities, Venice specified the number of annual voyages and sold shares in them at auction based on a fixed price. This practice allowed big and small merchants to gain from the trade and encouraged all merchants to find other trading outlets.

Like its trade, Venetian government was also designed to disperse power. Although it was known as the Most Serene Republic, Venice was not a republic in the sense that we use the word; it was rather an oligarchy—a government by a restricted group. Political power was vested in a Great Council whose membership had been fixed at the end of the thirteenth century. All males whose fathers enjoyed the privilege of membership in the Great Council were registered at birth in the Book of Gold and became members of the Great Council when adults. From the body of the Great Council, which numbered about twenty-five hundred at the end of the fifteenth century, was chosen the Senate, a council about one-tenth the size, whose members served a one-year term. It was from the Senate that the true officers of government were selected: the doge, who was chosen for life, and members of a number of small councils, who administered affairs and advised the doge. Members of these councils were chosen by secret ballot in an elaborate process by which nominators were selected at random. Terms of office on the councils were extremely short in order to limit factionalism and to prevent any individual from gaining too much power. Though small groups exercised more power in practice than they should have in theory, the Venetian oligarchy was never troubled by either civil war or popular rebellion.

With its mercantile families firmly in control of government and trade, Venice created a vast overseas empire in the east during the thirteenth and fourteenth centuries. Naval supremacy allowed the Venetians to offer protection to strategic outposts in return for either privileges or tribute. But in the fifteenth century Venice turned west. In a dramatic reversal of its centuries-old policy, it began a process of conquest in Italy itself. There were several reasons for this new policy. First, the Venetian navy was no longer the unsurpassed power that it once had been. The Genoese wars had drained resources, and the revival of the Ottoman Turks in the east posed a growing threat that ultimately resulted in the fall of Constantinople (1453) and the end of Venetian trading privileges. Outposts in Dalmatia and the Aegean came under assault from both the Turks and the king of Hungary, cutting heavily into the complicated system by which goods were circulated by Venetian merchants. It was not long before Portuguese competition affected the most lucrative of all the commodities traded by the Venetians—pepper. Perhaps most importantly, mainland expansion offered new opportunities for Venice. Not all Venetians were traders, and the new industries that were being developed in the city could readily benefit from control of mainland markets. Most decisively of all, opportunity was knocking. In Milan Visconti rule was weakening and the Milanese territories were ripe for picking.

Venice reaped a rich harvest. From the beginning of the fifteenth century to the Peace of Lodi, the Most Serene Republic engaged in unremitting warfare. Its successes were remarkable. It pushed out to the north to occupy all the lands between the city and the Habsburg territories; it pushed to the east until it straddled the entire head of the Adriatic; and it pushed to the west almost as far as Milan itself. The western conquests in particular brought large populations under Venetian control which, along with their potential as a market, provided a ready source of taxation. By the end of the fifteenth century the mainland dominions of Venice were contributing nearly 40 percent of the city's reve-

nue at a cost far smaller than that of the naval empire a century earlier.

Florence: Spinning Cloth into Gold

Florentine prosperity was built on two foundations: money and wool. Beginning in the thirteenth century, Florentine bankers were among the wealthiest and most powerful in the world. Initially their position was established through support of the papacy in its long struggle with the Holy Roman Empire. Florentine financiers established banks in all the capitals of Europe and the east. In the Middle Ages, bankers served more functions than simply handling and exchanging money. Most were also tied to mercantile adventures and underwrote industrial activity. So it was in Florence where international bankers purchased high-quality wool to be manufactured into the world's finest woven cloth.

The activities of both commerce and cloth manufacture depended on external conditions, and thus the wealth of Florence was potentially unstable. In the mid-fourteenth century instability came with the plague that devastated the city. Nearly 40 percent of the entire population was lost in the single year 1348, and recurring outbreaks continued to ravage the already weakened survivors. Loss of workers and loss of markets seriously disrupted manufacturing. By 1380 cloth production had fallen to less than a quarter of preplague levels. On the heels of plague came wars. The property of Florentine bankers and merchants abroad was an easy target, and in this respect the wars with Naples at the end of the fourteenth century were particularly disastrous. Thirty years of warfare with Milan, interrupted by only a single decade of peace (1413–23), resulted in total bankruptcy for many of the city's leading commercial families. More significantly, the costs of warfare, offensive and defensive, created a massive public debt. Every Florentine of means owned shares in this debt, and the republic was continually devising new methods for borrowing and staving off crises of repayment. Small wonder that the republic turned for aid to the wealthiest banking family in Europe, the Medici.

As befitted a city whose prosperity was based on manufacturing, Florence had a strong guild tradition. The most important guilds were associated with banking and cloth manufacture but they included the crafts and food-processing trades as well. Only guild members could participate in government, electing the nine *Signoria* who administered laws, set tax rates, and directed foreign and domestic policy. Like that of Venice, Florentine government was a republican oligarchy and like Venice, it depended upon rotated short periods in office and selections by lot to avoid factionalism. But Florence had a history of factionalism longer than its history of republican government. Its formal structures were occasionally altered so that powerful families could gain control of the real centers of political power, the small councils and emergency assemblies through which the Signoria governed. Conservative leadership drawn from the upper ranks of Florentine society guided the city through the wars of the early fourteenth century. But soon afterward the leaders of its greatest families, the Albizzi, the Pazzi, and the Medici, again divided Florentine politics into factions.

The ability of the Medici to secure a century-long dynasty in a government that did not have a head of state is just one of the mysteries surrounding the history of this remarkable family. Cosimo de' Medici (1389–1464) was one of the richest men in Christendom when he returned to the city in 1434 after a brief exile. His leading position in government rested upon supporters who were able to gain a controlling influence on the *Signoria*. Cosimo built his party carefully, banishing his Albizzi enemies, recruiting followers among the craftsmen whom he employed, and even paying delinquent taxes to maintain the eligibility of his voters. Most importantly, emergency powers were invoked to reduce the number of citizens qualified to vote for the Signoria until the majority were Medici backers.

Cosimo was a great patron of artists and intellectuals. He collected books and paintings, endowed libraries, and spent lavishly on his own palace, the Palazzo Medici. Cosimo's position as an international banker brought him into contact with the heads of other Italian city-states, and it was his personal relationship with Francesco Sforza that finally ended the Milanese wars and brought about the Peace of Lodi.

It was Cosimo's grandson, Lorenzo (1449–92), who linked the family's name to that of the age. He held strong humanist values instilled in him by his mother, Lucrezia Tornabuoni, who organized his education. He brought Michelangelo and other leading artists to his garden; he brought Pico della Mirandola and other leading humanists to his table. Lorenzo's power was based on his personality and reputation. His diplomatic abilities were the key to his survival. Almost immediately after Lorenzo came to power, Naples and the papacy began a war with Florence, a war that was costly to the Florentines in both taxation and lost territory. In 1479 Lorenzo traveled to Naples and personally convinced the Neapolitan king to sign a separate treaty. This restored the Italian balance of power and ensured continued Medici rule in Florence.

There is some doubt whether Lorenzo should be remembered by the title "the Magnificent" that was bestowed upon him. His absorption in politics came at the expense of the family's commercial enterprises, which were nearly ruined during his lifetime. Branch after branch of the Medici bank closed as conditions for international finance deteriorated, and the family fortune was dwindling. Moreover, the emergency powers that Lorenzo invoked to restrict participation in government changed forever the character of Florentine republicanism, irredeemably corrupting it. There is no reason to accept the judgment of his enemies that Lorenzo was a tyrant, but the negative consequences of his rule cannot be ignored. In 1494, two years after Lorenzo's death, the peninsula was plunged into those wars that turned it from the center of European civilization into one of its lesser satellites.

Lorenzo de' Medici. His patronage of artists and philosophers made Florence the leading Renaissance city.

Italy, 1494

rentine merchant, gave his name to the newly discovered continents.

But it was not in Italy that the rewards of innovation or the satisfactions of achievement were enjoyed. There the seeds of political turmoil and military imperialism, combined with the rise of the Ottoman Turks, were to reap a not-unexpected harvest. Under the cover of the Peace of Lodi, the major city-states had scrambled to enlarge their mainland empires. By the end of the fifteenth century they eyed one another greedily and warily. Each expected the others to begin a peninsula-wide war for hegemony and took the steps that ultimately ensured the contest. Perhaps the most unusual aspect of the imperialism of the city-states was that it had been restricted to the peninsula itself. Each of the major powers shared the dream of recapturing the glory that was Rome. Long years of siege and occupation had militarized the Italian city-states. Venice and Florence balanced their budgets on the backs of their captured territories. Milan had been engaged in constant war for decades and even the papacy was militarily aggressive.

And the Italians were no longer alone. The most remarkable military leader of the age was not a Renaissance *condottiere* but an Ottoman prince, Mehmed II (1451–81), who conquered Constantinople and Athens and threatened Rome itself (see chapter 15). The rise of the Ottomans, whose name is derived from Osman, their original tribal leader, is one of the most compelling stories in world history. Little more than a warrior tribe at the beginning of the fourteenth century, a hundred and fifty years later the Ottomans had replaced stagnant Byzantine rule with a virile and potent empire. First they gobbled up the towns and cities in a wide arc around Constantinople. Then they fed upon the Balkans and the eastern kingdoms of Hungary and Poland. By 1400 they were a presence in all the territory that stretched from the Black Sea to the Aegean. By 1450 they were its master. (See Special Feature, "The Fall of Constantinople," pp. 374–375.)

Venice was most directly affected by the Ottoman advance. Not only was its favored position in eastern trade threatened, but during a prolonged war at the end of the fifteenth century the Venetians lost many of their most important commercial outposts. Ottoman might closed off the markets of eastern Europe, and by 1480 Venetian naval supremacy was a thing of the past.

The Italian city-states might have met this challenge from the east had they been able to unite in opposing

The End of Italian Hegemony, 1450–1527

In the course of the Renaissance western Europe was Italianized. For a century the city-states dominated the trade routes that connected East and West. Italian manufactures, such as Milanese artillery, Florentine silk, and Venetian glass, were prized above all others. The ducat and the florin, two Italian coins, were universally accepted in an age when every petty prince minted his own. The peninsula exported culture in the same way that it exported goods. Humanism quickly spread across the Alps, aided by the recent invention of printing (which the Venetians soon dominated), while Renaissance standards of artistic achievement were known worldwide and everywhere imitated. The city-states shared their technology as well. The compass and the navigational chart, projection maps, double-entry bookkeeping, eyeglasses, the telescope—all profoundly influenced what could be achieved and what could be hoped for. In this spirit Christopher Columbus, a Genoese seaman, successfully crossed the Atlantic under the Spanish flag, and Amerigo Vespucci, a Flo-

Manuscript illustration of the siege of Constantinople. The tents of Turkish invaders are seen in the foreground, while their ships surround the city.

*T*he Fall of Constantinople

The prayers of the devout were more fervent than ever on Easter Sunday, 1453. The Christians of Constantinople knew that it was only a matter of time before the last remaining stronghold of the Byzantine Empire came under siege. For decades the ring of Ottoman conquests had narrowed around this holy city until it alone stood out against the Turkish sultan. Constantinople, the bridge between Europe and Asia, was tottering. The once teeming center of Eastern Christianity had never recovered from the epidemics of the fourteenth century. Dwindling revenues matched the dwindling population. Concessions to Venetian and Genoese traders reduced customs while Ottoman conquests eliminated tribute money.

Perhaps it was this impoverishment that had kept the Turks at bay. Constantinople was still the best-fortified city in the world. Two of its three sides faced the sea, and the third was protected by two stout rings of walls and a trench lined with stones. No cannon forged in Europe could dent these battlements and no navy could hope to force its way through the narrow mouth of the Golden Horn.

A siege of Constantinople hardly seemed worthwhile as long as there were conquests to be made in eastern Europe and Asia Minor. Thus an uneasy peace existed between sultan and emperor. It was shattered in 1451 when a new sultan, the nineteen-year-old Mehmed II, came to the throne. Mehmed's imagination was fired by the ancient prophecies that a Muslim would rule in all of the territories of the east. Only Constantinople was a fitting capital for such an empire, and Mehmed immediately began preparations for its conquest.

In 1452 Mehmed had constructed a fortress at the narrow mouth of the Bosporus and demanded tribute from all ships that entered the Golden Horn. The Byzantine emperor sent ambassadors to Mehmed to protest this aggression. Mehmed returned their severed heads. The Turks now controlled access to the city for trade and supplies. An attack the following spring seemed certain. The emperor appealed far and wide for aid for his beleaguered city. But the Europeans were in no hurry to pledge their support, as it was inconceivable that the Ottomans could assemble the army necessary to besiege Constantinople before summer.

But they reckoned without Mehmed. While the Italians bickered over their share of the expedition and Christians everywhere made ready to celebrate Holy Week, the Ottomans assembled a vast army of fighters and laborers and a huge train of weapons and supplies. Mehmed's forces, which eventually numbered more than 150,000, of which 60,000 were soldiers, assembled around the walls of Constantinople on April 5. During the next week a great flotilla sailed up the Bosporus and anchored just out of reach of the Byzantine warships in the Golden Horn. A census taken inside the city revealed that there were only 7,000 able-bodied defenders, about 5,000 Greek residents and 2,000 foreigners, mostly Genoese and Venetians. The Italians were the only true soldiers among them.

Though the defenders were vastly outnumbered, they still held the military advantage. As long as their ships controlled the entrance to the Golden Horn, they could limit the Ottoman attack to only one side, where all of the best defenders could be massed. The Byzantines cast a boom—an iron chain supported by wooden floats—across the mouth of the bay to forestall a naval attack. By the middle of April the Turks had begun their land assault. Each day great guns pounded the walls of the city and each night residents worked frantically to repair the damage. The Turks suffered heavily for each attempt to follow a cannon shot with a massed charge. But the attack took its toll among the defenders as well. No one was safe from the flaming arrows and catapulted stones flung over the city's walls. Nevertheless, in the first month of siege the defenders held their own.

The vigorous defense of the city infuriated Mehmed. As long as there was only one point of attack, the defenders could resist indefinitely. The line of assault had to be extended, and this could only be done by sea. With the boom effectively impregnable and with Italian seamen superior to the Turks, the prospects seemed dim. But what could not be achieved by force might be achieved by intelligence. A plan was devised to carry a number of smaller ships across land and then to float them behind the Christian fleet. Protected by land forces, the ships could be used as a staging point for another line of attack. Thousands of workmen were set the task of building huge wooden rollers, which were greased with animal fat. Under cover of darkness and the smoke of cannon fire, seventy-two ships were pulled up the steep hills and pushed down into the sea. Once they were safely anchored, a pontoon bridge was built and cannon were trained on the seaward walls of the city.

Moving ships across dry land was not the only engineering feat that sapped the defenders. One night a tower higher than the city's battlements was assembled in front of the landward walls. From there archers pelted the city and sorties of attackers sallied forth. The attacks and bombardments were now relentless. The city had withstood siege for nearly six weeks without any significant reinforcement. At the end of the month there was a sudden lull. A messenger from the sultan arrived to demand surrender. The choice was clear. If the city was taken by force the customary three days of

unrestricted pillage would be allowed, but if it yielded, the sultan pledged to protect the property of all who desired to remain under his rule. The emperor replied feebly that no one who had ever laid siege to Constantinople had enjoyed a long life. He was ready to die in defense of the city.

On May 30 the final assault began. Mehmed knew that his advantage lay in numbers. First he sent in waves of irregular troops, mostly captured slaves and Christians, who suffered great losses and were finally driven back by the weakened defenders. Next, better-trained warriors attacked and widened the breaches made by the irregulars. Finally came the crack Janissaries, the sultan's elite warriors, disciplined from birth to fight. It was the Janissaries who found a small door left open at the base of the wall. In they rushed, quickly overwhelming the first line of defenders and battering their way through the weaker second walls. By dawn the Ottoman flag was raised over the battlements and the sack of Constantinople had begun.

There was no need for the customary three days of pillage. By the end of the first day there was nothing left worth taking. The churches and monasteries had been looted and defaced, the priests and nuns murdered or defiled, and thousands of civilians had been captured to be sold into slavery. Large areas of the city smoldered from countless fires. The desolation was so complete that not even Mehmed could take joy in the ceremonial procession into the new capital of his empire. The bastion of Eastern Christendom was no more.

it. Successive popes pleaded for holy wars to halt the advance of the Turks. The fall of Constantinople in 1453 was an event of epochal proportions for Europeans, many believing that it foreshadowed the end of the world. Yet it was Italians rather than Ottomans who plunged the peninsula into those wars from which it never recovered.

The Wars of Italy (1494–1529) began when Naples, Florence, and the Papal States united against Milan. At first this alliance seemed little more than another shift in the balance of power. But rather than call upon Venice to redress the situation, the Milanese leader, Ludovico Sforza, sought help from the French. An army of French cavalry and Swiss mercenaries, led by Charles VIII of France (1483–98) invaded the peninsula in 1494. With Milanese support the French swept all before them. Florence was forced to surrender Pisa, a humiliation that led to the overthrow of the Medici and the establishment of French sovereignty. The Papal States were next to be occupied, and within a year Charles had conquered Naples without engaging the Italians in a single significant battle. Unfortunately, the Milanese were not the only ones who could play at the game of foreign alliances. Next it was the turn of the Venetians and the pope to unite and call upon the services of King Ferdinand of Aragon and the Holy Roman Emperor. Italy was now a battleground in what became a total European war for dynastic supremacy. The city-states used their foreign allies to settle old scores and to extend their own mainland empires. At the turn of the century Naples was dismembered. In 1509 the pope conspired to organize the most powerful combination of forces yet known against Venice. All of the mainland possessions of the Most Serene Republic were lost, but by a combination of good fortune and skilled diplomacy Venice itself survived. Florence was less fortunate, becoming a pawn first of the French and then of the Spanish. The final blow to Italian hegemony was the sack of Rome in 1527.

The sense of living in a new age, the spirit of human achievement, and the curiosity and wonderment of writers and artists all characterized the Renaissance. The desire to re-create the glories of Rome was not Machiavelli's alone. It could be seen in the palaces of the Italian aristocracy; in the papal rebuilding of the Holy City; and in the military ambitions of princes. But the legacy of empire, of "ancient and heroic pride," had passed out of Italian hands.

SUGGESTIONS FOR FURTHER READING

GENERAL READING

Ernst Breisach, *Renaissance Europe 1300–1517* (New York: Macmillan, 1973). A solid survey of the political history of the age.

* Denys Hay, *The Italian Renaissance* (Cambridge: Cambridge University Press, 1977). An elegant interpretive essay. The best first book to read.

J. R. Hale, ed., *A Concise Encyclopedia of the Italian Renaissance* (Oxford: Oxford University Press, 1981). A treasure trove of facts about the major figures and events of the era.

* P. Burke, *Culture and Society in Renaissance Italy* (Princeton, NJ: Princeton University Press, 1987). A good introduction to social and intellectual developments.

RENAISSANCE SOCIETY

* M. Aston, *The Fifteenth Century: The Prospect of Europe* (London: Thames and Hudson, 1968). A concise survey of Continental history; well written and illustrated.

* J. R. Hale, *Renaissance Europe: The Individual and Society* (Berkeley, CA: University of California Press, 1978). A lively study that places the great figures of the Renaissance in their social context.

* Carlo Cipolla, *Before the Industrial Revolution: European Society and Economy, 1000–1700* (New York: Norton, 1976). A sweeping survey of social and economic developments across the centuries.

* Harry Miskimin, *The Economy of Early Renaissance Europe 1300–1460* (Englewood Cliffs, NJ: Prentice Hall, 1969). A detailed scholarly study of economic development.

D. Herlihy and C. Klapische-Zuber, *The Tuscans and Their Families* (New Haven, CT: Yale University Press, 1985). Difficult but rewarding study of the social and demographic history of Florence and its environs.

* Christiane Klapische-Zuber, *Women, Family, and Ritual in Renaissance Italy* (Chicago: University of Chicago Press, 1985). A sparkling collection of essays on diverse topics in social history from wet-nursing to family life.

RENAISSANCE ART

* Michael Baxandall, *Painting and Experience in Fifteenth Century Italy* (Oxford: Oxford University Press, 1972). A study of the relationship between painters and their patrons, of how and why art was produced.

Frederick Hartt, *History of Italian Renaissance Art* (Englewood Cliffs, NJ: Prentice Hall, 1974). The most comprehensive survey, with hundreds of plates.

* Michael Levey, *Early Renaissance* (London: Penguin Books, 1967). A concise survey of art; clearly written and authoritative.

* Rudolph Wittkower, *Architectural Principles in the Age of Humanism* (New York: Norton, 1971). A difficult but rewarding study of Renaissance architecture.

Roberta Olson, *Italian Renaissance Sculpture* (New York: Thames and Hudson, 1992). A brief, up-to-date guide with good illustrations.

* Linda Murray, *High Renaissance and Mannerism* (London: Thames and Hudson, 1985). The best introduction to late Renaissance art.

* Howard Hibbard, *Michelangelo* (New York: Harper & Row, 1974). A compelling biography of an obsessed genius.

RENAISSANCE IDEALS

* Hans Baron, *The Crisis of the Early Italian Renaissance* (Princeton, NJ: Princeton University Press, 1966). One of the most influential intellectual histories of the period.

* Ernst Cassirer, ed., *The Renaissance Philosophy of Man* (Chicago: University of Chicago Press, 1948). Translations of the works of Petrarch, Valla, and Pico della Mirandola, among others, with excellent introductions.

George Holmes, *The Florentine Enlightenment* (New York: Pegasus, 1969). The best work on the successive generations of Florentine humanists.

Albert Rabil, ed., *Renaissance Humanism* (Philadelphia: University of Pennsylvania Press, 1988). A multi-authored multivolume collection of essays on humanism, with all of the latest scholarship.

* Quentin Skinner, *Machiavelli* (Oxford: Oxford University Press, 1981). A brief but brilliant life.

THE POLITICS OF THE ITALIAN CITY-STATES

* Lauro Martines, *Power and Imagination: City-States in Renaissance Italy* (New York: Alfred A. Knopf, 1979). An important interpretation of the politics of the Italian powers.

* Frederic C. Lane, *Venice: A Maritime Republic* (Baltimore: Johns Hopkins University Press, 1973). A complete history of Venice, which stresses its naval and mercantile developments.

* Gene Brucker, *Renaissance Florence, 2d ed.* (Berkeley, CA: University of California Press, 1983). The best single-volume introduction to Florentine history.

* J. R. Hale, *Florence and the Medici* (London: Thames and Hudson, 1977). A compelling account of the relationship between a city and its most powerful citizens.

* Eugene E. Rice, Jr., *The Foundations of Early Modern Europe 1460–1559* (New York: Norton, 1970). The best short, synthetic work.

*Indicates paperback edition available.

CHAPTER 13

The Religious Reformation in Europe, 1500–1555

SOLA SCRIPTURA

"In the beginning was the Word, and the Word was with God, and the Word was God." In no other period of European history was this text of the apostle John so appropriate. Men and women shared a consuming desire to hear and to read the Word of God as set down in the Bible. In the early sixteenth century, Europeans developed an insatiable appetite for the Bible. Scriptures rolled off printing presses in every shape and form, from the great vellum tomes of Gutenberg, pictured here, to pocket Bibles that soldiers carried into battle. They came in every imaginable language. Before 1500 there were fourteen complete Bibles printed in German, four each in Italian, French, and Spanish, one in Czech, and even one in Flemish. There were hundreds more editions in Latin, the official Vulgate Bible first translated by Saint Jerome in the fourth century. Whole translations and editions of the Bible were only part of the story. Separate sections, especially the Psalms and the first books of the Old Testament, were printed by the thousands. There were twenty-four French editions of the Old Testament before an entirely new translation appeared in 1530. When Martin Luther began his own German translation of the Bible in 1522, it immediately became an international best-seller. In twenty-five years it went into 430 editions. It is estimated that one million German Bibles were printed in the first half of the sixteenth century—at a time when Europe had a German-speaking population of about 15 million people, 90 percent of whom were illiterate.

Bible owning was no fad. It was but one element in a new devotional outlook that was sweeping the Continent and that would have far-reaching consequences for European society during the next 150 years. A renewed spirituality was everywhere to be seen. It was expressed in a desire to change the traditional practices and structures of the Roman church. It was expressed in a desire to have learned and responsible ministers to tend to the needs of their parishioners. It was expressed in a desire to establish godly families and godly cities and godly kingdoms. Sometimes it took the form of sarcasm and bitter denunciations; sometimes it took the form of quiet devotion and pious living. The need for reform was everywhere felt; the demand for reform was everywhere heard. It came from within the Roman church as much as from without.

The inspiration for reform was based on the Word of God. Scholars, following humanist principles, worked on biblical translations in an attempt to bring a purer text to light. Biblical commentary dominated the writings of churchmen as never before. Woodcut pictures, depicting scenes from the life of Jesus or from the Old Testament, were printed in untold quantities for the edification of the unlettered. For the first time common people could, in their own dwellings, contemplate representations of the lives of the saints. Many of the Bibles that were printed in vernacular—that is, in the languages spoken in the various European states rather than in Latin—were interleaved with illustrations of the central events of Christian history. Preachers spoke to newly aware audiences and relied on biblical texts to draw out their message. Study groups, especially in urban areas, proliferated so that the literate could read and learn together. Bible reading became a part of family life, which mothers and fathers could share with their children and their servants. *Sola Scriptura*—by the Word alone—became the battle cry of religious reform.

The Intellectual Reformation

Nothing is as powerful as an idea whose time has come. But the coming of ideas has a history as complex as the ideas themselves. In the early sixteenth century reformers throughout western Europe preached new ideas about religious doctrine and religious practice. At first these ideas took the form of a sustained critique of the Roman Catholic church, but soon they developed a momentum of their own. Some reformers remained within traditional Catholicism; others moved outside and founded new Protestant churches. Wherever this movement for religious reform appeared, whether Catholic or Protestant, it was fed by new ideas. This was made possible by the development of printing, which appeared in Germany in the late fifteenth century and rapidly spread across Europe in the succeeding decades. Yet printing was as much a result as it was a cause of the spread of ideas. The humanist call for a return to the study of the classics and for the creation of accurate texts, first heard in Italy, aroused scholars and leaders in all of the European states. Their appetite for manuscripts exhausted the abilities of the scribes and booksellers who reproduced texts. Printing responded to that demand.

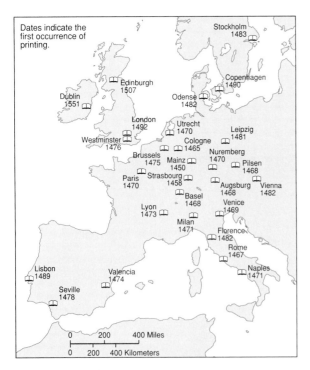

The Spread of Printing

The Print Revolution

The development of printing did not cause religious reform, but it is difficult to see how reform would have progressed in its absence. The campaign to change the doctrine and practice of Catholicism was waged through the press, with millions of flyers and pamphlets distributed across Europe to spread the new ideas. But the ways in which printing came to be used by religious reformers could hardly have been foreseen by the artisans, bankers, and booksellers who together created one of the true technological revolutions in Western history.

Printing was not invented. It developed as a result of progress made in a number of allied industries, of which papermaking and goldsmithing were the most important. Scholars and university students needed copies of manuscripts. Their need led to the development of a trade in bookselling that flourished in almost every university town. The process of reproduction was slowed by difficulties in obtaining the sheep and calf skins on which the manuscripts were written. In the early fifteenth century, copyists began to substitute paper made from linen rags for the expensive vellum skins. A number of German craftsmen experimented with using movable metal type to make exact reproductions of manuscripts on paper. In the 1450s in Mainz, Johannes Gutenberg (ca. 1400–1468) and his partners succeeded and published their famous Bibles.

The association of early printing with goldsmithing resulted from the high level of technical skill that was necessary to create the hard metal stamps from which the softer metal type was produced. Printing was an expensive business. Only the press itself was cheap. Any corn or wine press could be used to bring the long flat sheets of paper down upon a wooden frame filled with ink-coated metal type. Booksellers initially put up the capital needed to cast the stamps, mold the type, and buy the paper. They bound the printed pages and found the markets to distribute them. At first sales were slow. Printed books were considered inferior to handwritten manuscripts. Nor at first were printed books less expensive. Bibles, like those printed by Gutenberg, were major investments, equivalent to purchasing a house today.

Still, once it was begun, printing spread like wildfire. By 1480 over 110 towns had established presses, most in Italy and Germany. After that the pace quickened. By the beginning of the sixteenth century Venice and Paris were the centers of the industry, with the Paris presses producing over three hundred new titles annually. Most of the early printed works were either religious or classical. Bibles, church service books, and the commentaries of the Church Fathers were most common. Cicero topped the list of classical authors.

What is most amazing about the printing revolution is how rapidly printing came to be a basic part of life. In the first forty years after the presses began, perhaps as many as twenty million books were produced and distributed. Printing changed the habits of teachers and students and therefore the possibilities of education. It altered the methods by which the state conducted its business. It affected both legal training and legal proceedings. Compilations of laws could now be widely distributed and more uniformly enforced. Printing had a similar effect on the development of scientific study. The printing press popularized the discoveries of the New World and contributed to the reproduction of more accurate charts and maps, which in turn facilitated further discovery. Printing also helped standardize language, both Latin and vernacular, by frequent repetition of preferred usage and spelling. Perhaps most importantly, printing created an international intellectual community whose ideas could be dispersed the length and breadth of the continent. The printing press enhanced the value of ideas and of thinking. Nothing could be more central to the reform of religion.

Christian Humanism

Many of the ideas that spread across Europe as the result of the printing revolution originated in fifteenth-century Italian humanism (see chapter 12). The revival of classical literature, with its concern for purity in language and eloquence in style, was one of the most admired achievements of the Renaissance. Students from all over Europe who descended upon Italian universities to study medicine and law came away with a strong dose of philology, rhetoric, moral philosophy, and the other liberal arts. By the beginning of the sixteenth century, the force of humanism was felt strongly in northern and western Europe. The combination was a powerful intellectual movement known as Christian humanism.

Though the humanism of the north differed from that of the Italian city-states, this is not to say that northern humanists were Christians and Italian humanists were not. But Italian intellectual interests were in secular subjects, especially in mastering classical languages and in translating classical texts. Italian humanists had established techniques for the recovery of accurate texts and had developed principles for compiling the scholarly editions that now poured forth from the printing presses. Christian humanists applied these techniques to the study of the authorities and texts of the Church. Most of the new humanists had been trained in Italy, where they devoted themselves to the mastery of Greek and Latin. They had imbibed the idea that scholars, using their own critical faculties, could establish the authority of texts and the meaning of words. Building upon the patient work of their predecessors and the advantages offered by printing, this new generation of humanists brought learning to educated men and women throughout Europe.

Christian humanism was a program of reform rather than a philosophy. It aimed to make better Christians through better education. Humanists were especially interested in the education of women. Thomas More (1478–1535) raised his daughters to be among the educated elite of England. Renowned women scholars even held places at Italian universities. Humanist educational principles posed an implicit challenge to Roman Catholicism. Schools had once been the monopoly of the Church, which used them to train clergymen. Literacy itself had been preserved over the centuries so that the gospel could be propagated.

By the sixteenth century these purposes had been transformed. Schools now trained many who were not destined for careers in the Church, and literacy served the needs of the state, the aristocracy, and the merchant classes. More importantly, as the humanists perfected their techniques of scholarship, the Church continued to rely on traditional methods of training and on traditional texts. The dominant manner of teaching at the schools and universities was known as Scholasticism. Passages of biblical texts were studied through the commentaries of generations of Church Fathers. Rote memorization of the opinions of others was more highly valued than critical thinking. Argument took place by formal disputation of questions on which the Fathers of the Church disagreed. The Vulgate Bible was used throughout Western Christendom. It was now a thousand years old.

The Humanist Reform Movement and Erasmus

Many humanist criticisms of Church teaching focused on its failure to inspire individuals to live a Christian life. Humanist writers were especially scathing about popular practices that bordered on superstition, like pilgrimages to holy places or the worship of relics from the early history of the Church. Such beliefs became the butt of popular humor: "If the fragments [of the Lord's Cross] were joined together they would seem a full load for a freighter. And yet the Lord carried his whole cross."

This map by Ambrosius Holbein was published in Thomas More's Utopia, *1518. The mythical island's capital, Amaurote, is shown in the center.*

Utopia

large common halls to abolish jealousy. "A man would be stupid to take the trouble to prepare a worse meal at home when he had a sumptuous one near at hand in the hall." To abolish greed, Utopians scorned gold and silver. "Criminals who are to bear through life the mark of some disgraceful act are forced to wear golden rings on their ears, golden bands on their fingers, golden chains around their necks, and even golden crowns on their heads." Utopians lived harmoniously in planned cities, honored their elders, cared for their sick, and brought up their children to love learning and respect hard work. They "lead a life as free of anxiety and as full of joy as possible." There were many ways in which Christian humanists attempted to instruct their contemporaries to lead a joyful life. None has proved more enduring than the imaginary community Sir Thomas More created in *Utopia*, a social satire so convincing that a Catholic priest sought to become its bishop and sea travelers tried to learn its location. More's creation has proven so compelling that it has given its name to the entire genre of dreamworlds that followed in its wake, although in Greek *Utopia* means "nowhere." His vision of a carefully planned and permanently contented society has passed into our language, but in a way that would not have pleased the author. Now, *utopian* has a wistful ring. It is a label for impractical ideals that will never come to pass, a name for well-meaning but misguided daydreams. For More, as for his generation of humanists, the goal of teaching Christians to lead a Christian life was neither wistful nor impractical.

Sir Thomas More was a London lawyer by vocation but a humanist

"It is a general rule that the more different anything is from what people are used to, the harder it is to accept." So warned the imaginary traveler Raphael Hythloday as he described Utopia, a fabulous society he had visited in the New World. Utopian society was different indeed. In Utopia, all property was held in common—there were no social classes; families were extended to include grandparents, in-laws, and flocks of children; and all work and most social activities were regulated by the state. Utopians were rarely tempted to sin. Everyone wore the same practical clothes to abolish vanity. "No matter how delicate the thread, they say a sheep wore it once and still was nothing but a sheep." Everyone ate the same food in scholar by avocation. His father practiced law, and planned a similar career for his son. But Thomas's stay at Oxford University coincided with the first flush of humanist enthusiasm there, especially in the study of Greek. More proved so exceptionally able that his father removed him to London in fear that reading Greek would turn him away from Catholicism. More proved as able at law school as he had at the university, and he was soon singled out as one of the best lawyers of his day. But in his spare time he continued to study the classics and became part of the growing humanist circle in London. There he met Erasmus, who became his lifelong friend.

More wrote *Utopia* in 1516, before he embarked upon the public career that would result in his becoming Chancellor of England, Speaker of the House of Commons, Privy Councilor and companion to Henry VIII, and finally a victim of the king's divorce and assumption of the title Supreme Head of the Church of England. More ended his life on the chopping block, and his death was mourned by humanists throughout Europe.

Utopia is written in the form of a dialogue in which the author pretends to be one of the charac- ters. On a visit to Antwerp, the character More is introduced to an imaginary traveler named Raphael Hythloday. During a long evening, Hythloday relates a tale of a remarkable society that he encountered on his voyages. Utopia was a self-sufficient island, protected from invasion by the sea and thus able to develop its social customs without interference.

Hythloday contrasted the practices of the Utopians with those of contemporary Europeans and confounded the character More's objections that such arrangements were impractical. For example, where European peasants or craftsmen worked for fourteen hours a day, Utopians worked for only six. But all Utopians worked. There were no idle aristocrats with their marauding retainers, no priests and monks and nuns, no beggars unable to find jobs. Moreover, there was no surplus of workers in one field and shortage in another. For two years, each Utopian worked on the farm. After that, Utopians worked at a craft according to the needs of the city. Both males and females were educated to be of service to their community. Women were trained in less strenuous but no less essential trades like weaving or spinning. The population of cities was strictly controlled so that there was neither poverty nor homelessness. In their spare time Utopians engaged in uplifting activities like music, gardening, or artistic pursuits. Severe punishment awaited transgressors, but in contrast to the European practice of executing thieves, Utopian criminals were enslaved so that they could work for the restitution of the wrongs that they committed. Though they had not the benefit of Christian religion, the Utopians believed in a single divinity as well as an afterlife and their worship was simple and natural.

By ironic contrast with the unfulfilling life led by Europeans, grasping for riches, dominated by vanity, motivated by pride, the peaceful and simple life of the Utopians held great attraction. By contrasting the success of heathen Utopians with the failure of Christian Europeans, More called upon his contemporaries to reform their own lives. The purpose of *Utopia* was not to advocate the abolition of wealth and property or the intervention of the state in the affairs of the individual but to demonstrate that a society founded upon good principles would become a good society.

This ironic strain in humanist writing is most closely associated with the great Dutch humanist, Desiderius Erasmus, but it is also visible in the humanist social criticism of Sir Thomas More's *Utopia* (See Special Feature, "Utopia," pp. 382–383). Christian humanists wanted to inspire Christians.

Christian humanism was an international movement. The humanists formed the elite of the intellectual world of the sixteenth century, and their services were sought by princes and peers as well as by the most distinguished universities. In fact, monarchs supported the humanists and protected them from their critics. Marguerite of Navarre, sister of King Francis I of France (1515–47), was an accomplished writer who frequently interceded on behalf of the leading French humanists. Ferdinand of Aragon, Henry VIII of England (1509–47), and the Holy Roman Emperors Maximilian I (1486–1519) and Charles V (1519–56) all brought humanists to their courts and aided their projects. Maria of Hungary and Henry VIII's daughters, Mary and Elizabeth Tudor, were trained in humanist principles and participated in humanist literary achievements. This support was especially important for educational reforms. Under the influence of the French humanist Jacques Lefèvre d'Etaples (ca. 1455–1536), Francis I established the Collège de France; under the direction of Cardinal Jiménez de Cisneros, the University of Alcalà was founded in Spain. Throughout northern Europe professorships in Greek and Latin were endowed at universities to help further the study of classical languages.

The centerpiece of humanist reforms was the translation of Christian texts. Armed with skills in Greek and Latin, informed by scholars of Hebrew and Aramaic, humanist writers prepared new editions of the books of the Bible and of the writings of the early Church Fathers. The Polyglot Bible—literally "many languages"—that was produced in 1522 at the University of Alcalà took a team of scholars fifteen years to complete. They rigorously compared texts of all known biblical manuscripts and established the principle that inconsistencies among Latin manuscripts were to be resolved by reference to Greek texts and difficulties in Greek texts by reference to Hebrew texts. The result was six volumes that allowed scholars to compare the texts. The Old Testament was printed in three parallel columns of Hebrew, Latin Vulgate, and Greek. The New Testament was printed in double columns of Greek and Vulgate. The Greek edition of the Bible and its establishment as a text superior to the Vulgate caused an immediate sensation throughout humanist and Church circles.

Engraving of Erasmus by the German master Albrecht Dürer. The title, date, and signature appear behind the philosopher. The Greek inscription reads "His writings depict him even better."

Though the Polyglot Bible contained the first completed Greek edition of the New Testament, it was not the first published one. That distinction belongs to the man whose name is most closely associated with the idea of Christian humanism, Desiderius Erasmus of Rotterdam (ca. 1466–1536). Orphaned at an early age, Erasmus was educated by the Brothers of the Common Life, a lay brotherhood that specialized in schooling children and preparing them for a monastic life. Singled out early for his extraordinary intellectual gifts, Erasmus entered a monastery and was then allowed to travel to pursue his studies, first in France and then in England.

In England Erasmus learned of new techniques for instructing children both in classical knowledge and in Christian morals, and he became particularly interested in the education of women. While in England, Erasmus decided to compose a short satire on the lines of his conversations with Thomas More, extolling what was silly and condemning what was wise. The result was *In Praise of Folly* (1509), a work that became one of the first best-sellers.

Before his visit to England, Erasmus had worked solely on Latin translations, but he came to realize the

FROM *IN PRAISE OF FOLLY*

■ In Praise of Folly *was a witty satire on the abuses to be found in the Catholic church. Desiderius Erasmus wrote it on a lark to be presented to his friend Sir Thomas More, on whose name its Latin title puns. It was probably the first best-seller of the age of printing.*

These various forms of foolishness so pervade the whole life of Christians that even the priests themselves find no objection to admitting, not to say fostering, them, since they do not fail to perceive how many tidy little sums accrue to them from such sources. But what if some odious philosopher should chime in and say, as is quite true: "You will not die badly if you live well. You are redeeming your sins when you add to the sum that you contribute a hearty detestation of evil doers: then you may spare yourself tears, vigils, invocations, fasts, and all that kind of life. You may rely upon any saint to aid you when once you begin to imitate his life."

As for the theologians, perhaps the less said the better on this gloomy and dangerous theme, since they are a style of man who show themselves exceeding supercilious and irritable unless they can heap up six hundred conclusions about you and force you to recant; and if you refuse, they promptly brand you as a heretic,—for it is their custom to terrify by their thunderings those whom they dislike. It must be confessed that no other group of fools are so reluctant to acknowledge Folly's benefits toward them, although I have many titles to their gratitude, for I make them so in love with themselves that they seem to be happily exalted to the third heaven, whence they look down with something like pity upon all other mortals, wandering about on the earth like mere cattle.

importance of recovering the Greek texts of the early Church Fathers. At the age of thirty he began the arduous task of learning ancient Greek and devoted his energies to a study of the writings of Saint Jerome, the principal compiler of the Vulgate, and to preparing an edition of the Greek text of the Bible. Erasmus's New Testament and his edition of the writings of Saint Jerome both appeared in 1516.

Erasmus devoted his life to restoring the direct connection between the individual Christian and the textual basis of Christian doctrine. Although he is called the father of biblical criticism, Erasmus was not a theologian. He was more interested in the practical impact of ideas than in the ideas themselves. His scathing attacks upon the Scholastics, popular superstition, and the pretensions of the traditionalists in the Church and the universities all aimed at the same goal: to restore the experiences of Christ to the center of Christianity. Though his patrons were the rich and his language was Latin, Erasmus also hoped to reach men and women lower down the social order, those whom he believed the Church had failed to educate. "The doctrine of Christ casts aside no age, no sex, no fortune or position in life. It keeps no one at a distance."

In his life Erasmus encapsulated the intellectual reformation of the early sixteenth century. Taking advantage of the new technology of printing, Erasmus became a best-selling author able to influence thousands beyond his northern European home. He learned Greek, translated scripture, and wrote in the vernacular. Erasmus championed educational reforms, as did his friend Sir Thomas More, and a new spirit of critical thinking. The greatest of the Christian humanists, Erasmus imparted a vision that extended from the reorganization of the principles of scholarship to the reorientation of life in the Church, a vision that made possible religious reform.

The Lutheran Reformation

On the surface the Roman Catholic church at the end of the fifteenth century appeared as strong as ever. The growth of universities and the spread of the new learning had helped create a better-educated clergy. The printing press proved an even greater boon to the Church than it had to the humanists by making widely available both instructional manuals for priests and up-to-date service books for congregations. In Rome successive late medieval popes had managed to protect Church interests in the wake of the disintegration of the autonomous power of the Italian city-states. Popes had become first diplomats and then warriors in order to repel French and Spanish invaders. Rome was invaded, but never conquered. And it was more beautiful than ever as the great artists and craftsmen of the Renaissance built and adorned its churches. On the surface all was calm.

Yet everywhere in Europe the cry was for reform. Reform the venal papacy and its money-sucking bishops. Reform the ignorant clergy and the sacrilegious priests. Raise up the fallen nuns and the wayward friars. Wherever one turned one saw abuses. Parish livings were sold to the highest bidder to raise money. This was simony. Rich appointments were given to the kinsmen of powerful Church leaders rather than to those most qualified. This was nepotism. Individual clergymen accumulated numerous positions whose responsibilities they could not fulfill. This was pluralism. Some priests who took the vow of chastity lived openly with their concubines. Some mendicants who took the vow of poverty dressed in silk and ate from golden plates.

The cry for reform at the beginning of the sixteenth century came at a moment when people from all walks of life demanded greater spiritual fulfillment and held to higher standards those whose vocation it was to provide such fulfillment. Expectation rather than experience powered the demands for reform.

The Spark of Reform

Europe was becoming more religious. Cities hired preachers to expound the gospel. Pilgrims to the shrines of saints clogged the roadways every spring and summer. Rome remained the greatest attraction, but pilgrims covered the continent. The shrine of the apostle Saint James at Compostela in Spain was believed to cure the ill. Endowments of masses for the dead increased. Henry VII of England provided money for ten thousand masses to be said for his soul. In the chantries, where such services were performed, there were neither enough priests nor enough altars to supply the demand.

People wanted more from the Church than the Church could possibly give them. Humanists condemned visits to the shrines as superstitious; pilgrims demanded that the relics be made more accessible. Reformers complained of pluralism; the clergy complained that they could not live on the salary of a single office.

Civic authorities demanded that the established Church take greater responsibility for good works; the pope demanded that civic authorities help pay for them.

Contradiction and paradox dominated the movements for reform. Though the most vocal critics of the Church complained that its discipline was too lax, for many ordinary people its demands were too rigorous. The obligations of penance and confession weighed heavily upon them. Church doctrine held that sins had to be washed away before the souls of the dead could enter heaven. Until then they suffered in purgatory. Sins were cleansed through penance, the performance of acts of contrition assigned after confession. But the ordeal of confession kept many people away. "Have you skipped mass? Have you dressed proudly? Have you thought of committing adultery?" These were just a few of the uncomfortable questions that priests were instructed to pose in confession. In towns merchants were asked about their trading practices, shopkeepers about the quality of their goods.

Thus it is hardly surprising that the sale of indulgences became a popular substitute for penance and confession. An indulgence was a portion of the treasury of good works performed by righteous Christians throughout the ages. They could be granted to those who desired to atone for their sins. Strictly speaking, an indulgence supplemented penance rather than substituted for it. It was effective only for the contrite—for sinners who repented of their sins. But as the practice of granting indulgences spread, this subtle distinction largely disappeared. The living bought indulgences to cleanse the sins of the dead, and some even bought indulgences in anticipation of sins they had not yet committed.

By the sixteenth century, to limit abuses by local Church authorities, only the pope, through his agents, could grant indulgences. Popes used special occasions to offer an indulgence for pilgrimages to Rome or for contributions to special papal projects. Other indulgences were licensed locally, usually at the shrines of saints or at churches that contained relics.

The indulgence controversy was a symptom rather than a cause of the explosion of feelings that erupted in the small German town of Wittenberg in the year 1517. In that year the pope was offering an indulgence to help finance the rebuilding of Saint Peter's Basilica in Rome. The pope chose Prince Albert of Brandenburg (1490-1545) to distribute the indulgence in Germany, and Albert hired the Dominican friar Johann Tetzel (ca. 1465-1519) to preach its benefits. Tetzel offered little warning about the theological niceties of indulgences

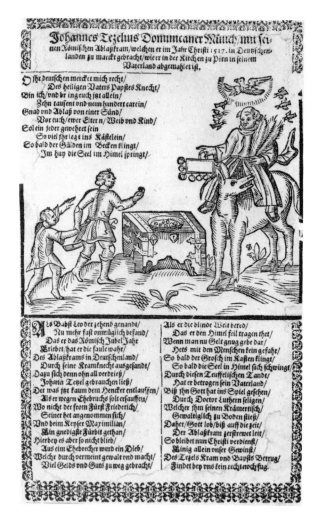

An anonymous caricature of Johann Tetzel, whose preaching of an indulgence inspired Martin Luther's Ninety-five Theses. Tetzel answered with 122 theses of his own, but was rebuked and disowned by the Catholics.

to those who paid to mitigate their own sins or alleviate the suffering of their ancestors in purgatory.

Enthusiasm for the indulgence spread to the neighboring state of Saxony, where the ruler, Frederick III, the Wise (1463–1525), banned its sale. Frederick's great collection of relics carried their own indulgences and Tetzel offered unwelcome competition. But Saxons flocked into Brandenburg to make their purchases, and by the end of October, Tetzel was not very far from Wittenberg Castle, where Frederick's relics were housed. On All Saints' Day the relics would be opened to view and, with the harvest done, one of the largest crowds of the year would gather to see them. On the night before, Martin Luther (1483–1546), a professor of theology at Wittenberg University, posted on the door of the castle church ninety-five theses attacking indulgences and their sale.

Other than the timing of Luther's action, there was nothing unusual about the posting of theses. In the Scholastic tradition of disputation, scholars presented propositions, or theses, for debate and challenged all comers to argue with them in a public forum. Luther's theses were controversial, but as that was the whole point of offering them for discussion, they were meant to be. Only circumstance moved Luther's theses from the academic to the public sphere. Already there was growing concern among clergy and theologians about Tetzel's blatant sale of indulgences. Hordes of purchasers believed that they were buying unconditional remission of sin. Individual priests and monks began to sound the alarm: an indulgence without contrition was worthless.

Luther's theses focused this concern and finally communicated it beyond the walls of the church and university. The theses were immediately translated into German and spread throughout the Holy Roman Empire by humanists who had long criticized as superstitious such practices as the sale of indulgences. Prospective buyers became wary; past purchasers became angry. They had been duped again by the Church and by the Italian pope who cared nothing for honest hard-working Germans.

The Faith of Martin Luther

Martin Luther was not a man to challenge lightly. Although he was only an obscure German professor, he had already marked himself out to all who knew him. In his youth Luther was an exceptionally able student whose father sent him to the best schools in preparation for a career in law. But against the wishes of his father he entered an Augustinian monastery, wholeheartedly followed the strict program of his order, and was ordained a priest in 1507. He received his doctorate at the university in Wittenberg and was appointed to the theology faculty in 1512.

Luther attracted powerful patrons in the university and gained a reputation as an outstanding teacher. He began to be picked for administrative posts and became overseer of eleven Augustinian monasteries. His skills in disputation were widely recognized and he was sent to Rome to argue a case on behalf of his order. He fulfilled each task beyond expectation. In all outward appearances Luther was successful and contented.

But beneath this tranquil exterior lay a soul in torment. As he rose in others' estimation, he sank in his own. Through beating and fasting he mortified his flesh.

Through vigil and prayer he nourished his soul. Through study and contemplation he honed his intellect. Still he could find no peace. Despite his devotion, he could not erase his sense of sin; he could not convince himself that he could achieve the righteousness God demanded of him.

Knowledge of his salvation came to Luther through study. His internal agonies led him to ponder over and over again the biblical passages that described the righteousness of God. In the intellectual tradition in which he had been trained, that righteousness was equated with law. The righteous person either followed God's law or was punished by God's wrath. It was this understanding that tormented him. "I thought that I had to perform good works till at last through them Jesus would become a friend and gracious to me." But no amount of good works could overcome Luther's feelings of guilt for his sins. Almost from the moment he began lecturing in 1512 he searched for the key to the freedom of his own soul.

Even before he wrote his Ninety-five Theses, Luther had made the first breakthrough by a unique reading of the writings of Saint Paul. "I pondered night and day until I understood the connection between the righteousness of God and the sentence 'The just shall live by faith.' Then I grasped that the justice of God is the righteousness by which through grace and pure mercy, God justifies us through faith. Immediately I felt that I had been reborn and that I had passed through wide open doors into paradise!" Finally he realized that the righteousness of God was a gift freely given to the faithful. It was this belief that fortified Luther during his years of struggle with both civil and Church powers.

Over the next several years, Luther refined his spiritual philosophy and drew out the implications of his newfound beliefs. His religion was shaped by three interconnected tenets. First came justification by faith alone—*sola fide*. An individual's everlasting salvation came from faith in God's goodness rather than from the performance of good works. Sin could not be washed away by penance, and it could not be forgiven by indulgence. Second, faith in God's mercy came only through the knowledge and contemplation of the Word of God—*sola scriptura*. All that was needed to understand the

LUTHER ON THE RELATIONSHIP OF HUSBAND AND WIFE

■ *Martin Luther wrote thousands of pages of theological and devotional literature in establishing a new religious movement. His simple style and everyday examples made his message accessible to hundreds of thousands of ordinary people. In this selection from his tract* On Good Works *(1520) he compares the relationship of the husband and wife to that of the Christian and Christ.*

We can understand this whole matter [of good works] by an obvious human example. When husband and wife are fond of one another and live together in love and in confidence in one another, and each believes truly in the other, who shall teach them how they should act, what they should do or leave undone, say or not say, think or not think? Their own insight tells them all that need be, and more too. There is no distinction in their "works" for one another. They do the long, hard, and heavy tasks as willingly as the slight and easy things, and moreover they act with glad, peaceful, and secure hearts and are altogether free and unconstrained. But when doubt comes they begin to ask what is best, and begin to distinguish between their acts in order to gain the other's favor, and go about with troubled and heavy hearts, perhaps well-nigh in despair or driven to downright desperation.

So the Christian who lives in confidence toward God knows what things he should do, and does all gladly and freely, not with a view to accumulating merit and good works, but because it is his great joy to please God and to serve him without thought of reward, contented if he but do God's will. On the contrary, he who is not at one with God, or is in doubt, will begin to be anxious how he may satisfy God and justify himself by his works. He runs off on a pilgrimmage to St. James of Compostella, to Rome, to Jerusalem,—here, there, anywhere; prays to St. Bridget, or some other saint, fasts this day and that, confesses here and confesses there, asks this man and that, but finds no peace.

From Martin Luther, *On Good Works.*

justice and mercy of God was contained in the Bible. Reading the Word, hearing the Word, expounding upon and studying the Word, this was the path to faith and through faith to salvation. Finally, all who believed in God's righteousness and had achieved their faith through the study of the Bible were equal in God's eyes. The priesthood was of all believers. Each followed his or her own calling and found his or her own faith through Scripture. Ministers and preachers could help others learn God's Word, but they could not confer faith.

Luther's spiritual rebirth and the theology that developed from it posed a fundamental challenge to the Roman Catholic church. Though for centuries the Church had met doctrinal challenges and had absorbed many seemingly unorthodox ideas, Luther's theology could not be among them. It struck too deeply at the roots of belief, practice, and structure. Yet for all of the transforming power of these apparently simple ideas, it was not Luther alone who initiated the reform of religion. Justification by faith alone provided an alternative to the combination of works and faith that many Roman Catholics found too difficult to fulfill. Luther's insistence that faith comes only through the study of the Word of God was facilitated by the new learning and the invention of printing. The printing press prepared the ground for the dissemination of his thought as much as it disseminated it. This was a contribution of the Renaissance. Luther's hope for the creation of a spiritual elite, confirmed in their faith and confident of their salvation, readily appealed to the citizens of hundreds of German towns who had already made of themselves a social and economic elite. This was a contribution of the growth of towns. The idea of the equality of all believers meant that all were equally responsible for fulfilling God's commandments. This set secular rulers on an equal footing with the pope at a moment in Western history when they were already challenging papal power in matters of both church and state. For all his painful soul-searching, Luther embodied the culmination of changes of which he was only dimly aware.

From Luther to Lutheranism

The first to feel the seriousness of Luther's challenge to the established order was the reformer himself. The head of his order, a papal legate, and finally the Emperor Charles V all called for Luther to recant his views on indulgences. Excommunicated by Pope Leo X in 1521, Luther was ordered by Charles V to appear before the diet, or assembly, in Worms, Germany, in April of that year. The emperor demanded that Luther retract his teachings. To all he gave the same infuriating reply: if he could be shown the places in the Bible that contradicted his views he would gladly change them. Charles V declared Luther an enemy of the empire. In both church and state he was now an outlaw.

In fact, during the three years between the posting of his theses and his appearance before the Diet of Worms, Luther came to conclusions much more radical than his initial attack on indulgences. He came to believe that the papacy was a human rather than a divine invention. Therefore he denounced both the papacy and the general councils of the Church. In his *Address to the Christian Nobility of the German Nation* (1520) he called upon the princes to take the reform of religion into their own hands.

Martin Luther (far left), Zwingli, Melancthon, and other dissenters surround their protector, Elector John Frederick the Magnanimous.

But Luther had attracted powerful supporters as well as powerful enemies. Prince Frederick III of Saxony consistently intervened on his behalf, and the delicate international situation forced Luther's chief antagonists to move more slowly than they might have wished. The pope hoped first to keep Charles V off the imperial throne and then to maintain a united front with the German princes against him. Charles V, already locked in his lifelong struggle with the French, needed German military support and peace in his German territories. These factors consistently played into Luther's hands.

While pope and emperor were otherwise occupied, Luther refined his ideas and thus was able to hold his own in the theological debates in which he won important converts. More importantly, as time passed Luther's reputation grew, not only in Germany, but all over Europe. Between 1517 and 1520 he published thirty works, all of which achieved massive sales. Yet Luther alone could not sustain what came to be called Lutheranism. The Roman Catholic church had met heresy before and knew how to deal with it. What turned Luther's theology into a movement, which after 1529 came to be known as Protestantism, was the support he received among German princes and within German cities.

There were many reasons that individual princes turned to Luther's theology. First and foremost was sincere religious conviction. Matters of the hereafter were a pressing concern in a world in which the average life span was thirty years and nearly all natural phenomena were inexplicable. And they were more pressing still among the educated elites infected by the new learning and self-confident of their power to reason critically. Yet there were secular reasons as well. The formation of large states had provided a model for civil government. On a smaller scale, German princes worked to centralize their administration, protect themselves from predatory neighbors, and increase their revenues. Taxes and gifts flowed south to a papacy dominated by Italians. Luther's call for civil rulers to lead their own churches meant that civil rulers could keep their own revenues.

The Reformation spread particularly well in German cities, especially those that the emperor had granted the status of freedom from the rule of any prince. Once Protestant ideas were established entire towns adopted them. Many cities had long struggled with the tension of the separate jurisdictions of state and church. Much urban property was owned by the Church, and thus exempt from taxation and law enforcement, and the clergy constituted a significant proportion of urban populations. Reformed religion stressed the equality of clergy and laity and thus the indisputable power of civil

authorities. Paradoxically, it was because the cities contained large numbers of priests that Luther's ideas reached them quickly. Many of his earliest students served urban congregations and began to develop doctrines and practices that, though based on Luther's ideas, were adapted to the circumstances of city life. The reform clergy became integrated into the life of the city in a way that the Catholic clergy had not. They married the daughters of citizens, became citizens themselves, and trained their children in the guilds. Moreover, the imperial free cities were also the center of the printing trade and home to many of the most noted humanists, who were initially important in spreading Luther's ideas.

Luther's message held great appeal for the middle orders in the towns. While it was necessary for the leader of a state to support reform if it was to survive, in the cities it was the petty burghers, lesser merchants, tradesmen, and artisans who led the movements that ultimately gained the approval of city governments. These groups resented the privileges given to priests and members of religious orders, who paid no taxes and were exempt from the obligations of citizenship. The level of anticlericalism, always high in Germany, was especially acute in cities that were suffering economic difficulties. The evangelism of reforming ministers created converts and an atmosphere of reform. Support from members of the ruling oligarchy both mobilized these pressures and capitalized upon them. Town governments secured their own autonomy over the church, tightening their grip upon the institutions of social control and enhancing the social and economic authority of their members. Once Protestant, city governments took over many of the functions of the religious houses, often converting them into schools or hostels for the poor. Former monks were allowed to enter trades. Former nuns were encouraged to marry. Luther himself married an ex-nun after the dissolution of her convent.

Religious reform appealed to women as well as men, but it affected them differently. Noblewomen were among the most important defenders of Protestant reformers, especially in states in which the prince opposed it. Marguerite of Navarre (1492–1549), sister of Francis I, frequently intervened with her brother on behalf of individual Lutherans who fell afoul of Church authorities. She created her own court in the south of France and stocked it with both humanists and Protestants. Her devotional poem, *Mirror of the Sinful Soul* (1533), inspired women reformers and was translated into English by Elizabeth I. Mary of Hungary (1505–58) served a similar role in the Holy Roman Empire. Sister

Portrait of Marguerite de Valois, queen of Navarre, the cultured and talented sister of King Francis I.

of both Charles V and Ferdinand I, queen of Hungary and later regent of the Netherlands, Mary acted as patron to Hungarian reformers. Though she was more humanist than Protestant, Luther dedicated an edition of Psalms to her, and she read a number of his works. Her independent religious views infuriated both of her brothers. Bona, wife of Sigismund I of Poland, was especially important in eastern reform. An Italian by birth, Bona (1493–1558) was a central figure in spreading both Renaissance art and humanist learning into Poland. She became one of the largest independent landowners in the state and initiated widespread agricultural and economic reforms. Her private confessor was one of Poland's leading Protestants.

Luther's reforms also offered much to women who were not so highly placed in society. The doctrine of the equality of all believers put men and women on an equal spiritual footing even if it did nothing to break the male monopoly of the ministry. But the most important difference that Protestantism made to ordinary women was in the private rather than the public sphere. Family

life became the center of faith when salvation was removed from the control of the Church. Luther's marriage led him to a deeper appreciation of the importance of the wife and mother in the family's spirituality.

By following humanist teaching on the importance of educating women of the upper orders and by encouraging literacy, the reformers did much that was uplifting. Girls' schools were founded in a number of German cities and townswomen could use their newly acquired skills in their roles as shopkeepers, family accountants, and teachers of their children. But there were losses as well as gains. The attack upon the worship of saints and especially of the Virgin Mary removed female images from religion. Protestantism was male-dominated in a way that Catholicism was not. Moreover, the emphasis upon reading the Bible tended to reinforce the image of women as weak and inherently sinful. The dissolution of the convents took away the one institution that valued their gender and allowed them to pursue a spiritual life outside marriage.

The Spread of Lutheranism

By the end of the 1520s the empire was divided between cities and states that accepted reformed religion and those that adhered to Roman Catholicism. Printing presses, traveling merchants, and hordes of students who claimed—not always truthfully—to have attended Luther's lectures or sermons spread the message. Large German communities across northern Europe, mostly founded as trading outposts, became focal points for the penetration of reformist ideas. In Livonia the Teutonic Knights established a Lutheran form of worship that soon took hold all along the shores of the Baltic. Lutheran-inspired reformers seized control of the Polish port city of Gdansk, which they held for a short time, while neighboring Prussia officially established a Lutheran church. Polish translations of Luther's writings were disseminated into Poland-Lithuania, and Protestant communities were established as far south as Kraków.

Merchants and students carried Luther's ideas into Scandinavia, but there the importance of political leaders was crucial. Christian III (1534–59) of Denmark had been present at the Diet of Worms when Luther made his famous reply to Charles V. Christian was deeply impressed by the reformer and after a ruinous civil war, confiscated Catholic church property in Denmark and created a reformed religion under Luther's direct supervision.

Paradoxically, Lutheranism came to Sweden as part of an effort to throw off the yoke of Danish dominance.

Cartoon showing Martin Luther carting a host of former priests away from their vows of chastity, followed by his wife, the former nun Katharina von Bora.

Here, too, direct connection with Luther provided the first impulses. Olaus Petri (1493–1552) had studied at Wittenberg and returned to preach Lutheran doctrine among the large German merchant community in Stockholm. He was a trained humanist who used both Erasmus's Greek New Testament and Luther's German one to prepare his Swedish translation (1526). When Gustav I Vasa (1523–60) led a successful uprising against the Danes and became king of Sweden, he encouraged the spread of Protestant ideas and allowed Petri to continue his translations of the mass and the Lutheran service. Luther's impact extended into central Europe.

Bohemia had had a reforming tradition of its own that antedated Luther. Though the teachings of Jan Hus (1373–1415) had been condemned by the Catholic church, Hussitism was in fact the all but established religion in most parts of Bohemia. Ferdinand I, king of Bohemia, was bound by law to allow its moderate practice. Hussites had already initiated many reforms, for Luther had been influenced by Hus. The mass was said in Czech, and the Bible had been translated into the vernacular. Hussites believed that communion in both forms was mandated by the Bible. This was the real issue that separated them from Roman Catholics, for the Hussites refused to accept the traditional view that the authority of either the pope or the general council of the Church could alter God's command. On all these issues, Hussites and Lutherans shared a common program. But the Hussites were conservative in almost everything else. While the German communities in Bohemia accepted the core of Lutheran doctrine, most Czechs rejected justification by faith alone and maintained their own practices.

As important as Protestant ideas were in northern and central Europe, it was in the Swiss towns of the empire that they proved most fertile. Here was planted the second generation of reformers, theologians who drew from Luther's insights radical new conclusions. In the east, Huldrych Zwingli (1484–1531) brought reformed religion to the town of Zurich. Educated at the University of Basel and deeply influenced by humanist thought early in his career, Zwingli was a preacher among the Swiss mercenary troops that fought for the empire. In 1516 he met Erasmus in Basel and under his influence began a study of the Greek writings of the Church Fathers and of the New Testament. Zwingli was also influenced by reports of Luther's defiance of the pope, for his own antipapal views were already developing. Perhaps most decisively for his early development, in 1519 Zwingli was stricken by plague. In his life-and-death struggle he came to a profoundly personal realization of the power of God's mercy.

These experiences became the basis for the reform theology Zwingli preached in Zurich. He believed that the Church had to recover its earlier purity and reject the innovations in practices brought in by successive popes and general councils. He stressed the equality of believers, justification by faith alone, and the sufficiency of the gospel as authority for church practice. He attacked indulgences, penance, clerical celibacy, prayers to the Virgin, statues and images in churches, and a long list of other abuses. He also stressed that the mass was to be viewed as a commemorative event rather than one that involved the real presence of Christ. He preferred to call the service the Lord's Supper. His arguments were so effective that the town council adopted them as the basis for a reform of religion.

The principles Zwingli preached quickly spread to neighboring Swiss states. He participated in formal religious disputations in both Bern and Basel. In both places his plea for a simple, unadorned religious practice met widespread approval. Practical as well as theological, Zwingli's reforms were carried out by the civil government, with which he allied himself. This was not the same as the protection that princes had given to Lutherans. Rather, in the places that came under Zwingli's influence, there was an important integration of church and state. He stressed the divine origins of civil government and the importance of the magistrate as an agent of Christian reform. "A church without the magistrate is mutilated and incomplete." This theocratic idea—that the leaders of the state and the leaders of the church

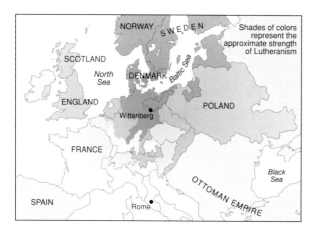

The Spread of Lutheranism

were linked—became the basis for further social and political reform.

The reformation that had begun with the personal struggles of an individual German priest had now spread across Europe. Luther's quest for salvation transformed religious life for millions of people. His insistence on reading the Scriptures, preaching the word, and living through faith struck a responding chord everywhere. Though he was excommunicated and banished from the Holy Roman Empire, Luther was protected by princes who were soon labeled Protestant. The conversion of princes and the spread of Lutheranism in towns ensured that the new religion would become a powerful political force even beyond the boundaries of the empire. In Scandinavia, Bohemia, and the Swiss cantons the message received a ready reception. In barely more than a decade a new religion had been established.

The Protestant Reformation

By the middle of the 1530s Protestant reform had entered a new stage. Luther did not intend to form a new religion; his struggle had been with Rome. Before he could build he had to tear down—his religion was one of protest. Most of his energy was expended in attack and counterattack. The second generation of reformers faced a different task. The new reformers were the church builders who had to systematize doctrine for a generation that had already accepted religious reform. Their challenge was to draw out the logic of reformed ideas and to create enduring structures for reformed churches. The problems they faced were as much institutional as doctrinal. How was the new church to be governed in the absence of the traditional hierarchy? How could discipline be enforced when members of the reformed community went astray? What was the proper relationship between the community of believers and civil authority? Whatever the failings of the Roman Catholic church, it had ready answers to these critical questions.

Geneva and Calvin

The Reformation came late to Geneva. In the sixteenth century Geneva was under the dual government of the Duchy of Savoy and the Catholic bishop of the town, who was frequently a Savoy client. The Genevans also had their own town council, which traditionally struggled for power against the bishop. By the 1530s the council had gained the upper hand. The council confiscated Church lands and institutions, secularized the Church's legal powers, and forced the bishop and most of his administrators to flee the city. War with Savoy inevitably followed and Geneva would certainly have been crushed into submission except for its alliance with neighboring Bern, a potent military power among the Swiss towns. Geneva was saved and was free to follow its own course in religious matters. In 1536 the adult male citizens of the city voted to become Protestant. But as yet there was no reformer in Geneva to establish a Protestant program and no clear definition of what that program might be.

Martin Luther had started out to become a lawyer and ended up a priest. John Calvin started out to become a priest and ended up a lawyer. The difference tells much about each man. Calvin (1509–64) was born in France, the son of a bishop's secretary. His education was based on humanist principles, and he learned Greek and Hebrew, studied theology, and received a legal degree from the University of Orléans. Around the age of twenty he converted to Lutheranism. Francis I had determined to root Protestants out of France, and Calvin fled Paris after one of his close friends was burned for heresy. These events left an indelible impression upon him. In 1535 he left France for Basel, where he wrote and published the first edition of his *Institutes of the Christian Religion* (1536), a defense of French Protestants against persecution. Calvin returned briefly to France to wind up his personal affairs, and then decided to settle in Strasbourg, where he could retire from public affairs and live out his days as a scholar.

To Calvin, providence guided all human action. He could have no better evidence for this belief than what happened next. War between France and the empire clogged the major highways to Strasbourg. Thus Calvin

This painting shows a Calvinist service in Lyon, France, in 1564. The sexes are segregated and the worshipers are seated according to rank. An hourglass times the preacher's sermon.

and his companions detoured through Geneva, where Guillaume Farel (1489-1565), one of Geneva's leading Protestant reformers, implored Calvin to remain in Geneva and lead its reformation. Calvin was not interested. Farel tried every means of persuasion he knew until, in exasperation, Farel declared "that God would curse my retirement if I should withdraw and refuse to help when the necessity was so urgent." For a quarter of a century, Calvin labored to bring order to the Genevan church.

Calvin's greatest contributions to religious reform came in church structure and discipline. He had studied the writings of the first generation of reformers and accepted without question justification by faith alone and the biblical foundation of religious authority. Like Luther and Zwingli he believed that salvation came from God's grace. But more strongly than his predecessors he believed that the gift of faith was granted only to some and that each individual's salvation or damnation was predestined before birth. The doctrine of predestination was a traditional one, but Calvin emphasized it differently and brought it to the center of the problem of faith. "Many are called but few are chosen," Calvin quoted from the Bible. Those who were predestined to salvation, the "elect," were obliged to govern; those who were predestined to damnation were obliged to be governed.

Calvin structured the institution of the Genevan church in four parts. First were the pastors who preached the Word to their congregations. While the pastors preached, the doctors, the second element in Calvin's church, studied and wrote. Deacons, the third element in Calvin's four-part structure, were laymen chosen by the congregation to oversee the institutions of social welfare, such as hospitals and schools, run by the church. The last element were the elders of the church, who were its governors in all moral matters. They were the most controversial part of Calvin's establishment and the most fundamental. They had the power to discipline. Chosen from among the elite of the city, the twelve elders enforced the strict Calvinist moral code that extended into all aspects of private life. Sexual offenses were the most common. Adultery and fornication were vigorously suppressed and prostitutes, who had nearly become a recognized guild in the early sixteenth century, were expelled from Geneva.

The structure that Calvin gave to the Genevan church soon became the basis for reforms throughout the Continent. The Calvinist church was self-governing, independent of the state, and therefore capable of surviving and even flourishing in a hostile environment. Expanded in several subsequent editions, *Institutes of the Christian Religion* became the most influential work of Protestant theology. It had begun as an effort to extend Protestantism to Calvin's homeland, and waves of Calvinist-educated pastors returned to France in the mid-sixteenth century and established churches along Calvinist lines. Calvinism spread north

CALVIN ON PREDESTINATION

■ *John Calvin was born in France but led the reformation in the Swiss town of Geneva. He was one of the leaders of the second generation of reformers, whose task was to refine church doctrinal structure. Calvinism was propounded in* Institutes of the Christian Religion *(1534), from which this section on the doctrine of predestination is taken.*

We must be content with this,—that such gifts as it pleased the Lord to have bestowed upon the nature of man he vested in Adam; and therefore when Adam lost them after he had received them, he lost them not only from himself but also from us all . . . Therefore from a rotten root rose up rotten branches, which sent their rottenness into the twigs that sprang out of them; for so were the children corrupted in their father that they in turn infected their children . . .

And the apostle Paul himself expressly witnesseth that therefore death came upon all men, because all men have sinned and are wrapped in original sin and defiled with the spots thereof. And therefore the very infants themselves, since they bring with them their own damnation from their mothers' womb, are bound not by another's but by their own fault. For although they have not as yet brought forth the fruits of their own iniquity, yet they have the seeds thereof inclosed within them; yea, their whole nature is a certain seed of sin, therefore it cannot be hateful and abominable to God . . .

Predestination we call the eternal decree of God, whereby he has determined with himself what he wills to become of every man. For all are not created to like estate; but to some eternal life and to some eternal damnation is foreordained. Therefore as every man is created to the one or the other end, so we say that he is predestinate either to life or to death.

From John Calvin, *Institutes of the Christian Religion.*

to Scotland and the Low Countries, where it became the basis for Dutch Protestantism, and east, where it flourished in Lithuania and Hungary. It reached places untouched by Luther and revitalized reform where Lutheranism had been suppressed. Perhaps its greatest impact was in Britain, where the Reformation took place not once but twice.

The English Reformation

The king of England wanted a divorce. Henry VIII had been married to Catherine of Aragon (1485–1536) as long as he had been king, and she had borne him no male heir to carry on his line. She had given birth to six children and endured several miscarriages, yet only one daughter, Mary, survived. Nothing so important as the lack of a male heir could happen by accident, and Henry came to believe that it was God's punishment for his marriage. Catherine had been married first to Henry's older brother, who had died as a teenager, and there was at least one scriptural prohibition against marrying a

brother's wife. A papal dispensation had been provided for the marriage, and now Henry wanted a papal dispensation for an annulment. For three years his case ground its way through the papal courts. Catherine of Aragon was the aunt of the Emperor Charles V, and the emperor had taken her side in the controversy. With imperial power in Italy at its height, the pope was content to hear all of the complex legal and biblical precedents argued at leisure.

By 1533 Henry could wait no longer. He had already impregnated Anne Boleyn (ca. 1507–36), one of the ladies-in-waiting at his court, and if the child—which Henry was certain would be a boy—was to be legitimate a marriage would have to take place at once. Legislation was prepared in Parliament to prevent papal interference in the decisions of England's courts, and Thomas Cranmer (1489–1556), archbishop of Canterbury, England's highest ecclesiastical officer, agreed to annul Henry's first marriage and celebrate his second. This was the first step in a complete break with Rome. Under the guidance of Thomas Cromwell (ca. 1485–1540), the

English Parliament passed statute after statute that made Henry supreme head of the church in England and owner of its vast wealth. Monasteries were dissolved, and a Lutheran service was introduced. On 7 September 1533, Anne Boleyn gave birth not to the expected son, but to a daughter, the future Queen Elizabeth I.

Henry's reformation was an act of state, but the English Reformation was not. There was an English tradition of dissent from the Roman church that stretched back to the fourteenth century. Anticlericalism was especially virulent in the towns, where citizens refused to pay fees to priests for performing services like burial. And humanist ideas flourished in England, where Thomas More, John Colet, and a host of others supported both the new learning and its efforts to reform spiritual life. Luther's attack on ritual and the mass and his emphasis on Scripture and faith echoed the lost Lollard program and found many recruits in London and the northern port towns.

Protestantism grew slowly in England because it was vigorously repressed. Like Francis I and Charles V, Henry VIII viewed actual attacks on the established church as potential attacks on the established state. The first published English translation of the New Testament, made by William Tyndale in 1525, had to be smuggled into England. As sensitivity to the abuses of the Church grew and Lutheran ideas spread, official persecution sharpened.

Henry's divorce unleashed a groundswell of support for religious change. The king's own religious beliefs remained a secret, but Anne Boleyn and Thomas Cromwell sponsored Lutheran reforms and Thomas Cranmer put them into practice. Religion was legislated through Parliament, and the valuable estates of the Church were sold to the gentry. These practices found favor with both the legal profession and the landed elites and made Protestantism more palatable among these conservative groups. It was in the reign of Edward VI (1547–53), Henry's son by his third wife, that the central doctrinal and devotional changes were made. Church service was now conducted in English and the first two English Prayer Books were created. The mass was reinterpreted along Zwinglian lines and became the Lord's Supper, the altar became the communion table, and the priest became the minister. Preaching became the center of the church service and concern over the education of learned ministers resulted in commissions to examine and reform the clergy.

Beginning in the 1530s, state repression turned against Catholics. Those who would not swear the new oaths of allegiance or recognize the legality of Henry VIII's marriage suffered for their beliefs. Thomas More and over forty others paid with their lives for their opposition. An uprising in the north in 1536, known as the Pilgrimage of Grace, posed the most serious threat to the English Crown since the Wars of the Roses. Henry's ability to suppress the Pilgrimage of Grace owed more

Henry VIII confers the royal succession on Edward VI,
his son by his third wife, Jane Seymour. The birth of
a male heir was seen as Henry's triumph over the pope,
who is seen lying defeated at Edward's feet.

to his political power than to the conversion of his governing classes to Protestantism. Catholicism continued to flourish in England, surviving underground during the reigns of Henry and Edward, and reemerging under Mary I (1553–58).

Mary Tudor was her mother's child. The first woman to rule England, she held to the Catholic beliefs in which Catherine of Aragon had raised her, and she vowed to bring the nation back to her mother's church. She reestablished papal sovereignty, abolished Protestant worship, and introduced a crash program of education in the universities to train a new generation of priests. The one thing that Mary could not achieve was restoration of monastic properties and Church lands. They had been scattered irretrievably and any attempt at confiscation from the landed elite would surely have been met with insurrection. Catholic retribution for the blood of their martyrs was not long in coming. Cranmer and three other bishops were burned for heresy.

Nearly 800 Protestants fled the country rather than suffer a similar fate. These Marian exiles, as they came to be called, settled in a number of reformed communities. There they imbibed the second generation of Protestant ideas, especially Calvinism, and from there they began a propaganda campaign to keep reformed religion alive in England. It was the Marian exiles who were chiefly responsible for the second English reformation, which began in 1558 when Mary died and her half-sister, Elizabeth I (1558–1603), came to the throne.

Under Elizabeth, England returned to Protestantism, but what was reestablished was not what had come before. Even the most advanced reforms during Edward's reign now seemed too moderate for the returning exiles. Against Elizabeth's wishes, the English church adopted the Calvinist doctrine of predestination and the simplification (but not wholesale reorganization) of the structure of the church. But it did not become a model of thoroughgoing reformation. The Thirty-nine Articles (1563) continued the English tradition of compromising points of disputed doctrine and of maintaining traditional practices wherever possible.

The Reformation of the Radicals

Schism breeds schism. That was the stick with which the Catholic church and civil authorities beat Luther from the beginning. By attacking the authority of the established church and flouting the authority of the established state he was fomenting social upheaval. But he insisted that his own ideas buttressed rather than subverted authority, especially civil authority under

whose protection he had placed the Church. As early as 1525 peasants in Swabia appealed to Luther for support in their social rebellion. They based some of their most controversial demands, such as the abolition of tithes and labor service, on biblical authority. Luther instructed the rebels to lay down their arms and await their just rewards in heaven. But Luther's ideas had a life of their own. He clashed with Erasmus over free will and with Zwingli over the mass. Toward the end of his life he felt he was holding back the floodgates against the second generation of Protestant thinkers. Time and again serious reformers wanted to take one or another of his doctrines further than he was willing to go himself. The water was seeping in everywhere.

The most dangerous threat to the establishment of an orthodox Protestantism came from groups who were described, not very precisely, as Anabaptists. Though it identified people who practiced adult baptism—literally "baptism again"—the label was mainly used to tar religious opponents with the brush of extremism. Anabaptists appeared in a number of German and Swiss towns in the 1520s. Taking seriously the doctrine of justification by faith, Anabaptists argued that only believers could be members of the true church of God. Those who were not of God could not be members of his church. As baptism was the sacrament through which entry into the church took place, Anabaptists reasoned that it was a sacrament for adults rather than infants. But infant baptism was a core doctrine for both Catholics and Protestants. It symbolized the acceptance of Christ and without it eternal salvation was impossible. Unbaptized infants who died could not be accepted in heaven, and infant mortality was appallingly common.

Thus the doctrine of Anabaptism posed a psychological as well as a doctrinal threat to the reformers. But the practice of adult baptism paled in significance to many of the other conclusions that religious radicals derived from the principle of *sola scriptura*—by the Word alone. Some groups argued the case that since true Christians were only those who had faith, all others must be cast out of the church. These true Christians formed small separate sects. Many believed that their lives were guided by the Holy Spirit who directed them from within. Some went further and denied the power of civil authority over true believers. Some argued for the community of goods among believers and rejected private property. Others literally followed passages in the Old Testament that suggested polygamy and promiscuity.

Wherever they settled, these small bands of believers were persecuted to the brutal extent of the laws of heresy. Catholics burned them, Protestants drowned them, and they were stoned and clubbed out of their communities. There was enough substance in their ideas and enough sincerity in their patient sufferings that they continued to recruit followers as they were driven from town to town, from Germany into the Swiss cities, from Switzerland into Bohemia and Hungary.

There on the eastern edges of the empire the largest groups of Anabaptists finally settled. Though all practiced adult baptism, only some held goods in common or remained pacifist. Charismatic leaders such as Balthasar Hubmaier (1485–1528) and Jacob Hutter (d. 1536) spread Anabaptism to Moravia in southern Bohemia, where they converted a number of the nobility to their views. They procured land for their communities, which came to be known as the Moravian Brethren. Independent groups existed in England and throughout northwest Europe, where Menno Simons (1496–1561), a Dutch Anabaptist, spent his life organizing bands of followers who came to be known as Mennonites.

The reformation begun by Luther was spread by different hands. The second-generation reformers, led by John Calvin, deepened theological and social changes. Calvin's emphasis upon predestination generated a vanguard of Protestant saints who believed it was their duty to govern on earth. They reordered church government and redefined moral discipline. Calvinism spread in Switzerland and France, but most importantly in England, where it was adopted as the foundation of the Elizabethan church. Though Calvinism was the most influential of the new forms of Protestantism, it was not the only one. Anabaptists could be found in a number of Swiss and German towns, and they were especially influential in Bohemia and Hungary. Together with the Lutherans, these groups and their churches constituted a potent new religious force in Europe.

The Catholic Reformation

Like a rolling wave Protestant reform slapped up across the face of Europe, but the rock of the Roman Catholic church endured. Though pieces of the universal church crumbled away, in northern Germany, Switzerland, Bohemia, Scandinavia, England, and Scotland, the dense mass remained in southern Germany, Italy, Poland-Lithuania, Spain, France, and Ireland. Catholics felt the same impulses toward a more fulfilling religious life as did Protestants and complained of the same abuses of clerical, state, and papal powers. But the Catholic re-

sponse was to reform the Church from within. A new personal piety was stressed, which led to the founding of additional spiritual orders. The ecclesiastical hierarchy became more concerned with pastoral care and initiated reforms of the clergy at the parish level. The challenge of converting other races, Asians and Native Americans especially, led to the formation of missionary orders and to a new emphasis on preaching and education. Protestantism itself revitalized Catholicism.

The Spiritual Revival

The quest for individual spiritual fulfillment dominated later medieval Roman Catholicism. Erasmus, Luther, and Zwingli were all influenced by a Catholic spiritual movement known as the New Piety. It was propagated in Germany by the Brethren of the Common Life, a lay organization that stressed the importance of personal meditation upon the life of Christ. *The Imitation of Christ* (1427), the central text of the New Piety, commonly attributed to Thomas à Kempis (1379–1471), was among the most influential works of the later Middle Ages. The Brethren taught that a Christian life should be lived according to Christ's dictates as expressed in the Sermon on the Mount. They instructed their pupils to lead a simple ascetic life with personal devotion at its core. These were the lessons that the young Erasmus found so liberating and the young Luther so stifling.

The New Piety, with its emphasis on a simple personal form of religious practice, was a central influence upon Christian humanism. It is important to realize that humanism developed within the context of Catholic education and that many churchmen embraced the new learning and supported educational reform or patronized works of humanist scholarship. The Polyglot Bible was organized by Cardinal Jiménez de Cisneros (1436–1517), Archbishop of Toledo and Primate of Spain. Without any of his famed irony, Erasmus dedicated his Greek Bible to the pope.

This combination of piety and humanism imbued the ecclesiastical reforms initiated by Church leaders. Archbishop Jiménez de Cisneros, who also served as Inquisitor-General of the Spanish Inquisition, undertook a wide-ranging reorganization of Spanish religious life in the late fifteenth century. Though not every project was successful, Jiménez de Cisneros's program took much of the sting out of Protestant attacks on clerical abuse, and there was never a serious Protestant movement in Spain.

The most influential reforming bishop was Gian Matteo Giberti (1495–1543) of Verona. Using his own frugal life as an example, Giberti rigorously enforced vows, residency, and the pastoral duties of the clergy. He founded almshouses to aid the poor and orphanages to house the homeless. In Verona Giberti established a printing press, which turned out editions of the central works of Roman Catholicism, especially the writings of Augustine.

The most important indication of the reforming spirit within the Roman church was the foundation of new religious orders in the early sixteenth century. Devotion to a spiritual life of sacrifice was the chief characteristic of the lay and clerical orders that had flourished throughout the Middle Ages. In one French diocese, the number of clergy quadrupled in the last half of the fifteenth century, and while entrants to the traditional orders of Franciscans and Dominicans did not rise as quickly, the growth of lay communities like the Brethren of the Common Life attested to the continuing appeal of Catholic devotionalism.

Devotionalism was particularly strong in Italy where a number of new orders received papal charters. The Capuchins were founded by the Italian peasant Matteo de Bascio (ca. 1495–1552). He sought to follow the strictest rule of the life of Saint Francis of Assisi, a path that even the so-called Observant Franciscans had found too arduous. In contrast, the Theatines were established by a group of well-to-do Italian priests who also wished to lead a more austere devotional existence than was to be found in the traditional orders. Like the Capuchins they accepted a life of extreme poverty, in which even begging was only a last resort.

This spiritual revival spread all over Catholic Europe and was not limited to male orders. In Spain, Saint Teresa of Avila (1515–82) led the reform of the Carmelites. She believed that women had to withdraw totally from the world around them in order to achieve true devotion. Against the wishes of the male superiors

FROM *THE LIFE OF SAINT TERESA*

■ *Teresa of Avila was a Carmelite nun whose life became a model of spirituality for Spanish Catholics in the seventeenth century. She founded a number of monasteries and convents and wrote popular devotional literature. Her autobiography was published after her death.*

My love of, and trust in, our Lord, after I had seen Him in a vision, began to grow, for my converse with Him was so continual. I saw that, though He was God, He was man also; that He is not surprised at the frailties of men; that He understands our miserable nature, liable to fall continually, because of the first sin, for the reparation of which He had come. I could speak to Him as a friend, though He is my Lord, because I do not consider Him as one of our earthly lords, who affect a power they do not possess, who give audience at fixed hours, and to whom only certain persons may speak. If a poor man have any business with these, it will cost him many goings and comings, and currying favour with others, together with much pain and labour before he can speak to them. Ah, if such a one has business with a king! Poor people, not of gentle blood, cannot approach him, for they must apply to those who are his friends; and certainly these are not persons who tread the world under their feet; for they who do this speak the truth, fear nothing, and ought to fear nothing; they are not courtiers, because it is not the custom of a court, where they must be silent about those things they dislike, must not even dare to think about them, lest they should fall into disgrace.

O my Lord! O my King! who can describe Thy Majesty? It is impossible not to see that Thou art Thyself the great Ruler of all, that the beholding of Thy Majesty fills men with awe. But I am filled with greater awe, O my Lord, when I consider Thy humility, and the love Thou hast for such as I am. We can converse and speak with Thee about everything whenever we will; and when we lose our first fear and awe at the vision of Thy Majesty, we have a greater dread of offending Thee—not arising out of the fear of punishment, O my Lord, for that is as nothing in comparison with the loss of Thee!

of her order she founded a convent to put her beliefs into practice and began writing devotional tracts like *The Way of Perfection* (1583). In 1535 Angela Merici (ca. 1474–1540) established another female order. The Ursulines were one of the most original of the new foundations, composed of young unmarried girls who remained with their families but lived chaste lives devoted to the instruction of other women.

Loyola's Pilgrimage

At first sight Saint Ignatius of Loyola (1491–1556) appears an unlikely candidate to lead one of the most vital movements for religious reform in the sixteenth century. The thirteenth child of a Spanish noble family, Loyola trained for a military life in the service of Castile. In 1521 he was one of the garrison defenders when the French besieged Pamplona. A cannonball shattered his leg, and he was carried home for a long enforced convalescence. There he slowly and carefully read the only books in the castle, a life of Christ and a history of the saints. His reading inspired him.

Loyola was not a man to do things halfway. He resolved to model his life on the sufferings of the saints about whom he had read. He renounced his worldly goods and endured a year-long regimen of physical abstinence and spiritual nourishment in the town of Manresa. He deprived himself of food and sleep for long periods and underwent a regimen of seven hours of daily prayer, supplemented by nearly continuous religious contemplation. "But when he went to bed great enlightenment, great spiritual consolations often came to him, so that he lost much of the time he had intended for sleeping." During this period of intense concentration he first began to have visions, which later culminated in a mystical experience in which Christ called him directly to his service.

Like Luther, Loyola was tormented by his inability to achieve grace through penance, but unlike Luther he redoubled his efforts. At Manresa Loyola encountered the *Imitation of Christ*, which profoundly influenced his conversion. He recorded the techniques he used during this vigil in *The Spiritual Exercises*, which became a handbook for Catholic devotion. In 1523, crippled and barefoot, he made a pilgrimage to Jerusalem. He returned to Spain intent upon becoming a priest.

By this time Loyola had taken on a distinctive appearance that attracted a following but also suspicion. Twice the Spanish ecclesiastical authorities summoned him to be examined for heresy. In 1528 he decided to complete his studies in France. Education in France

St. Teresa of Avila, the Carmelite reformer. The personal example and devotional works of this mystic and visionary inspired a rebirth of Catholicism in Spain.

brought with it a broadening of horizons that was so important in the movement that Loyola was to found. He entered the same college that Calvin had just left, but given his own devotional experiences, Protestantism held little attraction. While in France, Loyola and a small group of his friends decided to form a brotherhood after they became priests. They devoted themselves to the cure of souls and took personal vows of poverty, chastity, and obedience to the pope. On a pilgrimage to Rome, Loyola and his followers again attracted the attention of ecclesiastical authorities. Loyola explained his mission to them and in 1540 won the approval of Pope Paul III to establish a new holy order, the Society of Jesus.

Loyola's Society was founded at a time when the spiritual needs of the church were being extended beyond the confines of Europe. Loyola volunteered his followers, who came to be known as Jesuits, to serve in the remotest parts of the world. One disciple, Francis Xavier (1506–52), made converts to Catholicism in the Portuguese port cities in the East and then in India and Japan. Other Jesuits became missionaries to the New World, where they offered Christian consolation to the Native American communities. By 1556 the Society of Jesus had grown from ten to a thousand and Loyola had become a full-time administrator in Rome.

Loyola never abandoned the military images that had dominated his youth. He enlisted his followers in military terms. The Jesuits were "soldiers of God" who served "beneath the banner of the Cross." Loyola's most fundamental innovation in these years was the founding of schools to train recruits for his order. Jesuit training was rigorous. Since they were being prepared for an active rather than a contemplative life, Jesuits were not cloistered during their training. Jesuit schools were opened to the laity and lay education became one of the Jesuits' most important functions. Loyola lived to see the establishment of nearly a hundred colleges and seminaries and the spread of his order throughout the world. He died while at prayer.

The Counter-Reformation

The Jesuits were both the culmination of one wave of Catholic reform and the advance guard of another. They combined the piety and devotion that stretched from medieval mysticism through humanism, diocesan reforms, and the foundations of new spiritual orders. But they also represented an aggressive Catholic response that was determined to meet Protestantism head on and repel it. This was the Church militant. Old instruments like the Inquisition were revived, and new weapons like the Index of prohibited books were created. But the problems of fighting Protestantism were not only those of combating Protestant ideas. Like oil and water, politics and religion failed to combine. The Holy Roman Emperor Charles V and the hierarchy of the German church, where Protestantism was strong, demanded thoroughgoing reform of the Catholic church; the pope and the hierarchy of the Italian church, where Protestantism was weak, resisted the call. As head of the Catholic church, the pope was distressed by the spread of heresy in the lands of the empire. As head of a large Italian city-state the pope was consoled by the weakening of the power of his Spanish rival. Brothers in Christ, pope and emperor were mortal enemies in everything else. Throughout the Catholic states of Germany came the urgent cry for a reforming council of the Church. But the voices were muffled as they crossed the Alps and made their way down the Italian peninsula.

At the instigation of Charles V, the first serious preparations for a general council of the Church were made in the 1530s. The papacy warded it off. The complexities of international diplomacy were one factor—the French king was even less anxious to bring peace to the Holy Roman Empire than was the pope—and the complexities of papal politics were another. The powers of a general council in relation to the powers of the papacy had never been clarified. In fact, Catholic reformers were as bitter in their denunciations of papal abuses as were Protestants. The second attempt to arrange a general council of the Church occurred in the early 1540s. Again the papacy warded it off.

These factors ensured that when a general council of the Church did finally meet, its task would not be an easy one. The northern churches, French and German alike, wanted reforms of the papacy; the papacy wanted a restatement of orthodox doctrine. Many princes whose states were divided among Catholics and Protestants wanted compromises that might accommodate both. Ferdinand I, king of Bohemia, saw the council as an opportunity to bring the Hussites back into the fold. Charles V and the German bishops wanted the leading Protestant church authorities to offer their own compromises on doctrine that might form a basis for reuniting the empire. The papacy wanted traditional Church doctrine reasserted.

The general council of the Church that finally met in Trent from 1545 to 1563 thus had nearly unlimited potential for disaster. It began in compromise—Trent was an Italian town under the government of the emperor—

Spanish wood carving showing St. Ignatius Loyola, the founder of the Society of Jesus.

but ended in total victory for the views of the papacy. For all of the papacy's seeming weaknesses—the defections of England and the rich north German territories cut into papal revenues, and Italy was under Spanish occupation—an Italian pope always held the upper hand at the council. Fewer than one-third of the delegates came from outside Italy. The French looked upon the council suspiciously and played only a minor role, and the emperor forbade his bishops to attend after the council moved to Bologna.

Yet for all of these difficulties, the councillors at Trent made some real progress. They corrected a number of abuses, of which the sale of indulgences was the most substantive. They formulated rules for the better regulation of parish priests and stressed the obligation of priests and bishops to preach to their congregations. They ordered seminaries to be founded in all dioceses where there was not already a university so that priests could receive sufficient education to perform their duties. They prepared a new modern and uniform Catholic service and centralized and updated the Index of prohibited books to include Protestant writings from all over the Continent.

The Council of Trent made no concessions to Protestants, moderate or radical. The councillors upheld justification by faith and works over justification by faith alone. They confirmed the truth of Scripture and the traditions of the Church against Scripture alone. They declared the Vulgate the only acceptable text of the Bible and encouraged vast bonfires of Greek and Hebrew Scriptures in an effort to undo the great scholarly achievements of the humanists. They reaffirmed traditional Catholic doctrines. They upheld clerical celibacy. The redefinition of traditional Roman Catholicism drew the doctrinal lines clearly and ended decades of confusion. But it also meant that the differences between Catholics and Protestants could now be settled only by the sword.

The resolutions of the Council of Trent demonstrated the vitality and self-confidence of Roman Catholicism. The pietistic movements that had founded new spiritual orders for men and women, the zealotry that had inspired Ignatius of Loyola and his Jesuits—these could be seen in every Catholic nation. Protestantism had issued a challenge, and Catholicism had responded. Catholics, too, felt the need for spiritual regeneration, but they found its source not in breaking away from the universal church of Rome but by reforming from within. There could be no doubt that by the middle of the sixteenth century the Catholic church had a stronger hold on the hearts of its practitioners than it had had fifty years earlier.

The Council of Trent, painted by Titian in 1586. Despite interruptions and delays, the Council arrived at a definitive restatement of Catholic doctrine, even though it failed at the original goal of reconciliation with the Protestants.

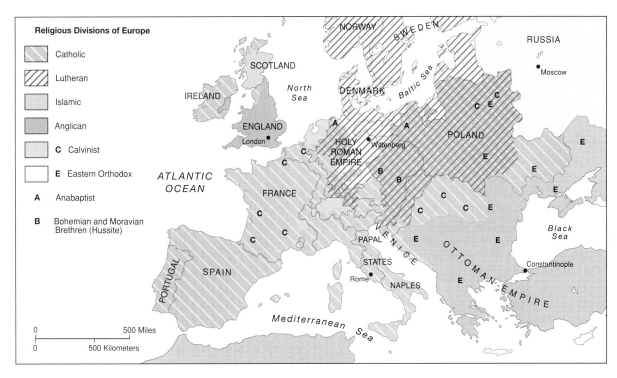

Religious Divisions of Europe, 1555

The Reformation and the Counter-Reformation

1517   Luther writes his Ninety-five Theses

1521   Luther is excommunicated and declared an enemy of the empire

1523   Zwingli expounds his faith in formal disputation

1533   Henry VIII divorces Catherine of Aragon, marries Anne Boleyn, and breaks with the church of Rome

1536   Calvin publishes *Institutes of the Christian Religion*

1540   Loyola receives papal approval for Society of Jesus

1545–63   Council of Trent

1553   Mary I restores Catholicism in England

1563   Elizabeth I enacts the Thirty-nine Articles, which restores Protestantism to England

The Empire Strikes Back

Warfare dominated the reform of religion almost from its beginning. The burnings, drownings, and executions by which both Catholics and Protestants attempted to maintain religious purity were but raindrops compared to the sea of blood that was shed in sieges and on battlefields beginning in the 1530s. The Catholic divisions were clear. The Holy Roman Emperor continued to be engaged in the west with his archenemy France, and in the south with the ever expanding Ottoman Empire. Charles V needed not only peace within his own German realms, but positive support for his offensive and defensive campaigns. He could never devote his full resources to suppressing Protestant dissent.

Yet there was never a united Protestant front to suppress. The north German towns and principalities that accepted Lutheranism in the 1520s had had a long history of warfare among themselves. Princes stored up grievances from past wars and contested inheritances, cities stored up jealousies from commercial rivalries and special privileges. Added to this was the division between Luther and Zwingli over doctrinal issues that effectively separated the German and Swiss components of the reformation from each other.

Though both the Protestant and the Catholic sides were internally weak, it was the greater responsibilities of Charles V that allowed for the uneasy periods of peace. Each pause gave the Protestant reformers new life. Lutheranism continued to spread in the northern part of the empire, Zwinglian reform in the south. Charles V asked the papacy to convoke a general council and the Protestants to stop evangelizing in new territories. But Protestant leaders were no more capable of halting the spread of the reformation than were Catholics. Thus each violation of each uneasy truce seemed to prove treachery. In 1546, just after Luther's death, both sides raised armies in preparation for renewed fighting. In the first stage of war Charles V scored a decisive victory, capturing the two leading Protestant princes and conquering Saxony and Thuringia, the homeland of Lutheran reform.

Charles V's greatest victories were always preludes to his gravest defeats. The remaining Protestant princes were driven into the arms of the French, who placed dynastic interests above religious concerns. Again Europe was plunged into general conflict, with the French invading the German states from the west, the Turks from the south, and the Protestant princes from the north. Charles V, now an old and broken man, was forced to flee through the Alps in the dead of winter and was brought to the bargaining table soon after. By the Peace of Augsburg in 1555 the emperor agreed to allow the princes of Germany to establish the religion of their people. The Peace of Augsburg ended forty years of religious struggle in Germany, but it settled nothing.

In 1547 the then-victorious Charles V stood at the grave of Martin Luther. He had been buried in the shadow of the church in which he had been baptized, and now other shadows darkened his plot. Imperial troops were masters of all Saxony and were preparing to turn back the religious clock in Luther's homeland. The emperor was advised to have the body exhumed and burned, to carry out twenty-five years too late the Edict of Worms that had made Luther an outlaw from church and state. But Charles V was no longer the self-confident young emperor who had been faced down by the Saxon monk on that long-ago day. Popes had come and gone, and his warrior rivals Francis I and Henry VIII were both dead. He alone survived. He had little stomach for the petty revenge that he might now exact upon the man who more than any other had ruined whatever hope there might have been for a united empire dominant over all of Europe. "I do not make war on dead men," Charles declared as he turned away from the reformer's grave. But the ghosts of Luther and Zwingli, of Calvin and Ignatius of Loyola were not so easily laid. For another century they would haunt a Europe that could do nothing else but make war on dead men.

Fishing for Souls, by Adriaen Van De Velde, 1614. This allegorical painting shows Protestants (on the left) and Catholics (on the right) vying for the souls of Christians. In the water, parties from both banks try to drag naked men and women into their boats. Overhead, uniting them all, shines the unheeded rainbow of God.

SUGGESTIONS FOR FURTHER READING

GENERAL READING

* G. R. Elton, ed., *The New Cambridge Modern History, Vol. II, The Reformation 1520–1559* (Cambridge: Cambridge University Press, 1958). A multi-authored study of the Protestant movement with sections on social and political life.

* Owen Chadwick, *The Reformation* (London: Penguin Books, 1972). An elegant and disarmingly simple history of religious change.

* Steven Ozment, *The Age of Reform 1250–1550* (New Haven, CT: Yale University Press, 1980). An important interpretation of an epoch of religious change.

* Evan Cameron, *The European Reformation* (Oxford: Oxford University Press, 1991). The most up-to-date survey of the Reformation period. Difficult but rewarding.

THE INTELLECTUAL REFORMATION

Lucien Febvre and Henri Martin, *The Coming of the Book* (Atlantic Highlands, NJ: Humanities Press, 1976). A study of the early history of bookmaking.

* E. Eisenstein, *The Printing Revolution in Early Modern Europe* (Cambridge: Cambridge University Press, 1983). An abridged edition of a larger work that examines the impact of printing upon European society.

R. W. Scribner, *For the Sake of Simple Folk* (Cambridge: Cambridge University Press, 1981). A study of the impact of the Reformation on common people. Especially good on the iconography of reform.

* Richard Marius, *Thomas More* (New York: Knopf, 1984). A recent reinterpretation of the complex personality of England's greatest humanist.

* Roland Bainton, *Erasmus of Christendom* (New York: Charles Scribner's Sons, 1969). Still the best starting point and the most compelling biography.

Richard L. DeMolen, *Erasmus* (New York: St. Martin's Press, 1974). Selections from Erasmus's writings.

THE LUTHERAN REFORMATION

* Francis Oakley, *The Western Church in the Later Middle Ages* (Ithaca, NY: Cornell University Press, 1979). A study of the spiritual and intellectual state of the Roman Catholic church on the eve of the Reformation.

* Hajo Holborn, *A History of Modern Germany, Vol. I, The Reformation* (New York: Knopf, 1964). A widely respected account in a multivolume history of Germany. Especially strong on politics.

* Roland Bainton, *Here I Stand* (New York: New American Library, 1968). The single most absorbing biography of Luther.

* John Dillenberger, *Martin Luther: Selections From His Writings* (New York: Doubleday, 1961). A comprehensive selection from Luther's vast writings.

* Eric Erikson, *Young Man Luther* (New York: Norton, 1958). A classic psychoanalytic study of Luther's personality.

* Heiko Oberman, *Luther, Man Between God and the Devil* (New York: Doubleday, 1992). English translation of one of the best German biographies of Luther. Sets Luther within the context of late medieval spirituality.

* Bernd Moeller, *Imperial Cities and the Reformation* (Durham, NC: The Labyrinth Press, 1982). A central work that defines the connection between Protestantism and urban reform.

R. Po-chia Hsia, ed., *The German People and the Reformation* (Ithaca, NY: Cornell University Press, 1988). A collection of essays exploring the social origins of the Reformation.

G. R. Potter, *Huldrych Zwingli* (New York: St. Martin's Press, 1977). A difficult but important study of the great Swiss reformer.

THE PROTESTANT REFORMATION

E. William Monter, *Calvin's Geneva* (London: John Wiley & Sons, 1967). A social and political history of the birthplace of Calvinism.

T. H. L. Parker, *John Calvin: A Biography* (Philadelphia: Westminster Press, 1975). The classic study.

William Bouwsma, *John Calvin* (Oxford: Oxford University Press, 1987). A study that places Calvin within the context of the social and intellectual movements of the sixteenth century.

* John Dillenberger, *John Calvin: Selections From His Writings* (New York: Doubleday, 1971). A comprehensive collection.

* J. J. Scarisbrick, *Henry VIII* (Berkeley: University of California Press, 1968). The classic biography of the larger-than-life monarch.

* A. G. Dickens, *The English Reformation* (New York: Schocken Books, 1964). An important interpretation of the underlying causes of the English Reformation.

* Rosemary O'Day, *The Debate on the English Reformation* (London: Methuen, 1986). A survey of conflicting views by eminent scholars.

George H. Williams, *The Radical Reformation* (Philadelphia: Westminster Press, 1962). A comprehensive synthesis of the first generation of radical Protestants.

Claus-Peter Clasen, *Anabaptism, A Social History 1525–1618* (Ithaca, NY: Cornell University Press, 1972). A study of the Anabaptist movement.

Steven Ozment, *Protestants: The Birth of a Revolution* (New York: Doubleday, 1992). An accessible study of the origins of Protestant beliefs and the impact of Protestant ideas among ordinary people.

THE CATHOLIC REFORMATION

Jean Delumeau, *Catholicism Between Luther and Voltaire* (Philadelphia: Westminster Press, 1977). A reinterpretation of the Counter-Reformation.

* John C. Olin, *The Autobiography of St. Ignatius Loyola* (New York: Harper & Row, 1974). The best introduction to the founder of the Jesuits.

* A. D. Wright, *The Counter-Reformation* (New York: St. Martin's Press, 1984). A comprehensive survey.

* A. G. Dickens, *The Counter Reformation* (London: Thames and Hudson, 1968). An excellent introduction, handsomely illustrated.

*Indicates paperback edition available

CHAPTER 14

World Encounters, 1350–1700

THE VIRGIN OF GUADALUPE

The Virgin of Guadalupe is perhaps the best known and the most important symbol of the Mexican nation. Her image reflects the complexity of the encounter between European and Indian cultures. Every year hundreds of thousands of people visit her shrine in Tepeyac just north of Mexico City. The most common version of the shrine's origin is that in 1531, barely a decade after the Spaniards had destroyed the Aztec capital of Tenochtitlán, the Virgin Mary appeared at Tepeyac to Juan Diego, a humble Indian, and spoke to him in his native language, Nahuatl. The Virgin ordered Juan Diego to tell the archbishop of Mexico that she desired a church to be built in her honor at Tepeyac. Of course, the Indian could not gain an audience with the great churchman. The Virgin then sent Juan Diego to gather roses in a place where only cactus grew, to put the roses in his cloak, and to present them to the archbishop. When the Indian unfolded his cloak, the image of the Virgin was stamped upon it. Acknowledging the miracle, the archbishop ordered the shrine built where Mary had appeared.

Over the following centuries the Virgin of Guadalupe was the subject of controversy, adoration, and manipulation. She came to illustrate much of the process and impact of colonial rule following the European encounters of the sixteenth century: the syncretization of folk religion and Catholicism; the flexibility of Spanish government; the conflicts within the Church over the plight of the Indian; the mestization, or mixture, of the native and European populations; and both the fierce and passive resistance of the Indians to the whites. The Virgin represented the "forging of the cosmic race," the Mexican people. It signified too the emergence of a sense of nationality among whites born in the New World. The Virgin became an important symbol of the new Mexican nation, and under her banner Father Miguel Hidalgo rallied the masses during the revolt for independence in 1810.

The site at Tepeyac exemplified the syncretic relation between native and Catholic religions, for it had previously been sacred to Tonantzin, the goddess of fertility. In the early years of the Christian shrine, the Indians may well have come to worship Tonantzin, and called out to her rather than to the Virgin Mary in their prayers. With the fusion of Indian and Spanish culture, the Virgin gradually integrated into the popular culture. The Virgin of Guadalupe may have served to restore the hope of salvation to the Indians, who had suffered in the conquest the death of all their old beliefs. The return of Tonantzin, through the Virgin of Guadalupe, rescued their gods.

The picture of the Virgin shown here from the seventeenth century is typical. She is usually represented standing on a crescent moon, surrounded by a crown of sunrays, which in turn is encompassed by clouds. She is clothed in a rich robe, ornamented with stars. Often a little cherub bears her on his head. The Virgin is dark-skinned.

Even before their encounters with the New World, the Virgin Mary, or Our Lady of the Immaculate Conception, was an important figure among Spaniards. One widely known version of her in Spain was the Virgin of Estremadura, which was coincidentally the birthplace of many of the *conquistadores*, or conquerors. Hernán Cortés's campaign banner carried a picture of Mary, who was a "symbol of Spanish power."

At first some clerics opposed the Virgin of Guadalupe cult. Their opposition ended, however, when during the first decades of the seventeenth century, the Virgin's intervention protected New Spain from desperate crises. Most notably, in 1629 displaying her image at the head of a procession protected Mexico City from inundation by floods. During the eighteenth century the Virgin became *patrona*, or patron saint, of New Spain.

The Guadalupe myth was important because it showed that Indians were capable of salvation; in other words, they could be Christians. This factor was crucial in the sixteenth-century debate over the humanity of the Indians. Some churchmen thought the Indian incapable of conversion and therefore rightfully exploited. Others maintained the Indians' humanity and resisted their oppression. For the Indian the most important aspect of the legend was that the Virgin appeared dark-skinned like an Indian. To rural Mexicans, the Virgin of Guadalupe was a "protectress" and an intermediary. In her were absorbed the ancient rites of agriculture. In the

harshness of Christianity as it was imposed on the Indians by crusading clerics, the Virgin Mary, depicted as "the approachable little woman," mediated, praying for them to the Father and the Son. She was a "modest house-wife," who as such eased the way to the acceptance of colonial authority. The Guadalupe myth also provided a place for the *mestizo* in the new order that emerged during the seventeenth century.

In one image, then, Indian, *mestizo*, and white were brought together. In their enthusiasm for her, they shunted aside class and racial differences. At a time when the Indians' world seemed destroyed by conquest and disease, when they were helpless and terrified, they gained comfort and hope in the Indian Virgin of Guadalupe. Later, when it was time to throw off the burden of Spanish colonial rule, Mexicans again called on the Virgin to unite and protect them.

Europe and the Encounters

In the history of the world, the fifteenth and sixteenth centuries were an age of encounters. Europeans, led by the Portuguese and the Spanish, set out to explore the world known to them in Africa and Asia and wound up discovering a world totally unknown to them—America. There were many reasons why this was the moment that Europeans would look beyond their own shores. Technological changes made long sea voyages possible, and the demands of commerce provided incentives. This was especially true in the trade for eastern spices, long dominated by Italian merchants but now gradually opening to traders along the Atlantic seaboard. Spices were rare and expensive, but they were not merely luxuries. Some acted as preservatives, others as flavorings

to make palatable the rotting foodstuffs that were the fare of even the wealthiest Europeans. Some spices were used as perfumes to battle the noxious gases that rose from urban streets and invaded homes and work-places. The drugs of the East, the nature of which we can only guess at, helped soothe chronic ill health. The demand for all of these "spices" continued to rise at a rate greater than their supply.

It was the Portuguese who made the first dramatic breakthroughs in exploration and colonization. In the early fifteenth century, they gained a foothold in northern Africa and used it to stage voyages along the continent's unexplored western coast. Like those of all explorers, the motives of the Portuguese were an unselfconscious mixture of faith and greed. Establishing bases there would enable them to surround their Muslim enemies while also giving them access to the

African bullion trade. The Portuguese navigator Bartolomeu Dias (ca. 1450–1500) summarized these goals succinctly: "To give light to those who are in darkness and to grow rich."

But those who were "in darkness" turned out to have rich cultures of their own. The cultures of the African peoples encountered by Dias and succeeding generations of Portuguese, Dutch, English, and French explorers and traders challenged many of the assumptions that Europeans made about non-Christians and initiated an encounter that transformed both European and African civilization. The Portuguese came to Africa seeking a passage to India and the gold that Africans were rumored to possess. Though they ultimately found both, they also found something that would prove more valuable still: slaves. At first, Europeans participated in the indigenous slave trade among the Africans, but soon they transformed it into an organized commercial activity that uprooted hundreds of thousands of black Africans to work plantations in the New World and on Atlantic and Indian Ocean islands.

While the Portuguese were the first Europeans to encounter African civilization, the Spaniards were the first to encounter the native populations of America. Queen Isabella of Castile was persuaded to take an interest in an expedition to the Indies led by a Genoese adventurer, Christopher Columbus (ca. 1446–1506). Like all well-informed people of his day, Columbus believed the world was round. By carefully calculating routes and distances, he concluded that a western track would be shorter and less expensive than the path the Portuguese were breaking around Africa. Because Columbus's conclusions were based on erroneous calculations, the land he reached on 12 October 1492 was not Japan, as he believed, but a hemisphere entirely unknown to Europeans.

Successive voyages by Columbus and others established that vast tracts of rich lands lay to the west of Europe. Indeed, in 1519 Ferdinand Magellan (ca. 1480–1521), a Portuguese mariner in the service of Spain, began a voyage that resulted in the circumnavigation of the globe. By then the globe had been divided between the Spanish and the Portuguese by the Treaty of Tordesillas (1494). The Portuguese were given the right to the eastern route to the Indies as well as to any undiscovered lands east of an imaginary Line of Demarcation fixed about 1,250 miles west of the Cape Verde Islands. This entitled Portugal to Brazil. The Spaniards received whatever lands lay west of the line.

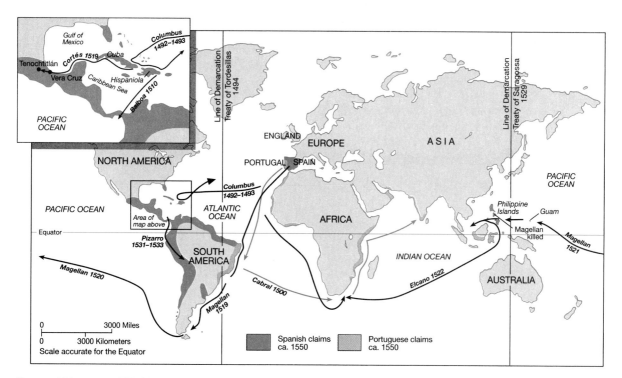

Voyages of Discovery and World Empires

CHRISTOPHER COLUMBUS, LETTER FROM THE FIRST VOYAGE, 1493

■ *Christopher Columbus seemingly needs no introduction. His name has forever been associated with the European discovery of the New World, although the meaning of that discovery has been continually contested. In the summer of 1492 Columbus sailed west from the Canary Islands, believing that he would reach the coast of China. Instead he landed on an island in the Caribbean. This passage from a letter addressed to the royal treasurer of Spain contains his first impressions of the people he encountered.*

A Letter addressed to the noble Lord Raphael Sanchez, Treasurer to their most invincible Majesties, Ferdinand and Isabella, King and Queen of Spain, by Christopher Columbus, to whom our age is greatly indebted, treating of the islands of India recently discovered beyond the Ganges, to explore which he had been sent eight months before under the auspices and at the expense of their said Majesties.

The inhabitants of both sexes in this island, and in all the others which I have seen, or of which I have received information, go always naked as they were born, with the exception of some of the women, who use the covering of a leaf, or small bough, or an apron of cotton which they prepare for that purpose. None of them are possessed of any iron, neither have they weapons, being unacquainted with, and indeed incompetent to use them, not from any deformity of body (for they are well-formed), but because they are timid and full of fear.

They carry however in lieu of arms, canes dried in the sun, on the ends of which they fix heads of dried wood sharpened to a point, and even these they dare not use habitually; for it has often occurred when I have sent two or three of my men to any of the villages to speak with the natives, that they have come out in a disorderly troop, and have fled in such haste at the approach of our men, that the fathers forsook their children and the children their fathers. This timidity did not arise from any loss or injury that they had received from us; for, on the contrary, I gave to all I approached whatever articles I had about me, such as cloth and many other things, taking nothing of theirs in return: but they are naturally timid and fearful. As soon however as they see that they are safe, and have laid aside all fear, they are very simple and honest, and exceedingly liberal with all they have; none of them refusing any thing he may possess when he is asked for it, but on the contrary inviting us to ask them. They exhibit great love towards all others in preference to themselves: they also give objects of great value for trifles, and content themselves with very little or nothing in return.

Such are the events which I have briefly described. Farewell.

Lisbon, the 14th of March. Christopher Columbus, *Admiral of the Fleet of the Ocean.*

West of the line lay the ancient cultures of the Americas. The Spanish encounters with the Native Americans—the peoples they dubbed "Indians"—were no less momentous than were those of the Portuguese in Africa. Among the Aztecs and the Incas the Spanish beheld unimaginable marvels, at once appealing and repulsive. But the Spaniards came as conquerors and brought with them deadly microbes that took the lives of millions of native peoples. European diseases proved far more potent than European weapons in destroying the mighty American empires.

Africa and the Encounters

At the beginning of the fifteenth century two of sub-Saharan Africa's three "coasts" had long been frontiers of change. For centuries, Muslim traders and preachers had crossed to the Sahel, the southern shore of the Sahara, using camels as their "ships of the desert." Their influence, both economic and religious, had penetrated southward from the Sahel into the West African forest zone. Similarly, trade and Islam, borne on the

This woodcut of Christopher Columbus landing on the island of Hispaniola accompanied the first illustrated edition of a letter that Columbus wrote about his first voyage. The ship is inaccurately depicted as a Mediterranean galley.

The Portuguese Pursuit of African Pepper and Gold

Changes in the economy of northern Europe that occurred at the end of the fourteenth century prompted Portugal's early leadership in European explorations along Africa's Atlantic coast. Through its exports of fish and sugar Portugal had had commercial connections with northern Europe for some time. But northern Europe's economic recovery from the Black Death after 1380 stimulated demands for other commodities that Portugal's rulers felt Portugal might also fill. Northern Europeans, for example, were raising more animals for meat. Lacking fodder to feed all of them through the winter, however, they had to slaughter many more animals in the autumn than they could consume immediately. To prevent the meat from spoiling, they needed tremendous quantities of preservatives. One commonly used preservative was malagueta pepper, known at the time as "Grains of Paradise" and obtained from West Africa through the trans-Saharan trade. Europe's reviving economy also demanded more and more gold, another commodity long supplied through the trans-Saharan trade.

Portugal's rulers therefore decided to attempt to sail along the Atlantic coast of Africa to reach the actual sources of the pepper and gold south of the Sahara. Perhaps, they thought, they might even establish direct links with the fabled trading center of Timubuktu by striking overland from the west coast of Africa, eastward along the Sahel zone. If they succeeded in establishing such a direct trade link, they would both eliminate the North African middlemen from the profitable trade and, as Christians, also strike a blow against Islam by undermining the prosperity of Muslim states. They knew that Portugal was well placed to attempt such a strategy. Most obviously, its location at the edge of Europe, facing outward toward the Atlantic, had given Portuguese fishermen ample experience with its currents and winds, making them among Europe's best mariners. At the start of the fifteenth century Portugal also had a centralized government at a time when most other parts of Europe were politically fragmented, and hence the state could be directly involved in explorations. Moreover, it was a small country with a serious lack of land to provide estates for a group of fairly well-educated younger sons of the nobility, who were thus forced to search for new ways to make their fortunes. Finally, through earlier investments in Portugal, Genoese bankers had established links with it that ensured that capital would be available for profitable overseas ventures.

Indian Ocean's predictable monsoon winds, had affected the East Coast of Africa and helped create its Swahili culture. But the Atlantic coast had remained almost wholly unaffected by outsiders and almost purely African. This situation was soon to change.

After centuries of political disunity, by 1400 a new Europe was stirring. As a consequence, led by the Portuguese, but with Spanish, English, Dutch, and French merchants close behind, Europeans began to visit Africa's Atlantic coast. These visits began a process of change that affected large areas of Africa. They also created new kinds of relationships with Africans living along the west coast that gradually came to be overshadowed by a single factor: the growing need of New World plantation owners for African slaves.

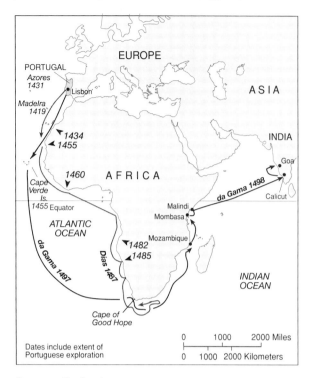

Portuguese Explorations

As a small country in Europe, Portugal's future seemed to require overseas expansion. In 1415 this expansion began with the seizure of Ceuta, a wealthy Moroccan city on the Mediterranean coast, as the Portuguese sought access to Moroccan grain, cloth, and Berber slaves.

But very real technical problems had to be solved if Portuguese mariners were to overcome the barriers that had prevented them from sailing south of Cape Bojador, on the coast of the western Sahara, into the "Ocean Sea," as the Atlantic was then called. Northeast trade winds that blow in the same direction throughout the year dominate the ocean to the south of Cape Bojador. The Canary Current is strong and constant, and it flows in roughly the same direction as the winds. This meant that, while a vessel found it easy to sail south as it was pushed along by both currents and winds, it was almost impossible to sail back to Europe against these forces. Theoretically, mariners could sail into an adverse wind by tacking back and forth, but doing this was exceedingly difficult when they were opposed by a strong current as well.

Prince Henry, known as "the Navigator" (1394–1460), brother of the king of Portugal, was the person who sought to discover the solution to this technical problem and thereby open the way for serious Portuguese expansion. Henry's interests were many. He was

administrator of the Order of Christ, a religious order dedicated to anti-Muslim crusades, and he continued to make war on Morocco. He possessed plantations and other lands. He was closely linked to Portuguese trading interests and invested much of his and his order's money in overseas trading ventures. And every year after 1419 Prince Henry sponsored one or two expeditions to explore how to sail beyond Cape Bojador and return safely. The crucially important knowledge of tides, currents, and wind patterns he accumulated encouraged Henry to establish a formal center for his work on the south coast of Portugal in 1433. In 1434, Gil Eanes, a Portuguese sailor, ventured south past Cape Bojador and then, using the new understanding of the Atlantic's wind patterns, sailed westward into the Atlantic to return home, discovering the islands of Madeira on the way.

Eanes's discoveries encouraged the Portuguese to combine elements of navigational technology from around the world into a new synthesis. From the Arabs they learned about the compass and the lateen sail, a type of sail shaped so as to create a vacuum on its leeward side, effectively causing the vessel to be pulled along even when sailing very close to the wind. From northern Europe they took the single-piece keel and other elements of hull construction, changes that allowed the building of smaller shallow-draft boats known as caravels that were well suited to move into dangerous uncharted waters. These adaptations created almost limitless possibilities for exploration. And so, after 1433, the Portuguese, followed closely by Castilians from Spain, sailed farther and farther down the west coast of Africa, making steady progress toward their ultimate goal of gaining direct access to gold and pepper and other exotic products such as ivory. In the process they gathered additional valuable information about the lands and peoples they encountered.

Prince Henry died in 1460. But the decade after his death witnessed continuing Portuguese explorations along Africa's Guinea coasts, with the most promising discoveries coming at decade's end. In 1469, Portuguese navigators passed the bulge of West Africa and coasted southeastward to what later came to be known as the Ivory, Gold, and Slave Coasts. In 1471, the Portuguese discovered in the Gulf of Guinea two islands with rich volcanic soils, São Tomé and Principe. The warm and wet regions of the Guinea coasts had many more people living in them than did the desert coasts the Portuguese had encountered north of the Senegal River. The area's people produced pepper and hunted for ivory. But best of all, the people of the Gold Coast, known today as

Ghana, produced gold. At last, the Portuguese had reached a major source of the ancient trans-Saharan gold trade. In 1482 they built the fortress of São Jorge da Mina—Elmina—as a base for their trade there.

Sugar and the Rise of Plantation Slavery

In 1443, in the process of their trading explorations, the Portuguese had added a new commodity to their shopping list. Sailing one of the new lateen-rigged caravels, Nuno Tristão landed on Arguin, an island off the north coast of Mauritania, and, extending Portuguese practices in Morocco, he purchased some African slaves in the course of his trading. He sold them in Portugal. In 1444 six vessels set sail from Portugal specifically seeking slaves to be taken home as well as other items. So great were the profits of the new trade for human cargo that in 1445 no fewer that twenty-six ships participated in it as part of their larger trading enterprise. To dispel any doubts about its propriety, in 1452 Pope Nicholas V promulgated a bull, *Dum Diversas*, sanctioning the enslavement of pagans and infidels. While the slaves traded in the years before 1500 were of distinctly secondary importance in the context of the overall trade, numbering only about 1,800 to 2,000 annually, and while gold remained the primary interest for the Portuguese, the establishment of the new trade in slaves nonetheless inaugurated an activity that was to characterize for centuries European activities on Africa's Atlantic coast.

That there were slaves available for the Portuguese to purchase was hardly surprising. Virtually every precapitalist society in human history has used slaves to perform arduous work for little cost. Those in Africa were no different. Significantly, a slave was defined as a person without relatives to protect him or her and, after being acquired, a slave was usually viewed as being in the process of being incorporated into the acquiring family as a subordinate relative. There were three basic categories of people who could find themselves "without relatives" and hence slaves. First, there were those given by one family to another as a way of redressing an injury. For example, if a man killed another man in a hunting accident, the dead man's family could be placated by the killer's family ceding a woman or young girl to the family of the dead man to compensate for his loss. Rather quickly, this slave would become a member of the new family, probably with a new name to signal her new social identity.

Second, families could sever ties of protection for criminals and other social misfits and then sell them into slavery. Disinheritance and the resulting status of slavery were mechanisms to punish serious criminal offenses or blatantly antisocial behavior in societies generally lacking prisons. Finally, and of special importance in the large states that were in time to become the main sources for the full-blown Atlantic slave trade, slaves were produced by warfare when enemies were captured. Such war captives might be treated badly and forced to do only menial work at first, but, if sold to a family, even they might be absorbed gradually into it. In short, considering the shortage of labor power in precapitalist Africa, it was quite natural that slavery was a social institution and that there were many ways of becoming a slave.

When the Portuguese appeared on the West African coast, therefore, they found Africans who were already slaves and who were available for purchase. But the destiny of those unfortunates was different from that which most slaves had experienced within Africa. In Africa there was a tendency to absorb slaves into the families that acquired them, but no such destiny awaited slaves purchased by the Portuguese and other European traders. For the most part, they became chattel slaves, who remained without kin and who were destined to labor long and hard on the plantations that were being developed in the Atlantic basin. The increase in the slave trade from West Africa and the development of the plantation as a system of production were linked inextricably. And it was sugar production that underlay both.

Sugar had had a long history. It was in India, around 500 C.E., that the discovery of a process for turning sugarcane juice into granulated sugar had made sugar

The Portuguese fortress of São Jorge da Mina was built with labor and materials imported from Portugal.

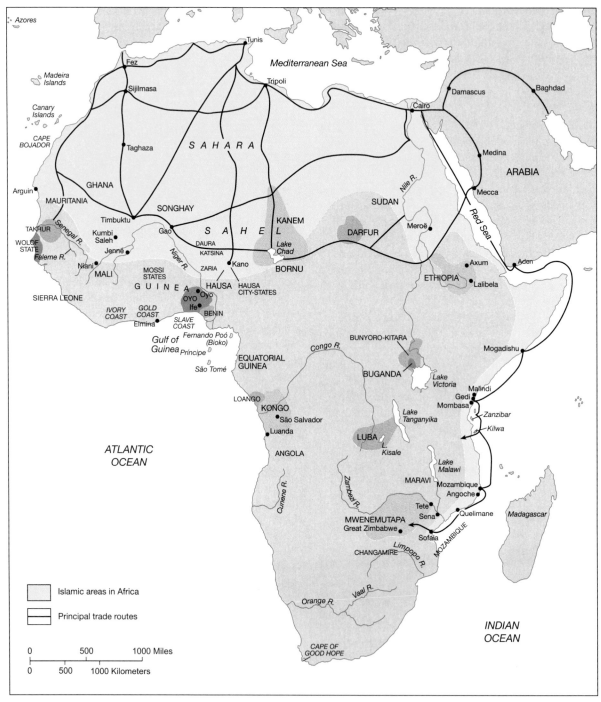

Africa, ca. 1400–1600

commercially important, for it could be stored indefinitely and traded over long distances. A luxury item valued widely for its many uses—medicinal, preservative, decorative, and as a sweetener—sugar was also highly profitable. Because all stages of its cultivation, harvesting, and processing required large numbers of highly disciplined workers, it was a crop ideal for production by slaves.

When the Crusaders from western Europe occupied Palestine in the eleventh century, they operated

Gender and Culture

VESPUCCI "DISCOVERING" AMERICA

Figure 1

The European encounter with the cultures of the western hemisphere posed a problem for visual artists. Prior to the voyages of discovery, the peoples of the world were represented according to Ovid's scheme of the *triplex mundus* or triple world, including Asia, Europe, and Africa. However, by the sixteenth century, the concept of a four or even five part world emerged, requiring a new and expanded symbolic mode. The allegory of the four continents first appeared in Abraham Ortelius's *Theatrum Orbis Terrarum*, published in Antwerp in 1570. Using the classical form of personification, a female figure bearing appropriate attributes signified a geographic location, and a new symbolic entity—America—was forged. The iconography confirmed fears about the strange new world, and long after Europe gained familiarity with the cultures of the indigenous peoples of America and elsewhere, the language of the arts retained the fantastic forms invented to describe the earliest encounters.

In the first depictions of new world allegories, "civilized" Europe contrasted with "savage" America. Theodor Galle's engraving *Vespucci "Discovering" America* (late sixteenth century, after a painting by Jan van der Street; Figure 1), seen on the preceding page, portrays the cartographer as a man of breeding, position, and science. He is stylishly dressed, and he holds the banner of the Southern Cross and an astrolabe. America, a massive woman, dressed in a scant feathered skirt and crowned with a feathered cap, springs from her hammock to greet him. Her domain is exotic and frightening. Odd animals, only the tapir and sloth can be identified, lurk in the lush foliage of her jungle home. In the distance, native people prepare a human leg on a spit. Cannibalism remained a persistent theme in the allegory; well into the seventeenth and eighteenth centuries, figures of America presided over grisly feasts, holding a severed head as an attribute.

The elegant interpretation of *America* by Giovanni Battista Tiepolo (1753, Italy; Figure 2) seems far removed from Galle's naive engraving. Painted in the stairwell of the Wurzburg Residenz of Prince-Bishop Carl Phillip von Greiffenklau, Tiepolo's handsome personification commands a procession of exotic people and extraordinary goods. She is presented with similar images of Africa and Asia, all bringing the wealth of their lands to Europe. Her trappings are magnificent. Decked in gold and multicolored feathers, she rides on the back of an alligator. Her tributes include powerful stags, bundles of brazil wood, and a cornucopia of ripe fruit. However, her savage heritage is not forgotten. Inconspicuously placed on

Figure 2

THE INDIAN WIDOW

Figure 3

the ground to the right of her retinue is a pile of severed heads, gruesomely pierced with arrows.

In the course of the eighteenth century, knowledge of the culture of the Americas increased. But, other inventions colored new world imagery. Rousseau's vision of the "Noble Savage," coupled with rising ethnographic interest about the beliefs and habits of the native Americans, informed a new ideal: the heroic Indian. Stories that proved the valor and nobility of the indigenous people provided the subjects for romantic painting. These works were a curious hybrid. Although often inspired by authentic lore, the artistic interpretation presented European values as Native American instinct. *The Indian Widow* by Joseph Wright of Derby (1783–85, England; Figure 3) praises the stoicism of indigenous women. According to tradition, on the first full moon after a chief is slain, his wife displays his war trophies and commemorates the day in silent reflection. Wright of Derby places the hero's widow in a potentially dangerous setting. Ominous clouds darken the sky, lightening crackles near the shore, and in the distance, smoke pours from an erupting volcano. Her quiet

BEAUTY ON A PALACE TERRACE

Figure 4

vigil becomes an act of bravery; she will fulfill her duties to her slain husband even at the risk of her own life.

Europe was not alone in projecting their ideas on other cultures. Asians and Americans similarly recorded the strange appearance and bizarre habits of the new people they encountered. A Moghul painting, *Beauty on a Palace Terrace* (late seventeenth century, Indian; Figure 4), depicts three European visitors, two women and a man, attended by an Indian serving girl. Their origins are distinguished by position and clothing rather than by facial features. But the daring necklines of the women's dresses, otherwise cut in a European fashion, are pure fantasy. Such decolletage would never be acceptable in Europe.

hundreds of sugar plantations using both free wage and slave labor. After the fall of their small Crusader kingdoms in the late twelfth century, Europeans moved sugar production onto Mediterranean islands such as Cyprus, again using a mixture of free and slave labor. It then moved steadily westward from island to island, often financed by Genoese bankers, until it finally reached Spain and Portugal. Sugar was, however, a crop that demanded special types of soils, which it quickly exhausted, as well as ample water. It was also a commodity that seemed to have an unlimited market in Europe. Therefore, while they continued their search for African gold, the Portuguese and their Castilian competitors also eagerly established new sugar plantations on the Atlantic islands of Madeira, which Portugal had claimed, and the Canaries, claimed by Castile. It was for these new sugar plantations that many African slaves were purchased, firming the link between plantation slavery and sugar production.

Clearly, the best sites for the Portuguese to obtain slaves were also best for them to trade for the other things they sought, places where African leaders had established states that could mobilize the labor needed for producing not only gold and ivory but also numbers of war captives. One should remember that the Portuguese were primarily traders in sub-Saharan Africa, not colonial settlers, and that they did not initially seek to obtain large pieces of territory. But they did need African partners to deliver the goods they wanted and to provide them with security while they were in the area. Quite naturally, therefore, they found it easiest to trade with powerful figures in large states. As a French visitor to the Lower Guinea coast reported, all aspects of the local slave trade were "the businesses of kings, rich men, and prime merchants exclusive of the lower sorts of blacks." Where powerful African states did not exist, trade could still be carried out, but only with greater difficulty and risk.

As they moved down the West African coast, the Portuguese found that the leaders of the peoples of the Lower Guinea coast were especially eager to deal with them. Not only did the Portuguese bring items from Europe that the rulers valued, such as hardware, alcohol, and cloth, but with their superior maritime skills, the Portuguese could also provide a useful service to the African elite by carrying a complex regional coastal trade on their caravels. Thus, for example, kola nuts were purchased for cloth and alcohol at Sierra Leone and then exchanged for slaves at the mouth of the Gambia River. Or, as the leaders of the Gold Coast sought labor to mine their gold, they became the annual purchasers of about

500 slaves whom the Portuguese obtained from the rulers of the states of Oyo and Benin, farther east, and whom they then exchanged for gold at the Portuguese trading post at Elmina.

In the process of their explorations and trading, the Portuguese also transplanted plantation agriculture to São Tomé. This occurred at the start of sixteenth century. Using African slaves obtained from nearby coastal areas of Africa, São Tomé became the world's largest single producer of sugar by the 1510s and 1520s. The combination of rich volcanic soils, disciplined slave labor, and the technological superiority of Portuguese transportation meant that sugar produced at this isolated outpost of empire could be delivered profitably to Lisbon and Genoa despite the long distance it had to be shipped.

Portuguese Success and Failure in the Indian Ocean Basin

Portugal's commercial successes along Africa's Guinea coasts inspired King John II (1455–95), the spiritual descendant of Henry the Navigator, to press on along the West African coast in search of yet greater successes. After a war between Portugal and Castile (1475–79) over the succession to the throne of Castile, the peace treaty recognized the Canary Islands as Castilian in exchange for the recognition of all African continental territory south of Cape Bojador as being within Portugal's commercial sphere. In the 1480s the Portuguese pressed onward to take advantage of this agreement. But by the 1480s it was really Asia, not Africa, that lay at the core of royal dreams. West Africa had been rewarding, but its trade was limited to a few commodities, and the amount of gold the Portuguese could obtain annually was stalled between 13,000 and 14,000 ounces. With the European economy improving steadily, Europeans more and more wanted to reach the fabulous riches of Asia directly, by sea, thereby eliminating middlemen located in eastern Europe and western Asia. In the context of the debate at the time over how best to reach Asia, John firmly believed the best route to Asia lay southward along the coast of Africa and was determined that his own fleets would pioneer it.

As part of this quest, in 1482, the explorer Diogo Cão arrived at the mouth of the Congo River and, somewhat surprisingly, was warmly welcomed by the leaders of the Kongo state, many of whom converted to Catholicism and asked for a Portuguese presence in their country.

THE NATURE OF THE PORTUGUESE PRESENCE IN WEST AFRICA: ELMINA, 1523

■ *King John III of Portugal well understood that Portugal was on the Guinea Coast to trade. The factory at Elmina, to which much West African gold gravitated, was crucially important for Portugal's success. By 1523 it had become a little city-state, with many local Africans having abandoned their earlier ties of loyalty and now living as Christian clients of the Portuguese governor. The governor had, however, expelled some people as punishment for alleged crimes. The king knew that successful trading required a contented population and peaceful conditions. In this letter he writes to the governor of Elmina admonishing him that his policy of harsh punishments is undermining the Portuguese's very purpose in being there to trade for gold.*

We have been informed that you are treating the knights of our village of Mina there harshly, in such a manner that the village is depopulated and men are going away to other parts; and we regard it as a matter very prejudicial to our interest and primarily to the welfare of that city and its trade. Since they are Christians and have received the water of baptism, they must be defended, protected and instructed, and not banished; and this also, since they are our vassals, and live there in obedience to us, serving in our name everything ordered them for our service, and with their people and their canoes conveying to the chiefs the wood for all our ships, and, furthermore, since many of them buy on a large scale in that factory, and all generally make purchases of old linen, which is bought by them and sold in their markets. Moreover, we are told that there are rich men among them, and that slaves may be had from them, and all of them are at our command, or may be, should they be treated well and protected with that moderation in punishment and also in instruction, which is meet and proper for our service and their security; then men tell us that for all their services, they neither have, nor expect, from us any other reward than we should protect them and command them to be maintained in justice. For this reason, it seems to us that you should not take it for granted that our interest would be promoted by your expelling them abroad. We command you, therefore, to treat them better and to dispense with banishments, otherwise, besides losing them and the service which we receive from them, the merchants will not come with similar new things [to trade].

From King John III to Affonso de Albuquerque, Governor of São Jorge da Mina, 13 October 1523.

(See Special Feature, "The Ambiguity of First Encounters: The Portuguese and the Kongo," pp. 418–419.) The Portuguese pressed onward, and in 1488 Bartholomeu Dias set sail from Portugal under orders to sail to the end of Africa to see if he could reach the Indian Ocean. Dias's ship was overtaken by a storm and blown far to the southwest. When the storm abated, Dias sailed eastward, expecting to strike the African coast. Without realizing it, he sailed past Africa into the Indian Ocean. At this point, however, his men mutinied and forced him to return to Portugal. As he sailed for home, he glimpsed the tip of South Africa and called it the Cape of Storms. When King John heard his story, the king aptly decided to rename it the Cape of Good Hope, for he saw it as a hopeful sign of future Portuguese successes in the Indian Ocean.

In 1492 Christopher Columbus, seeking Asia, discovered the New World of the Americas instead. In 1497, John's successor, King Manuel I (1495–1521), sent out the explorer Vasco da Gama (ca. 1460–1524) with four ships to enter the Indian Ocean and trade there. Engaging a Swahili pilot to guide him, da Gama succeeded in his venture, opening the Indian Ocean to Europeans for the first time. The Indian Ocean presented a far different situation from that which the Portuguese had been encountering for decades on the uncharted Atlantic coast of Africa. Romans, Persians, Arabs, Chinese, and others had sailed it for centuries and its sea-lanes were well mapped. Silks and spices, gold and jewels, ivory and slaves—all were available, and their presence seemed to testify to the wisdom of the Portuguese state's persisting with their explorations along the West

African coast. When Da Gama's ships returned home in 1499, the king was delighted, and he determined to use Portugal's naval power to try to dominate the Indian Ocean by force.

In the 1480s, after Spain had recognized Portugal's trading monopoly on the West Coast, Portugal became far more aggressive as they explored and traded. The king, for example, decreed that any non-Portuguese traders encountered along the coast were to be thrown into the ocean. When Vasco da Gama sailed into the Indian Ocean, he brought with him this new royal vision of a total Portuguese monopoly over important aspects of trade. In pursuit of this goal, he traumatically disrupted the region's flourishing trade, which was highly vulnerable to the superior Portuguese naval armaments. Portugal moved quickly to dominate the region's commercial life, trying to turn the trade in some items, such as pepper, ginger, cinnamon, and silk, into royal monopolies and charging merchants dealing in other commodities protection money. In 1505 the Portuguese captured the valuable flow of gold out of Zimbabwe from Swahili traders by seizing both the port of Sofala and the pivot of the gold trade, the city of Kilwa. In 1507, they constructed a fortress on Mozambique Island as their trading post in the area. In the following years the Portuguese continued their conquests and after defeating Muslim naval forces at the battle of Diu, off the coast of India, in 1509, the Portuguese ruled the seas, gradually adding to their list of fortified trading posts such places as Goa, in India (1510); Malacca, in Malaysia (1511); Hormuz, at the mouth of the Persian Gulf (1517); Macao, in China (1557); and Mombasa, in East Africa (1594).

But despite its striking naval successes, rather surprisingly the Portuguese state's share in the trade soon stagnated. This stagnation occurred for several reasons. First, its monopolies over the most lucrative trade items discouraged investments from private enterprises in Portugal because they could not legally trade in the commodities most likely to enrich them. Many individual Portuguese evaded the state's control by participating in a complex web of private deals that did the state little good. A second reason was fiscal. The Portuguese had few desirable manufactured goods to offer the sophisticated peoples of Asia in exchange for the commodities they sought. Forced, therefore, to purchase Asian products with gold and silver, Portugal soon found itself drained by a troubling balance of payments deficit to Asia. Finally, the Portuguese were never wholly unchallenged in their attempts to dominate the Indian Ocean. Their navies

had failed to take Aden, in southern Arabia, and this failure gave their Muslim rivals a base from which to attack Portuguese shipping in the Indian Ocean. The Portuguese usually responded effectively to such attacks, but their responses were costly and badly taxed their resources.

In short, while impressive for their rapid establishment, the series of trading posts that the Portuguese state established in the Indian Ocean was equally striking for their failure to transform or create much of anything new or enduring in the region. As a consequence of the growing problems in the middle of the sixteenth century, Portuguese leaders began to think of fresh and perhaps more satisfactory venues for their energies. Their thoughts turned to the New World.

Growing Links Between Africa and the New World

In 1494, soon after Columbus's first voyage, Spain and Portugal negotiated the Treaty of Tordesillas, formally dividing the world between themselves in order to forestall conflict. On one of Portugal's voyages of exploration, in 1500, Pedro Alvares Cabral (ca. 1468–1520) sailed out into the Atlantic far to the west and landed in Brazil. When he consulted his instruments, he discovered that this surprising piece of the New World was east of the line of division and hence belonged to Portugal. Aside from gathering some dyewoods there, however, the Portuguese largely ignored their new possession. Only in 1549 did the crown finally take direct control over some of Brazil's coastal areas and begin to send thousands of Portuguese settlers, government officials, and missionaries to occupy them.

The discovery that sugar grew extremely well in Brazil and that it could be the base of a prosperous economy motivated this change of policy. Gradually, a sugar industry was built up with Native Americans used as slave labor. But its major expansion occurred in the 1570s when an increase in Dutch investment and a decline in slave prices in Africa allowed large numbers of African slaves to be imported from across the Atlantic on the dreaded "Middle Passage." The new Brazilian sugar industry soon undercut the already established Spanish sugar industry on the island of Hispaniola as well as the older Portuguese industries on Madeira and São Tomé.

The success of Brazilian sugar affected West Africa greatly by demonstrating once again how profitable a plantation system based on highly disciplined slave labor could be. The specific parts of Africa to which the

An engraving of São Salvador (1686), illustrates an idealization of the capital of the Kingdom of Kongo.

The Ambiguity of First Encounters: The Portuguese and the Kongo

It is commonly believed that Europeans, with their superior military technology, have always been able to dominate Africans. Yet, in fact, before the late nineteenth century African leaders were generally able to act independently, in what they saw as their own best interests, when dealing with Europeans. It is in the revealing ambiguities embedded in such African dealings with Europeans that one can discover the contradictory self-interest and flawed humanity of all participants. None is more interesting than the Kongo welcome of the Portuguese between 1483 and 1543.

When the explorer Diogo Cão arrived at the mouth of the Congo River in 1482, he expected a cool reception similar to those his countrymen had earlier received from West African leaders farther north. But this was not the case. Instead, the Kongo king welcomed the Portuguese with startling enthusiasm. Over the next several decades, Kongo leaders converted to Roman Catholicism, took Christian names, made Catholi-cism a state religion, renamed their capital São Salvador, enthusiastically embraced reading and writing, gave rich gifts to the Portuguese, and clamored for westernization. One Kongo prince became a Catholic bishop.

Why? Some have suggested that the Kongo were overawed by the Portuguese and the magic of their technology. This answer is unconvincing for it ignores African motivation. Other African leaders encountered Europeans without acting as the Kongo did. Why were the Kongo different? The explanation lies in the nature of Kongo politics when Cão appeared on the scene.

The people of Kongo were typical of other African peoples. Although sharing a common culture, they had long been fragmented geographically and politically, with the local extended family being the main social unit. But, as among other peoples, a family's head, if powerful enough, was known as a "big man" because of his links of clientage with people not actually of his family. One such big man, who was situated at the crossroads of two important trade routes, had been able to levy tolls on the trade in cloth, salt, and copper, build up his power, and extend his authority over neighboring areas and fellow big men. Finally, he had assumed the title of *maniKongo* and become the "king" of all the Kongo.

Yet his position was not a dictator's, for he ruled within a complex system of checks and balances. His own family appointed influential counselors to advise him. The state's bureaucracy often acted independently. Religious leaders were prepared to oppose him. Groups on the fringe of the state sought opportunities to resist him or even secede from his control. In short, when Diogo Cão dropped anchor, the *maniKongo* was searching for allies, which would grant him greater independence, legitimacy, and freedom of action. When the Portuguese said that they wanted to be his friends, the *maniKongo* accepted them as allies who could supply him with European weapons. When Catholic missionaries arrived, the *maniKongo* also made them his allies, believing that they would give him a source of independent religious legitimacy he currently lacked.

The *maniKongo's* initial dependence on Portuguese support continued. When the *maniKongo* died in 1506, one of his sons,

Afonso, was ambitious to succeed him. According to Kongo custom, however, the kingship should have gone to a nephew. Convinced that European primogeniture was appropriate, the Portuguese supported Afonos, an old friend and ardent Catholic, and he was able to usurp the throne after a "miracle" enabled his army to defeat his rival's force and execute the rightful heir. Afonso rewarded the Portuguese by giving them access to the copper, ivory, cloth, and slaves that they sought.

Did the *maniKongo's* policies work? To the extent that the Portuguese strengthened his position, they clearly did. When Afonso died in 1543, the central government was still going strong and the economy was thriving.

Yet once established in Kongo territory, the Portuguese proved difficult to control. This was because they split into various factions, each with its own aims and strategies. Many of these Portuguese sought to expand slave trading for their own private benefit. Seeking slaves for sugar production on São Tomé, however the Portuguese crown tried to win Afonso's favor by sending him presents in 1508 and 1512. In response, he yielded to the crown a monopoly in buying war captives as slaves. The other Portuguese were outraged, for they wanted to participate in the lucrative trade, and they successfully pressured the crown to abandon its monopoly. All Portuguese in Kongo were then granted the right to trade for

slaves. But there were not enough war captives to supply the demand, and the Portuguese sought slaves wherever they could, trading arms to anyone who could provide them, legally or not, and ignoring Afonso and his interests. This situation endangered the *maniKongo's* position in two ways. First, ambitious local big men acquired arms from the Portuguese and, once they had established their own private armies, they pursued their own political goals. Second, the illegal enslavement of Kongo citizens led to popular discontent with Afonso's government for its inability to guarantee public safety. Ironically, then, only with the support he obtained from the Portuguese did he survive the problems precipitated by the Portuguese. In time, during the 1530s, the focus of the slave trade moved inland beyond the state's borders. This eased the pressures on the Kongo state and even permitted Afonso to increase his income by levying tolls on the new slave trade to the coast.

Clearly, the nature of the Kongo reception of the Portuguese can be explained only in terms of Kongo politics. But, as with most political initiatives, it was filled with ambiguities. The Portuguese shored up the *maniKongo* by supplying guns and bringing Catholicism. But they also brought the growing international slave trade, and, with its corrosive impact on society, it could not but lead to profound troubles in the long run not only for the Kongo leadership, but for the Kongo people as a whole.

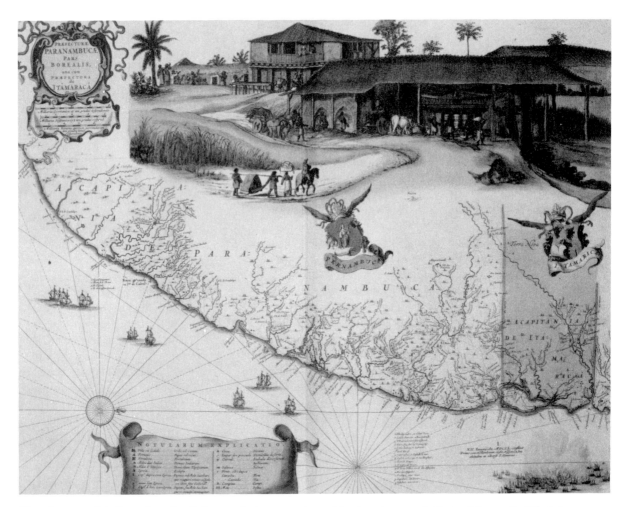

View of a sugar mill in Pernambuco, Brazil. Sugar and tobacco were the two labor-intensive crops that fostered the growth of plantation agriculture and of slave labor in the New World.

Portuguese turned most for slaves for their Brazilian enterprises were Kongo and Angola, an area to the southwest of Kongo. The story of the new phase in the extraction of slaves from these areas is filled with contradictions.

After the 1540s, the *maniKongo* had ended relations with the Portuguese because of their interference in local affairs. During the 1560s and into the 1570s internal political problems had plagued the *maniKongo* Alvaro I, however, and it was only through accepting renewed Portuguese military support that he had survived the challenges from ambitious rival leaders within the state. The price tag for this military support was that the Portuguese be allowed to increase the level of slave trading from the Kongo region to supply labor to São Tomé and to Brazil's expanding plantations.

In later decades, the Brazilian demand grew more insistent as the plantation economy increased and as the slave population in Brazil did not reproduce itself. This was so for several reasons. The high mortality rate of slaves, plantation owners' discouragement of marriage and family life, psychological stress, the use of abortifacients, and being simply worked too hard all hindered tropical slave societies from reproducing themselves, and Brazil was no different. Furthermore, the trade was mostly in young men, with the number of women always far, far below that of men. As long as slaves could be obtained relatively cheaply in Africa, it made good economic sense for plantation owners to obtain young males, work them to death, and then replace them. If a slave lived for a minimum of four years, he had paid for the cost of his acquisition, transport, and food.

As elsewhere in Africa, despite the appalling suffer-ings of those enslaved, the burgeoning slave trade through Kongo and Angola greatly increased the power of the participating elites and, in the process, transformed the very nature of the Kongo state as it also changed the nature of slavery within the state. More and more societies of the interior, to the east beyond the Kongo state, became involved in catching people to supply the Portuguese demand. As a con-sequence, the *maniKongo* was able to increase his tolls on the trade from the interior to the coast. As the trade grew, the *maniKongo* invested much of the state's growing income from the tolls in acquiring slaves for his own state.

The state's leadership used these slaves in two wholly new ways. First, they provided the labor for large plantations established to grow food to be supplied to the Portuguese port of Luanda, founded in 1575 on the coast of Angola, and to the ships involved in the trans-atlantic slave trade. The introduction of maize and cas-sava (manioc), new crops from the New World, made this novel use of slave labor especially attractive. These crops yielded far more calories per unit of land than older native crops and hence produced far more income to plantation owners who grew them.

Second, the state also employed slaves as civil ser-vants and, especially, as soldiers. In this way, the gov-ernment of the *maniKongo* was able to reduce its former dependence upon subsidiary leaders for military sup-port. With his own loyal army of an estimated 20,000 troops, the *maniKongo* effectively curtailed the indepen-dence of local big men and expanded the boundaries of his state. As a result of these changes, while in 1550, before the expansion of the slave trade to Brazil, there had been very few slaves in Kongo, by 1650 there were more slaves than free people.

But it was not only in the realms of economic pros-perity and military power that the increased Portu-guese presence aided the *maniKongo*. For example, lit-eracy was used to strengthen bureaucratic efficiency in Kongo as written Arabic had done in the Sudanic region, with written records allowing for greater exactitude in levying taxes. The use of written letters also permitted the *maniKongo* to communicate directly with people both in his country and in Europe. And making Cathol-icism a state religion guaranteed that Catholic mission-aries would become involved in the day-to-day admin-istration of the state and helped to legitimize the power of the central government.

As a consequence of all this, between 1578, when Alvaro I received renewed support from the Portuguese

after the long period of estrangement, and 1614, when Alvaro II died, the Kongo state reached new heights of centralization and prosperity. The *maniKongo* skillfully used the Portuguese to overcome and blunt tendencies within the Kongo political structure to fragment and shatter. Yet support from the Portuguese had become an addiction for the *maniKongo*, and it, like all addictions, was dangerously unpredictable. This was so particularly as the Portuguese developed interests that conflicted with those of the *maniKongo*.

Such conflicting interests arose as a result of Portu-guese activities in Angola, to the southwest of the Kongo state. In 1568 a Portuguese adventurer, Paulo Dias de Novais (d. 1589), had landed on Angola's coast. Sebas-tian (1557–78), the new Portuguese king, a romantic youth of fourteen, had ordered him to conquer the area, a radical departure from past Portuguese policy, which had relied upon cooperation with West African leaders and the maintenance of only small fortified posts such as Elmina. Novais's instructions were different because Portugal wanted direct access to two commodities thought to exist in the interior: silver and slaves. At the time of Novais's landing, there were a number of refu-gees also entering the area, fleeing the political instabil-ity in the Kongo state to the north. These refugees allied themselves with Novais and used Portuguese-supplied arms to raid for slaves for markets in Brazil, São Tomé, and elsewhere.

There was an element of perpetual motion in the slave raiding that came to typify the area, with new groups of people acquiring arms and carrying a slave-raiding frontier deeper and deeper into the interior. And with it came the Portuguese—some government officials and other adventurers working on their own—establishing their fortresses in the interior in the decades after 1600. By 1640 the interior of Angola had become an area of very real and expansive Portu-guese military and economic activity, a situation up to then unknown on the West Coast of Africa.

This new situation to the south undermined the Kongo state in two ways. First, much of the earlier trade in slaves that had enriched the *maniKongo's* government for so long was drawn southward through Matamba, an area claimed by the Kongo, toward the Portuguese port of Luanda, on the Angolan coast. Using the income drawn from this new trade, the leaders of this area were able to break free from the overlordship of the Kongo and declare their independence under a remarkable queen, Nzinga. She then outfitted a strong army with Portuguese arms, and by the 1640s, virtually all 13,000 slaves annually exported to Brazil from Luanda were coming through Matamba, cutting off one of the *mani-Kongo's* main sources of income and enriching Nzinga's coffers.

A type of shell known as *nzimbu* was used in the region as a currency. Harvesting them from Luanda Bay, the Portuguese introduced immense quantities of these shells into the Kongo economy. The result was as if unlimited counterfeit money had been placed in circulation. A huge surge of inflation occurred at the very moment that the Kongo leadership was losing its control over the profitable slave trade from the interior. The inflation and the loss of control over its lucrative trade was a combination that the Kongo leadership could not long endure. When the Kongo state was challenged by Nsoyo, a rival coastal state to its west whose leaders had begun to strengthen themselves through trade with British and Dutch merchants challenging Portuguese commercial dominance in the region, the Kongo state entered upon a period of prolonged decline, defeat, and dismemberment. At last, in 1649, after a military defeat, the *maniKongo* surrendered his southern territories to the Portuguese, yielded them a trade monopoly, agreed to stop taxing the slave trade, and sent hostages to Lisbon as guarantors of his good behavior. The state of Kongo, long famous in Europe for its wealth and its adoption of many European customs, quickly collapsed. São Salvador, the Kongo capital, which had had tens of thousands of people living in it at the start of the century, was finally abandoned in 1678, with its people returning to the countryside.

A Portuguese delegation meets the formidable Queen Nzinga of Matamba. When the Portuguese governor refused her a chair, she sat down on one of her attendants.

Portuguese and Africans in Mozambique

During the sixteenth century the Portuguese also expanded their presence on the East Coast, in Mozambique, where gold was their main motivation. At the start of the century, they thought they could remain in their coastal settlements at Sofala and on Mozambique Island and that the gold trade would flow naturally down to them as it had long done in West Africa, at Elmina. These expectations were not fulfilled, however, and gradually the Portuguese felt that they had no choice but to intervene in the interior. One reason for such involvement was that they encountered stiff competition. Portuguese naval forces were too weak to prevent Swahili merchants from developing new inland trade routes for Zimbabwe's gold, bypassing the Portuguese settlements, and arriving at the coast at Angoche, a new Swahili port at which they offered better deals than the Portuguese did. The Portuguese quickly realized that if they were to prosper, they would have to compete by sending their own agents inland to seek direct access to the gold and cut out the Swahili competition.

Competition also came from individual Portuguese beyond official control. In establishing their empire, Portugal's rulers had largely relied upon a group of people whom they felt Portugal itself could well do without. Many of the foot soldiers of empire were criminals, not people from whom much loyalty to the Portuguese state could be expected. Once beyond Lisbon's direct control, these people often struck out on their own, seeking their fortunes by venturing beyond governmental control into the interior. As they pushed up into the hot and humid Zambezi valley in search of gold, they formed a second group of competitors to the official traders in coastal settlements. As time passed, more and more of these Portuguese adventurers traveled into the interior, married local African women, and settled down as Africanized *sertanejos*, or "backwoodsmen." As had happened earlier along the Guinea coast and was to happen later in Angola, an Africanized group of people of mixed race and culture developed in Mozambique after 1580.

That the Swahili merchants and Portuguese sertanejos were welcome in the interior was largely because of a situation there remarkably similar to that in Angola during the same period. Successors of the Great Zimbabwe state occupied the area, but none was as unified or powerful as its predecessor. Instead, several states competed with each other over access to gold and other resources. One of these was "Monomotapa," named after its ruler, the *Mwene Mutapa*. Other substantial states in the area included Changamire and a set of Maravi kingdoms north of the Zambezi River. Changamire posed an especially severe threat to the Mwene Mutapa, and so he welcomed outsiders to come into his area to trade and be his allies.

It was in this political context that Portuguese officials reluctantly moved up the Zambezi valley to compete more effectively for gold and other products. In the 1530s they established trading stations at Sena and Tete, both on the south bank of the Zambezi River. In 1544 they founded the coastal town of Quelimane as a commercial alternative to the Swahili port of Angoche. By 1560 the official Portuguese settlements were flourishing, but by then, too, their English, French, and Dutch rivals were beginning seriously to challenge the Portuguese naval dominance of the Indian Ocean basin.

A portrait of a Mwene Mutapa. *The Portuguese artist depicts the king with a European-style scepter and crown.*

The Portuguese began to think that it would be wise for them to consolidate their still tenuous position in Mozambique by taking direct control over the mines of the interior. Perhaps Mozambique was destined to become "the Brazil of Africa" and, if so, it should remain Portugal's.

During this period of reevaluation, in 1568, Sebastian, the new Portuguese king, became convinced that God had chosen him to lead a crusade against the Muslims. He decided that the Muslim Swahili traders competing with the Portuguese in Mozambique were ideal targets for his wrath. He dispatched an army to conquer the Mwene Mutapa and his Swahili allies and to seize Monomotapa's mines for Portugal. Things went well initially, and in 1569 the Portuguese handily defeated an African army and massacred Muslims they encountered. But soon malaria began to kill the Portuguese, sleeping sickness killed their horses, and the army gradually evaporated.

In the midst of this action, the Mwene Mutapa, both concerned with the Portuguese military advance into the interior and eager to gain their aid against his African enemies, especially the state of Changamire, executed several Muslim merchants at his capital to show his good intentions. In 1575 he concluded a treaty of friendship with the Portuguese. The treaty gave them the right to trade freely in his lands, to build churches, to mine gold, and to expel any Muslims that they might encounter. In subsequent years, as the Mwene Mutapa sought additional Portuguese arms, he made more concessions and further undermined the integrity of his state. As in the case of the Kongo, a situation was fast developing from which the African elite had no real escape. On the one hand, the Mwene Mutapa felt that Portuguese support was necessary for his campaigns against his local enemies. On the other hand, however, with the expulsion of the Muslims, he now had no one to balance against the Portuguese and their demands for concessions.

The dependency of the Mwene Mutapa on the Portuguese grew. In 1607 he signed a treaty that turned over to them the area's gold, copper, and iron mines and yielded five of his children as hostages, so that they might be trained as Catholics and educated as Portuguese. While these concessions kept the Portuguese state at bay, more and more unruly Portuguese sertanejos were coming to live in the interior beyond the reach of Portuguese officials and as laws unto themselves, frequently ignoring the Mwene Mutapa and his laws. At the death of the old Mwene Mutapa in 1624, a succession dispute occurred, which was marked by efforts by

Portugal and Africa, 1415–1650

1415	Seizure of the Moroccan city of Ceuta
1434	Discovery of the Madeira Islands in Atlantic Ocean
1444	First slaves traded from Argiun, on Mauritanian coast
1482	Fortified trading station built at Elmina, Guinea coast; Diogo Cão welcomed by the king of Kongo
1494	Treaty of Tordesillas divides the world between Spain and Portugal
1498	Vasco da Gama enters Indian Ocean
1509	Battle of Diu, near India, establishes Portugal as dominant naval power in Indian Ocean basin
1531	Portugal establishes trading station of Sena, in Mozambique's Zambezi valley
1549	Portugal decides to build sugar industry in Brazil
1568	Sebastian, an intense anti-Muslim, becomes king of Portugal
1569	Portugal's first serious invasion of inland Mozambique
1575	Establishment of colony at Luanda to facilitate slave trade from Angola
1629	*Mwene Mutapa* becomes "vassal" of Portuguese king and cedes concessions in Mozambique to Portugal
1649	*ManiKongo* cedes concessions of Portugal and Kongo state begins final collapse

a pretender, Kaparidze, to bring the Portuguese under control. He first seized some Portuguese trading stations and demanded tribute from the Portuguese government. In response, the Portuguese supported another pretender, whom they placed on the throne in 1629. He then signed an agreement with the Portuguese that formally made him a vassal of the Portuguese king and opened his country without any restriction to Portuguese traders and prospectors.

Monomotapa's people were unhappy to see their independence disappear in this way, and in 1631, Kaparidze organized a campaign of resistance to the Portuguese takeover. Missionaries, traders, prospectors, and Africans identified as collaborators with the Portuguese were killed, with the final death count reportedly running into the thousands. The Portuguese government sent an army to reestablish order, and through the army's successes in 1632 the Portuguese government secured a powerful position in the whole Zambezi valley. Once established there, the Portuguese went to work in succeeding decades to dismantle further the Mwene Mutapa's state as well as those of other Africans. Perhaps the greatest threat, however, came not from the Portuguese state itself but from the Portuguese sertanejos, who used slaves to create private mercenary armies that allowed them to rule over large tracts of the Zambezi valley utterly heedless of Lisbon and its laws and largely beyond the control of local Africans as well. In this way, large areas of Mozambique's interior experienced the same sort of changes then occurring in Angola's interior, with local Africans being drawn into an economic system largely dominated by Portuguese adventurers and with the Portuguese state laying the foundations of a colony destined to remain Portugal's until 1974.

The impact of Portuguese trade and intervention in the internal affairs of regions in the African hinterland was highly contradictory. Initially, for rulers who were able to supply what the Portuguese wanted, there were real benefits, and their governments were able to strengthen themselves. But one of Portugal's demands—for slaves to work sugar plantations—had especially negative consequences. It not only brought misery to the unfortunates who were enslaved and forced to experience the harrowing "Middle Passage" to the New World, but Portugal's demand for slaves also created extreme difficulties for African rulers, especially in places such as Kongo where the needs of the newly established Brazilian plantations prompted the Portuguese to intervene actively in the procurement of slaves. By the start of the seventeenth century, however, other European nations had decided to challenge Portugal's hegemony along all the coasts of Africa, beginning an era of far greater African contact with other European powers, far greater challenges for Africans, and far greater changes within Africa itself.

America and the Encounters

The regions of Mesoamerica and the central Andes underwent enormous changes during the half millennium between the mid-thirteenth and eighteenth centuries. Two powerful peoples, the Aztecs of the Valley of Mexico and the Incas of the Andean highlands, moved into the void left by the collapse of classic civilizations and constructed vast empires. At the zenith of their achievements they in turn fell before the Spanish *conquistadores* (conquerors).

The reaction of the peoples of Mesoamerica and the Andes to the Europeans framed the history of the succeeding two centuries. They resisted the imposition of European rule and the intrusion of European culture, particularly religion—fiercely and violently on occasion, passively and relentlessly most of the time. The conjunction of the two groups, combined with a third, the African peoples brought forcefully to work in the New World, forged a hybrid culture and produced new peoples of mixed blood (*mestizos*, the offspring of European and Indian; mulattos, or *pardos*, the progeny of European and African; *zambos*, the offspring of Indian and African).

The Spanish and Portuguese succeeded in controlling the vast territory from the Californias south to the Strait of Magellan at the tip of South America. Their success was due to a combination of their own administrative flexibility and the effects of the catastrophic decline in native population that resulted from the introduction of European diseases.

The Rise of the Aztec and Inca Empires

Mesoamerica and the Andes produced artistic, intellectual, and political accomplishments that rivaled and sometimes surpassed those of the Old World. (See Chapter 1.) The Olmec, Chavín, and Maya civilizations produced magnificent achievements. But these societies crumbled under circumstances that we only partially understand, leaving both the central Andes and Mesoamerica fragmented. After 200 to 300 years, in the fourteenth and fifteenth centuries, powerful new empires arose, the Aztec in Mesoamerica and the Inca in South America, unifying vast expanses of territory and millions of people. Both Aztecs and Incas rose meteorically; the Incas built their domain in the short span of thirty years. Neither had been in power long enough to consolidate and stabilize their conquered lands. Each faced the Europeans with a divided empire. Their vulnerabilities became all too apparent when they were confronted with the challenge of the Spaniards.

The Aztecs were one of the barbarian peoples called Chichimecas who migrated from the north to the Valley of Mexico. The Mexicas, as they were also known, arrived in the region and settled at Chapultepec on Lake Texcoco around 1250 C.E. Because of their extreme brutality, they were unwelcome neighbors, and in 1319 an alliance of city-states expelled them. The Mexica worked as mercenaries, eventually finding safe haven on an island in the middle of the lake, where in 1345 they founded what was to be Tenochtitlán. Borrowing the technology of the valley dwellers, they built an ingenious hydraulic farming system based on floating gardens, called *chinampas*, which enabled the city to grow to a population that exceeded 200,000 at its height.

The road to empire began between 1429 and 1433 when the Triple Alliance of Tenochtitlán and two neighboring city-states, Texcoco and Tlacopán, defeated the dominant power in the Valley of Mexico, Atzcapotzalco. The alliance conquered the Valley of Mexico and its neighboring regions, then set about to unify the high plateau under its rule and extend the empire south and east into what is now the state of Veracruz and then west to the Pacific Coast. To ensure the food supply, devastated in a four-year-long famine at mid-century, the alliance constructed an extensive system of irrigation and flood control for the lakes in the valley. The unprecedented series of military victories ended when the Aztecs attempted unsuccessfully to defeat the Tarascans in what is now Michoacán. Further defeats followed. In 1502 Moctezuma II (1466–1520) took power. He presided over the destruction of the empire by the Spanish.

Historians vary widely in their interpretations of the Aztec empire. The differing views focus on the nature of the relationship between the Aztecs and their subject peoples and on the extent of and the reasons for the practice of human sacrifice. There is substantial agreement that the Aztecs erected no significant bureaucracy, that they used marriage to link the city-states of the valley, and that they kept lesser local rulers in power as long as they paid the required tribute. The Aztecs maintained military control not by occupation but through threats and reconquest. No such consensus exists about the nature of the relations between the Aztecs and neighboring states. The nature of the "flowery wars" fought between the Triple Alliance and five city-states just over the mountains in the Puebla Valley, southeast of Tenochtitlán, is at the heart of the debate. Why did the Aztecs allow these states, most

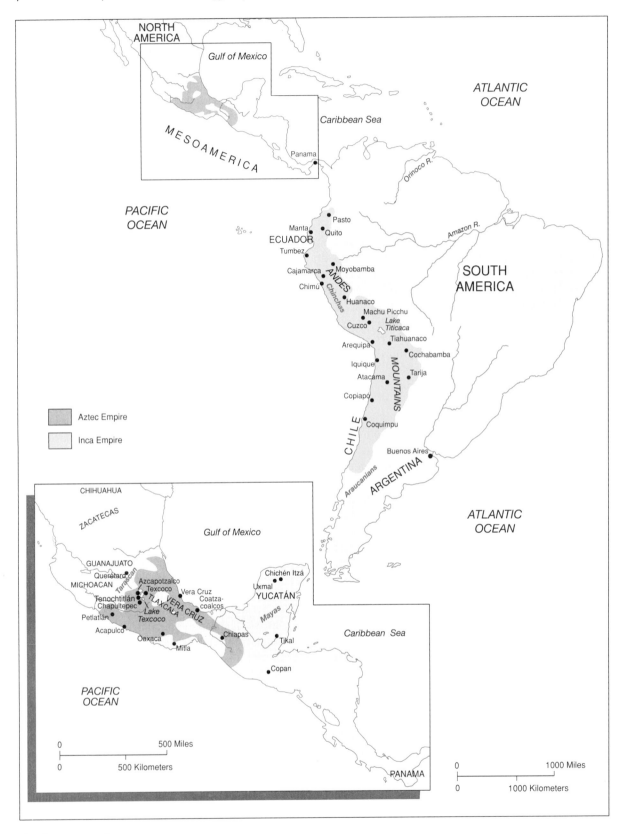

notably Tlaxcala, to maintain their autonomy, when Aztec military might should have brought easy victory over them? One possible answer is that these were phony wars used to provide a guaranteed supply of captives for human sacrifice. Another possible reason is that the Aztecs used these conflicts to furnish much-needed high-level military training for their young soldiers. The overall question of just how much control the Aztecs exerted over their empire is still only partially answered.

The extent of and motivation for human sacrifice by the Aztecs is perhaps the most controversial topic. Undoubtedly, human sacrifice was an integral part of Aztec religion. According to Aztec tradition, the world had gone through four previous stages or Suns, each destroyed by catastrophe. In order to maintain the Fifth Sun in place and ward off the predicted next disaster, the Aztecs sought to keep their deities satisfied. This required human blood obtained from bloodletting and sacrifice. Some observers see human sacrifice as an invention of imperial rule, aimed at terrorizing military foes into quick surrender and subject peoples into submission. The extent of the practice is also much debated. The Spanish chroniclers, who recorded the conquerors' exploits and who tried to compile a version of the Aztecs' history after their defeat, told of extensive sacrifice. At the dedication of a new temple in Tenochtitlán in the late fifteenth century, Aztec priests supposedly sacrificed tens of thousands of lives. Others believe the practice existed on a far more modest scale and that the chroniclers exaggerated the numbers to enhance the glory of the Aztec empire and, thus, the glory of its conquerors.

The Aztec capital, Tenochtitlán, rivaled the great cities of Europe. The city was laid out like Venice, and its canals furnished the major means of transportation. Although the chinampas were extremely productive, most supplies had to be brought in from the mainland on three causeways. Consequently, Tenochtitlán was a bustling commercial center. An extensive system of aqueducts transported drinking water. Large temples and palaces rose from the lake, forming a magnificent skyline.

The basic social unit of Aztec society was the *calpulli*, a kin-based community with landholding, religious, and military functions. At the top was the *tlatoani* or chief speaker (emperor). Originally elected by the calpulli, by the time of Moctezuma II the chief speaker reached the status of deity. As Aztec conquests expanded, society stratified; what began as bureaucratic and citizen military meritocracies became a hereditary nobility and a

The founding of Tenochtitlán, from Codex Mendoza. *The drawings at the bottom depict the early Aztec conquests of Colhuacan and Tenayucan.*

professional military. In the middle of the social scale were merchants and artisans. Merchants occupied perhaps the most precarious position in society, not only because they risked death as military spies for the Aztec armies, but because, if too successful and ostentatious in their display of wealth, they were subject to drastic punishment by their rulers. Artisans were assured an important status, for they crafted the gold and feather ornaments for the chief speaker and nobility, providing them with the necessary conspicuous consumption their exalted positions required. The common people, called *macehualtin*, were members of the calpulli and owned land. Beneath them were the *mayeques*, or bondsmen, who comprised perhaps as many as one-third of the population. We know very little about them other than that they were probably landless people attached to the lands of the nobility. The *tlacotin*, or slaves, made up roughly five percent of the population. One could become a slave by committing a crime, through debts, or by selling oneself. As society grew more hierarchical and social classes more stratified, women experienced less independence. Nonetheless, they could own their own property, conduct business such as trade (through traders), and practice quite autonomous professions like midwife, healer, or priestess. Women who died in childbirth were revered equally with those males who died in battle, the greatest glories an Aztec could attain.

There is little historical evidence about the rise of the other great American empire, the Incas. They had no writing, and archaeological discoveries in the Andes, especially in the environs of Cuzco, the Inca capital, are limited. Most likely, the Incas arrived in the region of Cuzco around 1250 C.E. For nearly two hundred years, they lived as one of numerous tribes in the region. They began their meteoric rise to mighty empire in 1438, when Inca Yupanqui, a disinherited son of the reigning Inca Viracocha, saved them from defeat by a local rival. Legend has it that, unable to gather enough recruits to battle, he turned stones into soldiers. The new ruler, now known as Pachacuti, began an unprecedented series of conquests. During the next thirty years, he and his successors carried the empire south to the region of Lake Titicaca and into what is now Argentina and Chile and north as far as Ecuador. They controlled the central Andean highlands and the Pacific Coast. Only the Amazonian jungles proved an impenetrable barrier.

In an extraordinarily short period, the Incas built an empire that rivaled in territory and population the great conquests of the Greeks and Romans. The expansion depended more on persuasion than on military prowess. Inca policies were meant to give subject peoples a stake in the empire and to foster loyalty to it. Whereas Aztec armies were composed of professional soldiers from the Triple Alliance, Inca armies consisted primarily of peasants from the most recently conquered states mobilized as part of their tribute obligations to the empire. Including subject peoples in the new military campaigns served two practical purposes. Since there were far too few Incas to carry out large-scale conquest, it furnished needed soldiers. In addition, it gave conquered people a stake in the empire. Local elites retained their power. The Incas also realized the need for at least the threat of coercion behind their persuasion. Consequently, they established a clear record of atrocities to back up their material incentives.

The Incas controlled their empire by means of a vast bureaucracy and tax system, more remarkable because they lacked a written language and because the Andes presented enormous difficulties in transportation and communication. They built their rule on existing polit-

An Inca "accountant." The Inca lacked writing, but they used the quipu, *knotted strings of different lengths and colors, to keep accurate and detailed records.*

ical structures. They were very flexible, treating small-scale chiefdoms differently from complex city-states. The Incas rewarded subject peoples with participation in the glory and spoils of new conquests, shrewdly taking advantage of regional rivalries, pitting a newly conquered people against an old, neighboring enemy. Moreover, the Incas provided other benefits, such as irrigation works, terraces, and roads.

The Incas closely administered conquered peoples. They resettled much of their subject population. The sons of the rulers of conquered states were sent to school in Cuzco, partly as hostages to assure cooperation, but also to indoctrinate them into Inca language and ideology. The Incas sought to spread their language, Quechua, and their religion. But they also absorbed other deities and beliefs into their pantheon. As always their inclusiveness and openness had a purpose. They often brought the idols of subject peoples to Cuzco to hold as hostages. The Incas' primary form of retribution against rebels was deportation, not death.

When they began their conquests, the Incas relied on peasant soldiers. As the empire grew, however, there evolved a professional military centered in specialized ethnic groups. Inca-led armies did not plunder or forage, but rather used provisions stored in warehouses along their famous road system.

By the early sixteenth century the Inca military campaigns slowed or ended. There was no method to maintain the satisfaction of peripheral subject peoples, and they frequently rebelled. When two rivals for leadership clashed in 1525, an underutilized military proved restless and dangerous and moved easily to civil war.

Inca social organization revolved around the family unit, called the *ayllu*. The ayllu distributed land among its members every two years. Its members cared for the old and infirm by working common lands. As in the case of the Aztecs, the social structure became more stratified as the empire grew. At the top of society was the Sapay-Inca, or emperor. By the time of the Spaniards' arrival, his position had evolved from tribal leader to god-king. Originally a council of ayllu elected the Sapay-Inca, but after the conquests, the ruler chose his successor. Below the Sapay-Inca was the hereditary nobility, the ruling Inca clan. Underneath them were the ayllus of Cuzco and the chieftains of conquered peoples. There was also a class of bondsmen called *yanacona*.

The Inca capital, Cuzco, was not nearly as elaborate as Tenochtitlán, but it had more than 100,000 residents. Each inhabitant had to wear the costume of his or her home tribe or city-state. Cuzco was an administrative and religious center, but unlike Tenochtitlán it was not a hub of commerce. The Inca state controlled trade in the Andes, and the medium of trade was barter.

Despite better administration and more benevolent rule, the Inca empire, like the Aztec, was in crisis in the years before the Spaniards arrived in Peru. The Inca Huayna Capac, who reigned from 1493 to 1525, had taken a number of measures that led to civil war. He moved his capital from Cuzco to Ecuador in the far northern reaches of the empire, which led to a geographic split between north and south. In addition, the emperor fostered rivalry between his legitimate heir and successor, Huáscar, and his son by a concubine, Atahuallpa. When Huayna Capac died, Atahuallpa refused to recognize his half-brother as Sapay-Inca and civil war ensued. With northern support, the rebel won. But the bloody civil war left wounds that never healed.

The Fall of the Aztec and Inca Empires

By the first decade of the sixteenth century the great empires were weakened and divided, having apparently reached their limits. The Aztecs had encountered the fierce resistance of western Tarascans and northern Chichimecs; bitter old enemies like Tlaxcala festered in their hate. There is evidence too that when slowed conquest diminished the supply of luxury items and sacrifice victims, internal dissension arose. Moreover, the population of the Valley of Mexico may have reached its ecological limits. In the mid-fifteenth century, when a massive famine struck, the Aztecs had trouble feeding a smaller version of the empire. Based on tribute, which often was in the form of sacrifice victims, the Aztec empire elicited no loyalty. Tlaxcalans, after a nasty defeat at the hands of the Spaniards, and imbued with old grudges against Tenochtitlán, allied with the newcomers. If the Aztec empire was held together by the terror of human sacrifice, it was not a lasting bond. The empire of the Incas tore itself apart by civil war between north and south. Hence, on the eve of the encounters, both empires were vulnerable.

The stories of the conquests of Mexico and Peru are epic tales told by the victors. Glorified by the chronicles of their companions, the *conquistadores*, or conquerors, especially Hernán Cortés (1485–1547), emerged as heroes larger than life. In 1517 the Spaniards sent a scouting expedition to the region of Veracruz. Cortés landed in the same region in 1519. He scuttled his ships and set off westward. After soundly thrashing a Tlaxcalan army and inducing the losers to join them against the Aztecs, the Spaniards marched to Tenochtitlán. They quickly captured and publicly humiliated Moctezuma, forcing him to rule as their puppet. Cortés had to return to the coast to head off an expedition led by Pánfilo de Narváez (ca. 1480–1528), sent to arrest him for insubordination to the governor of Cuba, under whose auspices the expedition had sailed. Cortés defeated Narváez, incorporating Narváez's remaining soldiers in his army, now numbering 1,300. While Cortés was away from Tenochtitlán, his second-in-command, Pedro de Alvarado (ca. 1485–1541), provoked a bloody confrontation with the Aztecs, leading to the overthrow of Moctezuma, who fell victim to a lethal stone thrown by one of his subjects. When Cortés returned, he realized he must retreat from the city. This he did on the night of 30 June 1520, known as *La Noche Triste*, the Night of Sorrows. The retreat cost the conquistador two-thirds of his men and most of his horses. The Aztecs, however, did not pursue the Spaniards, who fled to Tlaxcala. The Aztecs

THE MASSACRE AT THE CANAL OF THE TOLTECS

■ *The Aztecs and Incas did not relinquish their rule without persistent, fierce resistance to the Spaniards. As this passage from* The Broken Spears *indicates, the natives defeated the conquerors rather badly. If not for the ravages of disease on the population of Tenochtitlán, especially on the Aztec leadership, and the alliance of other cities once subordinated or allied with the Aztecs, the Spaniards might have perished.*

When the Spaniards reached the Canal of the Toltecs . . . they hurled themselves headlong into the water, as if they were leaping from a cliff . . .

The canal was soon choked with the bodies of men and horses; they filled the gap in the causeway with their own drowned bodies. Those who followed crossed to the other side by walking on the corpses . . .

The dawn was breaking as they entered the village. Their hearts were cheered by the brightening light of this new day: they thought the horrors of the retreat were all behind them. But suddenly they heard war cries and the Aztecs swarmed through the streets and surrounded them. They had come to capture the Tlaxcaltecas for their sacrifices. They also wanted to complete their revenge against the Spaniards.

remained in Tenochtitlán and reconstituted their forces. The Spaniards returned to besiege Tenochtitlán, now ruled by the emperor Cuauhtémoc. The Aztecs held out miraculously for nearly three months, during which time the city was almost completely destroyed by bombardment from ships on the lake and house-to-house fighting. The end of the siege came on 13 August 1521 with the capture of Cuauhtémoc. The resistance of native peoples did not end then, however.

Francisco Pizarro (ca. 1475–1541) arrived in Cajamarca, Peru, in November 1532. Like Cortés, he sought to capture the emperor, cutting off the head of the empire. This he did on 16 November, when the haughty Atahuallpa fatally miscalculated his military power. The Spaniards executed Atahuallpa and conducted an appalling slaughter of the Inca army. Pizarro needed a puppet to act as titular head of the Inca empire. Manco Capac, son of Huayna Capac, began as a collaborator. From 1533 to 1536 he acted as the Spaniards' stooge, humiliated and imprisoned. Finally, after the Europeans raped his wives in front of him, he escaped, gathered an army, and began the Inca resistance. Despite a numerically superior army—over 40,000 against 200 Spaniards—Manco was unable to successfully besiege Cuzco. When his army dissipated, Manco established a mountain retreat, from which he harassed the conquerors until betrayed by Spaniards to whom he had offered refuge. His son Sayri Tupac, only ten years old, succeeded him, only to surrender in 1555 to the enticements of a royal life under Spanish rule. When he died in 1560, another son of Manco, Titu Cusi, rekindled the resistance and ten years of guerrilla war ensued, ending with his death. The Spanish viceroy, Francisco de Toledo, penetrated the Inca redoubt, capturing the last Inca, Tupac Amarú, in 1572.

After the initial shocks of losing their leaders and their capitals, the Aztecs, Incas, and other native peoples fiercely resisted the Spaniards. They quickly learned how to fight against the guns and horses. Throughout the three hundred years of colonial rule, they resisted, if not by shedding blood then passively, day by day, to maintain their language and customs. Some fought into the twentieth century. Latin American culture today remains a testimony to their persistence.

The native population of Brazil was composed of nonsedentary and semisedentary peoples, who also fiercely resisted the incursions of the Europeans. Because of their mobility and the vastness and harshness of the land into which they could escape, they proved difficult to defeat permanently, though their numbers were decimated by disease.

The Portuguese in many ways obtained Brazil much as the British were later said to have acquired their empire—"in a fit of absence of mind." In 1500 Pedro Alvares Cabral, en route to Asia via the coast of Africa, was blown far off course across the Atlantic and landed

The Spanish attitude toward the Indians is demonstrated in this sixteenth-century drawing of a Spaniard kicking an Indian. Spanish colonial society was divided into classes on the basis of birthplace and race.

on the coast of what is now Brazil. He discovered, evidently to his surprise, that under the terms of the Treaty of Tordesillas, which was signed in 1494 by Spain and Portugal and divided the world between them, the territory he landed on belonged to Portugal. At the time, however, the Portuguese were preoccupied by trade with Asia. Aside from gathering brazilwood—from which the colony derived its name—for use in dyes, they largely ignored their new possession. Since no precious metals were readily available, there was no pressing need for attention.

Controversy as well as curiosity abounds about the reasons for the Spanish conquest, which was decisive and relatively swift. Vulnerable or not, the great Aztec and Inca empires were formidable foes and vastly outnumbered the Europeans. They had the advantage of knowing the land. They were brave, brilliant warriors.

How then did barely four hundred Spaniards under Hernán Cortés and perhaps one hundred with Francisco Pizarro destroy them?

The Spaniards recognized weakness and division and exploited both. Native soldiers comprised the preponderance of the army that Cortés led against Tenochtitlán. Pizarro allied with the losing side in the Inca civil war, the followers of Huáscar. Cortés and Pizarro provided brilliant leadership compared to the Aztecs and Incas. Early in the struggles the Spaniards captured both Moctezuma II and Atahuallpa, leaving a vacuum in these highly centralized empires.

The Spaniards had a number of advantages in the war against the Aztec and Inca empires. At first glance they appear to have enjoyed superior weaponry; they had guns, cannon, and metal armor. They also had horses, which added speed and mobility and frightened their opponents. Ultimately, though, their technology may not have been advantageous. The Spaniards quickly discarded their heavy armor, which in tropical climates or high altitudes was burdensome, and adopted the natives' woven cotton. Archers could reload faster than gunners. Although the noise of the cannon terrorized the native troops at first, they quickly got used to it. The initial advantage of the horses was soon lost, as they were a distinct hazard in closed spaces like Tenochtitlán.

The Spaniards' greatest advantage, perhaps, lay in their persistence and ruthlessness and in the profound cultural misunderstanding between them and their opponents, especially the Aztecs. The Spaniards, deeply motivated by greed and ambition, employed vicious tactics. Cortés's scuttling his ships in order to prevent any turning back clearly indicates the extent of the Spaniards' desperate motivation. The Spaniards also benefited from their view of warfare. To the Aztecs, war was a sacred undertaking, in which the goal was to capture the bravest, most capable opponents for sacrifice. At its utmost, war was one man against another, face to face. Aztec warriors did not retreat, did not hide behind walls or horses, did not kill civilians indiscriminately. The Spaniards did all of these, for their concept of war was quite different. To them, as to all Europeans, the goal of war was victory at any cost. This helps explain why the Spanish suffered so few casualties.

Another example of the radically different and mutually misunderstood worldviews of Aztecs and Spaniards was their respective perceptions of the gifts Aztec emperor Moctezuma II sent to Cortés after the latter landed in the region of Veracruz in 1519. These opulent presents were meant by the Aztecs as a haughty display

Aztec Indians suffering from smallpox during the conquest. The disease took a terrible toll among the inhabitants of Mexico, who had no immunity to the plagues of the Old World.

of their power; they were insults to the Spaniards. The Spaniards interpreted the gifts as a sign of Aztec weakness, attempted bribes to keep them from Tenochtitlán.

Perhaps the crucial factor in the defeat of the Aztec and Inca empires, however, was neither the military prowess of the Spaniards nor the internal weaknesses of the American empires, but rather the rapid spread of diseases like smallpox, measles, and plague, which devastated the native population. There is little question that disease preceded the arrival of the Spaniards to both Mesoamerica and Peru. Early landings had spread smallpox to Tenochtitlán. Several important leaders fell to the disease, weakening Aztec war-making power. In the Andes, half the population may have perished even before Pizarro arrived. So badly weakened, the Incas were easier prey for the Spaniards.

Spanish and Portuguese Colonial America, 1550–1700

Once the initial military victories in Mesoamerica and the Andes were complete, the Europeans, thousands of miles from their homelands across the Atlantic Ocean, confronted a vast extent of territory, with a population far larger than that of the Iberian Peninsula. The problems of ruling such an enormous domain were as vast and complex as the land and the people. The natives resisted fiercely, and rebellions punctuated the sixteenth century; some less sedentary peoples continued to fight for three hundred years to avoid the colonial yoke. Moreover, the New World colonies were constantly threatened by European rivals. English pirates, Dutch merchants, and French adventurers nibbled at Iberian hegemony. In Europe the Spanish crown engaged in continual warfare, with unfortunate consequences for its colonies.

The Spanish and Portuguese ruled their New World empires with utmost flexibility, bare-bones administration, and minimal use of force. The Spaniards, especially, centered their efforts on the extraction and removal of gold and silver, which the crown used to finance its European involvements.

A complex mixture of motivations, which historians have characterized as gold, glory, and God, comprised the psyche of the conquerors and colonists. They were exceptionally greedy and ruthless in their pursuit of riches and—particularly the earliest arrivals—fervent in their desire to Christianize the natives. They believed that military conquest and religious proselytization would bring honor to them and to the crown. To Ferdinand and Isabella, the first Spanish rulers of the New World, and their successors, Charles I and Philip II, the defense and spread of Christianity were paramount considerations. They were literally the defenders of the faith, second only to the pope. But it was enormously expensive to defend Christianity and the huge Spanish empire in Europe, which expanded when King Charles I of Spain became Holy Roman Emperor Charles V in the mid-sixteenth century. Spanish kings' demands for revenues from the New World were aggressive and unending. When faced with conflict between Christian virtue and treasure, the crown most assuredly chose the latter.

The administrative and economic complex of Spanish colonial rule evolved around the extraction of precious metals, such as gold and silver. For three hundred years the crown managed to walk a tightrope between meddling in the smallest matters involving revenue and

Spanish and Portuguese Colonial America

The phrase *obedezco pero no cumplo*, which means "I obey but do not comply," aptly describes the ability of the colonists to refuse laws that they opposed.

There is considerable debate over the size of the population of the New World at the time of the arrival of the Europeans. For Mesoamerica in 1519, estimates range from 4.5 to 25.2 million, and for Peru from 3 to 32 million inhabitants. The best current estimates are probably 12 to 25 million for Mesoamerica, 9 million for Peru, and 2.4 million for Brazil. But there is no question that the population underwent a catastrophic decline. One estimate based on postconquest tribute (taxation) records posits that the population of Mesoamerica stood at 25.2 million in 1519 and then fell to 16.8 million in 1532; 6.3 million in 1548; 2.65 million in 1568; 1.9 million in 1580; 1.375 million in 1595; 1.075 million in 1605; 0.75 million in 1622. The destruction took place in successive epidemics, first of smallpox and measles, later influenza. In the mid-seventeenth century yellow fever and malaria arrived from Africa. By 1650 contact with Europeans had eliminated 90 to 95 percent of the native population. (Accepting the lower range of estimates for Mesoamerica in 1519, the percentage loss is over 80 percent for a population of 12 million.)

The demographic collapse changed landholding patterns, crop production, ecology, labor systems, and methods of administration. Formerly dense populations of native peoples disappeared, replaced by Europeans, Africans, and migrants from other regions. The decline was uneven, some areas were harder-hit than others. However, the devastating physical and psychological toll did not destroy the indigenous cultures.

Given the scarce resources and manpower and the vast distances between Spain and its empire, the first impulse of the Spanish was to merely take over the top ranks of the hierarchical indigenous societies. The native elite would remain in place, retaining most of its privileges, and ensuring that their subjects furnished tribute in the form of taxes and labor. However, the drop in population forced the Spaniards to involve themselves more extensively with the native people.

Because the revenues from Peru and New Spain, as the Spaniards named the Mesoamerican part of the empire, were so important, the crown constructed a large bureaucracy to administer them. These Spanish bureaucrats, with their propensity for paperwork, generated tons of laws, regulations, reports, and correspondence, which historians have used to study the period. Much of importance that happened was unrecorded, however.

At the top of the administrative pyramid, just below the Spanish king and based in Spain, was the Council of

pushing the colonists to rebellion. Colonial administration functioned differently in the regions central to mining than in those in the periphery. The central mining regions were highly regulated, while the far regions were left for the most part to rule themselves. The entire economic system, including commerce, landholding, and labor organization, was based on a complex of mining center, city, and *hacienda* (a large landed estate). A similar situation existed in Brazil, where the Portuguese concentrated their efforts on the production of sugar, with interludes for gold and diamonds.

Two practical considerations shaped Iberian governance in the New World. First, the precipitous and catastrophic decline of the native population forced constant readjustments of Spanish policies. Demographic recovery resulting not only from increased immunities of the native peoples to European diseases after the mid-seventeenth century but also from the growing population of mixed-bloods (*mestizos* and mulattos) and white immigrants also forced important shifts. Second, the great distances between Spain and Portugal and their colonies and the inability of either to station large number of soldiers in the New World meant that flexibility was crucial. Colonists were in a favorable position to oppose onerous laws or policies.

III.
INDI, QVA ARTE AVRVM EX
MONTIBVS ERVANT.

E X POTOSI montanis, aurifodinis omnium ditiſſimis per o-
mnem Indiā, aurum Indi hac arte effodiunt, qua in noſtris ferè
regionibus itidem factitant. Nā ex rupibus excindenda omnia
ſunt. Operarios in duos ordines diſpeſcunt. Quorum hi de die la-
borantes, noctu quieſcunt: illi noctu operis vacantes, interdiu dormiunt.
Quamuis nec diurnam nec nocturnam cæli facem videat, ſed vniuerſim ſuc-
cenſis cereis opus habeant: Cum vltra 150. orgias infra terram ſeſe demittant.
Nec tamen iſta tàm immenſa fodinarum profunditas impedit, quò minus
omne effoſſum as ſuis dorſis foras efferre cogantur. Quem in vſum ſcalas ad-
hibent, ita ſtructas parataſq́, vt bina ſibi ſemper cöiuncta hæreant. Scalæ verò ex intortis boum coriis confectæ ſunt, qua tranſuerſis radiis ligneis ſuffir-
mantur ita, vt ternis viris ſemper ex ordine deſcenſu vno latere, altero verò
totidem aſcenſus ſit. Cumq́, in aſcenſus labore vtraq́, manu ſcalas corripere
cogantur, ideo, qui illorum primus eſt, cereum ardentem de pollice religatum
geſtat. Porrò, quia meta aſcenſuris nimis longa eſt, iccirco in media via ſur-
recta quædā ſcamna ſunt, quibus onera ſua quadamtenus deponere poſſunt.

*A silver mine at Potosí, in Peru. The mine provided enormous wealth
for the Spaniards, but many of the Indian laborers lost their lives in
the harsh working conditions.*

the Indies. It was responsible for the legislative, judicial, and consultative functions of colonial administration, both recommending the appointment of officeholders and scrutinizing their work. Unfortunately, very few members of the Council had any experience in the colonies. The crown's ranking representatives in the Americas were the viceroys. Initially, there were two viceroys, one for New Spain and one for Peru. Each viceroy was responsible for general administration, tax revenues, public works, social order, defense, and protection of the native peoples. Although in theory they were substitute kings, in practice the viceroys were limited in power by the overlapping jurisdictions of the crown's financial officers and the Church. Because the viceroyalties proved far too large to administer, the crown divided them into smaller units known as *audiencias* (the equivalent of provinces). These in turn were divided into even smaller, local units known as *corregimientos,*

alcaldías mayores, and *gobernaciones* (the equivalent of districts). And finally, at the lowest level were the municipalities. The viceroy headed the audiencia in his capital; in the other regions they were headed by captain-generals. The *cabildo* (or city council) administered the municipalities. Each of these organizations had legislative and judicial as well as administrative functions.

The crown bureaucracy was meddlesome, corrupt, and inefficient. Because Spanish kings were always short of funds, they resorted to selling colonial offices. This practice had one positive and one negative effect. In the first instance, it enabled American-born Spaniards, known as *criollos* (creoles), to obtain offices, and thus presumably assured that colonial administration, especially at the municipal level, would be more responsive to local needs. In the second instance, however, the initial cost of acquiring office and the poor salaries offered forced officeholders to use their positions for profit-making enterprise. This situation ensured a high degree of corruption and suffering for subject people. The crown's colonial bureaucracy closely regulated all aspects of society and economy, often to the smallest detail. The rules and regulations were not always based on colonial realities and therefore were often widely ignored. The discrepancy between law and practice, then, became so large that it discredited law and government.

The introduction of sugar into Brazil made that colony a money-making enterprise and led to building permanent settlements. The native population, for the most part comprised of nonsedentary and semisedentary peoples, proved quite unwilling to subject themselves to the harsh labor conditions on sugar plantations. Resisting such work, they fled into the interior out of their tormentors' reach. Like their brethren in Spanish America, they lacked immunity to European diseases and died in great numbers. The Portuguese then turned to the importation of African slaves to work the sugar plantations and *engenhos,* or sugar mills.

The Portuguese were somewhat more relaxed in their governance than the Spanish. Their administration began as private enterprise in the form of vast grants of land by the crown, known as donatory captaincies. The recipients in turn had wide latitude to grant land to settlers and name officials, in return for which they were obligated to pay revenue to the crown. Most of the captaincies failed from the lack of capital, inability to attract enough colonists, or poor management. The danger of French intrusions in the mid-sixteenth century forced the crown to take a more formal role in the administration of Brazil. For this purpose, the Portuguese crown established the Overseas Council, which

LETTER OF VICEROY FRANCISCO DE BORJA TO HIS SUCCESSOR, 1621

■ *On the occasion of the completion of their term, the viceroys reviewed their terms in* memorias *or* memoirs *to their successors. This selection clearly indicates that Borja's priorities lay in the extraction of silver. It also reveals his deep-seated contempt for the native peoples. The Indians reported for work in the mines as part of a system of forced labor known as the* mita.

The Indians assigned for the labor [in the mines] are supposed to enter on Monday morning, and for this they assemble at a place called Guaina at the foot of the hill. Here the corregidor reviews them and delivers them to the recipients . . . and they work through the following Saturday. In fact, given their laziness and drunkeness that appears on holidays, it has always been difficult to get them rounded up before Monday afternoon, or even Tuesday morning . . . The holidays that they are supposed to observe are few . . . and the mineowners have tried to make them work on the holidays that the councils have left open, it has not seemed convenient to concede this. For they are miserable people and recently converted, and the labor of those few is hardly worth considering.

functioned like the Council of the Indies. The Portuguese equivalent of the viceroy in Spanish America was the governor-general. Both Spanish and Portuguese decentralized governance, with regions and localities operating quite independently in routine matters. Powerful family groups arose to rule over these geographic fragments.

Both crowns paid close attention to revenue-producing areas. In New Spain the central corridor extended from Parral in Chihuahua, through Zacatecas and Guanajuato into Mexico City, and then to Veracruz, the major Caribbean port. This corridor was intensely monitored because it included the most important mining camps and trading routes. The same was true for the highland mining centers in Peru. The Spanish crown demanded one-fifth of the value of all ores mined in its empire. It also maintained a monopoly over the production and supply of mercury, which was essential for silver extraction. Both Iberian colonial empires tried to limit their colonies' trade to the mother country. Spain went further, restricting New World trade to only one port in Spain, Seville, and two in the Americas, Veracruz and Panamá, and allowing goods to be transported on only one or two heavily guarded convoys sent back and forth across the Atlantic each year. (This was known as the *flota*, or fleet system.) Constructed to maximize crown revenues, the overbearing economic system added greatly to the cost of living in the colonies and resulted in widespread smuggling. The most notorious example of the adverse effects of the system was the

prohibition of direct trade between Spain and Buenos Aires (in what is now Argentina). The colonial administration required goods to be shipped from Spain to Panamá, then to Peru, then across the Andes and Pampas to Buenos Aires on the Atlantic coast. The extra cost of this wayward route was large. Obviously, these rules were made to be broken. Crown customs officials were easily bribed, and smuggling in the vast underadministered territory was easy and rampant. Corruption and inefficiency made the system less onerous.

It was crucial for the Iberians to integrate the native peoples into their economic system, for without their labor, the colonies could not have survived. The two most important institutions for this acculturation were the Catholic church and the *hacienda*, or large landed estate.

The Church came early to the Americas to convert the native peoples to Christianity. A small number of regular clergy, composed of members of the Franciscan, Dominican, Augustinian, and later Jesuit orders, often heroically led the way into new territories. Initially, they tried to destroy the vestiges of the heathen religions. Unfortunately, in doing so, they erased much of the historical and cultural record of pre-Columbian times. But the friars quickly realized that they had to learn native cultures, religions, and languages in order to teach the people the word of their god. The regular clergy also sought to protect the native peoples from the rapacious European settlers. The resulting conflicts often led to violence. In one case in northern Brazil, several regular priests were forcefully put to sea in a raft;

the raft capsized and the passengers drowned, to the great satisfaction of the Portuguese settlers.

The most famous Spanish protector of the native peoples was friar Bartolomé de las Casas (1474–1566). In the early sixteenth century he gained the ear of the Spanish crown, who at his behest prohibited Indian slavery. Later in the colonial era the regular clergy were replaced by secular clergy, who were often American-born, far more pragmatic, and less solicitous of the native population. However, the crown itself was rarely willing to sacrifice mineral production for the spiritual well-being of the natives. In a choice between religion and the need for native labor, gold and silver took precedence.

By indoctrinating the native peoples into Catholicism, the priests taught them obedience and passivity. The misery of this world would be rewarded by heaven in the next. Any deviance from the norm was expurgated by the Inquisition, the Church's investigative arm.

Most native and mixed-blood (*mestizo*) people blended their folk culture and religion with Christianity to produce a unique form of Catholicism. Especially in the countryside, Catholicism was only imperfectly absorbed. There were never very many regular clergy. As a result, they touched the people of the periphery only lightly. The nomadic peoples fiercely resisted any incursions. In the cities many more priests presided and Catholicism was more conventional.

The Church also functioned as an important financial institution. It became enormously wealthy because many rich colonists bequeathed their funds and estates, others purchased penance in the form of indulgences, and the entire population was supposed to pay the tithe, usually a ten percent assessment on their income. Collectively, the Church was the largest rural property holder and urban landlord in New Spain and operated as the most important commercial and mortgage banker.

The hacienda evolved as a consequence of population decline in the demographic disaster, which caused a severe shortage of labor and the abandonment of large tracts of land. Originally the Spaniards adopted an institution from the Iberian Peninsula, later adapted to the Caribbean, the *encomienda*, which was a grant of tribute from the native people of a specified geographic entity, usually paid in the form of labor. The encomienda, however, presented serious problems for the Spanish crown. The owners of the encomiendas showed every indication of turning themselves into a New World hereditary nobility, a development the crown vigorously resisted. Most important, the decline in population wiped out the basis of the grant—people. Next the Spaniards turned to *repartimiento*, a forced labor system, but there

were not enough natives to fill the work quotas. The hacienda proved a solution to the shortage of labor, for it attracted native workers by offering to pay their tribute and church fees (for marriage, baptism, funeral). Hacienda laborers accumulated large debts that were passed on unpaid to their children. This system of debt peonage, however, offered some advantages, for it protected laborers from oppressive taxation or other obligations and provided an opportunity for security. In areas such as northern Mexico, indebtedness was more of an advance in wages than a burden. The evolution from encomienda to hacienda occurred unevenly. In some areas encomienda lasted centuries; in others different labor systems existed side by side.

The decline in native population caused both Spanish and Portuguese to turn to Africa to supply labor needed for New World plantations and mines. Large numbers of slaves were imported into Brazil, Mexico, and Peru. By 1800 2.5 million African slaves had been brought to the Americas, three-quarters of them to Brazil. The most profound impact was in Brazil. Because of a seemingly unending potential supply from Africa, the plantation owners of Brazil determined it was cheaper to work slaves to death than to feed or treat them well.

Life in Latin America Under Colonial Rule

The influx of Iberians, the loss of native population, and the realignment of landholding brought vast changes to life in the New World. The Europeans demanded different foods, most importantly wheat, olives, and wine. They brought with them new plants and animals. Their cattle, sheep, and goats required a completely altered pattern of land ownership and land usage. In an effort to better acculturate and administer the native peoples, the Spanish colonial government often tried to congregate or resettle them. Agriculture reorganized to supply markets in the mining camps and cities.

The great empires that preceded the Iberians were socially stratified, and colonial society was no different, but the Europeans added the new dimension of race. Under Spain and Portugal, whites were at the top of the social pyramid. Being white did not by any means assure one such an exalted position, however. There were poor and middle-class Spaniards. Moreover, there were two types of Spaniards, those born in the New World, known as *criollos* (creoles), and those born in Spain, *peninsulares*, or as they were known disparagingly, *gachupines* (greenhorns). Occupationally, the colonial elite were

This painted wooden beaker from Spanish colonial Peru is decorated with a multiracial portrait of a Spanish trumpeter, an African drummer, and a Native American official.

large landowners, miners, merchants, upper-level clergy, and government officials. These categories often overlapped, for example, when successful merchants and miners purchased large estates. In the middle were artisans, retail merchants, intermediate-level bureaucrats, and priests in the cities and, though their ranks were few in number, small farmers and ranchers in the countryside. Racially the middle comprised whites and some mixed-bloods, most likely *mestizos* or less often, *pardos*. The vast majority of the population, which included mestizos, pardos, Indians, and free Africans, was poor and lived in a continual state of deprivation. Most of the lower class lived in rural areas. At the very bottom were the African slaves, commodities to be bought and sold. Economically, urban and household slaves may have at times been better off than their mestizo or Indian counterparts, for their masters generally guaranteed them a minimal subsistence. Those who depended on market forces to determine their wages had no such guarantee. The distribution of wealth was extremely unequal, for the rich had almost all the resources and the poor virtually none. There was minimal chance for upward mobility. Mestizos and pardos were known to have purchased certificates of purity of blood that attested to their whiteness. Money could sometimes buy social standing, but rarely was the opportunity available.

The primary institution for the survival of Indian culture was the village, enduring through the demographic losses, the overbearance of the hacienda, and resettlement. It was most resilient in the regions on the periphery outside Spanish centralized rule. Communal landholding persisted, but most Indians had to work outside the village to obtain merchandise unavailable there. Hacienda and village developed a complex relationship, which was symbiotic when the hacienda needed labor and the villagers needed to supplement the subsistence yield of their individually or communally owned land, and which conflicted when the two fought over scarce land and water resources. Many Indians moved to towns and cities to escape tribute exactions. They earned a bare subsistence as day laborers or in textile factories.

In a society obsessed with matters such as honor and manhood, women were repressed by a double standard of behavior. There were, however, various ways to escape these constraints. Indeed, entrance into a convent was an important means for wealthy women to obtain their independence. Widows also obtained considerable autonomy, especially if they were beyond childbearing age and thus free of pressure to remarry, because they were entitled to one-half their husbands' estates.

Rural and urban working-class women worked, for few families could survive without their income. In the countryside they planted and harvested. In the cities and towns the market vendors were often women. Other employment was available as domestic servants for the rich and as factory workers, particularly in the textile mills.

For men and women of the lower classes, life was a struggle to subsist. One of the most remarkable statistics of Latin American history is the fact that wages on the haciendas on the central plateau of Mexico stayed the same from 1650 to 1800, at a level that was not sufficient to provide the basics of food and shelter for a family. Wages rose only in areas such as the northern mining districts where labor was scarce.

The population of Latin America began to increase in the second half of the seventeenth century, when at last the Indian population, having developed immunities to European diseases, began to recover and the number of mixed-bloods and whites grew, the latter through immigration. This growth added to the general misery of the people and presented colonial rulers with a new set of difficulties. When these new pressures combined with a series of external events in Europe, they caused a crucial political realignment in the New World empires.

From 1519 to 1700 the great empires of the New World fell to the onslaught of internal dissension,

America and the Encounters

1325	Aztecs settle on Lake Texcoco
1427	Triple Alliance: Tenochtitlán, Tlacopán, Texcoco
1438-71	Reign of Sapay-Inca Pachacuti
1471-93	Reign of Sapay-Inca Topa Inca Yupanqui
1492	First voyage of Columbus
1493-1525	Reign of Sapay-Inca Huayna Capac
1500	Cabral discovers Brazilian coast
1516	Charles I ascends Spanish throne
1519	Hernán Cortés lands in Veracruz
1521	Tenochtitlán destroyed by Spanish-Tlaxcalan siege
1525	Civil war between Inca factions led by Huáscar and Atahuallpa
1527	First *Audiencia* and bishopric established in New Spain
1531	Francisco Pizarro reaches Peru
1555	Philip II succeeds to Spanish crown
1572	Execution of Tupac Amarú ends Inca resistance
1650	Low point of native population in Mexico, less than one million

Iberian arms, and European diseases. The new rulers, intolerant of the conquered, tried mightily to destroy indigenous culture and religion. They achieved only limited success. The vanquished did not succumb easily, fighting for centuries to preserve their ways. The Spanish and Portuguese never conquered all of Latin America, but rather succeeded only in occupying crucial areas. Flexible but authoritarian, meddlesome but inefficient, religious but ruthless, both Spanish and Portuguese colonial rule comprised a series of paradoxes.

The changes wrought by the encounter between Europeans and the native peoples of the Americas were extensive and profound. The very face of the land changed: where corn had once sprouted, wheat grew and cattle grazed. Where once the temples of Aztec gods had stood, Catholic churches dominated the skyline. But in many respects, life for most native people changed little with the coming of the Europeans. The Aztecs were feared and loathed throughout Mesoamerica. They were cruel conquerors, who at times demanded terrible tribute in the form of victims for human sacrifice, and who at the very least required the payment of luxury commodities while contributing little to their subjects. Though the Incas offered opportunity to share in the spoils of conquest and the benefits of tribute labor, such as roads and emergency food stores, they too exacted a high price from their subjects, who were forcibly resettled, held hostage, deprived of their gods, and forced to work for no recompense. The Spaniards who replaced the Aztecs and Incas were also takers. Those who defend the Iberians claim that religion, language, and peace were considerable contributions, but the Spaniards and Portuguese brought little to improve the lives of their subjects. They ruled for so long because the calamitous population decline of the native peoples made sustained resistance impossible for two centuries. But after the mid-seventeenth century, when the population began to recover, unrest recurred. As we will see (in Chapter 28), in the eighteenth century colonial rule became so burdensome to Latin America that it threw off its Iberian shackles.

In the centuries following the discovery of America and a passage to the East Indies by the Cape of Good Hope, a worldwide marketplace for the exchange of commodities emerged—a living symbol of the mixture these encounters had engendered. First the Dutch and then the English established monopoly companies to engage in exotic trades in Asia. First the Spanish and Portuguese, then the English and French established colonial dependencies in the Atlantic, which they carefully nurtured in hope of economic gain. Protected trade flourished beyond the wildest dreams of its promoters. Luxury commodities became staples; new commodities became luxuries. Trade enhanced the material life of all European peoples, though it came at great cost to the Asians, Africans, and Latin Americans whose labor and raw materials were converted into the new crazes of consumption. The consequences of black slavery and the destruction of native populations had as significant an impact on the modern world as the discoveries and encounters themselves.

SUGGESTIONS FOR FURTHER READING

EUROPE AND THE ENCOUNTERS

Felipe Fernández-Armesto, *Columbus* (Oxford: Oxford University Press, 1991). The best of the new studies. Reliable, stimulating, and up-to-date.

Felipe Fernández-Armesto, *Before Columbus: Exploration and Colonisation From the Mediterranean to the Atlantic 1229-1492* (London: Macmillan, 1987). A comprehensive survey. Difficult but rewarding.

C. R. Boxer, *The Portuguese Seaborne Empire 1415-1825* (London: Hutchison, 1968). A comprehensive history of the first of the explorer nations.

* Samuel Morrison, *Christopher Columbus, Mariner* (New York: New American Library, 1985). A biography by a historian who repeated the Columbian voyages.

* Dan O'Sullivan, *Age of Discovery 1400-1550* (London: Longman, 1984). Best short, synthetic work.

* J. H. Parry, *The Age of Reconnaissance* (New York: New American Library, 1963). A survey of technological and technical changes that made possible the European discovery of America.

* Eugene Rice, *The Foundations of Early Modern Europe 1460-1559* (New York: Norton, 1970). An outstanding synthesis.

AFRICA AND THE ENCOUNTERS

* Philip Curtin, *The Rise and Fall of the Plantation Complex: Essays in Atlantic History* (New York: Cambridge University Press, 1990). A highly readable survey of the context in which the African slave trade arose.

* Sidney W. Mintz, *Sweetness and Power: The Place of Sugar in Modern History* (New York: Viking Penguin, 1985). A fascinating history of sugar's impact on historical development.

* J. F. Ade Ajayi and Michael Crowder, eds., *History of West Africa*, 3d ed., Vol. I (New York: Longman, 1985). An encyclopedic treatment of all West African history.

A. F. C. Ryder, *Benin and the Europeans, 1485-1897* (New York: Humanities Press, 1969). A detailed discussion of one important West African state and its relationship with Europeans.

* David Birmingham and Phyllis Martin, eds., *History of Central Africa*, Vol. I (Harlow, UK: Longman, 1983). An edited survey of the history of a broadly defined central Africa in the precolonial era.

Anne Hilton, *The Kingdom of Kongo* (Oxford: Oxford University Press, 1985). A recent, comprehensive, but somewhat controversial analysis of the Kingdom of Kongo.

John Thornton, *The Kingdom of Kongo: Civil War and Transition, 1641-1718* (Madison, WI: University of Wisconsin Press, 1983). A standard survey of the decline of the Kongo state.

M. D. D. Newitt, *Portuguese Settlement on the Zambesi: Exploration, Land Tenure and Colonial Rule in East Africa* (London: Longman, 1973). A dense, extremely thorough analysis of Portuguese activity in Mozambique.

David Beach, *The Shona and Zimbabwe, 900-1850* (London: Heinemann, 1980). A historical analysis of the region of the Mwene Mutapa.

AMERICA AND THE ENCOUNTERS

Mark A. Burkholder and Lyman L. Johnson, *Colonial Latin America*. (New York: Oxford University Press, 1990). This comprehensive introduction to colonial history incorporates the latest research on social history.

Inga Clendinnen, *Ambivalent Conquests: Maya and Spaniard in Yucatan, 1517-1570* (New York: Cambridge University Press, 1987). Innovative look at the interaction of Spanish and Indian.

Inga Clendinnen, *Aztecs* (New York: Cambridge University Press, 1991). Broad interpretation using Aztec texts.

Hernán Cortés. *Five Letters of Cortes to the Emperor*, trans. J. Bayard Morris (New York: Norton, n.d.). Illuminating propaganda.

Alfred W. Crosby, Jr., *The Columbian Exchange: Biological and Cultural Consequences of 1492* (Westport, CT: Greenwood, 1972). Standard study of the plants, animals, and diseases exchanged by new world and old.

Charles Gibson, *Spain in America* (New York: Harper, 1966). Classic examination of the institutions of Spanish rule.

Ramon A. Gutierrez, *When Jesus Came, the Corn Mothers Went Away: Marriage, Sexuality, and Power in New Mexico, 1500-1846* (Stanford, CA: Stanford University Press, 1991). Brilliant and provocative view of the interchange of Spanish and native societies from the native perspective.

Miguel Leon-Portilla, *The Broken Spears: The Aztec Account of the Conquest of Mexico* (Boston: Beacon, 1969). Gripping story of the conquest from the Aztec side.

James Lockhart and Stuart B. Schwartz, *Early Latin America: A History of Colonial Spanish America and Brazil* (New York: Cambridge University Press, 1983). This is a sophisticated analysis of Iberian colonial rule.

Alfred Metraux, *The History of the Incas* (New York: Schocken Books, 1969). Comprehensive study.

R. C. Padden, *The Hummingbird and the Hawk* (New York: Harper, 1970). A provocative and controversial view of the Aztecs, it presents a brilliant picture of a terroristic state.

Thomas C. Patterson, *The Inca Empire* (New York: Berg, 1991). An up-to-date survey.

Caio Prado, Jr., *The Colonial Background of Modern Brazil*, trans. Suzette Macedo (Berkeley, CA: University of California Press, 1971). Standard introduction to Brazilian colonial history.

Jacques Soustelle, *Daily Life of the Aztecs*, trans. Patrick O'Brian (Stanford, CA: Stanford University Press, 1961). Thorough examination of life in the Aztec empire.

Stuart B. Schwartz, *Sugar Plantations in the Formation of Brazilian Society, 1550-1835* (New York: Cambridge University Press, 1985). Comprehensive study of the most important aspect of Brazilian economy during the colonial era.

Karen Spalding, *Huarochi: An Andean Society under Inca and Spanish Rule* (Stanford, CA: Stanford University Press, 1984). Insightful view of the interchange of conquerors and conquered.

Stanley J. and Barbara H. Stein, *The Colonial Heritage of Latin America* (New York: Oxford University Press, 1970). The classic exposition of the burden of colonial rule on the new nations of Latin America.

Steven J. Stern, *Peru's Indian Peoples and the Challenge of the Spanish Conquest* (Madison, WI: University of Wisconsin Press, 1982). Provocative examination of the ways in which the native people of Peru resisted their oppressors.

* Indicates paperback edition available.

THE OLD *BEZESTAN:* MARKETS, MERCHANTS, AND PATRON SAINTS

Evliya Chelebi, a Turkish traveler born in 1611 in Istanbul, the capital of the Ottoman Empire, writes of the Old *Bezestan* (shown here), the oldest part of the central marketplace in his native city: "It is a great warehouse like a fortress, where the goods of all the military men and viziers are deposited . . . [with] six hundred shops." Evliya enumerates twenty-five kinds of merchants and artisans who work in the Old *Bezestan* or in the uncovered markets that surround it, which together employ several thousand people. An example of the professions enumerated are the satin merchants, of whom he says: "They are three hundred men, with one hundred and five shops. Their patron is Mansur, from Islamic Spain, who was girded [for his saintliness] by Salman [a companion of the Prophet Muhammad] . . . They are for the most part Jews."

With its lofty vaults and well-lit avenues, the Old *Bezestan,* built by the Ottoman sultan Mehmed the Conqueror after his acquisition of the Byzantine capital in 1453, was an impressive monument for the sultan's new seat of government. Evliya's description suggests areas of dependency between the market and the government. The market was used by government officials as a secure place to store goods and to deposit money with large merchants, who were the bankers of this world. Yet the government's attempts to control these merchants and artisans had limits. In the reign of the Ottoman sultan Murad III (1574–95), when the government's attempts to fix meat prices ran counter to all real economic conditions, wholesale butchers simply disappeared from Istanbul and the government was ultimately forced to relent.

The marketplace and mosque were the two breathing spaces of the Islamic town—large public spaces in which people gathered freely, exchanged information and formed public opinion. But the central mosque served this function principally on Friday when attendance at the noonday prayer was obligatory and men and women were separated, whereas the markets were open most or all days of the week, and in them men and women, and Muslims and non-Muslims, circulated freely, although certain sections of the market—or, in large cities, small separate markets such as the "thread market"—tended to be dominated by women.

The culture of the marketplace in the early modern Islamic empires—the Ottoman, Safavid, Sharifian, and Moghul empires—shows both continuity and change. As in earlier Islamic regimes, the area of the marketplace was considered a legal entity, although its boundaries were defined by custom, since there were distinctions between sales made in and outside the market. As in earlier centuries, the wholesale merchants rented or owned space in vast caravansaries, secure buildings on which the ground or lower floors had space for pack animals, offices, and storage, and the upper floors space for travelers and artisans. And, as in previous centuries, an official market inspector, an official sanctioned by Islamic law, supervised weights and measures.

Yet the changed functions of the market inspector in the Ottoman and Safavid empires show the ambitions of central governments to regulate society in these new empires much more closely. The tax system canonized in Islamic law was fairly rigid about taxes on agriculture but specified very few taxes on trade.

But, although the law forbade tolls within the Islamic world, in practice Islamic governments had always maintained toll stations to collect such noncanonical taxes.

The new empires owed their strength in significant part to an increased volume of world trade, and they used the market inspectors to organize the professions into guilds and to tax the guilds and the merchants. In the Safavid empire the market inspector was also supposed to fix prices on basic commodities such as food; the Ottomans did the same, more effectively, through other officials.

The early modern empires were not, however, very successful in acquiring deep commitment from the merchant community to their regimes. While some categories of merchants might be treated as a unit for tax purposes, they viewed their collective nature as coming from some saintly figure who, like the Mansur of the satin merchants, had practiced their profession in the past. In general, societies looked to themselves and not to their ruling centers for their identity. The merchants, like the religious experts, preserved their distance from the powerful ruling establishments of these new empires, and remained a truly international community in the premodern Islamic world.

The Islamic World Before the Early Modern Empires

By the end of the thirteenth century, Muslims had more reason than ever to regard their world, the Islamic world, as the center of civilization. Muslims inhabited and ruled a vast band of territory from Spain to northern India, prominently positioned between the other major land areas of the Old World—sub-Saharan Africa, East and Southeast Asia, and Europe. Throughout this vast territory the great majority of governments relied on elite slave soldiers to control their subjects and protect their interests. The populations they ruled adapted to this institution, nearly unique in world history. They did so partly because their more vivid loyalties were not to governments but to many overlapping groups, some of them truly international. These multiple group identities wove societies together and made them flexible enough to survive violent invasions and changes of regime. Two of the most important groups, the large merchants and the religiously learned, wove together the basic fabric of the entire Islamic world. The merchants created networks of trade, credit, and agreed forms of contract. The religiously learned interpreted the laws of contract and fostered the study and exchange of written culture, thereby giving the Islamic world a surprising degree of intellectual unity. Thanks largely to these groups, cultural life in the Islamic world flourished even in periods of political turmoil.

The Emergence of New Rulers: 1100–1400

For the Islamic world of the Middle East in the premodern world, there were two great physical and moral lineages: Muhammad, the prophet to whom the revelation of Islam came in the seventh century, and Genghis Khan, the Mongolian conqueror and military genius who convinced the peoples of Central Asia in the thirteenth century that he and his descendants had a mandate from heaven to rule all the known world. Of the two, lineage from the Prophet, his clan and his tribe, proved the more durable; and even today the royal families of Jordan and Morocco claim direct descent from Muhammad. But the later claim of Genghis Khan that he had a God-given grant of rulership was able not only to legitimize many lines of royal descent but also to create a style of rulership that survived from the thirteenth to the eighteenth century.

Central Asian people first entered the Middle East as slaves. By the eleventh century many of the people of Central Asia spoke Turkish languages. (While "Turkish" can be used in its modern political sense for things related to the nation of Turkey, it is used in this chapter for the family of closely related languages that includes modern Turkish and the peoples who speak them.) Like their ancestors—peoples such as the Huns—they were superb horsemen. The 'Abbasid caliphs, the descendants of Muhammad's uncle who ruled the Islamic empire from 750, began in the ninth century to buy young Turkish slaves to raise as the elite cavalry needed to control their vast territories. On the completion of their training, in the course of which they invariably converted to Islam, these slaves, somewhat like successful Roman gladiators, were freed. But rulers and commanders had strong personal bonds to their former slaves because freed slaves were legally clients of their former owners who had often acted as foster parents to them while young. Usually, these owners became their employers when they were freed.

In the long run, however, the Turkish soldiers of the 'Abbasids proved more interested in enriching themselves from the caliph's treasuries or in ruling the caliph's provinces as independent governors than in saving the empire. But they did not dare assume formal independence because, to their Muslim subjects, legitimacy came only from the governors' recognition of an overlord, such as a caliph, whose lineage was connected with the Prophet. Therefore, most such soldier-rulers, who were in effect kings of their own lands, acknowledged the nominal overlordship of the 'Abbasid caliphs. Consequently, though the 'Abbasids lost the last fragment of real power when a Turkish commander took over their capital city of Baghdad in the 930s, they were preserved for three more centuries because, like the emperors of Japan, the caliphs gave legitimacy to the dynasties that inherited their empire. Even as a fiction, the claim that most of the Islamic world remained united under a caliph meant that Muslims had freedom of movement within that world. And, more important, the contracts Muslims formed, for marriage or for sale of goods, were recognized throughout the Islamic world, regardless of the temporary borders and changes of regime created by the caliphs' nominal governors.

One of the most important dynasties descended from Turkish military slaves was the Ghaznavids, named after their capital Ghazna, in what would later become Afghanistan, overlooking the mountain passes

to India. The Ghaznavid king Mahmud (998–1030) took advantage of his position to conquer over half of the Indian subcontinent. These conquests were rarely permanent, but they had many consequences. Mahmud, like future Muslim rulers, gained admiration and legitimacy by succeeding in his chosen role as a *ghazi*, a warrior who fought for Islam. He also opened the road for Muslim expansion into India. And the enormous amount of booty he brought back allowed him to be even more independent of his subjects than the kings before him. He even took the title *sultan*, which meant "dominion" or "authority" in Arabic; he was, literally, "Mr. Authority."

This separation between the people (often called the *ra'aya*, the "flocks") and a government headed by a military commander, was characteristic of most Middle Eastern Islamic regimes until the nineteenth century. The governments might be founded by tribes or, occasionally, even religious leaders, but they soon had to resort to slave and former slave soldiers as the mainstay of their rule. These slaves were expensive to buy, train, maintain, and equip in the most effective armor and weapons of the period. But, unlike tribes, they formed standing armies. Moreover, these military slaves were almost always from outside the Islamic world, not only because Islamic law forbade the enslaving of Muslims or protected peoples—such as the Christians and Jews—but also because rulers knew that outsiders were less likely to collude with the indigenous population.

The Arrival of The Turkish and Mongolian Tribes

Turks did not enter the Middle East only as slave soldiers. From the eleventh to the fifteenth centuries, whole tribes of Turkish nomads entered the Middle East in great waves of migration. The first wave entered in the eleventh century under the leadership of a royal clan called the Seljuqs. These Seljuq Turks, who were pious Muslims, preserved much of the social and cultural life of the area and created new forms of patronage, which in turn fostered Islamic Middle Eastern culture. They began using the developing Islamic law for pious endowments to found *madrasa*s (colleges), mosques, hospitals, and libraries.

Yet the foundations of Seljuq rule were far from stable. Despite their use of a large army of Turkish slave soldiers to rein in their unreliable army of Turkish tribes, they were defeated by these tribes in 1153. Disorder prevailed for about eighty years until a force appeared mightier than any seen in the Middle East since the Islamic conquests: the Mongols under Genghis

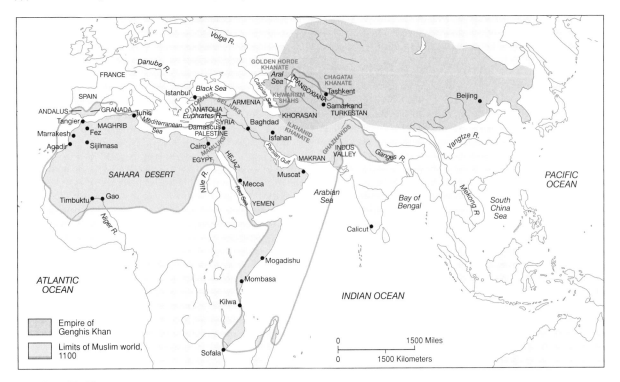

The Islamic World, 1100-1500

Khan. In 1219 Genghis launched an attack on the Islamic regime that ruled Transoxiana and Persia. His forces easily swept aside all Muslim opposition while they unleashed on many of the great cultural centers a wave of killing and destruction from which some never recovered; in Nishapur, for example, whose madrasas and men of learning were famous throughout the Islamic world, the Mongol troops carried out an order that neither a human of any age, nor "even cats and dogs should be left alive"; and the army returned several times to kill any inhabitants who might have survived in hiding.

As conquests continued under the descendants of Genghis Khan, who were, like him, not Muslims, the Mongol empire soon stretched from Hungary to Korea. But the real unity of the Mongol empire soon disappeared; and almost all of their Muslim subjects were ruled by the Mongols of Iran, the Il-Khans, or the Mongols of Russia, the Golden Horde. The Il-Khans ruled western Asia and their kingdom, whose rulers and troops eventually converted to Islam, lasted until the early fourteenth century. Toward the end of that century the Il-Khans were replaced by an empire that began with a wave of destruction rivaling the early Mongols: the em-

pire of Tamerlane. A Muslim of Mongolian descent, Tamerlane (1370–1405) reconstituted the empire of the Il-Khans, often with horrifying and very public demonstrations of his violence, such as the towers of skulls he made from the victims of his massacres. Tamerlane married a descendant of Genghis Khan and carried along a Genghisid puppet *khan* to give himself legitimacy. His far less warlike descendants ruled over dwindling kingdoms, as nomadic Turkish peoples divided the bulk of Tamerlane's lands between tribal rulers.

The influx of Turkish and Mongolian peoples had dramatic effects on the history of the Middle East. In their own historical tradition the people of the Middle East portrayed the Mongols as the villains of this great historical change, partly because most of the early Mongol rulers were hostile to Islam, now the religion of the overwhelming majority of the population. In contrast, the equally bloody conquests of the Muslim Tamerlane, who with few exceptions chose other Muslim powers as his victims, received a far better press.

The Mongols put a lasting stamp on the character of succeeding centuries of Turkish rule. Since so many of the troops the Mongols brought into or enlisted in the Middle East were Turks, the language of the Mongol ruling families of the Il-Khans and the Golden Horde soon became Turkish. And the long-term movement of the Slavic peoples south and east was halted for centuries as Turkish-speaking peoples dominated a great band of Asia from the area north of the Black Sea to the Pacific Ocean. Correspondingly, Turkish peoples regarded as nearly sacred descent from Genghis Khan and the customary law established by the Mongols. The universal mandate claimed by Genghis—"One sun in heaven, one lord on earth"—had such a dazzling effect both in creating the world's largest premodern empire and in momentarily uniting most of the Turks of Eurasia, that it was long remembered among Turkish peoples.

The Mongols had a strong tradition of unwritten law that originated in the decisions and maxims of tribal leaders. Genghis Khan's word weighed as that of no previous figure in Turco-Mongolian history had done, and gradually the story took hold that he had laid down a code called the Great Yasa. Before the Mongols, customary law and royal administrative law had existed uneasily alongside Islamic law. The Yasa was not fundamentally more acceptable to the specialists in Islamic law than any earlier form of customary law. However, it had greater authority than earlier non-Muslim law, and it was seen as a cumulative body of royal law that existed apart from the personality of the ruler, one that a ruler could change or amend but not cancel. Even Tamerlane, for all the authority he acquired as a world conqueror, reaffirmed the allegiance of his dynasty to the Yasa.

A fifteenth-century Egyptian painted leather figure in the form of a riverboat containing three archers. The figure was used in the shadow plays of the Mamluk period.

A Slave Aristocracy Rules Egypt and Syria

In Cairo in 1250, the freed slave soldiers of Saladin's much-weakened dynasty thrust aside their former masters and began to rule in their own right. They were called *Mamluks*, which literally means "those owned," and they represent a further step in the evolution of elite slave armies in the Middle East. Occasionally father-son successions appeared among these former slaves, but usually whichever Mamluk commander was most powerful would succeed his predecessor through persuasion or open warfare. This "slave" aristocracy bought its future commanders and sultans as boys from Turkish areas of Central Asia and from the Caucasus. The Mamluks recalled their Central Asian roots, even invoking the Yasa to settle disputes, although they remained free of Mongol rule.

In fact, the role of the Mamluks as champions of Islam against the Mongols was an important part of their success. In 1260 the Mamluk sultan handed the Mongols their first significant defeat in the Islamic world at a battle at Ain Jalut in Syria. Despite repeated attempts by the Mongol Il-Khans and their successors to conquer Syria, the Mamluks maintained control of Syria as well as Egypt for most of the next two and a half centuries. With non-Muslim Mongols ruling the Muslim east until 1295, Muslims came to see the Mamluk empire to their west both as a place of refuge and as a bastion of true belief. The Mamluks campaigned hard and successfully to drive the last Crusaders from the eastern Mediterranean. And, under the Mamluks, the emerging system of recognizing four schools of Islamic law as equally legitimate was established as a lasting element of orthodox Sunni Islam, the form of Islam accepted by the majority of Muslims.

People, Trade, and Culture in the Premodern Islamic World

The subjects of these Islamic regimes—perhaps half of whom had converted to Islam by the time of Mahmud of Ghazna—also found advantages in this system of military rule by outsiders, even though these military regimes often extorted heavy taxes in order to maintain themselves and sometimes acted like occupying armies. After the moral and military failure of the first two dynasties of caliphs, the Umayyads and 'Abbasids, Muslim subjects seldom felt committed to any regime; they settled for governments that at best kept violence restricted to fights within the military elite or against neighboring regimes.

Madrasa of the Shah's Mother in Isfahan, Iran.

The College with the Gilded Cage

In 1694, Shah Sultan Husayn (1694–1722) at age twenty-six emerged from the harem to rule the Safavid empire. Raised in the harem—where rulers sometimes kept their sons to prevent rebellions—Shah Sultan Husayn had little knowledge of the world. He was by nature quiet and studious, and when his mother built the college shown here he had a gilded cage prepared for himself so that he could take part in discussions among the religiously learned faculty who taught and studied at the college. Shah Sultan Husayn showed no aptitude for kingship and, while at first violently against the drinking of alcohol, soon became addicted to it. A weak man, he quickly found himself caught in a struggle between the court eunuchs and the specialists in religious learning, the ulama, who in the Safavid empire belonged to the Shi'ite branch of Islam. The empire more or less spontaneously disintegrated as subject peoples and neighbors became aware that no one was minding the throne, and in 1722 Shah Sultan Husayn gave his insignia of office to a former subject, an Afghan leader, who occupied the capital city of Isfahan.

Around the central courtyard of the *Madraseh-ye Madar-e Shah* (Madrasa of the Shah's Mother) are arcades of cells or rooms for students as well as rooms and recesses for classes. The *madrasa* contains a prayer hall and a library. Like many madrasas, it has nearby property, the income from which was dedicated by the founder to its upkeep. In this case, a building rented to merchants for offices, storage space, and even sleeping space helps maintain the college. It was not unusual for a woman to found a madrasa. Wealthy women, especially of royal families, often endowed madrasas and mosques, in part because of ties to leading religious figures.

Madrasas were colleges for training the ulama. With curricula centered on religious subjects, the madrasas are sometimes called theological colleges. But their curricula varied and might even include subjects such as astronomy, important for determining the time of prayer and its direction, since Muslims face Mecca to pray. Usually the terms of the endowment determined the curricula, although over time the number of subjects taught tended to increase and many subjects, such as philosophy were offered in private classes.

Even the public classes were not as formal as in modern schools. The students entered the madrasa with a basic literacy gained at a Qur'an school and sometimes, as in the Azhar, the major college of Cairo, memorization of the Qur'an was a prerequisite to entrance. Students in good standing could count on a bread ration to keep them alive during their years at the madrasa. Classes at the madrasa were largely based on reading and interpreting set texts until the highest levels of education, when the students engaged in open debate on subjects determined by the teacher. Students had a great deal of freedom, for there were seldom any formal degrees, only "permissions" granted by a reputable teacher for a student to teach a book or, at the highest level, to give a legal opinion.

Despite variations, in the thirteenth and fourteenth centuries a body of widely recognized classics on grammar, law, and kindred subjects began to emerge. After that time madrasa education gave a remarkable unity to the educated elite of the Islamic world. The ulama were not part of any church that could unify their opinions; but they wanted to prevent religious opinion from diverging in many directions, and the madrasas helped them. Ibn Battuta, probably the most traveled man in the world before the

fifteenth century, during the years between 1325 and 1349 found employment among Muslims as a judge or religious authority in many areas he visited—from sub-Saharan Africa to India, Central Asia, and even China—because Muslims recognized that the education he had received in his native Tangier in Morocco was similar to the education of Islamic learned men everywhere. Similarly, many of the bureaucracies of Islamic governments were staffed by men who had received some madrasa training and shared a common background.

In Persian and in many languages influenced by Persian, such as Urdu, the ulama were also called *mullahs*—one of whom is seen here entering a vestibule of the madrasa. The Shi'ite mullahs lived in an uneasy symbiosis with the Safavid monarchs. They were hungry for royal patrons but, at the same time, were never quite sure of the legitimacy of Safavid claims to rule. The proximity of this madrasa to the royal palace facilitated the Shah Sultan Husayn's participation and, at the same time, emphasized the building's royal patronage. The power of the Shi'ite mullahs at the end of the Safavid period encouraged them to develop the theory that they should run the government, a theory realized in the Iranian Revolution of 1978.

The nonmilitary elites also accommodated themselves to these regimes. The upper level of bureaucrats, among whom the vizier was most important as the public face of the sultan and the head of the civil bureaucracy, played a high-risk game in which they could become rich or lose their lives overnight. In contrast, the lower bureaucracy, as long as it remained appropriately faceless, often survived great upheavals in government unharmed. Like the upper level of bureaucrats, the wealthiest merchants were subject to arbitrary confiscation when governments had urgent need for money. But, as they were the only subjects of the sultan with large sums of cash the government could borrow, a sultan who was too greedy might lose all his credit in the marketplace and even be faced with the migration of his leading merchants. By and large the rest of the merchant community was left alone.

The situation of large landlords was more precarious. Like the lower bureaucrats, they were important to the governments because they often had a role in tax collection. But, unlike the lower bureaucrats, they were more exposed to the economic changes brought by the new regimes. From the tenth century the government began to assign land-tax revenues to soldiers, especially officers. This method of payment—in which the assignment was called *iqta'*—suited both soldiers and sultans so well that until the nineteenth century it was as characteristic of Islamic regimes as military slavery. Landlords were seldom directly harassed by the central government, but they were frequently harassed and sometimes replaced by the soldiers and their bailiffs who descended on the countryside to collect the revenues assigned to them. This system tended to discourage investment in improving the land, and most landlords chose to live in the cities to the further disadvantage of the countryside. The iqta' loosely resembled the European fief, but there was no hierarchy among fiefholders as in western Europe; and, while some iqta's did become hereditary, the government could always step in and reassign them to different holders.

Islam had no priesthood, but specialists in religious learning gradually became a semiprofessionalized elite and were collectively called *ulama*, "knowers" (See Special Feature, "The College With the Guilded Cage," pp. 446-447). But even after the foundation of special schools to train the ulama in the last half of the eleventh century, religious learning continued to be cultivated in various degrees by men who were also landlords, merchants, and bureaucrats.

In fact, almost all groupings in society overlapped: a craftsman who made silk brocade, lived in the quarter next to the citadel, subscribed to the Shafi'i version of Islamic law and the Ash'ari school of Islamic theology, and participated in the Qadiri order of Sufi mystics, would have a real loyalty to each of the groups to which he belonged. And each group would connect him with other groups: some makers of silk brocades might be Jews and some members of his Qadiri Sufi order might be wholesale grain merchants. Moreover, from the tenth to the nineteenth centuries in many Middle Eastern cities the population was also divided into two roughly equal factions that, although named after a profession such as the butchers or, more often, after a law school, included members of the community from other professions and law schools. The feuding between these factions became fierce at times when central government was weak, and it resembled the feuding between rival factions in some Italian city-states of the late Middle Ages. The majority of the population knew that if people did not maintain their multiple and overlapping identities they would become involved in factionalism of quarter, profession, or citywide groups to a degree that would inspire arson, murder, and other forms of destructive violence. This fear gave them yet another reason to want the rule of alien peoples such as slave-soldiers who, while commanding no vivid loyalty from their subjects, would act as arbiters generally more interested in order than in siding with any faction among the local population.

Middle Easterners were, more than ever, a "middle" people. An unwitting achievement of the Mongols was to bring to the Middle East a better knowledge of the Old World than any people had previously possessed. A vizier of the Il-Khans, Rashid ad-Din (1247-1318), wrote in Persian the most informed account of his time of all the cultures of Europe and Asia, including China. This was possible because the Pax Mongolica had for the first time created a continuous and busy overland traffic between the Mediterranean, the northeast European world, and East Asia. This overland trade continued with surprising vigor until the eighteenth century. Although western Europeans, especially Italians, continued to dominate merchant shipping in the Mediterranean, as they had since the eleventh century, Byzantine and Muslim participation in this trade was far from negligible.

The Indian Ocean was quite another matter. From the ninth century a network of Muslim traders spread all the way from East Africa to China. They came to dominate this area through daring, but they maintained their control through sound commercial practice. Islamic law had developed a sophisticated law of sale and partnership adaptable to a variety of market conditions. Thanks in significant part to a fairly uniform commercial law, Muslim traders knew what to expect of each other. The rise of Egypt under the Mamluks to preeminence among the centers of Islamic culture in the Arabic-speaking world owed a great deal to its position as an intermediary between the trade of the Indian Ocean and the Mediterranean.

In Islamic lands to the north and east of the Mamluks, an important feature of Turco-Mongolian rule was its cultural allegiance to the Persian tradition. Turkish tribes entered the Middle East through an area in which Persian was spoken. This meant that the leaders of these Turkish peoples saw Islamic Middle Eastern culture through a Persian filter. For many centuries the only major alternative to Arabic as a vehicle of written expression was Persian. Used principally in Iran, Afghanistan, and Central Asia, Persian appeared in the tenth century as a language of lyric poetry and became in the eleventh century the language of epic poems, historical chronicles, and administrative correspondence, including most of the correspondence between Turkish-speaking rulers.

From India to Anatolia, Turkish-speaking rulers carried Persian court culture. This culture included a taste for long poems, unlike Arabic literature, which excelled in the short poem of praise and lamentation. Persian poetry was the vehicle for long imaginative epics on the semilegendary Iranian past, on romantic themes, and on mystical themes. These epics became the focus of a tradition of extraordinarily beautiful book illustration that spread to India, Anatolia, and Central Asia. Not only the descendants of Genghis Khan but also Tamerlane—who tried to save people of talent from the general slaughters he ordered—and his descendants were discriminating patrons of literature, the arts, and even the scholastic sciences (such as logic and jurisprudence), which were usually written about in Arabic.

Islamic lands west of the Mamluks—Arabic-speaking like Mamluk Egypt and Syria—were called by their inhabitants the Maghrib (roughly, Morocco, Algeria, Tunisia, and Libya) and Andalus (Islamic Spain and Portugal). Nowhere in the Muslim West did cultural life develop more brilliantly than in Andalus. Here, under tolerant Muslim rulers, Christians, Jews, and Muslims exchanged ideas freely. Europeans received their first extensive knowledge of Aristotle through Latin translations from the Arabic, along with the ingenious commentaries of the Muslim scholar Ibn Rushd (in Latin, Averroës, often called by the Europeans simply The Commentator). And here, as in many other places, Muslims brought about a "green revolution" by introducing crops such as cotton, sugarcane, and oranges (all three English words were borrowed from the Arabic). But Christian zeal for the reconquest of the Iberian Peninsula, officially considered to be a "crusade," proved too strong for the Muslim kingdoms; after the Muslim defeat at Las Navas de Tolosa in 1212, it was all downhill for the Muslims. Granada, the last Muslim kingdom in Spain, hung on until 1492. Its conquest was considered so important that the inscriptions around the tombs of Ferdinand and Isabella, which have no reference to the discovery of the New World, mention as their great achievement the capture of Granada and the expulsion of the Jews from Spain.

A curious complement to the history of the Iberian Peninsula of Spain and Portugal is the history of the Anatolian Peninsula, which was to become the backbone of the Ottoman Empire. In both peninsulas—one European, the other Asian—a holy war, waged by the

Life in the City, *a Persian watercolor miniature of the sixteenth-century by Mir Sayyid 'Ali, ca. 1540. The scene, showing preparations for a betrothal feast, was painted to illustrate a story.*

FROM THE *TRAVELS OF IBN BATTUTA*

■ *Ibn Battuta, the fourteenth-century Moroccan traveler who, by virtue of twenty-five years of travel in Asia, Africa, and Europe, was probably the most widely traveled person in premodern times, wrote a detailed account of his travels that is a fundamental source for its period. Here he relates an incident that began in the Turkish-speaking part of the Middle East and ended in China.*

My purpose in traveling to these mountains was to meet a notable saint who lives there, namely Sheikh Jalal al-Din of Tabriz. At a distance of two days journey from his abode I was met by four of his disciples, who told me that the Sheikh had said to his dervishes who were with him: "The traveler from the west has come to you: go out to welcome him." He had no knowledge whatever about me but this had been revealed to him. I went with them to the Sheikh and arrived at his hermitage, situated outside the cave. There is no cultivated land there, but the inhabitants of the country, both Muslim and infidel, come to visit him, bringing gifts and presents, and the dervishes and travelers live on these offerings. The Sheikh, however, limits himself to a single cow, with whose milk he breaks his fast every ten days. It was by his labors that the people of these mountains became converted to Islam, and that was the reason for his settling among them. When I came into his presence he rose to greet me and I embraced him. He asked me about my native land and my travels, and when I had given him an account of them he said to me: "You are the traveler of the Arabs." Those of his disciples who were there said: "And the non-Arabs, too, our Master." "And of the non-Arabs too," he repeated, "so show him honor." Then they took me to the hermitage and gave me hospitality for three days.

On the day when I visited the Sheikh I saw that he was wearing a wide mantle of goatshair. It took my fancy and I said to myself: "I wish the Sheikh could have given it to me." When I visited him to bid him farewell, he . . . took off the mantle and placed it upon me . . . The dervishes told me that the Sheikh was not in the habit of wearing this mantle and had put it on only when I arrived, saying to them: "This mantle will be asked for by the Moroccan, and it will be taken from him by an infidel king, who will give it to our brother Burhan al-Din of Sagharj, whose it is, for whom it was made."

Now it came about a long time afterwards that I visited China and eventually reached the city of Khansa . . . [The king summoned me and] questioned me about the Muslim sultans and when I replied to his questions, he looked at the mantle and took a liking to it. The *wazir* said to me: "Take it off," and I could not resist his order.

This incident roused my anger, but afterwards I recalled the Sheikh's saying that an infidel king would seize it and I was deeply amazed at the fulfillment of the prediction.

The following year I entered the palace of the king of China at Khan-Beliq [Beijing] and sought out the convent of the Sheikh Burhan al-Din of Sagharj. I found him reading and wearing that identical mantle . . . "This mantle," he went on, "was specially made for me by my brother Jalal al-Din, who wrote me saying: 'This mantle will reach you by the hand of so and so.' " Then he brought out the letter and I read it and marvelled at the Sheikh's perfect knowledge.

From *Travels of Ibn Battuta in Asia and Africa, 1325–1359.*

majority religion of the continent to which they were attached, eventually triumphed: Christianity in Iberia and Islam in Anatolia. In both peninsulas a sense of historical mission carried the conquerors far beyond their original homeland, and lent legitimacy to their ruling families. Both the Habsburgs, who succeeded Ferdinand and Isabella, and the Ottomans needed the economic and military resources of subject peoples to sustain their enterprise of expansion. By the second half of the sixteenth century the Habsburgs and the Ottomans were the two mightiest powers of the European and Mediterranean world.

The Islamic World Divides Into Four Empires

In the sixteenth century most of the Islamic world belonged to four empires, generally known after their ruling families: the Sharifians, the Ottomans, the Safavids, and the Moghuls. Morocco, the most westerly part of the Maghrib, was the seat of the Sharifian empire. The rest of the Maghrib and the lands immediately to its east, namely Egypt, Palestine, Syria, many parts of Arabia and Iraq, and the great peninsula known as Anatolia, or Asia Minor, belonged to the Asian part of the Ottoman Empire. Iran was the seat of the Safavid empire, which controlled much of what is modern Afghanistan as well as areas of the Caucasus, the knot of mountains to the west of the Caspian Sea, and areas further east that are now considered parts of Central Asia. The Indian subcontinent was the seat of the Moghul empire.

The Ottomans, Moghuls, Safavids, and Sharifians, often called the early modern Islamic empires, created a degree of order that the Islamic world had not known for some centuries, and for periods succeeded in controlling their realms more effectively and at deeper social levels than had any Islamic governments prior to them. In this respect the Ottomans were the most successful and the three other empires were influenced by their example. These empires (with the exception of the Moghuls) made new use of the established practice of creating slave elites, and they all got more use out of their (often non-Muslim) vassals. They represented themselves as warriors for Islam, whether fighting for the extension of their governments into non-Muslim areas or defending Islamic governments against an increasingly aggressive Europe. Their success was in part due to the ability of their populations to produce for—and act as middlemen in—a considerably intensified world trade. At their height, the stability and wealth of their central governments enabled the material culture of these areas to reach new heights.

The Ottomans: From Border State to Mightiest Empire of Islam

The Ottomans enter world history around 1300 as leaders of a small group of Turks in charge of the area of Anatolia closest to the Byzantines. As a border state fighting the most venerable opponent of Islam, they considered themselves *ghazi*s, fighters for Islam, and consequently were joined by volunteers who also wanted the honor of being ghazis. Like other border people they shared many cultural traits with their opponents so that, when they began to have modest success in acquiring nearby territory, Byzantine nobles often joined them. And, like many border peoples, they were not subject to the scrutiny of orthodox scholars of their religion and could take advantage of the enthusiasm of various slightly heterodox groups such as the Anatolian devotees of Sufism, the mystical tradition of Islam.

From very small beginnings the Ottomans expanded rapidly. By the 1350s they had a permanent foothold in Europe. Soon after, the Ottoman ruler assumed the style of Sultan. The reaction in western Europe to Ottoman success was mild, but in eastern Europe a coalition including Serbs, Hungarians, and Bulgarians took on the Ottomans at Kosovo Polje in Serbia in 1389. In the ensuing battle—famous in Serbian history for the heroism shown by their side—so many Serbs were killed that it was a foregone conclusion that the Ottomans would, as they did, soon occupy and control Serbia and the rest of the Balkans.

At the end of the fourteenth century, western Europeans woke up to the threat the Ottomans posed. With the support of the papacy a large army of crusaders, composed not only of the nobility of areas neighboring the Ottomans but also of the knighthood of England, France, and Germany, proceeded with great pomp under the leadership of the king of Hungary and Bohemia down the Danube toward the Ottomans. Despite their bravery, the crusaders were completely overwhelmed by the Ottoman sultan Bayazid, in 1396 at Nicopolis in Greece. The Ottomans now had the best ghazi credentials of any ruler since Mahmud of Ghazna.

Anatolia, however, still consisted of a welter of dynasties, most of them Turkish; and when the Ottoman sultan Bayazid annexed their territories, these rulers appealed to Tamerlane. Bayazid, known in Turkish as "the Lightningbolt," did not hesitate to face this latest world conqueror as he entered Anatolia. In 1402 at Ankara, Tamerlane dealt Bayazid a resounding defeat and—according to one story—after taking him prisoner carried him around in a cage until the hapless Ottoman died in captivity.

Defeat at the battle of Ankara showed the weaknesses and strengths of the Ottoman system. A major Ottoman weakness was dependence on an army that included many Turkish tribes, who could be fickle and undisciplined, and many troops led by Christian vassal rulers, some of whom would throw aside their allegiance to the Ottomans in the moment of the sultan's weakness. However, the anti-Catholic sentiment of the

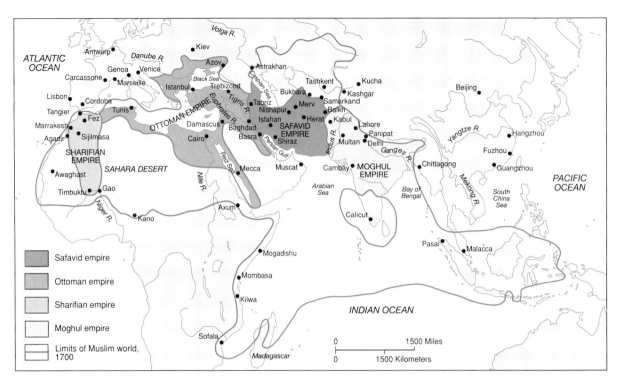

The Four Early Modern Islamic Empires, ca. 1700

Greek Orthodox church, which predominated in the Balkans, continued to help Ottoman rule and echoed the feeling of the Orthodox Patriarch, who said he would rather see in Constantinople the turban of the Turk than the mitre of the pope.

Nevertheless, the strengths of the Ottoman Empire were real enough to allow it to weather the storm. Very prominent among these strengths was the *timar* system, the Ottoman version of the Seljuk *iqta'*, upon which the Ottomans would increasingly depend after the defeat at Ankara. As they moved territory from vassalage to direct rule, they painstakingly recorded each region in registers listing the ownership of land and the number of households in the region. Then they assigned the tax revenues of the region to the sultan's loyal military supporters, including a fair number of Christians. These assignments or timars were at least large enough to support a single well-equipped mounted soldier, and sometimes large enough to support several other soldiers who fought alongside the timar-holder. Regional commanders had even larger assignments and acted both as provincial administrators and as field commanders. Timar-holders had a strong interest in keeping the Ottoman Empire a conquest state; for, as long as there was conquest, there were new territories to be divided into timars for relatives and retainers and new revenues to

keep the government from interfering with the income of timar-holders from existing timars.

By the reign of Bayazid's grandson, Murad II (1421–51), the Ottomans had developed significant new institutions that rendered them capable of creating the greatest Islamic empire in the Mediterranean since the early Caliphate of the eighth and ninth centuries. The Ottomans found that they needed, just as previous Islamic dynasties had needed, a standing army of freed slaves like the Mamluks; but in a bold innovation they domesticated the *mamluk* system. In contradiction to Islamic law, which guarantees the safety and possessions of Christians and Jews as long as they pay the taxes required of them, the Ottomans began a periodic levy of Christian boys inside their empire. They raised these boys as Muslims and trained them for service in the newly formed Janissary army corps and the Ottoman civil service. The prominence of this levy under Murad II opportunely fitted in with the new importance he gave to guns and artillery and his need to strengthen the central government against local heroes, especially renowned ghazis. The well-armed Janissary infantry protected the sultan in his palaces and surrounded him in battle; well-trained Janissary cannoneers gave his armies an advantage over Christian and Muslim opponents alike; and those in training for the Janissary corps who were spotted for administrative talent were separated and specially trained for high office in the sultan's administration. Gradually the training of the boys collected by the levy became the most elaborate and well-organized education ever created for soldiers and bureaucrats in Islamic history; and from 1453 most of the grand viziers, officials second only to the sultan, came from this background. Celibate until their "graduation" (usually in their twenties), slaves of the sultan and subject to his whim, the boys harvested by the levy were nevertheless offered a career with dazzling prospects. Bosnian Muslims were guaranteed a quota in the levies, and sometimes other Muslims tried to bribe levy officers to accept their children.

With its revived and new institutions, the Ottoman Empire saw over a century of nearly uninterrupted expansion. In 1453 Sultan Mehmed II, the son of Murad II, took Constantinople, the symbol of Christian resistance to Islamic conquest for seven centuries; and he rebuilt the city—usually called Istanbul by the Ottomans—with great splendor to give the empire a permanent capital worthy of his accomplishments. Mehmed gave to the Greek patriarch, the Grand Rabbi, and to other religious leaders theoretical and—often—real authority over the internal affairs of their people. The Ottomans not only tolerated religious diversity but also welcomed the Jews expelled from Spain.

On land the Ottomans carried all before them, and their European empire included Hungary, Croatia, Serbia, Bosnia, Albania, Greece, Bulgaria, Romania, and almost all of the districts of modern Russia and Ukraine adjacent to the Black Sea. In 1475, with the loss of Kaffa in the Crimea by the Genoese, the last route to Asia not in Muslim hands passed under Ottoman control. This loss contributed to the long-standing western European determination to reach East Asia by circumnavigating Africa (as Vasco da Gama did) or by finding a westerly

Venetian drawing of Suleiman the Magnificent leading a procession of Janissaries.

route (as Christopher Columbus attempted to do). The Ottomans acquired the largest segment of their Middle Eastern empire in one blow when they defeated the Mamluks in Syria at Marj Dabiq and then occupied Cairo in 1517. Not only did the Ottomans fall heir to the Mamluk role as guardian of the two holy places, Mecca and Medina, but they also gained responsibility as a sea power both on the Mediterranean and in the Indian Ocean, which had been newly invaded by the Portuguese. As rulers of the Arabic-speaking heartlands of the Middle East, the Ottomans inevitably came to see the Islamic tradition as much through Arab as Persian eyes.

The energies of the Spanish and Portuguese that had gone into the "reconquest" of the Iberian Peninsula were now fiercely directed toward North Africa, and a papal bull of 1494 required the faithful to help Spain in this "crusade." In 1497 the Spanish occupied the port of Malila in Morocco and subsequently took a whole string of ports including Algiers, which they occupied in 1510. Resistance to the Spaniards found its champions in an assortment of fearless North African sea captains, the most famous of whom was Khayr ad-Din Barbarossa (d. 1546). Barbarossa was by origin an Ottoman subject and a brilliant naval commander who lacked only the material support that the Ottomans could offer. With Barbarossa's help all of the North African coast except Morocco fell under Ottoman rule with its center at the recaptured port of Algiers. The interior, however, was seldom under Ottoman control and remained largely autonomous.

The acquisition of North Africa took place largely under Suleiman the Magnificent, whose reign from 1520 to 1566 has been considered the height of the empire. In Turkish Suleiman is known as Kanuni, the giver of *kanun*, or nonreligious law. Even the *shari'a*, the Islamic religious law, allowed some room for the ruler to dispense justice at his own discretion, and in practice most rulers in the Islamic world had taken a great deal of the law into their own hands and the hands of their officials rather than allowing it to remain in the hands of the *qadi*s, the judges appointed to adjudicate according to the shari'a. The Ottomans integrated the two systems of royal and religious law, and it was Suleiman who gave the combined system its fully mature form. The Ottomans even obliged the qadis to apply royal law alongside Islamic law in their courts.

This integration of royal and religious law reflects the degree to which the Ottomans penetrated and regulated society. The Ottomans were heirs to the Turco-Mongolian heritage of dynastic royal law and also to late-Roman traditions of law and bureaucracy preserved by the Byzantines. Like the Byzantines the Ottomans

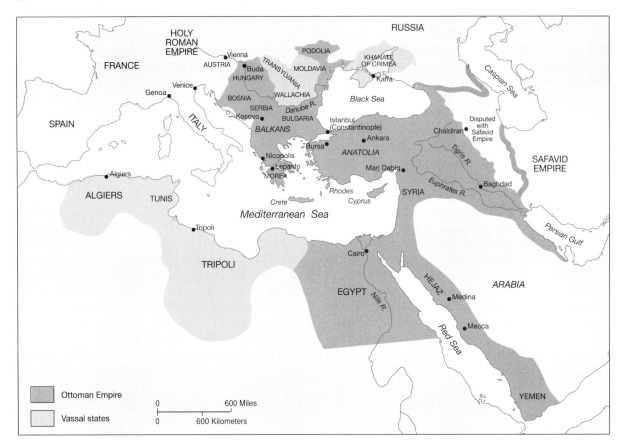

The Ottoman Empire at Its Peak in the 17th Century

organized the professions into guilds, counted households, and established supreme religious officials in their capital. While the Ottomans very often failed to control society to the extent that they wished, they came nearer to achieving such control than had any previous Islamic regime.

By the end of Suleiman's reign the empire had reached its natural limits. The Ottomans were never as successful at sea as on land. With their conquest of Egypt in 1517 they inherited the Mamluk struggle to push the Portuguese out of the Indian Ocean. For a while the Ottoman navy kept open the old route through Egypt, although they could never decisively defeat the Portuguese; and in the seventeenth century, when the larger fleets of the Dutch and English entered the Indian Ocean, these routes too were lost, and consequently the eastern Arab provinces of the Ottoman Empire became impoverished.

In the Mediterranean the Ottomans did not have the commercial fleet that the major Christian powers possessed; and they were dependent on the seafaring skills of such Ottoman subjects as Barbarossa in North Africa.

But the Ottomans had commercial interests, new provinces to protect and logistical needs to meet for further expansion in the Mediterranean, along which they controlled more than half the coast. They built a mighty navy and the Spaniards and Venetians, often enemies, allied themselves for a major confrontation. In 1571 at the battle of Lepanto off the coast of Greece in a ferocious fight with over two hundred galleys on each side, the Ottomans were defeated. Although the Ottomans rebuilt their fleet with amazing rapidity and although the Spaniards and Venetians quarreled and were unable to build upon their success, Lepanto was one of the great victories in the history of Christian Europe. The Ottomans had reached the limits of their expansion at sea. After Lepanto, seaborne Ottoman conquest in the Mediterranean was limited to the conquest of islands off their territories. And, as a further consequence, the independence of Morocco, the most distant part of North Africa and the only part of the Arab world to remain free of Ottoman rule, was assured.

Ottoman land expansion in Europe also reached its limit at this time. The Ottomans were hampered by the overland distance between Istanbul and Vienna, in miles and in time. They were also trapped by the rise of a formidable power immediately to their east in Persia, the Safavids. The Ottomans could neither move their army's barracks westward toward Vienna nor concentrate on their western front. These weaknesses grew out of a more serious weakness in Ottoman government: the central government remained too narrowly based on personal loyalty to the sultan, and any vital initiative—military or otherwise—required the personal commitment and attention of the sultan or his public face, the grand vizier.

The Safavids: From Sufi Mystics to Persian Emperors

In less than a decade the Safavid family rose from relative obscurity to world prominence, largely due to their long-established role as spiritual leaders of a Sufi religious order in Azerbaijan, the Turkish-speaking northwestern province of Iran. The mystical tradition of Islam known as Sufism holds that disciples of organized Sufi orders achieve spiritual advancement through complete obedience to their spiritual masters, who were believed to be powerful intercessors in heaven for those venerating them or their tombs. Usually Safavid rule is dated from 1501 when Isma'il (1501-24), a handsome youth, assumed the title of Shah of Iran. But the seed of Safavid rule had been planted over two centuries earlier when a Sufi leader in Azerbaijan established a Sufi mystical order that grew in respect and influence under his descendants, called Safavids. Such orders had increased after the appearance of the Mongols, partly because they offered points of social cohesion in times of political disruption and partly because Turco-Mongolian rulers respected holy men as seers and welcomed Sufis into their courts.

The Safavids soon acquired authority as spiritual leaders beyond Azerbaijan. At some point in the largely unrecorded history of the Safavid leaders before 1500, a large number of Turkish—and a few Kurdish—tribes in eastern Anatolia, northern Iraq, and eastern Iran were converted by Safavid propagandists and became fervently devoted to the Safavid leadership. The Safavids, while remaining Sufi leaders, also gained credit as ghazis by leading expeditions against the Georgian Christians in the Caucasus. With the advent of Shah Isma'il, the Safavids emerged as a genuine government with an unexpectedly effective army.

Isma'il stepped forward with virtually all the cards of legitimacy in his hand: He was a ghazi; a mystical leader who was owed total obedience; a near-divine being who fulfilled the esoteric speculations of Turkish nomads and others who awaited a Messianic leader; and a supposed descendant of the Prophet through the Prophet's son-in-law 'Ali, who was seen as the font of all wisdom. He reunited the area of the Iranian plateau and became the "Shah of Iran" and therefore heir to the royal tradition most deeply respected in western Asia. Lastly—and to the ultimate unmaking of his dynasty—he was the actual heir of the working tradition of tribally oriented Turco-Mongolian administration, which had existed continuously in Iran, while the Ottomans had only inherited certain attitudes toward statecraft from this tradition.

With his army of devoted followers Isma'il soon united most of the area that had constituted the empire called Iran before the coming of Islam. A latent identification of the linguistically varied people of this area as Iranians worked in Isma'il's favor. Isma'il proclaimed Twelver Shi'ism the only publicly acceptable form of Islam in his empire; and he and his followers set about systematically imposing this form of Shi'ism in the parts of the Safavid realm most firmly under their control. Twelver Shi'ism holds that the leadership rests with a line of descent in the Prophet Muhammad's family, the first of whom was 'Ali and the twelfth of whom had disappeared in the ninth century and would reappear as the Messiah at the end of time. Under the Safavids, being an Iranian gradually became identified with being a Twelver Shi'ite. The identification was never complete, however: significant communities in the Arab world and India were (and remain) Twelver Shi'ites, and significant minorities in Iran clung to the Sunni version of Islam espoused by the majority of non-Iranian Muslims. Meanwhile, the Turkish nomadic followers of Isma'il devotedly believed their leader to be infallible, even though Twelver Shi'ite ulama were horrified at such a claim; and Isma'il's Turkish poetry, which found an audience among Turks everywhere, implied that Isma'il saw himself as more than human.

The rise of the Safavids posed a threat to the Ottomans very different from the threat of the European powers. Many elements in the Ottoman Empire, especially the Turkish tribesmen of Anatolia and Syria, admired Isma'il and shared some of the religious beliefs of his closest followers. Turkish-speaking tribes had played a role in earlier Ottoman conquests but were no longer a significant part of the Ottoman army. They were still, however, a warlike presence in central and eastern Anatolia, and the Ottomans could not afford to have them rally to the new Shi'ite power on their eastern flank. The Ottomans marched on Azerbaijan and in

1514 the two new empires of the Middle East faced each other in battle at Chaldiran. Shah Isma'il's smaller force of mounted archers, convinced of his invincibility, charged repeatedly at the Ottomans, shouting (in Turkish) the battle cry: "My spiritual leader and master, for whom I sacrifice myself"! The handguns of the Ottoman infantry were effective against these troops but even more so was the Ottoman artillery, for which the Safavids had no counterpart. It did not matter that the individual bravery of Safavid horsemen carried some of them through the Ottoman lines to hack at the chains that held the Ottoman gun carriages together: Ottoman numbers, discipline, and technological superiority carried the day.

The battle of Chaldiran was as least as decisive as the battle of Lepanto for the future of the Middle East. As befitted a power that was far wealthier and more experienced in the new technologies of war, the Ottomans kept the upper hand in their confrontations with the Safavids and the Iranian powers that would succeed them. And Shah Isma'il lost his aura of invincibility.

LETTER FROM THE SULTAN

■ *This letter was sent by the Ottoman sultan Selim shortly before the battle of Chalidiran in 1514 to the Safavid ruler, Shah Isma'il.*

I, sovereign chief of the Ottomans, master of the heroes of the age, who unites the force and power of Feridun [a legendary king of ancient Persia], the majesty and glory of Alexander the Great, the justice and clemency of Khusraw [the famous king of Persia, in whose reign the Prophet Muhammad was born]; I, the exterminator of idolators destroyer of the enemies of the true faith, the terror of the tyrants and pharaohs of the age; I, before whom proud and unjust kings have humbled themselves, and whose hand breaks the strongest sceptres; I, the great Sultan-Khan, son of Sultan Bayezid-Khan, son of Sultan Muhammad-Khan, son of Sultan Murad-Khan, I address myself graciously to you, Amir Isma'il, chief of the troops of Persia, comparable in tyranny to Zahhak and Afrasiab [legendary tyrants mentioned in the Persian national epic], and predestined to perish like the last Darius, in order to make known to you that . . . it is He [the Almighty] who has set up Caliphs on earth . . . it is then only by practicing the true religion that man will prosper in this world and merit eternal life in the other. As to you, Amir Isma'il, such a recompense will not be your lot; because you have denied the sanctity of the divine laws; because you have deserted the path of salvation and the sacred commandments; because you have impaired the purity of the dogmas of Islam; because you have dishonored, soiled and destroyed the altars of the Lord, usurped the sceptre of the East by unlawful and tyrannical means; because coming forth from the dust, you have raised yourself by odious devices to a place shining with splendor and magnificence; because you have opened to Muslims the gates of tyranny and oppression; because you have joined iniquity, perjury and blasphemy to your sectarian impiety; because under the cloak of the hypocrite, you have sowed everywhere trouble and sedition; because you have raised the standard of irreligion and heresy . . . you have dared . . . to permit the ill-treatment of the *ulama*, the doctors and amirs descended from the Prophet, the repudiation of the Koran, the cursing of the legitimate Caliphs. Now as the first duty of a Muslim and above all of a pious prince is to obey the commandment, "O, you faithful who believe, be the executors of the decrees of God!" the ulama and our doctors have pronounced sentence of death against you, perjurer and blasphemer, and have imposed on every Muslim the sacred obligation to arm in defense of religion and destroy heresy and impiety in your person and that of all your partisans.

Animated by the spirit of this *fetwa*, conforming to the Koran the code of divine laws, and wishing on one side to strengthen Islam, on the other to liberate the lands and peoples who writhe under your yoke, we have resolved to lay aside our imperial robes in order to put on the shield and coat of mail, to raise our ever-victorious banner, to assemble our invincible armies.

But the Safavids survived, and Ottoman occupation of parts of Iran after Chaldiran did the occupiers little good because of the scorched-earth policy of the retreating Safavids and the hostility of the local population. Moreover, the Ottoman troops, which included elements secretly sympathetic to the Safavids, disliked these campaigns and grumbled that they would prefer to fight non-Muslim powers in Europe. In any case, it took the Ottoman central army as long or longer to reach the Safavids as it did to reach Vienna. Ottoman expansion had reached its physical and its ideological limits in the east as well as in the west.

For the Safavids the consequences were even more dramatic. Isma'il was not invincible, and normative Twelver Shi'ism (which had regarded him as a mere human all along) increasingly set the religious tone for the Safavid court. The most devoted followers of Shah Isma'il commonly called him "the friend and representative" of God; and it was possible for ordinary Twelver Shi'ites to accept the more conservative claim of the Safavids to be the representative of the Messiah, a claim that still allowed them ample authority.

The Safavids wanted infantry troops on the Ottoman model; and, thanks to their efforts in the sixteenth century to increase the extent of crown lands, they were able by the seventeenth century to buy slaves from the Caucasus and create their own version of the Janissaries. In the seventeenth century, under the long reign of Shah Abbas I (1587–1629), the Safavid dynasty reached its political apogee. The Turkish tribal supporters of the Safavids were assigned to specific provinces where, somewhat in the style of the Seljuk *iqta'*, they received the revenue of the provinces in exchange for providing a tribal levy for major campaigns. A small force chosen from these tribes was the original element in the standing army, to which Shah Abbas added cavalry, infantry, and artillery. Some of these troops were of slave origin, but some were recruited from very diverse elements, including—most exceptionally in the history of the pre-modern Islamic Middle East—the Iranian peasantry.

In Abbas's stunningly beautiful new capital of Isfahan in the center of Iran, the court language changed from Turkish to Persian, and Persian-speaking bureaucrats directly supervised taxation and expenditure in the central provinces. The luxury products of the central provinces, especially silk textiles, had an avid market and gave the crown significant income. By the early seventeenth century Safavid Iran was acknowledged by its far larger and richer neighbors, in particular the Moghuls of India, to have a certain cultural hegemony within the Islamic world.

Miniature of Shah Abbas I as a young man by an unknown Moghul painter.

The Moghuls: Tamerlane's Descendants Seize India

The Moghuls of India were the true biological heirs of Genghis Khan and of Tamerlane. Babur, the founder of the Moghul dynasty, was a great-great grandson of Tamerlane and, on his mother's side, a direct descendent of Genghis Khan. Babur wandered through Central Asia and Afghanistan, winning and losing parts of the heartland of Tamerlane's empire until, having gained control of the Afghan city of Kabul, he found himself overlooking the passes to India. In his engaging—and amazingly candid—memoirs, he wrote: "India is a wonderful country . . . [for, while it] is a land of few charms . . . the pleasant things of India are that it is a large country and has masses of gold and silver." At the battle of Pa-nipat in 1526 Babur defeated the far more numerous forces of the Muslim kings of Delhi with an Ottoman tactic, placing a barrier of carts linked by chains behind which musketeers fired at repeated cavalry charges. Shortly afterward he defeated the leader of the Rajputs, who formed a powerful Hindu military confederacy. His grandson Akbar (1556–1605) continued his conquests, uniting the greater part of India under one rule for the first time since the Buddhist emperor Asoka in the third century B.C.E. Indians used the term "Mongols" to describe Central Asians, and they called the largely Turkish dynasty of Babur the Moghuls, a Persian form of the word *Mongols*.

India on the eve of the Moghul invasion was divided into numerous kingdoms, very few of which were truly centralized. In the fifth century Indian rulers had as-signed hereditary rights to land in exchange for the ser-vices of the assignees in collecting taxes and keeping order at a local level. As many of these assignees were members of the Hindu religious elite called the Brah-mans, they also controlled the extensive lands owned by Hindu temples. This hereditary group worked, gener-ally without much commitment, for the many changing rulers of following centuries, who usually came from low-caste groups—that is, groups of low social sta-tus—or from foreign invaders. Rulers were therefore not considered to be divinely appointed; they were sup-posed to maintain the norms of society, which meant maintaining the local control of traditional elites. As long as they did so, they had more to fear from each other than from the people they ruled; and, in fact, they very often did not seek to replace each other but only to become the head of confederacies of king-doms, or the "great" king from whom lesser kings derived their greatness.

This image of society and kingship was only slightly altered by the invasion from the northwest of Turkish and Afghan rulers from the Muslim world. Occasionally, a Muslim ruler took the position that Hindus were poly-theistic pagans and should be given a choice of Islam or death. But the overwhelming majority of Muslim rulers agreed with an early Muslim commander that Hindus were a "people of the book" and therefore should be tolerated just as Jews and Christians were. By and large, the Muslims left local administration intact and wel-comed the military support of warlike Hindu elites such as the Rajputs. The Rajputs were a social category, or caste, of northern and central India whose traditional occupation was warfare and who exalted the virtues of a courageous death on the battlefield.

Akbar at the siege of the great Rajput fortress of Ranthambhor in 1568.

The Moghuls immediately understood their situa-tion: without the support of the Hindu Rajputs they could never maintain an extensive empire in India. Babur's grandson, Akbar, the true organizational founder of the Moghul empire, married several Rajput princesses (though only after defeating their fathers and/or brothers), and used a Rajput stronghold as the base from which his armies would establish a vast em-pire. By his death in 1605 the Moghul empire stretched from the heart of Afghanistan on the west to the Bay of Bengal on the east, and from The Himalaya on the north to the center of the Deccan plateau. Under Babur's successors, the Moghuls gained control of almost all remaining parts of India.

The administration created by Akbar was remarkably durable, and important aspects of it survived during the period of direct British rule of India after 1858. Akbar gave all the great officials of the empire the title of *mansabdar*, meaning "holder of a position of rank," and arranged the mansabdars into a hierarchy of thirty-three grades. The mansabdars held their position at the pleasure of the emperor and received payment through *jagirs*, assignments of revenues, the Moghul equivalent of iqta's. In the time of a vigorous emperor like Akbar, much of the actual revenue collection was performed by treasury officials, who used surveys to control revenues down to the village level and who dispensed salaries to the mansabdars. The system was open to both talent and favoritism: Muslim warriors and administrators from other Islamic regions were welcomed, and of Indian-born officials and officers a very high percentage were Hindus.

The Sharifians: The Islamic "Far West" Becomes an Empire

Morocco also emerged as a reconstituted political unit at the time of the founding of the three larger early modern Islamic empires. In the late fifteenth and early sixteenth centuries the Portuguese acquired direct or indirect control of most of the Atlantic coast of Morocco, as well as such strategic Mediterranean ports as Tangier. The Portuguese not only tried to extract as much tax as they could from their Moroccan subjects and tributaries but also raided the interior for plunder and slaves. It is often forgotten that the North African seafarers depicted as "pirates" in the literature of early modern Europe were mirror images of many of their Christian European counterparts.

The Moroccans reacted violently, and an upswell of religious sentiment shaped the destiny of Morocco to the twentieth century. Much of this sentiment found its focus in Sufism. Moroccans of all classes showed greater devotion than Muslims in other parts of the Arab world to their local Sufi leaders, who were seen as healers and miracle workers. Thanks to the contributions they received and the trade routes they dominated, many of these Sufi leaders were more independent of sultans than the ulama.

In the eighth century a *sharif*, or descendant of the Prophet Muhammad, had fled the caliphs of the Islamic Middle East and founded a minor but long-lived dynasty in Morocco. Sharifian lineage acquired particular prestige in this area, and sharifs continued to emigrate to Morocco over the centuries. In 1511 one line of sharifs agreed to lead the people of southern Morocco against the Portuguese; and the Sufi leaders, greatly empowered by the new religiosity of Moroccans, rallied to support their cause. In 1550 Muhammad (who adopted the regnal title al-Mahdi, "the Messiah"), took the greatest town of the interior, Fez.

This line of Sharifians (as the rulers of Morocco are known up to the present day) reunified Morocco and gradually expelled the Europeans. Since an important goal of European expansion along the Atlantic coast was to trade for gold (and, later, slaves) from the sub-Saharan interior, to compete with them the Sharifians moved overland far to the south, conquering Timbuktu in 1590; and, for half a century, they were the predominant power in a vast region of Africa immediately to the south of Timbuktu.

The first line of Sharifians, the Sa'dians, created a government more centralized than Morocco had experienced in some centuries and added to their tribal support a standing army of European renegades—Muslims expelled from Spain, and black troops trained by Ottoman deserters. The new state apparatus, much influenced by the Ottoman example, managed to survive in spite of continually disputed successions, competing tribal powers, and, finally, the disaffection of the Sufi leaders.

The Early Modern Islamic Empires Compared

The great Islamic empires of the early modern period shared many points of origin and of ongoing contact. In their appeal for legitimacy they all looked back to sacred history or sanctified lineages. The Moroccan rulers used the titles "caliph" and "commanders of the faithful," implying that they were rightful successors to the Prophet in temporal affairs, because they were descendants of the Prophet through 'Ali. The early Ottomans such as Bayazid, used the title caliph, as well as sultan, as did the Ottomans of the eighteenth and nineteenth centuries. The Moghuls also called themselves caliphs. The Safavid claim—quite probably false—that they were descended from the Prophet through 'Ali was generally accepted. None of the dynasties turned its back on the longing among Muslims for a universal Islamic state led by a descendant of the Prophet and/or a rightful political successor to the revered caliph or caliphs that had directly succeeded the Prophet. In a sense, the Islamic world continued to be a unit within which intellectual, mercantile, and artisanal elites moved freely.

For all these dynasties except the Moroccans, succession to the Turco-Mongolian heritage was of immense importance. Naturally, they used the title sultan, which had represented authority ever since

Mahmud of Ghazna. The grandiose title *khaqan*, originally reserved for the leader of the descendants of Genghis Khan, was used very commonly by the Ottomans, who also designated the khans of the Crimea, direct descendants of Genghis Khan, as their successors in the unlikely event that all members of the Ottoman house should expire. The Safavids, who used few titles in addition to their regnal names, nevertheless constructed a hierarchy of military officials using the Central Asian Turkish titles *khan* and *beg*, as did the Moghuls and Ottomans—for these titles carried immediate authority with their Turkish-speaking troops. Just as distinctive as the titles used by the Safavids, Ottomans, and Moghuls was their use of the Persian title shah or padishah (king) or shahanshah (king of kings). Safavid territory closely corresponded to the territory of the Sassanian shahs who ruled Iran before Islam; hence their use of the title shah. The centuries-old Iranian tradition of court culture remained the archetype to which not only the Safavid dynasty but also the more distant Ottoman and Moghul dynasties looked back.

All four early modern Islamic dynasties gained as much or more from their reaction to the contemporary world as from their association with the great physical and spiritual lineages. All four gained legitimacy by their fight against non-Muslim powers and therefore proudly bore the title of ghazi. They arose at a time when European Christian powers were assuming control of the sea, and they survived into periods of vigorous European onslaughts by land; thus, their role as ghazis carried great respect.

All four empires made use of the Sufi orders, which had emerged as huge brotherhoods with endowed lodges and teaching institutions supervised by hierarchies of leadership. The Safavid dynasty sprang directly from Sufi leadership to imperial rule. The connection of the Sharifian dynasties of Morocco to local Sufi saints often provided their most vital link to the masses. In Ottoman society, all of the rulers as well as most of the elite were interested in or affiliated with a Sufi order. The Moghuls maintained Sufi leaders as favored members of their court; and Sufi mysticism acted as a bridge to the Hindu mysticism espoused by many of their non-Muslim subjects.

Why did so much of the early modern Islamic world compose itself into fairly stable empires around 1500? For the Ottomans, Safavids, and Moghuls a reinterpretation of the Turco-Mongolian heritage played an important role. All three governments aspired to give legal authority to royal commands and to control the traditional experts of religion more than previous Islamic

dynasties. All three drew upon the tradition represented by the Yasa, ascribed to Genghis Khan, which gave a special aura to royal law. The Ottomans did this most successfully; their courts applied Islamic law as well as royal law. All three tried to standardize Islamic law (which ideologically resisted standardization because it accepted an established variety of interpretations). The Ottomans and the Safavids tried to supervise the affairs of the ulama. These attempts at organizing the religiously learned—their legal functions and their assets—did not always work; but they showed an ambition to control and standardize with few precedents in Islamic history.

This drive for central control manifested itself in other areas of government. All three empires, partly in the Mongol tradition, attempted extraordinarily careful surveys of their resources. Nevertheless, all three empires turned their backs on the fairly frequent Turco-Mongolian practice of dividing an empire between royal sons. But, ironically, the Safavids, inheriting the actual personnel and practices of the Turco-Mongolian tradition of administration, at first continued the tradition of assigning provinces to tribal peoples as hereditary "fiefs." Although they later attempted to suppress this system, they were unable to do so; and their failure severely undermined their attempts to build a central army and administration on the Ottoman model.

The Ottomans, Safavids, Moghuls, and Sharifians also owed their origins and ability to endure in part to the economic vitality of their greatest rivals, the Christian Europeans. The growing population and increasing sophistication of the European market gave an advantage to large centralized empires that controlled a significant part of the trade. It was no accident that Bursa, near the Sea of Marmara, a major depot for luxury goods crossing to the Mediterranean world, was for half a century the capital of the infant Ottoman government. The Sharifian dynasties of Morocco pushed hundreds of miles southward to control Timbuktu, the collection point for the gold from the rich West African mines. The Iranians controlled overland trade between the Persian Gulf and the Caspian Sea; in addition, their strong artisanal traditions made their products widely sought and gave them significant exports. The far more numerous Indians also had strong artisanal traditions and, from Roman times on, seem to have had a highly favorable balance of trade with areas to the west. As a result India, which has few sources of precious metal, was probably the most monetized large economy in the world in the sixteenth century; and truly astonishing sums of gold and silver passed through the Indian treasury. The new empires were fiscal empires, interested in enriching royal treasuries, as they sought to wring advantage out of a world market greatly increased by improvement in travel, growth of population, and the rise of Europe.

One European export proved essential to the centralizing activities of the later Islamic empires: guns. It is hard to imagine that the Ottoman Empire would have emerged as *the* Middle Eastern state without gunpowder weapons. The Mamluks were among the world's finest cavalry forces in the fifteenth century, and the Safavid Shah Isma'il had an army completely and selflessly devoted to him; but neither could stand up against Ottoman weapons. The Safavids and Moghuls learned to imitate the Ottoman tradition of gunnery. This achievement not only enabled them to withstand external threats but made them very different kinds of regimes internally. Thanks to guns, they subdued their own realms with unprecedented thoroughness. Whereas earlier empires had to come to terms with the local leaders in remote areas, the new empires could and often did gain direct rule, in some cases replacing small local dynasties whose origins dated back many centuries.

These empires also survived because they became emblematic of the cultural area they ruled. Their territories constituted a cultural area that their subjects felt would exist less fully or even disappear if their dynasties disappeared. Although far from modern nationalism, this sense of a culturally shared identity endured in both the Sharifian and Safavid empires. By the seventeenth century, the Ottoman-Safavid struggle had produced a border that has with small modification lasted to the present.

The Ottomans and Moghuls ruled empires far more ethnically and religiously diverse, but they nevertheless produced distinctive cultural styles, which their elites aspired to imitate. In the Ottoman case, this cultural style implied the knowledge of certain revered and/or admired classics of the Persian and Arabic traditions, the ability to speak and write the ornate form of Ottoman Turkish, and the observance of elaborate norms of polite behavior as defined by court culture. Properly trained, almost any people of the Ottoman Empire, Slavs, Arabs or Turks, could become "Ottomans." In the Moghul case, a distinctively Indian cultural synthesis emerged at the Moghul court. From this synthesis came Urdu, which is a northern Indian dialect written in characters like Persian and sprinkled with words borrowed from Persian, the official language of the Moghul court. Together with its sister language Hindi, essentially the same language but with an alphabet ultimately derived from Sanskrit and with somewhat fewer Persian words, Urdu was to become the most important intercommunal language of the Indian subcontinent.

Seventeenth-century allegorical representation of Shah Abbas I and Jahangir, emperor of India (1605–27). The two rulers embrace while standing on the symbols of peace on a globe of the world.

Artistic Refinement in the Early Modern Islamic Empires

The early modern Islamic dynasties were great patrons of culture, partly by individual whim and partly by political design. Court culture of this period shone most brilliantly in the production of material objects, both of practical and of aesthetic intent. Architecture throughout the region reached an astonishing refinement from the Sa'dian tombs in Morocco to the madrasas of Central Asia. In the central Islamic lands, above all Iran, color-tiled decoration gave buildings a visual brilliance and unity almost unrivaled to this day. The richer Ottomans and Moghuls were able to build enormous stone structures of great dignity, the best known of which is the Taj Mahal in India. Court patronage of painting brought the Persian miniature, with its slightly magical atmosphere, and Moghul painting, with its dramatic realism, to their highest points of perfection. Similarly, textiles such as brocades and rugs, some manufactured in royal workshops, became luxury items widely sought for their beauty on the international market.

The intellectual world did not flourish to the same degree. Practical items were imported and practical skills learned, but mainly to enhance existing cultural forms or to defend against European onslaught. Large numbers of grandfather clocks were imported for mosques, and European seafaring techniques were adopted; yet the more abstract sciences needed to understand and develop technologies were still cultivated largely along traditional Middle Eastern lines with little awareness of European developments. Ibn Khaldun (1332–1406), a North African Muslim scholar who was a highly original social thinker, reflects the difficulty faced in the Islamic world between about 1400 (when he wrote) and about 1800 by those persons curious about European thought and intellectual achievement: "We hear now that the philosophical sciences are greatly cultivated in western Europe . . . Existing systematic expositions of them are said to be comprehensive, the people who know them numerous and the students of them many. God knows best what exists there."

The Resilience of Islamic Societies

From the thirteenth to the eighteenth centuries Islam continued to spread as a world religion. In Central Asia it became the predominant religion, even among the Mongols, whose "paganism" had once seemed such a threat to the Islamic Middle East. Under the Moghuls the numbers of Muslims increased dramatically until Muslims accounted for over one-fifth of the inhabitants of the Indian subcontinent. The East Indies (modern Indonesia) became predominantly Muslim due to the continuing influence of Muslim traders in the Indian Ocean and to the persistence of Indian influence in Southeast Asia. The success of the Mamluks and Ottomans in controlling the Nile Valley and of the Moroccans in extending their state southward contributed to the conversion of a large area in sub-Saharan Africa. The presence of the Ottomans in the Balkans facilitated the conversion to Islam of Albania, Bosnia, and other areas.

The empires cared far more about the extraction of taxes than religious affiliation, however. Conversions were overwhelmingly the result of lay activity such as trade and, above all, the spread of the Sufi brotherhoods. The great majority of Muslims had some Sufi connection, whether they belonged to a Sufi order or merely visited the tombs of Sufi "saints," which existed throughout the Islamic world. Sufi themes dominated

Islamic poetry. Sufism's success at directly reaching the masses also accounts for the use of writing in a host of hitherto largely unwritten languages, such as Pushtu in Afghanistan. And international Sufi orders, with chapter houses all the way from the Ottoman Empire to China, facilitated the movement of believers traveling throughout the Islamic world, who found like-minded Sufi "brothers" to give them shelter.

Local elites persisted, although religion often connected local life to much larger units. For example, the tomb of a Sufi saint might connect the villagers living nearby to more important saints' tombs around which yearly pilgrimages and organized Sufi life were centered. And the village Qur'an teacher might send humble boys of great talent to a distant madrasa, where they could rise to the top of the ulama hierarchy. The position of village headman, however, would most likely be hereditary in one of the richer families. As a rule, pastoralists and farmers remained interdependent. The pastoralists would use marginally cultivable land when regimes allowed them to do so, and often villages had long-standing agreements with tribal pastoralists in which food and seasonal land use was exchanged for protection of the village. In the Middle East proper a surprisingly large percentage of the population would alternate between full or part-time pastoralism and full or part-time farming according to political and ecological conditions. Pastoralists, particularly fully nomadic ones, could play an important role in the distribution of power.

In many parts of the Islamic world of this period members of the local elite were called *a'yan*, "notables." The notables usually consisted of landlords, prominent merchants, and locally distinguished religious scholars. This group tended to view themselves as hereditary; they intermarried and claimed ancient origins, but, in fact, people of new wealth became notables fairly easily. The notables had often played an important role as intermediaries between the government and the local community in earlier regimes, but when the new empires were at their strongest, the central governments often bypassed them and instead used bureaucrats assigned to local administrators. Nonetheless, the notables survived, their numbers often strengthened by the addition of former officials, civil and military, or their sons; and by the eighteenth century they had assumed the importance they once held under previous dynasties.

The life of cities was more volatile, reflecting the variety of their interest groups and the presence of government. Most cities were networks of narrow alleyways, overlooked by houses with grilled windows. Large cities were divided into quarters, often with their own

A sixteenth-century drawing of the Turkish city of Bitlis shows a typical Islamic townscape.

gates. The large and more open spaces regularly included the citadel or the governor's residence, the principal mosque (often called the Friday mosque, since Muslims of the region were all expected to gather at one specially designated mosque on Fridays) and the marketplaces. Outside many towns was an enormous area especially designated for the entire local community of Muslims to gather for such communal religious events as the yearly feast of sacrifice and the prayer for rain in times of extreme drought. Imperial cities also had parade grounds, some portion of which might be incorporated into the heart of the city as a central square and, upon occasion, as a royal polo field.

Town and city organization varied greatly, but a number of features recurred. Near the principal mosques, the ritually "cleanest" professions existed, such as the cloth trade; and since wholesale cloth sales were such an important element in big business, other professions that dealt with large sums, such as jewellers and money changers were located nearby. The madrasas and the court of the *qadi*, or judge, were also located near this more desirable part of the market quarter. Since ritual and physical cleanliness were obviously associated, the public baths were there as well. In contrast, professions involving the use of ritually unclean materials (such as animal dung for tanning leather) were placed on the outskirts of town, since these workers had to wash themselves in a specified way before they could pray.

The market inspector supervised the town market, enforcing a variety of rules considered essential to the proper function of the market, such as the use of proper weights or the wearing of proper garments. The market inspector could order summary punishments, some trivial and some intended to terrify, such as nailing a grossly

dishonest shopkeeper by his ear to his shop door. In general, the operation of market forces set prices, and the saying ascribed to Muhammad, that "God sets prices" was widely quoted. In fact, a customer could return goods within three days if she or he could prove that the object sold had hidden defects or that the price was above the prevailing market price. There were also very strict injunctions against hoarding, which amounted to a demand that all goods held by merchants for sale should be offered immediately so that no merchant gain an "unjust" profit margin. The merchant communities generally respected the market inspectors, and so valued their services that in formerly Muslim parts of Spain the Christian merchants perpetuated the office. The Ottomans and Safavids gave new functions to the market inspectors, and their governments tended more and more to control retail prices (see p. 466).

The legal official of highest prestige was the qadi. The qadi not only rendered judgments in his court but also acted as the eyes and ears of the sultan in the maintenance of all the major functions of government. In the case of the Ottomans this included the levy of boys and, in later centuries, the regulation of market prices. Usually a select group of local notables worked closely with the qadi and served as witness-notaries, attesting to important legal acts such as the signature of contracts, manumission of slaves, the establishment of *waqf*s (pious endowments) and the like.

Pious endowments were an enormously important instrument for the recirculation of wealth. They maintained street fountains, hospitals, libraries, madrasas, hostels, tomb gardens, baths, free kitchens, and often all manner of public and semipublic institutions. Through such endowments rulers memorialized their names on earth and won a place in heaven. The endowments also fulfilled the contract by which God gave them sovereignty in exchange for their good and just care of their subjects. In fact, people at all levels of society established endowments out of communal feeling. These pious endowments (guarded for perpetuity by the record in the qadi's court) helped keep social peace in large cities with extremes of wealth and poverty, such as Istanbul, which, in the seventeenth century, had a population of at least seven hundred thousand, larger than its nearest competitors in Europe—London and Paris.

The economic elites, however, held on tenaciously to the basic sources of their wealth, often using the waqf to set up family trusts and keep money in the family. The ranks of the ulama, although open to talented students of humble background, tended to form a hereditary class, who passed on judgeships and teaching positions to their more talented children and the supervision of waqfs to less talented children. Large merchants still maintained networks that reached around the world because—in a world without banks—they were the principal source of risk capital and could invest as silent partners with ship captains and other small traders, who would settle for a relatively limited percentage of the profit. These and other elites held their own and flourished as the empires flourished; but in the seventeenth and eighteenth centuries, when signs of imperial decay appeared and the price revolution disoriented the economies of many parts of the world, both the governments and the elites of the Islamic empires found themselves on the defensive.

Political Decline and Transformation in the Seventeenth and Eighteenth Centuries

The seventeenth and eighteenth centuries saw an end to the expansion of these empires and to their organization as conquest states. Not surprisingly, by the eighteenth century positions tended to become hereditary: the central governments lacked the income to buy and/or train military elites, and they also needed the continuity offered by groups willing to exchange loyalty for the prestige of imperial recognition. But that loyalty was weak, and rebellions were a chronic danger in all the empires. Moreover, the loss of transit trade to Europeans and other economic setbacks shrank the empires' economies. Increasingly, they lost territory to the more able European powers. Yet, despite losses and periods of chaos, the early modern Islamic empires or their successors retained their core territories, which formed the basic elements of later nation-states. Furthermore, the social categories through which they administered society retained a greater degree of institutionalization, even under weak imperial governments, than they had achieved under earlier regimes. The decline of these empires in military power did not necessarily imply the decline of their society and cultures.

The Sharifians and the Safavids Confront Turmoil

Both the Sharifians of Morocco and the Safavids of Iran owed their rule to Sufi backing, sanctified lineage, and a regional cultural identification. Both governments tried to imitate the Ottoman example; both were undone by tribal forces. Paradoxically, the Sharifians of Morocco, who were far less successful at creating central institutions, survived; the Safavids did not.

The first family of Sharifians, the Sa'dians, for all their success in reconstituting a Moroccan political unit between the Ottomans and the Spanish, were too weak to sustain their balancing act between the rivalries of the tribes, the cities, and even the different branches of their family. It was rare when the ulama of Fez and of Marrakech agreed on the successor to any Sa'dian ruler. And if the two most important internal cities of Morocco disagreed, the people on the periphery and even the Ottomans and the Spaniards found ways of interfering in nearly every succession. The weakness of the dynasty resulted in Christians gaining control of port cities, as the Spanish did in 1610. The Sufi holy men whose support had been so vital to the rise of the Sa'dians, now became hostile to them.

Finally, from this disorder, in the mid-seventeenth century, a Sharifian family called the Alawis reconstituted the empire. Their most powerful leader, Moulay Isma'il (1672–1727) created a large new army of black slaves. He also presided over the ejection of Europeans from several port cities, including Tangier, and gained prestige as a great defender of the faith. But ultimately his resources were so slender and the consequent weight of his taxation so heavy, that without his forceful leadership this centralizing process proved impossible to continue. Continual turmoil from Moulay Isma'il's death until the late eighteenth century limited the authority of the central government over its subjects and made the Sharifian the least powerful of the early modern Islamic empires.

The Safavids, as we have seen, succeeded in building an impressive imperial bureaucracy and army under Shah Abbas I. His successors were for the most part mediocre, and it is a tribute to the structures Shah Abbas created that the empire survived at all. After a century of struggle to keep southern Iraq, the Safavids lost this province more or less permanently to the Ottomans in 1638. In the center of the empire the Shi'ite ulama grew more powerful, while in the empire's outer provinces the tribes grew more independent. When Shah Sultan Husayn (1694–1722), who succeeded to the throne in 1694, tried to impose Shi'ism on his distant Sunni Afghan subjects, the Afghans defeated his armies and marched virtually unopposed to Isfahan, the Safavid capital in the heart of Iran, in 1722. A decade of disorder ensued, in which Peter the Great of Russia, the Ottomans, descendants of the Safavids, and Afghan leaders all attempted unsuccessfully to take over the remnants of the Safavid empire.

Then, in the 1730s a Turkish leader named Nader Shah not only reconstituted the empire but soundly beat the powers surrounding Iran. The Russians withdrew from the southern Caspian shores, both Turks and Russians lost hegemony over most of the Caucasus, the Uzbeks were driven from the nearer parts of Central Asia, and—most spectacular of all—Nader Shah in 1739 defeated the Moghuls, sacked Delhi, levied an indemnity of millions of gold pieces, and carried home the world's most elaborate throne—the Peacock Throne—and the world's most famous diamond, the Koh-i-noor. All of this did little to create a durable government because Nader Shah relied on tribal armies, whose loyalty was sustained only by success, and on extortionate taxation. When he was murdered by one of his own tribesmen, Iran again reverted to anarchy until the end of the eighteenth century, only briefly relieved by the benevolent rule of Karim Khan Zand, who controlled much of Iran from his southern capital of Shiraz from 1750 to 1779.

The Slow Decline of the Ottomans

At the death of Suleiman the Magnificent in 1566 it was far from clear to the Ottomans that they had reached the limits of their expansion; if the Ottoman Empire had failed to grow significantly for over a century, it had not shrunk. The Ottomans succeeded in capturing two important islands from the Venetians: Cyprus in 1571 and Crete in 1669. An Ottoman victory against the poorly organized Poles in 1676 made the Ottomans immediate neighbors to the growing power of eastern Europe—Russia. Most of these Ottoman victories were possible because their European opponents were locked in deadly struggles or were undergoing decline within the European system. Ottoman sultans seldom led their troops in battle anymore, and sometimes took little interest in the affairs of state. Fortunately, the grand viziers to whom they confided much of their power were often men of great ability, notably the Koprulu family, who ran the empire for much of the last half of the seventeenth century.

FROM A REGISTER OF PIOUS ENDOWMENTS

■ *The following passage is an entry in the register of the pious endowments of Tangier in Morocco, consisting in the most part of copies of deeds written in the second half of the eighteenth and throughout the nineteenth century.*

When Ahmad ibn Muhammad Al-Susi was named overseer of the pious endowments of the students [attached to] the Great Mosque, he did not find any document establishing these pious endowments. In fear that they might be confused with those of the Great Mosque he decided to make a list of them. The pious endowments of the students consist of a small hostel sharing a wall with the Great Mosque, consisting of fourteen rooms with a fig tree in the middle; the large weavers' workshop opposite the hostel; a room opposite the room for funerals; a room near the shops of the witness-notaries; another room above it; the house Khadda; the oven of the mosque, above which, two apartments; the house of Hajj Abdullah al-Katib; a weavers' workshop in the Aqbal quarters; a shop in the grocers' market; two shops in the perfumers' market; a shop above that of the sons of Ibn Jallul; [another] shop in the perfumers' market; the shop of Haddu; the oven of Zaghmuri; two shops opposite that of Haddu; a shop in the cobblers section; another shop at the end of the cobblers' section; a shop in which is found a shoeing smith and a maker of packsaddles, against the wall of the city; a shop on the small square; a little apartment in ruins at the same place . . . three-quarters of a weavers' workshop, called the workshop of Isa ibn Muqaddin; a weaving loom in the possession of Abd al-Qadir Misbah; a loom in the possession of Ali Azyad; three salt caves in the salt mines of [the district] old Tangier. First of the month Jumada ath-Thaniya 1183 [1769 C.E.]. Witnessed by two witness-notaries.

From *Archives Marocaines XXIII* (1914).

FROM A MANUAL ON SAFAVID ADMINISTRATION

■ *The following passage is from a manual on Safavid administration written about 1726. The author is unknown to us but he was thoroughly acquainted with the tradition of later Safavid administration and compiled this manual to explain it to the Afghan leaders who had recently overthrown the Safavids.*

The duties of the exalted Market Inspector of the Entire Kingdom. Every month [an official] obtains from the elders of each guild an undertaking concerning the prices of the goods [in which they deal]. Having satisfied himself [as to the accuracy of the document] he seals it and hands it to the Market Inspector of the Entire Kingdom. The latter must confirm every point of it and send it to the Overseer of the Royal Workshop. The latter too considers it and, if he feels satisfied, seals it and passes it on to the Heads of the Departments, in order that, in accordance with it, the Supervisors may draw up the documents for the goods to be bought.

As regards the pricing of the goods sold by guilds to the inhabitants of the town, if any of the artisan-merchants eludes the Market Inspector's regulations, the latter makes him wear a transportable pillory, that he may serve as an example to others.

The Market Inspector of the Entire Kingdom appoints Deputies everywhere in the God-protected provinces. In every place, the traders, month by month, sell goods to people in accordance with the Deputy's certificate [of prices], so that tranquility may reign among the people [the *ra'aya* or "flocks"] and the inhabitants and residents [of towns], and that the latter may pray for the most sacred person of the King.

The Ottoman system had entered a period of internal transformation which, by the seventeenth century, was apparent to intelligent Ottoman statesmen and thinkers. Officials of the empire were no longer devotees of the Ottoman house and the Ottoman way who owed their advancement to the favor of the sultan, but men who owed as much to their family as to their ruler. The Janissary corps had swollen in numbers from about 8,000 in 1527 to about 38,000 in 1609, in part because a larger infantry was needed to use increasingly heavy firearms. They had become unruly, extravagantly expensive, and—in part because of relaxation of the celibacy requirement—a partly hereditary and far less effective military force. A quick turn in Ottoman fortunes revealed their basic military weakness within a decade. In 1683, when the Ottomans marched on Vienna to stop the alliance of the Austrian Habsburgs, the Russians, and the Poles, they were repulsed and repeatedly defeated as they retreated to Istanbul. In 1687 the defeat of the Ottomans at Mohacs ended a century and a half of direct Ottoman rule of Hungary. Further defeats followed, and only the outbreak of war between France and Austria saved the Ottomans. In the landmark Treaty of Karlowitz in 1699, the Ottomans conceded a large part of the Balkans, almost all of Hungary, and even a part of Greece to their enemies. The initiative had passed into the hands of the Europeans, who were checked only by their own rivalries, the rivalries between the European Christian subjects of the Ottomans, and by a modest recovery of Ottoman abilities in the first half of the eighteenth century.

The second half of the eighteenth century was even less favorable to the Ottomans. Russia as the leading Eastern Orthodox power posed as the champion of the Christian population of the Ottomans and stirred up trouble inside the Ottoman Empire while attacking from outside. Ottoman control of local administration had grown so weak that even in Anatolia holders of timars had become semi-independent and these "lords of the valleys" had to be coerced to send the soldiers and taxes they owed the central government. An important point in the Ottoman-Russian duel was the Treaty of Kuchuk Kainarji in 1774, which established the Russians firmly on the Black Sea with rights to navigate past Istanbul to the Mediterranean. Just as important for the future was recognition in the treaty that the Russians had some kind of protectorate over certain Eastern Orthodox institutions in the Ottoman Empire in exchange

More than a century before the 1687 battle of Mohacs, an army of Janissaries led by Suleiman the Magnificent routed the Hungarians under their young king Louis II at the "first battle of Mohacs" in 1526. In this miniature of the battle, Suleiman directs the army from behind a row of cannon.

for a recognition of the Ottoman sultan as the "caliph" of the Muslims with some kind of protectorate over the Muslims of the Crimea. The new extraterritorial character of the Russian-Ottoman confrontation as well as the revival of a hitherto little-regarded Ottoman claim to the caliphate was to have dramatic consequences in the next century and a half.

The Costly Expansion of the Moghuls

After the death in 1605 of Akbar, the administrative founder of the empire, the Moghuls, unlike the Ottomans, had a series of able and energetic leaders. Of these the most militarily successful was Akbar's great-grandson, Aurangzeb. Early Moghul emperors had sparred with the Safavids over control of Qandahar, in what is now southwestern Afghanistan, or led campaigns toward Central Asia, with which—as descendants of Ta-

merlane and Genghis Khan—they felt a natural link. In his long reign from 1658 to 1707 Aurangzeb turned his attention southward and was able to conquer or reduce to vassalage virtually all of the Indian subcontinent, as well as the surrounding northern mountainous regions of the Hindu Kush and The Himalaya. Only Kerala at the southern tip of India and the strongholds of Marathas, warlike tribal people of central India who threw off Moghul rule, successfully resisted Aurangzeb's attacks.

The situation of the Moghuls was fundamentally different from that of the other Islamic empires in that they alone had a population that was overwhelmingly not Muslim. Of all the Moghul emperors, Akbar, a stocky, burly man with a hearty laugh but a regal presence, went the furthest toward making a synthesis of Islamic ideas and non-Islamic Indian culture and religion (much of which we loosely associate under the name of Hinduism). From early in his reign Akbar tried to remove all stigma from being non-Muslim. His only problem was that while a policy of tolerance made sense, and was followed by his son and grandson, it convinced almost none of the Hindu, Muslim, Zoroastrian, Jewish, Jain, and Jesuit holy men he brought to his court, who disliked each other as bitterly after Akbar as before.

Although both emperors were men of great military ability, Aurangzeb was markedly different from his celebrated great-grandfather. Whereas Akbar had a poor education (though an open and extremely keen mind) and was barely literate, Aurangzeb was well-educated and wrote a handsome Persian style, as befitted a Moghul monarch. Aurangzeb was thin and ascetic and had, as one Italian observer wrote, "a craze for being held a saint." He partly reversed Akbar's policy of toleration. He made some Hindus serving in his army pay the poll tax prescribed in Islamic law for non-Muslims in exchange for military exemption. He even showed intolerance for Muslims, such as Shi'ites, who did not fit his vision of religious orthodoxy. He was wise enough, however, to limit most of these acts of intolerance on the grounds of expediency. Through his gift of leadership and strategy, through his lavish bestowal of jagirs to buy the loyalty of his many hesitant vassals, and through sheer doggedness—he was carried in his litter to battles whenever possible right up to his death in his eighty-eighth year—he created an empire that under its surface unity had already begun to unravel.

Aurangzeb had given some of his most intractable enemies, the Maratha leaders, large *mansab*s, or assignments of revenues in order to buy their loyalty. As the empire stopped growing, however, and Aurangzeb spent fortunes to subdue rebels, there were fewer sources of

Portrait of a Great Mogol, *a drawing of Aurangzeb from a seventeenth-century English "Voyage to East India."*

revenue and the mansab holders found that the system could no longer work for them. Moreover, where the Moghul government maintained direct control, it reduced cultivators to misery by attempts to extract higher taxes. On Aurangzeb's death the mansab holders fell to quarreling with one another and supported rival Moghul pretenders.

Older Hindu lineages such as the Rajputs, Marathas, and Jats, and the newer non-Muslim adherents of the Sikh religion asserted their right to autonomy. Like the Muslim-ruled areas around Hyderabad and Oudh, they became self-contained governments. The breakdown of political unity led to disorder in the countryside, a situation that allowed European trading stations to become semi-independent states. By 1764 the British, who had driven the French and Dutch from most of India a few years earlier, had uncontested control of the Bengal and Bihar, which they ruled as nominal governors of the powerless Moghuls. A surprising feature of this political scene was that many participants in the hurly-burly of Indian politics maintained the fiction that a Moghul empire still existed. This attitude continued right up to the great rebellion of 1857–1858, often called the Sepoy Rebellion, against the British, who were then in overwhelming control. During this uprising the Delhi rebels declared the Moghul ruler Bahadur Shah II emperor of India. The British consequently deposed him and put an end to all vestiges of Moghul rule. The Moghuls represented a claim that the subcontinent was an interrelated system with a center; they also represented the memory that the center had once been the carrier of a high court culture toward which all directed their gaze. That claim and that memory had sustained the twilight of Moghul rule for a remarkably long time.

Society and Culture in the Seventeenth and Eighteenth Centuries

The apparent decline of the four Islamic empires in the late seventeenth and eighteenth centuries can be explained only in part by the internal weaknesses of those empires. Earlier empires—even earlier phases of these early modern Islamic empires—had gone through periods of decentralization and then pulled themselves together. But the military and economic onslaught of Europe had brought about an altogether new situation. It was not only that Europeans were gobbling up the edges of Islamic regimes, but there was a growing awareness among Muslims that the Islamic world could no longer unthinkingly believe itself to be the central civilization of mankind. From the Treaty of Karlowitz in 1699 there were permanent European embassies in Istanbul. All Islamic powers became enmeshed in European patterns of diplomatic relations, hitherto alien, in large part so that they could use the rivalry of European powers to survive.

The Europeans used these diplomatic relations to good advantage in advancing European commercial penetration. Following a Byzantine custom, the Ottomans and other empires issued special rights to foreigners to trade and to govern their own traders abroad in treaties called "regimes of capitulation," which initiated a growing loss of trade to Europeans and—with the growth of foreign trader communities—a loss of sovereignty. Moreover, non-Muslim minorities often had trading partners of the same religious and ethnic affiliation throughout Europe and the Middle East. For example, the Armenians developed a network of trade in Persian

Suleiman receives the Austrian ambassador. Not until 1683 was the Turkish threat removed from Vienna.

silks that extended from India to Amsterdam. These minorities often knew European languages and acted as middle men in the trade between Europeans and the Islamic empires. By the eighteenth century European missionaries had come to educate Middle Eastern Christians, and the Greeks and Armenians of Istanbul often sent their children to the University of Padua in Italy. The rise of non-Muslim trading elites was yet another sign of the degree that the Islamic world was becoming enmeshed in a world economy.

This sense of no longer being in control of their destinies had a different effect on royal courts than it had on the ulama. The courts experienced a great vogue for European objects such as eyeglasses, telescopes, and pocket watches. But the growing gap in scientific development meant that technology could not be imported so easily. The Ottomans and Moghuls were still striving to make huge cannons at a time when Europeans were developing more mobile and accurate cannons. The trade in luxury objects was turning in favor of Europe.

Nevertheless, European objects were one of the important influences on many of the minor arts of the Islamic world, which reached their greatest sophistication in the seventeenth and eighteenth centuries.

Although taste in architecture and miniature painting often degenerated into a cloying cuteness and sentimentality in the eighteenth century, the everyday possessions of the wealthy—such as hair scissors, pen cases, and formal clothing—were of a sumptuous and yet not gaudy beauty. Similarly, some of the less-grandiose buildings of the period, such as the summer houses of the Ottoman nobility along the Bosporus, reflect a uniquely happy marriage of traditional Ottoman style with European rococo taste. Interestingly, while the older literatures of the Middle East, Arabic and Persian, produced few memorable works in this period, Ottoman Turkish poetry, as well as the poetry of newly written languages such as Pushtu and Urdu, produced lyrics of great beauty, in part because this poetry was closer to living vernaculars.

The ulama by and large reacted to European encirclement by becoming more hostile to European influence. In this they partly reflected the mood of the Muslim masses. They also reflected the disgust of many Muslims at the debauchery of the court. Selim II (1566–74), the son and successor of Suleiman the Magnificent, who bore the sobriquet "the Sot," was not the only drunkard among Muslim rulers. All four Safavid rulers who ruled from 1629 to 1722 were enthusiastically given to drinking—forbidden, of course, by Islamic law. Not only did they drink, but many of these seventeenth- and eighteenth-century rulers were patrons of miniature painting of great sensuality, which endeared them even less to the guardians of religion. When in 1727 an Ottoman statesman opened the first printing press owned by a Muslim in the Ottoman Empire, he wisely chose to print only books related to secular matters such as geography and the natural sciences. In the seventeenth century some of the Ottoman ulama waged a war against popular practices such as the use of tobacco and coffee, which was then becoming enshrined in the coffeehouses that would become a basic feature of local life in the Middle East. But in this instance the "consensus of the community," a principle of Islamic law, overwhelmed learned opposition and the ulama acquiesced.

Other influences, not necessarily related to European presence, also profoundly affected the orientation of Muslim religious thought in the eighteenth century. Many Muslims, both Sunni and Shi'ite, both ulama and lay believers, reacted against the highly scholastic Islamic sciences taught in madrasas and called for a renewal of direct imitation of the piety of the Prophet through a study of his sayings. Many Muslims also suggested the pious should take direct action to restore piety and not wait for governments to do so. One such movement to rid Islam of "false" accretions, called

The Islamic World Under the Turkish Dynasties and the Early Modern Empires

998–1030	Mahmud of Ghazna raids over half of the Indian subcontinent
11th–15th c.	Tribes of Turkish nomads enter the Middle East
13th–14th c.	Mongol empire under Genghis Khan and his descendants, the Il-Khans in Iran and the Golden Horde in Russia
1212	Defeat of Muslims at Las Navas de Tolosa begins their loss of Iberia to the Spanish and Portuguese
1260	Mamluks defeat Mongols at Ain Jalut in Syria
end of 14th c.	Tamerlane reconstitutes empire of the Il-Khans
1389	Battle at Kosovo Polje in Serbia
1492	Fall of Granada; expulsion of Muslims and Jews from Spain
1453	Ottoman sultan Mehmed II takes Constantinople from the Byzantines
1501	Safavid ruler Isma'il assumes title Shah of Iran and later proclaims Twelver Shi'ism the only acceptable form of Islam in his empire
1516	Babur founds Moghul dynasty in India
1517	Ottomans defeat Mamluks at Marj Dabiq in Syria
1520–66	Height of the Ottoman Empire under Suleiman the Magnificent
1550	Sharifian leader Muhammad al-Mahdi captures Fez in Moroccan interior
1571	Spanish and Venetians defeat Ottomans at battle of Lepanto
1587–1629	Safavid dynasty reaches apogee under Shah Abbas I
1590	Sharifians conquer Timbuktu
1672–1727	Reign of Alawi Sharifian leader Moulay Isma'il, who expels Christian powers from port cities of Morocco
1683	Ottomans besiege Vienna but are repulsed
1722	Afghans march unopposed to the Safavid capital Isfahan
1699	Treaty of Karlowitz
1658–1707	Aurangzeb extends Moghul control to virtually all of the Indian subcontinent as well as the Hindu Kush and The Himalaya
1730s	Nader Shah reconstitutes Safavid empire, defeats Moghuls, sacks Delhi
1774	Treaty of Kuchuk Kainarji

Wahhabism after its leader Muhammad 'Abd al-Wahhab (1703–92), grew steadily in political power in Arabia and in intellectual influence throughout the Islamic world, where its austerity was seen as an answer to corruption and decline. Sufi leaders also adapted to the more activist climate of the eighteenth century and took a direct role in politics. The vigor and hope created by these pietistic movements was to persist well into the nineteenth century.

Broadly viewed, the decline of the great empires may have been accompanied by an impoverishment of their peoples and much local disorder, but this by no means meant a decay of the social order. Without doubt, in the eighteenth century the rulers of the great empires lost control of many of their provinces for long periods. Even the Ottomans, the stablest of the empires, had only a hazy control of Egypt and Iraq, which were effectively ruled by local Mamluks. However, all of these early modern Islamic empires, though not states in the modern sense, created or reinforced local structures that persisted through periods of weak central rule and maintained their collective existence even without government supervision. Somehow, the Islamic world emerged from the eighteenth century with its constituent social communities alive and intact.

The important changes that transformed the governments of the Middle Eastern and Islamic world in the period from the Mongol invasions in the thirteenth century to the eve of European colonization in the late eighteenth century were only partly responsible for changes in society and culture. Governments were more centralized, more accustomed to maintaining a body of royal law, more inclined to interfere in the application of Islamic law, and more prone to exact stock taking and exploitation of the resources of their domains. Governments moved toward creating institutions that might have an impersonal life apart from the ruler or his representatives. But government remained largely personal, and neither the reconfiguration of "fiefs" nor the restructuring of military slavery produced categories of people—even in the hearts of these empires—who felt permanently invested in maintaining the central governments' control.

Nevertheless, the empires helped define cultural areas that continued long after central governments failed. Moreover, many aspects of cultural life, in particular material culture, reached their highest development during this period. This high development was due not only to court patronage but also to the activity of certain categories of the population, such as traders and the ulama, who continued to form international elites. In this sense of belonging to an international community, they were joined by ordinary Muslims who felt less encapsulated in imperially defined "states" and more a part of a worldwide Islamic community. Therefore, while some aspects of what in Europe would be considered the "state" had emerged in these empires, by and large society looked to itself and not to its ruling centers for its identity. These early modern empires had respectably long lives—from two centuries among the Safavids to five centuries among the Ottomans. But even when the empires broke down, society proved remarkably resilient, perhaps because society and government, although closer in this period than in earlier periods of Islamic history, were still living together without being married.

SUGGESTIONS FOR FURTHER READING

GENERAL READING

* P. M. Holt, A. K. S. Lambton, and B. Lewis, eds., *Cambridge History of Islam* (Cambridge: Cambridge University Press, 1970). Excellent chapters on each of the early modern Islamic empires along with good surveys of major topics; a standard book in the field and a useful place to find basic historical facts.
* Ira M. Lapidus, *A History of Islamic Societies* (Cambridge: Cambridge University Press, 1988). A fine survey of Islamic history with good chapters on the early modern empires and thoughtful consideration of the role of Islam in shaping Islamic societies.

Francis Robinson, *Atlas of the Islamic World Since 1500* (New York: Facts on File, 1982). Not only an atlas but also a very imaginatively conceived social and cultural history of the period with magnificent illustrations.

THE ISLAMIC WORLD BEFORE THE EARLY MODERN EMPIRES

Ibn Battuta, *The Travels of Ibn Battuta* (Cambridge: Hakluyt Society, 1958–62). A translation—still not complete—of the memoirs of this fourteenth-century world traveler, which gives an unmatched view of the world of Islamic courts, colleges, holy men, and merchants.
* R. Stephen Humphreys, *Islamic History: A Framework For Inquiry* (Princeton: Princeton University Press, 1990). An astute guide to the major themes and problems facing historians of this subject with an expert review of bibliography of the field.

THE ISLAMIC WORLD DIVIDES INTO FOUR EMPIRES

R. M. Savory, *Iran Under the Safavids* (Cambridge: Cambridge University Press, 1980). The best book on the Safavids, with extensive treatment of cultural subjects such as literature.
S. A. A. Rizvi, *The Wonder That Was India*, Vol. II (London: Sidgwick and Jackson, 1987). While waiting for the new volume on the Moghuls in the *Cambridge History of Islam*, this study, which treats the entire subcontinent from 1200 to 1700, gives a useful panorama of most aspects of Moghul history.
Halil Inalcik, *The Ottoman Empire: The Classical Age 1300–1600* (London: Weidenfeld and Nicolson, 1973). A masterly treatment by the doyen of specialists on the Ottomans, strong on administration, trade, learning, and royal law.
* Jamil M. Abun-Nasr, *A History of the Maghrib* (Cambridge: Cambridge University Press, 1975). The standard history of the Maghrib and Andalus with good chapters on the Sa'dians, Alawis, and Ottoman provinces, and a helpful bibliography.

POLITICAL DECLINE AND TRANSFORMATION IN THE SEVENTEENTH AND EIGHTEENTH CENTURIES

Annemarie Schimmel, *The Mystical Dimension of Islam* (Chapel Hill: The University of North Carolina Press, 1975). The best general treatment of Sufism, which was probably the religious orientation of most Muslims during the period covered, with excellent chapters on its intellectual and literary traditions.
Thomas Naff and Roger Owen, eds., *Studies in Eighteenth Century Islamic Society* (Carbondale, IL: Southern Illinois University Press, 1987). A pioneering collection of articles that show that the old paradigm of decline does not fit the continuing vitality of Islamic society in the eighteenth century.

* Indicates paperback edition available.

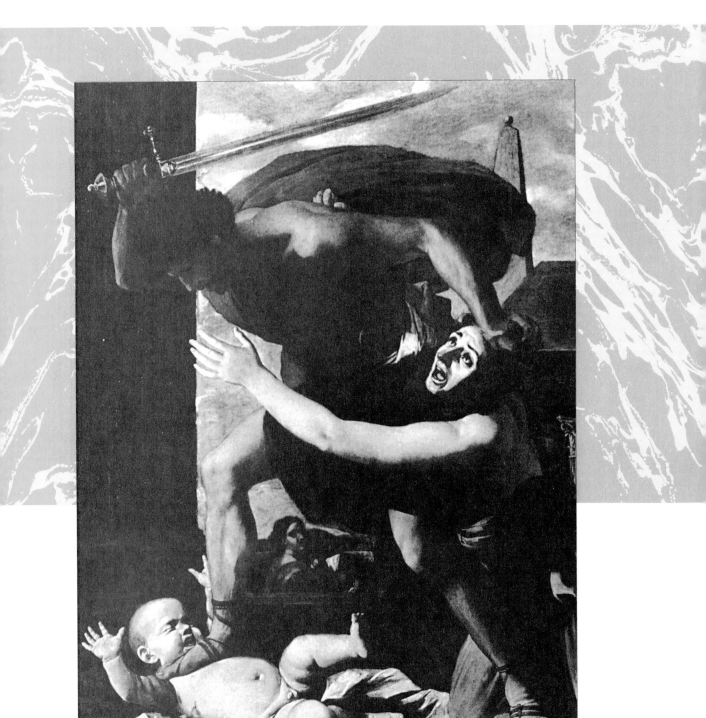

THE MASSACRE OF THE INNOCENTS

"War is one of the scourges with which it has pleased God to afflict men," wrote Cardinal Richelieu (1585–1642), the French minister who played no small part in spreading the scourge. War was a constant of European society and penetrated to its very core. It dominated all aspects of life. It enhanced the power of the state, it defined gender roles, it consumed lives and treasure and commodities ravenously. War affected every member of society from combatants to civilians. There were no innocent bystanders. Grain in the fields was destroyed because it was food for soldiers; houses were burned because they provided shelter for soldiers. Civilians were killed for aiding the enemy or holding out against demands for their treasure and supplies. Able-bodied men were taken forcibly to serve as conscripts, leaving women to plant and harvest as best as they could.

Neither the ancient temple nor the Roman costume can conceal the immediacy of the picture on the facing page. It is as painful to look at now as it was when it was created over 350 years ago. Painted by Nicolas Poussin (1594–1665) at the height of the Thirty Years' War, the *Massacre of the Innocents* remains a horrifying composition of power, terror, and despair. The cruel and senseless slaughter of the innocent baby that is about to take place is echoed throughout the canvas. Between the executioner's legs can be seen a mother clasping her own child tightly and anticipating the fall of the sword. In the background on the right another mother turns away from the scene and carries her infant to safety. In the foreground strides a mother holding her dead child. She tears at her hair and cries in anguish. To a culture in which the image of mother and child—of Mary and Jesus—was one of sublime peacefulness and inexpressible joy, the contrast could hardly be more shocking.

The picture graphically displays the cruelty of the soldier, the helplessness of the child, and the horror of the mother. By his grip on the mother's hair and his foot on the baby's throat, the warrior shows his brute power. The mother's futile effort to stop the sword illustrates her powerlessness. She scratches uselessly at the soldier's back. Naked, the baby boy raises his hands as if to surrender to the inevitable, as if to reinforce his innocence.

To study Europe at war, we must enter into a world of politics and diplomacy, of issues and principles, of judgment and error. There can be no doubt that the future of Europe was decisively shaped by the century of wholesale slaughter from 1555 to 1648, during which dynastic and religious fervor finally ran its course. The survival of Protestantism, the disintegration of the Spanish empire, the rise of Holland and Sweden, the collapse of Poland and Muscovy, the fragmentation of Germany—these were all vital transformations whose consequences would be felt for centuries. We cannot avoid telling this story, untangling its causes, narrating its course, revealing its outcome. But neither should we avoid facing its reality. Look again at the painting by Poussin.

The Formation of States

The early sixteenth century was the age of the prince, the first great stage of nation building that would last for the next three hundred years. The New Monarchies, as they are sometimes called, consolidated territories that were divided culturally, linguistically, and historically. The states of Europe are political units and they were forged by political means: by diplomacy, by marriage, and most commonly by war.

It was Machiavelli who identified the prince as the agent of change in the process of state formation. He believed that the successful prince could bring unity to his lands, security to his borders, and prosperity to his subjects. The unsuccessful prince brought nothing but ruin.

A process as long and as complex as the formation of nations is not subject to the will of individuals, even princes. Factors as diverse as geography, population, and natural resources are all decisive. So too are the structures of human activity. The ways in which families are organized and wealth is transmitted from generation to generation can result in large estates with similar customs or small estates with varying ones. The manner in which social groups are formed and controlled can mean that power is centralized or dispersed. The beliefs of ordinary people and the way they practice them can define who is a part of a community and who is apart from it. All these elements and many others influence the way European states began to develop from medieval monarchies at the end of the fifteenth century. Despite these complexities, we should not lose sight of the simple truth of Machiavelli's observations. In the first stages of the consolidation of European nations, the role of the prince was crucial.

Indeed, in the middle of the fifteenth century there were many factors working against the formation of large states in Europe. The most obvious involved simple things like transportation and communication. The distance that could be covered quickly was very small. In wet and cold seasons travel was nearly impossible. Large areas were difficult to control and to defend. Communication was subject not only to the hazards of travel but also to the distinct languages or dialects of small states. Separate languages meant separate cultures. Customary practices, common ancestry, and shared experiences helped define a sense of community through which small states defined themselves.

In addition to these natural forces that governed the existence of small units of government, there were in- vented ones. To succeed, a prince had to establish supremacy over a number of rivals. For the most part, states were inherited. In some places it was customary to follow the rule of primogeniture, inheritance by the eldest son. In others, estates were split among sons, or among children of both sexes. Some traditions, like the French, excluded inheritance through women; others, like the Castilian, treated women's claims as equal to men's. Short lives meant prolonged disputes about inheritance. Rulers had to defend their thrones from rivals with strong claims to legitimacy.

So, too, did rulers have to defend themselves from the ambitions of their mightiest subjects. The constant warfare of the European nobility was one of the central features of the later Middle Ages. To avoid resort to arms, princes and peers entered into all manner of alliances, using their children as pawns and the marriage bed as the chessboard. Rulers also faced independent institutions within their states, powerful organizations that had to be won over or crushed. By the end of the fifteenth century, the long process of taming the Church was about to enter a new stage. Fortified towns presented a different problem. They possessed both the manpower and wealth necessary to raise and maintain armies. They also jealously guarded their privileges. Rulers who could not tax their towns could not rule their state. Finally, most kingdoms had assemblies representing the propertied classes, especially in matters of taxation. Some, like the English Parliament and the Spanish Cortes, were strong; others, like the Imperial Diet and the French Estates-General, were weak. But everywhere they posed an obstacle to the extension of the power of princes.

In combination, these factors slowed and shaped the process of state formation. But neither separately nor together were they powerful enough to overcome it. The fragmentation of Europe into so many small units of government made some consolidation inevitable. The practice of dynastic marriage meant that smaller states were continually being inherited by the rulers of larger ones. If the larger state was stable, it absorbed the smaller one. If not, the smaller state would split off again to await its next predator or protector. As the first large states took shape, the position of smaller neighbors grew ever more precarious.

This was especially true by the end of the fifteenth century because of the increase in the destructive power of warfare. Technological advances in cannonry and in the skills of gunners and engineers made medieval fortifications untenable. Gunpowder decisively changed battlefield tactics. It made heavy armor obsolete and allowed for the development of a different type of warfare. Lightly armored horses and riders could not only inflict more damage upon one another, but they were now mobile enough to be used against infantry. Infantry armed with long pikes or small muskets became the crucial components of armies that were growing ever larger. What could not be inherited, or married, could be conquered.

Eastern Configurations

The interplay of factors that encouraged and inhibited the formation of states is most easily observed in the eastern parts of Europe. There the different paths taken by Muscovy and Poland-Lithuania stand in contrast. At the beginning of the sixteenth century, the principality of Muscovy was the largest European political unit. Muscovy had established itself as the heir to the ancient state of Russia through conquest, shrewd political alli-

The sixteenth century saw the introduction of new and powerfully destructive weapons. Many felt that these "murderous engines" would destroy the virtues of chivalry. In this woodcut from 1521, the bows and arrows, lances, and heavy armor of the Middle Ages are challenged by the new cannon.

ances, and the good fortune of its princes to be blessed with long reigns. Muscovy's growth was phenomenal. Under Ivan III, "the Great" (1462–1505), Muscovy expanded to the north and west, annexing Novgorod and large parts of Livonia and Lithuania. Its military successes were almost unbroken, but so too were its diplomatic triumphs. Between 1460 and 1530, Muscovy increased its territory by 1.5 million square miles.

A number of factors led to the rise of Muscovy. The deterioration of the Mongol empire and the fall of Constantinople significantly diminished external threats. And internally, Ivan the Great was fortunate in having no competitors for his throne. He was able to extend power to others to administer the new Muscovite territories without fear of setting up rivals to power. Ivan expanded the privileges of his nobility and organized a military class who received land as a reward for their fidelity. He also extended his sovereignty to cover all lands to which there was an ancient Russian claim and combined it with the religious authority of the Orthodox church. Both he and his successors ruled with the aid of able Church leaders who were normally part of the prince's council.

What made the expansion of Muscovy so impressive is that land once gained was never lost. The military and political achievements of Ivan the Great were furthered by his son Vasili and his more famous grandson Ivan IV, "the Terrible" (1533–84). Ivan IV defeated the Mongols on his southeastern border and incorporated the entire Volga basin into Muscovy. But his greatest ambition was to gain a Livonian port on the Baltic Sea and establish a northern outlet for commerce. Nearly three decades of warfare between Muscovy and Poland-Lithuania, with whom Livonia had allied itself, resulted in large territorial gains, but never the prized Baltic port. And Ivan's northern campaigns seriously weakened the defense of the south. In 1571 the Crimean Tartars advanced on Muscovy's southwestern border and inflicted a powerful blow when they burned the city of Moscow. Although the Tartars were eventually driven off Muscovite soil, expansion in both north and south was at an end for the next seventy-five years.

By the reign of Ivan IV, Muscovite society was divided roughly into three groups: the hereditary landed nobility known as the boyars, the military service class, and the peasantry who were bound to the land. There was no large mercantile presence in Muscovy and its urban component remained small. The boyars inherited their lands and owed little to the tsar. Members of the military class, however, depended on the success of the crown for the possession of their estates, which were granted out of lands gained through territorial expansion.

Europe, ca. 1500

Gradually the new military service class grew in power and prestige, largely at the expense of the older boyars. Ivan IV used members of the military service class as legislative advisors and elevated them in his parliamentary council (the Zemsky Sobor), which also contained representatives of the nobility, clergy, and towns.

Unlike his grandfather, Ivan IV had an abiding mistrust of the boyars. They had held power when he was a child and it was rumored that they had poisoned his mother. It was in his treatment of the boyars that he earned the nickname "the Terrible." During his brutal suppression of supposed conspiracies, several thousand boyar families were massacred by Ivan's orders, and thousands more were forcibly relocated. This practice made the boyars' situation similar to that of the military service class, who owed their fortunes to the tsar.

All of these measures contributed to the breakdown of local networks of influence and power and to a disruption of local governance. But they also made possible a system of central administration, one of Ivan IV's most important achievements. He created departments of state to deal with the various tasks of administration, such as revenues and the military. He created new boyars, who owed their positions and loyalty to him. Both boyars and the military benefited from Ivan's policy of binding the great mass of people to the land. Russian

peasants had few political or economic rights in comparison to western peasants, but during the early sixteenth century even their meager rights were curtailed. Binding the peasants in serfdom to the land made possible the prolonged absence of military leaders from their estates and contributed to the creation of the military service class. But in the long term, serfdom retarded economic development by removing incentive from large landholders to make investments in commerce or to improve agricultural production.

Following the death of Ivan the Terrible in 1584, the Muscovite state began to disintegrate. Ivan had murdered his heir in a fit of anger and left his half-witted son to inherit the throne. This led to a vacuum of power at the center as well as a struggle for the spoils of government that lasted for thirty years. When Michael Romanov (1613–45) was chosen tsar by an assembly of landholders, he only gradually restored order.

The growth of an enlarged and centralized Muscovy stands in contrast to the experiences of Poland-Lithuania during the same period. At the end of the fifteenth century Casimir IV (1447–92) ruled the kingdom of Poland and the grand duchy of Lithuania. His son Vladislav II ruled Bohemia (1471–1516) and Hungary (1490–1516). Had the four states been permanently consolidated, they could have become an effective barrier to Ottoman

A delegation of Russian boyars bearing gifts visited the Holy Roman Emperor Maximilian II in 1576 to seek his aid against Poland-Lithuania.

expansion in the south and Russian expansion in the east. But the union of crowns had never been the union of states. It had taken place over the previous century by political alliances, diplomatic marriages, and the consent of the nobility. Such arrangements kept peace among the four neighbors, but it kept any one of them from becoming a dominant partner.

There were many reasons why a unified state did not appear in east central Europe as it did in Muscovy. In the first place, external forces disrupted territorial and political arrangements. Wars with the Ottomans and the Russians absorbed resources. Second, the princes faced internal rivals to their crowns. Though Casimir IV was able to place his son on the thrones of both Bohemia and Hungary, his success necessitated concessions to leading citizens, which decreased the ability of the princes to centralize their kingdoms or to effect real unification among them. The nobility of Hungary, Bohemia, and Poland-Lithuania all developed strong local interests that increased over time. In Bohemia, Vladislav II was king in name only, and even in Poland the nobility won confirmation of its rights and privileges from the monarchy.

Until the end of the sixteenth century, Poland-Lithuania was the dominant power in the eastern part of Europe. The permanent union of the two separate states in 1569 made it economically healthy and militarily powerful. Through its Baltic ports, especially Gdansk, Poland played a central role in international commerce and was a leader in the northern grain trade. Matters of war and peace, of taxation, and of reform were placed under the strict supervision of the Polish Diet, a parliamentary body that represented the landed elite. But the failure of the Jagiellon monarchy in Poland to produce an heir ended that nation's most successful line of kings and forced the Polish nobility and gentry to

peddle their throne among the princes of Europe. Successively, a French duke, a Hungarian prince, and finally in 1587 the heir to the Swedish throne, Sigismund III (1587–1632), were elected. As in Muscovy, the absence of strong rule led to military and economic decline by the beginning of the seventeenth century.

The Western Powers

Just as in the east, there was no single pattern to the consolidation of the large western European states. They, too, were internally fragmented and externally imperiled. While England had to overcome the ruin of decades of civil war, France and Spain faced the challenges of invasion and occupation. Western European princes struggled against powerful institutions and individuals within their states. Some they conquered, others they absorbed. Each nation formed its state differently: England by administrative centralization, France by good fortune, and Spain by dynastic marriage. Yet in 1450 few imagined that any one of these states would succeed.

The Taming of England. England was the only European state that suffered no threat of foreign invasion during the fifteenth century. This island fortress might easily have become the first consolidated European state were it not for the ambitions of the nobility and the weakness of the Crown. For thirty years the English aristocracy fought over the spoils of a helpless monarch. The Wars of the Roses (1455–85), as they came to be called, were as much a free-for-all among the English peerage as they were a contest for the throne between the houses of Lancaster and York. At their center was an attempt by the dukes of York to wrest the crown from the mad and ineffective Lancastrian king Henry VI (1422–61). All around the edges was the continuation of local and family feuds that had little connection to the dynastic struggle.

Three decades of intermittent warfare virtually destroyed the houses of Lancaster and York. Edward IV (1461–83) succeeded in gaining the crown for the House of York, but he never wore it securely. When he died, his children, including his heir, Edward V (1483), were placed in the protection of their uncle Richard III (1483–85). The two boys disappeared, reputedly murdered in the Tower of London, and Richard declared himself king. Richard's usurpation led to civil war, and he was killed by the forces of Henry Tudor at the battle of Bosworth Field in 1485. By the end of the Wars of the Roses the monarchy had lost both revenue and prestige, and the aristocracy had stored up bitter memories for the future.

Henry Tudor picked up the pieces of the kingdom, as legend has it he picked up the crown off a bramble bush. The two chief obstacles to his determination to consolidate the English state were the power of the nobility and the poverty of the monarchy. No English monarch had held secure title to the throne for over a century. Henry Tudor, as Henry VII (1485–1509), put an end to this dynastic instability at once. He married Elizabeth of York, and their children were indisputable successors to the crown. He also began the long process of taming his overmighty subjects. Traitors were hung and turncoats rewarded. He and his son Henry VIII (1509–47) adroitly created a new peerage, who owed their titles and loyalty to the Tudors. They were favored with offices and spoils and were relied upon to suppress both popular and aristocratic rebellions.

The financial problems of the English monarchy were not so easily overcome. An English king was supposed to live "of his own," that is, off the revenues from his own estates. Only in extraordinary circumstances were the king's subjects required to contribute to the maintenance of government. This principle was defended through the representative institution, the Parliament. When the kings of England wanted to tax their subjects, they first had to gain the assent of Parliament. Though Parliaments did grant requests for extraordinary revenue, especially for national defense, they did so grudgingly. The English landed elites were not exempt from taxation, but they were able to control the amount of taxes they paid.

The inability of the Crown to extract its living from its subjects fostered the efficient management of the royal estates. Thus English state building depended upon the growth of centralized institutions that could oversee royal lands and collect royal customs. Gradually, medieval institutions like the Exchequer were supplanted by newer organs that were better able to adjust to modern methods of accounting, record keeping, and enforcement. Whether Henry's reputation for greed and rapacity was warranted, it was undeniable that he squeezed as much as possible from a not very juicy inheritance. His financial problems limited both domestic and foreign policy.

Not until the middle of the next reign was the English monarchy again solvent. As a result of his dispute with the papacy, Henry VIII confiscated the enormous wealth of the Catholic church, and with one stroke solved the Crown's monetary problems (see chapter 13). But the real contribution that Henry and his chief minister, Thomas Cromwell (ca. 1485–1540), made to forming an English state was the way in which this windfall was administered. Cromwell accelerated the centralization of government that had begun under Edward IV. He created separate departments of state to handle the various administrative functions—record keeping, revenue collection, law enforcement, etc. Each had a distinct jurisdiction and a permanent, trained staff. Cromwell coordinated the work of these departments by expanding the power of the Privy Council, which included the heads of these administrative bodies and which came to serve as the king's executive.

ANNE BOLEYN'S SPEECH FROM THE SCAFFOLD (1536)

■ *Anne Boleyn was the second wife of Henry VIII and the mother of Elizabeth I. Henry's desire to have a son and his passion for Anne resulted in his divorce from Catherine of Aragon and England's formal break with the Roman Catholic church. When Anne bore only a daughter she too became dispensable. She was convicted of adultery and incest and executed in 1536. Here are her last words.*

Good friends, I am not come here to excuse or to justify myself, for as much as I know full well that aught that I could say in my defense doth not appertain unto you, and that I could draw no hope of life from the same. But I come here only to die, and thus to yield myself humbly to the will of the King my Lord. And if in my life I did ever offend the King's grace, surely with my death I do now atone for the same. And I blame not my judges, nor any other manner of person, nor anything save the cruel law of the land by which I die. But be this, and be my faults as they may, I beseech you all, good friends, to pray for the life of the King my sovereign lord and yours, who is one of the best princes on the face of the earth, and who hath always treated me so well that better could not be; wherefore I submit to death and with a good will, humbly asking pardon of the world.

Holbein's last portrait of Henry VIII, 1542. Henry made England into one of the world's greatest naval powers but embroiled the kingdom in a series of costly foreign wars. He married six times in an effort to produce a legitimate male heir.

Cromwell also saw the importance of Parliament as a legislative body. Through Parliament, royal policy could be turned into statutes that had the assent of the political nation. If Parliament was well managed, issues that were potentially controversial could be defused. Laws passed by Parliament were more easily enforced locally than were proclamations issued by the king.

The Unification of France. Perhaps the most remarkable thing about the unification of France is that it took place at all. The forces working against the consolidation of a French state were formidable. France was surrounded by aggressive and powerful neighbors with whom it was frequently at war. Its greatest nobles were semi-independent princes who were constant rivals for the throne and consistent opponents of the extension of royal power. The French people were deeply suspicious of the pretensions of the monarchy and fiercely loyal to their province and its local customs and institutions. And France was splintered by profound regional differences. The north and south were divided by culture and by language (the *langue d'oc* in the south and the *langue d'oïl* in the north).

The first obstacles that were overcome were the external threats to French security. For over a century the throne of France had been contested by the kings of England. The so-called Hundred Years' War (1337–1453) originated in a dispute over the inheritance of the French crown and English possessions in Gascony in southern France (see chapter 10).

The problems posed by the Hundred Years' War were not just those of victory and defeat. The struggle between the kings of England and the kings of France allowed French princes and dukes, who were nominally vassals of the king, to enhance their autonomy by making their own alliances with the highest bidder. When the English were finally driven out of France in the middle of the fifteenth century, the kings of France came into a weakened and divided inheritance.

Nor was England the only threat to the security of the French monarchy. On France's eastern border, in a long arching semicircle, were the estates of the dukes of Burgundy. The dukes of Burgundy and the kings of France shared a common ancestry; both were of the House of Valois. Still, the sons of brothers in one generation were only cousins in the next, and the two branches of the family grew apart. The original Burgundian inheritance was in the southeast, centered at Dijon. A good marriage and good fortune brought to the first duke the rich northern province of Flanders. For the next hundred years, by marriage and through force, the dukes of Burgundy managed to unite their divided estates in one long unbroken string. But it was a string stretched taut. The power of Burgundy threatened its neighbors in all directions. Both France and the Holy Roman Empire were too weak to resist its expansion, but the confederation of Swiss towns to the southwest of Burgundy was not. In a series of stunning military victories Swiss forces repelled the Burgundians from their lands and demolished their armies. Charles the Bold, the last Valois duke of Burgundy, fell at the battle of Nancy in 1477. His estates were quickly dismembered. France recovered its ancestral territories, including Burgundy itself, and through no effort of its own was now secure on its eastern border.

The king most associated with the consolidation of France was Louis XI (1461–83). He inherited an estate exhausted by warfare and civil strife. More by chance than by plan he vastly extended the territories under the dominion of the French crown and, more importantly, subdued the nobility. Louis XI was as cunning as he was peculiar. In an age in which royalty was expressed through magnificence, Louis sported an old felt hat and a well-worn coat. His enemies constantly underestimated his abilities, which earned him the nickname "the Spider." But gradually during the course of his reign, Louis XI won back what he had been forced to give away. Years of fighting both the English and each other depleted the ranks of the French aristocracy and the stocks of fathers and sons ran low. Estates with no male heirs fell forfeit to the king. In this manner the crown absorbed Anjou and Maine in the northwest and Provence in the south. And by brilliant political marriages for his son and daughter, Louis XI ultimately obtained control of the two greatest independent fiefs, Brittany and Orléans. When in 1527 the lands of the duke of Bourbon fell to the crown, the French monarch ruled a unified state.

The consolidation demonstrated how a state could be formed without the designs of a great leader. Neither Louis XI nor his son Charles VIII (1483–98) were nation builders. Louis's main objective was always to preserve his estate. And considerable good fortune saved him from the consequences of many ill-conceived policies. But no amount of luck could make up for Louis's failure to obtain the Burgundian Low Countries for France after the death of Charles the Bold in 1477. The marriage of his daughter and heir Mary of Burgundy to Maximilian of Habsburg initiated the struggle between France and Spain for control of the Low Countries that endured for over two centuries.

These long years of war established the principle of royal taxation, which was so essential to the process of state building in France. This enabled the monarchy to raise money for defense and for consolidation. Because of the strength of the nobles, most taxation fell only on the commoners, the so-called third estate. The *taille* was a direct tax on property, from which the nobility and clergy were exempt. The *gabelle* was a consumption tax on the purchase of salt in most parts of the kingdom, and the *aide* was a tax on a variety of commodities including meat and wine. These consumption taxes were paid by all members of the third estate no matter how poor they might be. In spite of complaints, the French monarchy established a broad base for taxation and a high degree of compliance long before any other European nation.

Along with money went soldiers, fighting men necessary to repel the English and to defend the crown against rebels and traitors. Again the French monarchy established a first, the principle of a national army,

raised and directed from the center but quartered and equipped regionally. Originally towns were required to provide artillery, but constant troubles with the nobility had led the kings of France to establish their own store of heavy guns. The towns supplied small arms, pikes, and swords and later pistols and muskets. By the beginning of the sixteenth century the French monarch could raise and equip an army of his own.

Taxation and military obligation demanded the creation and expansion of centralized institutions of government. This was the most difficult development in the period of state formation in France. The powers of royal agents were constantly challenged by the powers of regional nobles. It is easy to exaggerate the extent of the growth of central control and to underestimate the enduring hold of regional and provincial loyalties. Even the crown's absorption of estates did not always end local privileges and customs. But despite continued regional autonomy, a beginning had been made.

The Marriages of Spain. Before the sixteenth century there was little prospect of a single nation emerging on the Iberian Peninsula. North African Muslims called Moors occupied the province of Granada in the south, while the stable kingdom of Portugal dominated the western coast. The Spanish peoples were divided among a number of separate states. The two most important were Castile and Aragon. Three religions and four languages (not including dialects) widened these political divisions. And the different states had different outlooks. Castile was, above all, determined to subjugate the last of Islamic Spain and to convert its large Jewish population to Christianity. Aragon played in the high-stakes game for power in the Mediterranean. It claimed sovereignty over Sicily and Naples and exercised it whenever it could.

A happy teenage marriage brought together the unhappy kingdoms of Castile and Aragon. When Ferdinand of Aragon and Isabella of Castile secretly exchanged wedding vows in 1469, both their homelands were rent by civil war. In Castile, Isabella's brother Henry IV (1454–74) struggled unsuccessfully against the powerful Castilian nobility. In Aragon, Ferdinand's father, John II (1458–79), faced a revolt by the rich province of Catalonia on one side and the territorial ambitions of Louis XI of France on the other. Joining the heirs together increased the resources of both kingdoms. Ferdinand took an active role in the pacification of Castile, while Castilian riches allowed him to defend Aragon from invasion. In 1479 the two crowns were united and the Catholic monarchs, as they were called,

An idealized portrait of Ferdinand and Isabella shows the Catholic monarchs reigning in Renaissance style surrounded by richly costumed courtiers.

ruled the two kingdoms jointly. But the unification of the crowns of Castile and Aragon was not the same as the formation of a single state. Local privileges were zealously guarded, especially in Aragon, where the representative institutions of the towns, the Cortes, were aggressively independent. The powerful Castilian nobility never accepted Ferdinand as their king and refused him the crown after Isabella's death.

But Ferdinand and Isabella (1479–1516) took the first steps toward forging a Spanish state. Their most notable achievement was the final recovery of the lands that had been conquered by the Moors. For centuries the Spanish kingdoms had fought against the North African Muslims who had conquered large areas of the southern peninsula. The *reconquista* was characterized by short bursts of warfare followed by long periods of wary coexistence. The final stages of the reconquista began in 1482 and lasted for a decade. It was waged as a holy war and was financed in part by grants from the pope and the Christian princes of Europe. It was a bloody undertaking, but in 1492 Granada, the only remaining Moorish stronghold, finally fell and the province was absorbed into Castile.

The reconquista helped create a national identity for the Christian peoples of Spain. In order to raise men and money for the war effort, Ferdinand and Isabella mobilized their nobility and town governments and created a central organization to oversee the invasion. The conquered territories were used to reward those who had aided the effort, though the crown maintained control and jurisdiction over most of the province. But the idea of the holy war also had a darker side and an unanticipated consequence. The Jewish population that had lived peacefully in both Castile and Aragon became another object of hostility. Many Jews had risen to prominence in government and in skilled professions. Others, who had accepted conversion to Christianity and were known as *conversos*, had become among the most powerful figures in the Church and the state.

Both groups were now attacked. The conversos fell prey to a special Church tribunal created to examine their sincere devotion to Catholicism. This was the Spanish Inquisition which, though it used traditional judicial practices—torture to gain confessions, public humiliation to show contrition, and burnings at the stake to maintain purity—used them on a scale never before seen. Thousands of conversos were killed and many more families had their wealth confiscated to be used for the reconquista. In 1492 the Jews themselves were expelled from Spain. Though the reconquista and the expulsion of the Jews inflicted great suffering upon victims and incalculable loss to the Castilian economy, both events enhanced the prestige of the Catholic monarchs.

In many ways, Ferdinand and Isabella trod the paths of the medieval monarchy. They relied upon personal contact with their people more than upon the use of a centralized administration. They frequently dispensed justice personally, sitting in court and accepting petitions from their subjects. Queen Isabella was venerated in Castile, where women's right to inheritance remained strong. Ferdinand's absences from Aragon were always a source of contention between him and the Cortes of the towns. Yet he was careful to provide regents to preside in his absence and regularly returned to visit his native kingdom.

Ferdinand and Isabella consciously sought to bring about a permanent union. Ferdinand made Castilian the official language of government in Aragon and even appointed Castilians to Aragonese posts. He and Isabella actively encouraged the intermarriage of the two aristocracies and the expansion of the number of wealthy nobles who held land in both kingdoms. Nevertheless, these measures did not unify Spain or erase the centuries-long tradition of hostility among the diverse Iberian peoples.

Heroic portrait of the Emperor Charles V by Titian, 1547. The emperor is shown at the battle of Mühlberg, which paved the way for the Peace of Augsburg of 1555.

It was left to the heirs of Ferdinand and Isabella to forge together the Spanish kingdoms, and the process was a painful one. The hostility to a foreign monarch increased dramatically at the accession of their grandson, who became the emperor Charles V (1516–56) and who had been born and raised in the Low Countries, where he ruled over Burgundy and the Netherlands. Through a series of dynastic accidents, Charles was heir to the Spanish crown with its possessions in the New World and to the vast Habsburg estates that included Austria. Charles established his rule in Spain gradually. For a time he was forced to share power in Castile and to suppress a disorganized aristocratic rebellion.

Because of his foreign obligations, Charles was frequently absent from Spain. During those periods he governed through regents and royal councils that helped centralize administration. Charles V realized the importance of Spain, especially of Castile, in his empire. He established a permanent bureaucratic court, modeled on that of Burgundy, and placed able Spaniards at the head of its departments. This smoothed over the long periods when Charles was abroad.

Yet neither his personal efforts to rule as a Spanish monarch, nor those of his able administrators were the most important factor in uniting the Spanish kingdoms of Iberia. Rather it was the fact that Charles V brought Spain to the forefront of European affairs in the sixteenth century. Spanish prowess, whether in arms or in culture, became a source of national pride that helped erode regional identity. Gold and silver from the New World helped finance Charles's great empire. In Italy he prosecuted Aragonese claims to Sicily and Naples; in the north he held on firmly to the kingdom of Navarre, which had been annexed by Ferdinand and which secured Spain's border with France. In the south he blocked off Ottoman and Muslim expansion. The reign of Charles V ushered in the dawn of Spain's golden age.

The process by which European kingdoms became states was long and involved. The first steps were taken all over the continent at the end of the fifteenth century. Inheritance, dynastic marriages, and wars of conquest expanded territory under the domination of a single monarch. Bureaucracy, the spread of legal jurisdiction, and the extraction of resources through taxation expanded the monarch's internal control. In kingdoms as diverse as Muscovy and Spain, Poland-Lithuania, and England a similar process was under way, a process that would define European history for centuries to come.

The Dynastic Struggles

The formation of large states throughout Europe led inevitably to conflicts among them. Thus the sixteenth century was a period of almost unrelieved warfare that took the whole Continent as its theater. Advances in technology made war more efficient and more expensive. They also made it more horrible. The use of artillery against infantry increased the number of deaths and maiming injuries, as did the replacement of the arrow by the bullet. As the size of armies increased, so did casualties.

Power and Glory

The frequency of offensive war in the sixteenth century raises a number of questions about the militaristic values of the age. Valor remained greatly prized—a Renaissance virtue inherited from the crusading zeal and chivalric ideals of the Middle Ages—and princes sought to do valiant deeds. Ferdinand of Aragon and Francis I

(1515–47) of France won fame for their exploits in war. Charles the Bold and Louis II of Hungary were less fortunate. Their battlefield deaths led to the breakup of their states. Wars were fought to further the interests of princes rather than the interests of national sovereignty or international Christianity. They were certainly not fought in the interests of their subjects. States were an extension of a prince's heritage; what rulers sought in battle was a part of their historical and familial rights, which defined themselves and their subjects. The wars of the sixteenth century were dynastic wars.

Along with desire came ability. The New Monarchs were capable of waging war. The very definition of their states involved accumulating and defending territories. Internal security depended upon locally raised forces or hired mercenaries. Both required money, which was becoming available in unprecedented quantities as a result of the increasing prosperity of the early sixteenth century and the windfall of gold and silver from the New World. Professional soldiers, of whom the Swiss and Germans were the most noteworthy, sold their services to the highest bidders. Developments in transport and supply meant campaigns could take place far from the center of a state. Finally, communications were improving. The need to know about potential rivals or allies strengthened the European system of diplomacy. Princes installed agents in all the European capitals, and their dispatches were the most reliable sources of information about the strengths of armies or the weaknesses of governments, about the birth of heirs or the death of princes.

Personality also influenced the international warfare of the early sixteenth century. The three most consistent protagonists, Charles V, Francis I, and Henry VIII, were of similar age and outlook. Each came unexpectedly to his throne in the full flush of youth, eager for combat and glory. The three were self-consciously rivals. Henry VIII and Francis I held wrestling bouts when they met in 1520. Francis I challenged Charles V to single combat

after the French king's humiliating imprisonment in Madrid in 1526. As the three monarchs aged, their youthful wars of conquest matured into strategic warfare designed to maintain a Continental balance of power.

Habsburg and Valois

The struggle for supremacy in Europe in the sixteenth century pitted the French House of Valois against the far-flung estates of the Habsburg empire. In order for one house or the other to succeed, it was necessary to construct alliances among the various Italian city-states and most especially with England, whose aid both Charles and Francis sought in the early 1520s. Henry VIII was eager to reconquer France and cut a figure on the European scene. Despite the fact that his initial Continental adventures had emptied his treasury without fulfilling his dreams, Henry remained hungry for war. Charles V made two separate trips to London, while Henry crossed the Channel in 1520 to meet Francis I in one of the gaudiest displays of conspicuous consumption that the century would witness, appropriately known as the Field of the Cloth of Gold.

The result of these diplomatic intrigues was an alliance between England and the Holy Roman Empire. English and Burgundian forces would invade northern France while Spanish and German troops would attempt to dislodge the French forces from Italy. The strategy worked better than anyone could have imagined. In 1523 Charles's forces gained a foothold in Milan by taking the heavily fortified town of Pavia. Two years later Francis was ready to strike back. At the head of his own royal guards, he massed Swiss mercenaries and French infantry outside Pavia and made ready for a swift assault. Instead, a large imperial army arrived to relieve the town, and in the subsequent battle the French suffered a shattering defeat. Francis I was captured.

The Field of the Cloth of Gold, the lavish setting for the meeting between Henry VIII and Francis I in June 1520. The fountain in the foreground provides free wine for all.

Portrait of Mary, Queen of Scots.

The Monstrous Regiment of Women

"To promote a woman to bear rule, superiority, dominion or empire above any realm, nation, or city is repugnant to nature, contumely to God, and the subversion of good order, of all equity and justice." So wrote the Scottish theologian John Knox (1513-72) in *The First Blast of the Trumpet Against the Monstrous Regiment of Women* (1558). Though he made his points more emphatically than many others, Knox was only repeating the commonplace notions of his day. He could quote Aristotle and Aquinas as well as a host of secular authorities to demonstrate female inadequacies:

"Nature, I say, doth paint them forth to be weak, frail, impatient, feeble, and foolish." He could quote Saint Paul along with the ancient Fathers of the Church to demonstrate the "proper" place of women—"Man is not of the woman, but the woman of the man."

But no stacking up of authorities, no matter how numerous or revered, could erase the fact that all over Europe in the sixteenth century women could and did rule. In the Netherlands Mary, Queen of Hungary (1531-52) and Margaret of Parma (1559-67) were successful regents. Jeanne d'Albret

(1562-72) was queen of the tiny state of Navarre, territory claimed by both France and Spain but kept independent by this remarkable woman. Catherine de Médicis (1560-89), wife of one king of France and mother of three others, was the effective ruler of that nation for nearly thirty years. Mary, Queen of Scots (1542-87) was the nominal ruler of Scotland almost from her birth. England was ruled by two very different women, the Catholic Mary I (1553-58) and her Protestant half-sister Elizabeth I (1558-1603).

The problems faced by this long list of queens and regents were more than just the ordinary cares of government. The belief that women were inherently inferior in intelligence, strength, and character was so pervasive that for men like Knox, a woman ruler was almost a contradiction in terms.

Yet this was not the view taken by everyone, and female rule had its defenders as well as its detractors. One set of objections was overcome by the traditional medieval theory of the two bodies of the monarch. This argument was developed to reconcile the divine origins and functions of monarchs with their very real human frailties. In the theory of the two bodies, there was the body natural and the body politic. Both were joined together in the person of the ruler but the attributes of each could be separated. Rule of a woman did nothing to disrupt this notion. In fact, it made it easier to argue that the frailties of the body natural of a woman were in no way related to the strengths of the body politic of a monarch.

While such ideas might help a female ruler to be accepted by her subjects, they did little to invigorate her own sense of her role. Female rulers often strained against the straitjacket that definitions of gender placed them in. When angered, Elizabeth I would proclaim that she had more courage than her father, Henry VIII, "though I am only a woman." Mary, Queen of Scots, once revealed that her only regret was that she "was not a man to know what life it was to lie all night in the fields or to walk with a buckler and a broadsword." Some queens assumed masculine traits, riding in armor or leading forces to battle. Other women rulers mixed together characteristics that were usually separated by gender definitions. Margaret of Parma was considered one of the most accomplished horse riders of her day. After leading her courtiers through woods and fields at breakneck speed, she would then attend council meetings and work on her needlepoint. Mary, Queen of Scots, loved hawking, a traditional kingly sport in the Scottish wilds. After relishing the hawk's destruction of its prey, she liked to negotiate matters of state by beginning with tears and entreaties and ending with accusations and threats. The effect was more than discomforting.

Women were no more nor less successful as rulers than were men. Women's achievements, like men's, depended upon strength of character and the circumstances of the times. All the women rulers of the sixteenth century had received outstanding educations. Whether raised Catholic or Protestant, each was trained in Latin as well as modern languages, in the liberal arts, and in fine arts.

Mary, Queen of Scots, was the only one of these female rulers born to rule. She was the sole survivor of her father, who died shortly after her birth. Mary and Elizabeth Tudor came to their thrones after the death of their younger brother Edward VI; Mary of Hungary and Margaret of Parma came to theirs as princesses of the House of Habsburg. The rule of Catherine de Médicis was the most unexpected of all. Her vigorous husband, Henry II, died during a jousting tournament and her eldest son, Francis II, husband of Mary, Queen of Scots, died the following year. Instead of retirement as a respected queen dowager—the widow of a previous king—Catherine de Médicis was forced into the vortex of French politics to protect the rights of her ten-year-old son, Charles IX.

Unfortunately, the accomplishments of women rulers did little to dispel prejudices against women as a whole or to alter the definition of gender roles. Except for Mary, Queen of Scots, whose principal achievement was to provide an heir to the English throne, all the queens and regents of the sixteenth century were successful rulers. Margaret of Parma steered the careful middle course in the conflict between Spain and the Netherlands. She opposed the intervention of the Duke of Alba, and had her advice been followed, the eighty years of war between Spain and the Netherlands might have been avoided. Catherine de Médicis held the crown of France on the heads of her sons, navigated the treacherous waters of civil war, and provided the model for religious toleration that finally was adopted in the Edict of Nantes. Elizabeth I of England became one of the most beloved rulers in that nation's history. A crafty politician who learned to balance the factions at her court and who turned the aristocracy into a service class for the crown, she brought nearly a half-century of stability to England at a time when the rest of Europe was in flames.

The victory at Pavia in 1525 occurred on Charles V's twenty-fifth birthday and seemingly made him master of all of Europe. His ally Henry VIII urged an immediate invasion and dismemberment of France and began raising an army to spearhead the attack. But Charles's position was much less secure than it appeared. The Ottomans threatened his Hungarian territories, and the Protestants threatened his German lands. He could not afford a war of conquest in France. His hope now was to reach an agreement with Francis I for a lasting European peace, and for this purpose the French king was brought in captivity to Madrid.

It is doubtful that there was ever any real chance for peace between Habsburg and Valois after the battle of Pavia. Francis's personal humiliation and Charles's military position were both too strong to allow for a permanent settlement in which Habsburgs ruled in Milan and Naples. Charles demanded that Burgundy be returned to him. Though Francis was hardly in a position to bargain, he held out on this issue for as long as possible and he secretly prepared a disavowal of the final agreement before it was made. By the Treaty of Madrid in 1526, Francis I yielded Burgundy and recognized the Spanish conquest of Navarre and Spanish rule in Naples. The agreement was sealed by the marriage of

Francis to Charles's sister, Eleanor of Portugal. But marriage was not sufficient security for such a complete capitulation. To secure his release from Spain, Francis was required to leave behind as hostages his seven- and eight-year-old sons until the treaty was fulfilled. For three years the children languished in Spanish captivity.

No sooner had he set foot upon French soil than Francis I renounced the Treaty of Madrid. He even gained the sanction of the pope for violating his oath. Setting France on a war footing, he began seeking new allies. Henry VIII, disappointed with the meager spoils of his last venture, switched sides. Most importantly, Francis I entered into an alliance with the Ottoman sultan, Suleiman the Magnificent (1520–66), whose armies were pressing against the southeastern borders of the Holy Roman Empire. In the year following Pavia, the Ottomans secured an equally decisive triumph at Mohács, captured Budapest, and threatened Vienna, the eastern capital of the Habsburg lands. Almost overnight Charles V had been turned from hunter into hunted. The Ottoman threat demanded immediate attention in Germany, the French and English were preparing to strike in the Low Countries, and the Italian wars continued. In 1527 Charles's unpaid German mercenaries

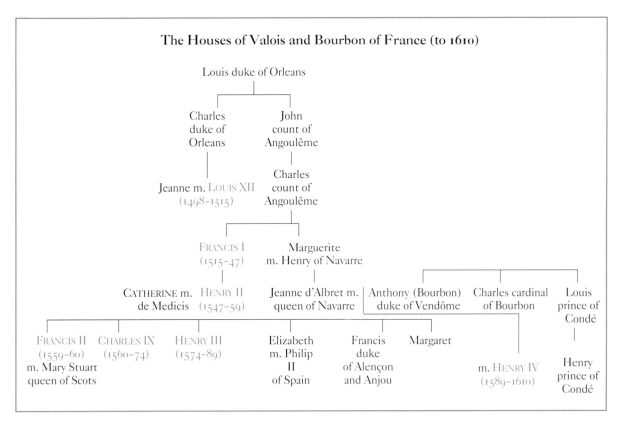

The Houses of Valois and Bourbon of France (to 1610)

stormed through Rome, sacked the papal capital, and captured the pope. Christian Europe was mortified.

The struggle for European mastery ground on for decades. The Treaty of Cateau-Cambrésis in 1559 brought to a close sixty years of conflict that had accomplished little. The great stores of silver that poured into Castile from the New World were consumed in the fires of Continental warfare. In 1557 both France and Spain declared bankruptcy to avoid foreclosures by their creditors. For the French, the Italian wars were disastrous. They seriously undermined the state's financial base, eroded confidence in the monarchy, thinned the ranks of the ruling nobility, and brought France nearly to ruin. The fiasco ended with fitting irony. After the death of Francis I, his son Henry II (1547–59) continued the struggle. Henry never forgave his father for abandoning him in Spain, and he sought revenge on Charles V, who had been his jailer. He celebrated the Treaty of Cateau-Cambrésis with great pomp and pageantry. Among the feasts and festivities were athletic competitions. Henry II entered the jousting tournament and there was killed.

In 1555 Charles abdicated all of his titles and retired to a monastery to live out his final days. He split apart his empire and granted to his brother, Ferdinand I (1558–64), the Austrian and German lands and the mantle of the Holy Roman Empire. To his son, Philip II (1556–98), he ceded the Low Countries, Spain and the New World, Naples, and his Italian conquests. The cares of an empire that once stretched from Peru to Vienna were lifted from his shoulders. On 21 September 1558, he died in his bed.

The wars for European supremacy between France and Spain dominated the politics of the first half of the sixteenth century. The quest for glory involved the Continent's two greatest kingdoms in unrelenting warfare, warfare that bankrupted both fiscally and emotionally. The humiliation of Francis I in prison in Madrid was ultimately matched by that of Charles V fleeing across the Alps as the Ottomans advanced on his German territories. For decades the two states poured all of their resources into warfare and made it a more deadly and more expensive venture than ever before.

The Crises of the European States

In the sixteenth century, society was an integrated whole, equally dependent upon monarchical, ecclesiastical, and civil authority for its effective survival. A European state could no more tolerate the presence of two churches than it could the presence of two kings. But the Reformation had created two churches. The coexistence of both Catholics and Protestants in a single realm posed a stark challenge to accepted theory and traditional practice.

The problem proved intractable because it admitted only one solution: total victory. There could be no compromise for several reasons. Religious beliefs were profoundly held, and religious controversy was a struggle between everlasting life and eternal damnation. The practical solution of toleration was still unacceptable. To the modern mind, toleration seems so logical that it is difficult to understand why it took over a century of bloodshed before it came to be grudgingly accepted by those countries most bitterly divided. But toleration was not a practical solution in a society that admitted no principle of organization other than one king, one faith.

The French Wars of Religion

Protestantism came late to France. It was not until after Calvin reformed the church in Geneva and began to export his brand of Protestantism that French society began to divide along religious lines. By 1560 there were over two thousand Protestant congregations in France, whose membership totaled nearly 10 percent of the French population. Calvin and his successors had their greatest success among the middle ranks of urban society, merchants, traders, and craftsmen. They also found a receptive audience among aristocratic women, who eventually converted their husbands and their sons.

The wars of religion, however, were brought on by more than the rapid spread of Calvinism. Equally important was the vacuum of power that had been created when Henry II (1547–59) died in a jousting tournament. Surviving Henry were his extraordinary widow, Catherine de Médicis, three daughters, and four sons, the oldest of whom, Francis II (1559–60), was only fifteen. Under the influence of his beautiful young wife, Mary, Queen of Scots, Francis allowed the noble Guise family to dominate the great offices of state and to exclude their rivals from power. The Guises controlled the two most powerful institutions of the state—the army and the Church.

The Guises were staunchly Catholic and among their enemies were the Bourbons, a family with powerful Protestant members and a direct claim to the French throne. The revelation of a Protestant plot to remove the king from Paris provided the Guises with an opportunity to eliminate their most potent rivals. The Bourbon Duc de Condé, the leading Protestant peer of the realm, was sentenced to death. But five days before Condé's execution, Francis II died and Guise power evaporated. The new king, Charles IX (1560–74), was only ten years old and firmly under the grip of his mother, Catherine de Médicis, who now declared herself regent of France. (See Special Feature, "The Monstrous Regiment of Women," pp. 484–485.)

Condé's death sentence convinced him that the Guises would stop at nothing to gain their ambitions. Force would have to be met with force. Protestants and Catholics alike raised armies and in 1562 civil war ensued. Once the wars began, the leading Protestant peers fled the court, but the position of the Guises was not altogether secure. Henry Bourbon, king of Navarre, was the next in line to the throne should Charles IX and his two brothers die without male heirs. Henry had been raised in the Protestant faith by his mother, Jeanne d'Albret, whose own mother, Marguerite of Navarre, was among the earliest protectors of the Huguenots, as the French Calvinists came to be called.

The early battles were inconclusive, but the assassination of the Duc de Guise in 1563 by a Protestant fanatic added a personal vendetta to the religious passions of the Catholic leaders. They encouraged the slaughter of Huguenot congregations and the murder of Huguenot leaders. Protestants gave as good as they got. In open defiance of Valois dynastic interests, the Guises courted support from Spain, while the Huguenots imported Swiss and German mercenaries to fight in France. Noble factions and irreconcilable religious differences were together pulling the government apart.

By 1570 Catherine was ready for reconciliation. She announced her plans for a marriage between her daugh-

The French Wars of Religion

1559	Death of Henry II
1560	Protestant Duc de Condé sentenced to death
1562	First battle of wars of religion
1563	Catholic Duc de Guise assassinated
1572	Saint Bartholomew's Day massacre
1574	Accession of Henry III
1576	Formation of Catholic League
1584	Death of Duc d'Anjou makes Henry of Navarre heir to throne
1585	War of the three Henrys
1588	Henry Guise murdered by order of Henry III
1589	Catherine de Médicis dies; Henry III assassinated
1594	Henry IV crowned
1598	Edict of Nantes

ter Margaret and Henry of Navarre, a marriage that would symbolize the spirit of conciliation between the crown and the Huguenots. The marriage was to take place in Paris during August 1572. The arrival of Huguenot leaders from all over France to attend the marriage ceremony presented an opportunity of a different kind to the Guises and their supporters. If leading Huguenots could be assassinated in Paris, the Protestant cause might collapse and the truce that the wedding signified might be turned instead into a Catholic triumph.

Saint Bartholomew was the apostle that Jesus described as a man without guile. Ironically it was on his feast day that the Huguenots who had innocently come to celebrate Henry's marriage were led like lambs to the slaughter. On 24 August 1572 the streets of Paris ran red with Huguenot blood. Though frenzied, the slaughter was inefficient. Henry of Navarre and a number of other important Huguenots escaped the carnage and returned to their urban strongholds. In the following weeks the violence spread from Paris to the countryside and thousands of Protestants paid for their beliefs with their lives.

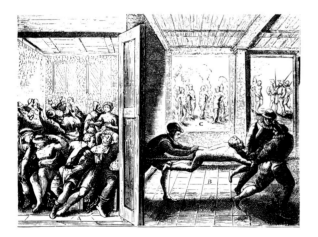

This scene depicts the mistreatment of French Catholics by the Protestants in the town of Angoulême. They were deprived of all nourishment, dragged over a taut rope, and then slowly roasted at the stake.

After Saint Bartholomew's Day, a genuine revulsion against the massacres swept the nation. A number of Catholic peers now joined with the Huguenots to protest the excesses of the crown and the Guises. These Catholics came to be called the *politiques* from their desire for a practical settlement of the wars. They were led by the Duc d'Anjou, next in line to the throne when Charles IX died in 1574 and Henry III (1574–89) became king. Against them, in Paris and a number of other towns, the Catholic League was formed, a society that pledged its first allegiance to religion. The League took up the slaughter of Huguenots where the Saint Bartholomew's Day massacre left off. Matters grew worse in 1584 when the Huguenot Henry of Navarre became next in line for the throne. Catholic Leaguers talked openly of altering the royal succession and began to develop theories of lawful resistance to monarchical power. By 1585, when the final civil war began—the war of the three Henrys, named for Henry III, Henry Guise, and Henry of Navarre—the crown was in the weakest possible position. Paris and the Catholic towns were controlled by the League, the Protestant strongholds by Henry of Navarre. King Henry III could not abandon his capital or his religion, but neither could he gain control of the Catholic party. The extremism of the Leaguers kept the politiques away from court, and without the politiques, there could be no settlement.

In December 1588 Henry III took matters into his own hands. He summoned Henry Guise and Guise's brother to a meeting in the royal bedchamber. There they were murdered in an attempt to destroy the League. The politiques were blamed for the murders—revenge was taken on a number of them—and Henry III was forced to flee his capital. He made a pact with Henry of Navarre and together royalist and Huguenot forces besieged Paris. Only the arrival of a Spanish army prevented its fall. In 1589 a fanatic priest avenged the murder of the Guises by assassinating Henry III.

Now Henry of Navarre came into his inheritance. But after nearly thirty years of continuous civil war it was certain that a Huguenot could never rule France. If Henry was to become king of all France, he would have to become a Catholic king. It is not clear when Henry made the decision to accept the Catholic faith—"Paris is worth a mass," he reportedly declared—but he did not announce his decision at once. Rather he strengthened his forces, tightened his bonds with the politiques, and urged his countrymen to expel the Spanish invaders. He finally made his conversion public and in 1594 was crowned Henry IV (1589–1610). In 1598 Henry proclaimed the Edict of Nantes, which granted limited toleration to the Huguenots. It was the culmination of decades of attempts to find a solution to the existence of two religions in one state.

The World of Philip II

By the middle of the sixteenth century Spain was the greatest power in Europe. The dominions of Philip II (1556–98) of Spain stretched from the Atlantic to the Pacific: his Continental territories included the Netherlands in the north and Milan and Naples in Italy. In 1580 Philip became king of Portugal, uniting all the states of the Iberian Peninsula. With the addition of Portugal's Atlantic ports and its sizable fleet, Spanish maritime power was now unsurpassed. Philip saw himself as a Catholic monarch fending off the spread of heresy. He was particularly hostile toward England,

From the Edict of Nantes

■ *The Edict of Nantes (1598) was a milestone in the development of religious toleration in Europe. It was granted by King Henry IV to the Huguenots at the end of the French wars of religion. The Edict of Nantes established the rights of Protestants and was in effect for nearly a century.*

We ordain that the Catholic, Apostolic and Roman religion shall be restored and re-established in all places and districts of this our kingdom and the countries under our rule, where its practice has been interrupted, so that it can be peacefully and freely practiced there, without any disturbance or hindrance. We forbid very expressly all persons of whatever rank, quality or condition they may be, under the aforesaid penalties, to disturb, molest or cause annoyance to clerics in the celebration of the Divine worship.

where he had briefly been married to the Catholic Queen Mary I (1553–58). But her Protestant successor, Queen Elizabeth I (1558–1603), encouraged piracy against Spanish treasure ships and covertly aided both French and Dutch Protestants. Finally in 1588 Philip decided upon invasion.

He assembled a fleet of over 130 ships, many of them the pride of the Spanish and Portuguese navies. The ships of the Spanish Armada were bigger and stronger than anything possessed by the English, whose forces were largely merchant vessels hastily converted for battle. But the English ships were faster and more maneuverable in the unpredictable winds of the English Channel. They also contained guns that could readily be reloaded for multiple firings, while the Spanish guns were designed to discharge only one broadside before hand-to-hand combat ensued. With these advantages the English were able to prevent the Armada from reaching port in the Netherlands and to destroy many individual ships as they were blown off course. The

defeat of the Spanish Armada was less a military than a psychological blow to Philip II. He could more easily replace ships than restore confidence in Spanish power.

That confidence was to be shaken more thoroughly by the greatest crisis of his reign: the revolt of the Netherlands. Though Philip's father, Charles V, amassed a great empire, he had begun only as the duke of Burgundy. Charles's Burgundian inheritance encompassed a diverse territory in the northwestern corner of Europe. The seventeen separate provinces of this territory were called the Netherlands or the Low Countries because of the flooding that kept large portions of them under water. The Netherlands was one of the richest and most populous regions of Europe, an international leader in manufacturing, banking, and commerce. The heavy concentration of urban populations in the Low Countries provided the natural habitat for Calvinist preachers, who made converts across the entire social spectrum. As Holy Roman Emperor, Charles V may have made his peace with Protestants, but as king of Spain he

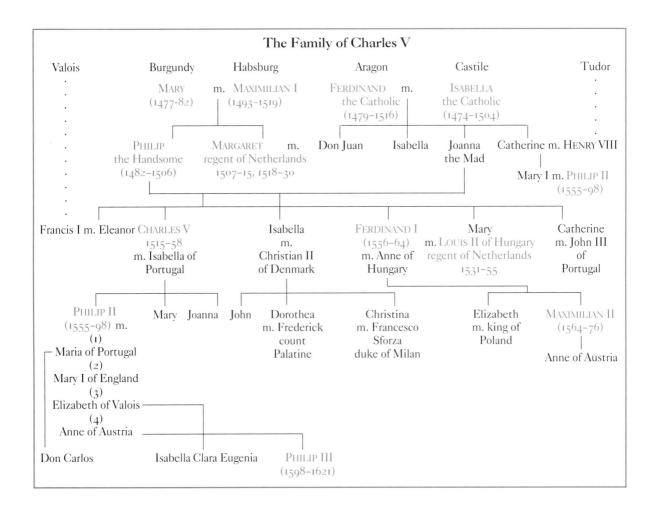

The Family of Charles V

The Spanish and the English Fleets Engaged, 1588, *by an unknown artist, ca. 1590. In the foreground, two English warships flank a Spanish ship bearing the standard of the pope.*

had not. Charles V had maintained the purity of the Spanish Catholic church through a sensible combination of reform and repression.

Philip II intended to pursue a similar policy in the Low Countries. With papal approval he initiated a scheme to reform the hierarchy of the Church by expanding the numbers of bishops, and he invited the Jesuits to establish schools for orthodox learning. The

Protestants sought the protection of their local nobility who, Catholic or Protestant, had their own reasons for opposing the strict enforcement of heresy laws. Provincial nobility and magistrates resented both the substance of Philip's policies and the fact that they disregarded local autonomy. Town governors and noblemen refused to cooperate in implementing the new laws.

The Revolt of the Netherlands

The passive resistance of nobles and magistrates was soon matched by the active resistance of the Calvinists. Unable to enforce Philip's policy, Margaret of Parma, his half-sister, whom Philip had made regent, agreed to a limited toleration. But in the summer of 1566, before it could be put into effect, bands of Calvinists violently attacked Catholic property, breaking stained glass windows and statues of the Virgin and the saints, which they claimed were idolatrous. Local authorities could not protect Church property and open revolt ensued. Fearing social rebellion, even the leading Protestant noblemen helped suppress these riots.

In Spain, the events in the Netherlands were treated for what they were: open rebellion. Philip II was determined to punish the rebels and enforce the heresy laws. He sent a large military force from Spain under the

The Revolt of the Netherlands

command of the Duke of Alba (1507–82). Alba fulfilled his mission with a vengeance, executing leading Protestant noblemen, harshly punishing participants in the rebellion, and destroying towns implicated in the revolt. As many as sixty thousand Protestants fled north beyond Alba's jurisdiction. By the end of 1568 royal policy had gained a sullen acceptance in the Netherlands, but for the next eighty years, with only occasional truces, Spain and the Netherlands were at war.

Alba's policies had driven Protestants into rebellion, and this forced the Spanish government to maintain its army by raising taxes from those southern provinces that had remained loyal. Soon the loyal provinces too were in revolt, not over religion, but over taxation and local autonomy. Alba was unprepared for the series of successful

assaults Protestants launched in the northern provinces during 1572. The Protestant generals established a permanent base in the northwestern provinces of Holland and Zeeland. By 1575 they had gained a stronghold that they would never relinquish. Prince William of Orange assumed the leadership of the two provinces, which were now united against the tyranny of Philip's rule.

Spanish government was collapsing all over the Netherlands. William ruled in the north, and the States-General, a parliamentary body composed of representatives from the separate provinces, ruled in the south. No one was in control of the Spanish army. The soldiers, who had gone years with only partial pay, now roamed the southern provinces looking for plunder. Brussels and Ghent both were targets, and in 1576 the worst atrocities of all occurred when mutinous Spanish troops sacked Antwerp. Over seven thousand people were slaughtered and nearly a third of the city burned to the ground.

The "Spanish fury" in Antwerp effectively ended Philip's rule over his Burgundian inheritance. The Protestants had established a permanent home in the north. The States-General had established its ability to rule in the south, and Spanish policy had been totally discredited. To achieve a settlement, the Pacification of Ghent of 1576, the Spanish government conceded local autonomy in taxation, the central role of the States-General in legislation, and the immediate withdrawal of all Spanish troops from the Low Countries. This rift among the provinces was soon followed by a permanent split. In 1581 one group of provinces voted to depose Philip II while a second group decided to remain loyal to him. Philip II refused to accept the dismemberment of his inheritance and refused to recognize the independent

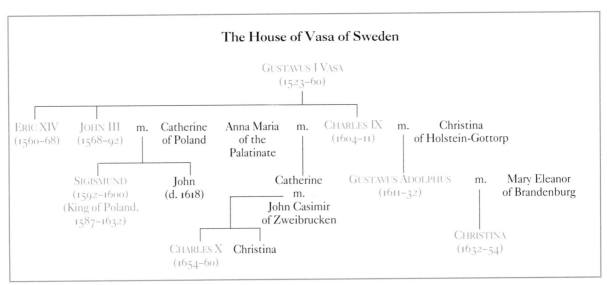

The House of Vasa of Sweden

Dutch state that now existed in Holland. Throughout the 1580s and 1590s military expeditions attempted to reunite the southern provinces and to conquer the northern ones. In 1609 Spain and the Netherlands concluded the Twelve Years' Truce, which tacitly recognized the existence of the state of Holland. By the beginning of the seventeenth century Holland was not only an independent state, it was one of the greatest rivals of Spain and Portugal.

The Thirty Years' War, 1618–1648

Though there was nothing new about warfare in Europe, the fighting that set the Continent ablaze from 1555 to 1648 brought together the worst of dynastic and religious conflicts. These wars were fought on a larger scale, were more brutal and more expensive, and claimed more victims, civilians and combatants alike. During this century war extended throughout the Continent. Dynastic strife, rebellion, and international rivalries joined together with the ongoing struggle over religion. Ambition and faith were an explosive mixture. The French endured forty years of civil war; the Spanish eighty years of fighting with the Dutch. The battle for hegemony in the east led to dynastic strife for decades on end, as Poles, Russians, and Swedes pressed their rival claims to each other's territory until the Swedes emerged victorious. Finally, in 1618, these separate theaters of war came together in one of the most brutal and terrifying episodes of destruction in European history, the Thirty Years' War.

The Rise of Sweden

Sweden's aggressive foreign policy began accidentally when the Baltic seaport of Reval requested Swedish protection. After some hesitation, Sweden fortified Reval in 1560. A decade later, Swedish forces captured Narva, farther to the east, and consolidated their hold on the Livonian coast, where they controlled a sizable portion of the Muscovite trade. As the Swedes secured the northern Livonian ports, more of the Muscovy trade moved to the south and passed through Riga, which would have to be captured or blockaded if the Swedes were to control commerce in the eastern Baltic. At the beginning of the seventeenth century the powerful Swedish navy blockaded Riga and entered into war against Poland.

A Livonian peasant. Livonia was conquered by Ivan the Terrible in his campaign of 1563, but was soon reclaimed by the Poles. In 1660 Livonia became part of the Swedish empire. Livonia was originally inhabited by the Livs, a Finnish people.

The blockade of Riga and the assembly of a large Swedish fleet in the Baltic threatened Denmark. The Danes claimed sovereignty over Sweden and now took the opportunity of the Polish-Swedish conflict to reassert it. In 1611, under the energetic leadership of the Danish king Christian IV (1588–1648), Denmark invaded Sweden from both the east and the west, threatening to take Stockholm. In the same year, during the Danish war, Sweden's king Charles IX died and was succeeded by his son Gustavus Adolphus (1611–32). Gustavus's greatest skills were military, and the calamitous wars inherited from his father occupied him during the early years of his reign. He was forced to conclude a humiliating peace with the Danes in 1613. For most of the next decade he rebuilt his armies and nursed his grievances. Then in 1621 he struck. He landed a force in Livonia and in two weeks he captured Riga, the capstone of Sweden's Baltic ambitions. Occupation of Riga increased Swedish control of the Muscovy trade and it deprived Denmark of a significant portion of its customs duties. Gustavus now claimed Riga as a Swedish port and successfully demanded that ships sailing from there pay tolls to Sweden rather than Denmark.

THE DESTRUCTION OF MAGDEBURG

■ No event of the Thirty Years' War had a greater effect on public opinion than the annihilation of the Protestant city of Magdeburg in 1631. Dozens of pamphlets and woodcuts detailed the slaughter of civilians and the devastation of property. It was commonly believed that neither a human nor an animal escaped the destruction.

Thus it came about that the city and all its inhabitants fell into the hands of the enemy, whose violence and cruelty were due in part to their common hatred of the adherents of the Augsburg Confession, and in part to their being imbittered by the chain shot which had been fired at them and by the derision and insults that the Magdeburgers had heaped upon them from the ramparts.

Then was there naught but beating and burning, plundering, torture, and murder. Most especially was every one of the enemy bent on securing much booty. When a marauding party entered a house, if its master had anything to give he might thereby purchase respite and protection for himself and his family till the next man, who also wanted something, should come along. . . .

Thus in a single day this noble and famous city, the pride of the whole country, went up in fire and smoke; and the remnant of its citizens, with their wives and children, were taken prisoners and driven away by the enemy with a noise of weeping and wailing that could be heard from afar, while the cinders and ashes from the town were carried by the wind to Wanzleben, Egeln, and still more distant places.

The rise of Sweden had two dramatic effects in the reorganization of power politics in northeastern Europe. In the first place, it signalled the permanent eclipse of Poland-Lithuania in the region. Once a territorial giant with pretensions of dominating all of eastern Europe, Poland-Lithuania now saw its territories shrink and its power diminish. With the Swedish capture of Riga, dominance over the Muscovy trade passed out of Polish hands, never to return. Secondly, and most importantly for the immediate future of Europe, the rise of Sweden created a Protestant counterbalance to the power of the Austrian Habsburgs. Sweden's domination of the Baltic ports placed its future firmly on German soil at just the moment that Germany was to explode into warfare.

Bohemia Revolts

The Peace of Augsburg had served the German states well. The principle that the religion of the ruler was the religion of the state complicated the political life of the Holy Roman Empire, but it also pacified it. Though rulers had the right to enforce uniformity on their subjects, in practice many of the larger states tolerated more than one religion. By the beginning of the seventeenth century Catholicism and Protestantism had achieved a rough equality within the German states, symbolized by the fact that of the seven electors who

chose the Holy Roman Emperor, three were Catholic, three Protestant, and the seventh was the emperor himself, acting as king of Bohemia. This situation was not unwelcome to the leaders of the Austrian Habsburg family, who succeeded Emperor Charles V and who were more tolerant than their Spanish kinfolk. The head of their house was elected king of Bohemia and king of Hungary, both states with large Protestant populations.

In 1617 Mathias, the childless Holy Roman Emperor, began making plans for his cousin, Ferdinand Habsburg, to succeed him. Ferdinand was Catholic, very devout and very committed. In order to ensure a Catholic majority among the electors, the emperor relinquished his Bohemian title and pressed for Ferdinand's election as the new king of Bohemia. The Protestant nobles of Bohemia forced the new king to accept strict limitations upon his political and religious powers, but once elected Ferdinand had no intention of honoring them. His opponents were equally strong-willed. When Ferdinand violated Protestant religious liberties, a group of noblemen marched to the royal palace in Prague in May 1618, found two of the king's chief advisers, and hurled them out of an upper-story window.

The Defenestration of Prague, as this incident came to be known, initiated a Protestant counteroffensive throughout the Habsburg lands. Fear of Ferdinand's policies led to Protestant uprisings in Hungary as well as

Bohemia. Those who seized control of the government declared Ferdinand deposed and the throne vacant. But they had no candidate to accept their crown. When Emperor Mathias died in 1619, Ferdinand succeeded to the imperial title as Ferdinand II (1619–37) and Frederick V, one of the Protestant electors, accepted the Bohemian crown.

Frederick was a sincere but weak Calvinist whose credentials were much stronger than his abilities. He ruled a geographically divided German state known as the Palatinate. One hundred miles separated the two segments of his lands, but both were strategically important. The Lower Palatinate bordered on the Catholic Spanish Netherlands and the Upper Palatinate on Catholic Bavaria.

Once Frederick accepted the Bohemian crown, he was faced with a war on three fronts. Ferdinand II had no difficulty enlisting allies to recover the Bohemian crown, since he could pay them with the spoils of Frederick's lands. Spanish troops from the Netherlands occupied the Lower Palatinate, and Bavarian troops occupied the Upper Palatinate. Frederick, on the other hand, met rejection wherever he turned. Neither the Dutch nor the English would send more than token aid—both had advised him against breaking the imperial peace. The Lutheran princes of Germany would not enter into a war between Calvinists and Catholics, especially after Ferdinand II promised to protect the Bohemian Lutherans.

At the battle of the White Mountain in 1620, Ferdinand's Catholic forces annihilated Frederick's army. Frederick and his wife fled to Denmark, and Bohemia was left to face the wrath of Ferdinand, the victorious king and emperor. The retribution was horrible. Mercenaries who had fought for Ferdinand II were allowed to sack Prague for a week. Elective monarchy was abolished and Bohemia became part of the hereditary Habsburg lands. Free peasants were enserfed and subjected to imperial law. Those nobles who had supported Frederick lost their lands and their privileges. Calvinism was repressed and thoroughly rooted out, consolidating forever the Catholic character of Bohemia. Frederick's estates were carved up and his rights as elector transferred to the Catholic duke of Bavaria. The battle of the White Mountain was a turning point in the history of central Europe, for it forced all Protestant nations to arm for war.

The War Widens

For the Habsburgs, religious and dynastic interests were inseparable. Ferdinand II and Philip III of Spain (1598–1621) fought for their beliefs and for their patrimony. Their victory gave them more than they could have expected. Ferdinand swallowed up Bohemia and strengthened his position in the empire. Philip gained possession of a vital link in his supply route between Italy and the Netherlands. Spanish expansion threatened France. The occupation of the Lower Palatinate placed a ring of Spanish armies around France from the Pyrenees to the Low Countries.

Frederick, now in Holland, refused to accept the judgment of battle. He lobbied for a grand alliance to repel the Spaniards from the Lower Palatinate and to restore the religious balance in the empire. Though his personal cause met with little sympathy, his political logic was impeccable, especially after Spain again declared war upon the Dutch in 1621. A grand Protestant alliance—secretly supported by the French—brought together England, Holland, a number of German states, and Denmark. It was the Danes who led this potentially powerful coalition. In 1626 a large Danish army under the command of King Christian IV engaged imperial forces on German soil. But Danish forces could not match the superior numbers and the superior leadership of the Catholic mercenary forces under the command of the ruthless and brilliant Count Albrecht

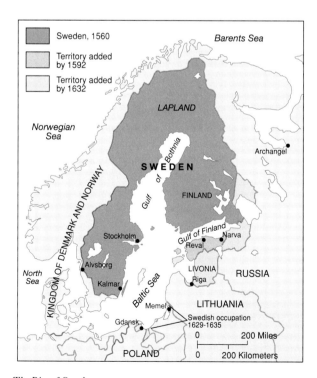

The Rise of Sweden

von Wallenstein (1583–1634). In 1629 the Danes withdrew from the empire and sued for peace.

If the Catholic victory at the White Mountain in 1620 threatened the well-being of German Protestantism, the Catholic triumph over the Danes threatened its survival. More powerful than ever, Ferdinand II determined to turn the religious clock back to the state of affairs that had existed when the Peace of Augsburg was concluded in 1555. He demanded that all lands that had then been Catholic but had since become Protestant must now be returned to the fold. He also proclaimed that as the Peace of Augsburg made no provision for the toleration of Calvinists, they would no longer be tolerated in the empire. These policies together constituted a virtual revolution in the religious affairs of the German states, and they proved impossible to impose. Ferdinand succeeded in only one thing—he united Lutherans and Calvinists against him.

In 1630 King Gustavus Adolphus of Sweden decided to enter the German conflict to protect Swedish interests. While Gustavus Adolphus struggled to construct his alliance, imperial forces continued their triumphant progress. In 1631 they besieged, captured, and put to the torch the town of Magdeburg—a turning point in Protestant fortunes. Brandenburg and Saxony joined Gustavus Adolphus, not only enlarging his forces, but allowing him to open a second front in Bohemia. In the autumn of 1631 this combination overwhelmed the imperial armies. Gustavus won a decisive triumph at Breitenfeld, while the Saxons occupied Prague.

Gustavus Adolphus lost no time in pressing his advantage. The Swedes marched west to the Rhine, easily conquering the richest of the Catholic cities and retak-

The Thirty Years' War	
1618	Defenestration of Prague
1619	Ferdinand Habsburg elected Holy Roman Emperor Frederick of the Palatinate accepts the crown of Bohemia
1620	Catholic victory at battle of the White Mountain
1621	End of Twelve Years' Truce; war between Spain and Netherlands
1626	Danes form Protestant alliance under Christian IV
1627	Spain declares bankruptcy
1630	Gustavus Adolphus leads Swedish forces into Germany
1631	Sack of Magdeburg Protestant victory at Breitenfeld
1632	Protestant victory at Lutzen; death of Gustavus Adolphus
1635	France declares war on Spain
1643	Battle of Rocroi; French forces repel Spaniards
1648	Peace of Westphalia

ing the Lower Palatinate. In early 1632 Protestant forces plundered Bavaria, but Wallenstein chose to chase the Saxons from Bohemia rather than the Swedes from Bavaria. Not until the winter of 1632 did the armies of Gustavus and Wallenstein finally meet. At the battle of Lutzen the Swedes won the field but lost their beloved king. In less than two years Gustavus Adolphus had decisively transformed the course of the war and the course of Europe's future. Protestant forces now occupied most of central and northern Germany.

The final stages of the war involved the resumption of the century-old struggle between France and Spain. When the Twelve Years' Truce expired in 1621, Spain again declared war upon the Dutch. Dutch naval power was considerable and the Dutch took the war to the far reaches of the globe, attacking Portuguese settlements in Brazil and in the East and harassing Spanish shipping on the high seas. In 1628 the Dutch captured the entire Spanish treasure fleet as it sailed from the New World. Spain had declared bankruptcy in 1627, and the loss of the whole of the next years' treasure from America exacerbated an already catastrophic situation.

The siege of Magdeburg, 1631. The sack of the city by the Imperial troops of Tilly's army was one of the most barbarous incidents of a brutal war.

Allegorical painting celebrating the Treaty of Westphalia. The shattered weapons of war lie in the foreground; at the right, the ship of peace carries the news to the capitals of Europe.

These reversals, combined with the continued successes of Habsburg forces in central Europe, convinced Louis XIII and his chief minister, Cardinal Richelieu, that the time for active involvement in European affairs was now at hand. Throughout the early stages of the war, France had secretly aided anti-Habsburg forces. Gustavus Adolphus's unexpected success dramatically altered French calculations. Now it was evident that the Habsburgs could no longer combine their might, and Spanish energies would be drained off in the Netherlands and in central Europe. The time had come to take an open stand. In 1635 France declared war on Spain.

France took the offensive first, invading the Spanish Netherlands. In 1636 a Spanish army struck back, pushing to within twenty-five miles of Paris before it was repelled. Both sides soon began to search for a settlement, but pride prevented them from laying down their arms. Spain toppled first. Its economy in shambles and its citizens in revolt over high prices and higher taxes, it could no longer maintain its many-fronted war. In 1643 Spain gambled once more on a knockout blow against the French. But at the battle of Rocroi, exhausted French troops held out and the Spanish invasion failed.

By now the desire for peace was universal. Most of the main combatants had long since perished: Philip III, ever optimistic, in 1621; Frederick V, an exile to the end, in 1632; Gustavus Adolphus, killed at Lutzen in the same year; Wallenstein, murdered by order of Ferdinand II in 1634; Ferdinand himself in 1637; and Louis XIII in 1643, five days before the French triumph at Rocroi. Those who succeeded them had not the same passions, and after so many decades the longing for peace was the strongest emotion on the Continent.

In 1648 a series of agreements, collectively known as the Peace of Westphalia, established the outlines of the political geography of Europe for the next century. Its focus was on the Holy Roman Empire and it reflected Protestant successes in the final two decades of war. Sweden gained further territories on the Baltic, making it master of the north German ports. France, too, gained

The Peace of Westphalia

THE HORRORS OF THE THIRTY YEARS' WAR

■ *No source has better captured the brutality of the Thirty Years' War than the novel* Simplisissimus. *In a series of loosely connected episodes, the hero (whose name means "the simplest of the simple") is snatched from his village to serve in marauding armies whose confrontations with local villagers are usually more horrifying than the episode narrated here.*

These troopers were even now ready to march, and had the pastor fastened by a rope to lead him away. Some cried, "Shoot him down, the rogue!" Others would have money from him. But he, lifting up his hands to heaven, begged, for the sake of the Last Judgment, for forbearance and Christian compassion, but in vain; for one of them rode him down and dealt him such a blow on the head that he fell flat, and commended his soul to God. Nor did the remainder of the captured peasants fare any better. But even when it seemed these troopers, in their cruel tyranny, had clean lost their wits, came such a swarm of armed peasants out of the wood, that it seemed a wasps'-nest had been stirred. And these began to yell so frightfully and so furiously to attack with sword and musket that all my hair stood on end; and never had I been at such a merry-making before: for the peasants of the Spessart and the Vogelsberg are as little wont as are the Hessians and men of the Sauerland and the Black Forest to let themselves be crowed over on their own dunghill. So away went the troopers, and not only left behind the cattle they had captured, but threw away bag and baggage also, and so cast all their booty to the winds lest themselves should become booty for the peasants: yet some of them fell into their hands. This sport took from me well-nigh all desire to see the world, for I thought, if 'tis all like this, then is the wilderness far more pleasant.

From Hans von Grimmelhausen, *Simplisissimus* (1669).

---

in territory and prestige. It kept the vital towns in the Lower Palatinate through which Spanish men and material had moved and, though it did not agree to come to terms with Spain immediately, France's fear of encirclement was at an end. The Dutch gained statehood through official recognition by Spain and through the power they had displayed in building and maintaining an overseas empire.

Territorial boundaries were reestablished as they had existed in 1624, giving the Habsburgs control of both Bohemia and Hungary. The independence of the Swiss cantons was now officially recognized as were the rights of Calvinists to the protection of the Peace of Augsburg, which again was to govern the religious affairs of the empire. Two of the larger German states were strengthened as a counterweight to the emperor's power. Bavaria was allowed to retain the Upper Palatinate, and Brandenburg, which ceded some of its coastal territory to Sweden, gained extensive territories in the east. The emperor's political control over the German states was also weakened. German rulers were given independent authority over their states and the imperial diet, rather than the emperor, was empowered to

settle disputes. Thus weakened, future emperors ruled in the Habsburg territorial lands with little ability to control, or influence, or even arbitrate German affairs. The judgment that the Holy Roman Empire was neither holy, Roman, nor an empire was now irrevocably true.

The Peace of Westphalia put back together the pieces of the map of European states. Protestantism and Catholicism now coexisted and there was to be little further change in the geography of religion. The northwest of Europe—England, Holland, Scandinavia, and the north German states—was Protestant; the south was Catholic. The empire of the German peoples was now at an end, the Austro-Hungarian empire at a beginning. Holland and Sweden had become international powers; Spain and Denmark faded from prominence. Muscovy began a long period of isolation from the west, attempting to restore a semblance of government to its people. But if the negotiators at Westphalia could resolve the political and religious ambitions that gave rise to a century of nearly continuous warfare, they could do nothing to eradicate the effects of war itself. The devastation of humanity in the name of God with which the reform of religion had begun was now exhausted. The costs were horrific. The population of Germany fell from 15 million in 1600 to 11 million in 1650. The armies brought destruction of all kinds in their wake. Plague again raged in Europe—the town of Augsburg lost 18,000 inhabitants in the early 1630s. Famine, too, returned to a continent that fifty years earlier had been self-sufficient in grain. The war played havoc with all of the economies that it touched. Inflation, devaluation of coinage, huge public and private debts were all directly attributable to the years of fighting. And the toll taken on the spirit of those generations that never knew peace is incalculable.

SUGGESTIONS FOR FURTHER READING

GENERAL READING

* J. H. Elliott, *Europe Divided 1559–1598* (New York: Harper & Row, 1968). An outstanding synthesis of European politics in the second half of the sixteenth century.

* Geoffrey Parker, *Europe in Crisis 1598–1648* (London: William Collins and Sons, 1979). The best introduction to the period.

* William Doyle, *The Old European Order* (Oxford: Oxford University Press, 1978). An important synthetic essay bristling with ideas.

* Jan de Vries, *The European Economy in an Age of Crisis* (Cambridge: Cambridge University Press, 1976). A comprehensive study of economic development, including long-distance trade and commercial change.

THE FORMATION OF STATES

J. H. Shennan, *The Origins of the Modern European State 1450–1725* (London: Hutchinson, 1974). An analytic account of the rise of the state.

Bernard Guenée, *States and Rulers in Later Medieval Europe* (London: Basil Blackwell, 1985). An engaging argument about the forces that helped shape the state system in Europe.

* Norman Davies, *God's Playground: A History of Poland, Vol. 1. The Origins to 1795* (New York: Columbia University Press, 1982). The best treatment in English of a complex history.

* Richard Pipes, *Russia Under the Old Regime* (London: Widenfeld and Nicolson, 1974). A magisterial account.

* Robert O. Crummey, *The Formation of Muscovy 1304–1613* (London: Longman, 1987). The best one-volume history.

* J. R. Lander, *Government and Community, England 1450–1509* (Cambridge, MA: Harvard University Press, 1980). A comprehensive survey of the late fifteenth century.

* S. B. Chrimes, *Henry VII* (Berkeley, CA: University of California Press, 1972). A traditional biography of the first Tudor king.

* C. D. Ross, *The Wars of the Roses* (London: Thames and Hudson, 1976). The best one-volume account.

* G. R. Elton, *Reform and Reformation, England 1509–1558* (Cambridge, MA: Harvard University Press, 1977). An up-to-date survey by the dean of Tudor historians.

Richard Vaughan, *Valois Burgundy* (Hampden, CT: Shoe String Press, 1975). An engaging history of a vanished state.

* Paul M. Kendall, *Louis XI: The Universal Spider* (New York: Norton, 1971). A highly entertaining account of an unusual monarch.

* R. J. Knecht, *French Renaissance Monarchy* (London: Longman, 1984). A study of the nature of the French monarchy and the way it was transformed in the early sixteenth century.

* J. H. Elliot, *Imperial Spain 1469–1716* (New York: Mentor, 1963). Still worth reading for its insights and examples.

THE DYNASTIC STRUGGLES

* J. R. Hale, *War and Society in Renaissance Europe* (Baltimore: Johns Hopkins University Press, 1986). Assesses the impact of war on the political and social history of early modern Europe.

M. E. Alvarez, *Charles V* (London: Thames and Hudson, 1975). An accessible biography of the most remarkable man of the age.

* R. J. Knecht, *Francis I* (Cambridge: Cambridge University Press, 1982). A compelling study by the leading scholar of sixteenth-century France.

* J. J. Scarisbrick, *Henry VIII* (Berkeley, CA: University of California Press, 1968). The definitive biography.

THE CRISES OF THE EUROPEAN STATES

J. H. M. Salmon, *Society in Crisis* (New York: St. Martin's Press, 1975). The best single-volume account of the French civil wars; difficult but rewarding.

Robert Kingdon, *Myths About the St. Bartholomew's Day Massacres 1572–76* (Cambridge, MA: Harvard University Press, 1988). A study of the impact of a central event in the history of France.

* Mark Greengrass, *France in the Age of Henri IV* (London: Longmans, 1984). An important synthesis of French history in the early seventeenth century.

Geoffrey Parker, *Philip II* (Boston: Little, Brown, 1978). The best introduction.

* Garrett Mattingly, *The Armada* (Boston: Houghton Mifflin, 1959). Still the classic account despite recent reinterpretations.

* Henry Kamen, *Spain 1469–1714* (London: Longmans, 1983). A recent survey with up-to-date interpretations.

* Geoffrey Parker, *The Dutch Revolt* (London: Penguin Books, 1977). An outstanding account of the tangle of events that comprised the revolts of the Netherlands.

W. E. Reddaway et al., eds., *The Cambridge History of Poland to 1696* (Cambridge: Cambridge University Press, 1950). A difficult but thorough narrative of Polish history.

Michael Roberts, *Gustavus Adolphus and the Rise of Sweden* (London: English Universities Press, 1973). A highly readable account of Sweden's rise to power.

THE THIRTY YEARS' WAR

* C. V. Wedgwood, *The Thirty Years' War* (New York: Doubleday, 1961). A heroic account; the best narrative history.

* Peter Limm, *The Thirty Years' War* (London: Longmans, 1984). An excellent brief survey with documents.

* Indicates paperback edition available.

CREDITS

Chapter 1

"The Code of Hammurabi." From "The Code of Hammurabi" in The Ancient Near East, edited by James B. Pritchard. Copyright © 1958 by Princeton University Press, renewed by Princeton University Press. Reprinted by permission of Princeton University Press.

"The Kingdom of Israel." Scripture quotations are from the Revised Standard Version of the Bible. Copyright 1946, 1952, 1971 by the Division of Christian Education of the National Council of the Churches of Christ in the USA. Used by permission.

"The Creation of the Universe in the Rig Veda." "Nadadiya," Creation Humn, from The Rig Veda, translated by Wendy Doniger O'Flaherty. Copyright © 1981 by Wendy Doniger O'Flaherty. Reprinted by permission of Penguin Books, Ltd.

"Early Chinese Oracle Bone." From Sources of Shang History: *The Oracle-Bone Inscriptions of Bronze Age China* by David Keightley. Copyright © 1978 The Regents of the University of California. Reprinted by permission by the University of California Press.

Chapter 2

"Hector and Andromache." From The Iliad of Homer, translated by Richmond Lattimore. Copyright 1951 by The University of Chicago. Reprinted by permission of The University of Chicago Press.

Chapter 4

"Summons of the Soul" by Zhao hun from The Songs of the South: *An Anthology of Ancient Chinese Poems*, translated by David Hawkes. Copyright © 1985 by David Hawkes. Reprinted by permission of Penguin Books Ltd.

From Records of the Grand Historian of China, translated from Shih Chi of Ssu-Ma Ch'ien by Burton Watson. Copyright © 1961 by Columbia University Press, New York. Reprinted by permission of the publisher.

"From *Questions of King Melinda.*" From Buddhist Scriptures, translated by Edward Conze. Copyright © 1959 by Edward Conze. Reprinted by permission of Penguin Books Ltd.

Quote by Li Xuequn in Eastern Zhou and Qin Civilizations, translated by K.C. Ghang, pp. 251–253. Copyright © 1985 by Yale University. Reprinted by permission of Yale University Press.

Chapter 5

"The Reforms of Tiberius Gracchus." From Roman Civilization Volume I by Naphtali Lewis and Meyer Reinhold. Copyright 1951 by Columbia University Press, New York. Reprinted with the permission of the publisher.

Chapter 6

"Augustus Describes His Accomplishments." From Roman Civilization: *Selected Readings, Vol. II*, edited by Naphtali Lewis and Meyer Reinhold. Copyright © 1955 by Columbia University Press, New York. Reprinted with the permission of the publisher.

Chapter 7

"The Justinian Code." From The Digest of Roman Law by Justinian, translated by C. F. Kolbert. Copyright © 1979 by C. F. Kolbert. Reprinted by permission of Penguin Books Ltd.

Chapter 8

"An Old Charcoal Seller" from Sunflower Splendor: Splendor: Three Thousand Years of Chinese Poetry, edited by Wu-Chi Liu and Irving Y. Lo. Reprinted by permission of Irving Y. Lo.

"Bharata's Treatise on Dramaturgy." Bharata. Natya Sastra, edited by Joanny Grosset. Paris: Ernest Leroux, 1898.

"Zhou Daguan's Recollections on the Customs of Cambodia." By Chou Ta-kuan, A.D. 1296. Translation from Pelliot, *Bulletin de l'Ecole Francaise d'Extreme Orient*, No. 1 (123), 1902, pp. 137–177.

"Observations on the Heian Capital." From Sources of Japanese History, Volume One by David John Lu. Copyright © 1974 by McGraw-Hill, Inc. Reprinted by permission.

"Autumn Meditation 4" by TuFu from Poems of The Late T'ang, translated by A.C. Graham. Copyright © 1965 by A.C. Graham. Reprinted by permission of Penguin Books Ltd.

"Written on a Monastery Wall" by Li-Shang-Yin from Poems of the Late T'ang, translated by A.C. Graham. Copyright © 1965 by A.C. Graham. Reprinted by permission of Penguin Books Ltd.

"Song of Woe" by Shen Yueh from Sunflower Splendor: Three Thousand Years of Chinese Poetry, edited by Wu-Chi Liu and Irving Y. Lo. Reprinted by permission of Irving Y. Lo.

"Thinking about him" by Ono no Komachi from the book Anthology of Japanese Literature by Donald Keene, Copyright © 1955 by Grove Press. Used with permission of Grove/Atlantic Monthly Press.

"The Southern Emperor Rules the Southern Land" by Ly Thurong Kiet in The Heritage of Vietnamese Poetry, edited and translated by Huynh Sanh Thong. Reprinted by permission of Huynh Sanh Thong.

"If you lean against the pillar of my little home" from the book The Wonder That Was India by A.L. Basham, Copyright © 1959 by A.L. Basham. Used with the permission of Grove/Atlantic Monthly Press.

"The farmers who harvest rice in the hot sun" from the book The Wonder That Was India by A.L. Basham, Copyright © 1959 by A.L. Basham. Used with the permission of Grove/Atlantic Monthly Press.

"Holy and mighty will be his form" from the book The Wonder That Was India by A.L. Basham, Copyright © 1959 by A.L. Basham. Used with the permission of Grove/Atlantic Monthly Press.

Chapter 9

"From Slave to Queen." Jo Ann McNamara and John E. Halborg, Sainted Women of the Dark Ages. Durham, North Carolina: Duke University Press, pp. 269–273. Copyright © 1992 Duke University Press. Reprinted with permission of the publisher.

"Two Missionaries." From A History of the English Church and People by Bede, translated by Leo Sherley-Price, revised by R.E. Latham. Copyright © 1955, 1968 by Leo Sherley-Price. Reprinted by permission of Penguin Books Ltd.

Chapter 10

"A Woman Before the Inquisition." From "Jacques Fournier, Inquisition Records" in Readings in Medieval History, edited by Patrick J. Geary. Copyright © 1989 by Broadview Press Ltd. Reprinted by permission.

Chapter 11

Excerpt from "Confessions of Lady Nijo" from Classical Japanese Prose. Compiled and Edited by Helen Craig McCullough. Copyright © 1990 by the Board of Trustees of the Leland Stanford Junior University. Reprinted by permission.

From The Columbia Book of Later Chinese Poetry, translated and edited by Jonathan Chaves. Copyright © 1986 by Columbia University Press, New York. Reprinted with the permission of the publisher.

"I Bound Up My Hair." From Five Hundred Years of Chinese Poetry 1150–1650 by Yoshikawa Kojiro, translated by John Timothy Wixted. Copyright © 1989 by Princeton University Press. Reprinted by permission.

"Prohibition Ordinance." Reprinted with the permission of The Free Press, a Division of Macmillan, Inc. from Chinese Civilization and Society: A Sourcebook by Patricia Buckley Ebrey. Copyright © 1981 by The Free Press.

"Tune: Green Jade Cup" from Sunflower Splendor: Three Thousand Years of Chinese Poetry, edited by Wu-Chi Liu and Irving Y. Lo. Reprinted by permission of Irving Y. Lo.

"Tune: As in a Dream: A Song" from Sunflower Splendor: Three Thousand Years of Chinese Poetry, edited by Wu-Chi Liu and Irving Y. Lo. Reprinted by permission of Irving Y. Lo.

Excerpt from "The Mind, the Nature, and the Feelings" from Self and Society in Ming Thought by William Theodore de Bary and the Conference on Ming Thought. Copyright © 1970 Columbia University Press. Reprinted with the permission of the publisher.

Excerpts from Self and Society in Ming Thought by William Theodore de Bary and the Conference on Ming Thought. Copyright © 1970 Columbia University Press. Reprinted with the permission of the publisher.

"Nichiren" from Self and Society in Ming Thought by William Theodore de Bary and the Conference on Ming Thought. Copyright © 1970 Columbia University Press. Reprinted with the permission of the publisher.

Chapter 12

Excerpt from Leon Battista Alberti, "On the Family" in The Family in Renaissance Florence by Renee Watkins. Reprinted by permission of Renee Watkins.

Chapter 14

"The Massacre of the Canal of the Toltecs." From The Broken Spears by Miguel Leon-Portilla. Copyright © 1962, 1990 by Beacon Press. Reprinted by permission of Beacon Press.

"The Nature of the Portuguese Presence in West Africa: Elmina, 1523." From "King John III to Affonso de Albuquerque, Governor of Sao Jorge da Mina, 13 October 1523" from Europeans in West Africa, 1450–1560 Volume I, translated and edited by John William Blake. Reprinted by permission of the Hakluyt Society.

Chapter 15

"From the Travels of Ibn Battúta." From Ibn Battúta: Travels in Asia and Africa 1325–1354, translated by H.A.R. Gibb. Reprinted by permission of Routledge & Kegan Paul.

"Letter from the Sultan." From the book The Muslim World on the Eve of Europe's Expansion, edited by John J. Saunders. Copyright © 1966 by Prentice-Hall, Inc. Reprinted by permission of the publisher, Prentice Hall, a division of Simon & Schuster, Englewood Cliffs, NJ.

Chapter 18

"The Trials of Galileo." From Discoveries and Opinions of Galileo by Galileo Galilei. Copyright © 1957 by Stillman Drake. Used by permission of Doubleday, a division of Bantam Doubleday Dell Publishing Group, Inc.

"Early History of the Dutch East India Company." Page 353 from The Low Countries in Early Modern Times: A Documentary History by Herbert Rowen. Copyright © 1972 by Herbert Rowen. Reprinted by permission of HarperCollins, Publishers, Inc.

Chapter 19

"Dutch East India Company's Attitude to the Xhosa, 1794."

"Report of H. C. D. Maynier to Commissary A. J. Sluysken, 31 March 1974" from Afrikaner Political Thought: Analysis and Documents, Vol. 1, 1770–1850 by Andre du Toit and Hermann Giliomee. Copyright © 1983 by A. du Toit and H. Giliomee. Reprinted by permission of the University of California Press.

"Lament on the French Conquest of Algiers." From "The French Entry into Algiers" by Saikh Abd al-Qadir in The French Conquest of Algiers, 1830: An Algerian Oral Tradition by Alf Andrew Heggoy, Ohio University Monographs in International Studies, Africa Series No. 48. Copyright © 1986 by the Center for International Studies Ohio University. Reprinted by permission of Ohio University Press.

"Islamic Modernist Statement on the Universality of Science." From "Lecture on Teaching and Learning" in An Islamic Response to Imperialism: Political and Religious Writings of Sayyid Jamal ad-Dın "al-Afghanı" by Nikki R. Keddie. Copyright © 1983 by The Regents of the University of California. Reprinted by permission.

Chapter 20

Excerpts from "Marshal Saxe's 'Reveries on the Art of War'" from War, Diplomacy, and Imperialism, 1618–1763 edited by Geoffrey Symcox. Copyright © 1974 by Geoffrey Symcox. Reprinted by permission of Geoffrey Symcox.

Excerpts from "Japan's Declaration of War" from World War II: Policy and Strategy by Hans Adolf Jacobsen and Arthur J. Smith, Jr. Reprinted by permission.

Excerpts from "Roosevelt's Request for Declaration of War on Japan" from World War II: Policy and Strategy by Hans Adolf Jacobsen and Arthur J. Smith, Jr. Reprinted by permission.

"Glittering Fragments" by Hara Tamiki (p. 221) from The Penguin Book of Japanese Verse translated by Geoffrey Bownas and Anthony Thwaite (Penguin Books, 1964) translation copyright © Geoffrey Bownas and Anthony Thwaite, 1964. Reprinted by permission of Penguin Books Ltd., Letters translated by Corinner Antezana-Pernet from La Seconda Guerra Mondiale, 6th Edition by Roberto Battaglia. Reprinted by permission.

Chapter 33
"I Am the Train of Sadness" by Qabbani Nizar from New Writing From the Middle East, edited by L. Hamilian and J.D. Yohannan. Copyright © 1969 by Qabbani Nizar, translation copyright © 1974 by Abdullah al-Udhari. Reprinted by permission of The Crossroad Publishing Company.

Excerpt from Harem Years: The Memoirs of an Egyptian Feminist by Huda Shaarawi. Translation copyright © 1986 by Margot Badran from the book Harem Years: The Memoirs of an Egyptian Feminist by Huda Shaarawi. Translated and introduced by Margot Badran. Published by The Feminist Press at The City University of New York. All rights reserved.

Chapter 34
"Winston Churchill, The Iron Curtain (1946)." Excerpt from "The Sinews of Peace" by Winston Churchill from Robert Rhodes James, Winston S. Churchill: His Complete Speeches 1897–1963 Volume VII 1943–1949. Copyright © 1983 by Chelsea House Publishers. Reprinted by permission of Chelsea House Publishers.

"Subterranean Homesick Blues" by Bob Dylan. Copyright © 1965 by Warner Bros. Music, copyright renewed 1993 by Special Rider Music. All rights reserved. International copyright secured. Reprinted by permission.

Excerpts from "Report to the Twentieth Party Congress" by Nikita S. Khrushchev reprinted from Current Soviet Policies II. The Documentary Record of the Twentieth Party Congress and Its Aftermath published by The Current Digest of the Soviet Press, Columbus, Ohio. Used by permission.

Excerpts from The Second Sex by Simone De Beauvoir, translated by H.M. Parshley. Copyright 1952 and renewed 1980 by Alfred A. Knopf, Inc. Reprinted by permission of the publisher.

Chapter 35
Ian Buruma, A Japanese Mirror: *Heroes and Villains of Japanese Culture.* London: Jonathon Cape, Ltd., 1984, p. 147.

Excerpt from "A Definition of the Japanese Film" from A Lateral View: Essays on Culture and Style in Contemporary Japan by Donald Richie (Stone Bridge Press, 1992). Reprinted by permission.

Excerpt from "One Page of a Diary" from One Day in China: May 21, 1936 translated, edited and introduced by Sherman Cochran and Andrew C.K. Hsieh with Janis Cochran. Copyright © 1983 by Yale University. Reprinted by permission of Yale University Press.

Photo Credits

Positions of the photographs are indicated in the abbreviated form as follows: top (t), bottom (b), center (c), left (l), right (r).

Unless otherwise acknowledged, all photographs are the property of ScottForesman.

Chapter 1

xxxiv Satellite image of the Earth. © Tom Van Sant, Science Source/Photo Researchers

xviii (Volume I) Satellite image of the Earth. © Tom Van Sant, Science Source/Photo Researchers

xxiv (Volume II) Satellite image of the Earth. © Tom Van Sant, Science Source/Photo Researchers

xviii (Volume A) Satellite image of the Earth. © Tom Van Sant, Science Source/Photo Researchers

xxx (Volume B) Satellite image of the Earth. © Tom Van Sant, Science Source/Photo Researchers

xxvi (Volume C) Satellite image of the Earth. © Tom Van Sant, Science Source/Photo Researchers

3 Kathleen M. Kenyon/Jericho Excavations

5 © Kazuyoshi Nomachi/Pacific Press Service

6 Courtesy Federal Department of Antiquities, Nigeria

13 Hirmer Fotoarchiv, Munich

15 Hirmer Fotoarchiv, Munich

18 Hirmer Fotoarchiv, Munich

19 The Metropolitan Museum of Art, Rogers Fund, 1931 (31.3.157)

23 Erich Lessing/Art Resource, NY

27 National Museum of India, New Delhi

28 Government of India Information Services

32 From *Sources of Shang History: The Oracle-Bone Inscriptions of Bronze Age China* by David N. Keightley. University of California Press, 1978. Copyright © 1978 by The Regents of the University of California

34 Courtesy of The Cultural Relics Bureau, Beijing and The Metropolitan Museum of Art

36 Emil Muench

41 Doug Bryant/D. Donne Bryant Stock

42 Peabody Museum, Harvard University

Chapter 2

44 Black-figure Hydria. *Achilles Dragging the Body of Hector around the Walls of Troy*, ca. 520 B.C. William Francis Warden Fund. Courtesy, Museum of Fine Arts, Boston

46 The Metropolitan Museum of Art, Rogers Fund, 1947 (47.100.1)

48 Hirmer Fotoarchiv, Munich

50 Copyright British Museum

52 Copyright British Museum

54 Bibliothèque Nationale, Paris

55 Staatliche Museen Preussischer Kulturbesitz, Antikenmuseum, Berlin

56 Alexander Tsiaras/Stock, Boston

59 Scala/Art Resource, NY

61 The Metropolitan Museum of Art, Fletcher Fund, 1932 (32.11.1)

62 Hirmer Fotoarchiv, Munich

63 Wadsworth Atheneum, Hartford, J. Pierpont Morgan Collection

66 Lee Boltin

Chapter 3

70 *Battle of Issus* and a detail showing Alexander the Great. Mosaic copy of a Hellenistic painting. (both) Alinari/Art Resource, NY

73 American School of Classical Studies at Athens: Agora Excavations

74 Staatliche Museen Preussischer Kulturbesitz, Antikenmuseum, Berlin

75 The Metropolitan Museum of Art, Fletcher Fund, 1931 (31.11.0)

78 Hirmer Fotoarchiv, Munich

80 Copyright British Museum

81 Martin-von-Wagner Museum, University of Würzburg

83 The Metropolitan Museum of Art, Rogers Fund, 1952 (52.11.4)

85 Hirmer Fotoarchiv, Munich

87 Copyright British Museum

90 Alinari/Art Resource, NY

93 Hirmer Fotoarchiv, Munich

95 The Metropolitan Museum of Art, Rogers Fund, 1911 (11.90)

Chapter 4

100 Halebid, Hoysaleśvara Temple: Draupadī about to wash her hair with the blood of Duhśāsana, offered to her by Bhīma. Photo by Helen Hiltebeitel, Courtesy of Alf Hiltebeitel

104 Seth Joel/Courtesy The Metropolitan Museum of Art

105 Shanghai Museum

106 From Lo Chen-yu, *Yin-hsu Shu-ch'i Ching-hua*, 1914

108 Field Museum of Natural History, Chicago

111 Worcester Art Museum

112 Seth Joel/Courtesy The Metropolitan Museum of Art

115 Shensi Provincial Museum

116 Courtesy of the Freer Gallery of Art, Smithsonian Institution, Washington, D.C.

117 Originally published by the University of California Press; Reprinted by permission of The Regents of the University of California

123 National Museum of India, New Delhi

124 The Seattle Art Museum, Eugene Fuller Memorial Collection

126 Copyright British Museum

128 Archaeological Survey of India

129 Government of India Information Services

Chapter 5

132 The Roman Forum. Istituto Geografico de Agostini, Milan. Photo: A. De Gregorio

137 Hirmer Fotoarchiv, Munich

139 Bibliothèque Nationale, Paris

142 Museo Nazionale, Naples

145 Alinari/Art Resource, NY

149 Giraudon/Art Resource, NY

150 Carbone & Danno, Naples

151 Alinari/Art Resource, NY

153 Römische-Germanisches Zentralmuseum, Mainz

155 Alinari/Art Resource, NY

158 Roger-Viollet

Chapter 6

Barbarian medallion (front and back) of Valentinian I and Valens. (both) Hirmer Fotoarchiv, Munich

165 Scala/Art Resource, NY

169 Alinari/Art Resource, NY

Bomb Survivors edited by The Japan Broadcasting Association. Copyright © 1977 by NHK. Reprinted by permission by Pantheon Books, a division of Random House, Inc.
1002 U. S. Navy
1004 Franklin D. Roosevelt Library, National Archives and Records Service

Chapter 33
1006 Mourners surrounding the flag-draped coffin of UAR President Gamal Abdel Nasser during his funeral procession. UPI/Bettmann
1012 UPI/Bettmann
1014 AP/Wide World
1016 N.R. Farbman, *Life* Magazine © Time Warner Inc.
1020 UPI/Bettmann
1023 East African Standard Newspapers Ltd.
1024 AP/Wide World
1026 Betty Press/Woodfin Camp & Associates
1029 Trustees of the Imperial War Museum, London
1033 Courtesy of United Jewish Appeal
1039 Ralph Crane, *Life* Magazine © Time Warner Inc.
1040 Reuters/Bettmann

Chapter 34
1044 *The Poster Scene*, 1967. Topham/Image Works
1048 UPI/Bettmann
1050 European Community Information Service
1054 UPI/Bettmann
1057 Erich Lessing/Magnum
1062 UPI/Bettmann
1065 Bruno Barbey/Magnum
1067 Peter Marlow/Magnum
1068 Vlastimir Shone/Gamma-Liaison
1069 DeKeerle/Grochowiak/Sygma
1070 AP/Wide World
1073 Leh/Saukkomaa/Woodfin Camp & Associates
1075 AP/Wide World
1076 AP/Wide World
1079 Reuters/Bettmann

Chapter 35
1082 Shanghai Sampan. Hiroji Kubota/Magnum
1086 UPI/Bettmann
1089 AP/Wide World
1093 UPI/Bettmann
1095 AP/Wide World
1098 UPI/Bettmann
1099 AP/Wide World
1101 AP/Wide World
1104 (l) AP/Wide World; (r) Reuters/Bettmann
1106 Courtesy of *Baseball Magazine Sha*
1109 T. Matsumoto/Sygma
1111 Andy Hernandez/Sygma

Color Essay 1 following page 126
1 Erich Lessing/Art Resource, NY
2 B. Norman/Ancient Art & Architecture Collection
3 TAP Service/National Museum, Athens
4 Hirmer Fotoarchiv, Munich

Color Essay 2 following page 222
1 Scala/Art Resource, NY
2 The Metropolitan Museum of Art, Purchase, Lita Annenberg Hazen Charitable Trust Gift, in honor of Cynthia Hazen and Leon Bernard Polsky, 1982 (1982.220.8)
3 The Board of Trinity College Dublin
4 Scala/Art Resource, NY

Color Essay 3 following page 318
1 Erich Lessing/Art Resource, NY
2 Scala/Art Resource, NY
3 Reproduced by courtesy of the Trustees, The National Gallery, London
4 Reproduced by courtesy of the Trustees, The National Gallery, London

Color Essay 4 following page 414
1 The Granger Collection, New York
2 Scala/Art Resource, NY
3 Derby Museums and Art Gallery
4 Werner Forman/Art Resource, NY

Color Essay 5 following page 590
1 Giraudon/Art Resource, NY
2 Courtesy of The Arthur M. Sackler Museum, Harvard University Art Museums, Private Collection
3 Colorphoto Hans Hinz
4 Reproduced by permission of the Trustees of the Wallace Collection

Color Essay 6 following page 718
1 Bridgeman/Art Resource, NY
2 Royal Academy of Arts, London
3 Erich Lessing/Art Resource, NY
4 Erich Lessing/Art Resource, NY

Color Essay 7 following page 814
1 Pablo Picasso. *Les Desmoiselles d'Avignon.* Paris (June–July 1907). Oil on canvas, 8′ × 7′ 8″. The Museum of Modern Art, New York. Acquired through the Lillie P. Bliss Bequest
2 M. Felix Collection, Brussels. Photo: Dick Beaulieux
3 Private Collection. Photo: Jeffrey Ploskonka
4 Frida Kahlo. *Self Portrait with Cropped Hair.* 1940. Oil on canvas, 15¾ × 11″. The Museum of Modern Art, New York. Gift of Edgar Kaufmann, Jr.

Color Essay 8 following page 1102
1 Kitagawa Utamaro, Japanese, 1753–1806, *Joshoku Kaiko Tewaza Gusa (Women's Work in Silk Culture),* woodblock print, c. 1802, 38.1 × 25.4 cm, Departmental Funds, 1925.3257, photograph © 1993, The Art Institute of Chicago. All Rights Reserved
2 Tate Gallery, London/Art Resource, NY
3 Library of Congress
4 From *Prop Art: Over 1000 Contemporary Political Posters* by Gary Yanker. Darien House, New York, distributed by New York Graphic Society, 1972. Copyright © 1972 by Gary Yanker

INDEX

Page numbers followed by *t* and *f* indicate tables and figures, respectively. pronunciation guidance is supplied in square brackets, [ ], after difficult words. The symbols used for pronunciation are found in the table below. Syllables for primary stress are *italicized*.

a	act, bat, marry
AY	age, rate
år	air, dare
ä	ah, part, calm
ch	chief, beach
e	edge, set
EE	equal, seat, bee
EER	here, ear
g	give, trigger
h	here
hw	which, when
i	if, big
I	bite, ice
ng	sing
o	ox, hot
O	hope, over
ô	order, ball
oi	oil, joint
oo	book, tour
ou	plow, out
sh	she, fashion
th	thin, ether
u	up, sum
zh	vision, pleasure
uh	*a*lone, syst*e*m, eas*i*ly, gall*o*p, circ*u*s
A	as in French *a*mi
KH	as in German a*ch*, i*ch*
N	as in French bo*n*
OE	as in French d*eu*x
R	as in French *r*ouge
Y	as in German f*ü*hlen

Aachen [*ä* kuhn, *ä* Huhn], 255, 258, 610
Abbas I (Safavid shah), 457, 457*f*, 461*f*, 464
'Abbas [uh *bä*, *ä* buh], 206
'Abbasid [uh *bas* id, *ab* uh sid] dynasty, 206–207, 211, 443, 445
Abbots, 276, 287
'Abd [ab d] al-Qadir (Algerian shaykh), 578
'Abdallah (Arab leader), 1030
'Abd ar-Rahman III, 206
'Abduh, Muhammad, 589

Abdullah Hassan (Somalian leader), 813
Abeokuta [ä bAY *O* koo tä], 19th-c., 855
Abolition movement
in British West Africa, 855
in Great Britain, 560, 565–567, 751
in United States, 751, 753
Abolition philosophy, and French Revolution, 665, 668
Abraham, 21, 24, 173
Abu Bakr [uh bU *bak* uhr, A bu Bekr], 203–204
Académie des Sciences, 538
Academies, in 18th-century Europe, 635
Academy (Plato's), 88
Achaemenid dynasty, 68
Acheson, Dean [*ach* uh suhn] (U.S. official), 1048
Achille Lauro, highjacking of, 1078
Achilles, 45, 92
Acropolis, 52, 65, 67, 86
Actium [*ak* tEE uhm, *ak* shEE uhm], battle of, 159, 164, 166
Acts of the Apostles, 173
Adam brothers, 623
Adbul Hamid II (Ottoman sultan), 830
Address to the Christian Nobility of the German Nation (Luther), 389
Aden, 417
19th-c., British acquisition of, 829
Adenauer, Konrad [*ad* n ou uhr] (West German chancellor), 1056, 1060
Adowa, battle of, 814, 815*f*, 825, 856
Adrianople, battle of, 182
Advancement of Learning (Bacon), 538
Advertising, 869–870. *See also* Press; Public opinion
Aeneas, 167 *Aeneid* [i *nEE* id], 167
Aeolians, 49
aeropagus, 66
Aeschylus [*es* ku luhs], 81, 84
Afghanistan, 443, 449, 457, 462, 467. *See also* Ghaznavids; Mahmud of Ghazna
19th-c., and Russia, 819
Hellenistic, 96
and Safavid Empire, 451, 466
Afghans, 447, 464–466
Afonso (Kongolese *maniKongo*), 419
Africa. *See also* East Africa; North Africa; *specific country or group*; West Africa
15th–16th-c., Catholicism in, 418–419, 421
15th–17th-c., Portuguese in, 408–424
17th-c., and European economy, 561–562
17th–19th-c., relationship with Europe, 560–575

19th-c., 568*f*, 573, 809–818, 821, 825, 851–856
20th-c., *map* 818, 822, 860–863, 866, 1017–1019, 1020–1021, 1065
agricultural/pastoral peoples in, 4–8
"big men" in. *See* Big men
Christianity in, 855–856, 864–866, 1017
climate of, 7
European exploration of, 410–424, 805
European settlers in. *See* Africa, 20th-c., European settlers in; Rhodesia; South Africa; Zambia; Zimbabwe
before European slave trade, economic structure of, 413
Islam in, 193, 211–219
Lower Guinea Coast, *map*, 562
map, 4, 414, 852, 1018
Neolithic food-production practices, diffusion of, 4–6
political policies and practices of. *See* Political policies and practices, of Africa; *specific country*
politics of kinship in, 7–8
regional politics in, 8–9
religion in. *See also* Christianity, spread, in Africa; Islam, spread, in Africa
social structure of, 413
sub-Saharan, early civilization in, to 700 c.e., 4–9
African National Congress, 1024–1025
Freedom Charter of, 1019, 1025
Africans
in Americas. *See* Llaneros; Pardos; Slaves
resistance to Portuguese intervention, 424
Western-educated elite, 855–856, 1022
Afrika Korps, 998
Afrikaner Nationalist Party, 1024
Afrikaners, 569–572, 814–818, 1024–1025
Afterlife, belief in
Chinese Buddhist, 226
Egyptian, 18–19
Han Chinese, 113
Vedic, 29
Agamemnon, 84
Agincourt, battle of, 297*f*
Agni [*ug* nEE, *ag* nEE] (god), 29
Agora, 52
Agricultural Revolution, 715–717
Agriculture. *See also* Collectivization; Ecology; Famine in Africa, 193, 421
ancient Andean, 39
Angkor (Khmer), 242

in Arabia, 200
in Austria, 18th–19th centuries, 735
in Carthage, 135
in China, 105–106, 117, 119–120, 223, 228, 231, 317, 321, 326, 329, 331, 682–683, 683*f*, 688–689, 945
collective, in Soviet Union, interwar period, 916–920
in colonized societies, 19th-c., 825
common farming system, 643
in Communist Yanan, 1086
development of, 3–4
double-cropping system, 128, 698
dry field system, 682
in eastern Europe, 18th-c., 643–644
Egyptian, 16–17, 577–578, 585
enclosed field system, 716–717
in England, 307, 511
equal field system, 228, 233, 245, 247
Etruscan, 137
in Europe, 263, 264*f*, 272–273, 302–303, 510–511, 638–639, 642*f*, 642–644, 643*f*, 714–717, 738, 885, 1047
European philosophy on, 18th-c., 631
fertilizers, 106, 128, 242, 643, 688, 706
flooded-field system, 317
fodder crop system, 716
four-course rotation system, 716
in France, 776
in Germany
in Great Britain
in Greece, 51, 75
Harappan (ancient India), 28
in Holland, 546
in Hungary, 18th-c., 644
Indian, 26, 28, 128
Indian philosophy regarding, 123
in Indonesia, 20th-c., 1091
invention of, in Chinese mythology, 103
in Iraq, 19th-c., 584
in Ireland, 643, 741
in Islamic empires, 207, 441–442, 462
in Japan, 250, 335–336, 340
in Java, 19th-c., 965
in Kenya, 19th-c., 821
in Korea, 244–245
in Latin America, 20th-c., 1009–1010, 1014, 1016
Longshan (ancient Chinese), 31
market, development in Europe, 644, 716–717
Mayan, 39
meadow-floating system, 716
Mesoamerican and ancient South American, 34–35, 41
in Mesopotamia, 9, 12